AMERICA'S POLITICS

AMERICA'S POLITICS
A Diverse Country in a Globalizing World

John T. Rourke

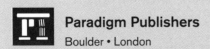

Paradigm Publishers
Boulder • London

Copyright © 2011 Paradigm Publishers

Published in the United States by Paradigm Publishers, 2845 Wilderness Place, Boulder, CO 80301 USA.

Paradigm Publishers is the trade name of Birkenkamp & Company, LLC, Dean Birkenkamp, President and Publisher.

Library of Congress Cataloging-in-Publication Data

Rourke, John T., 1945–
    America's politics : a diverse country in a globalizing world / John T. Rourke.
        p. cm.
    Includes bibliographical references and index.
    ISBN 978-1-59451-912-3 (pbk. : alk. paper)
    1. United States—Politics and government. 2. Cultural pluralism—United States. 3. Globalization. I. Title.
    JK275.R68 2011
    320.473—dc22

                                                                2010019003

Printed and bound in the United States of America on acid-free paper that meets the standards of the American National Standard for Permanence of Paper for Printed Library Materials.

14 13 12 11   1 2 3 4 5

Para mi amiga, mi amor, mi esposa—
Guadalupe Rodriguez

BRIEF CONTENTS

CONTENTS

PART ONE

SETTINGS FOR A DIVERSE AND GLOBAL GOVERNMENT 31

9 POLITICAL PARTIES   322

PART THREE

MAKING POLICY: CONVERTING DIVERSE AND GLOBAL INPUTS TO OUTPUTS 419

11 CONGRESS 420

WEB MATERIALS

Glossary

Bibliography

Powerpoint Slides of Figures in Text

www.paradigmpublishers.com/books/BookDetail.aspx?productID=274091

BOXES, TABLES, AND FIGURES

YOU DECIDE BOXES

TABLES

FIGURES

PREFACE

This is a different kind of American government text. It is more compact, less "busy," and best of all, more affordable than most other texts on the market. At the same time, it packs a lot of information into its pages, and is written in a way that is interesting to students and significant to professors. It speaks to two of the most important developments of our times: the increasing diversity of the American public and the greater globalization of America's politics. These trends are not coincidental, and they are not going away. With this book, it is my intent to offer a text that will provide solid grounding for an understanding of America's political past and its future—political, social, and economic.

To the Student

This book is written directly to you and for you. Its author is successful because he writes in a way that is informative without overload, entertaining without antics, and respectful without condescension. Most of all, the book is written about real politics in a realistic way. It doesn't dwell in the lofty region of normative idealism—the "shoulds" and "oughts" of politics. It also doesn't wallow in the troughs of academic realism—that's different from being realistic, as you will experience as you read this book. The author tells a good story and shows you the facts behind it. This book respects both your pocketbook and your intellect and leaves a lot up to you to deliberate and decide.

To the Professor

This book is also written for you—to help you cover a lot of ground in an efficient way, offering solid information on which you can expand and from which you can launch into new topics at will. It is data driven and interpretive at the same time. Its themes—globalization and diversity—are important as well as interesting. It is designed to form the core of your course without precluding additions, diversions, and specialties. It provides complete documentation of a wide variety of sources— far broader in reach than most American government texts because of the author's background in international relations as well as American government. It also offers teaching aids, among them consistent chapter pedagogy and instructor's materials, including a test bank.

Organization of the Text

This book is organized in a way that speaks to students and themes. It starts with the basics of American political history—how we got to where we are in a global and diverse America. Then it moves to the "inputs" into American government—political beliefs, interest groups, media, political parties, and elections: all the ways that students and citizens can get involved. Then it takes up the "conversion process" that absorbs the inputs and creates "outputs," the policies that emanate from the Congress, the presidency, the bureaucracy, and the federal courts. All chapters are freestanding and designed for consistent coverage from outline to summary to glossary so chapters can be rearranged in any way desired.

Features of This Text

- Presents themes of **globalization** and **diversity**, a first for an introductory American politics text.
- Written by an **experienced and successful textbook author** with a specialty in American foreign policy as well as international relations. He has received considerable positive feedback from students for writing *to* them and not *at* them.
- Includes **2010 midterm election results** for up-to-date coverage.
- Tells the **"story"** that makes politics fascinating while also ensuring that major theoretical political science approaches and controversies are covered.
- Includes unique feature boxes and insets: **You Decide**, **A World of Difference**, and **American Diversity**. Globalization and diversity **icons** denote relevant content.
- Provides numerous **tables**, **charts**, **figures**, **photos**, and additional illustrations to enliven the text, some with **icon-identified** thematic content reflecting the book's emphasis on globalization and diversity. **Color highlights** spotlight key data.
- Includes consistent elements for each chapter: Opening **chapter outlines**, closing **chapter summaries**, and end of **chapter glossaries** corresponding to **color highlighted key terms** throughout the text.
- **Designed simply**, avoiding multitudinous boxes and other specialized inserts that disrupt the flow of the main text and serve to promote the quintessential question: "Will this be on the test?"
- Offers the **extensive coverage** of a full-scale text with the **modest price** of a brief book.

Supplements to This Text

- Website ancillaries include **PowerPoint slides** of tables and figures from the text, a **full-text glossary**, a widely ranging **bibliography**, and **updates and additions** as they occur. See:
  www.paradigmpublishers.com/books/BookDetail.aspx?productID=274091

- An **Instructor's Manual with Test Questions** is available to professors reviewing or adopting the text.
- A full set of **supplementary texts** on key topics and institutions with special **package pricing** available. Topics include Congress, the Presidency, Media and Politics, Globalization, Ethnic and Minority Politics, and any other supplementary text from the Paradigm list. Email:

    examcopies@paradigmpublishers.com

    for more information.

To Conclude

In 1962, a reporter asked President John F. Kennedy this question: "Somewhere in our land today there is a high school or college student who will one day be sitting in your chair. If you could speak to this future president, what advice and guidance would you give him or her?" Kennedy sagely replied, "It will help you to know the country you seek to lead," adding: "If you find the opportunity to know and work with Americans of diverse backgrounds, occupations, and beliefs, then I would urge you to take eagerly that opportunity to enrich yourself." Kennedy also advised his successor to see the world because "the future of your own country is bound to your capacity to exercise leadership and judgment on a global scale."[1]

The year 2011 marks the 50th anniversary of Kennedy's inauguration, and in many ways, we are still only just beginning to realize the import and impact of these words. This book is designed to help carry us forward along these crucial trend lines.

---

1. Quoted in Fred Blumenthal, "How to Prepare for the Presidency," *Parade Magazine,* 1962. Reprinted in *The World Book Encyclopedia* (Chicago: Field Enterprises Educational Corporation, 1965), 678–79.

ACKNOWLEDGMENTS

Seldom is the well-worn, grammatically dubious phrase "I couldn't of done it without you" more appropriate than in writing a college-level text. "You" here is a plural noun, and I want to express my gratitude to the numerous people without whom, quite literally, this book would be a theory rather than a fact. During the genesis of this book, almost 20 scholars read various groups of chapters and gave me their suggestions on how to improve them. Such reviews are done anonymously, so for these contributors I have to confine myself to a "You know who you are!" and a thank you. What might be described as the ultimate review was taken on by Professor Marjorie Randon Hershey of the Department of Political Science at Indiana University in Bloomington. Professor Hershey's stellar career as both a scholar and teacher invaluably helped me ensure that both the academic content of this book and how it is presented to its student readers is on the mark. An April 2010 news release by Indiana University that highlighted Professor Hershey's contributions included one student's comment, "Professor Hershey is easily the best professor I have had. . . . Don't let Professor Hershey retire until she turns 90." I agree with that recommendation. I need her to read the revisions as this book moves through its second, third, and ongoing editions.

Another group of scholars who well deserve recognition are those who are listed in the section "Scholars Cited" toward the end of this book. The approximately 950 scholars listed are the authors or co-authors of the scholarly books and articles that together form the indispensable foundation of research on which this text rests. Their individual works are detailed in the bibliography, which is on this book's Website at

www.paradigmpublishers.com/books/BookDetail.aspx?productID=274091

A third group of people whose contributions I gratefully acknowledge consists of those who helped give this book its overall direction, who improved my prose, and who were instrumental in turning what might generously be called a diamond in the rough into the polished product it has become. Jennifer Knerr carries the august titles of Vice President and Executive Editor and Director of College Publishing at Paradigm Publishers, but instead of being above it all, she functioned much like a developmental editor and was involved in every detail of the text ranging from the scholarship to the kind of paper on which it is printed. Authors get their names on the cover, but DEs are the silent partners who make it all happen.

My thanks also go to Sharon Daugherty at Paradigm. She is the photo editor and creatively and industriously helped me find, select, and obtain the photographs, editorial cartoons, and maps that add visual interest as well as content to the book. Greg Draus of Scratchgravel Publishing Services has also added both educationally and visually to the book by turning its nearly 150 figures from my rough drafts into skilled representations of data, events, and ideas. The final stage in the process of creating a book is production. I have been very fortunate to be ably supported by four individuals. Two are Ann Whetstone, copyeditor, and Holly McLean-Aldis, proofreader, who saved me from numerous typos, grammatical errors, inconsistencies of usage, and other individually small but collectively important errors. Third is Carol Smith, Paradigm's Director of Editorial Production and in-house project manager for this text. Finally there is Aaron Downey, Senior Production Editor at Matrix Productions in Tucson, AZ. As we have moved from final manuscript through various stages of page proofs, with myriad final adjustments, Aaron has been a paragon of patience and skill in creating the book you are holding. Just one of the many testaments to Aaron's dedication is the number of emails I have received from his office dated Saturday or Sunday. Get some rest, Aaron. Watch a ball game or take a hike up Mount Lemmon.

With happy repetition, I say thank you, thank you all.

John T. Rourke

ABOUT THE AUTHOR

John T. Rourke taught for thirty years at University of Connecticut's Department of Political Science and served more than five years as its chair. His specialty, the American foreign policy process, encompasses both international relations and American politics, and he has taught courses and published in both areas. Among other works, his books include *You Decide: Current Debates in American Politics* (8 editions), *International Politics on the World Stage* (12 editions), and *Taking Sides: Clashing Views in International Politics* (15 editions).

AMERICA'S
POLITICS

1

YOU, AMERICAN POLITICS, AND THIS BOOK

YOU DECIDE: Women Warriors?

Women are increasingly among the young adults who make up the U.S. armed forces and face the dangers of war. One of these women, Private first class (Pfc.) Lori Piestewa, was among the U.S. troops who invaded Iraq in 2003. She was 23, a Hopi from Arizona, a single parent with a son (age 4) and a daughter (age 3), and serving her country, just as her father had in Vietnam and her grandfather had in World War II.

Soon after the war began, Iraqi troops attacked her unit, the 507th Maintenance Company, killing nine including Piestewa. Ten others were wounded or captured, including 30-year-old Pfc. Shoshana Johnson, an African American woman from Texas, and 19-year-old Pfc. Jessica Lynch, a white woman from West Virginia. The three were the first of many American female casualties (killed and injured) in Iraq, and they and their experiences encapsulate several concerns that are central to this book. First, their saga, like this book, is about the stake that they, you, and indeed all Americans have in your political system. Second, the story of these three racially diverse women is about the diversity of Americans and, increasingly, American politics. Third, why these women were in Iraq in the first place is about the place of Americans and their country in a culturally and politically diverse world.

What befell Piestewa, Johnson, and Lynch also raises the issue of women in combat. Many barriers to that have crumbled, and American women now serve as the pilots of warplanes and in many other roles that can put them in the line of fire. However, Pentagon regulations bar women from the primary ground combat units: artillery, armor, and infantry. Some want to eliminate these barriers as sexist. Doing so would give women more choice. But it would also give them less choice, because the military can assign troops to units involuntarily. Given that having combat experience is crucial for reaching the top ranks of the military, having women in combat positions would also increase their career prospects. That is, of course, if they survived. Having women in combat positions would also greatly increase their percentage of U.S. casualties, which has been 2.4% in Iraq. One poll found 52% of Americans in favor of putting women in all combat units, 46% opposed, and 4% unsure.[1] You decide! Does equal opportunity demand that G.I. Jane join G.I. Joe on the frontlines?

With the United States the leading power in a globalizing world, American forces are often sent into combat. These troops increasingly include women as sex-roles become more equal in the military and elsewhere. Military Police Sergeant Leigh Ann Hester, seen here, was the first woman to win a silver star in Iraq. When enemy insurgents attacked a convoy she was helping guard, Hester displayed great valor, killing at least three enemy and helping to lead a counterattack that drove them off. (DefenseImagery.mil SPC Jeremy D. Crisp, USA, photographer)

BEGINNING OUR JOURNEY

This chapter begins a journey that joins you, your classmates, your professor, and this text's author in an exploration of the American political system, the diversity within it, and its place in a diverse world. This introductory chapter lays out some important information that sets the stage for our exploration.

Our initial task is to explore why it is a good idea for you to increase your knowledge of government and politics in the United States. The explanation involves the immense size and power of **government** and its extensive impact on your life. Our second task in this chapter is to take up an overview of this book's organization and its main themes. Knowing these things will help you navigate your way as we proceed. *Global diversity* is the first theme. The global setting for U.S. politics and policy is a "world of difference," with diverse people, cultures, and political institutions and processes. That diversity remains extensive, but we shall also see that the accelerating globalization process is diminishing diversity in important ways. *Domestic diversity*, with particular attention to race and sex is the second theme. When these themes are present in boxes, charts, margin notes, and other such material you will find the logo for **World of Difference** or **American Diversity**.

One similarity between these two spheres of diversity is that each is playing an increasingly greater role in American politics and policy. Internationally, the United States is far less insular than it has ever been. Domestically, members of racial minorities and women have a growing presence in American politics. As this chapter proceeds, it makes the following key points:

★ The size, scope, and power of the American political system are awesome and expanding.
★ Politics affects you in many ways.
★ You can and should influence politics.
★ Americans live in an interdependent world amid advancing globalization, and that global setting influences U.S. policy and politics in many ways.
★ Perspective on the U.S. government and political process can be gained from comparing them with other countries.
★ Ethnic/racial minority groups are increasing as a percentage of the U.S. population.
★ Racial minorities and women are playing a larger role in American politics.

YOU AND POLITICS

A good way to begin this text and the course to which it is connected is to explain why its topic is important to you. This book generally does not try to tell you what to think, but it does preach one sermon: politics is very important to you and everyone else because of (1) the vast size and scope of government and (2) the government's imposing power and its impact on all of us. You cannot escape these realities even if you try. As heavyweight champion Joe Louis put it after knocking out a ducking and dodging Billy Conn in 1941, "You can run, but you can't hide." That would be pretty discouraging if the sermon ended there, but it does not. Instead, the message of hope is that (3) government can be made responsive to the public's needs and wishes and (4) there is a range of not terribly burdensome things you can to do to promote that end.

The Size and Scope of Government

It is daunting to realize how big and how omnipresent government is in the United States. The U.S. federal-state-local government triad is the largest organizational complex ever constructed. Moreover, government today is also involved in nearly every aspect of our activities.

U.S. taxes, at 28% of GDP in 2008, are the second lowest (after Japan, 27%) among the world's major industrialized countries, whose taxes average 38% of GDP.

The Size of Government

President Calvin Coolidge once observed, "The chief business of the American people is business."[2] Perhaps that was true in 1925, but in the twenty-first century it might be more accurate to say that the chief business of the American people is government. To begin to grasp the sheer size of the government complex in the United States, consider the following data for 2008:

- There are 89,527 governments (1 federal, 50 state, the rest local) with some level of autonomy in the United States. That is about one government for each 3,400 residents.
- Government revenue was $3.8 trillion (federal, $2.4 trillion; state and local, $1.4 trillion).
- Government spending was $4.2 trillion (federal, $2.7 trillion; state and local, $1.5 trillion), or about $480,000 an hour.
- Government spending accounted for 39% of the entire U.S. **gross domestic product** (GDP: all economic activity within the country).
- Federal government spending as a share of the GDP was 23%, up from 2% in 1792 and 7% in 1940.
- About 24 million people were public employees. They comprised 18% of all salaried workers. The breakdown was 13.9 million local employees, 5.1 million state, and 5.0 million federal (including civilian, postal, and military).
- Public employees earned $921 billion, accounting for 17% of all wages Americans earned.
- There were 116 civilian federal employees for every 10,000 U.S. residents, up from 5 per 10,000 residents in 1792.

One of the ways government affects the lives of many young adults is by partly determining the cost of their college education. This photograph shows a student from Kennesaw State University during a March 2010 rally at Georgia's Capitol building in Atlanta to protest cuts in the state's funding for higher education. (AP Photo/ Johnny Crawford, AJC)

The Scope of Government

The evolution of the U.S. political system has also included an expanding range of matters in which the government is engaged. At first the scope of government was quite limited. George Washington's cabinet had just four departments (State, War, Treasury, and Justice), and there was also the postal service. Now there are more than two dozen Cabinet departments and major independent agencies. As the country expanded internally, the Interior (1849) and Agriculture (1862) departments were added. Beginning in the early 1900s, integration of the national economy led the creation of such agencies as the Department of Commerce and Labor (1903) and the Federal Reserve Board (1913). Government's new role in social welfare brought the Social Security Administration (1935), then many other agencies such as the Department of Health, Education, and Welfare (1953). The list of agencies and the circumstances behind the creation of each is far too long to detail here, but the point to see is that the creation of each symbolizes the federal government expanding its reach into a new area of policy.

Government is now involved in all aspects of society including religion. Sometimes, the government restricts religion. In an early example, the Supreme Court in 1879 upheld prohibiting polygamy regardless of religion.[3] More recently, the Court in 1990 allowed Oregon to prosecute members of the Native American Church for using a small quantity of peyote, an illegal hallucinogenic drug, as part of a religious ritual.[4] Government can also benefit religion. Churches, synagogues, and other places of worship are routinely exempted from property taxes, donations to religious organizations can be taken as a tax deduction, and some types of public support for parochial schools is permissible.

Government Growth as a Global Phenomenon

At this point it is reasonable to ask why the size and scope of government have expanded so much. Before looking at specific reasons, it is important to note that this growth has been a global phenomenon. For example, spending by governments in Western Europe made up an average of 14% of their GDPs in 1913. In 2008, spending by these governments accounted for 49% of their respective GDPs. During the same period, government expenditures as a share of the GDP in Japan rose from 8% to 36%, and those in the United States grew from 8% to 39%.[5]

This global growth has occurred for several reasons that we can only touch on here. One has been the slow growth of democracy since the American and French revolutions in the late 1700s and the associated idea that governments have a responsibility for the general welfare of their people. Second, the age of industrialization beginning in the 1700s increasingly brought people together in urban areas, where in bad times their grievances could spark social unrest. Third, governments became more and more sensitive because of their need to have at least the passive economic and political support of their populations. Such considerations prompted Chancellor Otto von Bismarck to institute a series of social welfare programs in Germany in the 1880s that included government health and accident insurance and pensions for workers. Within a few decades this idea spread at least to some degree to all the industrialized countries.

The global Great Depression of the 1930s accelerated the growth of the welfare state even more, as governments used spending to support the needy. Following the ideas of British economist John Maynard Keynes, governments also spent vast sums to stimulate their economies. In subsequent years there has been a general push-pull process that has continued the growth of government. The push has been from people and interest groups pressing their governments for more and more services. The pull has come from governments, which add to their powers by increasing their revenues and expenditures and taking new areas of society into the realm of those subject to public policy. Keynesian economics also continues to play a role, as is evident in the stimulus packages and massive deficit spending favored by President Barack Obama in 2009 and 2010.

Finally, it should be noted that the globalization of threats from other countries in an era of nuclear weapons and now terrorism has also increased government spending. This has been more true for the United States than for other developed countries. But even for Americans, the growth of spending on national security has been much less important in the overall growth of spending since World War II than increased spending on social services.

The Power and Impact of Government

Anything that is as big and omnipresent as government is in the United States bears watching. This need to oversee it carefully is made doubly acute by government's power and impact.

The Power of Government

Most Americans consider themselves quite free, but the reality is that we are all subject to myriad laws and regulations that we must obey or suffer the consequences. The power of the government comes from its ability to make laws, to create regulations that have the force of law, and to enforce those laws and regulations. Some illustrative facts include:

- Since 1789 Congress has passed more than 48,000 laws.
- From 1973 through 2006, Congress enacted 9,783 public laws, an average of 280 a year.
- The 2009 *Federal Register*, the compendium of directives and regulations issued during the year by federal agencies, was 69,351 pages long. The 1940 *Federal Register* had 5,307 pages.

FIGURE 1.1 U.S. Law Enforcement and World Militaries

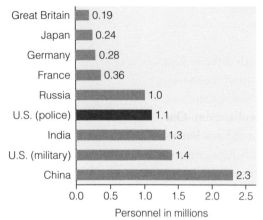

Personnel in millions

The federal, state, and local governments have great coercive power. If the 1.1 million people working for U.S. police agencies were a military force, they would be the world's fourth largest. Add in the 755,000 U.S. corrections officers, and the force would be the world's second largest.

Data sources: Center for Strategic and International Studies; Statistical Abstract of the United States

- There is no list of state and local laws enacted and regulations issued annually, but the laws certainly number in the tens of thousands and the regulations in the hundreds of thousands.
- To enforce their laws and regulations, federal, state, and local governments employ 1.1 million people in police agencies, 755,000 in correction departments, and 500,000 in the courts and prosecutors' offices. How this workforce compares to the world's largest military forces is shown in Figure 1.1.
- Fines are the mildest government penalty for violations of laws and rules. No national accounting exists, but in 2006 New York City and Los Angeles alone combined to collect more than $1 billion in fines.
- Jail is a more severe penalty. In 2008, some 2.3 million Americans—about 1% of the adult population—spent at least some time in jail.
- The ultimate penalty is a death sentence, and 52 inmates were executed in 2009. Another 3,207 waited on death row.

The Impact of Government

Statistics about the size, scope, and power of the government while impressive are somewhat abstract. So to give them life, it is important to look at how all this impacts Americans. The following commentary takes that up, with a particular eye to the impact on young adults, the most likely readers of this text. In each case there is but one example, but there could be dozens.

Spending decisions help shape key aspects of your life such as the cost of going to college. This is particularly true if you attend a state college. State governments have generally been reducing their share of the operating budgets of public colleges, forcing them to increase tuition and other fees. However, state spending decisions vary considerably. In 2008 New Mexico was the most student-friendly state, with tuition amounting to only 10% of the costs of running its public colleges. Vermont was at the other end of the scale, with tuition covering 73% of the costs.

Taxing decisions affect everyone directly through the payment of income and other taxes and indirectly though the included cost of taxes in the goods and services that we buy. Some details of tax policies are particularly important to students. For instance some states exempt textbooks from the sales tax; others do not. One potential change in tax policy that affects students is Barack Obama's proposal during the 2008 presidential campaign to allow students or their parents to take up to $4,000 a year in college expenses off their taxes (a tax credit) in exchange for 100 hours of community service.

Opportunity decisions are another area of government activity. Sometimes the government restricts equal opportunity, as the opening You Decide box relates with regard to women in the military. In other cases, the government expands opportunities for certain groups, including racial minorities and women, through affirmative action programs.

As of 2010, same-sex marriages were permitted by national law in Belgium, Canada, the Netherlands, Norway, Portugal, South Africa, Spain, and Sweden.

Personal relationship decisions are also within the government's realm. One current debate is over gay marriage. There are about 600,000 same-sex households, but under the Defense of Marriages Act (1996), the federal government refuses to recognize same-sex marriages. A few state legislatures have legalized gay marriages; courts in a few more states have declared that barring them is unconstitutional; and about 10 other states recognize civil unions with some or all of the same rights and responsibilities as marriages. *Personal conduct decisions* are also subject to regulation. One of these for most undergraduates is the decision about whether or not to drink alcoholic beverages between the ages of 18 and 21. This issue is taken up in the You Decide box, "Lowering the Drinking Age to 18."

YOU DECIDE: Lowering the Drinking Age to 18

In mid-2008, 130 university presidents caused a stir by releasing a petition they had signed calling for a national debate on whether the drinking age should be lowered from 21 to 18. "Our experience . . . convinces us that 21 is not working. A culture of dangerous, clandestine 'binge-drinking' . . . has developed," the educational leaders wrote.

Many groups such as Mothers Against Drunk Driving voiced strong opposition. First, they argue that since the national 21-year-old limit was instituted in 1984, traffic fatalities among drivers ages 18 to 20 have fallen 13%. Second, opponents of changing the drinking age note studies that show drinking adversely affects the health of young adults even more than it harms older adults. A third common argument against is that lowering the drinking age will make alcohol even more available to the next lower age group, the mid-teens, than it already is.

Groups such as Choose Responsibly and the National Youth Rights Association (NYRA) that favor change dispute some of the data. "Not all the evidence is on one side of the question," says John

M. McCardell Jr., former president of Middlebury College and founder of Choose Responsibility. Advocates of lowering the drinking age point out, for instance, that automobile fatalities are down across the board since the mid-1980s and the decrease might have any number of causes. Furthermore proponents argue that lowering the drinking age is about ending age discrimination, in this case against young adults. As the NYRA puts it, the issue is not "primarily about alcohol; rather it is an issue about equality, honesty, respect, discrimination and freedom."[6]

Congress was able to impose a uniform drinking age by threatening to withhold federal highway funds ($42 billion in 2010) from any state that had an alcohol-drinking age lower than 21. Thus any change in the drinking age would have to start in Congress, and that would be an uphill fight in light of strong public opposition. If you were a member of Congress, would you vote to repeal the 1984 law and once again leave the issue solely up to the states?

Life and death decisions, those that involve your very existence, are probably the most important area where the government limits your choices or may even mandate what you must do. One such decision that the government makes is to send its military forces into combat. This is particularly important to young adults because they make up the bulk of the armed forces. Of the American troops who have died in Iraq, three quarters have been under age 30, with 40% age 22 or less. Currently, military service is voluntary, but the government has resorted to the draft in the past and could well do so again in the future. Furthermore, the increasing range of dangerous military roles open to women will make it much harder to justify not drafting them along with men if a draft were to be reinstituted.

Controlling the Government

Given the size, scope, and power of government, it is vital that citizens keep general control over who serves in government and what policy is. This principle of democracy, that ultimate political power resides with the people, is called "the doctrine of **popular sovereignty**." A related principle is that democracy works well only if the citizenry is informed and active. English philosopher John Stuart Mill was correct when he wrote that democracy will fail "if, from indolence" the people "are unequal to the exertions necessary for preserving it."[7] Or in the blunt words of French philosopher Joseph Marie de Maistre, "Every country has the government it deserves."[8]

Americans and Their Democracy

Are Americans equal to the "exertions" that Mill thought necessary? On the positive side, Americans are strongly committed to the idea of democracy. Seventy percent believe that it is "appropriate" for textbooks and teachers in public schools to argue, "Democracy is the best form of government."[9] And 81% of Americans agree that whatever its faults, their country still has "the best system of government in the world."[10]

Yet for all this adulation of their system in theory, most Americans are skeptical about their government in application. Chapter 6 spends considerable time discussing how Americans view their political system and its responsiveness to their wishes, but for now we can say that less than one-third of Americans think they can trust the government to usually "do the right thing," and almost two-thirds believe that "what the people think doesn't count very much anymore."[11]

Whether this lack of trust in the government is justified is a controversial question addressed at several points in this book. What is important here is that the evidence shows that in general the president, members of Congress, and to a lesser degree even the bureaucracy and judges are concerned about public opinion and do react to it. It is also clear, though, that even elected government officials do not consistently respond to the public's will. There are many reasons why this occurs, but some have to do with the public not being politically interested and active enough to have voted and otherwise participated in campaign, to have informed views on policy, and to have conveyed them to policy makers. The extensive data on the public's limited interest, knowledge, and participation are covered in Chapters 6 and 10, but some indication is found the following: A smaller percentage of Americans vote than do people in most other established democracies, and a recent survey that asked Americans 23 questions about top U.S. officials and the news found that the average respondent correctly answered only 52%.[12]

What all this suggests is that who gets elected and the information about public preferences that they receive are likely to better reflect the whole population as the publc's interest in politics and participation pick up. That is where you come in.

Having an Impact on Politics

You can make a political difference if you want to and are willing to try! Moreover it is in your self-interest to do so given the size and power of government and its role in your daily existence. Not all of us can be elected to Congress, get appointed Attorney General, or become a widely respected opinion leader in the news media or blogosphere. There are, however, many smaller but in the aggregate important things that you can do to play a role in the political process. To illustrate that, we shall focus in this section on young adults (ages 18–24).

Getting better informed is a first step. Young adults are less likely than older adults to be interested in political news. For example, 42% of Americans aged 50–65 have a high interest in the news; only 16% of young adults do.[13] Comparative studies further reveal that American young adults tend to know less about politics than their contemporaries in many other countries, as Figure 1.2 illustrates. Being informed should be supplemented by taking action, but knowledge does make a difference. One study across 25 countries found a positive connection between how well informed a country's people are and how well it is governed.[14]

Voting is another influential form of political participation that young adults can and should do more. Historically, a much smaller percentage of young adults than older adults have voted and otherwise participated in politics. During the presidential elections between 1984 and 2008, for example,

FIGURE 1.2 Comparative Knowledge of the World

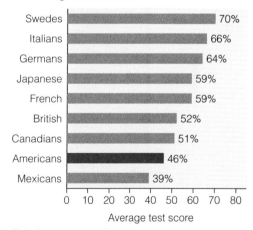

This figure shows the average score on a world affairs and geography test given to people aged 18 to 24 in nine countries. Note that Americans finished next to last, only ahead of Mexicans, who live in a poor country in which only about half of all youths graduate from high school.
Data source: National Geographic–Roper 2002 Global Geographic Literacy Survey, November 2002

FIGURE 1.3 Age Group and Voting Impact

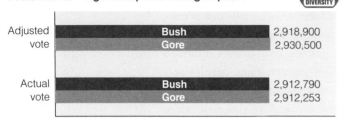

Actual/adjusted Florida vote 2000

Al Gore, not George Bush, would have won Florida's electoral votes and the presidency in 2000 if that state's young adults (ages 18–24), who were mostly pro-Gore, had voted at the same high level as Florida's voters age 65 and up, who mostly favored Bush. *Data source:* Exit polls, Florida Department of State

the average voter turnout among young adults (ages 18–24) was only 39% compared to 56% for the rest of the adult population.

One election when a better turnout of young adults would have made an important difference was that of 2000, when George Bush defeated Al Gore for president by winning Florida by just 537 votes out of more than 5.8 million cast. Polls in that state showed that 15% more young adults favored Gore than supported Bush. Among voters age 65 or more, Bush had a 6% edge. What made the difference in the election was that only 41% of the state's young adults voted, while 71% of its senior citizens did. If the same percentage of young adults as senior citizens had voted in Florida's 2000 election, then Al Gore, not George Bush, would have won the state's electoral vote and become president of the United States. What might have been is depicted in Figure 1.3.

A near record percentage of young adults (52%) turned out in the 2008 election, although they still trailed the turnout among all eligible adults (65%). However, the pro-Obama edge among young adults, 66%, versus 32% for John McCain, was one of the widest margins among all demographic groups and helped propel Obama to his sweeping victory. Moreover in at least two close states, Indiana and North Carolina, it was the under-30 vote that arguably ensured an Obama victory.

Getting more involved in campaigns and party politics is a third way that young adults can increase their impact on government. Brian Lawson, a 20-year-old student at St. Anselm College in Manchester, New Hampshire, set up the New Hampshire Presidential Watch blog. It got about 8,000 unique visitors every day prior to the state's January 2008 primary. David Gilbert-Pederson of Minneapolis began working for candidates in his state when he was 12. By 2008, when he joined Obama's field staff in Minnesota, Iowa, and New Hampshire, he was a veteran campaign worker. When he went to the Democratic National Convention in Denver as an Obama delegate, he was, at age 17, the youngest delegate there. Another route to the convention was as a "super delegate," those entitled to a seat based on their political position in the Democratic Party. The youngest of these delegates was Jason Rae, age 21, of Rice Lake, Wisconsin, who was dividing his time between being a political science student at Marquette University and being co-chairman of the Democratic National Committee's Youth Council.

Serving in office is a fourth of many routes to greater influence, and 2008 provided evidence that young adults can also make a difference this way. Jeremy

Yamaguchi, a 19-year-old political science major at Cal State Fullerton, led all other candidates in winning one of the city council seats in Placentia, California. Elsewhere in the state, 21-year-old Matt Hurst took office as mayor of LaFayette City. Voters in Grafton County, New Hampshire, elected Vanessa Sievers, a 20-year-old student at Dartmouth College, as their county treasurer. In neighboring Maine, Henry Beck, age 22, won a seat in the state House of Representatives, and in Illinois, 27-year-old Aaron Schock overcame the tide of Democratic votes in Barack Obama's home state and won a seat in the U.S. House of Representatives. Shock, a "long-time" politician, had been elected to the Peoria school board at age 19 and to the Illinois General Assembly at 23.

This concludes the book's only sermon. To recap, it has four parts: (1) The government is huge, powerful, and nearly omnipresent; (2) it therefore has important impacts on the lives of each of us; (3) each of us, therefore, has an important stake in controlling the government; and (4) it is possible collectively and individually to have an impact on our political system by being well informed about it and by being politically active.

Aaron Schock symbolizes what is possible for politically active young adults. He won his first election at 19 (to the Peoria, Illinois, school board), joined the state legislature at age 23, and was elected to the U.S. House of Representatives in 2008 at age 28. (Photo courtesy of GPO Access/U.S. Government Printing Office, http://www.gpoaccess.gov/)

NAVIGATING THIS BOOK

Hopefully the preceding call to be politically aware and active has added to your incentive to continue reading this book. To facilitate that, we shall now turn to an overview of the text.

Our first step is to create a mental map of our journey that will help you make sense of how we move from one chapter to the next. Organizationally, the book reflects the author's conceptual model of how the political system works. That model sees the country as an organization that in governing itself produces policy within the context of its settings, inputs, and conversion process, as discussed below.

Settings   The U.S. political system operates within three settings that help shape policy. *The legal setting* is one, and Chapters 2 (the constitution), 3 (the federal structure), 4 (civil liberties), and 5 (civil rights) are all part of that setting. There is also a *societal setting*. This involves political culture: Americans' beliefs about such basic issues as the proper relationship individuals and society. The first part of Chapter 6 addresses this topic. *The international setting* is the third context. Even though the United States is the world's most powerful country, its politics and policy are often influenced by the global realities of military and economic power and by the climate of international opinion. This is increasingly so in the current era of rapid globalization. Commentary on the international setting is dispersed throughout the book. Indeed, globalization is one of this book's themes.

Inputs   The text then takes up inputs into political system. *Supports* are one kind of input every organization needs. For a political system these include such acts as paying attention to politics, forming and voicing political opinions, voting, paying taxes, and serving in government. Because organizations have a purpose, they also operate in response to a second type of input, *demands.* These are pressures on the government to do something or to cease/refrain from doing something. Demands are made by citizens individually and by interest groups collectively by such methods and lobbying, protesting, and filing lawsuits. The second part of Chapter 6 takes up public opinion as a key input. Then other inputs are dealt with in Chapters 7 (interest groups), 8 (the media), 9 (political parties), and 10 (elections).

Conversion Process   Chapters 11 (Congress), 12 (the presidency), 13 (the bureaucracy), and 14 (the courts) detail the organization and operation of the institutions of government. They have the exclusive authority at the federal level to convert the inputs into outputs (policy).

Outputs   Policies are the outputs of the political process. Because of time constraints in a semester and because there are well over a dozen main areas of substantive policy areas, taking them up is beyond the scope of this book. You are encouraged to explore these topics in advanced courses on foreign policy, environmental policy, civil rights and liberties, and other offerings at your college.

The Process in Operation   Having laid out the process in neat order, it is important to add that in operation it is anything but neat. Instead, all three parts of the process are underway simultaneously and interactively. Moreover, putting political actors, such as the president, in one or another of the three steps is also too simple. Yes, presidents react to inputs and convert them into policy, but presidents are also a major input factor. Among other things, presidents bring public attention to issues and convey information and argumentation to the public and other political actors. Additionally, the political process is circular, because outputs or the lack of them influence supports and spark new demands.

Our next step in presenting our overview of this text is to introduce the two themes that appear throughout the text. These are (1) the diverse global setting in which the United States exists and (2) the domestic diversity that characterizes American society and politics.

INTRODUCING A WORLD OF DIFFERENCE

"No man is an island, entire of itself," English clergyman John Donne wrote in *Devotions Upon Emergent Occasions* (1624). Metaphorically much the same can be said about the United States. Even though it is the world's most powerful country, the United States, like every other country, exists in a global setting called "the **international system**." This concept encompasses the political, economic, technological, environmental, and cultural characteristics of the world. The system is important because it influences the international and sometimes even the domestic policies of countries. This has always been so, but in an era of rapid globalization, the impact of the international system on Americans and U.S. policy is growing quickly.

An Overview of Globalization

Globalization refers to the integration of the world's communications, culture, economics, and norms, thereby creating a much more interdependent world.[15] Globalization has existed throughout history, but the pace of change began to speed up considerably about two centuries ago and then went into overdrive beginning in the mid-twentieth century.

Causes of Accelerating Globalization

Modern technology is one cause of the rapid globalization. Our accelerating ability to extract resources, covert them into products, and ship them around the world has helped create a global economy. Transportation advances have expanded this process and have also enabled more people to travel more easily between countries. Modern communications technology has rapidly increased the ability of people to communicate with one another and to gather information globally. The Internet has been key here in recent years. The number of people using the Internet increased from 2.7 million in 1990 to 1.7 billion in 2009.

Government policy is the second cause of accelerating globalization. After two disastrous world wars, many came to believe that peace and prosperity for all countries depended on increased international cooperation and integration. To achieve this in the economic sphere, the United States led a drive to reduce barriers to international trade and investment by negotiating multilateral treaties such as the General Agreement on Tariffs and Trade (1947). Creating supporting **intergovernmental organizations** (IGOs), international organizations in which countries are the members, was also part of this drive. Among these IGOs are the International Monetary Fund (IMF, 1944), the World Bank (1946), and what is now the World Trade Organization (WTO, 1947). One indication of the impact of these moves to promote economic globalization is that world exports skyrocketed, as is evident in Figure 1.4. The belief that integration would promote peace also led the United States to champion the establishment of the United Nations (1945) and other IGOs to enhance international security and more generally to promote global and regional cooperation.

FIGURE 1.4 World Trade Growth

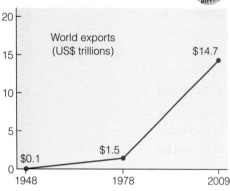

Skyrocketing trade in goods and services is one indication of increasing economic globalization and economic interdependence among countries.
Data source: World Bank

Impacts of Globalization

Economic globalization has led the way in "shrinking" the world and making countries and their people more *interdependent*. For example, countries increasingly rely on exports to employ their workers and otherwise generate domestic economic activity measured by GDP. In 1950, exports accounted for only 6% of the average country's GDP. By 2009, exports had grown to 25% of GDP globally.

Cultural globalization due to increased contacts by people across national borders through trade, travel, and communications is also a growing reality. It is premature to project a common world culture, but differences have narrowed. For example, English is now common among well-educated people globally, and its use is likely to spread rapidly. One indication is a 44-country survey that found a strong majority of people in every region of the world believes that children need to learn English to order to succeed. As part of cultural globalization, norms and other ideas now flow more easily among people and are reshaping their ways of thinking.

Issue globalization entails the idea that a growing number of issues are global in scope and therefore are best addressed through global cooperation. Global warming, for example, has global causes and global impacts. As such, the best way to deal with the problem is through a multilateral treaty reducing emissions of carbon dioxide (CO_2) and other greenhouse gases and having an IGO monitor compliance. Yet the issue is also domestic because each country will have to decide how to cut emissions and how to allocate the cost of doing so. The growing ties between global and national policy have persuaded some observers that it is often best to talk in terms of **intermestic issues**, those with both *inter*national and do*mestic* ramifications.

Political globalization has also increased. The concept of political globalization includes increased global governance, with states deciding policy collectively through IGOs and multinational treaties. Illustrating the spread of this approach, Figure 1.5 compares the number of IGOs in 1945 and in 2006. The number of multilateral treaties has grown even faster, with approximately 6,000 new ones having been concluded since 1945.[16]

Political globalization also includes a blurring of national boundaries in terms of policy making. For example, we shall see in Chapter 6 that global opinion influences the policy of even powerful countries such as the United States. Chapter 7 takes up the impact on

FIGURE 1.5 IGO Growth

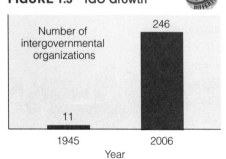

The number of intergovernmental organizations (IGOs) has grown as countries have looked for ways to solve problems collectively.
Data source: Union of International Associations

U.S. policy of a range of interest groups that operate across national boundaries. The key point is that countries are not sealed units when it comes to policy making. Inputs come from abroad as well as from domestic sources.

Globalization and Americans

As the world's leading country militarily, economically, and culturally, the United States is less affected by globalization than most countries. Nevertheless, the impacts of globalization on Americans are profound and growing. To show this we shall quickly survey several aspects of American lives and politics affected by globalization.

Economic Conditions

American prosperity is increasingly intertwined with international economic conditions and policy. Foreign trade and foreign investment provide two illustrations.

Foreign trade can help or harm the U.S. economy. U.S. exports are a plus. They provide jobs to some 18 million Americans, or about 13% of the total U.S. workforce. Imports have a mixed impact on the economy. On the plus side, low-cost imports allow Americans to buy goods for

China's government, corporations, and other investors owned 24% of all foreign-held U.S. Treasury bonds in 2009.

less than a domestic source could supply them. Imports also supply Americans with products they need, such as petroleum. On the negative side, imports can cost jobs. The number of Americans working in clothes manufacturing declined from 927,000 in 1990 to only 186,000 in 2006. Automation caused some of this plunge in employment, but many jobs were also lost to competition from cheaper imports from low-wage countries.

Foreign investment—the global flow of capital (money) to invest in businesses, real estate, and other assets—also has pluses and minuses. One upside is that more than 5 million Americans work for Japan's Honda making cars in Ohio, for China's Haier producing appliances in South Carolina, or for some other foreign company that has invested in U.S. operations. These companies pay Americans more than $300 billion in wages. On the downside, many American companies have closed some or all of their U.S. factories and moved production to other countries to take advantage of lower salaries and looser regulations.

Another foreign investment flow involves foreign investors buying U.S. Treasury bonds. These purchases help the U.S. government finance its budget deficits. The

Globalization has pros and cons. One disadvantage is that foreign imports can cost Americans their jobs as U.S. companies lose business to foreign competition. This reality is what sparked the protest in Granite City, Illinois, seen in this photograph, of some of the 2,000 steelworkers who had been laid off due to the use of imported steel to construct a pipeline. (AP Photo/Belleville News-Democrat/Steve Nagy)

downside is that foreigners collected more than $170 billion in interest in 2009. Given the massive budget deficits needed to fund the economic stimulus measures undertaken by the Obama administration, projections are that the federal debt will double between 2007 and 2014, propelling annual interest payments to foreigners to about $350 billion annually.

Environment

Environmental threats pay no attention to national borders. Annually, the United States suffers extensive damage to native species of flora and fauna and spends hundreds of millions of dollars trying to combat such foreign invaders as the Asian longhorn beetles and kudzu vines. The spewing of chemicals such as chlorofluorocarbons (CFCs) used in refrigerants and other products into the atmosphere has thinned the Earth's ozone layer, which helps shield us from cancer-causing ultraviolet rays. As a result, skin cancers among Americans have increased 250% since 1975. Global warming caused by the worldwide emission of 43 billion tons of carbon dioxide (CO_2) and other greenhouse gases into the atmosphere annually is altering climate conditions everywhere. One impact according to the U.S. Bureau of Land Management is "increasing fire problems because of global warming . . . [and the drought] conditions [that] will exist over the next 10 to 20 years."[17] California, many other parts of the West, and some parts of the South have been particularly hard hit, with billions of dollars in damages due to fires. Figure 1.6 shows the increase in wildfires in the United States.

FIGURE 1.6 **U.S. Wildfires**

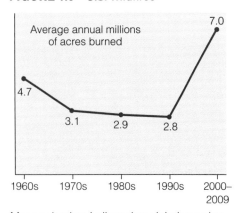

Average annual millions of acres burned

7.0

4.7

3.1

2.9

2.8

1960s 1970s 1980s 1990s 2000–2009

Many scientists believe that global warming has intensified the drought that has gripped parts of the United States, especially California, since the late 1990s and caused an upsurge in damage from wildfires due to the dry conditions.
Data source: National Interagency Fire Center

Health

Globalization is increasing the links between Americans' health and medical conditions in the rest of the world by the accelerating speed with which diseases can spread through modern transportation. It took the Black Plague about a decade to spread from China to Europe in the 1400s, where it killed at least a third of the population. It took only two years (1918–1919) for the Spanish flu to circumnavigate the globe, killing some 50 million people, including 650,000 Americans. The swine flu outbreak of 2009 turned out to be mild, but it spread from Mexico to more than 30 countries in a few weeks. Another global traveler, AIDs, has killed more than 27 million people, including 600,000 Americans, since 1981. Highlighting the threat of global diseases, the Central Intelligence Agency warns, "New and reemerging infectious diseases . . . pose a rising global health threat" and "complicate U.S.

and global security" because they "endanger U.S. citizens at home and abroad, threaten U.S. armed forces deployed overseas, and exacerbate social and political instability in key countries and regions in which the United States has significant interests."[18] Because the epidemics ignore territorial boundaries, global cooperation through such IGOs as the World Health Organization is crucial to combating such diseases.

Peace

Some analysts predict that globalization will be a force for peace. They argue that greater economic interdependence will make countries less willing or able to fight, that a growing common culture will make others seem more like us and less threatening, and that a sense of common problems needing global solutions will expand the willingness of countries to cooperate for the common good through IGOs.

There is some evidence to support this view, but there are also aspects of globalization that imperil peace.[19] *The global arms trade* ($58 billion in 2009) is one. *The proliferation of nuclear weapons and the long-range missiles* is a second threat. Nine countries now possess nuclear weapons and the ability to deliver them by missile. *Global terrorism* is a third threat. When a poll asked Americans to name their top foreign policy concerns in 1999, only 12% mentioned terrorism. Four years and 9/11 later, 75% of Americans saw terrorism as a critical threat.[20]

The global competition for natural resources is a fourth threat to peace, and we can focus on it to illustrate how globalization can endanger peace. Petroleum supplies and the Middle East are, of course, at center stage. The conflict with Iraq in the Persian Gulf War (1990–1991) was a testament to U.S. resolve not to let Iraq or any other power dominate the Middle East and its supply of "black gold." "The economic lifeline of the industrial world runs from the Gulf . . . [and] we cannot permit a dictator . . . to sit astride that economic lifeline," Secretary of State James A. Baker explained candidly.[21] The Middle East's oil also helped set the stage for the Iraq War, which since 2003 has cost Americans more than $700 billion and more than 4,000 U.S. troops killed. According to then Federal Reserve Board Chairman Alan Greenspan, "Whatever their publicized angst over Saddam Hussein's 'weapons of mass destruction,' American . . . authorities were also concerned about violence in an area that harbors a resource indispensable for the functioning of the world economy."[22] Similarly, Washington would probably be less alarmed about Iran's alleged nuclear weapons program if it were not also located in the oil-rich region. Notes former Secretary of State Henry A. Kissinger, "Iran simply cannot be permitted to fulfill a dream of imperial rule in a region of such importance to the rest of the world."[23]

FIGURE 1.7 U.S. Treaties and International Agreements

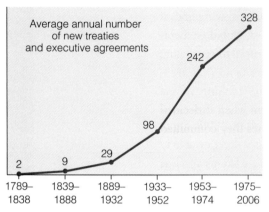

U.S. global interactions were once limited and required few international agreements, but the era of globalization since the 1940s has vastly increased the number and importance of these interactions, including agreements.

Data sources: Harold W. Stanley and Richard G. Niemi, *Vital Statistics on American Politics 2004–2005* (Washington, CQ Press, 2005); and Office of the Legal Adviser, Department of State for 2006.

Policy Making

Globalization is affecting U.S. policy and policy making in a variety of ways. These include the increasing importance of international governance, diplomatic interdependence, global norms, and direct international participation in the U.S. political process.

Global governance is playing a growing rule in American policy. The United States is a member of more IGOs than any other country and is party to more than 10,000 treaties. In addition, presidents make legally binding "executive agreements" with other countries. Figure 1.7 shows how quickly these law-making treaties and agreements have grown in number along with globalization.

These agreements and IGO memberships all restrict U.S. foreign policy, and many also impact U.S. intermestic and domestic policy. When the government moved in early 2009 to stimulate the economy and alleviate the economic crisis, some members of Congress proposed a ban on using funds in the stimulus package to purchase goods or services from outside the United States. These proposals were met by strong objections from the European Union, Canada, and other U.S. trading partners. They argued that favoring domestic suppliers violated the global world trade treaty overseen by the World Trade Organization. Some countries also hinted that they would retaliate with restrictions of their own on U.S. exports if Congress enacted the legislation. In the end, President Barack Obama and Congress gave way. "I don't want provisions that are going to be a violation of World Trade Organization agreements or in other ways signal protectionism," Obama explained to a reporter, adding that such a signal would be "a potential source of trade wars that we can't afford."[24]

Diplomatic interdependence also has an increasing impact on U.S. policy. As issue globalization and political globalization have expanded, even the powerful United States has found itself more and more dependent on the cooperation of other countries to achieve its goals. There are Americans, for example, who argue that the United States should use sanctions and other tools to pressure China to improve its poor human rights record or its unfair international trade practices. However, diplomatic interdependence limits how strong a stand Washington can take on any one issue. As noted, China has been a key source of foreign funding to finance the deficit spending needed by the Obama administration to pay for the more than $1 trillion economic stimulus package it put together in 2009.

China's help would be put at risk by cracking down too hard on either human rights or trade.

Global norms also help shape policy. One way this occurs is when global ideas influence American public opinion and eventually lead to changes in policy and law. Chapter 5, for example, traces the reciprocal links between the U.S. civil rights movement and attitudes about race and colonialism in other parts of the world. Changing world attitudes can even influence judicial thinking. In one example, the Supreme Court cited international public opinion when it decided in 2005 that it was unconstitutional to execute people for crimes they committed as a minor.

Direct international participation in the U.S. political process is also increasing because of globalization. As globalization advances, more and more countries, foreign companies, and other international actors have an important stake in U.S. policy. Reflecting this, more than 800 foreign entities such as Afghanistan's government, the Palestine Liberation Organization, Volkswagen, and the Dali Lama are registered to lobby the U.S. government.

Comparing Political Systems and Societies

Understanding the nature and impact of globalization is not the only way that Americans can profit from looking beyond their borders. Another worthwhile effort is to explore how other countries structure their government and pursue their politics. Even for the majority of Americans who believe, as we have noted, that they have the best system of government in the world, it is still possible to learn something from other political systems to correct whatever faults do exist and to improve international relations. With this goal in mind, this text regularly compares American institutions and processes with those of other countries.

We shall also compare other important political factors such as socioeconomic status across borders. There are, for one, thought-provoking parallels between the status of women and minorities in the United States and their circumstances globally. Poverty is one connection. Women are a majority of the poor in both the United States (57%) and

The average per capita gross national income in 2008 was $39,688 for high-income countries and $523 for low-income countries.

the world (70%, according to UN estimates.) Poverty is also related to race, with most predominantly European-heritage (Eurowhite) countries relatively wealthy and most countries populated primarily by people of color (non-Eurowhites) relatively poor. The World Bank classifies countries in four categories, ranging from high income, through upper-middle and lower-middle income, to low income. Of the 41 high-income countries, 76% have largely white populations. By contrast, only one (2%) of the 58 low-income countries, Moldova, is predominantly white.

INTRODUCING A DIVERSE AMERICAN PEOPLE

"We the people," as the Constitution begins, form the foundation of the U.S. political system. American political culture shapes both the structure and process of government. Therefore, an appropriate early focal point of any introductory study of American politics is the American people. We shall begin with an overall profile, then turn to our focus on Americans' diversity.

Profile of a People

More than 300 million people call the United States home. The U.S. Census Bureau's decennial census and its interim studies provide an ongoing demographic picture of the American people. Among the findings of the census:

- Of U.S. residents, 88% are native-born citizens, 5% are naturalized citizens, 4% are legal residents awaiting citizenship, and 3% are unauthorized immigrants.
- The annual U.S. population growth rate (0.94% in 2009) is well below the world average (1.17%), but higher than Western Europe (0.48%) and most other wealthy countries.
- Regionally, the South and West have a growing share of the population; the Northeast and Midwest have a declining share.
- Americans are more educated than ever. Among adults age 25 and older, 8% were college graduates in 1960; 19% had college degrees in 2006.
- Americans have become decidedly urban, with 77% living in metropolitan areas.
- Overall prosperity has increased, with Americans' per capita personal income increasing 35% in constant dollars (controlled for inflation) between 1990 and 2008.
- There is considerable economic disparity in the country, with the poorest 20% of Americans receiving 5% of the national income and the wealthiest 20% getting 59%.
- A big majority (80%) of American workers have jobs in the **services sector** doing intangible things for others, 18% are in manufacturing or construction, and 2% provide raw materials.
- Americans are getting older. The share of the population age 65 or older rose from 11.3% to 12.5% between 1980 and 2000, and is projected to reach 20.7% in 2050.
- Most Americans (50.7%) are females.
- The population is racially diverse. In 2006 it was: 65% white, 14% Latino, 13% black, 5% Asian American, 1% Native American, and 2% those identifying with multiple races or another not recognized by the census.

Focusing on American Diversity

The information in the last two bulleted items points out that slightly more than half the population is female and more than a third is minority group members. Those figures bring us to the second of this text's two themes: American diversity. A recent review of the portrayal of African Americans in introductions to American politics texts comments that a "significant percentage of the textbooks . . . treat the African American political experience as separate from mainstream American politics."[25] Much the same can be said about the treatment of other minority groups and of women. This text takes a different approach, viewing these groups as an ongoing and increasingly important element of the American political process. As a preview to the discussion of diversity throughout this text, here we shall briefly introduce the American nation's diverse racial and gender groups, look at the changing racial composition of the nation, and finally note the degree to which both women and racial minorities are becoming more active and influential in politics. We shall also see that groups can be divided by sex and race into two categories: **advantaged groups**, including men and whites, that have had and continue to have a disproportionately large share of political power, wealth, and other societal assets, and **disadvantaged groups**, including women and people of color, who have had and continue to have a disproportionately small share of these assets.

The Groups

It is common to identify someone as black, white, or of some other demographic group, and most of us have a general sense of what those terms mean. But these generalizations can obscure important complexities.

African Americans/Blacks   Most members of this group trace their roots to Africa through ancestors who were slaves in the United States. Increasingly, though, blacks also include two other groups. One traces its heritage to Africa through Haiti and other Caribbean islands, where its ancestors were slaves. The other group consists of blacks who (or whose family) immigrated freely to the United States from Africa, mostly in recent decades. As for the designations black and African American, 35% of the group prefers "black," 48% favor "African American," and 17% have no preference.[26] Following common usage, African American does not apply to people, such as Egyptian Americans, whose heritage is in North Africa.

Asian Americans   This group is largely made up of people who are ethnically linked to China, the Philippines, Japan, Korea, Vietnam, and the other countries of eastern Asia. About 20% of Asian Americans are linked to India, Pakistan, and elsewhere in western Asia. Some studies classify Arab Americans and others from the Near East including Iran, as Asian Americans, but most Americans tied to this region classify themselves as white or "other."

Hispanics/Latinos   These terms group together people of diverse cultural backgrounds. Mexican Americans are by far the largest group within the Hispanic community, as is evident in Figure 1.8, but national origins are varied. A majority (53%) of this group is equally comfortable with either term, 34% favor "Hispanic," and 13% prefer "Latino."[27] A final issue about terminology related to Hispanics is whether to refer to them as a racial or an ethnic group. Neither is fully correct. Latinos, whose origins range from Argentina to Cuba, have too many cultural differences to make ethnicity an accurate term. Race is not precise either because the racial heritage of Latinos is varied. Still, designating Latinos as a racial group is the choice here because the common American usage of the term racism includes discrimination against Latinos and because a majority see themselves as a separate racial group. When asked by one survey to identify themselves by race, a plurality chose either Latino/Hispanic (46%) or "some other race" (20%). Only a minority identified with another race, with 30% opting for white, 3% saying black, and 1% identifying as Asian.[28] Finally, note that data kept by U.S. agencies on the "U.S. population" does not include the approximately 4 million Puerto Ricans living on their home island or the largely Native American and Asian American populations in the U.S. Pacific Ocean territories. Data in this book necessarily follows that scheme.

FIGURE 1.8   **Latino Heritage**

Composition of the Latino Population

Latinos have a diverse ethnic background.
Data source: Sung-Chang Chun, "The 'Other Hispanics'— What Are Their National Origins? Estimating the Latino-Origin Populations in the United States," *Hispanic Journal of Behavioral Sciences,* 29/2 (2007): 133–155.

Native Americans   This group includes those descended from any of the indigenous people who, prior to the arrival of the Europeans, were living in the territories that became the United States. Thus the term "Native American," according to the Native American Rights Fund site, encompasses "all native people of the United States and its territories," including American Indians, the Inuits (termed "Eskimos" by the Census Bureau) and Aleuts of Alaska, and Native Hawaiians and other indigenous Pacific Islanders.

Whites   This book uses the term "white" to refer to those the Census Bureau calls "Non-Hispanic Whites." Almost all of these people trace their heritage to Europe—either directly or indirectly through largely European-heritage countries such as Australia, Canada, and New Zealand. The related term "Eurowhite" designates this group globally.

Mixed Race Identifiers About 2% of Americans identify themselves as having a multiracial heritage. These individuals tend to have political orientations that parallel the minority part of their heritage.[29]

Sex/Gender/Sexual Orientation Sex is perhaps the most obvious classification, but the identities of gay, bisexual, and transgender people mean that dividing people into males and females is less than precise. The terms "sex" and "gender" are used interchangeably herein, although gender can sometimes denote sexual orientation and role rather than physical traits. Heterosexual and homosexual are also used. Estimates of the bi, gay, and transgender population vary from 1% to 10%, but there are no definitive statistics. A recent clue was the 2008 presidential election exit polls, which found 4% of voters identifying themselves as gay.

Changing Demographics of the Population

The most important demographic change currently underway in the United States is that the share of the population made up by **racial minority groups** is increasing. This trend is projected to continue, as Figure 1.9 shows. The share of the population made up of women is projected to remain steady between 2000 and 2050 at 51%. However, because women live longer than men, voting age women are projected to be 51.5% of the adult population in 2050.

Diversity and Political Disparity

One thing that connects racial minority groups and women in the United States is that both are politically disadvantaged groups that exercise much less influence than warranted by their proportionate share of the population. By contrast, politically advantaged groups such as whites and males have political clout well beyond their share of the population. This text takes up political disparity in numerous places, but for now we can illustrate the gaps with the following:

- Historically, no minority or woman served as president or vice president until 2009.
- No women served in the U.S. Cabinet until 1933, no minority member until 1966.
- Of 112 U.S. Supreme Court justices, only 4 have been women and 3 minorities.
- Although about 35% of all Americans are members of a minority group, they are only 16% of the 112th Congress (2011–2012).

FIGURE 1.9 Recent and Projected Population Changes

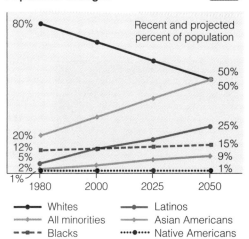

The demographic composition of the U.S. population is projected to change dramatically between 1980 and 2050.
Data source: U.S. Bureau of the Census

FIGURE 1.10 Increased Diversity in the House of Representatives

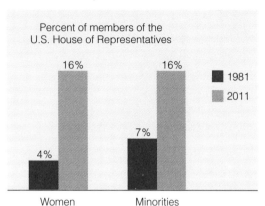

Percent of members of the
U.S. House of Representatives

1981
2011

Women   Minorities

The percentage of seats in the U.S. House of Representatives held by women and by minority representatives increased significantly between 1981 and 2009.

Data source: Clerk, U.S. House of Representatives

As the United States has become more diverse racially and as minority groups have become more active politically, the impact of minority groups on politics has grown. This change is clear in this image of Barack Obama, the first African American president, campaigning in 2008 at the League of United Latino American Citizens in Washington, D.C. (AP Photo/Jae C. Hong)

- Women are about 51% of the population but only 16% of the 112th Congress.
- Of the federal government's top career officials, members of the Senior Executive Service, just 14% are minority group members and only 25% are women.
- Of state governors, only 8% are minorities and 16% are women.
- Minorities make up just 12% of all the state legislators; 12% of state legislators are women.

Although these statistics are troubling, it is also important to note there are positive trends. Historically people of color and women voted less frequently than whites and men, respectively, but the gaps for minorities have closed, and women now vote more than men do. Similarly, minorities and women hold an increasing percentage of the country's political offices, and they are beginning to share political power more fully with men and with whites. Barack Obama's inauguration in 2009 as the first African American president was a huge step forward, and this positive trend is also evident in the U.S. House of Representatives, as Figure 1.10 shows.

What do these changes in political power portend for the future? There certainly will be change. Government is apt to become more proactive in trying to promote equality because women and people of color agree that considerable inequalities remain based on sex and race and that it is the proper role of government to ease and eliminate them. The United States may also be more cautious about using military force abroad. Women have historically been less willing to do so than men. Among other instances, women were less supportive than men of going to war against Iraq in both 1991 and 2003.[30] A similar pattern exists for whites and minorities. Blacks, for example, were less likely than whites to support either war with Iraq. There is less evidence about Latinos' attitudes on war, but they were 20% less likely than whites to support the invasion of Iraq in 2003.[31]

It is important to note, though, that the changes that will occur, while important, will not mean radical change. Instead, the shifts will be evolutionary rather than revolutionary because of numerous limiting factors. First, there is a high degree of consensus shared among all demographic groups on most core political values such as the rights of individuals and nationalism. Second, the opinions of women and minority groups are neither monolithic nor do they consistently differ with those of males and whites. There are issues on which women, blacks, Latinos, and other disadvantaged groups differ among themselves, with some agreeing with the advantaged groups (men, whites) and others disagreeing. Moreover, there are many factors, such as age, education, and income, that also influence opinion, often regardless of sex or race.

Diversity and Socioeconomic Disparity

Disparity among the races and between the sexes also exists in the socioeconomic realm. Whites and males have generally enjoyed a privileged place in society, while people of color and women have often suffered discrimination and relative deprivation.

Other parts of this text, especially Chapter 5, take up the history and current state of socioeconomic disparity. Therefore it will serve to simply note here the following data:

- The median income of full-time workers who are whites is about 60% higher than for either Latinos or blacks.
- The median income of full-time workers who are males is 29% higher than for women.
- Women and minorities are overrepresented among the ranks of the poor and underrepresented among the wealthy.
- The health of minorities is worse by many standards than that of whites, partly because of disparities in health insurance coverage. Only 15% of whites had no government or private medical insurance coverage in 2006 compared to 21% of blacks and 33% of Hispanics.

Fortunately, progress has been made to narrow and in some cases to close some socioeconomic gaps. For example, women are now a majority of those receiving college degrees, there is no longer a significant gap in male and female unemployment, and the income gap between men and women has been slowly closing. Many gaps between minorities and whites have also narrowed. In 1960, for example, whites over age 25 were 2.6 times more likely than blacks to have a college degree. Now the gap is 1.5 times. Income gaps have also narrowed, with, for instance, the white–black gap declining from 1.9:1 in 1990 to 1.4:1 in 2006. Latinos and other minority groups have also made educational and economic progress. Women and minorities have also advanced professionally. Since 1980, for example, the share of women lawyers is up from 8% to 32%, and the share of minority lawyers has increased from 4% to 12%. Health statistics also show progress. In 1970, the longevity gap between whites and blacks was 7.6 years; in 2005 it was 5.0 years.

Such advances should not be interpreted to mean that socioeconomic equality will soon arrive. In some cases,

The death rate for African American babies (1.4%) remains more than twice that of American white babies (0.6%) and is comparable to the infant mortality rate in poor countries such as Mexico (1.5%) and Sri Lanka (1.2%).

little or no progress has been made at all in erasing the racial and gender have and have-not gaps. Neither the male–female poverty gap nor the black–white unemployment gap has narrowed in decades, for instance. In other cases, progress is glacial. At the rate that the male–female income gap has been closing, for example, it will be almost a century and a half until it no longer exists.

SUMMARY

This chapter has two goals. One is to explain why you should read this book. The other is acquainting you with this text. Because this book is probably a course assignment, the obvious reason to read it is that doing so will improve your grade. An arguably more important reason to read this book is that it has two basic messages. First, government (federal, state, local) in the United States is an immense and powerful interconnected array of organizations whose extensive scope of activities touches on all aspects of American society. Each day you are impacted by a large number of government policies and regulations. Detailing the size of government, its vast power, and its multitudinous impacts on all Americans is a core undertaking of this chapter.

The second message is that all Americans should be part of controlling their government. Governments exist to benefit the people, but they do not do so naturally. Instead, every citizen needs to work to make sure the government's methods and policies are acceptable. At the very least, helping exercise control includes learning how the government works and staying up on current events. It is even better to be active in politics through a wide range of activities such as expressing your opinions, voting, working in an election campaign or to promote some issue, and running for office.

This chapter also discusses the text's organization in order to meet its second goal of familiarizing you with the rest of the book. Its organization is based on the idea that governance occurs within a political system. It is structured by rules and other boundaries that are taken up in Chapters 2 through 6 dealing with the Constitution, federalism, civil liberties, civil rights, and political culture. Within the system, there are also supports of it and demands on it, collectively called "inputs." These include public opinion, interest groups, the media, parties, and elections, and are taken up partly in Chapter 6 then in Chapters 7 through 10. These inputs are converted into policy, or outputs, by the government. This conversion process is examined in Chapters 11 through 14 on Congress, the presidency, the bureaucracy, and the courts. The outputs impact the demands and support in the system, thereby stimulating a new round in the circular system. This makes the process sound orderly, but in reality it is messy with all the various elements of the process continually in play and some political actors playing roles in more than one part of the process.

Another key focus of this text's organization is its two themes. One is the nation's diversity, with a particular focus on race and gender. Women and minorities have been underrepresented politically throughout U.S. history and remain so. However, change is underway, and the growth in the political power of women and minorities is a key trend in American politics.

The second theme is the global context in which American politics occurs. Increasingly rapid globalization is one part of that context. The world is becoming interconnected and interdependent economically, culturally, and in other ways at a quickening pace. This means that U.S. politics and world politics are increasingly intertwined. The global context also includes a comparative aspect. It focuses on contrasting and evaluating various aspects of the political system, such as having a federal system with power divided between the national and state governments, as the United States does, versus having a unified system with virtually all power resting with the national government, as most other countries do. Unless you assume the U.S. system is perfect, there may be valuable lessons to learn from seeing how other nations organize and conduct themselves politically.

CHAPTER 1 GLOSSARY

advantaged groups Those demographic groups that persistently exercise much greater political influence than is warranted by their proportionate share of the population and/or that have a disproportionately large share of the society's wealth and other assets. Whites and males are among the politically and socioeconomically advantaged groups in the United States.

disadvantaged groups Those demographic groups that persistently exercise a much smaller degree of political influence than is warranted by their proportionate share of the population and/or that have a disproportionately small share of the society's wealth and other assets. African Americans, Asian Americans, Latinos, Native Americans, and women are among the politically disadvantaged groups in the United States.

globalization A process by which the world's communications, culture, economics, and norms are becoming integrated and, to a degree, homogenized.

government Structures and processes established to make binding decisions regarding the conduct of the common business and service provisions of a society organized as a political unit, such as a country, state, or town.

gross domestic product (GDP) A measure of a country's economic activity that includes all revenue generated within a country by both that country's citizens and organizations (such as businesses) and by foreign individuals and organizations operating within the country. GDP does not include revenue generated by the country's citizens and organizations while operating in other countries.

intermestic issues Those issues with both *inter*national and do*mestic* ramifications.

international system The world's political, economic, technological, environmental, and cultural structure.

intergovernmental organizations (IGOs) International organizations whose membership consists of countries. Domestic governments can also have intergovernmental organization, such as state–federal task forces, and thus the global and regional varieties are often preceded by "international," as in "International IGO."

popular sovereignty A political doctrine that holds that ultimate political authority resides with the citizens of a country. According to this doctrine, citizens grant a certain amount of authority to the government, but do not surrender ownership of that authority, and thus retain the right to revoke it.

racial minority groups This text uses the common understanding of these groups in the United States, including African Americans/(blacks), Asian Americans, Latinos/Hispanics, and Native Americans (including American Indians, Native Alaskans, and Native Pacific Islanders).

services sector The part of the economy that includes sales, education, government administration, public safety, and other functions that provides support to people and does not produce anything tangibly material as the manufacturing and agriculture sectors do.

SETTINGS FOR A DIVERSE AND GLOBAL GOVERNMENT

PART ONE

THE CONSTITUTION

2

YOU DECIDE: What Would the Founding Fathers Think of America Today?

One has to wonder what George Washington, Thomas Jefferson, and the other luminaries dubbed the "founding fathers" who led Americans to independence and shaped their new government would think about the United States today. One thing that would certainly amaze them is the important political roles being played by people of color. After all, more than 90% of American blacks were slaves in 1790, and American Indians were not considered citizens or even counted in the official census. Imagine then the surprise of President Washington, himself a slaveholder, to find Barack Obama in the White House. Equally astounding to the men of the 1790s would be the political roles women now play. Jefferson surely spoke for his sex when he commented, "The appointment of a woman to office is an innovation for which the public is not prepared, nor I."[1] This is not to say that the founders would be necessarily dismayed to find Obama among the successors of the first president, Washington, or Hillary Clinton among those who have followed Jefferson, the first secretary of state. For example, Washington did say, "Among my first wishes [is] to see some plan adopted, by which slavery in this country may be abolished."[2] Furthermore, he put his wish into action when he provided in his will that his more than 100 slaves were to be freed after his wife Martha died.

Also fascinating to learn would be whether the country's founders were impressed or appalled by the way Americans have shaped their political system. One can only wonder what their reactions would be when they learned that the federal government now spends more money every 90 seconds than it spent an entire year when Washington was president, or that the United States is the world's reigning superpower despite Washington's caution to have "as little political connection as possible" with other countries.[3] Would those who fashioned the Constitution in 1787 be delighted or horrified by the federal government's substantial role supporting and regulating health care, welfare, education, the environment, and a variety of other subjects that were either the domain of state and local government or outside the government sphere altogether in 1790? Then there are the current interpretations of the Bill of Rights. For instance, would those who wrote and ratified the Constitution's first ten amendments applaud or be aghast to discover that the First Amendment now protects pornography but prohibits prayer in schools?

When one survey asked modern Americans what they supposed the early leaders would think of what has transpired, 76% answered that the founders would not be pleased. Only 16% thought Washington and the others would approve, 6% said that they would have mixed feelings, and 2% were unsure.[4] What do you think the leaders of the late 1700s would have to say about the United States in the early twenty-first century?

INTRODUCTION

This chapter takes up the Constitution as a key element in the **legal setting** in which the U.S. political system operates. Chapter 3 on federalism extends the discussion of how the U.S. political system is organized legally, and Chapters 4 and 5 take up two other central parts of the legal setting: civil liberties and civil rights. To begin our exploration of the legal setting, this chapter will make the following points:

★ American economic interests, growing nationalism, and an urge for democratic self-governance sparked the American Revolution. These motives also helped shape the Articles of Confederation, the first U.S. constitution.
★ The first American government, organized under the Articles of Confederation, was a failure.
★ Several motives, including economic self-interest, nationalism, and a desire to preserve liberty led the American upper class to favor creating a stronger central government under the second and current constitution.
★ The delegates to the Constitutional Convention of 1787 had to reach many compromises during the drafting of the new constitution.
★ However, the delegates generally agreed on the need to restrain both government and the direct role of the people in the conduct of government.
★ The attitudes, events, and documents that made up the evolution of the American political system between 1763 and 1789 continue to influence our current system of governance.

Additionally, as every chapter does, this one will pay particular attention to how our two themes, a world of difference and American diversity, intertwine with the history, structure, and conduct of the American political system.

Globalization and the Origins of the United States

The origins of the United States are tied to globalization. This historic process had begun to increase its pace by the 1400s. During that century, the search for trade routes to the east led Europeans south along the African coast, then eventually around the Cape of Good Hope and across the Indian Ocean to Asia. Other adventurers, including Christopher Columbus, sailed west and "discovered" the Americas. Thus, the arrival of Europeans in the Western Hemisphere was tied to globalization. Soon thereafter, an expedition led by Ferdinand Magellan circumnavigated the globe (1519–1522), presaging the advent of global trade, travel, and communications.

The search for trading rights, resources, and other advantages set off a quest for colonies among the European powers that included settlements in the future

United States. The linking of the world also saw several European countries, first Spain and later France and Great Britain, become the world's first truly global powers, with colonies, military forces, and interests around the world. Colonial and economic globalization also quickly led to clashes among the imperial powers.

The colonial rivalries intensified in the 1700s when the rise of industrialization in Europe made the struggle for colonies with their raw materials and markets even more important to the status and wealth of the home countries. Indeed, the colonial struggle during the 1700s between the British and French in North America and elsewhere played a key role in the later desire of Americans to break away from Great Britain and their success in doing so. One phase of the global struggle between Paris and London was waged in North America during four wars: King William's War (1689–1697), Queen Anne's War (1701–1713), King George's War (1740–1748), and the decisive French and Indian War (1754–1763). It was a contest over who would dominate North America: the French who held Canada and the Mississippi and Ohio river valleys in the mid-continent, or the British who were centered in their 13 colonies along the eastern seaboard.

A major cause of the onset of the French and Indian War was the desire of the American colonists to expand into French territory. When the French moved to push encroaching British colonials out of the Ohio River Valley, the colonial government in Virginia responded in 1754 by dispatching a small force commanded

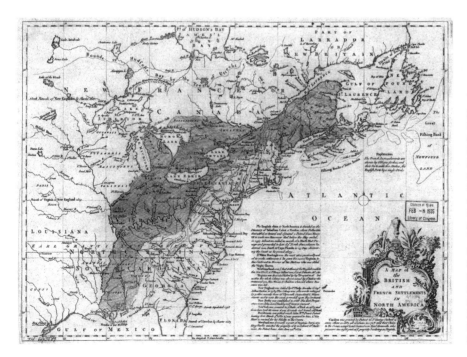

This map of territorial divisions prior to 1763 shows that the British colonies in North America (light shading along the coast) were hemmed in by France's territory (dark shading). The global rivalry between the British and French, extending from North America to India, led to the French and Indian War (1754–1763). The British acquisition of all of Canada to the north and, even more, most of the French land to the west in 1763 was an important factor in prompting the Americans to declare independence 13 years after the war's end. (Library of Congress)

by a 22-year-old militia colonel, George Washington. Even though unsuccessful, the campaign was enough to reignite British–French warfare in North America and to spread it to the European continent, India, and elsewhere. Later in this chapter you will see that this war of globalization led directly to a series of events and attitudes that soon spurred the colonists to declare their independence. The balance of the chapter will also highlight other ways that globalization influenced the formative course of the United States. These impacts ranged from ideas about democracy to military action, including an exploration of the roles of France, Spain, and Holland in supporting American independence.

American Diversity and the Limits of Democracy

When the first census was taken in 1790, the United States and its territories were already diverse demographically. The percentage of the population that was white then (66%) is about that same as it is today. The rest of the population of 4.7 million was split about evenly between blacks and American Indians. Although there is no record of Latinos or Asians in the United States of 1790, there were Spanish-speaking people in nearby Florida and other territories that soon became part of the United States, and Asians of Filipino descent were living near New Orleans as early as 1763.

Racial issues were already important in the politics of the late 1700s, just as they are now. The same globalization that sent Europeans farther and farther in search of trade also caused an increase in slavery. Those native peoples who the Europeans encountered in Africa, Asia, and the Americas were generally less advanced technologically and were easily defeated with European arms. This increased Europeans' sense of racial superiority. In turn, this sense seemingly justified enslaving people of color to meet an economic need: cheap labor to help develop the lands in the Western Hemisphere that the Europeans had seized as colonies. In some regions, the Europeans tried to meet their labor requirements by enslaving the native populations, but so many died from brutality or disease that it soon became necessary to import slaves, mostly blacks from sub-Saharan Africa. Thus, the rise of the Atlantic slave trade can be attributed in substantial part to economic globalization.

Between the 1600s and the mid-1800s, at least 10 million Africans were enslaved and shipped to the Americas. During its colonial period and then as an independent country, the United States received about 5% of this human traffic, or about a half million imported slaves. Natural reproduction expanded this number, and there were almost three quarters of a million blacks in the colonies when they declared their independence. Even at that time, the possession and treatment of slaves troubled a substantial part of the population and stood in particular contrast to the principle that "all men are created equal" in the Declaration of Independence. Nevertheless, as we shall see, the saga of dealing with diversity during early American history was not a proud one. Most blacks remained in chains for almost a century; American Indians were driven from their lands and died in the millions from wounds or diseases inflicted by the oncoming whites; and women, as Abigail Adams protested to her husband John in 1776, were "treat[ed] . . . only as the vassals of your sex."

REVOLUTION AND INDEPENDENCE

Why go back more than 200 years to study American politics? The answer is that how politics works today is related in part to the events, attitudes, and decisions that led to the American Revolution and otherwise shaped the U.S. political system before 1789.

Americans have long struggled with issues related to the diversity of the U.S. population. By the time of this advertisement of slaves for sale in Charleston, South Carolina, in the 1780s, the issue of slavery was already a sensitive national issue. Less than 80 years later, the corrosive slave issue led to civil war. (Library of Congress)

Prelude to Revolution

Fourth of July speeches tell us that the founding fathers who led the Revolution were brave patriots willing to risk their lives and fortunes to secure Americans' freedom from British tyranny. This image contains some truth, but it is only part of the story. More accurately, there were several factors, including the founding fathers' self-interests, that caused the American Revolution. The conflicts between the colonists and the British began to intensify with the end of the French and Indian War. Ironically, Great Britain's victory in that war led to its subsequent loss of its 13 colonies because (1) the cost of the war prompted London to increase taxes and political control over its colonies, thereby angering the colonists, and (2) by eliminating the French threat, the war made the colonists less dependent on the British for protection and, therefore, more willing to resist London's taxes and control. Economics, territorial expansionism, resistance to British rule, and the genesis of American nationalism each played a role during the ensuing 13 years on the road to revolution.

Economics and Revolution

Americans revolted in part because it benefited their economic interests. Until the end of the French and Indian War in 1763, the colonists had a sweet economic deal going with

Partly because of very low taxes, the economy of the 13 American colonies grew faster than that of any European country during the 1750s.

FIGURE 2.1 British Tax Revenues from the Colonies

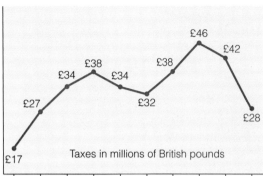

After the end of the French and Indian War in 1763, the British government sharply increased taxes on its 13 colonies. This sparked resentment that helped move the colonies to revolt in 1776. This figure shows the sums collected. The drop-off after 1772 partly represents increased tax evasion by the colonists.

Data source: Census Bureau, Historical Statistics of the United States

the British. For example, London provided defense and paid for much of colonial governance. As a result, Americans on average paid only about a third of the taxes that people in Great Britain paid. These policies helped create a prosperous class of Americans engaged in commerce and plantation agriculture.

The economic advantages Americans were enjoying ended when London sought to offset the high cost of waging the French and Indian War by raising Americans' taxes. The first measure to do so was the American Revenue Act (1764), which imposed new tariffs or increased existing ones on a range of goods that Americans imported. The steep increase in taxes is clear in Figure 2.1. Americans considered the taxes an affront, and retaliated with boycotts of British goods and other actions. As a result, the ensuing decade witnessed persistent economic struggle between London and the colonies. The details are less important than the fact that Americans came to believe that their prosperity was endangered rather than enhanced by their ties to Great Britain. Soon, talk of resistance to British rule began to be heard.

Perhaps the most famous act of disobedience to the British on the economic front came after the Tea Act (1773). In it London bailed out the nearly bankrupt East India Company by giving it a monopoly on supplying tea to the colonies. That was good for the British investors in the company, but it threatened ruin for John Hancock and other colonial merchants involved in the important tea trade. Moreover, the monopoly put the company in the position to sharply raise the price of tea. Colonial reaction was sharp. Among other actions, the **Boston Tea Party** saw protesting colonists dressed as Mohawk Indians board an East India Company ship and dump its cargo of tea into the harbor. This iconic act, soon supplemented with the coiled rattlesnake and accompanying "Don't Tread on Me" warning that first appeared on colonial military drums in 1775, came to symbolize American resistance to intrusive government, a tradition continued currently by the Tea Party movement.

Although British economic policy pinched most Americans, it was the **American gentry** who felt the most pain. This upper class of wealthy landowners, merchants, and others composed perhaps 10% of the population and controlled almost half the wealth. It was they who paid the lion's share of the taxes and who had businesses that were harmed by the taxes. Therefore, it was this group that led the way in fomenting anti-British sentiment and declaring independence. To be sure, many members of the gentry became the leaders of the new United States and were patriots in the best Fourth of July sense. But they were also heavily motivated by their economic self-interests. We shall see these interests once again play a key role when the gentry gathered in Philadelphia in 1787 to write the second U.S. constitution.

Expansionism and Revolution

More than any single immediate factor, the determination of the colonials to expand to the west into French territory had sparked the French and Indian War. With their victory in that war, the British gained control of all of Canada to the colonies' north and France's territory between the Allegheny Mountains to the Mississippi River to the west. Not surprisingly, the land-hungry colonies thought that the new British acquisition to the west would now be open to settlement, and many of the colonies asserted extensive claims in the region. For one, Virginia claimed a western boundary that reached as far as modern day St. Louis.

These territorial ambitions were soon frustrated by the British. They cared nothing for the native peoples living in these lands, but London was worried that a surge of settlers would spark conflict with the Indian tribes, requiring the expensive use of British troops to defend the colonists. To avoid this, London issued the **Proclamation of 1763** closing its newly acquired western territory to further settlement. This move particularly angered those members of the American gentry such as plantation owner George Washington who stood to profit from western land speculation, investment in the fur trade, and other economic activities. In any case, the colonists blatantly ignored the proclamation, thereby furthering tensions with London.

Resistance to British Rule and Revolution

What followed from the mid-1760s on was an escalating series of British attempts to tax and regulate the colonies, colonial resistance to these measures, British countermeasures to quell the colonies' obstreperousness, and even greater resentment in the colonies. Great Britain sent an increasing number of troops to its restive colonies and passed Quartering Acts (1765, 1774) requiring the colonies to provide barracks and supplies for the soldiers. Americans in turn became increasingly confrontational. Fighting had begun by 1770, with armed clashes in several cities between colonists and British troops. Most famously, in March of that year tensions led to the **Boston Massacre**. Although there were only five deaths (all colonists) and even though the soldiers were exonerated of any crime, the killings further inflamed anti-British feelings.

One of the five colonists killed at the Boston Massacre was former slave Crispus Atticus, whose father was black and whose mother was a Natick Indian.

AMERICAN DIVERSITY

Nationalism and Revolution

A growing sense among the colonists that they were not British also promoted separatism. This occurred for two reasons.

Demographic changes were one reason why people felt less British. By the 1760s, most colonists were no longer immigrants from Great Britain or elsewhere. Instead, they had been born in the colonies, and their **political identity**, their sense of who they were politically, focused increasingly on where they lived rather than the "mother country." Moreover, a growing number of those who were immigrants from the British Isles were Scottish, Welsh, and Irish, all people with a history of struggling against English rule.

Conflict with the British government also diminished the colonists' sense of being British. A few Americans had long criticized British rule and came to think of themselves as not British. Prominent among these critics was Sam Adams, an employee in his father's Boston brewery. As early as 1748, Adams began the *Public Advertiser*, a weekly publication with an anti-British theme. In time he became so strident in his opposition to the British that Royal Governor Thomas Hutchinson portrayed him as "the greatest incendiary in the Empire." At first Adams was on the fringe of colonial sentiments, but after 1763 the British taxes and other new measures led an increasing number of colonists to agree with his nationalist views.

Note, however, that this gradual change did not mean that most colonials felt "American." Small farmers, tradesmen, and others who had little reason to travel any great distance or to correspond with people in other colonies were more apt to see themselves as a New Yorker, a Virginian, or a resident of some other colony. By contrast, members of the gentry had the education, money, and often the business need to travel and correspond more widely. The ties they established across the boundaries of the 13 colonies made them more likely to identify politically with the embryonic nation, rather than simply with the colony in which they lived. Here again, then, it was the gentry who were at the forefront of the revolutionary movement.

In sum, there were crosscurrents of political identity in the colonies during the period preceding the Revolution. The sense of being American—or at least not British—helped clear the way for independence. However, the propensity of most people to identify first as a Virginian or citizen of another colony, rather than as an American, led the new country to adopt an initial political system marked by nearly sovereign states and a weak central government.

Revolution

London reacted to the disorders in the colonies with a series of punitive measures called the Coercive Acts (1774). Colonial delegates assembled in September 1774 in Philadelphia as the **First Continental Congress** to consider a unified response.

This was the first time an American legislature had met, and it marks the beginning of what might be called the **first American government**, the national political structure and process that existed from 1774 until the U.S. Constitution went into effect in 1789.

There was no turning back. In April 1775 a force of 700 British troops moved to seize munitions held by the colonials outside Boston. The Redcoats routed a group of seventy militiamen at Lexington, killing eight. Further fighting continued at Concord and elsewhere, and before the day was done, 4,000 colonial militia troops had engaged the retreating British, killing seventy-three of them. The next month the **Second Continental Congress** convened in Philadelphia, voted to create a Continental Army, and asked George Washington to command it. On June 17, British and colonial forces clashed at Breed's Hill and Bunker Hill near Boston. General Washington reached the city's outskirts on July 3, 1775, and took command of the 14,000 colonial troops besieging the British there. The Revolutionary War had begun.

American Diversity and Support of the Revolution

Not everyone living in the colonies supported the break with Great Britain. Indeed, John Adams later estimated that the white population was evenly split with one-third each revolutionaries, loyalists, and apathetic or uncertain. Most historians believe that Adams overestimated the proportion of loyalists, but at least 5,000 of these so-called Tories fought for the British, and about 100,000 fled the United States for Great Britain, Canada, and elsewhere after the war.[5]

Many blacks also found common cause with the British. For them, the Revolution created mixed feelings. Free blacks fought at Lexington and Concord and at Bunker Hill, and eventually at least 5,000 of them served in the Continental Army, even though General George Washington initially barred blacks from service. But a much larger number of blacks sided with the British. Lord Dunmore, the royal governor of Virginia, tried to disrupt the rebelling colonists in 1775 by offering freedom to any slaves owned by rebel masters who would serve the British forces. Because slaves were 46% of the state's population, the possibility of a massive defection was a serious threat, and Virginia's colonial legislature reacted by decreeing that "all Negro or other slaves, conspiring to [join the British] shall suffer death."

Despite such threats, about 30,000 slaves fled to freedom and joined the British cause. Some formed military units led by black officers. The most famous of these was an escaped slave, Titus, who adopted the *nom de guerre* Colonel Tye. He first led the Ethiopian Regiment of Virginia, whose members wore sashes proclaiming "Liberty to Slaves." Then he commanded the Black Brigade, a force of some 800 men fighting in New York and New Jersey, until he was killed in action in 1780.[6]

At the end of the war, the British betrayed some of the blacks who had sought freedom by supporting them. After surrendering at Yorktown, for example, British Lord Cornwallis turned over several hundred black troops in his command to the forces of General Washington and to an eventual return to slavery. In many other areas, the British did honor their pledge, however, and their ships carried some 15,000 blacks to freedom in Nova Scotia, the Bahamas, Jamaica, England, Sierra Leone, and elsewhere.

The American Indians' perspective on the Revolutionary War was also different from that of most white colonists. As noted, one cause of the Revolution was American anger over London's resistance to further colonial settlement of the western lands occupied by the Indians. Hence many Indians fought alongside the British. In fact, the last battles of the Revolutionary War had less to do with gaining American independence than with making the western tertories safe for white settlement. In an effort to protect their lands, a coalition of Wyandot, Shawnee, and other tribes aided by a small number of British loyalists attacked white settlements in the Ohio Valley and defeated a Kentucky militia force led, for one, by Daniel Boone at the Battle of Blue Licks in August 1782. Three months later, Continental Army troops sent to support the Kentuckians attacked and burned five Shawnee villages in a campaign to ensure, as the colonial commander General George Rogers Clark put it, that "everything they [the Shawnee] were possessed of [was] destroyed."[7] Thus the American Revolution's promise of liberty and justice for all did not include the country's native groups any more than it included its blacks.

Globalization and the Revolutionary War

Global forces helped determine the success of the Americans' campaign for independence, just as globalization had earlier played a role in Europeans first arriving in the Americas and later causing them to wage the global colonial conflicts, including the French and Indian War, that set the stage for the American Revolution.

Still smarting from their defeat in 1763, the French saw the American Revolution as a way to even the score. Writing to King Louis XVI in 1776, France's foreign minister advised aiding the Americans because their success would "diminish the power of England and increase in proportion that of France" and might even make it possible to recover "the possessions which the English have taken from us in America."[8] The king agreed, and France and its ally Spain each began to send secret military aid to the Americans. By war's end, the French had contributed more than $19 million (about $450 million in current dollars) to the American cause, and Spain had added several million more. Later, encouraged by the decisive American victory at the Battle of Saratoga in 1777, France openly sided with the Americans by signing a formal alliance. Spain soon joined the war formally

(1779), as did Holland informally the following year to protect its trade with the colonies. Dutch bankers then loaned the Americans almost $4 million.

Even more importantly than the flow of money, the alliance with France brought French troops to the United States to fight alongside General Washington's army. The decisive battle occurred in 1781 when 9,000 Americans led by Washington and 7,800 French troops commanded by the Count of Rochambeau trapped Lord Cornwallis and 7,500 British soldiers on a peninsula near Yorktown, Virginia. Even then, Cornwallis might have escaped had it not been for the arrival of a fleet of French warships and their victory over a British squadron trying to evacuate the trapped British army. When news of Cornwallis' surrender reached London, the prime minister resigned. His successor opened peace negotiations with the Americans.

This 1780 drawing depicts the Count de Rochambeau reviewing his troops as commander of the forces that France sent in 1780 to support the American Revolution. These troops played a key role in General George Washington's decisive victory over the British at Yorktown in 1781 that secured American independence. French willingness to aid the Americans financially and militarily was prompted by its global rivalry with the British rather than by any regard for the Americans. (Library of Congress)

Would there have been an independent United States without the aid of France and other European powers? Perhaps, but the Americans would have been lucky indeed to have survived unassisted. That assistance did not originate out of regard for the Americans. Rather it was forthcoming mostly because the French, Spanish, and Dutch all had a stake in weakening the British on the globalizing world stage.

The First American Government

At the onset of hostilities in 1775, the Continental Congress and Washington's army were the only two tangible elements of a country that was just beginning to form. The next step came on July 4, 1776, when the Continental Congress adopted the Declaration of Independence. Yet another step toward transforming thirteen colonies into a confederation of thirteen states involved creating a constitution and a government. To that end, the Continental Congress drafted the **Articles of Confederation** and in 1777 sent it to the states for ratification. In 1781, when Maryland became the thirteenth state to ratify the Articles, the Continental Congress declared them to be in force, and the first American government was fully established.

The Articles of Confederation

Under the Articles from 1781 to 1789, the states were "united" in name only. Reflecting concerns about exchanging oppression by London for domination

Who was the first U.S. president? Arguably, it was Samuel Huntington of Connecticut pictured here. He was president of "The United States in Congress Assembled" when the Articles of Confederation went into effect on March 1, 1781. The government under the Articles was weak, and Huntington and the other 14 presidents of Congress were not major figures because there was no president as we know the office today. A second contender for the title of first president is John Hancock, president of the Continental Congress on July 4, 1776. (Library of Congress)

by the newly formed national government in Philadelphia, the Articles declared that "each state retains its . . . independence" and created a decentralized form of government known as a **confederation**. In this arrangement, the states held every power that was not expressly delegated to the central government. Because the Articles gave the **Confederation Congress** very few powers and confined them mostly to foreign policy, almost all political power remained with the states.

However justified their motives might have been, the authors of the Articles of Confederation had created a central government unable to function effectively. The problems included:

- The Congress could not tax. The central government relied on voluntary contributions by the states to pay for its activities.
- Congress could not regulate commerce. By contrast, the states were free to establish tariffs, embargoes, and other trade regulations among each other and with other countries.
- There was no chief executive. Antipathy toward royal authority led to an American government without a leader. The president of the Congress was the highest-ranking U.S. official, but that office was more akin to today's Speaker of the House than the president.
- There was almost no executive branch. The few ambassadors and other executive officials that existed were appointed by the legislature and needed its approval for most actions.
- There were no national courts.
- Congress was prone to stalemate. Nine of thirteen states had to approve legislation.
- Congress was a revolving door. Members served one-year terms, were limited to three consecutive terms, and could be removed at any time by their state.
- Amending the Articles of Confederation was difficult, requiring the unanimous approval of all the states.

The Record of the First American Government

As a result of these problems, the central government was largely ineffective. Indeed, it was so weak that it is somewhat surprising that the United States survived at all. The war against the British had forced a level of cooperation among the states, but that largely ended with Washington's victory at Yorktown, Virginia, in 1781. Without a common enemy, there was little, including the Articles of Confederation, to hold the country together.

A key problem was that the central government was nearly destitute. The states sent less than 20% of the funds that the Confederation Congress requested. As a result, the central government was unable to meet its expenses or to pay the interest and principal on the huge amount of money it borrowed to operate. With no central economic authority, almost everything that could go wrong did.

FIGURE 2.2 Economic Inflation, 1774–1788

High inflation in the late 1770s undercut confidence in the first American government. Prices eased as the Revolutionary War wound down, but the damage done left the economy weak. This figure means that what cost $1 in 1774 would have cost $1.69 in 1778, $1.49 in 1782, and $1.10 in 1788. *Data source:* Bureau of the Census, *Historical Statistics of the United States, Colonial Times to 1970*

- Inflation was rampant. Both the national government and state governments simply printed money to meet their expenses and so currency rapidly lost its value. One indication of inflation is shown in Figure 2.2. As evident there, inflation had begun to decline after the war ended, but the damage to the economy and to faith in the currency had already been done.
- Foreign and domestic commerce plummeted. Each state also set its own laws governing tariffs, shipping regulations, and other trade matters and sometimes applied them to each other as well as to foreign countries.
- Economic depression gripped the country. Exports to Great Britain fell by two-thirds, farm wages declined 20%, many farmers lost their land to foreclosure, and other economic hardships beset the land.

These political and economic problems threatened the stability and perhaps the survival of the United States in the mid-1780s. The depression caused a deep split between the small farmers, tradesmen, and others who formed the **debtor class** and the gentry who formed the **creditor class. Populists** favoring the debtors gained controlled of several state legislatures. They passed laws issuing massive amounts of nearly worthless currency that could be used to pay debts and took other actions that undermined the financial stability of the country and the economic interests of the gentry.

Populist civil disturbances broke out. The worst of these was **Shays' Rebellion.** The uprising began in August 1786 when 1,200 destitute farmers led by Daniel Shays took up arms in western Massachusetts to press the state legislature for debt relief. The state appealed for help to the Confederation Congress, but that impoverished body was impotent. Finally, in February 1787, a force of 4,000 state militia troops defeated Shays' rebels.

Many of those who had led the independence movement blamed the mounting turmoil on the weaknesses of the Articles of Confederation. George Washington believed that "the disturbances in New England" and the "declining state" of the economy were "in a great measure" attributable to the lack of "proper authority" in the central government.[9] He and others also feared that Shays' rebellion and the populist efforts in many state legislatures to aid the debtor class at the expense of the creditor class would lead to virtual mob control of the country. "The evils we experience flow from the excess of democracy," Elbridge Gerry of Massachusetts fretted.[10] Such leaders urged immediate action to strengthen the central government. Responding to that call, the states sent delegates to Annapolis, Maryland, in September 1786 to discuss what to do. They soon called for a convention to revise the Articles of Confederation. The stage was set for creating a new constitution and a second American government.

CREATING A NEW CONSTITUTION

On May 25, 1787, the **Constitutional Convention** assembled in Philadelphia with 55 delegates in attendance. It was a time of anxiety. Shays' Rebellion had been suppressed only a few months before and turmoil continued in the country. Moreover, powerful voices in many states opposed the convention. Rhode Island had even refused to send delegates.

The delegates realized that their goal of creating a stronger central government might be doomed by the provision in the Articles that required the unanimous consent of the states to amend it. Therefore, the delegates ignored their charge to revise the Articles. Instead they drew up a new constitution and specified that it would go into effect after ratification by only nine states. Objections that this process violated the Articles were swept aside, and during the next four months the delegates wrote a new constitution. Many of them felt the country's future hung in the balance as they sent the document on to the Confederation Congress for referral to the states for ratifications. "Should the states reject this excellent Constitution," delegate George Washington warned, "the probability is that an opportunity will never again . . . [come] in peace—the next will be drawn in blood."[11]

Washington's fears did not come to pass. Within a year New Hampshire became the ninth state to ratify the Constitution. The Confederation Congress then established the procedures for electing a president, seating a new Congress, and otherwise beginning the **second American government**, the one that continues today, on March 4, 1789. The old Confederation Congress transacted its last business on October 10, 1788, and the first American government faded quietly into history. Those were the basics, but what this overview of the writing and adoption of the Constitution omits is the intricate maneuvering necessary to create it. We shall now turn our attention to this important subject.

The Framers and Their Motives

Thomas Jefferson once warned against considering constitutions "too sacred to be touched" or thinking their authors possessed "a wisdom more than human."[12] Heeding Jefferson's advice, it is important to see the Constitution as a political document, not scripture, and to view the founding fathers as pragmatic politicians, not patriotic prophets. It is also the case that the move to create a new constitution was not driven by widespread discontent with the Articles among Americans. To the contrary, even though the government under the Articles was weak, "it satisfied a great many—probably a majority—of the people."[13] The American gentry felt differently, however, and it was that group that pushed for constitutional reform. Most members of this small, atypical group of Americans shared four traits that influenced how they proceeded in Philadelphia. These commonalities included a sense of nationalism, wealth, a belief in liberty, and pragmatic political experience.

The Framers as Nationalists

As members of the gentry, the framers were more likely than most Americans to have a national rather than a state focus. Their businesses and education had led them to travel and correspond more widely than most Americans. The national orientation of the delegates was also evident in the fact that many had been revolutionary leaders, and 75% of them had served in the Continental Congress or the Confederation Congress.

Given their national exposure and service, most of the framers were disturbed by the possibility that the union would fall apart because of the combination of a weak central government and the civil unrest symbolized by Shays' Rebellion. To safeguard national stability, the framers therefore sought to strengthen the central government and to restrain the threat of populism. As one historian has put it, many of the delegates "were more interested in authority and stability than in popular liberty."[14]

The Framers as Self-interested Gentry

Economic self-interest was a second factor that motivated the framers. All of them were members of the gentry. They were at least well off, and many were wealthy members of the creditor class. Although the delegates had a range of specific economic concerns, most had two common interests: national economic stability and the protection of their property from the populists. As one study put it:

> Manufacturers . . . preferred a uniformly high national tariff to the varying state tariffs. Merchants and shippers preferred a single and effective commercial policy to thirteen different and ineffective ones. Land speculators wished to see the Indian

menace finally removed from their Western tracts, and creditors desired to stop the state issues of paper money. Investors in Confederation securities hoped to have the Confederation debt make good the value of their securit[ies]. Large property owners in general looked for reliable means of safety from the threat of mobs.[15]

According to some historians, the framers' common interests led them to seek to protect those interests at the Constitutional Convention by establishing a strong central government that could create a more uniform economic system and do away with the creditor-class friendly economic policies that many states had adopted. In one scholar's view, the resulting Constitution "was essentially an economic document" written by members of the "moneyed class" in order to preserve and advance their "economic advantages."[16]

The Framers as Proponents of Liberty

A third thing that motivated the framers was their belief that the shaky start to American self-governance under the Articles had created external and internal threats to the liberties Americans had so recently won. Externally, some feared that if the confederation fell into disunion the British might take the opportunity to regain control of part of their former colonies, especially the western territories. Internally, some feared that if the country collapsed, democracy would be lost as people sought a king or other strong leader to restore order. George Washington was one of those who saw this possibility as a reason to strengthen the national government. As he wrote:

> I am told that even respectable characters speak of a monarchical form of government without horror. . . . What a triumph for the advocates of despotism to find that we are incapable of governing ourselves, and that systems founded on the basis of equal liberty are merely ideal and fallacious! Would to God that wise measures may be taken in time to avert the consequences we have but too much reason to apprehend.[17]

The Framers as Pragmatic Politicians

Pragmatism was a fourth factor that influenced the framers. The delegates to the Constitutional Convention were practicing politicians more than political philosophers. Three-fourths of them had experience in the Continental/Confederation Congress. Almost all of them had served in colonial or state government, including seven who had been governors.

This common practical experience made writing the Constitution an exercise in political maneuver and compromise. Certainly, there was a common theme on which almost all the delegates agreed—creating a stronger central government. But there was little agreement on exactly how to accomplish that goal. As a result, the

Constitution is a patchwork quilt of compromises, rather than a whole cloth representing a single overarching thought.

Were the framers pragmatists who laudably compromised to achieve the possible? Or should they have insisted on their ideals even if that meant stalemate with other, equally determined opponents? These are questions we shall take up later in this chapter. Indeed, debate over the relative value of principle versus pragmatism extends throughout our American political history. For example, among the current issues of American politics is the strong ideological divide between the two parties in Congress. Is it a welcome relief from what some argue were once middle-of-the-road parties that gave voters little real choice? Others see the polarization of Congress as an unwelcome division into two very contentious camps that have difficulty working in a bipartisan way to bridge differences and move policy forward.

The Struggle over Ratification

Whatever the framers' motives were, many Americans did not share their views. Still others had no strong opinions either way.

Supporters, Opponents, and the Undecided and Uninterested

Those who favored ratifying the Constitution were called **Federalists**. Although they had some distinct advantages, including the support of most of the country's leaders, the Federalists recognized the need to convince the larger population of the benefits of the proposed constitution. Most importantly, the Federalists sought to do this through a series of 85 essays written by James Madison, Alexander Hamilton, and John Jay under the joint pseudonym Publius and published in the press and elsewhere. These essays, collectively called the *Federalist Papers*, were brilliantly argued and helped win ratification. While reading them today provides some insights into the thinking of the framers, the *Federalist Papers* should be read with caution because they were written as pro-ratification persuasive pieces—that is, advertising. As such, they put the best face on the Federalist argument and do not always reflect precisely the thoughts of the framers.[18]

Opposing ratification were the **Antifederalists**. The main thrust of their argument against the Constitution was that it would subvert liberty. They charged that the Constitution shifted too much power from nearby state capitals to a central government that would be too far away for the people to control effectively. Antifederalists also argued that there were no rules in the Constitution that would prevent the much stronger central government from subverting such basic rights as freedom of speech and religions. It was through this objection that the Antifederalists made their greatest contribution to the American political system. Their concern led the Federalists to promise that if the Constitution were ratified, the first order of business would be to offer a group of amendments to protect liberties. Thus, Americans can thank the Antifederalists for the **Bill of Rights**, the first ten amendments to the Constitution.

Economic self-interest also motivated many Antifederalists. The proposed constitution decidedly transferred economic power from the states to the national government, and that tended to work against the interests of the debtor class. As one study put it, "On the whole the . . . Antifederalists got their support from the poorer farmers, especially those who were in debt."[19] Rhode Island, whose legislature was at the forefront of the movement to institute policies benefiting the debtor class, refused to send delegates to the Constitutional Convention, refused to create a state ratifying convention, and only reluctantly joined the union more than a year after the new government had begun to operate.

For all the sound and fury generated by the Federalists and Antifederalists, there were others who were ambivalent about the document. Thomas Jefferson, for one, commented, "There are very good articles in it, and very bad. I do not know which preponderate."[20] There is also evidence that the debate over ratification did not rivet the country's attention. Most states elected delegates to special conventions to decide on ratification, but according to one estimate, "Something like three-fourths of the adult white males in the country . . . failed to vote for delegates, mainly because of indifference."[21]

State Ratification

In the end, the fate of the proposed new constitution rested in the hands of state ratifying conventions. The Federalists had the edge, but there were close votes in a number of states. Pennsylvania was the only key state that ratified by a large margin. Massachusetts leaned against ratification at first, but the promise of a bill of rights changed enough minds for the convention to narrowly approve the Constitution by a 187–168 vote. The ninth and deciding state, New Hampshire, favored the document by a vote of 57–47 in June 1788. Still, the pivotal states of New York and Virginia had not voted, and the union faced an uncertain future without them. Assurances that a bill of rights would be added to the Constitution once again turned the tide, and Virginia supported ratification by a vote of 89–79. The news that Virginia had voted yes tipped the balance in New York, which added its consent by a razor thin vote of 30–27. North Carolina waited until after the new Congress had sent the Bill of Rights to the states before it voted to ratify in late 1789. And in May 1790, Rhode Island, reluctant to the end, was the last of the former colonies to assent, with only two votes to spare, 34–32.

CHARACTERISTICS OF THE CONSTITUTION

How were the goals and efforts of the framers reflected in the Constitution in ways that continue to affect the structure and operation of the American political system? In fashioning the Constitution, the framers did six key things. They

- created a constitution noted for its durability and brevity.
- fashioned a much stronger central government.
- consolidated considerable economic power in the national government.
- structured the government according to a series of compromises.
- restrained governmental power by separating and dividing it among institutions.
- limited democracy by creating a republic partially insulated from popular control.

Durability and Brevity

The U.S. Constitution is an impressive document. It has existed longer than any other written constitution in the world. Moreover, it has survived for more than two centuries with relatively few written changes—only 27 amendments—while the country it governs and the world in which that country exists have undergone transformations that would leave any of the framers gaping in disbeief.

The Constitution is also notable for its brevity. With just seven main parts (articles) and 7,525 words, it is shorter than any of the 50 state constitutions or the constitution of any other country. The few words with which the Constitution structures the American political system mean that it is vague on many points. This trait has advantages and disadvantages.

India's constitution adopted in 1950 is the world's longest with over 117,000 words in 395 articles and 83 amendments.

Constitutional flexibility is the main *advantage* of this lack of precision. One reason that the Constitution has survived so long with so few amendments is that it has been possible to adjust the interpretation of the document as realities and attitudes have evolved over time. More than a century ago, an analyst commented, "The American Constitution has changed, is changing, and by the law of its existence must continue to change in its substance and practical working even when its words remain the same."[22] Some of that change has occurred through the formal process of judicial interpretation (described below). Other interpretive revisions have come about through usage, with new practices being informally accepted as reasonable and proper.

Constitutional conflict is the main *disadvantage* of the document's lack of precision. Scholar Edward Corwin has aptly commented that "the Constitution . . . is an invitation to struggle."[23] For example, the Constitution designates the president

The brevity and often vague language of the Constitution have made its meaning "an invitation to struggle." The demand by these students in front of the U.S. Supreme Court for free speech was sparked by a school in Juneau, Alaska, that suspended a student for holding up a sign reading "BONG HiTS 4 JESUS" during a public event that the school allowed students to leave class to attend. To the students' dismay, the Court ruled in Morse v. Frederick (2007) that the Constitution did not bar schools from punishing students who during school-sanctioned events seem to advocate using illegal drugs. (AP Photo/Evan Vucci)

as "commander in chief." But one is tempted to add the parenthetical comment "whatever that is supposed to mean," because the interplay between the authority of that title and the power of Congress to declare war has long been a source of controversy. Whether overall the Constitution's brevity is an advantage that allows for adjustments without constitutional crisis or a disadvantage that permits the corruption of its clauses without the requisite amendment process remains a hotly debated issue.

Strong Central Government

All Federalists agreed that the central government under the Articles was too weak. To remedy that, the Constitution increased the power of the central or **federal government** and reduced the authority of the states. Note that federal government means the national government, the one now centered in Washington, D.C. That is different from a federal system of government, a way of organizing the government that we shall discuss presently.

Enhanced Power for the Central Government

The second American government's structure and authority were significantly different than those of the first American government. In general, the Constitution increased the weight of the federal government in the American political system by adding two newly created branches, the executive and the judicial, to the existing legislative branch; by giving each branch a potent array of authority; and by establishing the doctrine of constitutional supremacy. Table 2.1 provides a summary of the differences between the Articles of Confederation and the Constitution.

The legislative branch, Congress, received impressive new grants of authority that made it a veritable powerhouse compared to what the Confederation Congress had been. Article I, Section 8 of the Constitution gives Congress 17 **enumerated powers**. Among these specific powers are the authority to declare war and the power to regulate interstate commerce. Section 8 further adds to the power of Congress by authorizing it to "make all laws which shall be necessary and proper" to exercise its enumerated powers and to carry out all the other powers that the Constitution gives to the federal government. This **necessary and proper clause** is the basis for a broad range of **implied powers**. For example, if an enumerated power allows Congress to regulate commerce among the states, then

TABLE 2.1 The Articles of Confederation and the Constitution Compared

Compared to the relatively weak central government under the Articles of Confederation, the Constitution empowered the national government by establishing a president and federal court system, by making it easier to pass laws and amend the constitution, and by centralizing many economic powers at the national level.

PROVISIONS	ARTICLES OF CONFEDERATION	CONSTITUTION
Location of sovereignty	States retain substantial sovereignty	Constitution supreme law of land; state sovereignty limited
Number of legislative houses	1	2
Basis of legislative seats	State equality	House of Representatives by population Senate by state equality
Legislative term	1 year, could be recalled by state legislature	House: 2 years, no recall Senate: 6 years, no recall
Selection of legislators	By state legislatures	House: Election by people. Senate: By state legislatures; direct election after 1913
Vote required to pass acts	9/13 on important issues; majority on lesser issues	Majority by both houses, except 2/3 for treaties by Senate alone
Legislative term limits	3 of every 6 years maximum	None
Chief executive office	None	President
Appointment of officials	By Congress	By President with Senate majority approval
National courts	None	Supreme Court; others as established by Congress
Amendment procedure	By 2/3 vote of Congress and unanimous ratification by the states	By 2/3 vote of Congress or Convention, and ratification by 3/4 of the states
Power to collect taxes	No	Yes
Power to coin/print money	Central government and states	Central government only
Power to regulate commerce	Limited	Extensive

it can be implied that Congress also has the authority to set hygiene standards for meat that is shipped from one state to another. The necessary and proper clause has been a major factor in expanding the realm of federal authority because what is necessary and proper is a matter of opinion, has expanded over time, and has rarely been restrained by the federal courts.

A chief executive and an independent executive branch had not existed under the Articles but did under the Constitution. Article II, which deals with the executive branch, accomplished three goals. First, it created a *central authority figure*, the president. Second, it ensured a *stable chief executive* by opting for a single president (rather than an executive council, as some delegates proposed), by setting the president's term of office at four years (many governors served just one year), by not limiting the terms a president could serve (most state governors had term limits), and by making it difficult to remove a president. Third, it gave the president *enumerated powers*, such as being commander in chief of the armed forces, negotiating treaties, and appointing executive branch officials. Article II also established the president as head of the executive branch, giving him a wide range of *implied powers* as chief administrator.

A judicial branch was also established. National courts had not existed under the Articles of Confederation. By contrast, Article III of the Constitution established a Supreme Court and allowed Congress to create subordinate courts. The Constitution also empowered these courts by giving them the jurisdiction to adjudicate all issues involving the Constitution, federal laws and treaties, and actions taken by executive branch officials. This authority includes the power of **judicial interpretation**, the authority of the courts to decide the meaning and intent of the Constitution and statutory laws. As New York Governor (and later U.S. Supreme Court Chief Justice) Charles Evan Hughes put it, "We are under a Constitution, but the Constitution is what the judges say it is."[24] Article III also gives the judicial branch the implied power of **judicial review**: the authority to decide whether laws passed by Congress and actions taken by the executive branch are constitutional. The **supremacy clause** in Article VI is yet another source of federal judicial authority. By declaring the Constitution to be "the supreme law of the land," it made state constitutions and laws subordinate to the federal Constitution and laws. Each of these powers is discussed extensively in Chapter 14.

Diminished Powers for the State Governments

The Constitution added further to federal authority by limiting the powers of the states. Under the Articles of Confederation, states were already barred from making agreements among themselves without the consent of Congress and from engaging in foreign affairs activities such as going to war and negotiating treaties with foreign governments. The Constitution retained these prohibitions and added an array of economic prohibitions described below.

National Economic Control

Most of the framers were convinced that national economic control would help cure the economic woes that they and the country were experiencing. Therefore, they wrote a constitution that shifted economic power away from the states and toward the central government. To do that, the Constitution contains numerous clauses about:

What the Federal Government May Do

- Levy and collect taxes
- Establish import tariffs
- Borrow money
- Regulate commerce with other countries, among the states, and with Indian tribes
- Establish bankruptcy law
- Coin money and regulate its value
- Fix weights and measures
- Punish counterfeiting
- Regulate patents

What the States May Not Do

- Coin money
- Emit bills of credit (print paper money)
- Set import or export tariffs
- Charge a duty on goods being shipped through a state
- Make anything but gold and silver legal tender (usable as money)
- Pass as a law impairing [modifying] the obligation of contracts

Many of these economic provisions worked to the particular benefit of the creditor class. A single system of national trade laws, compared to a multiplicity of state laws, tended to benefit manufacturers and merchants. Congress's exclusive authority to coin and print money helped tame inflation, which devalued the debts owed to the creditor class. Other constitutional provisions that worked to the advantage of the creditor class and against the immediate interests of the debtor class included prohibiting states from enacting easy bankruptcy laws, prohibiting anything but gold and silver as a basis for currency to pay debts, and prohibiting laws that changed contract obligations (such as debts and interest rates).

Many of the gentry also benefited from Article VI. It made the new government responsible for not only the debts of the old Confederation government between 1774 and 1789 but also the debt the states had amassed fighting the Revolutionary War. Much of this was owed to the gentry, and the new Constitution virtually guaranteed that they would be paid.

A Bundle of Compromises

The Constitution proves the old adage "politics is the art of compromise." Many of its key provisions reflect what was possible given political disagreements rather than what might have been ideal. To demonstrate these compromises, we can look at two contentious issues: the relative power of each state in Congress and the ongoing importation of slaves.

Compromise on Allocating Seats in Congress

One knotty issue was how to divide the seats in Congress among the states. Once it was clear that population was going to play a role in that distribution, a second debate raged over whether slaves should be counted as part of the population.

FIGURE 2.3 Legislative Seats According
to Different Representation Formulas

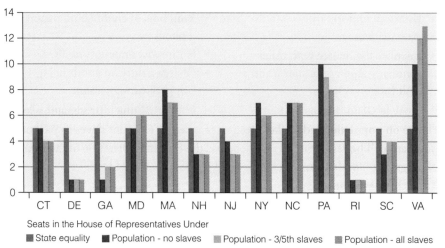

Seats in the House of Representatives Under
■ State equality ■ Population - no slaves ■ Population - 3/5th slaves ■ Population - all slaves

There were important consequences to the debate in the Constitutional Convention over (1) whether states should have representation based on equality or on population and (2) if by population, whether slaves should be counted. This figure shows the range of seats the 13 original states would have received under the various options.
Notes and data source: The figure is based on the number of seats (65) in the House of Representatives during the First Congress. Data from Census Bureau, Historical Data for 1790.

How to Allocate Seats in Congress   The first issue was whether to allocate seats among the states on the basis of equality among the states or by population. Not surprisingly, the more and less populous states disagreed. The **Virginia Plan** proposed a **bicameral legislature** (two houses) with seats in the first chamber allocated among the states based on population. This first chamber would then select a second one, and they together would select the chief executive and the national judiciary. Virginia, it should be noted, was the most populous state with 19% of the U.S. total counting slaves and 14% of the total not counting them.

New Jersey, which had only about half of Virginia's total population, offered an equally self-serving counterproposal. The **New Jersey Plan** called for a **unicameral legislature** (one house) in which each state would have equal representation, with that house selecting an executive council and the national judiciary.

Figure 2.3 shows the significance of the different formulas, including those involved with the dispute over counting slaves. Under the various plans, Virginia's seats would have ranged from 5 to 13 in the House of Representatives, assuming a 65-member chamber. By contrast, the seats of the least populous state, Delaware, would have varied between five under equal representation to one based on population.

After months of stalemated struggle, the **Great Compromise** (or Connecticut Compromise) engineered by Rogers Sherman of Connecticut resolved the matter by simply having one legislative house based on each formula. The House of Representatives would follow the formulation of the Virginia Plan and be based on population; the Senate would have an equal number of seats as favored by the New Jersey Plan.

Whether to Count Slaves as Part of the Population   Basing representation in the House on population led to the question of whether to count slaves as part of the population. The resolution of that debate is the clearest illustration of the triumph of pragmatic—in this case notorious—self-interest over the niceties of democratic theory in the writing of the Constitution. Predictably, the southern states (Georgia, Maryland, North Carolina, South Carolina, and Virginia), which had 91% of the slaves, wanted them counted. The other states did not. What makes these positions especially ironic is that it was northerners who were most likely to be critical of slavery, while most southerners argued that slaves were chattel (property), not people. In the end, the **Three-Fifths Compromise** settled the matter by counting five slaves as three people for determining representation. Figure 2.3 shows the seats in the House of Representatives based on equal representation and also under three approaches to counting slaves: not counting them, using the three-fifths formula, and counting slaves equally.

Compromise on Importing Slaves

Slavery was the most contentious issue that faced the United States for nearly a century. Speaking at the Constitutional Convention, James Madison perceptively noted that the country's greatest division was not between the most and least populous states. Rather, it was between the southern and northern states because of "the effects of their having or not having slaves."[25]

> The American debate over slavery reflected sentiments internationally. By the early 1800s, more and more countries were banning the slave trade, with the British prohibiting it in 1807.

There was little sentiment among the country's whites to abolish slavery, but many delegates in Philadelphia from northern states wanted to end importing slaves immediately. Most delegates from the southern states adamantly opposed any restriction.

Northern delegates feared that the southern states might not ratify the Constitution if it barred the slave trade or even if it left the decision to Congress. Particularly unthinkable was the absence from the union of Virginia (the wealthiest, most populous state and also the state with the greatest number of slaves). For their part, southern delegates knew they could not get a clause perpetually protecting the

YOU DECIDE: Principle or Union?

More than any other issue, slavery threatened to thwart the efforts of the delegates meeting in Philadelphia in 1787 to fashion a new constitution for the United States. Most delegates believed that failure here would cause the union to dissolve.[26] There was also considerable antislavery sentiment at the convention. Pennsylvania delegate Gouverneur Morris angrily condemned slavery as bringing a "curse of heaven" on states where it existed. He and like-minded delegates wanted to ban importing slaves.

The antislavery delegates probably had enough votes to add a provision to the Constitution barring the slave trade, but they feared that doing so might prompt some southern states to bolt the convention and even the union. South Carolina's John Rutledge warned of such a reaction by the South, declaring, "The people of those states will never be such fools as to give up so important an interest [as slavery]."

Place yourself in Philadelphia as a delegate. You abhor slavery, but you also fear for the union. Delegate Morris and others have introduced a motion to have the proposed constitution bar any further importation of slaves. Other antislavery delegates have proposed a compromise that will allow slaves to be imported for twenty years after the adoption of the Constitution. "Leave the matter [of the slave trade] as we find it," Connecticut's Roger Sherman urges you and the other delegates. As the time for a vote draws near, it is clear that your vote could decide the issue. Do you vote for the compromise and advance the cause of union, or do you stick to your principles, vote no, and risk dissolution of the United States?

slave trade. So the dispute was resolved by the **Twenty Year Compromise,** which protected the importation of slaves, but only until 1808. Whether that decision was one of laudable pragmatism or unprincipled shame is a matter for you to consider in You Decide: Principle or Union?

With the new constitution and government in place, Congress banned the export of slaves in 1794. Later it abolished the importation of slaves as of January 1, 1808, the first day possible under the Constitution. Led by the British, the international community increasingly acted to suppress the slave trade. The last place in the Americas to ban the importation of slaves was Brazil in 1853. Brazil was also the last in the hemisphere to abolish slavery, doing so in 1888.

Restrained Government

Although increasing the authority of the central government was the main purpose of the Constitution, its authors also were wary of the threat to liberty posed by concentrations of political power. To avoid that danger, the Constitution (1) separates the powers of the central government into three branches, (2) divides power between the central and state governments, and (3) places restrictions on the power of both levels of government.

Separation of Powers

One way the Constitution restrained the federal government was by separating it into three branches. This **separation of powers** is a key organizational concept in the Constitution. As Madison explained in *Federalist* No. 47, "The accumulation of all powers legislative, executive and judiciary in the same hands . . . may justly be pronounced the very definition of tyranny." To ensure the separation of powers, the Constitution provides for:

Independent selection: The president, House of Representatives, and Senate are selected independently of one another. Only the judiciary is picked by the other two branches.

Separate constituencies: Initially, the Electoral College chose the president, state legislatures selected senators, and voters picked members of the House. The Seventeenth Amendment (1913) transferred selection of senators to the public.

Fixed terms: Senators, representatives, and the president all serve fixed terms of between two and six years. Judges serve for life.

Difficult removal: Any official may be removed, but the removal process is difficult. Each house of Congress has the power to expel a member by a two-thirds vote; the president and judges can be removed by impeachment by the House (by majority vote) and conviction by the Senate (by a two-thirds vote).

Exclusive service: Simultaneous service in Congress and either of the other branches is prohibited. The single important exception is the vice president, who serves as president of the Senate. There is no language barring dual service in the executive and judicial branches, but practice has generally prevented that.

The Constitution also restrains the central government by granting countervailing powers to each of the branches. As part of the system of **checks and balances**, each of the branches has a range of countervailing powers that enable one branch to frustrate another. In *Federalist* No. 48, Madison argued that merely creating three distinct branches was insufficient to ensure against the possibility of a "tyrannical concentration of all the powers of government in the same hands." The solution, he suggested in *Federalist* No. 51, was to organize the government so that the various parts had "the means of keeping each other in their proper places." This meant, Madison went on to explain, creating overlapping functions among the three branches so that they could restrain one another. These checks and balances include the following:

- Congress can pass legislation but the president can veto it.
- The president can veto legislation; Congress can override the veto by a two-thirds vote.

- The executive branch may not spend money unless Congress appropriates it.
- The president appoints most officials, but the Senate must confirm them.
- The president negotiates treaties, but the Senate must ratify them by a two-thirds vote.
- Congress can impeach, convict, and remove the president, other executive officials, and judges.
- Congress declares war, but the president wages it as commander in chief.
- Congress passes laws, but the executive branch implements them.
- The courts can interpret law and can review the laws and actions of Congress and the executive branch and reject them as unconstitutional.
- Congress can organize the executive, other than the president and vice president, by creating agencies and defining their powers, by reorganizing agencies, and by disbanding agencies.
- Congress can organize the judiciary by creating, reorganizing, or eliminating courts (other than the Supreme Court), by defining jurisdiction to a degree, and by manipulating the judiciary's budget.

Division of Powers

In addition to separating powers within the federal government, the Constitution avoids an overconcentration of governmental authority through a **division of powers** between the federal and state levels. This restraint was not a product of democratic design by framers. Rather, it was the result of the forgone conclusion that the states would give up only a limited number of their powers. What occurred is that the Constitution transformed the political system from a confederation to a **federation**, with powers divided between the national and state governments.

Chapter 3 covers the creation and evolution of the federal system, but here we note that the authority of the states was established and protected in several ways including:

- States decide how to select the Electoral College that chooses the president.
- Until 1913, state legislatures selected their state's U.S. senators.
- Congress may not divide a state or merge one with another state without its permission.
- The Tenth Amendment, which was intended to limit federal authority and protect state authority by specifying, "The powers not delegated to the United States by the Constitution, nor prohibited by it to the states, are reserved to the states respectively, or to the people."
- Constitutional amendments must be ratified by three-fourths of the states whether the **amendment process** starts with a two-thirds vote of each house of Congress or is initiated by a constitutional convention that has been convened by Congress at the request of two-thirds of the states. This second option has never been used.

Limitation of Power

Yet another way that the Constitution seeks to restrain government is by forbidding certain actions by the central and/or state governments. For instance, Article I, Section 10 prohibits Congress from passing laws that penalize specific people **(bills of attainder)** or that make something illegal retroactively **(ex post facto laws)**. Still other language forbids any "religious test" for holding federal elective or appointed office, guarantees each state a republican form of government, and bars granting anyone a "title of nobility."

As noted, the debates in the state ratifying conventions made it clear that the provisions in the Constitution restraining the central government might not be strong enough to ensure ratification of the Constitution. To address that, the Federalists pledged that when the First Congress convened, it would propose amendments to further limit government. Twelve such amendments were sent to the states in September 1789. Of these, 10 were quickly ratified and became the Bill of Rights. These initially applied only to the federal government, but the courts later applied most of these amendments to the states also.

Restrained Democracy

Americans today value the concept of **democracy** and its grant to the citizenry of ultimate political authority, and they define the U.S. political system as a democracy. The framers of the Constitution did neither, at least not as they understood democracy back then.

Globalization and Concepts of Democracy

Democracy did not mean the same thing to the delegates in Philadelphia in 1787 that it means to most people today. For the delegates, democracy meant what we now call **direct democracy** (or pure democracy), a system in which laws are passed by popular vote, not by a legislative body. This is what had existed in ancient Athens and for a time in ancient Rome. The depictions of this form of democracy that had come down from ancient times painted a dark picture. Aristotle (*Politics*, 350 B.C.) defined democracy as "when the indigent . . . are the rulers" and govern "in view of the interest of . . . the needy" rather than "the common good of all." The result according to Aristotle was an "ochlocracy" (mob rule), in which public passion swept away reason and fomented tyranny by the mass (the majority) over people of property and other minorities. Similarly, Plato wrote in *The Republic* (370 B.C.) that "dictatorship naturally arises out of democracy, and the most aggravated form of tyranny and slavery out of the most extreme liberty." Alexander Hamilton, for one, commented in 1788, "The ancient democracies in which the people themselves deliberated never possessed one good feature of government. Their very character was tyranny."[27]

Concerns about Democracy in America

For many of the framers, events in the United States in the 1780s seemed to confirm the criticism of democracy by Aristotle and Plato. Although no state practiced direct democracy, many farmers, shopkeepers, and other representatives of the poorer classes had replaced members of the gentry as state legislators and had even gained a majority in the legislatures in Rhode Island and some other states. The gentry were also worried by populist measures, such as lenient state bankruptcy laws to make it easier for people to escape their debts, that these legislators had enacted. The gentry thought these policies would ruin the country economically and were also a form of tyranny by the mob over the property rights of the gentry. Armed uprisings by the needy, such as Shays' Rebellion, made the picture even scarier.

These concerns created a dilemma for the framers. On the one hand, most of them supported the idea that the people should have a voice in choosing their government. On the other hand, the framers wanted to stop the country from veering further toward a "mobocracy" that would trample the rights of various minorities and interest groups, or "factions," as Madison called them. As he argued in *Federalist* No. 10, democracies find that, "measures are too often decided, not according to the rules of justice. . . , but by the superior force of an interested and overbearing majority."

Of all possible factions, those organized around competing economic interests were foremost in Madison's mind. Writing further in *Federalist* No. 10, he contended that the most common source of division among groups was the "unequal distribution of property." It was beyond Madison's time to be concerned about factions based on race, gender, and ethnicity, but his efforts to protect the minority creditor faction against the majority debtor faction have important ramifications for civil liberties and rights today.

Restraints on Democracy

In the end, the framers sought to preserve both liberty and political stability by restraining democracy. Given their pessimistic view of democracy, the framers chose to institute a **republic**. This is an indirect democracy, a representative form of government that puts one or more insulating layers between the people and the elected and appointed officials who make policy. As Madison explained in *Federalist* No. 10, the purpose of a republic is to improve public policy by passing the preferences of the mass through "a chosen body of citizens, whose wisdom may best discern the true interest of their country." In other words, Madison thought that representatives are more apt to know what is in the public interest than is the public.

In order to put layers of "insulation" between the people and the government, the Constitution as written in 1787 took the following steps:

- The only officials the people chose directly were the members of the House of Representatives.
- Senators were chosen by their state legislatures (until 1913).
- All initiatives by the House must also pass the Senate. Madison called the Senate "the great anchor of the government" and a "temperate and respectable body of citizens" that would resist public passions "until reason, justice, and truth can regain their authority over the public mind."[28]
- Senators have terms of office that are three times longer than those of House members. Madison explained that the longer term of senators would make them less likely than members of the House to yield to the public's "sudden and violent passions."[29]
- The Senate confirms appointments and ratifies treaties; the House can do nothing unilaterally.
- The House can impeach (indict) presidents and other officials, but the Senate decides whether or not to remove an impeached official.
- The president is chosen by the Electoral College, which was appointed at that time by the state legislatures. Gradually, the states began to allow electors to be chosen by popular vote, and most did by 1824. The last state to appoint electors was Colorado in 1876.
- Judges were insulated from popular control by being nominated by the (then unelected) president and confirmed by the (then unelected) Senate.

This photo shows lawn signs in Portland, Maine, prior to the state's referendum in 2009 on whether to ban same-sex marriages. One limit on American democracy is that at the national level, unlike in many states, the voting public has no opportunity to directly decide policy issues. (AP Photo/Pat Wellenbach)

Democracy, Race, and Gender: The Forgotten Factions

Yet another way that democracy was limited resulted from the framers' very limited view of equality, rights, and democratic participation. The idea that women, blacks, and American Indians were equal to men and whites and had the same rights was not even raised at the Constitutional Convention, and would not have been taken seriously if it had been.

The issue of who should be able to vote and hold office was certainly part of the public discourse of the day. Even by the 1780s controversy was beginning to stir about whether free blacks, women, and tax-paying American Indians should be able to vote and hold office. Technically, by using the word "person" to describe who could hold federal office, the Constitution allowed women and other political minorities to serve. But most of the framers gave no thought to extending such freedoms to anyone but white males. So the Constitution avoided the issue of political participation by allowing the state legislatures to determine who could vote in federal as well as state elections.

By doing this, the Constitution in effect disfranchised most women, black freemen (emancipated slaves), and American Indians. Even many white males were barred from voting by state law. In 1790, only 3 of the 15 states (Vermont and Kentucky had joined the Union by then) allowed all adult white males to vote. The other states excluded men who did not have a certain amount of property and/or who did not pay taxes. Women were, as they are today, about half the population, but they could vote in only a few places and then only on local issues. The eighteenth-century attitude of men toward women is evident in Thomas Jefferson's observation that "Our good ladies . . . have been too wise to wrinkle their foreheads with politics. They are contented to soothe and calm the minds of their husbands returning from political debate."[30] Before the adoption of the Nineteenth Amendment in 1919, few women were allowed to vote or hold office.

By the 1780s, there were almost 60,000 free blacks in the country. Antislavery sentiment was rising and even attracting such eminent supporters as Benjamin Franklin, and a number of northern states had enacted emancipation laws. One of the few significant policies that the Confederation Congress had managed to enact was the Northwest Ordinance (1787), which organized the Northwest Territory (the present-day states of Ohio, Indiana, Illinois, Michigan, and Minnesota) and set the stage for its future division into states that would join the union. Among other provisions, the ordinance banned slavery in this extensive region. As noted earlier, Congress banned the export of slaves in the 1790s and the importation of slaves as of 1808. Thus, the movement to rid the country of slavery had begun, but it would be more than 80 years before the Civil War finally settled that matter.

In the meantime, blacks were prevented from playing significant political roles. Indeed, only a few states allowed so-called freemen to vote, and numerous secondary barriers such as property qualifications severely limited black participation even where it was legally allowed. The passage of the Fifteenth Amendment in 1870 ended these barriers in theory but made little difference in practice until the 1960s.

As for the Indian tribes, the thirteen states and the federal government continued to treat them much as they always had—as obstacles to settlement. The colonists' determination to expand westward across the Appalachians and the British resistance to that expansion by the Proclamation of 1763 had been among sore points that led to the Revolution. The colonies' independence had opened the west to increased white settlement, and the Northwest Ordinance indicated that the United States soon intended to incorporate these areas and others on the frontier as states. The problem was that American Indians inhabited these lands. The fundamental U.S. policy was to drive the tribes out of all these territories as well as the vast Louisiana Territory after it was acquired in 1803. As President Jefferson wrote, he hoped that Congress would authorize "the means of tempting all our Indians on the east side of the Mississippi to remove to the west."[31] If the tribes could not be tempted, then, Jefferson thought, "We have only to shut our hand to crush them."[32] As with African Americans, women, and demographic minorities, the struggle of American Indians to secure their civil liberties and rights would be a long one that continues even now. This sometimes sad, sometimes hopeful saga is related throughout this book.

SUMMARY

American political development is an ongoing story, not a series of isolated events. As such, it is valuable to explore the events that led to the European settlement of what is now the United States, to the eventual break between the American colonists and the British, and then to the formation of the U.S. political system.

Globalization played a role even in this early stage of American development. The search for trade routes to Asia led to Europeans settling in the Western Hemisphere. Clashing economic interests soon led to the first global struggles, as the European powers vied with one another for trade and colonies. One part of this clash, the British victory in the French and Indian War, initiated a chain of events that culminated in the Declaration of Independence 13 years later. Globalization also affected the outcome of the revolt, with France and other European countries aiding the rebels financially and militarily in order to bedevil the British.

Even during these early years, Americans wrestled with questions of diversity. It began when Europeans occupied the lands already held by indigenous peoples. Diversity increased as white Europeans brought in a vast number of black slaves from Africa. One diversity-related issue that led to the Revolution was the British policy that barred Americans from spreading into the western lands newly won from the French in 1763 but occupied by the American Indians. Diversity was also at the core of several contentious issues that arose during the founding of a new government. One was the debate over whether and, if so, how to count slaves in the population.

The educated, well-off class of Americans called the gentry was at the center of the movement toward independence. The gentry were more nationalistic than the average American. The wealth and associated economic stakes of the gentry also increased their desire to break with the British.

When the American colonies moved initially to cooperate with each other in 1774 at the First Continental Congress, they were a league, as Chapter 3 explains. The country became a somewhat more centralized confederation once the Articles of Confederation were adopted in 1781. That form of government soon proved ineffective, particularly in the view of the gentry. Many worried that the country would break apart. The state of the U.S. economy and the economic policies of some of the states also threatened economic stability and the interests of the gentry.

The gentry therefore moved to once again restructure the government, this time by gathering in 1787 at a convention in Philadelphia and writing a new constitution. The document they wrote created a federation by substantially adding to the powers of the national government and weakening those of the states. In particular, many decisions related to economic issues shifted from state to central control. The structure of the central government was strengthened by adding an executive and a judiciary. Doubts about the wisdom and stability of the citizenry led the gentry to insulate the government, except for the House of Representatives, from direct selection by the voters. The delegates also moved to avoid concentrations of power by separating power among the three branches of the national government and by dividing power between the states and the national government.

While these changes motivated the delegates, achieving them required considerable compromise. The delegates succeeded partly by not addressing many key issues, including voting rights. Therefore, the Constitution is best understood as a pragmatic political document and one with frequent gaps and vague language that have been both a bane and a boon to the country.

CHAPTER 2 GLOSSARY

amendment process The provision in the Constitution for adding amendments in one of two ways: (1) by passing both houses of Congress by a two-thirds majority in each and being ratified by three-fourths of the states, or (2) by a constitutional convention called by two-thirds of the states proposing amendments that are ratified by three-fourths of the states.

American gentry The upper class of American society whose members owed their position to wealth and the status of their families, rather than to noble titles.

Antifederalists The opponents to replacing Articles of Confederation with a new constitution granting greater power to the central government.

Articles of Confederation The first U.S. constitution. In effect from March 1, 1781, to March 4, 1789. The Articles featured a weak central government with no chief executive.

bicameral legislature A legislature such as the U.S. Congress with two chambers.

Bill of Rights The first ten amendments to the U.S. Constitution. Adopted in 1791.

bill of attainder A law penalizing specific people. Prohibited by the Constitution.

Boston Massacre A clash in Boston on March 5, 1770, between a few British soldiers and a small band of colonials who were taunting the British. Five Americans were killed.

Boston Tea Party An action taken on December 16, 1773, by colonial dissidents who, dressed as Mohawk Indians, boarded a British East India Company ship moored in Boston harbor and dumped its cargo of tea into the harbor.

checks and balances An underlying principle in the Constitution that gives countervailing powers to the executive, judicial, and legislative branches of government for the purpose of limiting the action of the other branches. See "separation of powers."

confederation A form of government in which authority is split between a central government and state (province, etc.) governments, with a weak central government and powerful, near-sovereign state units. The U.S. political system under the Articles of Confederation was a confederation. See "federal government."

Confederation Congress The legislative body of the United States from the adoption of the Articles of Confederation in March 1781 to the creation of Congress under the U.S. Constitution in March 1789.

constitutional conflict Disputes over the meaning of various clauses of the Constitution.

Constitutional Convention Meeting in Philadelphia beginning on May 25, 1787, with 55 delegates in attendance. Slightly less than four months later, the Convention agreed on a final draft constitution and sent it to Congress for referral to the states for ratification.

constitutional flexibility A trait of the U.S. Constitution that allows various interpretations of its meaning to meet changing times without the need to amend the document.

creditor class Bankers and other wealthy Americans who had extended loans to members of the debtor class and to the government. The creditor class in the 1780s favored a strong central government that could ensure financial stability and guard against laws that would reduce the value of their loans.

debtor class Artisans, small farmers, and others who tended to owe money to the creditor class for mortgages and other loans. The debtor class in the 1780s favored inflation, state currencies, and other policies designed to reduce the burden of their debts.

democracy A system of government in which the citizens have ultimate authority.

direct democracy Making policy and other governmental decisions by a vote of the people rather than through a legislature.

division of powers The underlying principle of a federal system of governance and the allocation of legal authority in the Constitution between the federal and state governments.

enumerated powers Authority of the federal government that is specifically mentioned in the Constitution, especially in Article I, Section 8.

ex post facto law A law that makes something illegal retroactively. Barred by the Constitution.

federal government The term widely used to designate the U.S. central government. See "federation."

Federalist Papers A series of 85 essays written by James Madison, Alexander Hamilton, and John Jay under the pseudonym Publius and published between October 1787 and August 1788 in the press and elsewhere. When published individually, each is referred to by a chronological number preceded by "*Federalist* No."

Federalists Those who favored abandoning the Articles of Confederation and replacing them with a new U.S. constitution enhancing the power of the central government. See "*Federalist Papers.*"

federation A (federal) system in which the national and the subnational governments (states, provinces, etc.) both have considerable authority that cannot be taken away or superceded by the other units.

first American government The government of the United States from 1774 to 1789 that declared independence and later operated under the Articles of Confederation.

First Continental Congress Meeting of delegates from 12 colonies (all except Georgia) from September 5 through October 26, 1774, in Philadelphia. Significant as the beginning of an American government, the Congress protested British policies and encouraged the colonies to resist them.

Great Compromise The solution to the dispute at the Constitutional Convention in 1787 over how to structure the government and select officials by having one house based on population, one house based on equal representation for the states, an independently elected chief executive, and a judiciary nominated by the president and confirmed by the Senate. See "Virginia Plan" and "New Jersey Plan."

implied powers Powers not specifically mentioned in the Constitution but logically derived from the authority that is specified. See "enumerated power" and "necessary and proper clause."

judicial interpretation The authority of the courts to decide on the meaning of language in the Constitution.

judicial review The authority of the courts to rule that legislation or actions of government are unconstitutional and void.

legal setting A context made up of the Constitution and other laws, the federal system, and civil rights and civil liberties in which day-to-day politics occurs and which helps shape what is likely or even possible.

necessary and proper clause Wording in Article I, Section 8 of the Constitution that gives to Congress the authority to "make all laws which shall be necessary and proper for carrying into execution the foregoing [enumerated] powers, and all the other powers vested by this Constitution in the government of the United Sates." See "enumerated powers" and "implied powers."

New Jersey Plan Proposed by delegates from New Jersey at the Constitutional Convention in 1787, the plan favored the least populous states by recommending (1) a legislature with a single house with seats allocated equally among the states and (2) selection of an executive council and the national judiciary by the legislature. See "Virginia Plan" and "Great Compromise."

political identity A sense of connection between an individual's various demographic, geographical, and other attributes and the political system. Nationalism (identification with one's country and its people) is one of the most common and strongest senses of political identification.

populists Those supporting a movement (populism) that alleges that "common people" are being oppressed and impoverished by a powerful elite and that favors taking strong actions to transfer power and wealth to those who are oppressed and poor.

Proclamation of 1763 An edict issued by King George III that designated all British territory between the crest line of Allegheny Mountains and the Mississippi River as Indian lands, required all settlers to leave the area, and forbade new white settlements.

republic A form of democratic government in which the people choose representatives to make laws.

second American government The United States government since the adoption of the Constitution in 1789.

Second Continental Congress Meeting of delegates from the 13 colonies in Philadelphia from May 10, 1775, through March 1, 1781, when it was succeeded by the Confederation Congress established by the newly ratified Articles of Confederation.

separation of powers The allocation of legal authority among the executive, judicial, and legislative branches of government, with each branch having some ability to limit the action of the other branches. See "checks and balances."

Shays' Rebellion A series of actions between August and December 1786 by debt-ridden farmers led by Daniel Shays that tried to prevent courts in Massachusetts from foreclosing on farms. The rebellion was put down by the Massachusetts militia.

supremacy clause Wording in Article VI of the Constitution that helps establish the dominance of the federal government over the states by declaring the Constitution to be the supreme law and that state as well as federal judges are bound to uphold it.

Three-Fifths Compromise Resolved the dispute at the Constitutional Convention in 1787 over whether and how to count slaves for the purpose of determining representation in Congress by counting every five slaves as three people.

Twenty Year Compromise Resolved the dispute at the Constitutional Convention in 1787 over whether or not to prohibit the importation of slaves by forbidding any law barring importing slaves until 1808 but not placing any barriers to exporting of slaves.

unicameral legislature A legislature with one chamber.

Virginia Plan Proposed by delegates from Virginia at the Constitutional Convention in 1787, the plan favored the most populous states by recommending that (1) seats in the lower house would be allocated among the states based on population, (2) the lower house would select the upper house, and (3) together they would select the chief executive and the national judiciary. See "New Jersey Plan" and "Great Compromise."

FEDERALISM

3

YOU DECIDE: Rape, Justice, and Federalism?

AMERICAN DIVERSITY

Christy Brzonkala learned a bitter lesson about federalism when the Supreme Court threw out her suit. In it, Brzonkala claimed that her civil rights had been violated when she had been raped on her college campus and state and local officials had been unwilling or unable to bring her assailant to justice. The Supreme Court dismissed her suit on the grounds that the federal law that allowed it was an unconstitutional violation of the division of powers in the federal system.

Brzonkala's path to the Supreme Court began in 1994 when she was a student at Virginia Tech. There, she alleged, another student, Antonio Morrison, raped her. He claimed the sex was consensual. A grand jury found too little evidence to indict Morrison, and for the same reason, Virginia Tech also declined to discipline him. Stunned, Brzonkala turned to the federal courts, suing the university and Morrison under the provisions of the Violence Against Women Act (VAWA). Congress had enacted the VAWA in 1992 based on its finding that women suffer economic losses due to violence against them, which, in aggregate, harms the nation's commerce. Therefore, Congress reasoned, its powers under the Constitution's **commerce clause** to regulate interstate commerce made it constitutional to legislate in the area of interpersonal violence even though such crimes normally fall within state jurisdiction. Morrison argued that (1) any relationship between rape and interstate commerce was tangential at best; (2) Congress had therefore stretched the meaning of interstate commerce too far in claiming the authority to enact the VAWA; and, therefore, (3) the provision of the VAWA allowing Brzonkala to sue in federal court was unconstitutional.

In *U.S. v. Morrison* (2000) the Supreme Court agreed with Morrison. Writing for the majority, Chief Justice William Rehnquist rejected Congress's authority to use the commerce clause to "regulate noneconomic, violent criminal conduct." Additionally, he depicted such a broad interpretation of interstate commerce as threatening to "obliterate the distinction between what is national and what is local and create a completely centralized government." Rehnquist wrote that he sympathized with Brzonkala "if the allegations here are true," but added, "Under our federal system [any] remedy must be provided by . . . Virginia, and not by the United States."

How would you have ruled had you been a justice on the Supreme Court in 2000? Remember, the issue before you is not whether Antonio Morrison raped Christy Brzonkala. It is whether rapes in college dormitories and other forms of violence against women should wind up in federal court or remain solely a matter of state jurisdiction. What say you, Mr./Madam Justice?

In 2000 the Supreme Court dismissed a suit filed in federal court by Virginia Tech student Christy Brzonkala against a man whom she accused of raping her on campus. She is shown here with her attorney speaking to reporters. The justices ruled that the U.S. law that allowed such suits violated the Constitution's division of powers in the federal system. Which should have prevailed: the principle of federalism or giving women who feel they have been denied justice at the state level an opportunity to seek justice in the federal courts? (AP Photo)

73

INTRODUCING FEDERALISM

The sad saga that began for Christy Brzonkala and Antonio Morrison in a college dormitory and wound up in the Supreme Court highlights three points that are important to this chapter. First, federalism is not an abstract theory. Instead, it applies to our lives, as Brzonkala learned. Second, disputes over where, if at all, to draw the line between the authority of the states and authority of the central government have often centered on the civil rights of women and people of color. Third, the line between federal and state jurisdiction is hazy, has changed over time, and continues to do so. This chapter reflects the unclear and dynamic aspects of U.S. federalism by presenting it as conflict between the central government and the states over the balance of power between them.

A good place to begin unraveling federalism's complexity is with a basic definition. **Federalism** is a system of government in which: (1) a country has two or more territorial subdivisions (commonly called states or provinces); (2) there is a central (national) government for the whole country and also state/provincial governments for each of the territorial divisions; (3) the national government has substantial and exclusive constitutional authority in some policy areas; and (4) the states/provinces have the constitutional authority to choose their own governments and to independently exercise substantial and exclusive authority in some areas of public policy.

What our definition of federalism does not do is to specify exactly what the **division of power** is between the national and subnational governments. There are three reasons for this. One is that there are usually policy areas in which the national and state governments share authority. Second, the division of power in the world's federal states varies greatly. Some countries are fairly decentralized, with the states having most of the authority. Other countries are fairly centralized, with the states possessing little autonomous authority. However, a federal system no longer truly exists if the states have no realm of exclusive authority and the decisions of the national government always prevail in the areas of shared authority. A third reason that exactly detailing the division of power is difficult is because a federal system creates two often-competitive power centers: a national government favoring centralization and the state governments favoring decentralization. As a result, the division of power in federal systems is always in flux, with some federations becoming more centralized and others more decentralized.

Before proceeding further it is also important to untangle some potential confusion about the word "federal." Somewhat oddly, when used as an adjective—as in the *federal* government, *federal* officials, or the *federal* courts—the word "federal" designates the national government in the United States, its officers, and its organizations. This is not the same as the federal system of national and state governments.

Our next two sections will continue our introduction to the U.S. federal system by putting it in the context of this text's themes of global and domestic diversity. Then we will take up the evolution of U.S. federalism. The ensuing discussion will emphasize the following points:

★ Conflict over the way federalism works dates back to the origins of the Constitution in 1787.
★ During each of several eras of federalism, the interplay between forces of centralization and the forces of decentralization has shaped the evolution of federalism.
★ Among the forces that have interacted to determine the nature of federalism are amendments to the Constitution, interpretations of that document by the courts, shifts in government finance, the increasing integration of the U.S. economy, the expanding role of government, and the civil rights movement.
★ Since 1776, the United States has changed from a highly decentralized league to a relatively centralized federation.
★ Whether this change is positive or negative and what the future course of federalism will be are subjects of lively debate.

Federalism in a World of Difference

As this chapter proceeds, it will be clear that the global setting in which U.S. politics occurs relates to federalism in several ways. One is the tension between globalization and federalism. The second is what we can learn from the comparative perspective of federalism as just one of a range of options for organizing a country's political system.

Globalization and Federalism

There is a tension between globalization and federalism. Globalization undermines federalism because "international legal integration" in trade and other areas of globalization "encourages the centralization of regulatory power" in national governments and discourages it in states and other subnational governments.[1] Recognition of this impact by the states was evident in a report, *International Trade "Primer"/What's at Stake for Vermont?*, by the Vermont Commission on International Trade and State Sovereignty. Among other "dangers" cited by the report is that "the federal government can preempt state laws by citing international trade commitments." One of the many restrictions on states that the report pointed out is that state contracts for goods and services are barred by international treaty from favoring in-state or even American contractors or suppliers.

Washington's ability to supersede the states through treaties and other international agreements stems from the Constitution's designation of treaties as part of the "supreme law of the land." The Supreme Court has repeatedly upheld this

As globalization draws the world together, the laws of states/provinces in countries with federal systems are increasingly likely to impact international relations. U.S.-Mexico relations took a downturn in 2010 after Arizona passed a bill (Senate Bill 1070) that significantly expanded police powers in checking people's immigration status. Here protesters in Mexico City hold signs reading in translation, "No to law SB1070." (AP Photo/Marco Ugarte)

status since 1796. Indeed, the court ruled in *Missouri v. Holland* (1920), a case involving a treaty protecting migratory birds, that treaties could even regulate areas (hunting in this case) traditionally beyond the normal range of federal authority.

Although globalization often limits state power, there are ways that it energizes them. For example, the international economy has become so important to the prosperity of every state that many operate abroad to promote trade and investment. Kentucky, for one, has opened offices in Europe, Japan, Mexico, South America, and China seeking investment (such as the Toyota plant in Georgetown, Kentucky) and promoting the state's exports. Globalization has also prompted growing state and local involvement in international affairs. One method has been for states and communities to refuse to do business with companies that invest in or otherwise do business with foreign governments that abuse human rights or are otherwise objectionable. Both the impact and constitutionality of such economic sanctions are discussed later in this chapter.

Comparing Federalism with Other Models of Political Organization

Creating a federal system was not preordained. Those who wrote the Articles of Confederation and the Constitution had options they could look to in world history and in other countries for structuring the United States. These choices ranged along a scale, as illustrated in Figure 3.1.[2] The most centralized option was a **unitary government,** one in which states are little more than administrative units whose authority is given by and can be revoked by the central government. Nearly all countries had

Only about one of every eight countries has a federal government. The others have unitary governments.

unitary systems in the late 1700s, and most still do. Less centralized is a *federation,* a system in which central and subnational governments each has considerable autonomous authority. The Swiss Federation (established in 1291) is the oldest federation. A *confederation* is even more decentralized. It has a weak central government and strong subnational governments. The United Arab Emirates provides an example, and the European Union, although not a country, is a second good example. Beyond that is a **league,** a system in which sovereign units sometimes make common policy and act together but there is little or no central authority.

Moreover, as Figure 3.1 illustrates, the division of power within a federation can range from highly decentralized, with subnational governments having most of the authority, to very centralized, with the subnational units possessing little autonomous authority. For example, Canada is more decentralized than is the

FIGURE 3.1 Comparative Government Organizations

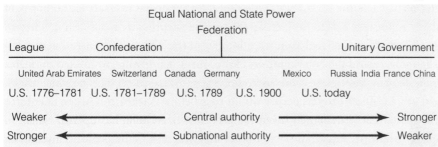

Government organization ranges along a scale from a league, in which there is no true central government, to a unitary form of government, in which territorial units have little or no independent authority. This figure places several countries along the scale for comparison with the United States both today and in history. Note that the U.S. system has become increasingly centralized over time.

United States, with Canada's 10 provinces having more autonomy from Ottawa than U.S. states have from Washington. Decentralization in Canada has also grown in recent decades. The province of Quebec, for instance, has adopted French as its first language, whereas the other provinces favor English. To the south of the United States, the 31 states in the federal system of Mexico were traditionally dominated by the central government, but they have become much stronger than they once were in recent decades as the country has become more democratic. By contrast, Russia is more centralized than the United States and in recent years has moved decisively to further subordinate its subnational governments. In 2005, for example, Russia changed the selection process of regional governors from popular election to appointment by Moscow.

Federalism and Diversity

From the earliest days of the republic, the protection of liberty and the rights of minorities have often been entwined with the U.S. federal system. James Madison believed that under the Articles of Confederation, the states were regularly committing alarming "aggressions . . . on the rights of minorities and of individuals."[3] To address this, he argued that the central government should have a "constitutional negative on the laws of the states" in order to protect individuals "against encroachments on their rights."[4] To be sure, Madison was concerned about the property rights of the small minority of wealthy Americans and not about women and people of color. Nevertheless, his belief that the central government should be the guardian of minority rights against state encroachments has generally come to pass, even if the minorities being protected have changed.

This intersection of federalism and the status of disadvantaged demographic groups began in the early 1800s when southerners began to assert the authority of states' rights as a way to protect slavery against the pressure to abolish it. Then in the aftermath of the Civil War, the adoption of the Thirteenth Amendment abolished slavery, and the Fourteenth and Fifteenth Amendments prohibited the states from denying the right to vote and other freedoms based on race, national origin, and other traits. Nearly a century would pass before Washington began to enforce these latter two amendments, but the seed had been planted. It finally began to sprout in the 1950s, when Washington first moved toward protecting minority rights against such violations by the states as mandating supposedly "separate but equal schools" for whites and students of color. The effort to promote equal rights was praiseworthy, but the process of achieving it further diminished the authority of the states in the federal system.[5] Similarly, we will see that the rights of women and federalism often intersected. The landmark Supreme Court decision *Roe v. Wade* (1973) diminished federalism by taking away most of the authority of the states to regulate abortions. By contrast, the court's decision in *U.S. v. Morrison* (2000) that Congress had overreached its authority in the federal structure when it enacted the Violence Against Women Act supported federalism.

ORIGINS AND EVOLUTION OF THE FEDERAL SYSTEM

As commonly happens in federal systems, the division of power between Washington and the state capitals has shifted considerably throughout U.S. history. These changes have usually been evolutionary rather than revolutionary, but in sum they have substantially changed the way the country is governed. Because of their importance, these shifts provide the organizing theme for most of the chapter, with the various phases of federalism styled as "rounds." Their outcomes have been determined by the interaction between the forces of centralization and the forces of decentralization. This saga continues, but we can say here that authority in the U.S. political system has flowed away from the states and toward the central government. It will become clear as we trace this ebb tide of state authority and flood tide of central authority in the federal system that two factors have been primarily responsible.

Successful legal assertions of expanded national authority are one way that Washington has been able to accumulate power in the federal system. Congress has passed laws, presidents have issued executive orders, and federal courts have made decisions that have eclipsed state power. Court challenges by the states to the federal government's assertions of new legal powers have usually been unsuccessful. Moreover, even when states have lost authority on very sensitive issues, federal authority has almost always been accepted peacefully. Finally, even when there has been resistance, the power of the federal government has ensured compliance. Later you will see, for example, that when the Supreme Court required school desegregation in the 1950s and 1960s and some states resisted, presidents twice sent U.S. Army units into the defiant states to enforce Washington's authority.

Financial sanctions and incentives are a second way that the national government has accumulated power. Washington has sometimes used federal funds to pressure states to follow federal rules in policy areas traditionally under state control. Setting speed limits is one example. To save fuel when an Arab oil embargo sparked a gasoline shortage in 1973, Congress acted to withhold federal highway funds from any state that did not adopt a maximum speed limit of 55 mph. Prior to the directive, only one state had a 55 mph or lower speed limit. Soon every state did. Once Congress began to allow higher limits beginning in 1987, almost all states immediately abandoned the 55 mph standard.[6] Washington also uses incentives to induce states to follow federal policy. The federal government has supplied states and localities with hundreds of billions in aid to mass transit since the 1960s, but that funding has come with numerous "strings," rules that states must follow to get the money. For example, they must practice affirmative action when hiring transit system personnel and provide access for the disabled.

Round 1: Federalism to 1789

Many studies of U.S. federalism begin with the writing of the Constitution in 1787. In reality, the origins of U.S. federalism extend back to the break of the 13 American colonies from Great Britain. At first, the rebellious colonies were a league. No constitution existed between 1776 and 1781. The states cooperated to achieve their common goal of ending British rule, but they were under no legal obligation to do so.

The United States as a league was only eight days old when the debate over national-state relations began. On July 12, 1776, a committee appointed by the Continental Congress presented its first draft of the Articles of Confederation. It envisioned a robust central government. States could have exercised authority only if it did not interfere with the powers of the national government. This plan was doomed. The heady atmosphere of newly declared independence favored the proponents of state power. Although the states had acted jointly in declaring their independence, each regarded itself as **sovereign**: legally free from higher authority. State sovereignty is evident in the words of the Declaration of Independence, "These united colonies are, and of right ought to be free and independent states."

This assumption of state sovereignty determined the structure of the United States under the Articles of Confederation (1781–1789). The document created a U.S. confederation, with a weak central government and powerful state governments.

Epitomizing that, the Articles stipulated that each state retained its "sovereignty, freedom, and independence" and possessed all governmental powers except those "expressly delegated to the United States" by the Articles. So in the contest between centralization and decentralization, Round One went to the states.

Round 2: The Constitutional Convention of 1787

The second round was held in 1787 at the Constitutional Convention in Philadelphia. As Chapter 2 details, most delegates believed that the country's marked decentralization under the Articles of Confederation imperiled national stability. Therefore, these delegates drafted a new constitution that shifted power toward the central government and away from the states. James Madison led this effort. He was an ardent nationalist and an opponent of substantial state power who derided the idea of sovereign states as "utterly irreconcilable" with having a strong United States. Therefore, he advocated the "supremacy of . . . national authority," while leaving "local authorities" in place only to the degree they could be "subordinately useful."[7]

Despite Madison's powerful role in writing the Constitution, he was unable to achieve all he wanted for two reasons: First, many delegates were less nationalistic than he and his supporters were and resisted centralizing the political system. As one opponent put it, "The defects of the confederation are extravagantly magnified."[8] Second, Madison knew that the states had to ratify the proposed constitution and would not agree to surrendering all or most of their power. Madison and his supporters did two things to overcome the opposition. First, the nationalists compromised with their opponents by adopting language that often left the exact division of powers between the two levels of government vague. "No great debate . . . occurred in the convention on the nature of . . . federalism," one scholar notes. Instead, the "critical decisions that established [the federal system] were made in an ad hoc fashion."[9] This political strategy moved the Constitution forward. However, it also resulted in so much imprecision about the national-state relationship that conflicting interpretations of federalism have been an ongoing source of struggle.

Second, the nationalists consciously and somewhat disingenuously soft-peddled the degree to which the new constitution strengthened the central government. As mentioned earlier, Madison, Alexander Hamilton, and John Jay wrote a series of essays called the *Federalist Papers* to promote ratification of the Constitution. Among other things, this "campaign document" downplayed the shift of power under the proposed constitution.[10] In *Federalist* No. 45, for instance, Madison soothingly told his readers that the central government's powers would be "few and defined," while the states' powers would be "numerous and indefinite."

Despite, or perhaps because of, their limited candor, the *Federalist Papers* achieved their goal, and the Constitution was ratified. It created a federal system by declaring itself the supreme law of the land, by giving extensive economic powers to the central government, by barring the states from exercising many economic powers, and by including expansive language authorizing Congress to take any action "necessary and proper" to exercise its authority. Thus, Round Two went to national government.

Round 3: Dual Federalism Emerges, 1789–1860

Round Three in the shaping of federalism began when the new constitution went into effect and lasted until the Civil War.[11] The division of power between the national and state governments that developed during this period has been labeled **dual federalism**. It designates a model in which the national government and the state government have their own distinct and mutually understood realm of authority with little overlap between them. Relations were never quite that simple, though, and the areas of uncertainty were sources of trouble.

The Forces of Centralization

Centralization advanced between 1789 and 1860. Almost all changes were the result of judicial decisions, especially those of the Supreme Court during the long tenure (1801–1835) of Chief Justice John Marshall, a strong nationalist. In ***McCulloch v. Maryland*** (1819) the court rejected a challenge to the authority of Congress to establish a national bank. Marshall wrote the court's opinion giving centralization a double victory. First, he held that the "necessary and proper clause" augmented the national government's *enumerated powers* (its specifically stated powers) by allowing *implied powers* (unspecified authority that logically flows from the enumerated powers). Therefore, Marshall concluded, the federal government's enumerated power to raise and spend revenue included the implied power to create a national bank. This doctrine of implied powers vastly expanded Congress's scope of authority and enabled it to legislate in areas that many had thought would be the exclusive dominion of the states. Second, Marshall's opinion advanced national authority by declaring that states may not regulate anything the federal government does. As Marshall put it, "The states have no power. . . . to retard, impede, burden, or in any manner control the operations of the constitutional laws enacted by Congress."

Gibbons v. Ogden (1824) was another important nationalist decision by the Marshall Court. The justices took an expansive view of the Constitution's commerce clause and Congress's ability to regulate commerce by finding that it "extends to every species of commercial intercourse between the United States

Under Chief Justice John Marshall from 1801 to 1835, the Supreme Court shaped federalism through a series of important decisions that advanced the power of the federal government at the expense of the authority of the states. (iStockphoto)

and foreign nations, and among the several states."[12] The implications of this decision were vast, and how far the national government can go under the interstate commerce clause remains a point of controversy in such cases as *U.S. v. Morrison* featured in the opening You Decide box.

As is true throughout U.S. history, issues about diversity and global affairs also played a role during this early period in advancing centralization. ***Worchester v. Georgia*** (1832) was a key case involving the treatment of minority groups. In that case, the Marshall Court ruled that Native Americans were a distinct political community whose affairs could be regulated only by the federal government, not by the states. Georgia ignored the court's ruling, and in an action unthinkable today, President Andrew Jackson refused to enforce the court's mandate. Not only that, he favored pushing many of the Indian tribes westward. During the ensuing few years Jackson and his successor, President Martin Van Buren, supported the state's efforts to push the Cherokee tribe off its lands in Georgia. The displaced Cherokee were then forced under U.S. Army guard to make a horrific march that killed about one-fourth of the 16,000 Cherokee along the "Trail of Tears" that led to what is now Oklahoma.

On the global front, the division of authority between the U.S. government and the state governments in dealing with the rest of the world was also clarified in a court decision that came down on the side of centralization. The case involved the refusal of a Virginia man to pay a debt he owed to a British citizen from the colonial period on the grounds that a Virginia law nullified debts owed to an "alien enemy." The British citizen sued in federal court, citing the Treaty of Paris (1783) between the American and British governments. As part of ending the war, the treaty had validated all debts owed by citizens of each country to citizens of the other. In *Ware v. Hylton* (1796), the Supreme Court issued its first of many rulings establishing almost exclusive federal authority in foreign affairs and affirming that treaties override state law.

The Forces of Decentralization

Several decentralizing factors helped offset centralization. These included constitutional amendments, assertions of state supremacy, and Supreme Court decisions beginning in the 1840s.

Constitutional Amendments   Concern about federal authority under the new Constitution prompted two quick amendments. The **Tenth Amendment** specified that the states retained those powers that the Constitution did not give to the federal government or deny to the states. This reservoir of authority constitutes the states' **reserved powers.** More than any other part of the Constitution, the Tenth Amendment became the basis of the now largely discredited **states' rights**

doctrine. It maintains that the Tenth Amendment should be read literally to mean that any power not given to the federal government or denied to the states is reserved for the states.

An early test of federalism arose when two South Carolinians sued Georgia in federal court over a property matter. Georgia argued that it could not be sued under the doctrine of **sovereign immunity**, which exempts sovereign units from oversight by the courts. When the Supreme Court ruled against the state in *Chisholm v. Georgia* (1793), states-right forces raised a storm of protest. Tempers in Georgia were so fevered that its legislature passed a law making enforcement of the *Chisholm* decision a crime punishable by hanging "without benefit of clergy."[13] Two important consequences followed. One was adoption of the **Eleventh Amendment** (1795). It overturned *Chisholm* by excluding from federal jurisdiction cases brought against a state by citizens of another state or another country.

Assertions of State Supremacy   The second and more extreme reaction to *Chisholm* was the **nullification doctrine.** This is the assertion that a state can void (nullify) any federal law or act that it believes to be unconstitutional. This concept was first advanced in 1798 after Congress passed the Alien and Sedition Acts. Among other things, those laws made it a crime to criticize federal officials in a way that would subject them to "the hatred of the good people of the United States."[14] In response, Thomas Jefferson and James Madison drew up the so-called Virginia and Kentucky Resolutions. They proclaimed the right of states to void federal laws that violated the rights of their citizens. Ironically, the nullification doctrine became best known as a basis for rejecting federal interference in slavery and, much latter, desegregation.

Judicial Decisions of the Taney Court   In contrast to John Marshall, Chief Justice Roger B. Taney (1836–1864), was a force for decentralization. In a series of decisions under his tutelage, the Court developed the idea of **concurrent powers**, those that can be exercised by both the federal and state governments. For example, the court allowed states to establish banks with the authority to issue monetary notes for public circulation, thereby temporarily eclipsing what had been the exclusive authority of the central government to print paper money.[15] In yet other cases, the Taney Court sought, as the chief justice put it, to identify "certain subjects as exclusively within the jurisdiction of the states and beyond the reach of the national government."[16] One such subject was the ownership of slaves. The Taney Court rejected attempts to apply federal jurisdiction to cases involving blacks who argued they had become free by virtue of having been taken to or having escaped to a state or territory where slavery was illegal. In *Strader v. Graham* (1851), the court ruled that the issue was entirely under the jurisdiction of the states.

An Overview of Federalism, 1789–1860

All in all, Round Three in the evolution of federalism was a draw with no clear winner. The early part of the period was dominated by a muscular assertion of national power, especially by the Marshall Court. It found 19 different state laws or actions to be unconstitutional. In the words of one scholar, "Marshall's constitutional jurisprudence pushed nationalism to the edge of the political envelope of his day."[17]

This nationalist trend was counterbalanced by strong assertions of states' rights. Even nationalists like James Madison argued for the nullification doctrine when faced with abhorrent federal laws like the Alien and Sedition Acts. After the mid-1830s, the Taney Court further restrained centralization. Moreover, a series of generally undistinguished presidents extending from Martin Van Buren (1837–1841) to James Buchanan (1857–1861) were unable to stem the decentralization tide as state resistance to national authority became ensnared in the bitter debate over slavery. All this set the stage "for a fratricidal contest over, in part, whether a nation-centered or states-centered theory of federalism would prevail."[18] The Civil War was about to begin.

Round 4: Dual Federalism Fades, 1860–1930

Round Four in the history of U.S. federalism began on the eve of the greatest political crisis in American history and ended on the eve of the worst economic crisis Americans have ever endured. Between the outbreak of the Civil War and the country's descent into the Great Depression, the division of authority between the national and state governments did not shift dramatically. Therefore, dual federalism survived largely intact. Still, despite victories for both the forces of centralization and those of decentralization, the foundation was laid for what would later be a major surge in national authority over the states.

The Forces of Centralization

Powerful changes were underway in the decades after the Civil War. Blacks were transformed from slaves into citizens, only to be reduced to second-class citizenship by racism and Jim Crow laws. The country also moved away from its rural, agricultural roots and became increasingly industrialized and urbanized. Transcontinental railroads, the telegraph, and, later, roads, radios, and telephones tied the country together. The national government went from taking a largely hands-off approach to what was a localized American economy before the Civil War to asserting increasing control over what had become a national economy by the beginning of the twentieth century. These broad trends and others played a role in advancing the forces of centralization.

The Civil War   The North's triumph in the Civil War was a victory for federalism. The authority of the federal government to impose its will on states in time of crisis was demonstrated repeatedly beginning with President Abraham Lincoln's decision to treat the claim of a sovereign right of secession by the southern states as treasonous rebellion. Later, the Supreme Court in *Texas v. White* (1869) gave judicial sanction to what Lincoln had established by force. The court ruled that states did not have the sovereign right to secede from "an indestructible union of indestructible states." Centralization was also advanced in 1863 when Lincoln issued the Emancipation Proclamation freeing the slaves in the 11 states of the Confederacy despite the dubious constitutionality of that executive order.

Also during this period, Congress passed three amendments to the Constitution. The Thirteenth Amendment (1865), which banned slavery, had little effect on federalism. By contrast, the other two amendments had major implications for federalism. The **Fourteenth Amendment** (1868) barred states from (1) violating the "privileges and immunities of citizens of the United States," from (2) depriving anyone of "life, liberty, or property without due process of law," and from (3) denying anyone the "equal protection of the laws." It took nearly a century, but the amendment eventually became a key tool of centralization, as we will discuss below. The **Fifteenth Amendment** (1870) prohibited states from interfering with the ability to vote "on account of race [or] color" and gave Congress the power to enforce this prohibition. Like the Fourteenth Amendment, however, it languished for a nearly a century before becoming a major force in ending state abuses of civil rights and liberties.

A Nationalizing Economy   The economic transformation of the United States in the second half of the 1800s had important consequences for federalism. The economy became truly national as an increasing number of businesses engaged in multistate operations, as more goods and services moved across state lines, and as national labor unions formed. These changes prompted the national government to extend its authority into areas that had once been the nearly exclusive domains of the states. To cite one example, the establishment in 1887 of the first U.S. regulatory agency, the Interstate Commerce Commission, supplanted the authority of 30 state railroad commissions and ended their existence. Congress took such actions under pro-centralization interpretations of the Constitution's interstate commerce clause and was sometimes supported by the Supreme Court.[19]

This photo shows the completion of the transcontinental railroad by the meeting of the Central Pacific and Union Pacific lines at Promontory Point, Utah, in 1869. The historic event advanced the rapid nationalization of the U.S. economy during the second half of the 1800s. This in turn led to greater centralization in the federal system through national economic regulations. (Library of Congress)

Changes in Government Finance   Two changes in government finance during Round Four of federalism had important implications. One was the beginning of federal **categorical grants**, the practice of the national government in giving money to states to fund specific programs. The first such legislation was the Morrill Act (1862). It let states sell federal land and use the proceeds to establish public colleges. Under the act and its revisions, including one in 1890 that pressured states to fund colleges for black students, 76 land grant colleges were established. From this beginning, the government slowly began to establish more such grant programs. By 1930, the number stood at 30. The amount of money distributed by these grants was still small, but grants would later become a major source of federal authority over the states.

Increased federal tax revenue was the second important change that occurred in government finance. The **Sixteenth Amendment** (1913) empowered the federal government to tax the proverbial golden goose of revenue: the earnings of individual Americans and corporations. Tax collections began modestly under this new authority, but in time they swelled and gave Washington the vast resources that let it become active in many areas of policy that had once been matters of state authority. The long-term implications of the Sixteenth Amendment were so important, according to one scholar, that the subsequent evolution of federalism can be explained entirely by the central government getting access to the "most lucrative of all public revenue sources."[20]

The Forces of Decentralization

Between 1861 and 1930, the forces of decentralization were fewer and had less long-term potency than those of centralization. Still, they slowed centralization down.

Jim Crow   Once Reconstruction ended in 1871 and federal forces withdrew from the southern states, a combination of poll taxes, literacy tests, and other Jim Crow policies along with sheer terrorist intimidation savaged the civil rights and liberties of African Americans and other disadvantaged groups. In Louisiana, for example, the number of registered black voters plummeted 90% between 1870 and 1906.[21] Yet the nation and its courts virtually ignored the Fourteenth and Fifteenth Amendments. Congress passed no legislation to enforce them, and the courts rejected attempts to "federalize" civil rights and liberties under the provisions of the amendments. The courts also turned a blind eye to state-legislated segregation. One important case involved a Louisiana law that required separate and supposedly equal railcar sections for blacks and whites and provided penalties for sitting in the wrong place. In 1892, Homer Plessy, a black man, was arrested for sitting in a white section. He appealed to the federal courts, arguing that Louisiana's law violated his rights under the Fourteenth Amendment. The Supreme Court rejected this argument in *Plessy v. Ferguson* (1896). The net effect of such attitudes and rulings was to leave most issues of civil and voting rights to the states.

Expanding State Government Decentralization was also buttressed by the general growth of state government. Although the federal government's relative power compared to that of the states grew, the absolute power of both levels of government expanded as all governments involved themselves in a widening scope of issues. Tax collections provide one indicator of the rapid growth of both levels of government. As Figure 3.2 shows, the increase in federal tax collections between 1902 and 1927 rose 556%, but that was nearly matched by a 536% increase in local taxes and was greatly outpaced by state tax hikes of 931%.

Reluctant Courts Although the courts sometimes supported greater federal activity under the commerce clause, they were still reluctant to adopt an expansive view of national authority when it impinged on traditional areas of state activity. Challenges by the states were usually unsuccessful, with federal courts upholding the state position in 83% of such cases between 1887 and 1910. As a result, the states continued to exercise nearly unfettered authority in such areas as family, criminal, and electoral law, and even extensive authority in commerce.

An Overview of Federalism, 1860–1930

Centralization began the period with a surge and then slowed, only to speed up again with the new powers that Washington gained in association with a nationalizing economy and its vast new taxing authority. This did not mean, though, that the state governments and their subsidiaries, local governments, withered. Instead, as has been true throughout U.S. history, the scope of government increased. Therefore, the activities of the states grew even while centralization advanced.

The changes between 1860 and 1930 were important but not profound. In part that is because many of the advances in centralization associated with the Fourteenth and Fifteenth Amendments, the advent of federal grants, and the growth of federal tax revenue after the passage of the Sixteenth Amendment did not occur fully until later. Thus, as the country approached 1930, dual federalism was still the prevailing model. However, the forces of centralization had won Round Four by a narrow margin, and dual federalism's days were numbered.

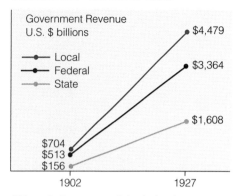

FIGURE 3.2 Growth of Taxes

Although the power of the federal government grew relative to the states between 1861 and 1930, the shift was partly offset by the absolute growth of all levels of government, as is illustrated by a comparison of taxes raised in 1902 and 1927.

Data source: David B. Walker, *The Rebirth of Federalism,* 2nd ed. (New York: Chatham House, 2000), p. 77.

Round 5: Cooperative Federalism, 1930–1960

Dual federalism's demise came quickly during Round Five. The model was demolished in the 1930s by dramatic events and political changes beginning with the country's greatest economic crisis, the Great Depression. The aggressive economic policies that President Franklin D. Roosevelt adopted to deal with that crisis, the increasing role of the federal grants in funding state programs, and the invigoration of the civil rights movement all worked during this 30-year period to supplant dual federalism with a new model.

Dubbed **cooperative federalism**, the new model featured overlapping federal and state authority in a wide range of governmental functions. Talk of exclusive state functions faded. During this era the federal government became involved in an array of policy areas that had been the exclusive domain of the states. In the end, the two levels of government came to cooperatively share responsibility for nearly all areas of governance other than national security and foreign policy. The difference between dual and cooperative federalism has been compared to two kinds of cake.

Dual federalism is akin to a *layer cake*, one with two distinct layers. Cooperative federalism resembles a *marble cake*, in which the two colors of cake wrap around one another in no fixed pattern.

The human impact of the Great Depression of the 1930s is captured by this 1936 photograph of a 32-year-old woman and two of her seven children outside their makeshift tent in California where her husband was working as a migrant farm laborer. The New Deal under President Roosevelt speeded economic recovery, but it also expanded the power of the national government and the centralization of the federal system. (Library of Congress)

The Forces of Centralization

Three factors played a major role in strengthening centralization during this 30-year period. One was the continued transformation of the U.S. economy from agricultural and local to industrial and national. The second factor was the growth of federal grants as a source of federal influence. And the third was an end of the Supreme Court's reluctance to use the Fourteenth and Fifteenth Amendments to protect the rights of Americans.

Economic Depression and Rejuvenation　The prosperous, socially exuberant decade of the 1920s ended on October 29, 1929, "Black Tuesday," when the stock market collapsed. The economy soon followed suit. Between 1929 and 1933, U.S. economic output plummeted more than 30% and unemployment soared sickeningly from 3% to 25%. Reaction to the onset of the Depression swept President Herbert Hoover and his belief that the federal government should not interfere in the economy from office and brought in a new president, Franklin D. Roosevelt, and a new philosophy of federal economic interventionism.

Roosevelt launched the **New Deal**, an economic recovery program that had the effect of weakening state authority in the federal system by involving Washington more than ever before in the domestic economy and in the welfare of individual Americans. For example, the National Industrial Recovery Act (NIRA) of 1933 required industries to adopt fair competition codes that were subject to the president's approval. At first, the Supreme Court, still rooted in the era of dual federalism, rejected such acts as an unconstitutional expansion of the authority of Congress to regulate commerce. In *Schecter Poultry Corporation v. U.S.* (1935), the "sick chicken case," the Supreme Court rejected the authority of the federal government to fine a Brooklyn, New York, poultry supplier for violating the NIRA's fair competition codes by selling chickens that were unfit for consumption. Because the company had sold all its fowl in New York, the court found that the foul chickens were not part of interstate commerce. Political feathers flew. Amid a huge outcry against the decision, an outraged Roosevelt responded with a "court packing" plan to increase the number of Supreme Court justices from 9 to 15. Arguably, the court "chickened out" in the face of this political pressure because the justices soon issued a series of decisions that reversed their previous positions and increased national authority under the commerce clause. The result of these and later decisions and of new laws and presidential executive orders was a dramatic and lasting enlargement of federal power.

Federal Grants and Revenue   The number and size of federal grants to the states accelerated rapidly during the 30-year period of cooperative federalism. The number of grant programs increased from 30 in 1930 to 132 in 1960. Annual federal grant dollars during this period shot up 3,173% to more than $6 billion, as indicated in Figure 3.3. These dollars had strings attached, however, and centralization increased as states increasingly had to accept more and more federal regulations in order to get or keep the money flowing.

Also, following the pattern that had begun in the 1920s, the revenue of the national government grew rapidly. This growth allowed it to control an increasing percentage of government spending on domestic programs. Federal spending accounted for only 17% of all such expenditures in 1929. By 1959, federal spending on domestic programs was 48% of the total. Not surprisingly, the ability to regulate these programs shifted substantially toward the federal

FIGURE 3.3   Growth of Federal Grants

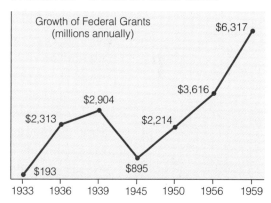

During the era of cooperative federalism, the federal government moved into many program areas once exclusively within the realm of the states by creating grant programs to support various state activities and attaching "strings" (regulatory requirements) to them. Except for a downturn during World War II, the dollar amount of the grants rose sharply throughout the period.

Data source: Walker, *Rebirth of Federalism*, p. 100.

government as its share of the funding rose and the share of the states and localities declined.

Initial Expansion of Civil Liberties and Civil Rights   After many decades of dormancy, the Fourteenth Amendment began to make a difference in the rights of Americans. During this period, the Supreme Court increasingly applied the language in the Fourteenth Amendment that bars states from violating "the privileges or immunities of citizens of the United States," from depriving people of "life, liberty, and property without the due process of law," and from denying them "the equal protection of the laws." According to the new view of the Court, these phrases meant that the Bill of Rights often applied to the states as well as to the federal government. These decisions are detailed in Chapters 4 and 5, but the important point here is that many of the decisions advancing civil liberties and rights did so by limiting the authority of the states and increasing federal supervision over them.

Of the cases that advanced civil rights and liberties during these years, the most important was ***Brown v. Board of Education of Topeka*** **(1954)**. In it, the Court unanimously reversed *Plessy v. Ferguson* (1896) and ruled that separate was inherently unequal. The South's reaction was reminiscent of the pre-Civil War advocacy of the nullification doctrine. Five southern legislatures passed resolutions saying their state would not enforce unconstitutional rulings. Georgia even made it a crime to implement school integration. The clash between states' rights and civil rights soon came to a head in Little Rock, Arkansas. Threatening mobs of whites blocked an effort to enroll nine black students, later called the "Little Rock Nine," in the city's Central High School in 1957. State and local officials refused to restore order. Enforcement thus came to rest in the White House. President Dwight D. Eisenhower did not agree with the *Brown* decision, but he also believed that in the face of the state's defiance of the Supreme Court, it would be "tantamount to acquiescence in anarchy and the dissolution of the union" if he failed to defend the Constitution.[22] To avoid that, he sent the Army's elite 101st Airborne Division to Little Rock. The racists' pledge that black and white children would go to school together only "over my dead body" took on a literal meaning. Integration proceeded. The specter of nullification was put back to rest.

An Overview of Federalism, 1930–1960

Round Five in the struggle between centralization and decentralization went decisively to centralization. Indeed, the scorecard for decentralization had so few points on it that the discussion of this period, unlike the discussion of the other eras, has no section entitled "The Forces of Decentralization." The country turned to Washington to deal with the crises presented by the Great Depression, then

World War II. Some of the authority that had flowed toward the center ebbed temporarily after the war. That retreat of national authority was a matter of budget though, and there was no significant counterbalance to the centralizing policy initiatives and the judicial decisions that marked most of the three-decades-long era.

A lopsided score in favor of federalism between 1930 and 1960 did not mean, however, that the states had withered away. In many ways they had grown as governmental units because of the absolute expansion of governmental activity in the United States. As a result, states took in significantly more revenue and spent more dollars than they had prior to the 1930s. In the changing political climate of the era, states also became involved in more policy realms than ever before through initiatives in areas that had once been local or even beyond the usual boundaries of government. But authority, not activity, is the true test of federalism. By the authority standard, the federal system weakened. First, the number of policy areas within the exclusive jurisdiction of state and local government declined dramatically. Second, the ability of states to make decisions that fell afoul of the political and judicial views of the national government was increasingly restrained. Thus the relative power of the states compared to the national government decreased. This trend would continue during Round Six.

ROUND 6: SEMI-SUBORDINATED FEDERALISM, 1960 TO THE PRESENT

Scholars of federalism have settled on the terms *dual federalism* and *cooperative federalism* to describe earlier eras of federalism, but there is no consensus on how to depict contemporary federalism. Some scholars discuss it in terms of the continuing development of cooperative federalism. "Creative federalism," "co-optive federalism," "new federalism," and other terms have also been used to describe some or all of what has occurred since the early 1960s. Recalling the culinary images of layer and marble cakes to represent earlier eras, yet another student of federalism has suggested with tongue in cheek that the great complexity and shifts of federal-state authority might be called "fruit cake federalism."[23]

Each of these characterizations of federalism has merit, but here we will use **semi-subordinated federalism** to describe the contemporary situation. According to this view of contemporary federalism, which has also been called "partially permissive federalism," the states have become extensively subordinated to the central government and exercise power in most areas only insofar as it does not conflict with national policy.[24] Note that "semi" and "partially" indicate that the process of subordination is not complete, only partially in place. Certainly, the overlapping, intertwining relationship between the national and state governments that characterized cooperative federalism still exists. But the power to make definitive judgments on policy has come to rest heavily with the federal government. Sometimes the states have latitude to tailor policy, but they have few areas of unfettered authority left. It remains the case that the struggle between centralization and decentralization continues, and there have been instances of resistance to the flow of power toward Washington that has prevailed since the beginning of the 1930s. However, these countervailing instances have been few and have done little to stem the tide of centralization.

The Forces of Centralization

In many ways the forces of centralization since the 1960s have been continuations of those that were at work between 1930 and 1960. Federal activity in domestic economic and social policy has continued to expand, as has the flow of federal grant money to state governments. Even more than between 1930 and 1960, the effort of Washington since 1960 to advance civil rights and liberties has often been accomplished by presidential executive orders, legislation by Congress, and decisions by the federal courts curbing the powers of the states. Further, the shift in the Supreme Court during the 1930s toward a greater willingness to support federal activity in traditional state policy realms has continued in most cases.

Expansive Domestic Policy Initiatives

With the Democrats controlling both the White House and Congress throughout most of the 1960s, there was an upsurge of federal spending on human resource programs. President Lyndon Johnson's **Great Society** initiative was of particular note. It included many new or greatly expanded programs that were funded by the federal government and largely operated under federal regulations. It is not necessary to detail these programs to make the point that they moved the central government increasingly into areas, such as housing and welfare, that had previously been mostly or exclusively state matters. The impact was to lessen the independent authority of the states because the national government established the rules, and the states most often followed them, either because they were legally obligated to do so or because they could not bring themselves to pass up the federal grants provided to fund the programs.

Education has been another such area. Schools were once almost exclusively the domain of state and local governments. In 1962, for example, the National Forensic League's topic for high school debate teams was whether there should be federal aid to education. Whatever the young debaters argued that year, the answer of the federal government was soon yes. Congress enacted the Higher Education Act and the Elementary and Secondary School Act in 1965 as steps toward President Johnson's Great Society goal. From that point, federal aid to elementary, secondary, and higher education has risen more than twentyfold, and numerous policy initiatives have come with the money. For example, Title IX of the Education Amendments Act of 1972 barred sex discrimination in schools getting federal funds directly or indirectly. Among other things, Title IX required schools to significantly increase the number of women playing organized sports, as Figure 3.4 shows for college athletics.

Perhaps the best overall measure of Washington's increased activity in education and the other human resource programs is funding. In 1960, the U.S. budget included $9.1 billion for education, health, and income security (not including Social Security or veterans' benefits). A decade later that amount had quadrupled to $30.4 billion, and by 2009 it had reached $1.6 trillion. Figure 3.5 shows the growth in the funding of these programs in terms of their percentage of the U.S. budget and the country's gross domestic product.

Washington's new or enhanced activity in a number of other policy areas has also served to undercut existing state authority. Environmental policy provides an example. The National Environmental Policy Act (1969) authorized formation of the U.S. Environmental Protection Agency (EPA). That act and other legislation, such as the Clean Air Act (1970) and the Clean Water Act (1972), either set specific standards that states had to meet or authorized the EPA to set standards. For instance, the Clean Air Act requires that states and localities, as well as private organizations, build sewage treatment plants, use pollution control technology, and get federal permission before discharging wastes into lakes and rivers or taking any other action (such as building roads) that might threaten to pollute bodies of water or watershed areas. These requirements are substantively desirable, but they also undercut state authority and thereby diminish federalism in many ways. For instance, a state may no longer build a highway where it wants without multiple federal clearances. Among these, the EPA must certify that wetlands and other environmentally sensitive areas are protected.

FIGURE 3.4 Women in College Sports

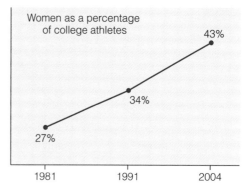

One impact of Title IX since its enactment in 1972 has been to vastly increase female participation rates in sports. This figure shows the increase for college athletics.
Data source: John Cheslock, *Who's Playing College Sports: Money, Race, and Gender,* Women's Sports Foundation Research Report (East Meadow, NY: September 2008).

FIGURE 3.5 Social Welfare Spending

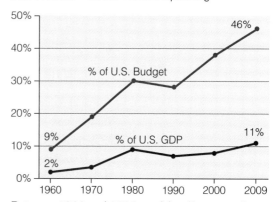

Between 1960 and 2009, social welfare spending on education, health, and income security rose substantially as both a percentage of the U.S. budget and GDP. The strong movement of the federal government into these policy realms has undercut state authority in them.
Notes and data source: Social welfare spending includes all categories listed in the U.S. Budget under "Human Resources" except Social Security and Veterans' benefits. Data from U.S. Office of Management and Budget.

FIGURE 3.6 Federal Grants to State and Local Governments

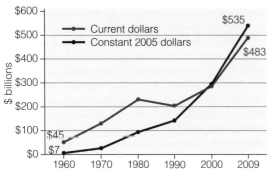

The money flowing from the federal government to state and local governments through various grant programs has increased substantially since 1960. With few exceptions, these programs carry provisions that have limited the ability or willingness of states to make policy decisions that do not adhere to Washington's standards.

Data source: U.S. Office of Management and Budget

A Flood of Federal Grants

The trickle of grants from Washington that began with the Morrill Act of 1862 and grew to a steady stream during the era of cooperative federalism (1930–1960) became a flood of funding beginning in the 1960s, as is evident in Figure 3.6.

Indeed, the flow of dollars and its impact became so central to the operation of the federal system that it became known as **fiscal federalism**. This is the one-way financial relationship that has Washington giving money with strings attached and the states getting the funds and administering the rules. To get a sense of the importance of federal grants and other support flowing to the states, consider the following:

- Federal grants to states rose from 0.8% of the GDP in 1960 to 3.8% of the GDP in 2009.
- Overall, each state received an average of $10.8 billion in federal funding.
- California got the most ($52 billion); Delaware got the least ($1.3 billion).
- In 1960, 16% of state spending came from federal grants; 25% came from grants in 2009.
- Mississippi was the state most dependent on federal grants, getting 47% of what it spent from them. Alaska (14%) was the least reliant state.
- On a per capita basis, the average state received $1,852 in federal funds.
- Wyoming got the most per person ($3,978); Virginia received the least ($939).

Fiscal federalism undermines the federal structure because the strings attached to the grants often impinge on areas traditionally in the realm of the states. Subsequent legislation and bureaucratic regulations often add to the skein of federal rules. However, states seldom can resist the lure of "free" money from Washington, and the impact of complying with these provisions has been the continued weakening of state autonomy in the federal system.

Federal funding for transportation provides a good example. Under the Highway Act of 1956 and later laws, the federal government gives the states up to 90% of their cost of constructing and maintaining interstate highways and mass transportation systems. Annual subsidies to the states have risen from an initial $1 billion in 1957 to $39 billion in 2009. With the money has come a bevy of federal laws and regulations that have in effect extended federal regulation deep into what was once an almost exclusive policy area of the states. For instance, as noted earlier,

Congress imposed a de facto national speed limit of 55 miles an hour by requiring federal officials to cut off the highway funds of states that did not adopt that standard. Such measures by Congress to pressure states to follow federal rules are highly controversial. The following You Decide box gives you a chance to weigh in on one such issue.

Burgeoning Civil Liberties and Rights

One of the most important traits of the 1960s and 1970s, and to a lesser degree the decades since then, was the rapid expansion of civil rights and liberties. African Americans, women, Latinos, and other groups became much more successful in asserting their rights. The courts strengthened their use of the Fourteenth Amendment to apply much of the Bill of Rights to the states. Similarly, federal judicial decisions and legislative action relying on the Fifteenth Amendment and the commerce clause also advanced civil liberties and rights. In 2009, for example, Congress relied in part on this authority under the commerce clause to make hate crimes committed against homosexuals a federal felony.

Because these changes are discussed fully in Chapters 4 and 5, it is not necessary to detail them here beyond a few examples to underline a basic point: federal support of expanding civil rights often occurred over the objections of states that the national government was violating their authority in the federal system. One example began when Congress passed the Civil Rights Act of 1964. It relied on

YOU DECIDE: Which Level of Government Should Decide the Drinking Age?

Chapter 1 contains a You Decide box debating whether the minimum "drinking age" should be reduced to 18, but that topic is also a federalism issue. States set the minimum age for buying and consuming alcoholic beverages until 1983 when Congress amended the Highway Act so that states with drinking ages below 21 would lose 10% of the money allocated to them. At that time 31 states had minimum ages between 18 and 20. By 1988 there was a nationally uniform age of 21 because of the federal pressure. Essentially, the authority to decide the drinking age had been removed from the states and taken by the federal government.

Unlike Chapter 1's You Decide box, what the drinking age should be is not the issue here. Instead, the focus is on who should decide. Irrespective of your opinion on the age issue, do you support Washington's use of its financial muscle to push the states to adopt the federal standard or was this an intrusion into state authority that unwisely weakened the federal system? Avoid letting your substantive opinion (what the drinking age should be) determine your procedural opinion (who should decide). If you favor letting the states decide *because* you favor lowering the age, you will be in a difficult position if, on another issue, you want the federal government to set a standard on an issue where you think your state or other states are falling short.

Decisions by the Supreme Court from the mid-1950s into the 1970s that allowed the federal government to intervene on the behalf of civil rights in the states advanced equality but also diminished federalism. The leader of the Court during this era was Chief Justice Earl Warren (left), seen here in 1968 talking with President Lyndon Johnson, whose Great Society program also advanced civil rights at the expense of state autonomy. (LBJ Library/National Archives)

the commerce clause to bar discrimination anywhere involved in interstate commerce. That turned out to be nearly everywhere, as illustrated by the refusal of Ollie's Barbecue in Birmingham, Alabama, to serve blacks. In an ensuing suit, the Supreme Court found against Ollie's.[25] Even though the eatery was locally owned and served local customers, the court reasoned that Ollie's use of products that had originated in other states permitted U.S. jurisdiction. The point here is not the social justice of Congress's legislation or the court's decision. Rather it is to see what the decision meant for federalism. If an establishment as peripheral to the national economy as Ollie's Barbecue is subject to federal regulation because some of its beef ribs came from Kansas cattle and its catsup contained Texas tomatoes, then there is probably no economic activity beyond federal oversight in an era of an integrated national economy. As one scholar notes, Congress's use of the commerce power to extend national authority and the willingness of the courts to support that trend has "transformed the commerce power into an almost unlimited federal grant [of authority]" and has raised questions about "what limits, if any, the requirements of a federal system place on national power."[26]

Unfunded Mandates

A separate outcome of the federal legislation has been the growth in the number and cost of **unfunded mandates**. These are federal laws and regulations that require the states to do things for which Congress supplies no or insufficient funding. According to the Mandate Monitor program of the National Conference of State Legislatures, Congress shifted at least $131 billion in costs to states between 2003 and 2008. Some mandates involve civil rights. The Americans with Disabilities Act (1990), for one, has required state and local governments to spend billions of dollars to install elevators, ramps, and curb cuts and to make many other changes to public property to make it more accessible to the disabled. This and other mandates, such as increasing the national minimum wage for workers, including those of state and local governments, have been domestic policy. Globalization has also added to unfunded mandates. One example is the REAL ID Act passed in 2004 ostensibly to make it harder for foreign terrorists to obtain U.S. identification documents. Among other things, the act required states to significantly upgrade their driver's licenses, but supplied no funding to pay the $4 billion that the National Governors Associated estimated that implementation would cost the states. In 2009 Secretary of Homeland Security Janet Napolitano, a former Arizona governor who had protested the 2004 act, proposed legislation to ease the burden, but even her substitute would still cost the states an estimated $2 billion.

The issue about these mandates with regard to federalism is not whether the program's goals were worthy or not. It is not possible to argue with the goals of the

ADA, for example. Rather the federalism issue is that by requiring states to spend money in certain ways, it forced the states to choose one of a number of possible fiscal responses, such as cutting spending on other programs, against its will.

Preemptive Laws and Regulations

Federalism has also been weakened by Congress passing and the presidents signing a record number of laws preempting state authority, as shown in Figure 3.7. Such laws substitute federal standards for state standards. Some preemptive acts and regulations establish minimum standards. Other laws and regulations bar state standards that are stricter. This second approach was common under President George W. Bush's administration when Congress was Republican-controlled during most of his first six years in office.[27] One Republican goal was to limit regulation, and that included stopping the states from setting environmental standards and other regulations higher than the federal level. The administration also claimed greater wisdom at the federal level. As an Office of Management and Budget official explained, state and local governments "often lack the information, expertise and staff that the federal agencies [have]," and, therefore, "having a single federal standard can be the best way to guarantee safety and protect consumers."[28]

Globalization was another factor.[29] Almost one quarter of the preemptive laws between 2000 and 2005 related to global terrorism, and several others involved international trade and communications. Yet other preemptions involved more traditional policy matters. For one, Bush's "No Child Left Behind" education policy greatly extended federal control over the nation's schools. In the words of one critic, Bush policies constituted a "somewhat breathtaking subordination of states rights, not a support of them as the president [had] pledged."[30]

Increased Federalization of Crime

Only three federal crimes are mentioned in the Constitution: counterfeiting, piracy, and treason. New federal crimes were soon added as the First Congress (1789–1791) taxed such items as imports and whiskey production and established penalties for not paying them. Over the years, though, the list of federal crimes grew slowly. That began to change in the 1960s as Congress increasingly used its implied power under the interstate commerce clause and also to a degree

FIGURE 3.7 **Preemptive Legislation**

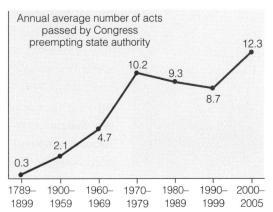

After a slight downturn in the 1980s and 1990s, the historic trend of Congress annually increasing the number of acts preempting state authority has resumed in recent years.
Data source: Joseph F. Zimmerman, "Congressional Preemption During the George W. Bush Administration," *Publius: The Journal of Federalism*, 37/3 (2007): 432–452.

under the Fourteenth Amendment to enact federal criminal laws in areas traditionally regulated by the states. There is no precise count of such laws, but former U.S.
Attorney General Dick Thornburgh told a congressional committee in 2009 that
"the current 'estimate' is a staggering 4,450 [federal] crimes on the books."[31] Most
of the increase in these laws since the Civil War has occurred since 1960.

Whether these laws have a laudable purpose is not the issue here. Most, perhaps all, do. For instance, a number of them are so-called hate crimes laws. The
first was passed in 1969 making it a federal crime to willingly injure or intimidate
anyone because of his or her race, religion, or national origin while doing such
things as voting. Since then, new laws have added to the groups that are protected.
Most recently, the law was expanded in 2009 to cover sexual orientation and disabilities. Hate crime laws now also cover any criminal act against someone in a
protected group, not just acts taken in specific circumstances.

The issue here is the degree to which such laws have moved the U.S. Department of Justice and the federal courts into an area, crimes against private persons
and private property, that was once almost exclusively within the realm of state
governments. According to a 1998 report by the American Bar Association, "Inap-
propriately federalized crime . . . generally undermines the state-federal fabric and
disrupts the important constitutional balance of federal and state systems."[32] Taking the same view, Chief Justice William H. Rehnquist warned that the "trend
to federalize crimes that traditionally have been handled in state courts not only
is taxing the [federal] judiciary's resources . . . , but it also threatens to change
entirely the nature of our federal system."[33]

A second issue related to the federalization of crime is that it narrows the Fifth
Amendment's protection against double jeopardy, not being tried twice for the
same crime. The reason is that double jeopardy does not include being tried
separately by state and federal courts for the same act. This was established in
1922 when the Supreme Court upheld the federal prosecution of bootlegger Vito
Lanza under the Volstead Act (1920) enforcing prohibition, even though Lanza
had already been convicted by a court in Washington state under its law.[34] This
principle also allows trials for the same act in Native American tribal courts and
federal courts.[35] To date, there have been few double jeopardy cases, but what
might occur is a concern.

Supportive Supreme Court Decisions

As they did in the Ollie's Barbecue case, the federal courts since 1960 have usually
supported the extension of federal authority at the expense of the states. Thus the
Supreme Court ruled in 1985 that federal minimum wage standards applied to
municipal (and presumably state) workers. Moreover, the court added in its major-

ity opinion that the justices were reluctant to impose "judicially created limitations on federal power."[36] We will see that there was a bit of an upsurge of the Supreme Court protecting federalism during the Rehnquist Court, but the Roberts court has not been as concerned about state authority.

The Forces of Decentralization

Centralization has not advanced unimpeded since the 1960s. Instead, several factors have had the intended or unintended impact of slowing the trend toward the nationalization of power. These decentralizing factors have been particularly prominent in recent years, leading some scholars and politicians to talk about **devolution**, the flow of power away from the central government and toward the states. However, other analysts consider the recent revival of decentralization to be little more than a rearguard action that has only slowed, not halted, the overall historical pattern of centralization.

Federal Grant and Mandate Reforms

Eliminating the strings attached to federal grants has been a primary goal of those opposed to increased centralization. **Revenue sharing**, whereby the central government passes funds to the states with no stipulations about how they can be spent, was initiated in 1972, then abandoned in 1985. More lasting has been the idea of **block grants**. These are funds given to the states to accomplish broad goals but which otherwise have few or no restrictions. Block grants were first enacted in 1966 and grew steadily as a percentage of grants for about a decade. They then tailed off, stood at about 15% of grants in the late 1990s, and remain at about that level.

Considerable political discord has occurred since the 1990s over efforts to expand block grants. The Aid to Families with Dependent Children (AFDC) program was reorganized in 1996 as a $16-billion block grant program, Temporary Assistance to Needy Families (TANF), but opponents have defeated other efforts to create block grants. Critics argue that such programs are ill-disguised efforts to eliminate the federal social welfare safety net by allowing state governments to lower benefits. It is also the case that even block grants usually have numerous strings. For example, the TANF program contains "workfare" restrictions that require states to force a percentage of recipients to engage in some work-related activity in order to receive benefits for more than a short time. Another provision bars giving TANF funds to all illegal immigrants and even to many legal immigrant families. The states have some discretion, but their leeway is limited. So most block grants are really "semi-block grants."

State complaints about unfunded mandates also moved Congress to try to control its urge to claim credit for passing programs without bearing the cost of paying for them by passing the Unfunded Mandates Reform Act (UMRA) in 1995. It required that the Congressional Budget Office estimate the unfunded costs of bills to the states and that any bill doing so by $50 million or more be subject to a parliamentary objection in either House. A majority vote is required to overcome the objection, thereby putting members' support of unfunded mandates on record. That was an advance, but speaking on the tenth anniversary of the reform's enactment, Senator (and former governor) Lamar Alexander (R-TN) lamented that it "hasn't done nearly as much as we might have hoped."[37] Among other limits are what critics say is an overly narrow definition in the act of what an unfunded mandate is and a weak barrier (the objection and majority vote) to passing such legislation. Supporting this view, a review of UMRA by the Government Accountability Office concluded that because "there are multiple ways that both statutes and final rules containing what [are arguably] 'unfunded mandates' can be enacted or published without being identified as [such]. . . . many statutes and final rules with potentially significant financial effects on [states] parties" had been enacted or implemented.[38]

Supreme Court Devolution Decisions

Although most assertions of federal control over the states have passed judicial scrutiny, not all have. Beginning in the mid 1990s, the Supreme Court with Chief Justice Rehnquist in the lead made a series of decisions that seemed to herald a new reluctance on the Court to permit federal preemption of state authority under the commerce clause and the Fourteenth Amendment.[39] The first of these decisions was *United States v. Lopez* (1995). In it the court ruled that the fact that guns moved in interstate commerce was not sufficient to justify a federal law making it a crime to possess a gun near a school. The court's decision upholding state autonomy in *U.S. v. Morrison* (2000), discussed in this chapter's opening You Decide box, was another of these decisions. Such decisions left supporters hailing what they hoped would be sustained judicial support of devolution. By contrast, critics fumed, with one characterizing the court's decisions as having "cast aside the text of the Constitution, ripped up precedent, and treated Congress with less respect than that due to an administrative agency."[40]

Do these and other recent pro-decentralization court decisions herald a devolution revolution? Scholars disagree, but the view here is probably not.[41] First, there have also been a number of court decisions that have supported federal authority in areas traditionally governed by the states. In *Lawrence v. Texas* (2003), for instance, the court applied the Fourteenth Amendment to strike down a Texas law making gay sexual contact illegal. Similarly, the court upheld the commerce clause as justification of the authority of the federal government to regulate or even deny the medical use of marijuana in *Gonzales v. Raich* (2005). Second, changes on the Supreme Court leave its future stand on federalism in doubt. Chief Justice Rehnquist died in 2005, and another frequent supporter of state authority, Justice Sandra Day O'Connor, retired in 2006. The still early records of their replacements, Chief Justice John Roberts and Justice Samuel Alito, indicate that they are fairly friendly toward federalism, but are less solidly pro-state than Rehnquist was.[42] This, plus the addition of Sonia Sotomayor in 2009 and Elena Kagan in 2010 to the Court, make predicting its direction unwise. As one review of Roberts' and Alito's impact on federalism put it, neither justice "endorses rigid viewpoints about federalism," and that makes it "uncertain if the Court will return to the type of aggressive new federalism which arguably defined the legacy of the Rehnquist Court."[43]

An Overview of Federalism, 1960 to the Present

The current round in the contest between the forces of centralization and decentralization in the federal system continues. To date the forces of centralization have been many and powerful. The shift of power toward Washington has left the states in a tenuous position as autonomous policy-making institutions. Congress, with the courts' support, has now interceded in all areas within the traditional realm of the states. Even where the federal government cannot constitutionally tell the states what policies to follow, the states are so dependent on federal grant money that Washington can usually coerce them into following its policy lead.

There have been some devolutionary steps by Congress, such as block grants, and through the courts in cases such as the *U.S. v. Morrison*. It is also the case that the growth of government has added to the sheer bulk of state and local governments, if not to their autonomy. Between 1960 when the current era of federalism began through 2009, spending increases by state and local governments (4,300%) outpaced even the meteoric rise of federal spending (3,600%). Third, the immense expanse and complexity of the U.S. system of government as an annual multitrillion-dollar enterprise has aided the autonomy of the states, albeit in an unintended way. During these years, the number of state and local employees nearly tripled while the number of civilian federal workers grew a more modest 17%. One implication is that Washington has come to rely heavily on the states and localities to administer its programs. This gives state and local officials considerable power to implement programs in ways that modify the intent of Congress and federal oversight agencies.

None of this, however, changes the fact that the scorecard for the current round of federalism shows centralization comfortably ahead since 1960. Policies such as block grants and cases such as *U.S. v. Morrison* have only slowed, not stopped, centralization. And the ability of states and localities to spend a mass of federal money on programs "out of sight, out of mind" of the federal government is not the same as having autonomy, much less sovereignty. When the national government decides to set policy and to focus on administration of one policy realm or another, it usually gets its way. As one study puts it, none of the "initiatives intended to . . . decentralize policy making authority to subnational governments have succeeded in igniting systemic, persistent devolution in American federalism." Instead, "the shift in power to the national level has been relentless [if] uneven."[44] The upshot of the ability of national officials to often circumscribe state authority, according to one scholar, makes "partially permissive federalism" or what we term here "semi-subordinated" federalism "the proper designation" for the national-state power relationship.[45]

THE FUTURE OF FEDERALISM

Since its founding in 1776, the United States has changed from a league to a confederation and then to a federation that has become increasingly centralized. Patrick Henry and some other early American leaders would be appalled by the state of U.S. federalism in the early twenty-first century. Other leaders like Alexander Hamilton would be pleased with the accumulation of power in the center. Modern opinion is similarly divided. Some scholars fret about "excessive nationalism."[46] Others criticize efforts to halt centralization as "extremely formalistic, taking state power as an end in itself rather than a means for promoting the rights and interests of the people."[47] Such opinions are valuable, but more important are attitudes in Washington about federalism, the views of the American people, and your own evaluation of the federal system of government.

Attitudes in Washington about Federalism

There is a gap between the rhetoric of presidents and leaders of Congress about federalism and reality. Typically, incoming presidents praise federalism and pledge to protect it. Presidents Richard Nixon and Ronald Reagan supported a series of proposals, collectively called New Federalism, designed to curb the federal government and strengthen the states. Reagan, for instance, expressed a desire to "restore a proper constitutional relationship between the federal, state, and local governments."[48] President George W. Bush also lauded federalism, creating a committee in 2001 to find ways to redress the balance of power between state and local governments. And then President-elect Barack Obama told a meeting of state governors that there is a "spirit [of federalism] that I want to reclaim. . . . One where . . . you and I are working together in partnership."[49] Similarly, congressional leaders have often lauded federalism and promised its rejuvenation. For one, Speaker of the House Newt Gingrich (R-GA) declared his commitment to "to getting power back to the states."[50]

Reality has been different. To accomplish their policy goals, presidents of both parties have often been willing to subordinate the principle of federalism when in practice state policies stood in the way of presidential policy preferences.[51] Congress has tended to behave similarly.

It remains to be seen how federalism will fare with Barack Obama in the White House and the Democrats in control of both houses of Congress. As noted earlier, Obama has followed tradition by hailing the virtues of federalism and pledging to nurture it. He even took to some early steps in that direction. For example, he sent a memorandum to all his agency heads in May 2009 telling them that the "general policy" in his administration would be that the "preemption of state law" should occur only after "full consideration of the legitimate prerogatives of the states."[52] Fans of federalism also cheered later that year when Obama's Attorney General announced his department would no longer prosecute those growing, distributing, and using medical marijuana in states where the practice is legal.

It should be noted though, that President Obama's directive to his agency heads defined preemption as applying only when agencies or laws deny the states the authority to exceed federal standard. What the president did not do is tell his agencies to honor state standards if they were more relaxed than federal requirements. The reason for the difference, he explained was because "state and local governments have frequently protected health, safety, and the environment more aggressively than has the national government." Thus, his commitment was to federalism when it fit his policy preferences, not to federalism as a principle.

The gap between President Obama's rhetorical and applied support of federalism was also evident in his advocacy of various initiatives that undermined federalism. Many educators and state and local officials had complained that the imposition of federal standards under President Bush's "No Child Left Behind" program had preempted a great deal of state and local control over their education systems and had hoped that the Obama administration would give the states more leeway. Instead, the education grants offered under Obama's stimulus plan generally demand compliance with federal standards. One California school superintendent characterized the rules proposed by the U.S. Department of Education as

The massive flow of federal grant money to the states has made them partially dependent on the national government and subject to its regulations. Governor Arnold Schwarzenegger (right) of California and the state's secretary of education (left) are happily holding a check for $24.7 million being presented by U.S. Secretary of Education Rod Paige to be used for California charter schools, but like virtually all federal money, it came with strings attached. (AP Photo/Rich Pedroncelli)

"overly burdensome" and giving "the impression that stimulus funds provide the federal government with unbridled capacity to impose bureaucratic demands."[53] Similarly, a scholar of education objected, "The Department of Education should respect the requirements of federalism and look to states to offer their best ideas rather than mandating policies that the current administration likes."[54] Again, the point here is not whether the federal standards are better than state ones. Instead, what is important to see is that, like other presidents, Obama's attitude toward federalism at any given moment is shaped more by how it coincides with what he wants to accomplish than by any particular regard for federalism as a principle of the U.S. political system.

As for Congress, it is unlikely that it will forgo the urge to make policy even if it preempts state powers. "It's not the way senators and congressmen think," one analyst advises.[55] Finally, as noted, the attitude of the Supreme Court remains unclear, but it is doubtful that any of the justices will emerge to champion state authority as resolutely as Chief Justice Rehnquist did.

Globalization, Federalism, and the Future

Globalization will also help shape the future of federalism. Federalism and globalization are incompatible in several ways. One problem is the increasing number of treaties and executive agreements that are part of U.S. integration into a globalizing world. These foreign pacts add to the body of federal law that under the supremacy clause overrides contradictory state laws and policies. This diminution of state authority has been so pronounced that the executive directors of the National Conference of State Legislators, the Council of State Governments, the U.S. Conference of Mayors, and the National League of Cities have joined to voice their concern. According to these officials, the "authority of states and local governments to regulate and interpret land-use, labor, health, safety, welfare, and environmental measures" is being "gradually diminished by competing language in international agreements."[56]

Global terrorism has also worked to weaken federalism. Responding to the 9/11 terror attacks, the Bush administration successfully sponsored 15 laws preempting state authority in some way. For instance, federal law now bars states from issuing a license to operate a motor vehicle transporting hazardous materials without first submitting the application to the U.S. Department of Homeland Security for a determination that the applicant is not a security risk.

Public Attitudes about Federalism

How do Americans feel about federalism? It depends. One factor is that Americans tend to have more confidence in governments that are closer to them physically. As indications of this:

- From an overall perspective, Americans have the most favorable opinion of local government, followed by state government, with the federal government third, as Figure 3.8 demonstrates.
- The closer-the-better pattern also holds for those expressing trust in the federal government (54%), state government (65%), and local government (69%).[57]
- Most Americans (66%) think the federal government has too much power, but only a few think that either state governments (20%) or local governments (5%) are too powerful.[58]
- When asked at which level government power should be concentrated, Americans chose the state level (64%) over the federal level (26%), with 10% unsure.[59]

The tendency to trust government more as it gets "closer" is shared among demographic groups, as Figure 3.9 shows. Notice that blacks evince the greatest difference in their level of trust among the three levels. By contrast, Hispanics draw the least distinction among the three. Also note that gender makes little difference in level of trust. A final point about the figure is that the markedly lower level of trust that blacks have in the national government is somewhat surprising given its role in advancing civil rights, often in opposition to state and local government policy.

However, the federal government does not always suffer in comparison to the state and local levels. Instead, Americans vary from issue to issue in their attitudes about the competency of the various levels of government. For

FIGURE 3.8   Attitudes Toward Levels of Government

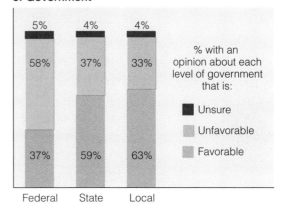

The overall positive opinion of most Americans about the three levels of government tends to increase the closer the level is to the person responding. This favors local government somewhat over state government and distinctly over the seemingly distant federal government.
Data source: Pew Research Center survey, April 2008

FIGURE 3.9   Trust in Level of Government by Demographic Group

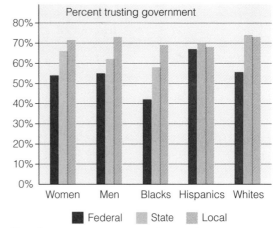

People across groups generally trust local government the most, followed by state government, then the federal government. One exception is that a small percentage of Hispanics trust their state government more than their local government.
Data source: Richard L. Cole and John Kincaid, "Public Opinion on U.S. Federal and Intergovernmental Issues in 2006: Continuity and Change," *Publius: The Journal of Federalism,* 36/3 (2006): 443.

example, James Madison would probably be glad to find that a majority of Americans agree with his view that the national government is the level most likely to protect minority rights. However, when it comes to fighting crime, most Americans are more confident in the efforts of state and local governments than the federal government. Another issue-related variable has to do with effectiveness in spending money. When asked which level of government provides them most for their tax dollar, Americans preferred local governments, but the federal government finished second, with state governments third. Demographically men and women agreed with this ranking, as did whites and Hispanics. However, blacks by a strong margin thought that they get more value for their tax dollars from the federal government, followed by their local and then state government.[60]

Deciding about Federalism

Deciding whether to support further centralization of the federal system, devolution, or the status quo is both important and difficult. The debate focuses on the relationship between federalism and democracy and on the value of policy diversity.

Federalism and Democracy

Those who favor halting or reversing centralization make a strong argument that federalism promotes and protects democracy. Proponents of robust federalism believe that dividing power among the various levels of government provides insurance against the United States being taken over, as other countries have been, by a despotic leader or movement. A second argument is that governments that are smaller and/or are closer to the people physically are easier for individuals to try to influence and more likely to be responsive to them. There is no clear evidence whether or not this is true. The few state-level studies show a good connection between public opinion and state policies, but other research indicates that national legislation also lines up with public opinion more often than not.[61] A third contention is that underrepresented groups are more likely to be able to gain positions of authority at the state and local levels than at the federal level. For example, 24% of state legislators were women in 2009, whereas only 17% of the members of Congress were. But there was little or no difference between the percentages of African Americans and Latinos in Congress and in the state legislatures.

Proponents of centralization reject the idea that a loose federal structure is more likely to protect democracy than a more centralized structure or even a unitary form of government. After all, the argument goes, the Union of the Soviet Socialist Republics was a totalitarian state despite the fact that on paper it was a confederation of 15 republics, while France, a unitary political system, has long been a democracy. A second argument from this viewpoint is that it has often been the national government, not the state and local governments, that has been at the forefront of protecting and advancing American democracy, especially for political minorities. Writing from the perspective of the 1960s, one critic of federalism observed, "If in the United States one disapproves of racism, one disapproves of federalism."[62]

Federalism and Policy

A second set of arguments for and against federalism centers on whether it promotes or detracts from good policy.

Proponents of strong federalism argue that states provide a way to try out policy ideas, with successful ones spreading and eventually becoming national and unsuccessful ideas being abandoned more easily than would be the case if Washington had enacted them. Capturing this idea, Justice Louis D. Brandeis wrote famously, "It is one of the happy incidents of the federal system that a single courageous state may, if its citizens choose, serve as a laboratory; and try novel social and economic experiments without risk to the rest of the country."[63] Some such experiments, like the right-turn-on-red (RTOR) traffic laws, have proven to be widely popular, with all states eventually adopting similar legislation. In 1947 California was the first state to pass such a law; by 1972 about a quarter of all states had done so. Then amid gasoline shortages in the 1970s and evidence from the states with RTOR laws that carnage did not ensue, the rest of the states quickly adopted RTOR policies, with Massachusetts being the last state to do so (1980).

Proponents of greater centralization contend that whatever the country may have been in the 1780s, the United States has become one country economically and socially, and policy should reflect that reality. Skeptics about the value of policy diversity wonder, for instance, why it is positive for 38 states to allow capital punishment and 12 states not to permit it. There is even a wide range of actual use of possible punishments among the states that permit them. During 2009, for example, 24 of the 52 inmates who were executed in the United States died in just one state, Texas. From this perspective, federalism often leads to uneven standards and even contradictory laws whose ill effects range from confusion to serious legal issues for citizens. The status of marriage provides a further example. The Constitution's **full faith and credit clause** (Article IV, Section 1) requires states to generally accept acts of other states, and all states have traditionally recognized a marriage under another state's laws as valid. This practice has been thrown into discord, though, by the issue of gay marriage, with most states refusing to recognize the marriages of same sex couples who have been married under the laws of the few states that permit that.

Ultimately, the argument is that whatever the country may have been in the 1780s, it has become a single nation and that multiple governments making often contradictory policies is an outmoded and unwieldy model of government. There is also an economic argument that Americans face higher costs as businesses struggle to meet often diverse state regulations regarding product safety, environmental standards, and other matters.

Finally, within the realm of public finance, critics of federalism argue that it has a number of drawbacks including allowing sometimes contradictory policies. During the domestic economic crisis that began in 2008, for instance, the federal stimulus bill cut taxes to give people more money to spend and increased federal spending. However, at least some of that effort was offset by states and localities increasing their taxes and using the federal stimulus money they received to support current services rather than by increasing spending to simulate new jobs. "Federalism has its points," one observer commented, "but in a growing number of ways, and especially during a recession, it makes no damn sense at all."[64]

SUMMARY

Federalism involves how power is divided between the national government and the state governments. Under the Articles of Confederation, there was a weak central government and powerful state governments. This arrangement proved unsatisfactory. The national government teetered on the edge of bankruptcy, and there were instances of civil violence. The upper class, the gentry, was worried that this state of affairs threatened both the stability of the country they had helped create and their personal economic interests. To ease these threats they favored a new constitution.

Most of the delegates to the Constitutional Convention came from the gentry. Some, including James Madison, preferred a dominant national government. However, they were restrained by a widespread fear that too much power in the hands of the national government might threaten liberty. From this perspective, the new federal system provided a barrier to potential tyranny. Additionally, the states had to ratify the new constitution, and many would not have done so if they had lost too much power. As a result, the Constitution created a federal system with a fairly even division of power between the national and state governments.

With national and state power centers, the federal system promotes a natural struggle between the two levels of power. This contest has also been prompted by the fact that the Constitution is very vague about the boundaries between national and state authority. Most of the phases, or rounds, in the evolution of federalism have seen an advance of federal power at the expense of state power. Numerous factors have accounted for this trend. One has been the frequent willingness of the

Supreme Court to interpret the Constitution, especially the interstate commerce clause and the Fourteenth Amendment, in ways that gave the national government new authority over the states. Part of this was due to pressure to give Washington increasing economic authority to manage an increasingly national economy. A second factor, especially since the 1950s, has been interpreting the Constitution in ways that empower the federal government to attack racial and gender inequality by allowing the Supreme Court to strike down discriminatory state laws and by allowing Congress to pass laws making discrimination illegal. Particularly since the advent of federal income taxes, national power has also been advanced by the ability of Washington to raise vast sums of money and to use that money to give grants to the states on the condition that they abide by various national restrictions on their policy.

The net result of these centralizing forces is that the federal system has changed from one in which there was an approximate balance of power between Washington and the state capitals to one in which the state governments have little left in terms of authority that they exercise exclusively. There have been a few recent moves by the courts, Congress, or the states to restore some of the states' earlier authority, but these efforts have been infrequent and much less important than the continuing diminution of the federal system.

Americans face an important choice about the federal system. It may be that it has been rendered obsolete by the changes that have created a national economy and society that are encumbered, not benefited, by having 50 states and the national government putting different, sometimes contradictory, laws and regulations into place. It also may be that the ebbing of federalism should be stemmed or even reversed. One of many arguments in favor of stronger federalism is that dividing power to prevent tyranny is as wise in the twenty-first century as it was in the eighteenth century.

CHAPTER 3 GLOSSARY

block grants Funds that are given by the central government to the states to accomplish broad goals but which otherwise have few or no restrictions.

***Brown v. Board of Education of Topeka* (1954)** The case in which the Supreme Court reversed its earlier decision in *Plessy v. Ferguson* (1896) and ruled that separate educational facilities are inherently unequal. The full name of the case is often shortened to *Brown v. Board of Education*.

categorical grants Money given by the national government to the states to fund specific programs according to the rules established by the national government.

commerce clause The provision in Article I, Section 8, of the Constitution that provides Congress with the power to "regulate commerce with foreign nations, and among the several states, and with the Indian tribes."

concurrent powers Those powers that can be exercised by both the federal and state governments.

cooperative federalism The model of federalism that existed for about 30 years beginning with the onset of the Great Depression in the 1930s and featured overlapping federal and state authority in an extensive range of governmental functions.

devolution The flow of power in a federal system away from the central government and toward the state governments in a process of decentralization.

division of power In a federal system, the specific distribution of authority between the national government and the state governments.

dual federalism A model of federalism that prevailed from 1789 to about 1930 in which the national government and the state governments have distinct realms of authority with little overlap between them.

Eleventh Amendment The amendment adopted in 1795 that excludes from federal jurisdiction cases brought against a state by citizens of another U.S. state or another country.

federalism A system of government with a central government and two or more territorially based subnational governments, each of which has some independent authority that cannot be revoked by the central government.

Fifteenth Amendment The amendment adopted in 1870 that prohibits interfering with a citizen's right to vote based on "race, color, or previous condition of servitude."

fiscal federalism The one-way financial relationship between the central government and the states characterized by the national government giving money with strings attached and the states getting the funds and administering the rules.

Fourteenth Amendment The amendment adopted in 1868 that bars states from violating the "privileges and immunities of citizens of the United States" and from depriving "any person of life, liberty, or property without due process of law" or the "equal protection of the laws."

full faith and credit clause Language in Article IV, Section 1, of the Constitution that specifies, "Full faith and credit shall be given in each state to the public acts, record, and judicial proceeding of every other state."

***Gibbons v. Ogden* (1824)** A key Supreme Court case that expanded the authority of Congress under the interstate commerce clause by ruling that commerce includes transportation as well as interstate transactions and that commerce means business done in more than one state, not just the movement of goods across state lines.

Great Society President Lyndon Johnson's vision of a more equitable society and the several domestic programs initiated to achieve that end.

league A political structure in which sovereign units sometimes make common policy and act together but in which there is little or no central authority structure.

McCulloch v. Maryland (1819) The Supreme Court case that established the doctrine of implied powers and the principle that states could do nothing to regulate the institutions or activities of the national government.

New Deal The economic recovery program of President Franklin D. Roosevelt in the 1930s that had the effect of weakening state authority in the federal system by involving the federal government in the domestic economy and in the welfare of individual Americans much more than previously.

nullification doctrine The assertion that a state could void (nullify) any federal law or act that it believed to be unconstitutional.

reserved powers The authority reserved in theory by the Tenth Amendment for the states and people, and thus outside the authority of the federal government.

revenue sharing A process in which the central government passes part of its revenue back to the states with no stipulations on how it is to be spent.

semi-subordinated federalism An image of the contemporary model of federalism characterized by the states exercising unfettered authority in most policy areas only as long as that authority does not conflict with national policy.

Sixteenth Amendment The amendment adopted in 1913 that empowered the federal government to tax the earnings of individual Americans and corporations.

sovereign Independent; not subject legally to any higher authority. Possessing sovereignty.

sovereign immunity The exemption of an independent (sovereign) government from civil suits without its permission. This immunity applies to the U.S. government and, to a substantial degree, to state governments.

states' rights doctrine The assertion that the Tenth Amendment should be read literally to mean that any power not specifically given to the federal government is reserved for the states.

Tenth Amendment The amendment that theoretically limits the authority of the central government by specifying that, "The powers not delegated to the United States by the Constitution, nor prohibited by it to the states, are reserved to the states respectively, or to the people." The courts have seldom used the amendment to overturn federal laws or actions.

unfunded mandates Programs that Congress requires the states to conduct but for which Congress supplies no or insufficient funding.

unitary government A system of government in which subnational units of government such as states are little more than administrative units operating only with authority granted to them by the central government.

Worchester v. Georgia (1832) A case in which the Supreme Court ruled that Native American tribes are distinct political communities whose affairs can be regulated by the federal government but not by the states.

CIVIL LIBERTIES

4

YOU DECIDE: Should Racist Speech Be Banned from the Public Airways?

The women of the Rutgers basketball team took center stage on April 3, 2007, when they played Tennessee for the NCAA championship. Although they lost the game, the Rutgers women were winners. Coach C. Vivian Stringer described the team as including not just gifted athletes, but also "valedictorians of their class, future doctors, musical prodigies and yes, even Girl Scouts."[1]

New York City-based "shock jock" Don Imus had a different view. On his nationally syndicated radio show the next day, he contrasted the "cute" women of the Tennessee team to the "rough girls from Rutgers." "Man, they got tattoos," Imus exclaimed, "That's some nappy-headed hos there." Amid a resulting storm of protest, Imus apologized, but he had earlier called the mostly African American members of the New York Knicks basketball team "chest-thumping pimps." Imus also targeted African American journalists, calling Gwen Ifill of PBS a "cleaning lady" sent to cover the White House and Bill Rhoden a "quota hire" at the *New York Times*. Members of other groups were also demeaned. To cite one, Imus called *Washington Post* reporter Howard Kurtz a "boner-nosed . . . beanie-wearing Jewboy."[2]

The reach of Imus's outbursts was extensive. Indeed, *Time* once named him to its 25 Most Influential People in America list. Most immediately, Imus's words wounded the Rutgers women. "Our moment to celebrate our success, to realize how far we had come, both on and off the court, as young women . . . was taken away," lamented team member Heather Zurich. Another player, Kia Vaughn, added, "I would like to [meet] him and . . . ask, 'After you've met me personally, do you still feel . . . that I'm a 'ho' as a woman and as a black, African-American'."[3] CBS soon fired Imus, but he sued for breach of contract and won a reported $20-million settlement. Before year's end, he was back on the air, broadcasting on WABC-AM and being syndicated nationally.

The issue here is whether the First Amendment should protect such speech, especially when aired over the public airways, which are governed by law and the Federal Communications Commission (FCC). In this case, the FCC declined to act. The reason, according to David Solomon, a former FCC Enforcement Bureau chief, is that the law does not ban racism on the airways. Additionally, Solomon notes, past "cases involving African Americans, Jews, [and others] . . . make it clear that the FCC views the First Amendment as protecting racist speech."[4] Moreover, Congress did nothing after the Imus episode to prevent similar future occurrences.

Do you agree that such speech, however distasteful, is properly protected by the Constitution? Or should Congress ban racist, sexist, and other such speech from the airways?

Nationally known radio show host Don Imus called Kia Vaughn, seen here, and other women basketball players at Rutgers University "nappy-headed hos" after they lost the 2007 NCAA championship game. This racial epithet broke no federal laws or regulations. Should such comments be protected by the First Amendment, or should they bring government sanctions? (AP Photo/Al Goldis)

INTRODUCING CIVIL LIBERTIES

Freedom is a core American value, with 96% agreeing that the "freedom of choice in how to live one's life" is the "American Dream."[5] That freedom is protected by civil liberties and civil rights, the subjects of this and the next chapter. Definitions of the two categories by scholars vary and overlap to a degree, but here **civil liberties** are the freedoms that people possess based on their individuality: their personal and political beliefs, their individual conduct, and how the government treats them as individuals. **Civil rights** are freedoms that people possess related to membership in a demographic group. Civil rights violations mostly involve government or societal discrimination against members of a disadvantaged group. One example is being barred from voting based on sex or race. This chapter focuses on civil liberties. Chapter 5 discusses civil rights. In this chapter's discussion of civil liberties you will find that:

★ Americans' civil liberties have evolved considerably.
★ Americans more strongly support civil liberties in theory than in practice.
★ There is no pattern of differences among demographic groups in their support of civil liberties.
★ Government activity cannot promote religion but need not be devoid of religious content.
★ People may have any religious belief, but the government can restrict some religious practices.
★ The courts have been the most willing to restrict free speech where public safety is involved.
★ The rights of citizens in the criminal justice system expanded greatly in the 1960s but have retreated somewhat since then.
★ People have a right to own a gun, but it is limited.
★ The idea of property rights has faded considerably since the Constitution was written.
★ There is a right to privacy based mostly on the Fourth and Fourteenth Amendments.

Civil Liberties and Demographic Diversity

Because most violations of the rights of disadvantaged groups are addressed in Chapter 5, this chapter focuses primarily on how different demographic groups view civil liberties. For example, blacks, Latinos, and Asian Americans are less confident than whites that their civil liberties will not be violated by the criminal justice system. This chapter additionally takes up the degree to which different demographic groups support civil liberties. Sometimes, the groups differ significantly. At other times, as shown in Figure 4.1, race and gender make little difference in attitudes about civil liberties.

Civil Liberties in a World of Difference

Globalization has had a growing impact on American civil liberties. As the world draws closer together, one debate is over whether universal civil liberties and other types of human rights exist and, if so, what they are. American perspective influences the world because of U.S. power in the international system and because U.S. foreign policy sometimes promotes democracy and, by extension, civil liberties. For good or ill, that is part of what prompted U.S. involvement in Iraq beginning in 2003. It is also the case, though, that foreign views on rights influence U.S. attitudes and policy. Capital punishment provides an example. The United States continues to execute more criminals than almost any other country, but the numbers are declining, and international attitudes against the death penalty are enhancing domestic opposition. Indeed, as we shall see, the Supreme Court recently cited global standards as one consideration when it barred the death penalty for crimes committed by juveniles.

Comparing American civil liberties to those in other countries also provides valuable insights. One is that different cultures vary in their views of civil liberties. The idea of the separation of religion and government is a powerful principle in the United States. It is also widely accepted in Western Europe and some other regions. Yet in the Middle East and to a degree in Muslim countries elsewhere, more people believe that the word of God and the rule of law should be one and the same. There are also comparative differences on the importance given to civil liberties as an aspect of democracy. People in some countries are not as convinced as are Americans that democracy is always the best form of government.

Yet another valuable comparative perspective is that Americans enjoy more civil liberties than do people in most countries (see Figure 4.2). It shows the percentage of countries in each of seven categories based on their protection of civil liberties. The United States is among the 26% of countries in the top rank.

AMERICANS AND THEIR CIVIL LIBERTIES

There are, as noted, divergent views in the world regarding what civil liberties should be and the degree to which they are protected. This

FIGURE 4.1 Opposition to Torture

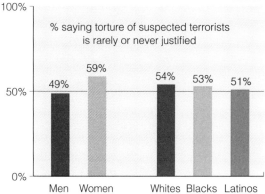

The percentage of those saying torture is never or rarely justified is fairly consistent across groups.

Notes and data source: Unsure responses not included. Data from Pew Research Center, "Foreign Policy Attitudes Now Driven by 9/11 *and* Iraq," 2004.

FIGURE 4.2 Comparative Civil Liberties

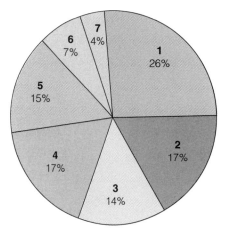

% of countries in each of seven rankings

Americans have more civil liberties than do people in most countries. Freedom House annually evaluates civil liberties around the world and ranks the records of countries from 1 (freest) to 7 (least free). The United States was among the 26% of countries that earned a rank of 1 in 2010.

Data source: Freedom House, 2010.

divergence makes it important to take up the American "version" of civil liberties in general before getting to their more specific aspects. To that end, we will first examine the evolution of Americans' civil liberties. Then we will turn our attention to American attitudes about them.

The Evolution of Civil Liberties

Many democratic countries such as Canada and Great Britain, do not have a bill of rights in their constitution. Indeed, the British have no single, written constitution.

Clashing views over various civil liberties have occurred throughout U.S. political history. This will be evident later in this chapter as we explore specific civil liberties. You will see that Americans' freedoms have often been assaulted and sometimes curbed, especially in the short term. More generally, Americans' civil liberties have expanded. This has occurred by constitutional amendment, by statutory law, by executive action, by specific court decisions, and more generally through the nationalization of the Bill of Rights by the Supreme Court.

Constitutional Amendments

Amending the Constitution is the most authoritative way to extend or restrict civil liberties. However, once the Bill of Rights was adopted in 1791, constitutional amendments ceased to play an important role in changing civil liberties. In fact, the only other amendments dealing specifically with civil liberties have been the Eighteenth and Twenty-First Amendments, which respectively established and repealed prohibition. All the other amendments related to freedom have addressed civil rights and are discussed in Chapter 5.

Statutory Laws

Because civil liberties are not absolute, Congress has some authority to define them. At times, Congress has tried to restrict civil liberties. As early as 1798, Congress passed the Sedition Act making it a crime to "write, print, utter, or publish . . . any false, scandalous and malicious" statements against members of Congress or the president. Among those imprisoned under the act was Matthew Lyon, a member of the U.S. House of Representatives from Vermont, who criticized President John Adams for "a continual grasp for power" and for an "unbounded thirst for ridiculous pomp." Although the Sedition Act soon expired (1801), it gives a sense of how far Congress has gone in restricting one or another civil liberty. At other times, Congress has expanded civil liberties. In the area of freedom of religion, for example, Congress has allowed religious conscientious objector (CO) exemption from military service since the Civil War.

Executive Actions

Decisions of the executive branch also shape civil liberties. Policy since the 9/11 terrorist attacks illustrates this. One controversy erupted when President Bush ordered the National Security Agency (NSA) to use wiretaps and other clandestine techniques without first getting a court order to intercept the electronic overseas communications of American citizens and others suspected of terrorist activity. Challenges to Bush's order were raised in the courts but were not successful. The Obama administration announced it was making reforms to Bush's surveillance methods, but continued many of them and took positions against challenges to them in several court cases in 2009. Presidents can also advance civil liberties. One instance occurred when President Bill Clinton signed an executive order in 2000 barring the federal government from using information from genetic testing in any hiring or promotion decision.

Global terrorism has sparked a debate in the United States about how much, if any, limits on civil liberties are necessary and/or desirable to increase safety. This 2006 photo shows a speech at Georgetown University Law School by U.S. Attorney General Alberto Gonzales, standing near the flag in the background. To protest limits on civil liberties by the Bush administration, audience members are holding a banner with a famous quotation from Benjamin Franklin. (AP Photo/Charles Dharapak)

Court Decisions

The courts have been particularly important in defining Americans' civil liberties. One way this has occurred is through individual decisions on a range of issues. Each year the courts make a large number of decisions that uphold or dismiss complaints about an alleged abridgment of civil liberties. Few such judgments by lower courts have an impact beyond the parties involved, but in sum, the mass of these court decisions constitutes a body of judicial thinking that helps shape civil liberties. Even more clearly, Supreme Court decisions often are crucial in defining civil liberties. These decisions are taken up later in the chapter.

Most importantly of all, the courts have shaped civil liberties through a series of decisions that together have nationalized the Bill of Rights by applying most of its provisions to the states as well as the federal government. This process is called the **incorporation doctrine**. Originally, the Bill of Rights applied only to the national government. The Supreme Court made this clear in *Barron v. Baltimore* (1833). In that case, an individual sued the city claiming it had violated the Fifth Amendment's ban on taking property "without just compensation." The Court rejected the suit on the grounds that, "These amendments [the Bill of Rights] contain no expression indicating an intention to apply them to the state governments."

This decision governed until *Chicago, Burlington, & Quincy Railroad v. Chicago* (1897), a property case similar to *Barron*. The *Chicago* case was the first time that the Supreme Court applied any of the protections found in the Bill of Rights to a state or local government. What changed the Court's mind was the adoption of the **Fourteenth Amendment** in 1868. It barred states from violating the "privileges and immunities of citizens of the United States" by depriving "any person" of either "life, liberty, or property without due process of law." Focusing on the **due process clause**, the Court in the *Chicago* case decided that "since the adoption of the Fourteenth Amendment, compensation for private property taken for public uses constitutes an essential element in 'due process of law'." Therefore, not paying, just compensation, "violate[s] the provisions of the federal constitution."

In the decades that followed, the Supreme Court moved very slowly to apply other parts of the Bill of Rights to the states and localities. Then beginning in the 1950s, the courts did so quickly and decisively in a series of civil liberties and civil rights cases. This shift marked an important expansion of the freedoms enjoyed by Americans, especially minorities. Requiring states and localities to abide by the protections enumerated in the Bill of Rights also was a major part in the ongoing shift of power in the federal system away from the states and toward the national government, as explained in Chapter 3.

Americans' Attitudes about Civil Liberties

How civil liberties are construed and applied also reflect public attitudes. These views include how Americans approach civil liberties in theory and in practice and also the degree of consistency among demographic groups in their attitudes about civil liberties.

Civil Liberties in Theory

Americans strongly support civil liberties in theory. For example, 85% say that their pride in country would decline if the Bill of Rights were to be repealed.[6] This sentiment stems from Americans' pronounced individualism, with its emphasis on the welfare and the freedom of the individual over such communitarian values as the public good (see Chapter 6). For example, individualism is why the judicial system sometimes releases criminals because the police have violated their civil liberties such as their freedom from unreasonable searches. As one scholar notes, Americans have stressed "liberty over authority, freedom over responsibility, [and] rights over duties" throughout history. Moreover, Americans feel secure in their rights. When asked, "Do you think the federal government threatens your . . . rights?" only 28% of Americans said yes. And of those people, 58% said the threats were "minor."[7] Most Americans, however, do not believe in unrestrained rights. To the contrary, when asked how far the freedoms in the Bill of Rights should go,

FIGURE 4.3 Attitudes on Civil Liberties and Terrorism

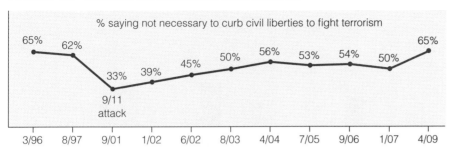

After 9/11, Americans were more willing to surrender some civil liberties to increase safety. Support for civil liberties soon began to grow again, but did not reach its pre-9/11 levels until eight years after the attack.
Data source: Pew Research Center.

only one-fourth say they should be "complete and absolute." Three-fourths reply that the rights "should also come with limits and responsibilities."[8]

Civil Liberties in Practice

Americans' support for civil liberties is less ardent in practice than it is in theory. For instance, only 42% favor having the Bill of Rights protect noncitizens as well as citizens.[9] Additionally, support for civil liberties often declines when a liberty such as free speech is being used to promote an unpopular cause. For example, 73% of the public believes that it should be illegal to burn an American flag as a political protest.[10]

Times of perceived danger also increase the percentage of Americans who are willing to curb civil liberties, even their own. This is evident in Figure 4.3. Yet the figure also shows that Americans have a core belief in civil liberties that gives way grudgingly and then soon reasserts itself. Thus, as an overall statement: (1) Many Americans are willing to restrict the civil liberties of those they dislike or (2) even limit their own liberties in the interest of perceived safety. Nevertheless, (3) most Americans generally have a broad commitment to civil liberties in practice as well as theory.

Demographic Groups and Civil Liberties

There is no consistent pattern among demographic groups in their support of civil liberties. Figure 4.1 shows fairly consistent opposition among groups to torture. Figure 4.4 reveals a different pattern for gay marriage, with opinion differences among various groups.

FIGURE 4.4 Support for Gay Marriage

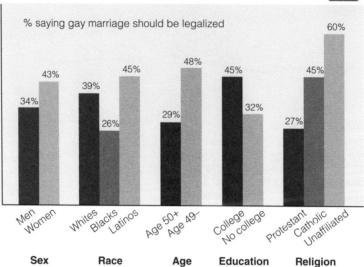

Support for gay marriage differs markedly by sex, race, and other demographic factors.

Notes and data source: Unsure responses not included. Data from Pew Research Center survey report, October 9, 2009.

FIGURE 4.5 Changes in Group Views on Civil Liberties

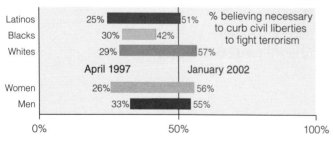

All groups were more willing to curb liberties to fight terrorism in stressful times (January 2002), soon after the 9/11 attacks, than in normal times (April 1997). But blacks remained steadiest and mostly opposed to doing so. Whites changed the most and were also the most willing to curb some liberties.

Data source: Pew Research Center survey report, November 5, 2003.

One factor in the variation among groups in their support of civil liberties in specific situations is whether an issue directly and negatively impacts a group. It is not surprising, for example, that more whites (63%) than blacks (53%) are willing to allow a racist to speak publicly. Indeed, what is surprising is that most blacks are willing to support the right of a racist to speak. Group experiences may also account for the differences shown in Figure 4.5. It shows that after the 9/11 terrorist attacks, minorities, especially African Americans were less likely than whites to change their views and be willing to accept fewer civil liberties in exchange for safety from future attacks. One explanation is that having had many civil liberties denied to them, blacks and other minorities were very reluctant to surrender any of their recent gains in this area.

RELIGION AND GOVERNMENT

There is an ongoing tension between religion and politics that stems from the clash between two powerful forces. One is the First Amendment, which separates "church and state" and also protects religious beliefs including atheism. The competing force is strong religiosity among Americans and the tendency of many of them to interject their religion-based values into public policy debates.

Most Americans say that religion plays a key role in their lives. This is somewhat surprising because as countries become more prosperous, their societies usually become more secular, with religion declining as a source of identity and values. As evident in Figure 4.6, American society has not followed this trend. The percentage of Americans who say that religion plays a very important role in their life more closely resembles poorer countries than other wealthy ones.

FIGURE 4.6 Comparative Religiosity

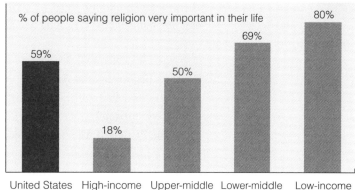

This figure compares religiosity in the United States with 43 other countries. People are usually less religious in wealthier countries than in poorer ones. As you can see, though, Americans deviate from this norm.
Data source: Pew Research Center, "Among Wealthy Nations, U.S. Alone in Its Embrace of Religion," 2002.

Furthermore, Americans are more willing to mix politics and religion than are people in many other countries. A majority of people in almost all countries supports keeping religion and public policy separate. But a substantial minority in many countries, including the United States, disagrees. A poll taken in 44 countries found that only a bit more than half of Americans said religion and government should be kept completely separate. This was slightly below the 57% who did in the median country.

The reluctance of many Americans to completely separate religion and politics impacts the application of both to the two clauses of the First Amendment dealing with religion. The first is the establishment clause; the second is the free exercise clause. Neither barrier is absolute.

Government and the Establishment of Religion

The **establishment clause** of the First Amendment specifies, "Congress shall make no law respecting the establishment of religion." This clause means that the federal government may not support a specific religion or even religion in general. Like most elements of the Bill of Rights, the courts have also applied the establishment clause to state and local government. It is, however, one thing to say that the government cannot promote religion. It is quite a different thing to say that all government functions must be devoid of any religious reference or content. An ongoing controversy is exactly where the line should be drawn.

Historical Government Support of Religion

From its beginning, the American government has been infused with a degree of religiosity, and that continues to be true. The motto "In God we trust," appears on all U.S. currency since the Civil War, and the words "one nation under God" are in the Pledge of Allegiance. December 25 is a national holiday, and President Obama's inauguration in 2009 began and ended with members of the Christian clergy giving an invocation and a benediction. Extending this list is not necessary to underline the point that American governments at all levels have traditionally promoted religion and, to a degree, Christianity. Such government-related religiosity persists because most Americans support it, but government support of religion has declined considerably from what it once was.

Limiting Government Support of Religion

For most of American history, blatant examples of government religiosity such as compulsory school prayer were practiced at the state and local level, which was beyond federal jurisdiction. This changed once the Supreme Court began to apply the First Amendment's clauses related to religion to the states. This shift first occurred in *Everson v. Board of Education* (1947), a case related to whether it was constitutional for New Jersey to help bus children to parochial schools. In that case, the Supreme Court seemed to set a strict standard by calling for an "impregnable . . . wall of separation between church and state."

Since then, the courts have restricted many forms of government religiosity. For example, the Supreme Court has struck down most forms of religious activity in public schools, including nondenominational school prayer and even prayer-like moments of reflection. The courts have also targeted religion-inspired curriculum decisions. One illustration is a Supreme Court decision in 1968 striking down an Arkansas law that made it illegal for schools to adopt science books that included Charles Darwin's theory of evolution, which contradicts "creationism," the religion-based theory that God created the Universe and everything in it.

Inconsistent Standards on Government Support of Religion

Even though the Supreme Court said in the *Everson* case that there should be an "impregnable" separation of church and state, later decisions have not always applied that strict standard. Indeed in *Everson* itself, the Court allowed transportation aid to parochial schools to continue. Since then, the Court has been inconsistent or complex (depending on one's view) in its thinking about what constitutes government support of religion. For example, the Court took a major step away from the "impregnable wall" standard in *Lemon v. Kurtzman* (1971), a case related to Pennsylvania's policy of giving some aid to parochial and other private schools. In that case, the Court ruled that such support does not violate the establishment clause if the aid: (1) has a "secular" purpose, (2) has a "primary effect . . . [that] neither advances nor inhibits religion," and (3) does not "foster excessive government entanglement with religion." These three standards are called the **Lemon test**.

Beyond the realm of education, the Supreme Court has even been less willing to enforce strict separation of religion and government. The result, according to one scholar, has been a "long line of inconsistent rulings."[11] Two recent Supreme Court decisions handed down on the same day provide an excellent illustration. In *Van Orden v. Perry* (2005) the Court held that having the Ten Commandments displayed outside Texas' capitol building was a permissible reflection of the country's culture. Taking the opposite view in *McCreary County v. ACLU* (2005), the Court ruled that displaying the Ten Commandments in Kentucky's courthouses served to promote religion and therefore violated the establishment clause. As if to underline what some see as the Supreme Court splitting legal hairs too finely, both decisions were 5 to 4, with four justices opposed to displaying the commandants in both cases and four other justices finding the displays acceptable in both cases. Only one of the nine justices, Stephen G. Breyer, saw any difference between the two cases, but that was enough for one display to survive and the other to be barred.

Some of the Court's inconsistency may be the result of the stormy criticism that the Court has often received from Congress and the public when the justices have barred prayers from school or otherwise enforced the establishment clause. The Senate Judiciary Committee, for instance, held hearings entitled in 2004 on "Hostility to Religious Expression in the Public Square" to emphasize, as one senator put it, that the Supreme Court's "unfortunate and unjustified hostility to religious expression is pervasive, and it must be stopped."[12] Most Americans arguably support his view, as Figure 4.7 indicates.

Government and the Exercise of Religion

The **free-exercise clause** of the First Amendment declares Congress can pass no law "prohibiting the free exercise" of religion. This applies to organized religions and also to the personal religious views of individuals.[13] Like many other civil liberties, the free-exercise clause has been

FIGURE 4.7 Opinion on Government Religiosity

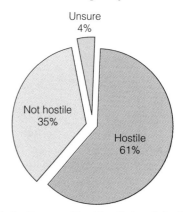

Is the Supreme Court hostile to religion?

Public opinion has generally disagreed with court decisions banning school prayer and otherwise limiting government religiosity. As evident here, most Americans think that the Supreme Court is hostile to religion.

Data source: Pew Research Center poll, November 2000. Data provided by The Roper Center for Public Opinion Research, University of Connecticut.

applied by the courts to the states as well as the federal government. This first occurred in *Cantwell v. Connecticut* (1940). In that case, the Court overturned the conviction of three Jehovah's Witnesses who, while proselytizing in a largely Catholic neighborhood, had been arrested for breach of peace and for violating a state law requiring a permit to solicit donations for religious causes. The free-exercise clause can be divided into three parts: freedom of belief, freedom to practice religion, and freedom to be exempt from laws and regulations.

Freedom of Belief

The least controversial aspect of the free-exercise clause is freedom of belief. Generally, every one is free to believe whatever they want without any negative legal repercussions. One of the few points of contention were clauses in numerous state constitutions that required a belief in a deity to hold a public office or even have a state job. The Supreme Court ruled all such requirements unconstitutional in 1961.[14] Based on that case, earlier requirements that witnesses in trials, office holders at swearing in ceremonies, and others be sworn in on a Bible or use phrases such as "so help me God" have also been eliminated or are ignored.

Religious practices are regulated in many ways. As early as 1878 the Supreme Court sanctioned such regulation by upholding legal barriers to polygamy. This Mormon woman, Mattie, who gave only her first name, was one of more than a dozen young women and girls from Utah polygamist families who spoke at a 2006 rally in Salt Lake City urging that they be given the right to practice their religious beliefs. (AP Photo/Douglas C. Pizac)

Freedom of Religious Practice

Even though the First Amendment protects the "exercise" of religion, the courts have usually upheld the law when it clashes with an activity that a religion dictates. The first instance was *Reynolds v. United States* (1878) when the Supreme Court upheld the conviction of a Mormon in the Utah Territory for violating a federal law barring polygamy. Describing polygamy as "odious among the northern and western nations of Europe" and limited mostly to "Asiatic and . . . African people," the Court held that the law validly protected a core cultural value.

The Supreme Court has abandoned such overt cultural bias, but it still holds that if a law is enacted for legitimate purposes and does not target religion, then the law supersedes religious practice. For example, the Supreme Court ruled in 1990 against two Native Americans who had used peyote, an illegal drug under Oregon law, during a religious ritual.[15] The Court conceded that the drug was part of a traditional religious ceremony but still upheld the Oregon law barring drug use.

There have been times, though, when the courts have sided with a religious practice that contravenes the law. In *Church of the Lukumi Babalu Aye v. City of Hialeah* (1993), the Supreme Court struck down the city's ban on animal sacrifice. The Court noted clear evidence that the city was targeting the practices of those who believe in Santeria, an Afro-Caribbean religious tradition with roots in West Africa.

Freedom to be Exempt from Legal Obligations

A third aspect of the free exercise clause involves claims by individuals or groups that their religion exempts them from obeying a law or regulation. As a rule, those making such a claim must show that the burden on religion is so great that it is more important than the interest that the government has in enforcing its law or regulation. Also, the courts have usually held that a claim to an exemption must be based on religion defined as having some presence of a deity and have generally not been willing to extend religion to include an individual's personal secular philosophy, no matter how profoundly held. One exception relates to the military draft, as discussed below.

When cases based on a religious claim first came before the Supreme Court beginning in the 1960s, it took an expansive view of the free exercise clause. In a 1972 case, for example, the Court allowed an Amish father to "home school" his daughter in violation of a state law requiring all children to attend an organized school.[16] Then beginning in the 1980s, the Supreme Court took a narrower view of claims for exemption. For instance, the Court ruled in 1986 that a Jewish Air Force officer could not continue to wear a yarmulke in violation of his service's military uniform regulations.[17] The following year the Court dismissed the case of several Muslim inmates who claimed that their prison's work routine on Fridays kept them from their prayers.[18] The Court has consistently held that government must show that its law or regulation has a legitimate and important purpose in the law or rule and is not targeting religion.

The Supreme Court has never directly ruled on whether a religious belief in pacifism could exempt an individual from being drafted into the military. This is because Congress has always exempted those who have a religious objection to killing from being drafted into the military and/or being assigned to a combat role. The Supreme Court has said, though, that conscientious objector status cannot be limited only to those with religious beliefs. Instead, it must also include objectors to combat based on a "sincere and meaningful belief which occupies in the life of its possessor a place parallel to that filled by the God of [religion-based objectors]."[19]

FREEDOM OF EXPRESSION

The First Amendment declares that "Congress shall make no law . . . abridging the freedom of speech, or of the press; or the right of the people peaceably to assemble, and to petition the government for a redress of grievances." As a starting point, these words:

- Protect freedom of expression: not just what is said, but also what is written and every other form of communication.

- Also protect individuals from having to express things, such as a loyalty oath against their will.
- Go beyond individuals and the press to protect all forms of media and also collective communications by groups.
- Not only protect words and other passive expressions, but also protect active expressions such as associating with political groups and attending political events.
- Have been applied to the states as well as the federal government.
- Do not provide absolute protection. Instead, government can limit some forms of expression.

This last point is at the heart of the ongoing struggle over what may or may not be regulated by law. We will take up this debate beginning with the question of when the government can restrict free expression in the interest of safety.

Freedom of Expression and Safety

One value of the Preamble to the Constitution is that it lays out five tasks that the government is supposed to accomplish. Two of those, "provide for the common defense" and "insure domestic tranquility," relate to safety. Unfortunately, ensuring it sometimes clashes with free speech.

National Security

Danger from abroad is perhaps the most common reason—or excuse—for restricting free speech. Only seven years after the Bill of Rights was adopted, Congress seemly ignored it by enacting the Sedition Act (1798). It limited speech and other freedoms for the claimed reason of improving country's safety and stability. President Abraham Lincoln made a similar claim when he jailed those who too vociferously opposed his war policy. When a group of officials in New York objected to one such arrest, he replied that the imprisoned individual's rhetoric "was damaging the army, upon the existence and vigor of which, the life of the nation depends."[20]

Despite such occasional restraints on free speech, there was no major test of its limits before the Supreme Court until *Schenck v. United States* (1919). In it the Court upheld the conviction of Charles Schenck for violating the Espionage Act (1917). That law prohibited trying to disrupt the military during wartime, and Schenk had distributed a pamphlet that opposed the World War I draft law and that urged inductees not to "submit to intimidation." The Court reasoned that the protections of the First Amendment did not extend to communications that created "a clear and present danger" of unleashing "evils that the [government] has a right to prevent." This is called the **clear and present danger test**. To illustrate an evil that was not protected, the Court's opinion famously noted that free speech would not include "falsely shouting fire in a theater and causing a panic."

Since the *Schenck* decision, the Supreme Court has varied in its willingness to find a clear and present danger that permits restricting free speech. During the 1920s, the Court upheld the convictions of several individuals who had urged the overthrow of the government or otherwise arguably endangered national security. Then during the seemingly less threatening 1930s, the Court became more reluctant to find a clear and present danger. In 1937, for example, the Supreme Court reversed the conviction of an individual convicted of endangering national security by distributing pamphlets that invited people to join the Communist Party. Altering course during the perceived dangers of the early cold war, the Court once again upheld the convictions of several communists. But by the late 1950s, as alarm eased, the Court continued the cycle, this time by again becoming more willing to defend free speech. Among other cases, the Court twice reversed convictions of communists who believed in the theory of overthrowing the government but who had not actively tried to do so. These cases were also important to the freedom of assembly, which includes the right of people to associate with ideas, organizations, interest groups, and political parties without government interference.

There have been fewer cases involving national security in more recent times, with the Supreme Court sometimes supporting free speech and sometimes upholding national security restrictions. For example, the Court refused in *New York Times Co. v. United States* (1971) to stop the newspaper from publishing secret documents about the U.S. diplomatic strategy in Vietnam. By contrast, the Court upheld the conviction of a man for violating federal law by burning his draft card. The Court ruled in 1968 that doing so amounted to destroying a government document that was important to raising military forces.[21]

Public Order

The Supreme Court has been very reluctant to limit free speech in cases where the government has prosecuted individuals for endangering domestic public order. For example, in *Brandenburg v. Ohio* (1969), the Court took up the conviction of a man charged with violating an Ohio law against promoting violence. Ultimately, the justices reversed the conviction even though Brandenburg had told a Ku Klux Klan rally that blacks should be sent back to Africa and Jews deported to Israel and had alluded to "revenge" against these groups. The Court reasoned that such utterances fell short of presenting a clear and present danger because they did not (1) intend to directly incite (2) a lawless action that was (3) likely to soon occur. This decision made it very difficult to restrict general calls for radical political activity.

In addition to the clear and present danger standard, a second test to determine if the government can restrict free speech is the **fighting words** standard. This was formulated in a case involving a Jehovah's Witnesses who was convicted of violating a state breach of the peace law after he had nearly started a riot by handing out a pamphlet in New Hampshire that condemned all other religions as "rackets." The Supreme Court upheld the conviction in 1942, arguing that the government could punish some types of speech, including obscenity, profanity, libel and slander, and insults that constituted "fighting words—those which by their very utterance inflict injury or tend to incite an immediate breach of the peace."[22]

Although the fighting words standard remains in place, the Court is very cautious about what fighting words are. For example, it has overturned several convictions for using vulgar language, including hurling the f word at police. The courts have also been reluctant to limit **hate speech**, hostile expressions based on religion or such innate characteristics as race. Illustrating this, the Supreme Court in 1992 overturned the conviction of a man who had mimicked KKK activity by burning a wooden cross in the yard of a black family.[23] The Court reasoned that because the law in question barred only hate speech related to race, the law therefore targeted specific content and by doing so violated free speech.

Despite the courts' propensity to allow most forms of expression, some restrictions are lawful. The Supreme Court has upheld several laws protecting people from direct intimidation. For instance, abortion opponents may be kept a reasonable distance away from abortion clinics, and protestors may not picket an individual's private residence. As for actions such as marches and protest rallies, the courts have tried to strike a balance between the freedom to assemble and the legitimate interest of the government to prevent situations that endanger people or prevent their freedom to go about their business. It is also noteworthy that the courts have been less willing to protect vulgarity and some other offensive or disruptive types of expression when they are not connected to political activity. Finally, the First Amendment does not protect fighting words or actions that are directed face-to-face at individuals or small groups.

General Freedom of Expression

There are several topics related to free speech that do not involve national security or public safety. These include patriotism, the press, partisan political activity, and nonpolitical speech.

Expressions of Loyalty

The government cannot force you to be patriotic. Saluting the flag is one example. In 1943, the Supreme Court struck down a school's requirement that its students salute the American flag and recite the Pledge of Allegiance. The majority opinion declared, "No official . . . can prescribe what shall be orthodox in politics, nationalism . . . or other matters of opinion."[24] In a related case, the Court held in 1977 that people had the right to cover up New Hampshire's motto, "Live Free or Die," inscribed on its license plates.[25]

The Press

Freedom of the press is covered extensively in Chapter 8. Therefore the following summary points suffice here:

- There is greater freedom of the press in the United States than most other countries, but there are some limits.
- Generally, the government may not exercise prior restraint of the press either by requiring it to be licensed or by reviewing or censoring it prior to publication or broadcast.
- Although the press has broad freedom to publish, it can be held liable if it violates certain standards. Most prominently, the press may not defame an individual by the spoken (libel) or written (slander) word.
- Proving defamation of a public figure must show malice, not just error and damage as for a private individual.
- Like all businesses, the news media are subject to taxation and certain kinds of regulation, such as labor laws, by government.
- The government may license radio and television stations that broadcast over the airwaves and otherwise regulate their use.
- Most states, but not the federal government, sometimes shield reporters from having to disclose anonymous sources for news stories. Shield laws usually apply to criminal investigations but not to civil cases, such as slander suits.
- Most Americans agree that a free press is important to democracy, but the public also supports some limits, especially in the area of national security.

Partisan Political Activity

Money has always played a powerful and, some believe, corrupting role in U.S. politics. In an effort to change that, there have been repeated efforts in recent decades to restrain the ability of wealthy individuals and groups to use their money to gain a greater say in who gets into office and the policies they favor. The issue is whether limiting what people and groups can spend to voice their views or to donate to a candidate or political party abridges their freedom of speech. This topic is covered extensively in Chapters 9 (political parties) and 10 (elections); therefore only a summary is needed here. The view of the courts under the law is that the government may:

- Restrict direct donations to candidates and political parties.
- Limit the flow of funds between and among the federal, state, and local level political parties.
- Bar candidates from helping to raise funds for groups other than political parties or their own campaign organization.
- Limit the ability of certain tax-exempt organizations to engage in all or specific types of political activity, such as using ads to specifically promote or oppose a candidate.

The government may not:

- Restrict what an individual or organization, including corporations, spends independently to support or oppose a candidate.
- Limit what individuals spend of their own money to campaign for office.
- Limit what interest groups can spend to advance their political goals.
- Limit the ability of certain tax-exempt organizations to identify candidate policy views in issue ads, even during an election.

Nonpolitical Expression

To decide what the First Amendment protects, the courts often distinguish between political speech and nonpolitical speech expression, such as obscenity and commercial expressions.

Obscenity   Obscene material in any form is generally not protected unless it can be considered a form of artistic or political expression. Determining what is obscene was historically left to local authorities until the Supreme Court first set standards in 1957.[26] During further litigation, the Court tinkered with these standards until formulating what remains as the basic standard for obscenity in *Miller v. California* (1973). What the Court said was that a "work" such as a movie was not obscene unless the average person applying local and contemporary "community standards" would find the work (1) to be "patently offensive," (2) to have a dominant theme that stimulated "prurient [lust-inducing] interests," and (3) when "taken as a whole," to lack "serious literary, artistic, political, or scientific value."

Commercial Speech   Advertising and other expressions designed to promote commercial gains may be limited by the government more than political, religious, and other forms of protected speech. Until the 1970s, the courts allowed almost unlimited regulation, but that has changed, with the courts extending some protections. Now the government can limit communications that are deceptive or promote illegal conduct. Beyond that, however, the government is required to show a compelling interest in regulating a commercial communication. This wiped away many restrictions on products such as tobacco and alcohol and generally made it more difficult to limit commercial speech.

THE RIGHT TO BEAR ARMS

One of the most controversial parts of the Bill of Rights has been the Second Amendment's words: "A well regulated militia, being necessary to the security of a free state, the right of the people to keep and bear arms, shall not be infringed." The key dispute has been whether the language about a militia meant that only members of state national guards under the control of the "people" as a collective

(As in "We the people") had the right to bear arms or whether "people" meant individuals. In that case, everyone would have the right to bear arms.

Until recently the Supreme Court avoided the core issue. That became increasingly difficult, however, because of contradictory decisions by different circuits of the U.S. Court of Appeals. In 2001 the Fifth Circuit held that individuals had a constitutional right to have weapons, and the D.C. Circuit took the same view in a 2007 decision. By contrast, the Ninth Circuit ruled in 2002 that the Second Amendment did not give individuals the right to possess arms. To rectify this split among the appeals courts, the Supreme Court took the issue up in *District of Columbia v. Heller* (2008). In it, the Court ruled by 5 to 4 that individuals do have the right to bear arms. The majority opinion by Justice Anton Scalia argued that an "inherent right of self-defense" is "central to the Second Amendment" and creates a right to possess self-defense weapons. Because the District of Columbia was involved, the *Heller* decision applied only to federal laws and jurisdictions, but in *McDonald v. Chicago* (2010) the Supreme Court added to the incorporation doctrine by extending the Second Amendment rights to the states as well.

Of U.S. homicides, 62% result from gunshot. The rate in some other countries: Canada 35%, France 39%, Germany 19%, Great Britain 8%, and Japan 3%. Turbulent Colombia (81%) has the highest percentage of homicides due to firearms.

Neither the *Heller* nor the *McDonald* decision means that anyone can have whatever kind of weapons he or she wants. To the contrary, both decisions qualified the right to bear arms in several ways. Scalia noted in *Heller*, for example, that "nothing in our opinion should be taken to cast doubt on longstanding prohibitions on the possession of firearms by felons and the mentally ill, or laws forbidding the carrying of firearms in sensitive places such as schools and government buildings." As for the types of weapons protected by the amendment, Scalia wrote that they were limited to the type reasonably needed for protecting oneself and one's home and did not include very powerful weapons such as those "specifically designed for military use." This left in place the Court's decision in *United States v. Miller* (1939) that the right of individuals to have weapons is not absolute. In that case, the Court upheld a federal law restricting the possession of machine guns and other fully automatic weapons and sawed-off shotguns. In the years and even decades to come there will be many cases aimed at finding out how far Second Amendment rights go. Within days of the *McDonald* decision, for instance, Chicago passed a new law attempting to limit the impact of the decision by, among other things, barring owners of

This woman advocating her views outside the U.S. Supreme Court is only partly right that the Second Amendment protects her right "to bear arms." The Supreme Court did decide that the amendment gives Americans a right to do so, but the Court's decision addressed only "self-defense" weapons and left it unclear exactly what types of weapons are included and when and where they may be kept or carried. (AP Photo/Jose Luis Magana)

a handgun from taking it out of their home, even onto their porch, without disassembling the weapon; requiring a city permit at $100 per weapon and registration of each weapon with the police at $15 each, and mandating classroom and firing range training before being eligible for a city permit, even though firing ranges are banned in Chicago. Which if any of these provisions or the countless other continuing or yet-to-be-enacted federal, state, and local restrictions on firearms are constitutional remains to be seen.

PROPERTY RIGHTS

Ownership of property is a civil liberty that receives little attention in many of today's analyses of Americans' rights. Yet it was a key concern of the country's early leaders.

Early Concern with Property Rights

Although the Constitution does not contain the words "property rights," it protects them. Article II prohibits states from interfering with existing contracts. The Fifth Amendment also addresses property rights. It declares that no one can be "deprived of . . . property without the due process of law" and also permits the government to take "private property" (real estate) only for "public use" and only after paying "just compensation" to the owner.

The country's leaders also regularly advocated property rights. Apart from any philosophical support of property rights, many of the country's early leaders vigorously supported property rights because they were members of the upper class that possessed most of the property. Moreover, as Chapter 2 details, the gentry had been alarmed in the 1780s by various efforts around the country to undermine their property rights. Their philosophical and pragmatic concerns led James Madison to argue that "government is instituted" to protect people's liberty, including their "right of acquiring and using property."[27] Similarly, John Adams declared in 1790, "property must be secured or liberty cannot exist."[28] The Supreme Court also took this view. Many of its early decisions involved enforcing the clause barring states from interfering with contracts. In one such case decided in 1829, the majority opinion held that the "maxims of a free government seem to require that the rights of personal liberty and private property should be held sacred."[29] This did not mean that the government could never take property. Taxes take property (money), and the Constitution specifically empowered the government to "collect" them. Moreover, the Fifth Amendment required only that the government follow the "due process of law" before taking property for public use and also pay for it.

CIVIL LIBERTIES | 133

Eminent Domain

After the right to own slaves was settled by the Thirteenth Amendment, the most contentious property rights issue has related to **eminent domain**, the right of the sovereign authority (once the monarch, now the country) to take real estate without the owner's consent. What has been controversial is the Fifth Amendment's clause specifying that eminent domain can be used to take land only for "public use." All agree that the government can take land to build a road, school, or public housing project. But how far can the government go in taking one individual's land and transferring it to another owner for a private use that the government believes is in the public interest?

Historically, the courts have given the government fairly wide latitude to do so. The most recent notable case began when New London, Connecticut, sought to take possession of over 100 pieces of aging, but not blighted private property in a waterfront area and turn them over to private developers to build hotels, office complexes, a marina, and an upscale condo complex. New London believed this would help revitalize the city and boost tax revenues. Several of the owners refused to sell their property and sued the city. They claimed that the intended use of their property did not meet the "public use" test. Ultimately, the Supreme Court upheld the city in *Kelo v. New London* (2005). The justices held that "public use" can be equated with "public purpose," and that the city had acted legally because, "There is no basis for exempting economic development from our traditionally broad understanding of public purpose."

The decision caused a sensation, with most of the commentary highly critical of the ruling. Subsequently, more than half the states enacted legislation related to eminent domain. Most tightened the meaning of "public use," but a few went in the opposite direction and gave public authorities more leeway to condemn property for development. A flurry of bills in Congress did not yield any national legislation, but in 2006 President Bush barred federal agencies from condemning property "for the purpose of advancing the economic interest of private parties." An ironic note to the story is that in the years since the *Kelo* decision, the former homes have been torn down but no development has taken place amid a struggling economy and disputes between New London and the prospective developers.

CIVIL LIBERTIES AND CRIMINAL JUSTICE

British tradition dating back to the **Magna Carta** (1215) and the English Bill of Rights (1689) holds that the law, especially criminal procedures, should be administered fairly through a regular process. The Magna Carta, for example, declared that fines had to be "in proportion to the gravity of their offense," and that no one

FIGURE 4.8 Public Opinion
on Criminal Rights

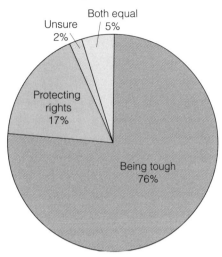

Which is more important:
being tough on criminals
or protecting the rights
of suspects?

When asked to choose between being
tough on criminals and protecting the
rights of suspects, a strong majority of
Americans favors being tough.
*Data source: Washington Post/Kaiser Family
Foundation/Harvard University poll, August 1998.
Data provided by The Roper Center for Public
Opinion Research.*

could be imprisoned "except by the lawful judgment of his equals."
Unfortunately, the crown often ignored these rights. Such transgressions in the colonies helped spark the American Revolution. Among other abuses, the Declaration of Independence charges King George III with "depriving us of the benefits of trial by jury."

What the crown had done in the colonies also helped shape the Constitution to ensure that no American government could replicate those abuses. Article I contains several rights related to the justice system. **Ex post facto laws**, those which make something illegal retroactively, are prohibited. So are **bills of attainder**, laws that make an individual guilty of a crime or impose punishment without a trial. The article also generally protects the ability of citizens who believe they are being illegally imprisoned to seek a **writ of habeas corpus**. This is an order by the court requiring authorities to justify the individual's detention. Concerns about the justice system also influenced the content of the U.S. Bill of Rights. Indeed, half of its 10 amendments (the Fourth through Eighth Amendments) deal almost exclusively with the rights of individuals vis-à-vis the legal system.[30] These rights, as noted, have largely been nationalized.

Before proceeding, it is also worth noting that of all civil liberties, those protecting suspects and criminals enjoy the least support among Americans. Surveys find 78% of the public thinks that protecting suspects' rights make law enforcement very difficult; 70% contend that the courts are more concerned with protecting the rights of criminals than the rights of victims; and as Figure 4.8 shows, a large majority prefers being tough on criminals than protecting the rights of those who have been accused or convicted.[31] We will discuss those rights in the order of a criminal justice procedure (investigation, arrest, pretrial, trial, and sentencing).

Investigation

The Fourth Amendment might well be nicknamed the "investigation amendment." It decrees that people have the right "to be secure in their persons, houses, papers, and effects" and bars the government from conducting "unreasonable searches and seizures" in these private spaces.

General Application of the Fourth Amendment

What is a reasonable search or seizure and who gets to decide that is the key to applying the Fourth Amendment. During the investigation of anything other than a crime in progress, police can generally conduct a search and seize material as evidence only if a judge has approved a search warrant. Even this cannot occur unless investigating authorities present the court with "probable cause": reasonable grounds to conclude that (1) a crime has occurred or is likely to take place and (2) that evidence exists at the site to be search related to the crime. Furthermore, a search warrant must be in writing and must detail the site to be searched and what the police are looking for and want to take as evidence. As technology has advanced, the courts have extended these standards beyond physical searches and seizures to include ones involving electronic and other forms of technology such as listening devices.

What gives the Fourth Amendment clout is the **exclusionary rule**: the inadmissibility in court of evidence that is obtained in violation of a suspect's civil liberties. The Supreme Court first applied the exclusionary rule to the federal government in 1914. The Court later partially extended the Fourth Amendment to the states in 1949, but did not fully apply the exclusionary rule to them until *Mapp v. Ohio* (1961). In that case, the Court overturned a Cleveland woman's conviction for possessing obscene material because the police had found it after forcing their way into her home using a bogus search warrant while seeking a fugitive from justice.

Exceptions to the Need for a Warrant

Despite the impressive language of the Fourth Amendment and the potency of the exclusionary rule, the amendment is not as formidable as its critics claim. First, judges quickly approve the overwhelming majority, perhaps 90%, of the warrants sought by the police.

Second, there are many exceptions to the rules regarding warrants and to the exclusion of evidence if warrants are absent, faulty, or exceeded by police. For example, the good-faith rule allows evidence taken by police while executing a warrant in "good faith," even if the judge who issued the warrant erred in some way, such as not requiring sufficient probable cause. The courts have also upheld warrants that contained technical errors. Seizures without a warrant of evidence in "plain view" are also acceptable. Thus, if the police look through an open door and see illegal drugs sitting on a table, they may seize the drugs without a warrant.

Police also have considerable authority to conduct searches and to seize evidence while making a valid arrest. This includes evidence for a crime other than the one that caused the arrest. Thus if police arrest a motorist for drunk driving and during the frisking process also discover that he or she has an illegally concealed weapon, then the gun may be seized and validly used as evidence of a further crime. The courts have also held that fleeing from police gives them probable cause to search someone and use anything found as evidence. Automobiles are yet another area of exception. The courts are less willing to protect them than residences. The Supreme Court has stopped short of allowing a full search during a police stop for a minor traffic violation, but the Court does allow a search if the stop produces other probable cause. For example, police can detain a motorist long enough to have a drug-sniffing dog brought to the scene, then use a positive reaction by the dog to search the vehicle. Objects outside the home are also generally not shielded from searches and seizures without a warrant. Examples include marijuana growing in a fenced backyard observed by a police helicopter and material in garbage cans placed by the curb for collection.

The Fourth Amendment and National Security

What is and is not allowed by the Fourth Amendment in the realm of national security is often different from the norm. The difference stems from the reluctance of Congress and the courts to restrict the national security powers of the president, especially in times of danger. This is well illustrated by President Bush's order to various intelligence agencies soon after the 9/11 attacks to monitor without warrant international telephone calls and other communications of people in the United States with suspected terrorist links. To justify his actions, the president relied on a range of existing laws and on his authority as commander in chief. The administration also asked for and got legislation that made it easier to get warrants and to monitor individuals' activities and communications. Despite charges that such activities violate the Fourth Amendment, neither Congress nor the Supreme Court has curtailed them to any great extent. Moreover, the Obama administration has continued many of these practices despite the president's campaign condemnation of them.

Arrest and Trial

Whereas the Fourth Amendment is the key to peoples' rights during the investigative phases of a criminal justice procedure, the Fifth and Sixth Amendments provide most of the constitutional guarantees during the arrest and trial phases. An initial point is that an indictment by a grand jury is required to bring someone to trial for a major crime at the federal level, but many states do not require this step. Moreover, the grand jury procedure is one of the few rights in the Bill of Rights that has not been applied to the states by the Supreme Court.

Self-Incrimination

Almost everyone who has watched a police drama on television has seen an arresting officer inform a suspect of his or her rights, beginning with, "You have the right to remain silent." This right is based on the Fifth Amendment. It forbids the government from compelling people to testify against themselves in a criminal case. This prohibition long held in federal trials, but the Supreme Court did not apply that right to the states until 1964.

The courts also extended the prohibition against involuntary self-incrimination to police interrogations. For example, the Supreme Court barred physically coerced confessions at the federal level in 1897, but did not extend that protection to the state level until 1936. Psychological coercion was disallowed in 1940. This trend culminated in *Miranda v. Arizona* (1966). The case involved an individual who was convicted of kidnap and rape after confessing to police. However, the Supreme Court overturned his conviction because police had not informed him of his right against self-incrimination and to have a lawyer. In its opinion, the Supreme Court established the **Miranda rights**. These require that upon arrest and before questioning, police must tell suspects that: (1) they may remain silent; (2) even if they choose to answer questions, they may stop at any time; (3) anything they say can be used against them in court; and (4) they may consult with a lawyer. A fifth stipulation, that the court will appoint an attorney for anyone arrested for a serious crime who cannot afford a lawyer, is based on the Sixth Amendment, as we shall see presently.

A suspect's "Miranda rights," which begin, "You have the right to remain silent," are named after Ernesto Miranda. He is pictured here during his 1967 trial. He appealed his conviction, and the Supreme Court overturned it because he had not been advised about his right as a criminal suspect. (AP Photo)

The *Miranda* decision appalled many. Americans opposed it by about a 2 to 1 margin. Congress passed legislation trying to weaken the ruling, but that act and subsequent ones have had little effect. In fact the Supreme Court in 2000 declared the Miranda rights to be part of fundamental due process and thus beyond modification by Congress.[32] Yet it is also the case that the Court itself has chipped away at the strict application of the rights. The most significant of these limits on the Miranda rule came in 2010 when the Supreme Court ruled 5-4 that after being advised or his or her rights, a suspect had to specifically invoke the right to be silent to prevent further interrogation and the potential use in court of anything the questioning revealed. Writing for the majority, Justice Anthony Kennedy reasoned that people who had been advised of their rights but then acted "in a manner inconsistent" with those rights, could be presumed to have waived them. Dissenting, Justice Sonia Sotomayor castigated the decision for turning "*Miranda* upside down" and undermining "the fundamental principles that *Miranda* protects."[33]

A historical note is that Ernesto Miranda was stabbed to death in a bar ten years after the Supreme Court freed him. The suspect who was arrested for killing Miranda was read his Miranda rights and took advantage of them by refusing to talk to police. Stymied by insufficient evidence, the suspect was released, and the murder remains officially unsolved.

Counsel

The Sixth Amendment provides that "during criminal prosecutions" those accused have a right to "the assistance of counsel" in their defense." Despite this simple language, many people accused of crimes were never defended by an attorney. One reason is that the right was long construed to mean the right to hire an attorney. Congress provided in 1790 that indigent defendants in federal death penalty cases had to have an attorney appointed by the court, but it was not until 1938 that the Supreme Court said that all defendants in federal felony cases had the right to counsel.

The courts also moved slowly to apply this right to the states. That first case involved the "Scottsboro boys," nine blacks, ages 12 to 21, charged with raping two white women. The defendants were tried with only cursory access to an attorney, convicted by an all-white jury, and (except for the 12-year-old) sentenced to death by a white judge. Eventually in *Powell v. Alabama* (1932) the Supreme Court vacated the convictions on a number of grounds including lack of an adequate legal defense. However, the impact of the ruling was limited because the Court applied its ruling only to death penalty cases. Further extension of the right to counsel did not occur until *Gideon v. Wainwright* (1963). After being tried without a lawyer and convicted of breaking into a pool hall, Clarence Gideon sent a hand-written appeal to the U.S. Supreme Court. It rarely accepts such *in forma pauperis* (pauper's) appeals, but Gideon's caught the justices' attention. They agreed to hear the case, appointed a distinguished attorney to represent him, and eventually ruled unanimously that all defendants in felony cases have the right to an attorney and that states are responsible for providing one if necessary. That right has been extended even to those facing misdemeanor charges that could result in a jail term.

Fair Trial

The Sixth Amendment also gives accused individuals the right to a fair trial, defined as one that: (1) is speedy, that is, not inordinately delayed; (2) occurs in public; (3) is conducted in the locality that the alleged crime occurred unless the defense asks for and is granted a "change of venue"; (4) allows the defense to cross-examine prosecution witnesses and to present and subpoena if necessary defense witnesses; and (5) is decided by an impartial jury unless the defendant chooses a trial by judge. Although not specifically listed in the amendment, various court decisions have added such requirements as an impartial and competent judge, and a guilty verdict that is based on proof "beyond a reasonable doubt." Yet another standard, competent counsel, has already been discussed. Each of these has been extended to cover the states by the Supreme Court in various decisions handed down for the most part in the 1960s.

Of these requirements, the one for a jury trial has been the most contentious. The Constitution does not specify the size of juries or that they must be unanimous to convict, and the Supreme Court has upheld state laws allowing as few as six jurors and convictions by lopsided majorities (such as 9 to 3) in some criminal cases.

By contrast, the Supreme Court has gradually reduced state discretion in determining jury composition. Although the phrase "jury of one's peers" does not appear in the Constitution, the courts use this historic standard to decide what constitutes an impartial jury. Generally, the courts require that a reasonable cross-section of a community be on the jury or at least in the jury pool. This bars any practice that excludes or limits jurors from any segment of society. For example, blacks and other nonwhites were once excluded from juries in the South by law, and women were also barred in many states. The Supreme Court disallowed such legal barriers as early as 1880.

However, some states then moved to informal tactics, such as keeping minorities off the voter registration lists used to select panels of prospective jurors. Once women got the right to vote, their presence on juries was still limited by many state laws that allowed women to decline to serve. Gradually, the courts have also declared such impediments unconstitutional. For example, the Supreme Court ordered new trials for the Scottsboro boys, as discussed above, not only because of inadequate legal representation but also because of the trial court's all-white jury system. In a 1954 Texas case, the Court made a similar decision related to the conviction of a Latino in a county that had never had a Mexican American juror. The Court ended allowing women to exempt themselves from jury duty in 1975. None of this means that a defendant has a right to have a jury with at least one person from any particular demographic group. Instead, what the Supreme Court has said is that no demographic groups of citizens can be excluded, exempted, or otherwise restricted from serving on juries.

Double Jeopardy

Another element of fairness in the Fifth Amendment is its prohibition of **double jeopardy**. This means that a person who has been acquitted of a crime cannot be tried a second time for the same offense. This right was applied to the states in 1969.[34] There are, however, many exceptions to the double jeopardy rule. The most important is that it does not exclude either the federal and a state government or two or more state governments for trying an individual for the same act if it violates the law in their respective jurisdictions. Dual prosecutions are rare, but as noted in Chapter 3, their number has risen because of the increased federalization of crime. This trend has occurred because of claims that some states have not always been willing to fully prosecute crimes against minorities and women. This concern has prompted the federal government to make many such acts federal criminal violations of civil rights standards. One example that drew national attention occurred in 1991 when videotape showed Los Angeles police officers unnecessarily beating a black man, Rodney King, during an arrest. After a state court jury with no black members acquitted three of the four officers, the federal government indicted all four of them for violating King's civil rights. Subsequently, the officer already convicted by the state and one other were found guilty of the federal charges and sent to prison.

Double jeopardy also does not exclude a retrial in most cases where an appeals court overturns a defendant's conviction. Although the evidence against them was shaky, most of the Scottsboro boys were retried after *Powell v. Alabama*, found guilty, and imprisoned. New trials may also be ordered if there is a hung jury or other reason to declare a mistrial. People can also be tried multiple times for "included acts" that are part of the same overall criminal activity. For example, it is possible to prosecute someone separately for manufacturing drugs, for possessing them, and for selling them.

Penalties

The Eighth Amendment protects people convicted of crimes against "excessive fines" and "cruel and unusual punishments." The Supreme Court has also held that bail must not be excessive. Whatever the language, the courts long left it up to Congress and legislatures to decide the parameters for bail, fines, and sentences. Then beginning in the late 1950s the Supreme Court began to set limits. The justices ruled in a 1958 case that a criminal penalty revoking a natural born American's citizenship was "more primitive than torture."[35] Then in a 1962 ruling, the Court nationalized the Eighth Amendment by striking down a state law that made it a criminal offense to be a drug addict, even if no possession could be proven.[36]

Nationalization of the Eighth Amendment soon moved the Supreme Court into the middle of the mounting debate over whether capital punishment constituted cruel and unusual punishment. The justices answered yes in a 5 to 4 decision, *Furman v. Georgia* (1972). But the decision was not definitive because every justice in the majority wrote a separate opinion, each of which differed from the others about why the death penalty as it was then being applied was unconstitutional. Moreover, only two of the five justices said the death penalty as such was cruel and unusual punishment. This left the door open for death-penalty reform, rather than abolition.

Soon thereafter, both the federal government and 35 states enacted reforms, setting the stages for more new executions and new challenges. Subsequently, the Court ruled in 1976 that executions as such were neither cruel nor unusual. Nevertheless, the justices have chipped away at the circumstances in which the death penalty is constitutional. For instance, the Court has disallowed laws that impose mandatory death sentences and death sentences for rapists, those who are accessories to murder, who are "mentally retarded," or who have become insane while awaiting execution. Age at the time of the offense has also become a factor. In 1988, the Court barred executing anyone for a crime committed while under age 16. Then the minimum age limit at the time of the crime was increased to age 18 in *Roper v. Simmons* (2005). In 2010, the Court further extended the protection of juveniles by ruling that those who committed crimes as juveniles that did not involve killing someone could not be sentenced to life without any possibility of parole.[37]

The *Roper* case also was notable for demonstrating the impact of globalization on American civil rights and liberties in particular and U.S. policy in general. Although in reaching its decision the Court relied on the Eighth and Fourteenth Amendments, it noted "the stark reality that the United States is the only country in the world" to execute people for such crimes and also the "overwhelming weight of international opinion against the juvenile death penalty." This reciprocal relationship between

Indicating how unusual capital punishment has become for any crime, there were legal executions in only 25 of the world's 193 countries during 2008. Of the 25 countries, 10 were in Asia.

what the world thinks and does and what Americans think and do is further in evidence in Figure 4.9. Another global perspective that makes the persistence of the death penalty in the United States somewhat puzzling is that the spread of democracy has been the key factor in the decline of legal executions worldwide. As one study put it after studying the global trend, in democracies "there is a growing acceptance to regard the death penalty as a violation of human rights."[38]

FIGURE 4.9   U.S. and World Death Penalty Statistics

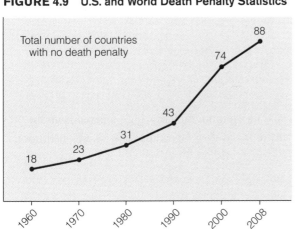

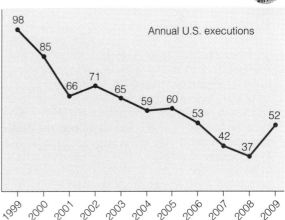

Comparing the figure showing the increasing number of countries that have abolished capital punishment with the figure showing the decline in its use in the United States suggests a connection between global thought and practice and U.S. policy.

Data sources: Amnesty International; U.S. Department of Justice.

Charges of racial bias provide another indictment of the death penalty. *McCleskey v. Kemp* (1987) was the first time this issue came before the Supreme Court. In that case, a black man convicted of killing a white police officer in Georgia appealed on the grounds of racial discrimination and cited a study showing that in Georgia, an African American convicted of killing a white was more than seven times more likely to be sentenced to death than a white convicted of murdering a black. By a 5 to 4 margin, the Supreme Court upheld the conviction, arguing that there was no evidence of intentional bias in either the law or its application and that it remained unclear whether even unintentional bias existed.[39] A historical note is that after Justice Lewis Powell, who voted with the majority in *McCleskey*, retired, a biographer asked if in retrospect there was any case on which he would change his vote. "Yes," Powell replied, "McCleskey v. Kemp."[40] Whether it was just or not, the *McCleskey* decision did not end the debate over whether race and the death penalty are connected. Your views on it are solicited in the You Decide box, "Is the Death Penalty Racially Motivated?

YOU DECIDE: Is the Death Penalty Racially Biased?

One indictment of the death penalty is that it is racially biased, particularly against blacks. The evidence is mixed. For example, blacks make up a much greater percentage of those executed than their share of the population. But it is also true that a greater percentage of those charged with murder are black than that group's share of the population. There is also off-setting evidence that finds: (1) of those charged with homicide, whites are slightly more likely than blacks to be convicted; (2) of those convicted, blacks are a bit more likely than whites to be sentenced to death; and (3) of those on death row, whites are a little more likely to be executed than blacks. Victims also make a difference, with those convicted of killing whites more likely to be sentenced to death than those who kill blacks.

To gain some further insights, data from Texas is helpful for two reasons. First, this one state carried out 52% of all U.S. executions between 2007 and 2009. Second, the usefulness of the national data reported by the U.S. Department of Justice is limited because it does not distinguish whites from Latinos.

Figure 4.10 shows that from 2007 through 2009 the percentage of blacks sentenced to death in Texas far exceeds their share of the state's population, and the percentage of whites was disproportionately low. The percentage of Latinos sentenced to death was about equal with their share of the population. Another important matter relates to victims and the charge that those who kill blacks are less likely to be condemned to death than those who murder whites. Blacks accounted for about 40% of all homicide victims in Texas 2007, yet only 4% of the inmates executed there that year were condemned for killing a black person. By contrast, 62% of those executed died for murdering a white person. The remaining 34% involved murders of other minorities. What do such data suggest to you? Is the application of the death penalty in the United States tainted by racial bias?

FIGURE 4.10 Death Penalty Statistics

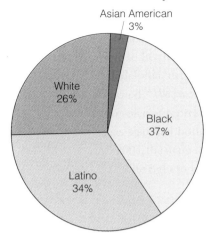

Texas death sentences 2007–2009

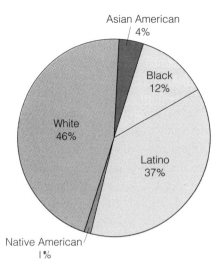

Texas population 2008

It is clear that blacks convicted of murder in Texas are much more likely to be sentenced to death than members of any other racial group, especially whites. Whether this is evidence of racial bias is very controversial.
Data sources: Texas Department of Criminal Justice; U.S. Census Bureau.

THE RIGHT TO PRIVACY

The Ninth Amendment is appealing yet vague. It states that in addition to the various rights mentioned in the Constitution, there are "others retained by the people." The idea of including such a catchall phrase dates back to the Magna Carta (1215), which contained more than 60 prohibitions on the monarchy and then added that the king also recognized "all the unwritten liberties" of the English people.

The question is: What are these other rights "retained by the people" that the Ninth Amendment suggests exist? Personal privacy is one answer than some people believe is included. Yet the Supreme Court has seldom cited the Ninth Amendment as a source of any right claimed by a petitioner. Moreover, even when an opinion has cited the amendment, the Court has never relied on it exclusively to find that a right exists. Instead, the Court has always also cited rights specified in other parts of the Constitution to make its rulings.

Indicative of the scant use of the Ninth Amendment is the fact that the Court did not use it even partly to uphold a right until *Griswold v. Connecticut* (1965). In that case, Estelle Griswold, director of the Planned Parenthood League of Connecticut, was appealing her conviction for violating the state's law against teaching how to use birth control devices. The Court ruled that Connecticut's law violated

Indicating how fast attitudes about government interference in contraception changed, the Supreme Court did not strike down state laws barring contraceptives until 1965. Just seven years later this U.S. stamp celebrating family planning was issued, and the year after that, in 1973, the Supreme Court in Roe v. Wade *severely limited the ability of states to restrict abortions. (iStockphoto)*

the right to privacy of married couples. However, the majority opinion mentioned the Ninth Amendment as only one of several that "imply zones of privacy." Subsequent privacy cases have followed the *Griswold* example by also including other amendments to secure a right of privacy. A notable example is *Roe v. Wade* (1973). In that case, the Court stated specifically it was relying primarily on the "Fourteenth Amendment's concept of personal liberty" and not the Ninth Amendment to rule that laws forbidding women to have abortions during their first two trimesters violated their right to privacy.

Sexual orientation is another intensely personal area that the courts now protect under the right to privacy. In *Lawrence and Garner v. Texas* (2003) the Supreme Court struck down a Texas law that classified homosexual acts as sodomy and a crime. Here again though, the Court ignored the Ninth Amendment and instead argued that the state's sodomy law violated the due process clause of the Fourteenth Amendment.

Whether there is a right to die is an additional sensitive subject related to privacy rights. In 1990, the Supreme Court ruled that patients have the right to refuse medical treatment even if that means they will die. Whether patients have the right to hasten their death with the aid of a physician has drawn a more cautious response by the Court. In 1997 it upheld state laws barring physician-assisted suicides in one case, but it refused to hear the appeal of a lower court decision upholding an Oregon law permitting such acts. Essentially, what the Court has said is that there is no constitutional right to assisted suicide. Instead, its legality rests with state law.

SUMMARY

The history of American civil liberties brings several descriptive words to mind. *Expansion* is one. What is protected by the First Amendment and the Constitution's other guardians of civil liberties has expanded over time. Many extensions, such as the right to have a lawyer if charged with a crime that could lead to prison, are accepted as progress by almost everyone. Other changes, such as protecting most forms of pornography, are less widely applauded. A second part of expanding civil liberties has been the incorporation process. This has involved the Supreme Court applying most parts of the Bill of Rights to state and local governments in addition to the federal government. Constitutional amendments, especially the Fourteenth Amendment, have been a third part of the expansion of civil liberties. Since the 1950s, the Supreme Court has used the amendment's "equal protection" and "due process" clauses to add to the list of civil liberties. Globalization has also played a role in expanding civil liberties. To a degree, the declining number of executions in the United States arguably reflects changing attitudes about capital punishment internationally and its decreasing use in other countries.

Inconsistent is a second word that describes the country's civil liberties history. When asked about civil liberties in theory, Americans are strongly supportive. That level of commitment declines in practice. The idea of denying a communist the right to speak in public may sound absurd today, but most Americans favored doing so in the early 1950s. Government policy has matched public attitudes. Some of the same legislators and officials who supported the Bill of Rights in 1789 also favored the Sedition Act of 1798. Similarly, the Supreme Court has been inconsistent in its application of the Bill of Rights. For instance, the Court may have declared that there is an "impregnable" wall between religion and state, but its subsequent decisions have hardly maintained that strict standard. Additional inconsistencies relate to the civil liberties of women, minorities, and other disadvantaged groups. Throughout most of U.S. history, women and minorities were barred from jury duty in many states.

Limited is a third word applicable to Americans' civil liberties. No liberty is absolute. Free speech is protected, but not when it presents "a clear and present danger" or contains "fighting words." Slavery has been abolished, but it is still possible to force people to serve in the military. Protections against searches and seizures by the government without a warrant are much weaker in the area of national security than in domestic affairs.

Debatable is a fourth word applicable to civil liberties. American history is an ongoing debate about where to draw the lines regarding free speech, free religion, the right to bear arms, the rights of the accused, and many other civil liberties. For example, the Supreme Court has recently ruled that people do have the right to possess weapons for self-defense, but what kinds of weapons, where they can be carried, and many other details are subject to debate.

Perishable is a fifth description of civil liberties. Freedom is never a given; it needs protection. There have been many times when foreign threats or domestic turmoil have led to restrictions on Americans' civil liberties. It is important to put the burden of proof on anyone who advocates limiting liberty and to be active in politics to ensure that any diminution of Americans' civil liberties is absolutely necessary, no greater than required, and reversed as soon as possible.

CHAPTER 4 GLOSSARY

bill of attainder A law that makes an individual guilty of a crime and imposes punishment without a trial.

civil liberties Freedoms that are possessed by individuals and that cannot be abridged by the government.

civil rights Freedoms that must extend to all people equally and that cannot be denied to any one group based on its race, gender, or other characteristics.

clear and present danger test A standard used by the Supreme Court to judge the constitutionality of a restraint on freedom of expression. It asks whether the restricted expression can reasonably be said to create a clear and present danger to public safety, or whether it causes some other evil that the government has a legitimate interest in preventing.

double jeopardy Trying a person who has been acquitted of a crime for a second time on the same charge.

due process clause An imprecise but important phrase found in the Fifth and Fourteenth Amendments that means that government may not take action, especially anything that restricts an individual's liberties, that (1) does not follow the prescribed processes established by law (procedural due process) or that is arbitrary or unreasonable (substantive due process).

eminent domain Based on common law, the authority of the government to take private property.

establishment clause The First Amendment clause, "Congress shall make no law respecting the establishment of religion," that has come to mean that government is barred from supporting any specific religion or even religion in general.

exclusionary rule The position of the courts that evidence that is obtained in violation of a suspect's civil liberties cannot be used in court.

ex post facto laws Those laws that make something illegal retroactively.

fighting words A standard set by the Supreme Court in *Chaplinsky v. New Hampshire* (1942) that denotes one class of speech, that is highly provocative, that is not protected by the First Amendment.

Fourteenth Amendment Adopted in 1868, this amendment ensured citizenship status for freed slaves by specifying that "all persons born or naturalized in the United States . . . are citizens of the United States and of the state wherein they reside. The amendment also included the due process clause barring states from depriving "any person of life, liberty, or property, without due process of law" and the equal protection clause saying that no state could "deny to any person within its jurisdiction the equal protection of the laws."

free-exercise clause The language in the First Amendment that bars Congress from passing any law "prohibiting the free exercise" of religion. Also applies to the states.

hate speech Hostile expressions based on religion or such innate characteristics as race, ethnicity, gender, or sexual orientation.

incorporation doctrine The idea that the "due process" language of the Fourteenth Amendment means that all or most of the Bill of Rights should apply to state governments as well as the federal government.

Lemon test Standard set in *Lemon v. Kurtzman* (1971) that government support for religious institutions and activities is constitutional if: (1) it has a "secular legislative purpose," (2) its "primary effect . . . neither advances nor inhibits religion," and (3) it does not "foster excessive government entanglement with religion."

Magna Carta A document that English nobles forced King John I to sign in 1215 that contains more than 60 prohibitions on the monarchy.

Miranda rights The requirements that upon arrest and before questioning, police must tell suspects that: (1) they have the right to remain silent; (2) even if they choose to answer questions, they can stop at any time; (3) anything they say can be used against them in court; (4) they have a right to consult with a lawyer; (5) if they cannot afford an attorney, the court will appoint one.

writ of habeas corpus An order issued by a court requiring government authorities to justify their detention of an individual.

CIVIL RIGHTS

5

YOU DECIDE: Affirmative Action Admissions?

Within the general debate over affirmative action, college admissions standards have been a particular flashpoint that has sparked numerous court cases. The Supreme Court ruled on two of these, both involving the University of Michigan, on the same day in 2003. The first, *Gratz v. Bollinger* (2003), challenged the school's undergraduate admissions process that gave applicants from some minority groups an extra 20 points on a 150-point admissions scale. The second case, *Grutter v. Bollinger* (2003), focused on the university law school's use of race as one factor in deciding admissions without assigning a particular weight to it. Those supporting and opposing the university made similar arguments in both cases. For example, Hillary Clinton (D-NY) and eight other U.S. senators filed a brief arguing that admissions policies promoting diversity "have strengthened our society, our economy, and our democratic institutions." Taking the other side, a brief by the Anti-Defamation League charged that the university's admissions policy denied "applicants who are not members of designated minority groups fundamental equal protection" by valuing "persons for their race, not for relevant individual characteristics."

If you had been a Supreme Court justice in 2003, how would you have voted in the two cases? You could have voted for the university in both cases or against it in both. Or perhaps you see differences in the two admission processes significant enough for you to uphold one and strike down the other? Most importantly, think about why you cast your two votes in terms of the value of diversity, what equal opportunity means, and how, if at all, affirmative action should work. As for what the Supreme Court decided, that is taken up later in the section on affirmative action in higher education. When you get there, see if you think the same way you do now.

INTRODUCING CIVIL RIGHTS AND EQUALITY

Equality is at the core **civil rights**. These rights include freedoms that should extend equally to everyone regardless of race, sex, or other characteristics. Violations of civil liberties usually target people based on their individual views or actions. By contrast, abridgements of civil rights tend to be motivated by one of the victim's demographic characteristics such as race.

This chapter takes up American civil rights with a primary focus on racial minority groups and women. Their rights fall into two categories. One consists of *political civil rights*, including the right to vote and otherwise participate in the political system. *Socioeconomic civil rights* make up the second cluster. These involve employment, education, and other areas of opportunity that help determine a person's well-being and status in society. During our exploration of civil rights, you will see that:

★ Equality is at the core of civil rights.
★ Advances in American civil rights have not occurred in international isolation.
★ Two key concepts are legal equality and societal equality.
★ Persistent inequality among races and genders has been a constant in American life.
★ American history is a saga of a long and significantly but not fully successful effort to reduce the inequality between and among whites and racial minorities, men and women, and society in general and other disadvantaged groups including gays, the disabled, and the elderly.
★ Despite progress, the groups that have been disadvantaged throughout American history remain so.

Civil Rights and Demographic Diversity

Civil rights and demographic diversity are closely linked. Political theory includes the idea of a **social contract**, a tacit agreement between people and their society as to what their relationship should be. Part of that agreement is that except for a weighty cause: (1) everyone should have an equal say in how the society governs itself; (2) society and its government should treat everyone equally; and (3) everyone should be equally free to achieve whatever their abilities and effort permit. None of these standards has been uniformly honored in American history. Instead, some demographic groups have been and remain disadvantaged politically and socioeconomically. Government has had a hand in limiting these groups, but society has played an even larger role.

Certainly the status of civil rights has improved over the last 50 years or so. Indeed, most government restrictions have been eliminated. Yet racial minorities, women, and some other groups remain disadvantaged.

Civil Rights in a World of Difference

American civil rights have not advanced in isolation from the rest of the world. Instead, efforts in the United States to expand civil rights have been linked to global thinking and global events. We will see, for example, that American abolitionism was part of an international effort to end the slave trade, then slavery altogether. Similarly, Americans were near but not at the front of the global effort to gain the right to vote for women. More recently, it was not a coincidence that Americans of color launched the modern civil right movement in the 1950s at about the same time that people of color in Africa, Asia, and elsewhere began to struggle against white colonial rule. The American women's movement was also part of a larger global effort. Moreover, there are parallels between people of color and women on the one hand and whites and males on the other in the United States and in the world. For example, Americans of color are persistently more likely to be poor than white Americans. Similarly, the populations of the world's most prosperous countries are predominantly white, while very poor countries are populated mostly by people of color.[1] Women are not yet equal in the United States, nor are they equal in any other country according to the UN's gender-related development index (GDI) and gender empowerment measure (GEM).[2]

Equality

Given that civil rights denote equal rights among groups, it is important to consider what "equal" means. *Legal equality* is one aspect. It means that everyone should have equal standing with the government, especially its courts. Legal equality also requires that laws and policies do not disadvantage any individual or group without overwhelmingly just cause. This is particularly true for restrictions on societal groups that are considered by the courts to be **protected classes**. These groups have been designated by law or court decisions as groups that have been/are subject to widespread discrimination. Therefore they warrant protection from being limited in any way that does not apply to all of society except in extraordinary circumstances. Most clearly, protected classes are those based on a religion/belief system, race/color, ethnicity/national origin, old age, and disability status. Note that all these traits except religion are inherent or otherwise not a matter of choice. However, despite being inherent, sexual orientation is not yet considered a fully protected class by the federal courts. The courts require that whoever wants to impose a restriction on a protected class must demonstrate that (1) there is an important, even compelling reason to single out the class for different treatment, and also that (2) there is no other less restrictive policy options available to address the vital interest.

Societal equality is a second key concept. This means that all groups must be treated equally by society in the many aspects of life that are difficult or impossible to regulate by law. The idea of **equal opportunity** provides an example. For equal opportunity to exist, there must be no legal barriers to members of any group voting, getting a job, finding housing, or otherwise being an equal member of society. Additionally, equal opportunity requires the virtual absence of prejudice in a society. In the United States, job discrimination based on race is illegal. Yet it continues because of prejudice. In 2003, for example, researchers responded to 2,500 want ads in the *Boston Globe* and Chicago *Tribune* with a pair of made-up resumes that were virtually identical except that one included an applicant's first name (such as Tamika or Tyrone) most commonly found among blacks. The other resume included a first name (such as Anne or Brett) most commonly found among whites. The result was that the resumes with white sounding names drew a 50% higher response rate than the resume with names associated with blacks.[3]

RACIAL INEQUALITY AND REFORM TO THE 1950s

Persistent inequality among races has been a constant in American life. Whites dominated in the newly created United States in 1776, and everyone else was marginalized or enslaved. From that point through the 1950s there were some improvements. Slavery ended, Native Americans achieved citizenship, living conditions for racial minorities improved somewhat, and some other limited advances occurred. Still, the fundamental political and socioeconomic realties had not changed. In the 1950s as in the 1770s, whites dominated the country politically and, on average, enjoyed a much higher standard of existence than members of other races.

It is tempting to detail the travails that people of color endured during this long period because that saga set the stage for what has occurred since. However, space limits us here to a mere glimpse of the history of American race relations.

African Americans and Inequality

Before the Civil War, most blacks were slaves with neither citizenship nor rights. Almost all these slaves lived in deplorable conditions, with marginal nutrition, housing, and health care the norm.

The few free blacks were not much better off. Even in the states that outlawed slavery, free blacks could rarely vote or hold property, most lived in poverty, and few had any education. Making matters worse, the Supreme Court in **Dred Scott v. Stamford** (1857) ruled that free blacks were not even citizens. The

 Aversion to slavery was one reason that the British and French did not support the Confederacy during the Civil War.

case involved the effort of a slave, Dred Scott, to gain his freedom after having been taken by his owner to a state where slavery was illegal. The Court not only rejected Scott's suit, but went out of its way to say, "Whether emancipated or not," blacks "are not included . . . under the word 'citizens' in the Constitution."

The Antislavery Movement and the End of Slavery

The country's first civil right effort was the antislavery movement that began in the late 1700s. The U.S. effort paralleled the larger international movement centered in Great Britain. Religion was a connection between the efforts in Britain and America, with the Quakers in both countries being among the first antislavery advocates. It is not coincidence that Great Britain banned the slave trade within its empire in 1807, and the United States barred the importation of slaves in 1808. It is also the case that British thought influenced the movement to end slavery altogether in the United States. Indeed, former slave Frederick Douglass, argued in 1846 that the scathing criticism of slavery in the United States by the English writer Charles Dickens in *American Notes* (1842) had done more to rally opinion against slavery "than all the books published in America for ten years"[4]

The Supreme Court ruled in 1857 that Dred Scott, pictured here, and other blacks, both slave and emancipated, were not American citizens. (Library of Congress)

Civil War Era Reforms

In the end, Civil War bullets, not books, ended slavery in the United States. Any chance for blacks to advance rested on three post-war constitutional amendments. The **Thirteenth Amendment** (1865) barred slavery. The **Fourteenth Amendment** (1868) voided the *Dred Scott* decision by its *jus soli* **clause**. It declared that all people born in the United States were citizens of both the country and the state where they lived. By law, the United States also recognizes *jus sanquinis*, a doctrine that connects an infant's citizenship to its parents.

The Fourteenth Amendment also included two clauses that would later have a major impact on civil rights. The **due process clause** barred states from depriving "any person of life, liberty, or property, without due process of law," and the **equal protection clause** said that no state could "deny to any person . . . the equal protection of the laws." Finally, the **Fifteenth Amendment** (1870) gave black males the right to vote by forbidding any barrier to voting based on race, color, or previous condition of servitude."

Racism Reverses Reform

For a time, the circumstances of blacks improved. For example, former Confederate states elected 16 blacks to Congress during Reconstruction, the period after the Civil War when the U.S. army occupied the South. These advances were short-lived, however. Soon after federal forces withdrew in 1877, the southern states began to enact **Jim Crow laws**. "Jim Crow" was a derogatory term used for blacks during the pre-Civil War period. Some of these laws created barriers to black voting. *Literacy tests* allowed white registrars of voters to decide that blacks and other minorities were not sufficiently literate to vote. *Poll taxes* created a financial barrier to voting. To exempt whites from such impediments, many states also enacted *grandfather clauses*. These gave exemptions to anyone who had voted before 1868 or whose ancestor had voted before then. *White primaries*, yet another racist tactic, barred blacks from voting in party primaries and thereby ensured that only white candidates would be nominated.

Jim Crow laws also legalized socioeconomic discrimination. Many states, southern and otherwise, legally required that schools, public transportation, and most other public facilities and accommodations be segregated. Mississippi even managed to revive quasi-slavery by leasing its prison inmates, most of whom were black, to planters and others as unpaid workers. Making matters worse, the Ku Klux Klan and other racist organizations sprang up to intimidate blacks and others who tried to vote or otherwise break the through the lines of bigotry. Beatings were routine, and murder was not uncommon. Among other horrors, white racists lynched or otherwise killed at least 3,000 blacks between 1882 and 1930.

When blacks and others sought judicial relief, the Supreme Court joined the rest of the federal government in abandoning them to racism. In *United States v. Cruickshank* (1876), a case involving the massacre of blacks by whites, the court ruled that the Fourteenth Amendment did not apply to private citizens and organizations that violated the civil rights of blacks and other minorities. Later in *Plessy v. Ferguson* (1896), the court upheld the conviction of Homer Plessy, a black man, for violating Louisiana law by sitting in a "whites only" railroad car. This legitimized the claim of the **separate but equal doctrine** that state-mandated segregation was constitutional if supposedly equal facilities were available to the "colored" races.

Most of this Jim Crow system lasted into the mid-twentieth century. At that time, for example, only 5% of Mississippi's black adults were registered to vote, and schools were segregated widely across the country. Moreover, most Americans still had a Jim Crow mentality. In 1945, 64% wanted to maintain white superiority or keep the races entirely separate, while only 33% favored more or equal rights for blacks.[5]

Other Racial Groups and Inequality

Other racial minorities also endured most or all of the race-based violations of their political and socioeconomic civil rights that blacks suffered during the century that followed the Civil War. Each minority group also had its own unique unsettling experiences.

Hispanics

Mexicans living in California, Texas, and much of the Southwest, had their land forcefully annexed by the United States. As a result, they lost their lands, were treated as racially inferior, and were the victims of racial violence. In its worst form, whites lynched about 600 Mexican Americans between 1848 and 1928.[6] They were also largely excluded from politics by literacy tests, poll taxes, white primaries, and similar tactics. Yet despite the racist resentments of many whites, Mexican immigration was simultaneously encouraged by white businessmen who sought cheap labor, thus increasing the Mexican Americans population and intensifying the racist sentiments of the general white population.

Puerto Ricans had a similar experience. Their homeland was seized from Spain as and became a U.S. colony in 1898 Initially, few Puerto Ricans came to the United States, but there were immigration surges during World War I and especially World War II when Washington recruited and even drafted more than 100,000 Puerto Ricans into the military and tens of thousands of others were lured to the mainland to work in industry. However, the end of the war diminished the need for workers on the mainland, and poverty spread rapidly among U.S.-based Puerto Ricans. In 1950, their unemployment rate was quadruple the national average, and their median income was about half the national average. Puerto Ricans also suffered from social prejudice. A 1971 survey recorded a plurality of Americans saying they would be concerned if a member of their family were dating a Puerto Rican.[7]

This sign from a diner window in Dimmit, Texas, in 1949 symbolizes the widespread discrimination against Hispanics in the Southwest and elsewhere. (© The Dolph Briscoe Center for American History, The University of Texas at Austin)

Asian Americans

As occurred with Latinos, U.S. employers encouraged an influx of Asians by bringing them in to work in mining, railroad construction, and agriculture in the early West. Also as befell Latinos, this inflow sparked a racist reaction among many whites. One can glimpse this racism in an 1879 editorial in the *Santa Cruz Sentinel* that depicted Chinese as a "half-human, half-devil, rat-eating . . . subspecies" of humans.[8] States routinely discriminated against Asians in such ways as by barring them from owing property or operating a business. Violence against Asians was common, and states abetted these crimes by not allowing Asians to testify in court and identify their white assailants. When a white mob in Los Angeles slaughtered 19 Asians in 1871, all the assailants were soon released because no white would testify against them and state law barred Asians from taking the stand.

Making the position of Asians and other nonwhite immigrants even more tenuous, the **Nationality Act of 1790** permitted only immigrants who were "white persons" to acquire citizenship. To further preserve white dominance, Congress passed a dozen **Asian exclusion laws** between the 1860s and 1930s that severely

The headlines from the San Francisco Examiner in February 1942 document the government order to confine all Japanese Americans on the West Coast in fenced camps guarded by the military. (Library of Congress)

limited or prohibited Asian immigration. The argument that immigrants from India and some other parts of Asia are Caucasians and therefore "white" and eligible for citizenship was rejected by the Supreme Court in 1923 when it ruled that "white person" and "Caucasian" were not synonymous.[9]

War with Japan precipitated the single most concentrated attack on Asian American civil rights. Following Pearl Harbor in 1941, the government declared the West Coast a military zone and expelled all 125,000 Japanese Americans living there as "subversive" members of "an enemy race."[10] Virtually all of them were forced into ill-equipped camps in the interior of the country. In addition to the psychological damage, most lost their homes, businesses, and other property. Washington called the camps "relocation centers," but as one official later admitted, "We gave the fancy name of 'relocation centers' to these dust bowls, but they were concentration camps nonetheless."[11]

When one detainee challenged the constitutionality of the policy, the Supreme Court in *Korematsu v. United States* (1944) accepted the government's argument that national danger justified confining an entire segment of the population based on ancestry. However, the racist underpinning of the internal deportation is obvious in the fact that no restrictions were imposed on white German Americans or Italian Americans even though their ancestral countries were also at war with the United States.

Native Americans

The largest group of Native Americans, American Indians, suffered what today would be called *ethnic cleansing*. The American Indian population declined at least 50% between 1500 and 1800 and by another 50% between then and 1900. Many died of diseases contracted from whites. Countless others were killed during ruthless campaigns to acquire their lands. Typifying the attitude of many whites, California Governor John McDougal pledged in 1851 that, "a war of extermination will continue to be waged . . . until the Indian race becomes extinct."[12] Most of those who survived were herded onto impoverished reservations on desolate land often far from their traditional tribal areas. There was also an effort to eradicate American Indian culture by forcing those living on reservations to send their children to boarding schools where, for example, they were forbidden to speak their native language. Justifying this policy, U.S. Commissioner of Indian Affairs

Thomas Morgan reasoned in 1889 that "Indians . . . do not have any right" to have their children "grow up like themselves, a race of barbarians and semi-savages."[13]

Other Native Americans suffered similarly. Native Alaskans were not even citizens of the territory until 1915 when its legislature grudgingly granted them citizenship, but only if they could find five whites willing to testify that they had abandoned their native culture. As for Native Hawaiians, their country, which had been recognized by the United States since 1853, was hijacked in 1893 when white American sugar planters backed by U.S. troops from the warship U.S.S. *Boston* overthrew the government of Queen Lili'uokalani. Instantly Native Hawaiians became second-class citizens in their own homeland, and they remain at the bottom of the state's socioeconomic structure, as evident in Figure 5.1.

FIGURE 5.1 Native Hawaiian Economic Data

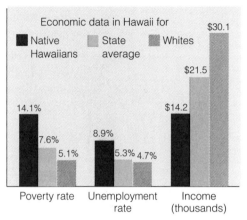

Native Hawaiians are more disadvantaged in their own state and former country than any other racial group.
Data source: U.S. Census Bureau.

Global Influences Promoting Racism

For many Americans, ideas from abroad seemed to help justify racism. English naturalist Charles Darwin argued in *The Origin of Species* (1859) that species evolved and improved themselves through natural selection. English scholar Herbert Spenser, who Columbia University President Frederick Barnard lauded as the "most powerful intellect of all time," then developed **social Darwinism** by applying Darwin's ideas to human society. Social Darwinism is the idea that some groups dominate because evolution has made them superior.[14] Spenser coined the term "survival of the fittest" in 1864 and defined it as "the preservation of favored races in the struggle for life."[15] Globally, Americans and Europeans used social Darwinism to justify their imperial domination over supposedly lesser, non-white people. Social Darwinism was also used to legitimize domestic racism in the United States and elsewhere. For example, Professor Joseph Le Conte of the University of California, Berkeley wrote in *The Race Problem in the South* (1892) that when two races lived in proximity, it was natural "that the higher race will assume control and determine the policy of the community."[16]

The Impacts of Discrimination

Legal barriers combined with physical intimidation effectively denied political rights to minorities. The modest gains during Reconstruction were lost. No black served in the U.S. Senate between 1881 and 1967, and only one served in the House between 1901 and 1945. Other minority groups fared no better. Between

1865 and 1945, only seven Hispanics and three Native Americans served in Congress. Asian Americans were shut out completely until 1956.

Socioeconomic conditions were also dismal. Some progress occurred in minority health, education, and economic circumstances in the latter 1800s and early 1900s. Yet glaring gaps between whites and minorities continued to exist. In 1950, for example, the average life span of whites was 15% longer than that of minorities, and their unemployment rate was about half that of minorities.

RACE, POLITICAL INEQUALITY, AND REFORM SINCE 1950

It was amid the Jim Crow laws and KKK violence in the later 1800s that the modern black civil rights movement was born. After several preliminary attempts in the 1890s to create national organizations, prominent African Americans founded the Niagara Movement in 1905 to press for their civil rights. It expanded, added sympathetic whites and others to its ranks, and adopted the name National Association for the Advancement of Color People (NAACP) in 1910. Somewhat later civil rights groups formed to defend other minority groups. Among the earliest were the League of United Latin American Citizens (LULAC, 1929), which began in Texas, and the California-based Japanese American Citizen's League (1929).

During their early years, civil rights groups concentrated on organizing and trying to devise strategies to attack legal and societal racism. Racial attitudes and the general absence of minority representatives in Congress and state legislatures made it nearly impossible to move antidiscrimination legislation forward. At the federal level, for example, the Dyer Anti-Lynching Bill (1922) would have made it a federal crime to participate in a lynching, to fail to protect someone from being lynched, or to fail to prosecute those who had lynched someone. President Warren Harding endorsed the bill, and it passed the House, but Southern Democrats in the Senate killed the bill in their chamber. It was a fate for which the Senate formally apologized in 2005.

Such defeats soon led many civil rights groups to adopt a strategy of attacking discrimination through lawsuits. This was more fruitful. Among other successes, Thurgood Marshall, chief counsel for the NAACP, successfully argued against segregated schools in the *Brown v. Board of Education* (1954) case before the Supreme Court. Thirteen years later, Marshall became the first black on the Supreme Court. Similarly, LULAC won a case in 1945 against the Orange County, California, schools, which had segregated Mexican children on the grounds that they were "more poorly clothed and mentally inferior to white children."[17]

The Civil Rights Movement in the 1950s and 1960s

Although the court successes of the NAACP, LULAC, and other organizations were important, the legal approach was slow. Spurred by growing frustration, new efforts arose. Baptist minister, Martin Luther King, Jr. led one of these new approaches. He advocated civil disobedience: peaceful acts designed to raise awareness for a cause and to create pressure for change. Symbolizing this approach, a black woman, Rosa Parks, refused to obey a city law and surrender her seat to a white person boarding a full bus in Montgomery, Alabama, in 1955. When she was arrested, blacks led by King began a yearlong boycott of the city's buses. Joining the effort, the NAACP filed suit and prevailed when the Supreme Court upheld a federal district court's ruling that the city's law violated the Fourteenth Amendment's equal protection clause.[18] The success established King as major civil rights leader. He went on to help found the Southern Christian Leadership Conference in 1957 and to shape its emphasis on nonviolent protest through such tactics as mass marches, boycotts, and sit-ins at segregated lunch counters.

King's well-crafted approach brought significant and favorable press coverage that raised whites' awareness and increased their sympathy. One 1965 poll found 94% of its respondents saying King had made a positive impact.[19] Attitudes also changed about the status of blacks. Between 1956 and 1963, the share of Americans who thought that blacks were being treated unfairly increased from one-third to two-thirds.[20]

Inadvertently, white racists assisted the civil rights movement by behaving like terrorists and thugs. In one infamous 1965 incident, state and local police used clubs, whips, and dogs to brutally attack a peaceful march in Selma, Alabama. It was being led by King to protest the fact that less than 2% of the city's adult blacks were registered to vote. The onslaught was a public relations disaster for the racists. Polls showed Americans siding by more than two-to-one with the marchers over the police.[21] Then in a horrific culmination of the violence, the Reverend King was assassinated in 1968 while in Memphis, Tennessee, supporting a strike for better pay by black sanitation workers.

Without King's leadership, the civil rights movement splintered and slowed. Factionalism was not the only reason. More positively, the civil rights movement was also the victim of its own successes, with its victories taking some of the steam out of African American discontent. This deceleration, however, did not mean the demise of the civil rights effort. Instead it became less reliant on major marches and other public events, although those have occurred, and again more focused on legal action, pressure on government, and efforts to empower minorities by increasing their voting turnout, representation in government, educational achievement, and other keys to power and equality. The civil rights movement also diversified as civil rights organizations associated with Latinos, Asian Americans, and Native Americans increasingly joined the effort.

The Global Context of the Civil Rights Movement

During the first half of the twentieth century, whites dominated the world. Except for Japan, the countries with most of the wealth and power were predominantly white in the European sense. Moreover, several of these *Eurowhite* countries, including the United States, held colonial empires in Asia, Africa, and elsewhere populated mostly by people of color.[22] The parallel between empowered and relatively prosperous whites and largely powerless and poor minorities both globally and in the United States is hard to miss.

Similarly, parallel changes began to occur in the racial equation globally and in the United States. One change was that human rights became a more prominent issue everywhere. The newly created United Nations (1945) set human rights as one of its main concerns. In this spirit, the UN General Assembly adopted the Universal Declaration of Human Rights (1948) enumerating more than two dozen "inalienable" rights, to which "everyone is entitled . . . without distinction of any kind, such as race. . . ." Later, as the global human rights and American civil rights movements simultaneously gathered strength in the 1960s, the UN sponsored such multilateral treaties as the International Convention on the Elimination of All Forms of Racial Discrimination (1966) and the International Covenant on Civil and Political Rights (1966) at virtually the same time as Congress was enacting the far-reaching Civil Rights Act (1964) and Voting Rights Act (1965).

Among their other impacts, the human rights treaties further fueled the growing discontent among people of color with their colonial status under white rule. What occurred with increasing speed was the collapse of colonialism and the establishment of many new countries, most of which were predominantly populated by people of color. Such countries grew from about half of all the world's countries in 1950 to about three quarters by 2000.

Kwame Nkrumah, Ghana's first president, and Thurgood Marshall, the first African American Supreme Court justice, attended college together at Lincoln University in Pennsylvania.

In turn, the birth of these new countries, especially in Africa, helped inspire the American civil rights movement.[23] The first of the black African countries to gain independence during this era was Ghana in 1957, and Martin Luther King and several other African American leaders traveled there to attend the independence ceremonies.[24] Soon after returning, King depicted Ghana's independence as symbolizing that an "old order of colonialism, of segregation, of discrimination is passing away."

King added that the change "would have worldwide implications and repercussions—not only for Asia and Africa, but also for America."[25]

King's belief in peaceful protest also had a strong global connection. He had studied the nonviolent practices of Mohandas K. (Mahatma, or "great soul") Gandhi, India's great philosopher and independence leader (1947). King acknowledged Gandhi as "the guiding light of our technique of nonviolent social change."[26] Further illustrating the global circulation of ideas, Gandhi had begun to develop his belief in pacifism when in 1909 he had read the essay "Civil Disobedience" (1849) by American transcendentalist thinker Henry David Thoreau.

ADVANCES IN POLITICAL EQUALITY AMONG RACES

Although Martin Luther King's dream of racial harmony and equality remains unfulfilled, progress has been made. We will examine the advances in minority political participation and power in this section and in the next take up advances in socioeconomic equality.

Eliminating Racial Restrictions on Immigration and Citizenship

One of Martin Luther King's models was India's pacifist independence leader Mohandas K. (Mahatma, or "great soul") Gandhi, whose picture is on the wall above King's desk. Gandhi was assassinated by a bigoted zealot in 1948; 20 years later King suffered the same fate. (©1976 Bob Fitch/Take Stock/The Image Works)

Ending citizenship requirements and immigration laws designed to keep the country overwhelmingly white provided some of the earliest civil rights advances. Asian Americans achieved one such early victory when the Supreme Court ruled in *United States v. Wong Kim Ark* (1898) that a child born to Chinese immigrants who were themselves ineligible for citizenship was nonetheless a U.S. citizen under the *jus soli* clause of the Fourteenth Amendment. This ruling also protected the citizenship rights of Latino children born in the United States, whatever the citizenship or immigration status of their parents. During the late 1800s and early 1900s, an increasing number of Native Americans also gradually acquired citizenship through various treaties and acts. Still, many American Indians and Native Alaskans could not claim citizenship until Congress passed the American Indian Citizenship Act in 1924. Even then it was another 24 years before the last state removed its barriers to voting by Native Americans.

The next major step toward opening the United States to greater diversity was the McCarren-Walter Act (1952). It repealed the 1790 law that barred people of color from becoming naturalized citizens. Another important step was the Immigration Act of 1965. It ended immigration quotas based on the ethnic heritage of Americans in 1890, a policy that had strongly favored European immigrants. Emphasizing the link between immigration laws and civil rights, Representative Philip Burton (D-CA) told his colleagues, "Just as we sought to eliminate discrimination in our land through the Civil Rights Act, today we seek by phasing out the national origins quota system to eliminate discrimination in immigration to this nation."[27]

Protecting Minority Electoral Rights

Other civil rights victories eliminated most of the Jim Crow limitations on minority political rights. Two early advances came when the Supreme Court rejected grandfather exemptions for voting in 1915 and struck down whites-only primaries in 1944.[28] Then Congress passed a series of acts in 1957, 1960, and 1964 somewhat improving the political civil rights of minorities. However, the most important legislation was enacted after the brutalization of the marchers in Selma in 1965.[29] Amid the ensuing uproar, Congress passed the Voting Rights Act (1965, VRA). It banned literacy tests and empowered the U.S. Attorney General to oversee the electoral systems of seven Southern states that had particularly poor civil right records. Later amendments to the VRA boosted its protections even more in such ways as extending its geographic coverage.

The VRA and similar acts had a major impact on African American political participation, particularly in the South. In the 11 states of the old Confederacy, black voter registration increased from 43% to 64% between 1965 and 1988, and the number of black elected officials in the region grew from about 100 to more than 3,000.[30]

The political rights blacks gained through the VRA and similar acts also benefited Asian Americans and Hispanics. For example, later amendments to the VRA boosted political participation by both these groups by requiring that ballots and voter information be available in Spanish, Chinese, and other languages as needed.[31]

Ensuring Fairer Electoral Districts

Jim Crow laws that kept minorities out of voting booths were paralleled by practices that made it very difficult for blacks or other minorities to be elected to office. Among these practices were racial gerrymandering and districting by geography, not population.

Racial Gerrymandering

After the VRA was passed, one way that southern whites attempted to limit its impact was by racial gerrymandering. This involves drawing electoral district lines to aid or hinder racial groups in the electoral process. In the post-VRA South, states adopted several racial gerrymandering techniques to minimize the influence of blacks or Latinos on elections. *Cracking* broke up concentrations of minorities, and *stacking* distributed them among larger white populations. If a minority concentration was too large to crack or stack, then *packing* put as many minority voters as possible into one district, leaving other districts abnormally white.

Not only did the Justice Department use its authority under the VRA to bar these practices, it turned racial gerrymandering around by pressuring states to create electoral districts in which a minority group was a majority of the population (a "majority–minority district") or near majority. This practice increased the chances of minority candidates being elected. It is a controversial practice, though, and the Supreme Court has sometimes found that a state has gone too far in using race to create a district. More generally, though, the court has allowed the practice as long as (1) a cohesive minority population exists (2) in a reasonably compact geographic area in a state where (3) a history of discrimination exists.

Whatever the legal considerations, racial gerrymandering has clearly increased minority representation. It remains true that very few African American or Latino legislators come from districts in which whites are a majority. Minority candidates won in only 35 of 6,667 congressional races held in white-majority districts between 1966 and 1996.[32] This pattern has continued, with 97% of white-majority congressional districts electing a white in 2008. Therefore, as is evident in Figure 5.2, districts with a high minority population remain crucial to minority representation.[33]

FIGURE 5.2   Representation and District Racial Characteristics

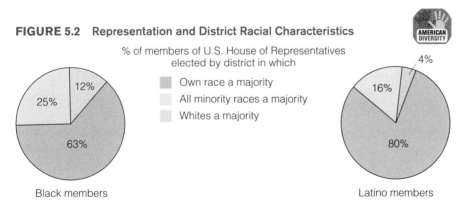

% of members of U.S. House of Representatives elected by district in which

- Own race a majority
- All minority races a majority
- Whites a majority

Black members: 12%, 25%, 63%

Latino members: 4%, 16%, 80%

Almost all blacks and Latinos elected to the U.S. House of Representatives in 2008 came from a district where whites were a minority.
Data source: Author's calculations.

Requiring Equal Population Voting Districts

Another change in districting that served to increase minority representation occurred when the Supreme Court ended the practice of states dividing their seats in the U.S. House of Representatives and in their own legislatures based on geographical units, such as counties. This approach overrepresented sparsely populated rural countries and underrepresented cities where blacks and other minorities were concentrated. In Georgia, for example, the Fifth Congressional district centered in Atlanta had a 1960 population of 824,000, while just 272,000 people lived in the state's rural Ninth Congressional District. In *Wesberry v. Sanders* (1964) and a series of other cases, the Supreme Court ruled that such disparities were unconstitutional in U.S. House districts and in all state and local legislative districts as well.[34] Now all election districts (except the U.S. Senate) must be apportioned according to population to meet the **one person–one vote principle**. The impact of this change was to increase the representation of urban areas, and by extension African Americans and other minorities.

The Status of Minority Political Participation

The inauguration of President Barack Obama in 2009 and the evidence in Figure 5.3 illustrate that increased minority registration and voting, fairer districting practices, and other factors have worked together since the 1960s to increase the number of minority elected officials. Particularly strong gains have been made by African Americans in the U.S. House of Representatives and in state legislatures, where their share of representatives is approaching their share of the population. Another indication of progress is the greater number of minorities who have been appointed to high office at every level of government. For instance, there had been no minority members of a president's Cabinet until an African American, Robert Weaver, became secretary of the Department of Housing and Urban Development in 1966. Since then, every president has had minorities as members of his Cabinet, and there have also been more appointments of minorities to other top executive positions and to the bench. Seven of President Obama's 19 initial appointments to the Cabinet or positions of Cabinet rank were members of minority groups. The representation of these groups on the federal bench has also grown, and there have been similar and in some cases greater advances at the state and local levels.

FIGURE 5.3   Minority Elected Officials

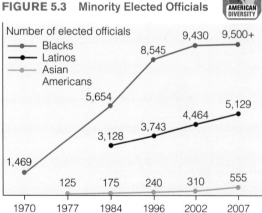

One indication of the gains in political rights that minorities have made is the increased number of minority elected officials at the local, state, and national levels of government.

Data sources: Joint Center for Economic and Political Studies; the National Association of Latino Elected and Appointed Officials; the *National Asian Pacific American Political Almanac*; and the Asian American Action Fund.

These advances have been laudable, but it is also true that no minority group's share of elected or appointed political offices at any level of government equals that group's share of the population. Indeed, the gaps remain significant in most cases. Thus political equality remains a goal, not an achievement.

ADVANCES IN SOCIOECONOMIC EQUALITY AMONG RACES

Along with increasing minority political participation and power, the civil rights movement sought to improve minority socioeconomic status (SES). SES includes such factors as income, health, and education. The first targets were the overt forms of bigotry such as segregated facilities. The centerpiece of this effort was the **Civil Rights Act of 1964**. Passed after an epic legislative battle, this far-reaching law gave the federal government powerful weapons to attack segregation by:

- Prohibiting as a restraint of interstate commerce racial, religious, or ethnic discrimination in public lodgings, food services, transportation, entertainment, retail sales, and fuel sales.
- Barring states and localities from segregating public facilities.
- Forbidding discrimination in any private or government organization or program that received federal funds.
- Banning employment discrimination by any company engaged in interstate commerce.
- Creating the Equal Employment Opportunity Commission to receive and investigate complaints alleging discrimination and to award damages to victims.
- Providing other federal agencies increased enforcement tools and enabling victims of discrimination to enforce the act's provisions by suing in federal court.
- Adding through later amendments further protections including housing discrimination to the list of prohibited practices in 1968.

The impact of the 1964 Act was rapid. Just five months after its passage, the Supreme Court handed down companion decisions that illustrate how deeply into society the government could reach. The decisions dealt with two private businesses that served only whites: the Heart of Atlanta Motel in Georgia and Ollie's Barbeque in Birmingham, Alabama. The Court found that both were engaged in interstate commerce and therefore subject to the 1964 act because the motel sometimes rented rooms to people traveling from state to state and 46% of the meat used by the restaurant came from out of state.

These and similar cases were each single battles in the increasing attack on discrimination, but their overall importance was immense. They stretched the meaning of the term "interstate commerce" in the Constitution well beyond previously accepted boundaries. This gave the federal government a powerful new weapon to attack discrimination. However, the new meaning of "interstate commerce" also undermined federalism (see Chapter 3). Given the reality that virtually every business relies partly on out-of-state goods, services, or customers to operate, the decisions nearly wiped away any distinction between interstate and intrastate commerce.

Another court-related change that advanced socioeconomic equality was the increasing use of the Fourteenth Amendment's due-process and equal-protection clauses to bar private and government discrimination and to nationalize the Bill of Rights by applying it to the states. In the *Heart of Atlanta Motel* case, for example, Justice William O. Douglas wrote in his concurring opinion that basing the Court's decision on the Fourteenth Amendment was even better than resting it only on the commerce clause because "the former deals with the constitutional status of the individual, not [just] with the impact on commerce" and therefore avoids "litigation over whether a particular restaurant or inn" is engaged in interstate commerce," and thus puts "an end to all obstructionist strategies and finally close[s] one door on a bitter chapter in American history."

Cases such as those requiring local diners and motels to integrate also took federal law and regulation yet a step further by beginning to apply federal authority to private business and organizations. Subsequent laws, such as those making "hate crimes" a federal felony have added still more to federal authority by applying it to individual actions that were once beyond the reach of Washington. Laudably, this has improved civil rights. But it has also vastly increased the reach of the federal government into civil society. Some civil libertarians worry what this reach could mean if the government began to use it for other, less laudable purposes.

Advancing Educational Equality among Races

Perhaps more than any single factor, equal education is the key to greater socioeconomic equality. Taking that view, the NAACP made attacking school segregation a top priority.

Demolition of the Separate but Equal Doctrine

Segregated schools were widespread in 1950, with 17 states requiring them and another 15 permitting them. Schools for minority children were often dilapidated, overcrowded, and less accessible than white schools. In Topeka, Kansas, for example, black third-grader Linda Brown lived near a white school but had to walk more than a mile to her black school. When Linda's parents sued with the help of the NAACP, the Supreme Court in *Brown v. Board of Education* (1954) unanimously found for the Browns. In doing so, the Court overturned *Plessy v. Ferguson*

(1896) and demolished the separate but equal doctrine by declaring, "Separate educational facilities are inherently unequal." It was the first major decision of the Court under its new chief justice, Earl M. Warren. During his tenure as chief justice between 1953 and 1969, the "Warren Court," championed a broad expansion of civil rights and liberties.

The year following the *Brown* decision, the Supreme Court ordered schools to desegregate "with all deliberate speed." Many did, but others, especially in the South, moved slowly. As mentioned earlier, this led to a crisis in 1957 when nine black students tried to enroll in an all-white high school in Little Rock, Arkansas. White mobs threatened the students, and local and state authorities refused to protect them. Then in one of the finer moments of his presidency, Dwight D. Eisenhower sent the Army's 101st Airborne Division to Little Rock to enforce the law.

Public School Integration after Brown v. Board of Education

Eisenhower's action in Little Rock was dramatically decisive, but that did not mean that school integration would proceed quickly and completely. At first, integration increased, especially for blacks in the South. But progress soon slowed, and then was reversed for blacks. The courts also ordered the integration of white and Latino students in a number of school districts. Despite this, the percentage of Latino students attending integrated schools has declined since 1968. Figure 5.4 shows these negative shifts. Some of this is due to the increased minority population, but more of it reflects the general racial segregation of communities caused by such factors as white flight from cities.

School integration stalled then began to decline principally because of the distinction the courts have made between two types of segregation: (1) *de jure segregation* due to intentional segregation policies and (2) *de facto segregation* based on informal factors such as housing patterns. Where the courts found de jure segregation existed, they struck it down. In some cases of de jure segregation where whites and minorities also lived in different areas, judges ordered school districts to integrate by busing children to schools other than the one nearest their home. The Supreme Court accepted busing in *Swann v. Charlotte-Mecklenburg Board of Education* (1971), but the remedy set off a storm of protest. More than 70% of Americans opposed it, and President Richard M. Nixon declared,

FIGURE 5.4 **Resegregation of Public Schools**

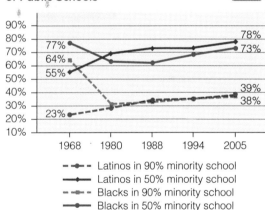

- - ◆ - - Latinos in 90% minority school
——— Latinos in 50% minority school
- - ■ - - Blacks in 90% minority school
——— Blacks in 50% minority school

Among black and Latino students, about three-fourths now attend "majority-minority" schools and almost 40% attend schools in which minorities are 90%+ of the students. Note that the percentage of black students in de facto segregated schools declined, then increased. For Latinos, enrollment has gotten steadily more segregated.

Data source: Gary Orfield and Chungmei Lee, *Historic Reversals, Accelerating Resegregation, and the Need for New Integration Strategies,* A report for the Civil Rights Project/Proyecto Derechos Civiles, University of California, Los Angeles, August 2007.

"I am against . . . the busing of our nation's schoolchildren to achieve a racial balance."[35]

Perhaps bending to this opposition, the Court soon began to curb busing. It ruled in 1973 that if schools were segregated only because of de facto housing patterns, then no constitutional violation existed, and by implication, neither busing nor any other remedy could be required.[36] Then in 1974, the Supreme Court dealt busing a further blow by rejecting court-ordered busing between Detroit and its suburban towns.[37] Even though de jure segregation existed in Detroit, the justice ruled that it did not justify forcing suburban towns to send students to and accept students from Detroit.

How far can a city go to voluntarily integrate? This was the issue in Seattle, Washington, which used race as one of three criteria to decide which school any given child would attend. When parents challenged the plan, the Supreme Court ruled in 2007 against Seattle's plan, leaving unclear if any voluntary busing plan could be valid to remedy de facto segregation.[38]

Easing Language Discrimination

Hispanic and Asian American children have had to face not only segregated schools but language barriers as well because many school districts refused to provide limited-English-proficiency (LEP) students with bilingual education. In *Lau v. Nichols* (1974), a case involving San Francisco's Chinese students, the Supreme Court found against the school district on the grounds that "There is no equality of treatment" if "students who do not understand English are effectively foreclosed from any meaningful education." The Court ordered the city to offer bilingual education and to increase programs to boost students' English proficiency.

Integration and Affirmative Action in Higher Education

Segregated colleges began to disappear wherever they existed once the courts began to apply *Brown v. Board of Education* to public higher education. Then the courts put pressure on segregated private colleges in a 1984 decision that ruled that they and their students could lose federal funding if they discriminated.[39]

What remains unresolved at the college level is what, if any, role affirmative action should or may legally play. This approach entails taking positive steps to provide equal opportunities to disadvantaged groups by (1) actively reaching out to them; by (2) recognizing the value of having a demographic balance in schools, work places, and other societal activities; and by (3) taking into account the past and, to a degree, continuing barriers these groups have faced. To elaborate on this third point, it is based on the view that recent positive changes cannot rapidly dispel the lingering impact of bigotry. President Lyndon B. Johnson made this point when he advised Americans, "You do not take a person, who for years, has been hobbled by chains and liberate him, bring him up to the starting line of a race and then say 'you are free to compete with all the others,' and still believe that you have been completely fair."[40]

Although affirmative action has impacted higher education in many ways, such as hiring minority faculty, student admissions programs have been particularly controversial. Most colleges have long used "soft criteria" such as athletic ability as well as "hard criteria" such as grades to decide which students to accept. This has not been very controversial. However, when schools added race to their soft criteria, some disappointed white applicants with better hard criteria scores sued claiming reverse discrimination.

In response, the Supreme Court has said that race may play a role in admissions but that applicants may not be treated differently based solely on race. The first test came when Allen Bakke, who is white, sued the University of California-Davis Medical School after it denied him admission while setting aside 16% of its positions for minority students, some of whom had lower grades and test scores than he had. In *Regents of the University of California v. Bakke* (1978), the Supreme Court ruled that quotas were unacceptable. Yet the Court left the door open to affirmative action by also saying that student diversity "is a constitutionally permissible goal" and that race could be a "plus" factor in admissions decisions.

The problem with such vague language was demonstrated by the two cases involving the University of Michigan featured in this chapter's opening You Decide box. By 5-4 in *Grutter v. Bollinger* the Court upheld the law school's affirmative action admission plan. It sought to improve diversity but left the specific steps vague. By contrast, the Court rejected the university's undergraduate admission plan in *Gratz v. Bollinger* by 6-3 because that plan added a specific number of points to the admissions scores of minority students. Arguably, the Court followed *Bakke* by rejecting the race-specific points awarded in *Gratz* while upholding the more subtle use of race in *Grutter*. Still, the Court's position remains uncertain because only two justices, John Paul Stevens and Sandra Day O'Conner, made that distinction between the two cases. Four other justices voted against the university in both cases and three voted for it. This pattern reflects the divided views on the Court and in society, with some finding any consideration of race objectionable and others believing that positively considering race is necessary and proper.

The Status of Educational Equality among Races

There has been considerable progress in advancing educational equality among racial groups, but substantial gaps remain. Progress has been best at the college undergraduate level. Other than Latinos, enrollment for minority groups is now about equal to their respective shares of the population. However, notable gaps for all minority groups other than Asian Americans remain at the graduate school level.

Progress has been even more mixed at the elementary and high school levels. Since 1971, the gaps between minority and white students in reading skills, dropout rates, and college admissions have decreased, yet problems remain. For example:

- Among 9-year-old students, 25% of whites but only 8% of blacks score at the highest reading skill level.
- For 17-year-olds, the top score numbers are 45% for whites and 20% for blacks.
- The percentage of black, Latino, and Native Americans who drop out of high school is at least twice that of whites.
- White high school seniors are 23% more likely to go on to college than black seniors.

Advancing Economic Equality among Races

Economic equality is a key goal of the civil rights movement. As the Leadership Conference on Civil Rights, a coalition of 192 civil rights organizations, puts it on its Website: "There has long been a close association between the struggle for civil rights and the fight against poverty in the United States. From its beginnings, the contemporary civil rights movement was as much about jobs as justice—indeed, the two were seen as inextricably linked."

For the most part, the movement to legally attack economic inequality based on race began in the 1960s with efforts to improve the employment situation of blacks, Latinos, and others. This effort came through legislation, executive orders, agency activity, and court decisions.

Advances by Legislation

Several pieces of civil rights legislation already mentioned included provisions designed to increase economic equality. For instance, the Civil Rights Act of 1964 outlawed race-based discrimination in virtually all employment practices in the public and private sectors. To enforce its provisions, the act also created the Equal Employment Opportunities Commission (EEOC). Amendments to the CRA and other laws have expanded or strengthened its coverage. For instance, a 1991 amendment allows victims of intentional job discrimination to sue for monetary damages.

Advances by Executive Orders

Presidents have issued numerous executive orders advancing equal economic opportunity. Franklin Roosevelt issued the first of these in 1941. It prohibited racist hiring policies by companies with federal defense contracts. Twenty years later, the term "affirmative action" was first used in an executive order when John Kennedy directed federal contractors to "take affirmative action to ensure that applicants . . . [and] employees are treated . . . without regard to their race, creed, color, or national origin." Since then many additional executive orders have addressed employment discrimination and encouraged affirmative action.[41]

Advances by Agency Activity

Several federal agencies oversee various aspects of the U.S. government's fair employment and affirmative action programs. With a staff of nearly 3,000 and an annual budget of about $350 million, the EEOC is the largest of these. Like most other agencies in this area, the EEOC has investigative authority. It can also receive complaints of unfair practices, conduct quasi-judicial hearings, and issue rulings. Between 2000 and 2009, the commission received an average of about 83,000 complaints a year. Of these, almost half involved alleged discrimination based on race or national origin. Contrary to any belief that the EEOC and other civil rights agencies are eager to find violations, the EEOC finds "no reasonable cause" in about 60% of the complaints it receives.

Advances by Court Decisions

The federal courts have helped shape the application of the Civil Rights Act and other legislation barring job discrimination legislation. The Supreme Court has ruled, for example, that all employment qualifications must be "reasonably related" to the job.[42] However, the court has also said that if qualifications are job related, then they are valid even if they adversely impact a minority group. The burden of proof, however, is always on the employer.[43]

As for affirmative action related to employment, the Supreme Court initially took a positive view. For example, the justices decided in 1979 that a company could establish a minority quota for the seats in a technical training class. Soon thereafter the Court also upheld a law setting aside 10% of federal public works contracts for minority contractors.

Then beginning in the 1980s, the Supreme Court changed course considerably and has often narrowed affirmative action practices. It rejected a suit by black firefighters in Memphis who were being laid off in greater numbers than white firefighters by a "last in, first out" policy. The Court also rejected a 30% set-aside for minority contracts, and derailed attempts to increase minority ownership in the media by forbidding the Federal Communications Commission to consider race or gender as a factor in deciding who would receive broadcasting licenses.

An even more recent case was *Ricci v. DeStefano* (2009). It drew national attention because of the involvement of Supreme Court nominee Sonia Sotomayor as an appeals court judge. Events began when the city of New Haven, Connecticut, voided a promotion examination for firefighters after no African Americans passed it. The city said that accepting the results would open it to suit by the unsuccessful African Americans and that the outcome of the test made it impossible to show that it was not somehow biased. This led Frank Ricci and 19 other white and Hispanic firefighters who had passed the test to sue mayor John DeStefano. A federal district court ruled for the city, as did a three-judge panel, including Sotomayor, of the Second Circuit of the Court of Appeals. The appeals judges thought the law so clear that they issued only a summary judgment: a ruling without explaining their legal reasoning. The Supreme Court took a different view, agreed to hear the case, and by a 5 to 4 vote reversed the decisions of the district and appeals courts.

However, not all recent decisions have gone against affirmative action. Faced with intentional discrimination, the Court has allowed quotas to remedy past practices. It has also protected those who file complaints. For example, the Court decided in 2008 that an African American manager at a restaurant who was fired after filing a racial discrimination complaint could sue for damages.[44] There have also been numerous cases dealing with discrimination based on age, disabilities, sex, and other factors, and these are discussed in a later section.

The Status of Economic Equality among Races

Clearly, the efforts to combat employment discrimination have had a positive impact. During the decade after the passage of the CRA in 1964, for example, the percentage of blacks in many industries and the wages of blacks rose notably, especially in the South.[45] Another hopeful sign is that the number of complaints charging racial discrimination sent to the EEOC has declined. After peaking at about 10 per 100,000 workers in 1974, the rate declined and is now about 5 per 100,000 workers. This probably reflects progress in race relations, although other factors account for some of the decline.[46] It is also the case, though, that if the EEOC were better funded and had more staff, it could better help workers deal with the bureaucratic complexities of pursuing a complaint against well-funded employers with legal staffs.[47]

Mitigating the good news are indications that after an economic upsurge during the late 1960s and the 1970s, progress has slowed down. For example, the black poverty rate fell from 55% in 1960 to 31% in 1973, but then stalled at about that rate for 20 years, and was still 25% in 2008. Moreover, this level was more than triple the white poverty rate. By other measures, the civil rights era had little visible impact. Unemployment is one example. African Americans were about twice as likely as whites to be unemployed in 1960, and that gap still exists.

One reason for the slowdown in economic change beginning in the 1980s is that by that time the most overt forms of employment discrimination had mostly been eliminated. Eliminating more subtle bias has proven much harder. Second, under the Republican presidents who have occupied the White House most of the time since 1981, there has been less emphasis on civil rights in general and on eliminating economic disparities among races in particular.[48] The general decline of the civil rights movement also decreased the pressure in the political system to continue to narrow economic gaps.[49]

The Global Context of the Effort to Advance Racial Equality

We have seen that the American movements to end the slave trade and then slavery itself were part of global efforts and that the U.S. civil rights movement in the 1950s and after was related to the struggle of people in Africa, Asia, and elsewhere to achieve independence from their largely white colonial masters. This link between U.S. domestic developments and international developments to advance racial equality has continued. Public attitudes are one area of parallel change. Just as opinion in the United States, international opinion is now much more likely to view racism as abhorrent, to support the goal of equality, and to favor a role for government in promoting that goal. Illustrating this shift in sentiment, a 2008 survey taken in 15 countries around the world found that overall 69% said that it is "very important" to treat different races and ethnic groups equally, and 79% said that government should take a role in preventing racial discrimination.[50]

Domestic Efforts to Promote Racial Equality

Policies in the United States to improve racial equality and policies globally have been another area of parallel change in race relations. Many countries, particularly such economically developed countries (EDCs) as Canada and those in Western Europe, have made policy changes similar to those in the United States to advance equality. In 2001 the European Union's Charter of Fundamental Rights prohibited all forms of social discrimination including racism. Many EDCs have adopted similar national legislation, and some have also instituted affirmative action programs akin to those in the United States. Canada's Employment Equity Act (1986), for instance, requires a wide range of employers to give preferential treatment to women, the disabled, aboriginal people, and "visible minorities," defined as "persons, who are non-Caucasian in race or non-white in color."

As it has been in the United States, progress toward narrowing the political and socioeconomic differences among races in the EDCs has been slow and uneven. Unemployment in Great Britain, for instance, was 8% for whites in 2009, 11% for people of Asian heritage, and 18% for Afro-Caribbean blacks. From a broader perspective, a study across 10 Western European countries found that, "Minorities . . . appear to be particularly disadvantaged in education, access to the labor market, and occupational attainment."[51] Taking the same view, the Organization for Economic Co-Operation and Development (OECD), which includes all the

EDCs, reports that, "Women and ethnic minorities still find it harder to get a good job than other workers in OECD countries, and are more likely to be paid less, despite impressive improvements in recent years." The OECD report goes on to explain, "One reason for this continuing problem is discrimination—unequal treatment of equally productive individuals because of gender or race."[52]

International Efforts to Alleviate Racism

The UN and other international organizations do not have the authority over countries that the U.S. government has over states. Still, there are some parallels between pressure from the organizations of global governance on countries to ease racism and the central role of the U.S. government in the federal system to eliminate racist state policies. Some of the global efforts have been symbolic, such as the series of global conferences on the problem of racism. The most recent was the World Conference against Racism, Racial Discrimination, Xenophobia, and Related Intolerance that met in Durban, South Africa, in 2001 and brought together official delegations from 160 countries.

International organizations have few coercive tools to use against racism, but these are slowly increasing. One early success involved South Africa. There, years of international economic sanctions under UN auspices finally compelled South African whites to surrender political power in 1994. This ended the apartheid system that had permitted 6.5 million whites to dominate 29 million black, Asian, and mixed-race people and brought the country's first black president, Nelson Mandela, to power after 27 years of imprisonment. Another advance came after the shocking "racial cleansing" in Rwanda in central Africa and in the Balkans region of southeastern Europe in the 1990s eventually led to military interventions in Bosnia, Kosovo, and elsewhere under the authority of the UN and the North Atlantic Treaty Organization.

Additionally, UN-authorized international tribunals were established to prosecute and try those responsible for ethnic cleansing and other war crimes that were committed in Rwanda and the Balkans. These two courts have convicted more than 100 individuals for crimes, including genocide, and have handed out stiff sentences, including life in prison. Even more recently, a world treaty created the International Criminal Court. Its charter defines both genocide and apartheid as crimes, and the court has already brought several indictments, including one against the president of the Sudan for oppression of his country's ethnic minority in Darfur. Certainly, these steps are insignificant compared to the problems they address, but they, like the first tentative moves of the U.S. government in the 1950s and 1960s to punish those guilty of racial violence, are an important break with the past.

GENDER AND CIVIL RIGHTS

Like the black civil rights movement with its roots in the early antislavery campaign, the effort of women to achieve equality is as old as the country. In 1776, for example, Abigail Adams wrote to her husband, John, then a delegate to the Constitutional Convention in Philadelphia, urging that the new constitution include rights for women. She also warned, "We [women] will not hold ourselves bound by any laws in which we have no voice or representation." During its history, the women's civil rights movement has also had both a political and a socioeconomic dimension. Through the early 1900s, the main thrust of the women's civil rights movement was advancing suffrage, or the right to vote, and that is where we will begin.

The Suffrage Movement Political

Somewhat ironically, the genesis of the suffrage movement was tied to sexism in the antislavery movement. Lucretia Mott and Elizabeth Cady Stanton were both active in the American abolitionist movement and traveled to London in 1840 to attend the World Anti-slavery Convention. There they encountered the same sexist attitudes that existed in the United States. The convention refused to seat Mott and Stanton as delegates, confining them to observing from a balcony behind a curtain. Offended, they discussed calling a convention on the status of women when they returned home. Eight years later, that goal was realized when Mott, Stanton, several hundred other women, and a few sympathetic men gathered in Seneca Falls, New York, in 1848.[53] They proclaimed, "All men and women are created equal," and adopted 12 resolutions, one of which called for women to have the right to vote.

> *A Vindication of the Rights of Woman* (1792) by British author Mary Wollstonecraft was the first book to argue that women are equal to men. It influenced such early American feminists as Lucretia Mott.

Progress toward women's suffrage was slow and there were numerous setbacks. Many women were angry, for example, when the Fifteenth Amendment guaranteed the vote to all men but ignored women. Another reversal came in 1875 when the Supreme Court rejected a Missouri woman's challenge to her state's law barring women from voting.[54] Women were also hampered, just as racial minorities had been, by the patina of scientific theory that social Darwinism gave to gender as well as racial subordination. Darwin had written in *The Descent of Man* (1871), for example, that his study of evolution indicated that "man is more courageous, pugnacious and energetic than woman, and has a more inventive genius."

Adoption of the Nineteenth Amendment

Progress toward the vote did occur, however. In 1878 suffrage leader Susan B. Anthony persuaded a member of the U.S. Senate to introduce a constitutional

In 1884, Belva Lockwood, candidate of the National Equal Rights Party, became the first woman to receive votes in a presidential election. Her total was about 4,000 in six states.

This 1909 drawing by opponents to giving women the right to vote argues that doing so will lead them to abandon their home duties and husbands. (Library of Congress)

amendment giving women the vote. During the ensuing 42 years it took to get the Nineteenth Amendment (1920) adopted, the suffragists waged a persistent campaign on its behalf. A breakthrough occurred in 1918 when President Woodrow Wilson endorsed the amendment. The following year, the House, then the Senate with just two votes to spare, passed the amendment and sent it to the states.

Within a year, 35 states had approved the amendment. Attention turned to Tennessee, considered the most likely of the remaining states to provide the thirty-sixth and final ratification needed for adoption. Amendment supporters at the capitol in Nashville wore yellow roses and opponents sported red ones in a fierce "war of the roses." Tennessee's Senate soon approved the amendment, but vote counters predicted a 48 to 48 tie in the state's House of Representatives. That would have defeated the amendment not only in Tennessee but perhaps also in the country. At the last moment, though, the legislature's youngest member, 24-year-old Harry Burn, voted "yea" despite the red rose in his lapel. A pro-ratification telegram from his mother had changed Burns's mind. "I know that a mother's advice is the safest for her boy to follow, and my mother wanted me to vote for ratification," he told reporters.[55]

The Global Advancement of Women's Political Rights

The American suffrage movement was part of an international effort. Women's activism in the late 1800s and early 1900s was centered in Western Europe, the United States, and a few other countries, and focused primarily on the vote and eligibility for office. New Zealand in 1893 became the first country to recognize the right of women to vote. By the time the United States followed suit in 1920, more than two dozen other countries had already done so. As for holding office, the world's first elected female national legislator took her seat in Finland's parliament in 1907. A decade later, Jeanette Rankin (R-MT) became the first woman elected to Congress. The next step was for women to head national ministries. Nina Bang achieved this first when she became Denmark's minister of education in 1924. Nine years later, the United States joined the ranks of countries with women cabinet ministers when Frances Perkins became secretary of labor.

Although Americans lagged behind these and other global political firsts for women by only a decade or two, a large time gap has developed with respect to the top leadership spot. The first democratically elected woman prime minister,

Sirimavo Bandaranaike of Ceylon (now Sri Lanka), took office in 1960. The first elected woman president was Vigdís Finnbogadóttir of Iceland in 1980. In the United States, despite the near miss of Senator Hillary Rodham Clinton (D-NY) for the Democratic presidential nomination in 2008, it will be at least 2013 before an elected woman U.S. president joins the ranks of world leaders.

Ireland became the first country to have successive woman presidents when Mary McAleese (1997–) succeeded Mary Robinson (1990–1997).

The Equal Rights Movement

Socal

Did not pass into law

After winning the right to vote, the women's rights movement stalled for a time. The **Equal Rights Amendment (ERA)** specifying, "Equality of rights under the law shall not be denied or abridged by the United States or any state on account of sex," was first introduced in Congress in 1923, but almost 50 years elapsed before Congress passed it and sent it on to the states.

Rejuvenation of the Women's Movement

In the 1960s the women's movement revived for several reasons. Women had flooded into the workforce during World War II, and while most gave up their jobs after the war, a seed of discontent with traditional roles grew. Then in the early 1960s, the birth control pill became widely available, giving women more freedom to focus on jobs and other activities rather than motherhood.[56] Women's freedom was also spurred by increasing access to higher education. Women jumped from 35% of college graduates in 1960, to 45% in 1975, to more than 50% in the early 1980s. The counterculture sentiments that were part of the Vietnam era turmoil added to the willingness of women to challenge tradition and made society more open to change. Finally, the black civil rights movement helped to inspire women and paved the way for the feminist movement.

Perhaps the first "shot across the bow" of tradition was Betty Friedan's book *The Feminine Mystique* (1963), detailing women's dissatisfaction with society's constraints. Three years later, Freidan and other feminists founded the National Organization for Women (NOW). Yet another noted feminist, Gloria Steinem, began *Ms.* magazine in 1971, which sold 300,000 copies in eight days.

Betty Friedan was the driving intellectual force behind the women's movement beginning in the 1960s. In this 1971 picture, she is addressing a conference on "Women: A Political Force" in Albany, NY. (AP Photo)

The Rise and Demise of the ERA

A priority of the women's movement was to add the ERA to the Constitution. At first the effort was successful. Both houses of Congress easily approved the ERA in 1972, and by the end of 1973, 30 of the required 38 states had ratified the amendment. Polls showed almost two-thirds of Americans in favor of ratification.

Then the tide turned. During the next three years, only five more states consented. However, 5 of the 35 states that had already ratified the ERA rescinded their approval. Whether that is constitutionally permissible is unclear.[57] Adding further to the ERA's woes, time became a factor. Congress, as it had for several other amendments, had set a seven-year time limit for ratification of the ERA. With time running out in 1979, Congress passed a three-year extension. It proved futile. No other state ratified the ERA, and in 1982 time expired.

Why did the ERA fail? The first thing to note is that there were no major differences in public opinion between men and women.[58] Nor was the voting split on ratification in state legislatures along sex lines.[59] Instead of a battle of the sexes, the divide in the country was along ideological lines, with social conservatives mostly opposing the amendment and social liberals mostly favoring it. To some degree this was reflected in a Republican–Democrat voting split in state legislatures. It is, however, also true that the conservative, still largely Democratic South was the most resistant to the ERA. Of the 11 former Confederate states, only Texas and Tennessee ratified the ERA, and Tennessee later rescinded its approval. Social conservatives in the South and elsewhere were more likely to be persuaded by the arguments of the ERA's opponents. Few people of any ideology paid heed to some of these objections, like predicting mandatory unisex toilets. Other issues such as whether the ERA would make women subject to the military draft concerned a much broader spectrum of Americans. The high hurdles to amending the Constitution also defeated the ERA. It was approved by 94% of the House, 91% of the Senate, 62% of the public, and 70% of the states. But under the Constitution that was not enough.

The Post-ERA Women's Movement

The demise of the ERA did not destroy the women's rights movement, but its intensity was diminished. This decreased energy also reflected gains that had been made on other fronts. Congress had outlawed sex discrimination in employment in 1964, and had prohibited sex discrimination in education in 1972. The Supreme Court had done away with most barriers to abortions in 1973. By 1982 20 states had adopted constitutional provisions barring sex discrimination. Reflecting such changes, a 1982 poll found that 88% of the public said women had made gains in the previous 10 years.[60] This sense of progress eased some of the urgency among women for reform. NOW and other multi-issue women's organizations still played an important role, but a greater prominence was given to specific women's issues, such as abortion rights, and to groups, such as the National Abortion Rights League, that concentrated on those issues.

Advancing Women's Political Equality

Getting the vote in 1920 did not make women politically equal. For a long time they turned out to vote less than men did. That gap narrowed somewhat over time, but it was still 11% during presidential elections in the 1950s. Women also continued to be a rarity in office. In 1950 there were no women governors or U.S. Cabinet members, and women held only 3% of the seats in Congress and 3% of the seats in state legislatures. Against this background, a core goal of the women's movement was to increase women's political clout by increasing the number of women who were voters, office holders, and otherwise politically active. Numerous women's groups, such as the nonpartisan White House Project, were organized to pursue this goal.

Such groups have been an effective part of the overall effort to increase women's political presence and power. By the 1980s, women were outvoting men by an average 1.3% in presidential elections. Since then voting advantage of women has continued to expand, averaging +4% in 2000, 2004, and 2008. Similarly, women have gained a greater share of political offices at every level of government. By 2011, as Figure 5.5 shows, women made up 16% of the House and were 17% of the U.S. senators. Women in 2011 also comprised 27% of President Obama's Cabinet, 14% of the country's governors, and 23% of its state legislators. All these percentages are significantly higher than they once were but remain much lower than women's 51% share of the population.

FIGURE 5.5 Women's Share of U.S. House Seats

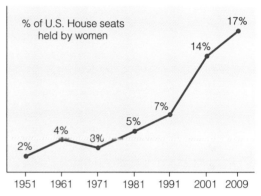

% of U.S. House seats held by women

The advances in women's political equality are symbolized by their increasing membership in Congress.
Data source: Clerk of the House.

Advancing Women's Socioeconomic Equality

Although suffrage was the focus of the early women's movement, it also worked to advance their socioeconomic rights and status. Progress was glacial, though, and in the mid-twentieth century socioeconomic status was still very much defined by sex. Then with the revival of the women's movement in the 1960s, efforts to increase socioeconomic equality among men and women strengthened. It would overtax the space available here to detail all the socioeconomic conditions for which sex was an important determinant. Therefore, to illustrate the issue, we will focus on education and economic opportunity.

Women and Educational Equality

Historically women made some of their greatest advances in the area of education. Enrollment differences at the elementary and high school levels had already disappeared by 1900. Equal enrollments at the undergraduate college level took much longer. Women were still only 19% of the undergraduates in 1900 and 39% in 1960. Spurred by changing laws and attitudes, female enrollment then grew to 50% of all undergraduates in 1977 and to 57% in 2005. Slowest to change has been the opportunities for

A review of 17 wealthy countries found that women went from being a majority of undergraduates in only 4 of the 17 in 1985 to 14 in 2002.

women in graduate schools, especially those leading to such high-pay, high-status professions as medicine and the law. Women were just 9% of the students in professional schools in 1970; by 2005 enrollments were about equal.

Still, problem areas remain in education. One is the gender distribution in areas of study. Of particular note, women's share of the bachelor's degrees awarded are only 28% in computer science and information technology, 20% in engineering, and 21% in physics. Explanations for these gaps vary, but most focus on the lack of women role models in these fields and other messages that tend to deter female students from pursuing those majors. The arguments of some that women are somehow not mentally suited to these fields or are more disposed to people-oriented disciplines such as education, the humanities, and social science are undermined by the fact that women earn almost half the undergraduate degrees in such fields as mathematics, statistics, and chemistry.

The most significant legal advance in expanding educational opportunities for women was the passage of Title IX, a 1972 amendment to the Civil Rights Act (CRA) of 1964. Initiated by Representative Patsy Mink (D-HI), the first Asian American woman in Congress, Title IX barred sex discrimination in any school receiving federal funds. Because virtually all schools at every level get federal money, Title IX's coverage has been sweeping. It has been instrumental, for example, in women going from 25% of all college full-time faculty members in 1976 to 42% in 2007. Virtually all schools also now have written policies against sexual harassment and procedures to deal with complaints. Title IX has also expanded the opportunities for women in athletics by requiring schools to create programs and scholarships for females. As a result, the number of females participating in sports has increased 900% at the high school level and 500% at the college level. And women's share of college athletic scholarships has risen from 0% to 45%.

Women and Economic Equality

Women's economic condition improved more slowly than their educational status in the 1800s and first half of the 1900s. In 1950, women were still distinctly disadvantaged compared to men. For example:

- Among full-time workers, women made only 60 cents for every dollar men made.
- Unemployment among women was 11% higher than men.
- Men dominated the highest paying professions such as engineers (99% men), attorneys (97%), and physicians (94%).
- Females made up 67% of those living in poverty.

Since 1950, several factors have combined to improve, although not equalize, the economic condition of women. *Education* is one. As noted, greater percentages of women have entered and graduated from college, and more women are also going to advanced professional schools that provide entry into the higher paying professions.

Legislation is the second factor. The Equal Pay Act of 1963 and the Civil Rights Act of 1974 bar sex-based job discrimination, sexual harassment, and other barriers to women competing equally in the workforce. These laws also give women the ability to file complaints with the EEOC and lawsuits in federal court.

Executive actions by presidents and various federal agencies have also benefited women. For example, Lyndon Johnson issued Executive Order 11375 adding women to those covered by affirmative action rules governing employment by the federal government and federal contractors. At the agency level, 30% of the complaints filed with the EEOC in 2007 related to job discrimination based on sex and sexual harassment, and the agency validated and took action on about 5,000 of these cases.

Court decisions have been a fourth factor that have advanced the economic condition of women. In 1974, for example, the Supreme Court rejected the practice of employers paying less to women because the "going market rate" for them was lower than for men. Then in 1986, the Court recognized sexual harassment as a form of job discrimination.[61]

How much have women benefited? The overall record related to improvements in the economic condition of women in recent years is mixed. Women have closed the gap with men in a few areas. Unemployment is one example. Since 1990 there has usually been little difference in the average male and female unemployment rates. Indeed, women fared better than men during the sharp economic downturn that began in 2008. As of mid 2010, 10.3% of American men age 20 or over were unemployed compared to only 9.1% of their female counterparts.

More commonly than catching up to or surpassing men economically, women have somewhat closed the gap with men, but inequality remains. Females made up 67% of those in poverty in 1960, and by 2007 that share had narrowed to 55%. By another measure, Figure 5.6 shows that among full-time workers, women have narrowed the earnings gap with men since 1950. However, at the average improvement rate in the figure, it will be the year 2183 before earnings are equal. It may be, though, that the progress will be faster. One sign is that the gap is narrower among young adults. For all workers ages 25 through 34, women in 2009 made 81 cents for every dollar made by men, and for

FIGURE 5.6 The Gender Wage Gap

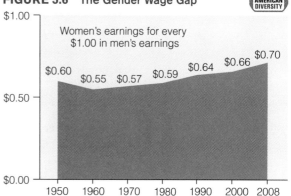

Like the wage gap shown here, most areas of economic disparity between men and women are narrowing, but only slowly.
Note and data source: Data for full-time workers. Data from U.S. Bureau of Labor Statistics.

those in that age bracket with at least a bachelor's degree, women made 90 cents for every dollar made by men.

The Global Context of the Women's Rights Movement

Like the suffrage movement, the modern American women's rights movement has been part of an international effort to improve women's rights and conditions. The global context is the "second wave feminism," which began principally in the United States, Western Europe, and other industrialized countries after World War II and first gained prominence in the 1960s.[62] French social critic Simon de Beauvoir sounded the call for the second wave in *The Second Sex* (1949), in which she wrote, "Men have presumed to create a feminine domain [the household], only in order to lock up women therein." American feminist leader Betty Friedan, would later laud *The Second Sex* as having "led me to whatever original analysis of women's existence I have been able to contribute."[63]

By the 1970s, the second wave had moved beyond the industrialized countries and had become a global phenomenon. A major symbolic step occurred when the United Nations declared 1975 as International Women's Year and the kickoff of a Decade for Women. Funding for projects to benefit women began to flow through such newly established structures as the UN Development Fund for Women (1976). The adoption of the **Convention on the Elimination of All Forms of Discrimination Against Women** in 1979 led the way in defining women's rights on an international level.

One effort to protect these rights has been through the aforementioned international tribunals for the Balkans and Rwanda and the new International Criminal Court (ICC). The tribunals have convicted and imprisoned numerous individuals for planning campaigns of rape and other atrocities against women, and the Charter of the ICC is the first global treaty to make it an international crime to commit "rape, sexual slavery, enforced prostitution, forced pregnancy, enforced sterilization, or any other form of sexual violence of comparable gravity."

Globally, 70% of the poor are females. Among American poor, 56% are women.

The UN also organized a series of global conferences on women. Perhaps the most important of these was the **World Conference on Women (WCW)** that met in Beijing in 1995 with 189 countries participating. U.S. ambassador to the UN Madeleine Albright led the U.S. delegation, and first lady Hillary Rodham Clinton addressed the meeting. In addition to the official conference, an unofficial one gathered with about 30,000 delegates representing the Global Fund for Women, MADRE, U.S. Women Connect, and more than 2,000 other private organizations involved with women's rights. At its conclusion, the WCW demanded an end to discrimination against and the abuse of women and called for their economic and political empowerment. These positions had no legal status, but they have had an effect. Evidence of those gains is clear in Figure 5.7. It shows two indices developed by the UN that compare the status of women relative to men. One is the Gender Development Index (GDI), which measures socioeconomic factors such as health, education, and income. The second is the Gender Empowerment Measure (GEM), which gauges relative power in a society through such indicators as each sex's share of seats in parliaments, national cabinets, and professional and technical positions. As you can see, the mean GDI and GEM scores both improved between 1995 and 2008, indicating that the world became somewhat more equalitarian. Reflecting on such advances, one scholar concluded, "What's happened . . . could not have happened without Beijing."[64]

FIGURE 5.7 Global Advances in Gender Equality

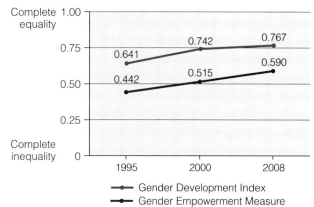

This figure shows the median score for the world's countries for two measures of the status of their women relative to their men. GDI gages socioeconomic factors; GEM measures societal and political power. No country measures perfect equality (1.0) on either, but the scores are improving.
Data source: UN Development Programme, Human Development Report, various years.

OTHER DISADVANTAGED GROUPS AND CIVIL RIGHTS

Although this chapter's discussion reflects our focus on race and gender, other groups have also had important civil rights issues—and gains.

Sexual Orientation

Gay males, lesbians, and transgender people have faced legal barriers since 1610 when Virginia made sex between men punishable by death. From that time until recently, government policy and its underlying societal biases have steadfastly restricted people whose sexual orientation differs from that of the majority.

An Overview of Gay Civil Rights

Gay rights was a virtual nonissue in American politics until fairly recently. During the last few decades, though, change has begun to occur as part of the general expansion of civil rights in the United States and around the world.

It is therefore not surprising that many aspects of the gay rights movement resemble those of racial groups and women. Like them, gays established national advocacy groups such as the National Gay and Lesbian Task Force (1973), Lambda Legal (1973), and the Human Rights Campaign (1980). Also like the other groups, some of the earliest civil rights victories for homosexuals came in the courts. In perhaps the first such case, a male student in Providence, Rhode Island, successfully sued his school in U.S. district court in 1980 to force it to allow him to bring a male date to the senior prom.

Since then public attitudes about homosexuals and their rights have become more accepting. Laws and as a general rule court decisions have paralleled these changes. As recently as 1978, for example, 59% of Americans rejected "homosexual relationships" as "unacceptable."[65] By 1999, most Americans had come to view "homosexual behavior" as "an acceptable lifestyle." The public also has become more willing to see gays in a wide range of roles. When asked in 1983 if they would vote for a gay candidate for president, only 29% of Americans said yes.[66] By 1999, 59% were saying yes.[67]

As of 2010, 35 countries including Canada, France, Great Britain, and Germany allow gays to serve openly in their armed forces.

Laws and policies also began to change. In 1994, for example, President Clinton ordered the military to stop asking its personnel about their sexual orientation. This "Don't Ask, Don't Tell" policy allowed gays to remain in uniform as long as they did not overtly acknowledge being gay or follow a gay lifestyle. Also in 1994, Massachusetts became the first state to prohibit discrimination against gay students in public schools. Other states have added laws barring discrimination in education and other areas, and perhaps a third of all states now have laws protecting gay civil rights. Yet other legal barriers to gays are almost certain to fall by legislative action. For example, President Obama asked Congress to remove all barriers to gays serving in the military, and one poll showed that 78% of the public supported the change.[68] In September 2010 a Republican-led filibuster in the Senate blocked the effort to fully open the military to gays, but proponents sought to amend a defense spending bill to enact the change.

These former members of the U.S. armed services, with Stacy Vasquez of Denton, Texas, in the foreground, are all gay and were all discharged from the military for openly acknowledging their sexual orientation. Here they are in Washington, D.C., in March 2010 to press Congress to let gays serve openly in the military. (AP Photo/Harry Hamburg)

Court decisions have been inconsistent, sometimes liberalizing, sometimes restraining gay rights. For example, the Supreme Court voided a law passed by Colorado in a referendum that barred any attempt by the state to protect gay rights.[69] By contrast, the Court ruled that as a private organization, the Boy Scouts could ban gay scoutmasters.[70]

Epitomizing the rapidly shifting view of the Court, it upheld a Georgia law criminalizing common gay sexual acts in *Bowers v. Hardwick* (1986), then just seven years later reversed itself in *Lawrence v. Texas* (2003) and declared a similar Texas law to be unconstitutional.

Gay Marriage

Same-sex marriage is the most controversial issue related to gay rights. It first gained national attention in 1996 when a judge in Hawaii ruled that prohibiting same-sex marriages violated the state constitution. Even though Hawaii soon amended its constitution to reinstitute the ban, an alarmed Congress passed the Defense of Marriage Act (1996). It barred federal recognition of same-sex marriages and allowed states not to recognize them either, even if legally performed in another state. Then in 1999, Vermont's Supreme Court ruled that the state constitution entitled same-sex couples to the same benefits and protections as married heterosexual couples. The following year, Vermont enacted a civil union law allowing gay couples to formalize their relationship. A **civil union** is a legal domestic partnership agreement that gives a same-sex couple all or most of the rights, benefits, and responsibilities that married couples have.

Counterattacking, numerous states passed laws and even state constitutional amendments barring gay marriages and/or civil unions. These limits are more than symbolic. The U.S. General Accountability Office has found that federal laws and regulations alone contain more than 1,000 benefits such as reduced taxes and added pension and Social Security benefits that are available to married heterosexual couples but not to gay couples even if they are married or part of a civil union under state law.

Initially, public and political reaction to gay marriage was overwhelmingly negative. However, that has began to moderate. You can see in Figure 5.8 that while most Americans still opposed gay marriage in 2010, that opposition had declined considerably.

The shift of public opinion toward a greater acceptance of gay rights has led several state legislatures to join Vermont in authorizing same-sex civil union. As of mid-2009, 10 states by either legislative enactment or judicial decision provided gay couples with some or all the benefits extended to married couples. For a time, there was a

FIGURE 5.8 Opinion on Same-sex Marriage in the United States

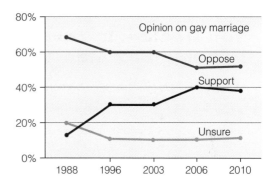

Americans' bias against gays has eased. Even on the sensitive question of same-sex marriage, opposition has declined and support has increased.

Note and data sources: This figure is suggestive only because the wording in the polls was not always the same. Data from the Roper Center for Public Opinion Research, the Pew Research Center, and PollingReports.com.

Six countries allow same-sex marriages, and another 17 permit gay civil unions.

movement to add an amendment to the U.S. Constitution to bar gay marriages, but its supporters have largely come to recognize that getting two-thirds of Congress and three-fourths of the states to agree would be nearly impossible. Thus for now, the mess of inconsistent state and federal laws is likely to grow until almost inevitably the Supreme Court is forced to sort things out by ruling on the constitutionality of barring same-sex marriages. Indeed, the case that may eventually do that was filed in a federal district court in San Francisco in 2010. The two gay couple plaintiffs in the case, *Perry v. Schwarzenegger,* are asking the federal courts to void as unconstitutional an amendment to California's state constitution barring gay marriage that was adopted by referendum in 2008. A federal district court judge ruled in August 2010 that the state's ban violated the Fourteenth Amendment, but the Ninth Circuit Court of Appeals kept the ban in place during the appeal that was immediately filed and will almost surely later go to the Supreme Court. The following You Decide box asks you to help the Court decide the issue.

You Decide: Is *Loving* Applicable to Same-Sex Marriage?

Those seeking to overturn state barriers to same-sex marriages argue that the laws deny a basic right that cannot be violated without a compelling public interest to do so. Most courts have rejected this argument. New York's highest court ruled in 2006 that the state's ban did not violate the due process clause because "The right to marry is unquestionably a fundamental right. . . . [but] the right to marry someone of the same sex . . . is not."[71]

Although the U.S. Supreme Court has not yet addressed gay marriage, it did hear an arguably similar case regarding state laws barring interracial marriages. Nearly half the states had such laws on their books in the 1950s. They were challenged after Richard Loving, a white man, and Mildred Jeter, a woman of African American and Native American descent, married, moved to Virginia, and were subsequently convicted in 1959 of violating that state's anti-miscegenation law. The judge in the case held that the law was valid because, "Almighty God cre-

ated the races white, black, yellow, malay and red, and he placed them on separate continents. . . . The fact that he separated the races shows that he did not intend for the races to mix."[72]

The Lovings appealed their conviction, and the Supreme Court unanimously overturned it in *Loving v. Virginia* (1967). In the majority opinion, Chief Justice Earl Warren described marriage as "one of the basic civil rights of man" and argued that denying such a "fundamental freedom on the basis of race" was "directly subversive of the principle of equality at the heart of the Fourteenth Amendment." Warren concluded that, "Under our Constitution, the freedom to marry, or not marry, a person of another race resides with the individual and cannot be infringed by the state."

The issue for you to decide here is whether the reasoning in *Loving v. Virginia* should also govern the Supreme Court in its decision on gay marriage.

The Disabled and Senior Citizens

As the civil rights movement expanded its scope beyond African Americans to other racial minorities, women, and other disadvantaged groups, the status of two further segments of the population—people with disabilities and people in the later stages of life—came into focus.

People with Disabilities

Whereas most of the barriers that traditionally faced racial minorities and women stemmed from racism, sexism, or other form of animus, most of the impediments to people with disabilities have been rooted in neglect. Lack of voting procedures for the visually impaired, public buildings with no ramps or elevators to make them accessible to those who cannot walk, schools with few or no programs to assist students with special needs, and a host of other barriers made for grossly unequal opportunities. Societal attitudes added to these impediments. Polio largely confined President Franklin D. Roosevelt to a wheelchair, and he went to great lengths and underwent significant pain to stand in order to hide his condition from the public. As one scholar explains, "He thought he couldn't get elected if people thought he couldn't walk. He was very, very clear that the nation didn't want a crippled president while they felt crippled by the economy."[73]

At the federal level, the first step toward leveling the playing field was the Rehabilitation Act of 1973. It barred discrimination against the disabled by those receiving federal funds. Even more important was the **Americans with Disabilities Act (ADA) of 1990.** As mentioned earlier, it barred discrimination against the disabled in employment, transportation, public accommodations, and communications and required "reasonable" actions be taken to remove barriers in these areas.

However, implementation of the laws enacted has often been delayed and limited by struggles over such issues as what constitutes a disability, how to measure degrees of disability, and how far an organization must go to eliminate barriers. Cost is at the core of many of these disputes. Most remedies cost money, and some are very costly. Soon after the ADA was passed, for example, Ohio estimated that it would cost $579 million just to increase physical access to its state buildings, public transportation systems, and universities and colleges. ADA proponents counter such cost complaints by arguing that they will be partly or completely offset in the long run by such positive changes as lowering the number of disabled people on welfare and allowing them to become productive, taxpaying workers.

What has been the impact of the ADA and other laws? A 2007 report by the National Council on Disability (NCD) conveyed a mixed message, finding much progress in some areas, but less progress and even backsliding in others.[74] On the up side, the NCD found that most disabled people say that their quality of life has improved due to the ADA. The NCD also reported significant improvements in access to public buildings and public transportation and improvements in educational opportunities and the ability to vote.

The NCD was less positive about other areas, including employment and economic circumstances. When compared to the fully able, the disabled who can work generally have higher unemployment and earn less at every level of education. Also testifying to continuing employment problems are the approximately 19,000 claims of job discrimination based on disabilities filed annually with the EEOC.

Senior Citizens

Older Americans face discrimination on a number of fronts. The declining physical and sometimes mental capabilities that come with advancing age have been one source of such barriers. The ADA and similar laws have helped address these. Additionally, though, older Americans are often not hired or, if employed, are fired because they often use more medical benefits and will soon earn a pension for which the employer would be responsible. Protection from such practices has been extended to all workers over age 40 by the Age Discrimination in Employment Act of 1967. Similarly, the Age Discrimination Act of 1975 prohibits discrimination on the basis of age in programs that receive federal funds. Despite these laws, the more than 16,000 complaints of age discrimination filed with the EEOC each year testify to the fact that "ageism" continues to be a problem.

SUMMARY

This chapter focuses on the struggle of women, people of color, and other disadvantaged groups to secure their civil rights. Other than eliminating slavery, little substantive progress was made until the twentieth century. Even then, the rate of progress did not pick up much speed until the 1950s. At that point the civil rights movement and the willingness of the federal government to support it both became much stronger.

At first the civil rights movement focused primarily on the demands of blacks for equal opportunities. However, this aspect of the civil rights movement was part of a larger context. Part of that context was domestic. African Americans were not the only group whose civil rights were being routinely violated. Latinos, Asian Americans, and Native Americans also began to assert their civil rights with more determination, as did women. Soon, gays, the disabled, and senior citizens followed suit. The second part of the context was global. Beginning with the independence of the Philippines from the United States in 1946 and accelerating during the next several decades, people of color in Asia, Africa, and elsewhere triumphed in their struggle to free themselves from predominantly white colonial countries.

Since the advent of the civil rights movement, there have been notable advances for minority groups. Most discriminatory laws and regulations have been eliminated. Various policies such as prohibiting workplace discrimination, encouraging affirmative action, and encouraging majority–minority legislative districts have helped advance equality.

For minorities, the quest for political equality has been the most successful part of the overall effort. Epitomized by President Barack Obama, efforts to improve minority political rights have resulted in more people of color being elected and appointed to top political posts. There have also been notable advances in the educational and socioeconomic condition of minorities, symbolized by the *Brown v. Board of Education* (1954) case that ended legal school segregation.

All the progress that has occurred does not mean that minorities have achieved anything near equality. Overall, they are still substantially underrepresented in the power positions in all branches of government at the federal and state levels. Socioeconomic equality is even more distant. Poverty and unemployment statistics, for example, continue to show that most minorities are significantly disadvantaged compared to whites.

The saga of women's civil rights has been similar to the history of minority civil rights. Like the campaign for racial civil rights, the cause of American women has been part of an international effort. Women had early victories in the United States, such as the Nineteenth Amendment (1920) guaranteeing women the right to vote. But, as with minorities, most advances in women's civil rights have occurred since the 1950s. On the political front, there have been marked increases in the number of women who are voters, hold high political office, and are otherwise politically active. The women's movement further sought to move women nearer to socioeconomic equality with men. Both areas of endeavor have achieved many successes. Women now commonly hold seats in Congress, are members of the Cabinet, and are governors. Yet it is also true that they will still hold fewer than half of all such positions of power than they would in a truly equal opportunity country. There have also been major advances for women in the socioeconomic area. In a few areas, such as getting into and graduating from college, women are even more successful than men. However, in many other areas, such as earnings and the percentage of people in poverty, women remain disadvantaged.

CHAPTER 5 GLOSSARY

affirmative action Taking positive steps to provide disadvantaged groups equal opportunities by (1) actively reaching out to offer them education, jobs, and other benefits; by (2) recognizing the value of having a proportionate demographic balance in schools, workplaces, and other societal activities, and by (3) taking into account the past and, to a degree, continuing opportunity barriers that have created the disadvantages these groups face.

American Indian Citizenship Act (1924) Granted citizenship to all Native Americans.

Americans with Disabilities Act (ADA) Enacted in 1990, this federal law barred discrimination against the disabled in employment, public transportation, public accommodations such as hotels, and communications; and required affirmative action be taken to remove barriers in these areas.

Asian exclusion laws A series of laws passed between the 1880s and 1930s that barred virtually anyone from Asia from entering the United States as an immigrant.

Brown v. Board of Education of Topeka (1954) The case in which the Supreme Court reversed its earlier decision in *Plessy v. Ferguson* (1896) and ruled that separate educational facilities are inherently unequal. The full name of the case is often shortened to *Brown v. Board of Education*.

civil disobedience Peaceful acts of individuals or groups of people that violate the law in an effort to raise awareness for a cause and to create pressure for change.

civil rights Freedoms that must extend to all people equally and that cannot be denied to any one group based on its race, gender, or other characteristic.

Civil Rights Act of 1964 This law and its amended versions gave the federal government powerful weapons to attack discrimination by using the Constitution's interstate commerce clause to bar discrimination in employment and in most services and by creating new and strengthening existing enforcement agencies.

civil union A legal domestic partnership agreement that gives a same-sex couple all or most of the rights, benefits, and responsibilities that a married couple has.

Convention on the Elimination of All Forms of Discrimination Against Women Adopted by the UN General Assembly in 1979 and subsequently accepted by 98% of all countries, the treaty defines what constitutes discrimination against women and sets an agenda for national actions to end it.

Dred Scott v. Stamford (1857) A case in which the Supreme Court rejected the claim of a slave, Dred Scott, to freedom after having been taken to a state where slavery was illegal. Part of the Court's decision rested on its finding that no black person, either slave or free, was a citizen of the United States entitled to sue in its courts.

due process clause Language found in the Fifth and Fourteenth Amendments that says that government may not restrict an individual's liberties (1) without following the prescribed processes established by law (procedural due process) or in a way that is arbitrary or unreasonable (substantive due process).

equal opportunity The concept that each individual's political and socioeconomic success should be based on his or her energy and ability, and not on class, race, sex, or some other demographic category.

equal protection clause The language in the Fourteenth Amendment that mandates that everyone in the United States, regardless of group, be treated equally by the law.

Equal Rights Amendment (ERA) Specified, "Equality of rights under the law shall not be denied or abridged by the United States or any state on account of sex." Congress passed the ERA in 1972, but it failed to win ratification by three-fourths of the states and died in 1982.

Fifteenth Amendment Adopted in 1870, this amendment prohibits interfering with a citizen's right to vote based on "race, color, or previous condition of servitude."

Fourteenth Amendment Adopted 1868, this amendment ensured citizenship status for freed slaves by specifying that "all persons born or naturalized in the United States . . . are citizens of the United States and of the state wherein they reside. The amendment also included the due process clause barring states from depriving "any person of life, liberty, or property, without due process of law" and the equal protection clause saying that no state could "deny to any person within its jurisdiction the equal protection of the laws."

Immigration Act of 1965 Eliminated national immigration quotas based on the ethnic heritage of Americans in 1890, a criterion designed to heavily favor West European immigrants.

Jim Crow laws Laws that instituted racially segregated public facilities and such practices as poll taxes and discriminatory literacy tests designed to prevent blacks, and later Latinos and others, from voting. "Jim Crow" was a derogatory term used for blacks during the pre-Civil War period.

***jus soli* clause** The language in the Fourteenth Amendment that makes anyone born in the United States both a U.S. citizen and a citizen of the state where he or she lives.

McCarren-Walter Act A 1952 law that repealed the Nationality Act (1790), under which only whites could become naturalized citizens.

Nationality Act of 1790 Specified that the only noncitizens who could become citizens were free white people.

Nineteenth Amendment Adopted in 1920, it declared that the right of citizens to vote could not be abridged based on sex. Applied to both federal and state elections.

one person–one vote principle The standard that all electoral districts for a given legislative chamber must contain approximately the same number of people. Mandated by the federal courts beginning in the 1960s. The only exception is the U.S. Senate because of the language of Article I of the Constitution.

Plessy v. Ferguson (1896) Case in which the Supreme Court legitimized the separate but equal doctrine that state-mandated segregation was constitutional if equal facilities were available to the "colored" races.

protected classes Societal groups designated in statutory law or by the courts as being shielded, except in extraordinary circumstances, from being limited in any way that does not apply to all of society. These groups are usually defined by religion/belief system, race/color, ethnicity/national origin, [old] age, and disability status.

racial gerrymandering Manipulating the minority population in one or more electoral districts to increase or decrease minority influence and representation.

separate but equal doctrine A theory that it was not unconstitutional discrimination if people of color were required to use separate facilities as long as they were said to be equal.

social contract The tacit agreement between people and their collective society as to what the relationship between the individual and society should be.

social Darwinism The belief that the writings of biologist Charles Darwin on evolution and the survival of the fittest justifies the definition and domination of "less advanced" races and ethnic groups by "more advanced" people.

Thirteenth Amendment Adopted in 1865, it eliminated slavery or involuntary servitude except as punishment for a crime.

Title IX Refers to a 1972 amendment to Title IX of the Civil Rights Act (1964). Title IX bars sex discrimination in any school receiving federal funding.

Voting Rights Act (1965) Barred states from imposing any voting qualification or procedure that limited the right of any citizen to vote on account of race or color. Provided federal examiners to oversee elections in states with a history of denying blacks and others the right to vote.

World Conference on Women (WCW) Sponsored by the United Nations and meeting in Beijing in 1995, this conference was the fourth in a series that highlighted the problems women face and called for actions to ease or eliminate them.

INPUTS INTO GOVERNMENT
Demands and Support for a Diverse and Global America

PART
TWO

POLITICAL BELIEFS

6

YOU DECIDE: What Should the Role of Public Opinion Be?

Seldom has a president more tenaciously followed a policy more solidly opposed by the public than when President George W. Bush increased the number of U.S. troops into Iraq in 2007. Bush was already in trouble with the public. Only 34% thought he was doing a good job as president. That was one of the lowest job ratings for a president in history. A major cause of this woeful evaluation was the war in Iraq. Two thirds of the public was opposed to the war, and 72% disapproved of how Bush was handling it. Most Americans (65%) wanted to withdraw U.S. troops from Iraq immediately or within a year.[1]

Bush chose to do the opposite. He announced during a January 10, 2007, televised address that he would soon "surge" an additional 21,000 troops into Iraq, and asked Americans for their support. They did not give it. A poll the next day found that two-thirds opposed the idea. Siding with the public, the House of Representatives passed a nonbinding resolution by a vote of 246 to 182 disapproving of the surge, and only a Republican filibuster prevented the Senate from also objecting. When a few days after Bush announced the surge, a reporter pointed out the broad opposition in the country against it, the president was undeterred. "I've made my decision, and we're going forward," he insisted.[2]

Are you satisfied that the president should be able to ignore two-thirds of the American people and a majority of Congress? After all, the United States is a democracy. Perhaps public opinion should prevail, especially when it is as lopsided against the policy preferences of the president (or Congress, or even both together). What should the role of public opinion be in the policy making process? The last section of this chapter again takes up this question, and when you are finished reading it, ask yourself if you still agree with the view you have now. A final note is to be careful not to base your answer on your view of President Bush and/or the Iraq War. Presidents and wars change. The important point is how much public opinion should affect policy.

INTRODUCING AMERICAN POLITICAL BELIEFS

"I think, therefore I am," French philosopher René Descartes (1596–1650) once observed.[3] This wisdom also applies to Americans and their politics. In this chapter we will explore three concepts related to how we think about politics.

Political culture is the first. It is the sum of a society's widely held and long-held basic values. To explore American political culture, we will look at its orientation toward individualism, tolerance, equality, trust, and nationalism. The idea of a national political culture supposes a general consensus, but it is also true that each individual has his or her own array of attitudes toward individualism and other aspects of political culture.

Political ideology is the second basic mind-set. It denotes a set of ideas about the proper purposes and conduct of government and how individuals relate to societies and their governments. Both political culture and ideology include core values, but the former relates to the overall values of a society and the latter is an individual pattern. Whichever term is used, it means that most people's opinions are usually influenced by underlying values rather than being random.

Political opinions, the third type of political belief, are the views of individuals about current issues, events, leaders, institutions, and other matters. In contrast to political culture and political ideology, which related to basic and long-term values, political opinions are about current events. How you feel about the trustworthiness of government is a long-term attitude related to political culture and ideology. Whether or not you think the current president is trustworthy is a political opinion. These two views may well be related, but they are not the same. You could, for instance, generally trust government but not trust the current president.

Political culture, ideology, and opinions are separate concepts, but they are linked. A country's political culture strongly influences its overall public opinion. We will see, for example, that Americans' strong sense of individualism limits how far they are willing to have the government go to narrow economic differences in their country. Similarly, each individual's basic ideological orientation plays an important role in determining his or her specific political opinions. As one scholar describes the links, "Research on public opinion and mass behavior has demonstrated repeatedly that citizens' attitudes on policy issues are determined primarily by their more general orientations and feelings."[4] During our discussion of Americans' political beliefs, we will find that:

★ Political culture sets the boundaries of what Americans accept or reject politically.
★ Americans are strongly individualistic and nationalistic, are fairly tolerant politically, believe equality should extend to opportunity but not necessarily circumstances, and tend not to trust the government.

★ Political culture is fairly consistent across gender and race.

★ Therefore, the ongoing demographic and political diversification will not radically reshape the American political system.

★ Dividing Americans' ideology between liberal and conservative misses many variations.

★ Who the "public" is and what "opinion" is are complex issues.

★ Getting informed about politics and forming opinions are types of political participation.

★ There are long-term and short-term factors that shape an individual's political opinions.

★ It is very difficult to measure public opinion accurately, and the results of even the best polls only approximate true public opinion.

★ There are differences in opinion among demographic groups on a range of issues, but these differences should not be overestimated.

★ Public opinion affects policy through elections and also because policy makers heed it.

★ The impact of public opinion on policy is neither dominant nor consistent.

★ The debate over what the role of public opinion on policy making should be involves the quality of public opinion, the accuracy of polls, and what the public wants.

American Political Beliefs in a World of Difference

Americans' political culture, ideologies, and political opinions are influenced by, and in turn influence, the rest of the world. The basic beliefs of Americans about what is right and wrong, their political culture, is drawn broadly from Judeo-Christian tradition and more particularly from the British heritage of most of those who founded and led the United States from its earliest days through the mid-twentieth century. For example, the rights enumerated in the U.S. Bill of Rights strongly reflect British tradition dating back to 1215 when England's barons forced the tyrannical King John I to sign the Magna Carta. It contained more than 60 prohibitions on the monarchy and began the evolution of the idea of rights and of democracy in England and, by extension, in the American colonies and later the United States. Similarly, English political philosopher John Locke (1632–1704) had a profound impact on the thinking of early American leaders. When Thomas Jefferson was writing the Declaration of Independence, for example, he borrowed such concepts as "unalienable rights" from Locke's *Second Treatise on Civil Government* (1690). And to this day, Locke's ideas remain important in American political culture.

Because public opinion is rooted in political culture, it is often possible to see connections between opinions in Great Britain and those in the United States and

FIGURE 6.1 Comparative Opinion on the Basis of Success

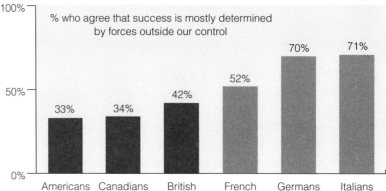

Because of political culture ties, American, Canadian, and British opinions are often similar to one another and different from opinions in continental Europe.
Data source: The Pew Research Center, Pew Global Attitudes Project, 2007.

in Canada with their largely British heritage. To illustrate that, notice in Figure 6.1 that (1) majorities of Americans, British, and Canadians share one view and (2) majorities of French, Germans, and Italians have a different view.

Figure 6.1 does not mean that American opinion is insulated from the views of mainland Europe and elsewhere. Modern social welfare policy began in Germany in the 1880s, spread in Europe, and then came to the United States in the 1930s as part of President Franklin Roosevelt's New Deal policies. Chapter 5 connects Americans' attitudes about the civil rights of minorities and women to changes in global opinion on those topics.

It is also the case that global opinion can have direct impact on U.S. policy and international outcomes. When the Supreme Court ruled in *Roper v. Simmons* (2005) that executing anyone for a crime committed when they were under age 18 was cruel and unusual punishment, and therefore unconstitutional, the Court's opinion acknowledged the "overwhelming weight of international opinion against the juvenile death penalty."

Global opinion also helps determine U.S. soft power. Soft power consists of the intangible traits of a country, such as its reputation, that influence the willingness of other countries to support it. Between 2001 and 2009, the foreign policies of the Bush administration, especially the invasion of Iraq, caused the U.S. favorability rating abroad to drop precipitously. The widespread belief that this made it more difficult for Washington to win international cooperation in many areas was reflected in Barack Obama's comment that the "mistakes" of the Bush presidency "have made our current task more difficult. World opinion has turned against us."[5] Such statements by Obama and other top officials in the new administration in 2009 led many foreign observers to sense a change in the U.S. foreign policy approach. As Australia's Defense Minister Joel Fitzgibbon, put it, "I think you'll see a greater [U.S.] emphasis on soft power rather than hard power, in other words, more emphasis on dialogue rather than military action."[6]

> A poll of 22 countries before the 2008 U.S. presidential election found that at least a plurality in all countries favored Barack Obama over John McCain. The average result was Obama 49%, McCain 12%, and 39% unsure.

American Political Beliefs and Diversity

Americans' political beliefs and the country's demographic and political diversity intersect in important ways. As a preview of the considerable attention that will be given to comparing the political culture of whites and minorities and of men and women, we can summarize the major points:

- Advantaged groups (men, whites) of Americans differ with disadvantaged groups (women, minorities) about whether there are equal opportunity and treatment regardless of sex or race.
- Minority groups differ among themselves on some policy issues. In the 2008 California referendum to amend the state constitution to ban gay marriages, most blacks and Latinos voted for the ban; most Asians, along with most whites, voted against it.[7]
- Minority groups can differ on issues that directly affect one or another of them. Most Latino and Asian American political leaders think that illegal immigrants should be able to get a driver's license. Most African American leaders disagree, as do most whites.[8]
- Many issues evoke little gender or racial division. When asked if the United States should remain the world's only superpower, 50% of women and 50% of men said yes. The differences among whites (51%), blacks (49%), and Latinos (61%) were fairly minor.[9]
- The race or gender of officials is just one of many factors that shape their policy choices. Barack Obama brought an African American's perspective to the presidency in 2009, but it vies with ideology, partisanship, public opinion, and other factors in shaping his positions.
- There is consensus across demographic lines on such core political beliefs as protecting individual liberties. Between 1976 and 2004 a survey has regularly asked if people would allow a racist to speak. On average a majority of blacks (53%) as well as whites (64%) support the First Amendment by letting the racist speak.

POLITICAL CULTURE

Americans' core political values form the nation's political culture, its widely accepted, long-held, and slow-to-change beliefs about fundamental matters such as the proper relationship between citizens and their government. Belief in democracy and its requirement for electoral contests to select the U.S. presidents are a matter of American political culture. Favoring John McCain or Barack Obama for president in 2008 was a matter of opinion. The relative stability of political culture and its focus on fundamental values make political culture a key element in any country's political process. It defines the boundaries of what is politically possible and what is not.

Although political culture is usually stable, it does change. This means that the increased political importance of minority groups and of women could significantly change the nation's prevailing values. However, the impact will probably be limited because the newly empowered groups have core belief systems that are not radically different from the prevailing values of men and whites. Therefore, the demographic and political diversification that is underway will impact policy but will not radically reshape the basic principles of the American political system.

Transmitting Political Culture

A nation's political culture is transmitted by **political socialization**, the process by which individuals acquire their basic political values and orientations. For the most part, political socialization occurs from early childhood through early adulthood.

Schools are an important agent of political socialization. Among other things, they tend to instill patriotism through such methods as having children recite the pledge of allegiance, which depicts an idealized America. (iStockphoto)

Family is one important agent of political socialization. Parents play a role in transmitting some basic attitudes. For example, children from families that encourage political discussion are later apt to be more interested and active in politics. Parents also transmit party identification. If, for instance, both parents identify with the same party, it is very probable that their children will also identify with that party.

Schools are another key agent of socialization. Nationalism is one aspect of political culture that schools transmit. Requiring young students to recite the Pledge of Allegiance makes them take an oath of support that they do not really understand to an idealized version of a country in which there is "liberty and justice for all." There is no precise data on how widespread the practice is, but when one survey asked parents how often their children recited the oath in school, 43% said daily, 11% thought occasionally, only 11% replied not at all, and the rest were unsure.[10] Moreover, people strongly support the practice, agreeing by an almost two-to-one margin that students should be required to recite the Pledge of Allegiance.[11] School curriculums also appear to play a role in political trust. Students who have taken civics courses are more likely to trust government than those who have not.

Media sources are a third agent of political socialization. The mainstream media tend to support the basic tenets of the American system and pass those values on to new generations of Americans. One study comments that this "may help to explain why Americans take pride in their country (patriotism), approve the basics of their political system, [and] prefer (modified) capitalism over other forms of economic organization."[12]

Experiences are a fourth agent. For example, those who grew up during the World War II era are likely to support using military force in foreign policy than are those whose formative years were during the Vietnam War. And no matter where they later live, those who lived in a competitive political district when they were youths are more likely to later be politically active than those who lived in noncompetitive areas.[13]

The Dimensions of Political Culture

It is possible to analyze the political culture of Americans or any other nation by exploring where that people's attitudes fall along each of several attitudinal scales.

Individualism ⟵⟶ Communitarianism

The first scale ranges between **individualism**, the belief that individual rights are more important than community needs or preferences, and *communitarianism*, the belief that the welfare of the community overrides what is good for any individual. Americans are strongly individualistic. Symbolizing this, the Declaration of Independence proclaims that individuals are "endowed with certain unalienable rights."

Americans' strong sense of individualism makes them likely (1) to hold individuals accountable for their actions, (2) to think individuals should be responsible for their own welfare, and (3) to oppose government intervention. These attitudes are one reason why polls in 2009 found that (1) 65% of Americans favor the death penalty; (2) 61% said that individuals should be "primarily responsible" for providing their own health insurance, while only 37% thought the government should be primarily responsible; and that (3) even amid disclosures of irresponsible corporate activity during the economic meltdown in 2009, 59% of Americans opposed and only 35% approved of having the government limit the pay of business executives.[14]

Globally, American political culture lies farther toward the individualism end of the scale than do the values of many other nations. That was evident when a dispute

A strong tendency toward individualism in American political culture is why most Americans agree with this woman and support physician-assisted suicide when an individual who is terminally ill or in uncontrollable pain requests it. (AP Photo/Charles Dharakpak)

erupted with Singapore after an American college-age man was convicted of vandalism there and sentenced to be caned. (This painful punishment involves beating a convict's bared buttocks with a rattan cane.) Many Americans were outraged by what they saw as cruel and unusual punishment. Officials in Singapore took a much more communitarian view. One noted the much higher crime rates in U.S. cities than in Singapore, claimed caning deterred crime, and asked, "Which is more important, the interests of the whole society or the interests of the individuals?"[15] Most Americans would reply the individual; most Singaporeans would say the community.

Tolerance ⟷ Intolerance

Nations also vary considerably in the degree to which they exhibit **political tolerance**. This is the willingness to accept the political participation of individuals from minority groups or people who are expressing highly unpopular opinions. Given the history of discrimination in the United States, it would be fatuous to label Americans as highly tolerant.[16] Yet Americans are now more tolerant toward minority groups than they have ever been. In 1958 only 37% of Americans said they would vote for their party's candidate for president if the nominee were black. By 2007, 92% said yes, and the following year the country elected its first black president.[17] Political tolerance of women has also progressed. Only 33% of Americans were willing to vote for a woman for president in 1937. That percentage rose to 54% in 1958 and to 86% in 2007.[18]

Americans are also more tolerant than are many other nations according to a study that asked people in 25 countries whether they believed certain minority groups in their country were a good or bad influence on the country. Americans were more tolerant toward minority groups (blacks and Latinos for the U.S.) than all but five of the other countries and were only about half as likely as the average country to view the designated minorities as a "bad influence."[19]

American tolerance also generally extends to unpopular opinions. After the 9/11 terror attacks, 88% of Americans supported military action against Afghanistan. Yet a mere 23% was willing to countenance banning antiwar protests.[20] By a slim margin Americans are even willing to preserve freedom-of-speech rights to those sympathetic toward terrorism.[21]

The general atmosphere of tolerance does, however, have boundaries. There are times when Americans find one or another group or point of view too odious to tolerate. In the tense cold war atmosphere of the 1950s, only about a quarter of Americans were willing to grant free speech to avowed communists.[22] More recently, a survey found less than 20% of either whites or Latinos willing to tolerate a member of the Ku Klux Klan holding public office.[23]

Hierarchy ←→ *Equalitarianism*

People's attitudes toward organizing society according to social classes ranges from a strict hierarchy based on birth, wealth, or some other trait to a classless society at the other end of the scale. Americans rebelled against Great Britain's markedly class-bound society in 1776 and instead espoused **equalitarianism**, the belief expressed by the Declaration of Independence that "all men are created equal." For 91% of Americans, though, equalitarianism extends only to supporting **equal opportunity**. This means the equal ability of people to achieve based on their talents and energy without the assumption that everyone will achieve equally.[24] This attitude is strongly held across demographic groups, with strong majorities of whites (94%), Latinos (88%), African Americans (86%), and Asian Americans (84%) all agreeing that employment decisions "should be based strictly on merit and qualifications other than race/ethnicity."[25] Equalitarianism does not, however, extend to equal circumstance. To the contrary, 89% of whites and 77% of blacks reject the idea of government "promoting equal outcomes."[26]

A key factor that determines this view is Americans' individualism and their associated belief that your circumstances in life largely reflect your efforts and ability. When asked whether hard work or luck is more important to success, 69% of Hispanics, 67% of blacks, and 66% of whites answered "hard work."[27] One policy outcome of this belief is that Americans have a strong sense that individuals should be able to amass and keep wealth. For example, majorities of whites (79%) and blacks (68%) reject capping incomes so that that no one can earn more than a million dollars a year."[28]

Other nations have different views, and these can have important policy implications. For example, Figure 6.2, an extension of Figure 6.1, shows that most Americans reject and most French agree with the notion that success for failure is pretty much determined by forces outside an individual's control. Note in the figure how these divergent views relate to the unwillingness of most Americans and the willingness of most French to agree with the idea that government should guarantee that nobody in the society is in need. One policy result of these differing attitudes, as the figure also shows, is that France spends more of its wealth than the United States does on social welfare programs.

Trust ←→ *Suspicion*

Another aspect of political culture is **political trust**, faith that the government and other individuals and groups in the political system are not generally conspiring to subvert your rights and basic needs, especially by such illicit means as violence and corruption. Trust is essential to democratic governance.

While Americans' political trust has declined, a 20-country survey found that they still ranked third highest in their trust in government.

FIGURE 6.2 French and American Attitudes
and Social Welfare Spending

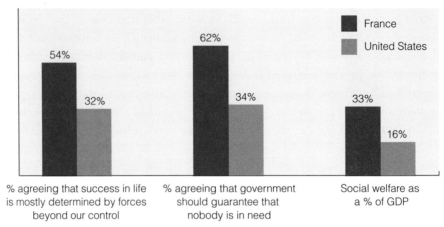

Americans and the French disagree about whether individual effort is the key to
success. These divergent views make the French more willing than Americans to favor
the idea that government policy should provide basic needs for everyone and to apply
that view by spending more on social welfare programs.
Data source: The Pew Research Center, "Views of a Changing World, 2003."

For one, trust engenders **political efficacy**, the belief that the government responds
to the will of the people and, therefore, that political participation can influence
government policy. Also, trust is necessary for people to be willing to compromise
or accept political defeat. Additionally, the willingness to be governed in a democracy rests in part on trust that the government is trying to do the right thing for
society.

Americans trust in their government has seriously eroded since the early 1960s,
when more than 75% said they trusted the government to try to do the right thing
"almost always" or "most of the time." From that point, Americans' political trust
plummeted beginning in the late 1960s amid an unpopular war in Vietnam and
the scandal that forced President Richard Nixon to resign. Trust then recovered
somewhat, as evident in Figure 6.3, with a majority once again expressing trust
in 2002 for the first time in almost 40 years. However, trust soon plummeted yet
again in response to the unpopular Iraq War, unrelenting partisanship in Washington, and other factors.[29]

Minority groups trust the government less than whites do, but the differences
are limited. As might be expected, whites (49%) are the most likely to trust the
government in one poll, but that level was only narrowly greater than Latinos
(47%) and Asian Americans (43%), and only moderately more than for African
Americans (33%). Differences in the level of trust expressed by women and men
are marginal.

FIGURE 6.3 Declining Political Trust

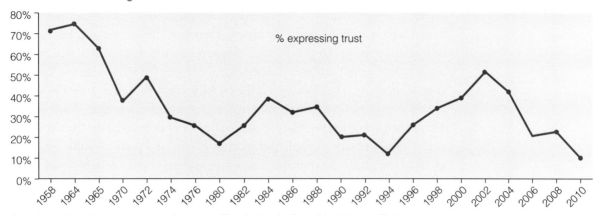

Americans' trust in government plummeted beginning in the mid-1960s, rallied beginning in 1996, then plunged again in 2002 and later.
Data source: See Chapter 6 endnote 29.

Nationalism ⟵⟶ Alienation

Americans have a strong sense of **nationalism**. Key elements of this important belief include (1) feeling loyal to and proud of your country and (2) seeing your country as the most important part of your **political identification** (your perception of who you are politically). President Lyndon Johnson captured this belief when he said, "I am an American, a Texan, and a Democrat, in that order." As one aspect of their nationalism, Americans are very proud of their country. One study that used a series of questions to measure national pride in 23 countries found Americans to be the proudest nation. For example, 80% of Americans compared to an average 48% in the other countries agreed with the statement, "My country is better than most others."[30] At its strongest, nationalism can take the form of **exceptionalism**: the belief that your country is not only good but also has had a special mission to spread its values globally for the world's good. There is a long tradition of exceptionalism among Americans. It was recently expressed by Secretary of Defense Robert Gates who told a reporter in 2010, "I am very much an American exceptionalist. I believe that we are, as a country, the greatest force for good in the history of the world."[31]

American nationalism cuts across racial and gender boundaries. Huge majorities of blacks, Asian Americans, Latinos, and whites and of females and males all describe themselves as patriotic. Majorities of each group also say they would rather live in the United States than anywhere else.[32] Furthermore, a study of 16 countries found that African Americans and Latinos were more likely to express pride in their country than were minority groups in any of the other 15 countries surveyed.[33]

The strong emotional tie between Americans and their country has a number of political consequences. Some American exceptionalists believe that the country should merely be an example for others. President Obama, for one, has said, "I believe in American exceptionalism."[34] However, he has characterized that as serving as "a beacon of freedom and justice for the world."[35] Other exceptionalists are more evangelistic. They believe it is the country's duty to spread American values abroad. President George W. Bush provides an example. In a 2002 White House document that laid out the "Bush Doctrine," the president noted the United States' unparalleled military strength and great economic and political influence," and declared that it should promote democracy and otherwise create a world order that "reflects the union of our values and our national interests."[36] This urge to spread democracy was one of the factors that led Bush to order the U.S. invasion of Iraq in 2003. Studies of the public's view find only a minority, 24% in a 2008 survey, want to make "building democracy in other countries" a top priority, but when the 43% who want to give that role "some priority" are added in, two-thirds of Americans show at least some propensity to evangelistic exceptionalism.[37]

Another impact of nationalism is the **rally effect.** This is the tendency of Americans to support their country and the president in times of a foreign crisis that involves potential or actual military action or other physical threats to Americans. This was evident at the time of the 9/11 attacks and again when its war with Iraq began in March 2003. In the first event, the public's approval rating of President Bush soared from 51% four days before the attack to 86% three days after it. Similarly, Bush's approval rating of 57% three weeks before the beginning of the war with Iraq jumped to 71% immediately after it.[38]

POLITICAL IDEOLOGY

It is common to divide Americans and others into two ideological camps: liberals and conservatives. **Liberals** favor government action to achieve a more even spread of wealth and other forms of opportunity and circumstance within a society. Liberals are also relatively comfortable with social change. **Conservatives** believe that government should only intervene in society to achieve a more even distribution of opportunity and circumstance caused by legal discrimination, not by the economic and social systems. Conservatives also are relatively uncomfortable with social change. Although this categorization has its benefits, it also has its limits. One problem in dividing ideology into two camps is that most Americans do not support an ideology or do so only tepidly. As Figure 6.4 shows, an average of 37% of Americans define themselves as moderates. Another 6% on average say they are unsure of their ideology. That increases the nonideologues to 43%. If you further add in the 28% of those who on average say they are "weak" liberals or conserva-

FIGURE 6.4 Americans' Ideological Self-Identification

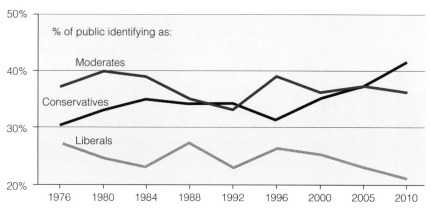

During the years covered in this figure an average of 37% of Americans characterized themselves as moderates ideologically. The percentage of those identifying as liberals declined slowly, while the percentage of conservatives increased slowly.

Note and data sources: Unsure respondents, usually 4% to 5%, not shown. General Social Survey polls; CBS polls provided by The Roper Center for Public Opinion Research.

tives, the share of the population that is not ideological or only slightly so grows to 69%. Moreover of those who are solidly ideological, few say they are "extremely" liberal or conservative. This group grew from an average of 4% before 2000 to 7% since then, but remains small.

The largely centrist orientation of Americans disposes them not to favor solutions to problems based on one or another ideology; many Americans have traditionally preferred a pragmatic approach to policy. They agreed with President Franklin Roosevelt in 1933 when he advised that to ease the Great Depression, "It is common sense to take a method and try it. If it fails, admit it frankly and try another. But above all, try something."[39] Americans still laud such pragmatism. When asked by a recent poll whether it is more important for elected leaders to have "strength of values and convictions" or a "willingness to find practical, workable solutions to the country's problems,"[40] most (59%) Americans chose practical.

Yet another problem with the notion of liberals and conservatives is that individuals may have value systems that vary from one aspect of policy to another. On domestic policy, for example, those who are liberal on economic issues are not always liberal on social issues, such as gay marriage. Many traditional New Deal Democrats, for instance, are economic liberals but social conservatives. Furthermore, the liberal-conservative dichotomy is not fully relevant to foreign policy. In that policy area, dimensions such as internationalism or isolationism (whether or not to participate actively in world affairs) and multilateralism or unilateralism

FIGURE 6.5 Ideology and Demographic Groups

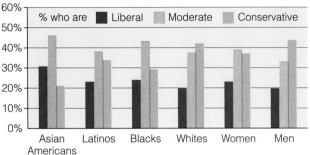

Minorities and women are less conservative and more liberal than whites and men.

Note and data source: Data on sex and race not directly comparable because the data on race are from a Gallup poll, February 3, 2010, and the data on sex are from a Gallup poll, June 15, 2009.

(whether to usually act in conjunction with other countries or to usually act independently) are more appropriate.[41] Devising a pattern of ideological groups that takes in both domestic and foreign policy is especially challenging, and despite several attempts, no consensus around an alternative has developed.

It is worth noting before leaving our discussion of ideology, that there are demographic differences in the liberal-moderate-conservative ideological divisions. As Figure 6.5 details, women are more liberal and less conservative than men. Similarly, minority groups, especially Asian Americans, are more liberal and less conservative than whites. Still, a plurality of minorities and women are moderate, and the conservative-moderate split in men is not wide, leaving the populace largely centrist.

THE NATURE AND FORMATION OF PUBLIC OPINION

Democracy is rooted in the principle of popular control of the government and requires some form of public participation.[42] However, what form that participation should take has long been controversial. Most early American leaders were skeptical of the public's wisdom. As a result, the Constitution of 1787 established a restricted republic by insulating much of the government from immediate public pressure (see Chapter 2). Since then, American political evolution has included increasing democratization in terms of who participates and how they do so. Public opinion polls and their role in the American political process are a relatively recent part of that evolution, and our goal here, as previewed in this chapter's opening You Decide box, is to think about what role public opinion should have on public policy. To lay a good foundation for that debate, we will look into the nature of public opinion and how it is formed before taking up what its role should be.

Defining Public Opinion

As used here, American **public opinion** means the distribution of views among those age 18 and older in the United States about contemporary issues, events, leaders, and institutions. There are two things to remember about this definition. First, public opinion could mean the pattern of opinions in any given "public," from everyone in the world to only those people in a defined population, such as Native Americans. Generally, though, public opinion is used here to designate the views of the national adult population of the United States, not just American citizens.

Second, the respondents who answer national surveys are meant to represent all adults, but every survey includes some error. All percentages reported by surveys should be read with the understanding that even the best polls claim to be accurate only to within about 3%. How valid even that claim is will be addressed later in this chapter. Thus, public opinion means what a poll reports the national distribution to be, not necessarily what it actually is.

This accuracy of public opinion is important because it counts in the political process. Because opinions count, this text takes the view that the process of forming and having political opinions is the most basic form of political participation. Moreover, with the rise of polling, blogging, tweeting, and other ways of transmitting opinions, forming and expressing them have become an even more important part of the political process. One description of public opinion as "the most important thing in American politics" is probably an overstatement, but it makes the point that public opinion does matter.[43]

How Public Opinion Is Formed

Political opinions neither form in a vacuum nor do they regularly come from one source. Instead opinions are rooted in such factors as political culture and ideology, experiences, the media, and opinion leaders. Often these sources work in combination.

Political Culture and Ideology

People partly evaluate new events and information according to their existing political culture and ideological values. Thus, when a new issue arises, say the treatment of illegal aliens, a person who is relatively more tolerant (political culture) and more liberal (ideology) and thus open to social change is more likely to favor amnesty and citizenship for undocumented residents than someone who is less tolerant and conservative and thus uncomfortable with social change.

Sometimes, however, values lead to seemingly contradictory positions. For example, it seems curious that American public opinion "has become much more liberal on . . . the ideals of the civil rights movement, but not on the implementation of those ideals."[44] Part of this gap between theory and practice exists because some whites say they support the idea of equal opportunity while cynically opposing government programs to achieve it. Yet the gap is also a function of the clash between two important aspects of political culture. One is equalitarianism and its idea that "all people are created equal" and should have an equal opportunity to achieve their goals. The other political culture value is individualism, which tends to reject government interference and to hold that each person's position in life is mostly based on his or her abilities and efforts rather than on outside forces.

At other times, values reinforce one another. Support for capital punishment as noted, provides an example. Americans' hard-nosed individualism, which holds individuals responsible for their actions, is one reason why American support for capital punishment is twice what it is in Western Europe, where people are more apt to feel that society bears considerable responsibility for people's actions and circumstances. The support for capital punishment among Americans based on individualism is reinforced in some people by low political tolerance, in this case racism. About 40% of those executed in the United States are black, and research indicates that "racial prejudice . . . [is] a comparatively strong predictor of white support for the death penalty."[45]

Experiences

Individual experiences and the experiences of groups with which a person identifies also shape opinions. For example, almost half of all African Americans and 31% of Latinos say that they, a family member, or a close friend has been denied employment because of their race.[46] By contrast only 13% of whites report having experienced or knowing someone who has suffered from race-based job discrimination. The differences in the shared experiences of minorities compared to whites gives African Americans and Latinos a sense of race-based barriers to equal opportunity that most whites find difficult to understand, as illustrated in Figure 6.6. Similarly, women are more apt to report job discrimination than men and less likely than men to believe that women have equal opportunities in the workplace. The result of these differing perspectives in turn lead to different opinions on whether the federal government should ensure that minority groups have equal job opportunities with a majority of minority group members and women believing the government should do so, but only a minority of whites agreeing.[47]

Other group experiences may be less directly connected to an issue but still influential. For example, Jewish support for the civil rights of African Americans and other minorities has been stronger than that of whites of other faiths.[48] This attitude also extends to such issues as gay rights, which also has strong support among American Jews.[49] Arguably their support of those suffering discrimination rests on the long Jewish history of also being discriminated against, discrimination that at its worst produced the Holocaust.

FIGURE 6.6 Racial Perceptions of Job Opportunities

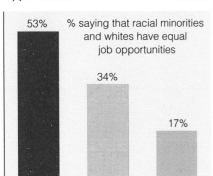

Most whites believe that racial minorities have equal job opportunities. Most blacks and Latinos disagree.
Data source: Gallup poll, June 2006, found at PollingReport.com.

Self-Interest

Americans also partly base their opinions on self-interest. In foreign policy, self-interest frequently translates to national interest. One survey that asked about sending U.S. troops to defend Saudi Arabia if it were invaded found just 19% of Americans favoring that option.[50] Yet in response to a second survey 3 months later, 49% favored sending U.S. troops to Saudi Arabia to counter an invasion when the survey question indicated that U.S. forces would be protecting the flow of oil to the United States.[51] In domestic politics, self-interest also often relates to individual or group interest.[52] For example, young adults are more apt than senior citizens to favor increasing government aid to education and low-income people are more supportive than wealthier individuals of expanding aid to the poor.

What is surprising is that self-interest does not determine opinions more than it does. Sometimes self-interest barely prevails. One study found that while parents were more likely than nonparents to support moderately higher taxes to fund increased school budgets, a majority of both groups favored the idea.[53] Another example of where perceived self-interest seems peripheral in opinion formation involves African Americans. They are more likely than whites to believe that immigrants compete with them for jobs, yet only a minority of African Americans compared to a majority of whites favor expelling all illegal immigrants from the country.[54]

Self-interest is an important factor in people's political opinion. Reflecting this, young adults, especially those enrolled in college like these two University of California, Berkeley, students demonstrating outside the capitol building in Sacramento in 2010, are more supportive of government aid to education than older Americans. (AP Photo/Rich Pedroncelli)

The Mass Media

Television, newspapers, the Internet, movies, and other media play important roles in transmitting values in the political socialization process and also in transmitting information and analysis during the political opinion formation process. It is possible to roughly divide the mass media into two categories. The first and more important of the two in the political process is the *news media* (the press: the organizations that transmit news to the public). Because the news media are the subject of Chapter 8, they warrant only a brief overview here. One quick point is that they serve as a link in political communications by transmitting information to the public from government officials and by carrying back feedback, such as polling results, from the public to the officials. This is not a passive role for the media, though, because journalists make decisions about what is news and how much detail gets covered. As we will see in Chapter 8, this gives journalists the ability to help set the *political agenda*: the issues that are being discussed in the country and in the government. The quantity and quality of the information the press provides also help determine how good the public's information is.[55]

The press also gives the public cues about how to interpret the information it receives by *framing* the way an issue is defined or put into context. Framing can have a significant impact on opinion. A story that frames the issue of illegal immigration in terms of how the supply of low-wage workers helps keep inflation down will have a very different impact on public opinion than a story that frames the issue in terms of the possibility of terrorists being among those who slip over the border.

The entertainment media make up a second category of the mass media These media include television shows, movies, music, and other types of public entertainment that oppose or support one or another political point of view. Television regularly broadcasts entertainment with a political message. Children's programs are a major source of values, as spending any time with Bert and Ernie and their messages of tolerance and nonaggression or the Wonderpets and their selfless assistance to those in need, will demonstrate. For adults, comedians are among those who often lead the way in political commentary on television, with Bill Maher and Jon Stewart two notable examples. Many films also have a conscious political message. For example, both the Oscar awards in 2006 for best picture, *Brokeback Mountain*, and in 2008 for best male actor, Sean Penn for his work in *Milk*, were supportive of the gay rights movement. Music provides a third example of the political content of the entertainment media. Songs, both patriotic and protest, are an American tradition.

Opinion Leaders

Political opinions in individuals usually evolve rather than emerge fully formed immediately after an individual learns about an event or issue. When an issue is relatively unfamiliar, an individual forms an opinion in part by listening to or reading the views of other individuals. In this process, people form a preliminary opinion based on such factors as how the issue fits with their values and how it has been framed by the news media. Often though, such opinions are still malleable, and people take cues from others that firm up their preliminary opinion, modify it, or—least likely—reverse it.

Not everyone is equal in this communications process, and those who regularly communicate with and persuade others are called **opinion leaders**. The president is perhaps the ultimate opinion leader, but this role extends down through the various levels of the population. Opinion leaders are often educators, members of the clergy, leaders of civic organizations, or those with other positions that have high status, carry an air of authority, and facilitate communications with numerous other people. Opinion leaders are also more interested in, knowledgeable about, and active in politics than the people they influence.[56]

The process by which opinion leaders mediate between events and public opinion has been called a "trickle-down flow." This image portrays a multistep process by which more influential leaders influence others, who in turn serve as opinion leaders to influence yet others, and so on. The channels of communications used in this process vary widely and, among others, include lectures, sermons, and other presentations; letters to the editor; conversations; appearances on radio or television; newsletters; and tweets, commentary on blogs, and e-mails.[57] Whatever the particulars, the idea of opinion leaders is that they provide cues that help opinion followers on the next level down interpret current events and form their views more fully and firmly. Ultimately, many of those opinions are surveyed and reported to the public and policy makers by polling organizations, to which we now turn.

The rapid expansion of tweeting, blogging, e-mailing, and other interpersonal communications through the Internet has altered the channels of political communication and increased the importance of the trickle-down process of public opinion formation. (iStockphoto)

MEASURING PUBLIC OPINION

Public opinion polls are a relatively recent political phenomenon. Some groups conducted pre-election polls as early as the 1880s, but these early polls were not reliable. The accuracy of polls improved beginning in the 1930s when a young market research expert, George Gallup, began to focus on opinions about politics rather than consumer goods.

The Amount of Polling

Polls have become an ever-present part of the American political process. Numerous U.S. polling organizations conduct and distribute information from thousands of surveys each year. The Gallup Poll alone has asked more than 136,000 questions since it was founded in 1935. A significant number of the questions that polling organization annually ask relate to the public's political opinions, and the press covers the results of these polls with increased frequency. Indeed, one study found that the number of stories reporting poll results increased 150% between 1992 and 2004, and the number of such stories on CNN rose 90% during that period.[58]

Criticism of the Amount of Polling

Some analysts criticize the upsurge in polling and the reporting of the results by the press. The increase in polling is "a case of more being less," writes one scholar.[59] "We've become poll crazy as a society," comments another scholar.[60] There are three basic concerns.

Quality of polling is the first of these concerns. Many, perhaps even most, but far from all of the hundreds of polling organizations in the United states subscribe to a code of ethics to be objective and also have the methodological expertise to produce scientific polls. Shoddy polling organizations are of two varieties. One type has a particular partisan, ideological, or issue viewpoint, and uses a variety of techniques to conduct polls in an effort to influence opinion rather than measure it. For instance, during the 2000 presidential primary contest in South Carolina, candidate George Bush conducted a **push poll,** one intended to spark a certain response. It included the question about his main rival. It went: "John McCain . . . raises money [from] and travels on the private jets of corporations. . . . In view of this, are you . . . likely to vote against him?"[61] The second type of shoddy polling comes from survey organizations that have an incompetent staff or too little money to conduct adequate polls.

Damage to the quality of the news is a second concern related to the amount of polling. One aspect of this worry (see Chapter 8) relates to the heavy focus by the press on "horse-race polls" during presidential elections and primaries. This type of poll indicates who is ahead, who is behind, and by how much.[62] Because the only "poll" that counts is the final election tally, reporting horse-race polls provides little other than entertainment value. Critics also point out that covering such polls takes up time and space that should be used to report the qualification of the candidates and their views on the issues.

The impact of polls is a third worry. We will address this issue later in this chapter, but for now we can say that some analysts worry that polls pressure uncertain voters to support whomever is ahead in the polls and pressure leaders to adopt unwise policies.

Defense of the Amount of Polling

Those who defend the extent of polling and poll reporting make several counterarguments. First, they argue that most of the polls that receive wide attention in the news are conducted by reputable organizations using techniques that have made polls much more accurate than they once were. Poll supporters also reject the argument that horse-race stories distract people and take away from the coverage of campaign issues and candidate qualifications. Instead, poll advocates argue, surveys can generate interest and excitement among voters about an election and prompt them to pay greater attention to the candidates and the issues. Regarding impact, there is considerable controversy, as we will see, about whether and how much polls affect elections and policy making and whether that influence is good or not. At the very least, one defender contends, "Policymakers need to be aware that Americans feel a sharp disconnection between how much influence they believe they actually have on government officials and how much they think they should have."[63]

Accuracy of Polling

Polling has progressed to the point that competent survey research firms can measure public opinion with considerable accuracy on such simple questions as for whom people will vote. One review of 15 national survey organizations showed that on average their polls conducted a week before the 2008 presidential election had Barack Obama leading John McCain by 7.6%, a scant 0.3% greater than the actual winning margin of 7.3%.[64]

Beyond such simple questions, though, there is controversy about how accurately polls measure public opinion. There is a multitude of factors, such as the order in which questions are asked, that can distort results.[65] It is far beyond our scope here to delve into the technical complexities of polling, but to give a flavor of the challenges facing polls, let us consider two difficulties: constructing the question and obtaining a representative sample of the population.

Crafting the Question

How to word a question is a key problem all polls face. Because the wording of a question can skew responses, writing good questions is the first step in designing a good survey. To see how difficult it often is to formulate a neutral question that will not influence answers, consider the following three questions that surveyed opinion about affirmative action.[66]

1. Do you generally favor or oppose affirmative action programs for racial minorities?
2. In order to overcome past discrimination, do you favor or oppose affirmative action programs designed to help blacks and other minorities get better jobs and education?
3. Do you favor or oppose affirmative action programs that give preferences to blacks and other minorities?

These three questions evoked very different responses. Question 1 drew the most evenly divided response: 49% for affirmative action and 43% against. Question 2 yielded the highest support for affirmative action (63%), and question 3 had the lowest support (38%). What caused the variations? Question 2 drew the most sympathetic response to affirmative action because it included the phrase "in order to overcome past discrimination." By contrast, question 3 brought the least support for affirmative action by using the phrase "give preferences to." Compared to the other two, Question 1 did not introduce elements that some people say would sway answers.

Even a single term can significantly change results. A 2010 poll that asked if "homosexuals" should be able to serve openly in the military found only 44% in favor. When the same poll substituted "gay men and lesbians" for "homosexuals" in the question, support for their serving openly rose to 58%.[67]

Lack of sufficient choice is another problem with many poll questions. Those that ask respondents for a simple yes/no-type response often miss the complexity of opinions on an issue. Abortion provides an example. If you ask people whether they agree with *Roe v. Wade* (1973), the Supreme Court decision granting women legal access to abortion, most say yes. The responses in one illustrative poll were yes 66%, no 25%, and unsure 9%.[68] However, the apparent strong support for abortion weakens when more choices are given. One poll asked whether abortion should (1) always be legal, (2) be legal most of the time, (3) be legal only in cases rape, incest, or to save the mother's life, or (4) never be legal. The responses were: always legal (25%), legal most of the time (24%), legal only in cases of rape, incest, and danger to the mother's life (37%), never legal (10%), and unsure (4%).[69] In this poll, only 49% were clearly pro-choice, while 47% were mostly pro-life.

Promoting random responses is a third problem with some questions. Because people do not like to appear uniformed or uninterested, many will express an opinion when asked for a yes/no response even if they have no knowledge of the issue or do not really care one way or the other. This generates random responses.[70] Such responses are evident in Figure 6.7 regarding the nomination of Samuel Alito to the Supreme Court in 2005. When asked, "Do you favor or oppose the nomination of Samuel Alito to the Supreme Court?" (left chart), 20% said they were unsure. When another poll at the same time (right chart) added the option "haven't heard enough . . . yet to have an opinion," 57% were unsure. The second poll made it seem less "dumb" to be unsure.

Just one reason random responses are important is that some groups are less willing than other groups to admit they do not know about an issue and, therefore, are more likely than others to give a random response. Men, for example, are 80% more likely than women to give an opinion on a survey even if they know little or nothing about the topic.[71]

Promoting misleading responses is a fourth problem of some questions. To a degree, respondents want to give socially acceptable answers.

FIGURE 6.7 Misleading Polling Responses on the Nomination of Samuel Alito

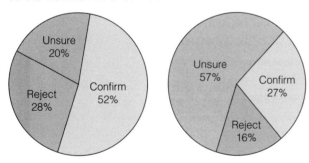

Should the Senate confirm or reject Samuel Alito as Supreme Court Justice?

The 37% difference in the unsure rate in these two surveys occurred because the question in the survey depicted in the right pie chart included an option to say unsure because of a need for more information and the other survey did not include an unsure option.

Note and data sources: Left chart from New Models poll, January 21–23, 2006; right chart from CBS News/*New York Times* poll, January 20–25, 2006, provided by The Roper Center for Public Opinion Research.

Voting is widely considered good, for example, and after an election more people claim to have voted than actually did. A poll taken a month after the 2008 election found 86% of the respondents saying they had voted.[72] In reality, only 57% of the voting-age population cast a ballot for president that year. Even the race or gender of the person conducting a survey interview can skew respondents' answers on questions related to such topics as equality. When a woman rather than a man is asking the questions, for instance, both male and female respondents are more likely to support women's rights and opportunities.[73] Another reason for misleading responses is that some people give the answer they think is most popular rather than what they really think. When asked, "In deciding where you stand on

One problem with opinion polls, as highlighted in this editorial drawing from the Hartford Courant, is that for a variety of reasons, some people do not reply to questions truthfully. (© 2008 Bob Englehart, the Hartford Courant, and PoliticalCartoons.com.)

important issues, how much attention do you tend to pay to what public opinion polls say the American public thinks?" 36% answered "a great deal" or a "fair amount."[74] One result of such thinking is evident in post-election polls. One survey in 2008 found that 57% said they had voted for the winner, Barack Obama, while only 37% admitted voting for John McCain, the loser. The real margin was Obama 53%, McCain 46%.[75]

Sampling

Even if a question is well crafted, it is difficult to accurately ascertain public opinion because it is virtually impossible to draw a **sample**, a subset of the population, that accurately represents the population in terms of race, sex, age, education, income, and other traits without questioning tens of thousands of people. But most national surveys take a sample of 1,000 to 2,000 people selected by a **random sampling** procedure such as using computers to randomly dial telephone numbers from their target area. That yields poll results that survey organization say are accurate within a **sampling error** of plus or minus 3% (±3%).

The problem begins with the fact that the respondents to most polls do not reflect the population. One 2008 national poll of more than 3,000 people recorded that 82% of its respondents were white, 9% were black, 6% were Hispanic, and 3% were "others."[76] Therefore, whites, compared to their share of the population, were overrepresented by 12% and blacks and Hispanics were underrepresented by 4% and 9% respectively. These gaps mean that the margin of error reported by the survey organization is only correct if it has devised a formula to accurately adjust the raw data to account for differences between the demographic characteristics of the sample and those of the actual population.

Because the permutations of all the possible relevant demographic traits are nearly endless, error is inevitable. These are important because they tend to somewhat suppress the input of disadvantaged groups: the poor, the less educated, and others who are less likely than the average person to have one or more household phones. Also underrepresented in polls are people who speak little or no English. As a result, surveys "tend to exclude precisely those people who are least likely to be heard in other ways."[77]

Public Opinion beyond Polls

Polls are the most common way that the public's opinion is brought to light, but they are not the only way. As a form of political participation, you can proactively bring your opinion to bear on the political process, rather than waiting to be called by a poll. One way to be heard is by getting involved in the ultimate poll, an election, by voting and otherwise participating. Between elections you can express your opinions by initiating direct communications with policy makers via letters, e-mails, telephone calls, or face-to-face conversations. You can also to try to act as an opinion leader by expressing your views to your personal contacts, to the news media through letters to the editor or op-ed pieces, or by using the Internet in such ways as writing blog entries to persuade those with whom you do not have immediate contact.

Direct action through participating in marches and other public demonstrations is also part of expressing public opinion. During the April 2006 debate on immigration in Congress, hundreds of thousands of Hispanics and others who supported guest-worker status and possible citizenship for illegal aliens demonstrated in cities around the country and won front-page coverage. Such efforts increase public awareness and also influence policy makers. As one Hispanic activist put it, "The message is 'Today we march, tomorrow we vote.'"[78]

DEMOGRAPHIC GROUPS AND PUBLIC OPINION

As noted, our opinions are shaped in part by being part of various societal groups defined by sex, race, age, education, income, and other traits because of the shared interests and experiences of those groups.[79] It is also true, though, that groups vary widely in their impact. *Strength of political identification* with the group is one such factor. We are all members of multiple demographic groups, but how strongly we identify with any one of them varies greatly. **Group consciousness** (group identification), our awareness that we are part of a group, tends to be stronger for minority groups than for those in the majority. Blacks, for example, are apt to be much more conscious of their race than are whites. The strength of group consciousness also varies by time and circumstance, increasing, for example, when there is a minority candidate in an election. Exit polls in 2008 showed that 9% of voters said race was an important factor in their choice, with some voting for Obama because he is black and some voting against him for that reason.

Degree of political salience is a second factor that helps determine the impact of any group on opinion. **Political salience** is the perceived connection that members of a group see between it and politics. People who are left-handed, for example, have a higher group consciousness than right-handed people, but there is little or no political salience between hand dominance and politics. That would change quickly, however, if the right-handed began to try to eliminate left-handed "deviance" by forbidding "lefties" from marrying. When there is strong group consciousness and perceived political salience, then the group plays an important role for most of its members in defining their political identification, their sense of who they are politically.

There are many possible groups that we could explore. However, to be consistent with our themes we will focus on race and gender, and then briefly take up some other groups., A note is that the opinions of Americans who define themselves as multiracial are apt to parallel those of the minority group to which they are linked most closely.[80]

Race and Public Opinion

A key point in our earlier discussion of political culture was that generally the attitudes of whites and minority group members are fairly similar on basic values. As for the specific issue opinions and other shorter-term views that we are focusing on now, greater dissimilarities between minorities and whites exist. Some examples and their policy impacts are obvious. We have seen, for example, that whites and Americans of color diverge on whether equal opportunity really exists and whether the government should be more active in narrowing the opportunity gap that most minorities believe exists and most whites deny.

Other group-opinion links based on race are less obvious. For example, feeling disadvantaged affected policy opinion related to Iraq. At the beginning of the war in 2003, 61% of African Americans opposed it, while most whites supported the war. One reason a majority of blacks opposed the war was their sense that it would distort what they thought the country's priorities should be. According to one African American scholar, "Black Americans are routinely told that there's not enough money for housing, medicine, education and rebuilding the inner city, but . . . considerable sums can be raised for war and rebuilding Iraq."[81] Latino opinion was also affected, although less strongly than black opinion. A plurality of Latinos (48%) supported going to war, but that level was still significantly below the majority support among whites.[82]

FIGURE 6.8 Race and Opinions on the Death Penalty

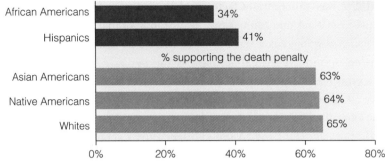

On some issues, whites and some minority groups are on one side and other minority groups are on the other.

Data source: JEHT Foundation and New California Media report, *Public Opinion Survey of California Ethnic Groups About Criminal Justice Issues*, January 8, 2004.

For all the differences in opinion, it would be an error to overemphasize these differences because majorities of whites and minorities agree on many other issues. A poll conducted in 2010, for instance, found that the legalizing of marijuana for medical use won majority support from whites, blacks, and Latinos. On yet other issues, the opinions of minority groups diverge from one another, with some groups aligned with white opinion and other groups not. One example, capital punishment, is illustrated in Figure 6.8. In sum, differences in public opinion based on race exist, but they are less profound than often portrayed. As one study put it with regard to Latinos, they "overall have very much the same policy agenda as most Americans, with perhaps a little more emphasis placed . . . [on some issue], and with a little less [on other issues]. . . . However, differences on the domestic agenda are minor compared to the similarities."[83]

Gender and Public Opinion

Much of what is true about the differences and similarities of minority and white opinions also applies to those of women and men. On the one hand, a gender gap certainly exists.[84] American women are almost always less supportive than men of using military force.[85] Just before the war started in Iraq in March 2003, 73% of men compared to 63% of women favored using force to oust Saddam Hussein.[86] The same gender gap exists globally. Surveys taken in 11 countries prior to the beginning of the Persian Gulf War against Iraq in 1991 found that in 10 of the countries a greater percentage of men than women were willing to use force.[87]

The gender gap between American men and women on military force is a microcosm of male–female attitudes toward violence in general. Responses of men and women to 285 questions related to military force, capital punishment, television violence, gun control, and other questions related to violence found that a greater percentage of men than women chose the more violent option in 87% of the cases. Women answered more aggressively than men on only 5% of the issues, with responses even on 8% of the issues.[88]

Women's opinions also tend to be similar to those of minority groups and different from the opinions of whites and males. For example, women (and minorities) are more likely than men (and whites) to say they would use a budget surplus to increase spending on public services, such as education, whereas men are more likely to favor using such surpluses to reduce taxes or reduce the national debt.[89] The sense of being discriminated against also makes women more likely than men to support policies to improve the lot of disadvantaged groups.[90]

For all the gender differences, though, it would be an error to think that majorities of men and women are usually opposed to one another. As one study concludes, "Saying gender is important [in opinion formation] does not mean that men and women are neatly divided into different camps when it comes to public opinion. . . . [To the contrary,] the differences often lie mostly at the margins."[91]

Other Groups and Public Opinion

Race and sex are not the only demographic categories that help determine an individual's opinions. Age, income, education, and religion, and many other traits also affect opinions. Volumes are written in an effort to sort out all the permutations of various group influences on opinion, but to give a snapshot we will use one point of opinion—the vote for president in 2008— to look at differences among demographic groups.[92]

- *General population.* For comparison with the groups below, bear in mind that in the exit polls on which all the data below is based, Barack Obama received 53% of the vote.
- *Race.* Almost all (95%) of African American voters chose Obama. So did 67% of Hispanics and 62% of Asian Americans. Only 43% of white voters favored Obama. The salience of race in 2008 increased black support for the Democratic candidate and decreased white support a few percentage points more than might otherwise have been expected.
- *Sex.* Support for Obama was markedly stronger among women (56%) than men (49%).
- *Sexual orientation.* Given the general views of the parties on gay rights, it was hardly surprising that 70% of gay voters went for Obama, compared to 53% of heterosexuals.
- *Age.* The generational contrast of Obama and McCain heightened the salience of age in 2008 and made it a good predictor of the vote. Obama was

supported by 66% of young adults (age 18–29). Then his support steadily dropped off among progressively older age groups and was only 45% among voters age 65 and up.

- *Income.* Given that the Democrats tend to favor more aid to and fewer taxes on lower income groups, support for Obama followed the expected pattern of decreasing as income levels rose. He drew 73% of the vote of those earning under $15,000 a year, and that support fell progressively, with only a minority of voters earning $50,000 or more supporting Obama.
- *Education.* A chart of Obama's support at increasing levels of education would look something like an inverted arc. His support was highest (63%) among those with less than a high school diploma, then fell among those with a high school degree (52%), some college (51%), and an undergraduate degree (50%). However Obama's support turned upward (58%) among the most highly educated, those with a postgraduate degree.
- *Religion.* The impact of religion was complex and is best understood by focusing on whites. Obama received weak support from white Protestants (34%) and white Catholics (43%), but was favored by Jewish voters (83%) in line with their traditional liberal and pro-civil rights leanings. Obama also received majority support from whites in other religions such as Muslims (67%), and whites who are atheists or who acknowledge no organized religion (71%). Strength of identification was also evident. Those whites attending religious services regularly were less likely to vote for Obama (43%) than those going only occasionally or never (67%). Similarly, white evangelical Protestants (27%) were less supportive of Obama than white mainline Protestants (44%).
- *Mutually supportive or conflicting group identifications.* Predictably, people with two or more group memberships aligned to support Obama were more likely to support him than people in either of the groups alone. For example, black women (96%) voted for Obama more than did all blacks (95%) or all women (56%). When group membership conflicted, the opposite sometimes occurred. White women (46%) voted for Obama less than all women (56%) but more than all whites (43%). And sometimes one group membership dominated when two conflicted. Despite the fall-off in support for Obama with each increasing age group in the population, black support for him was consistent between 94% and 96% at every age level.

Our work so far in exploring the nature and formation of public opinion, how it is measured, and its various demographic dimensions brings us to an even more important matter, the roles that polls play. One role is to entertain us and to satisfy our curiosity about what other people are thinking. Certainly it is neat to know that 43% of the public believes that pets go to heaven after they die, that 27% of Americans think they will be reincarnated, and that 48% believe in ghosts.[93] The second possible role is influencing public opinion. To examine that, we will look at what the role of public opinion is in the policy process, then ask what it ought to be.

PUBLIC OPINION AND PUBLIC POLICY: WHAT IS

Public opinion is neither absent from policy making nor its sole determinant. Between those extremes, however, there is no agreement on the impact of public opinion. The problem is that the links between what Americans think and whether policy subsequently changes or not are complex. Furthermore, the impact of opinion varies among policies and over time.[94] To explore how opinion affects policy, we will begin with the question of how public opinion influences policy makers. Then we will turn our attention to the impact of public opinion on policy makers' decisions.

How Public Opinion Influences Policy Makers

Elected and appointed policy makers stand between public opinion and policy in all cases except those decided by referendums and other direct democracy techniques. Public opinion influences these intervening policy makers through formal and informal means.

Voting

Voting is one means by which public opinion influences the policy process. *Determining who gets elected* is one impact. Rarely does an election give a clear indication of public sentiment on a specific issue. Nevertheless, policy issues do play a role in deciding elections and, by extension, which policies are implemented. Policy under President Barack Obama has been and will be different than it would have been under a President John McCain. Immediately after the election, for instance, McCain opposed the size of the economic stimulus program Obama proposed. Obama also sought to increase taxes on higher income groups, a step McCain opposed. On the foreign policy front, Obama made other decisions McCain would not have. These included ending President Bush's ban on giving U.S. international assistance funds to groups such as the International Planned Parenthood Foundation that promote or perform abortions overseas. Similarly, it makes a difference who serves in Congress. As Chapter 11 details, Republicans and Democrats usually vote on different sides of contentious policy issues.

Deciding policy through referendums is a second way that voting can impact policy. Although there are no national referendums in the United States, they are in common at lower levels. Such votes directly decide policy in states and localities.

Additionally, the pattern of votes on issues that are subject to referendums in several states serves as a gauge of opinion to political leaders at the national level. For example, more than 30 referendums on banning same-marriage have been held, and all of them but one (Arizona, 2006) has passed, usually by lopsided margins. This makes it unlikely that anyone at the federal level will push a gay marriage bill and even less likely that such a measure would pass Congress.

Policy Maker Reactions to Public Opinion

A second way that public opinion influences policy results from policy makers being sensitive to public sentiment. One indication of the attention politicians pay to polls is the fact that virtually all presidents since Franklin Roosevelt have both monitored the poll results reported in the press and conducted their own private polls.[95] Party leaders in both houses of Congress and some individual members also conduct polls, as do the national parties and many lower-level party organizations.

Polls, it should be noted, are not the only sources of public opinion for policy makers. In fact, polls are often not a satisfactory source of information for them. One of many reasons is that polls usually ask very general policy questions, while the choices policy makers face are often more specific and complex. Second, most elected officials are not as interested in what the country as a whole thinks as they are in the views of their constituents. Therefore, many policy makers often look beyond polls to determine the opinions of the public they care about.[96] Members of Congress cite attending public meetings in their districts, reading mail and e-mail from their constituents, talking to them on the phone, and similar channels as their main source of public opinion. Additionally, a growing number of legislators including Speaker of the House Nancy Pelosi now host blog sites. Members also frequently cite polls and the media as sources of information about public opinion. Political appointees and senior career officials in the executive branch rely very heavily on the media and to a lesser degree on personal contacts as sources of opinion. Political appointees also cite opinion polls as a key source, but civil servants do not.[97]

Whatever their sources of opinion, policy makers pay attention to public opinion because of a range of values. These values do not include a high regard for the public's wisdom. To the contrary, both elected and appointed officials are very skeptical about the quality of public opinion. When they were asked if "Americans know enough about issues to form wise opinions about what should be done" only 20% of policy makers said yes. Another 9% replied, "It depends."[98] Instead of heeding public opinion because it makes sense, most officials do so as a way of getting reelected, adhering to democratic principles, and achieving policy success.

The *electoral impulse* is one reason why officials often heed public opinion. Most elected officials are wary of taking policy stands that could jeopardize their reelection. This does not mean that elected officials slavishly follow opinion, but they do react to it. Research indicates, for example, that a president "typically does not support popular policies that he believes would harm society" but may bend to public opinion "when he is marginally popular and soon faces a contest for reelection."[99] As for members of Congress, 69% have said that public opinion pressures are a significant part of the legislative process.[100] Moreover, one study comments, "Legislators show greater attention to public opinion as election day looms than when the last election is just over."[101] Less directly, some political appointees heed public opinion because the continuation of their party in power is necessary for them to remain in office.

Belief in democracy is another reason that many policy makers pay heed to public opinion. Most officials reject the notion that public opinion should alone determine policy, but most of them say they believe that public opinion should be not ignored. Therefore, they try to balance their expertise and leadership role against the dictates of public opinion. President Gerald Ford was reflecting this approach when he suggested, "A president ought to listen to the people, but he cannot make hard decisions just by reading polls once a week."[102] Similarly, studies of the attitudes of legislators show that most waffle to some degree between two roles: being a *trustee* elected to make decisions and serving as a *delegate* who faithfully represents constituent opinions.[103] Belief in the democratic norm that public opinion should influence policy even extends to appointed officials. As one study of appointed officials put it, "the ideal of democratic accountability can be seen tugging many officials" in the direction of heeding public opinion.[104]

Desire for policy success is a third reason that many policy makers incorporate public opinion into their decisions. Officials commonly believe that public support and policy success are linked. Before ordering the invasion of Iraq in 2003, for instance, President Bush strove to win majority public support for the war because, he commented, "I am a product of the Vietnam era. I remember presidents trying to wage wars that were very unpopular and the nation split."[105]

In a globalizing world, clashing public opinions can create foreign policy tension. In 2010 American anger over the oil spill from a BP (originally known as British Petroleum) well in the Gulf of Mexico helped push President Obama into strident condemnation of BP, including a pledge to find out "whose ass to kick." Many British saw this rhetoric as scapegoating, with one British columnist portraying Obama as a "weak, complaining politician trying to blame a foreign bogeyman for a mishap which should be laid . . . at the door of his own oil industry and its regulators." (AP Photo/Drew Angerer)

The Impact of Public Opinion on Policy

We have seen thus far that policy makers tend to be concerned with public opinion. However, worrying about public opinion is not necessarily the same as following it. Therefore, the question is: To what extent does policy follow the preferences of the American people?

The Degree to Which Policy Follows Public Opinion

Studies of public opinion and subsequent policy making indicate that policy makers often do what the public wants by making changes in policy when the public is dissatisfied and by rejecting proposals to change policy when the public is satisfied with it.[106] One such analysis of policy over four decades found that it followed opinion 66% of the time.[107] Another study spanning 33 years concluded that policy followed the public's preferences 58% of the time.[108] This pattern of public opinion often playing a significant role in determining policy is also evident in other democracies worldwide.[109]

In addition to these observable impacts of existing opinion, public opinion plays a role in policy formation through the *anticipated reactions* of policy makers. This means that officials think twice about proposals that might upset the public. As one scholar explains, "Public opinion is influential" not just because of "how it *actually* responds" to events and policy, but also because "of how it *might* respond."[110] Or as another study concluded, "People [in the bureaucracy] would do kooky things perhaps if you didn't have the threat of public opinion."[111]

Differences in the Impact of Opinion on Policy

For all these indications that policy makers respond to public opinion, it is also clear that political leaders often do not follow the lead of public opinion. Six factors help determine when opinion is influential and when it is not.

Distribution of opinion is the first factor. Public opinion is least influential when it is closely split or evenly balanced. By contrast, few politicians are willing to go against public opinion that strongly favors one side or the other. This is true in democracies globally, according to one scholar who advises, "Policymakers in . . . democracies do not decide against an overwhelming public consensus."[112]

Opinion intensity is a second factor. Often what overall public opinion is on an issue is not as important as the opinion of its **issue public**. These are the individuals who are intensely interested in and likely to voice their opinions on a particular topic. For example, most Americans favor greater gun control. Yet passing legislation to do that is difficult to do because of the nature of the associated issue public. Within that group, intense opponents of gun control and their lobby groups such as the National Rifle Association outnumber and therefore outweigh avid control proponents. As one legislator put it, overall opinion on gun control has had less influence on Congress than the fact that the "pro-gun forces have been more effective politically in terms of generating votes and support" than anti-gun forces.[113]

Policy type is a third factor. Between 1960 and 1993, for example, policy related to environmental protection, education, relations with the then Soviet Union, and illegal drugs followed opinion in each of these areas at least 80% to the time.

By contrast, policy followed opinion 33% or less of the time in such policy areas as abortion, campaign reform, gun control, and welfare.[114]

Policy direction—whether to keep policy unchanged (the status quo) or to change it—is a fourth factor. Figure 6.9 shows that policy makers' decisions are much more likely to heed public opinion when it favors the status quo than when it wants policy to change.

Political circumstances constitute a fifth factor. Studies of policy during different periods have found that the degree to which policy followed opinion ranged between 75% and 54%. These studies also found that the strength of the link between opinion and policy declined from a high point in the 1970s to increasingly lower levels into the 1990s.[115] Why policy follows opinion more in some time periods than in others is not clear, but it may well be connected to such political circumstances as whether one party controls both Congress and the White House and the level of partisan intensity in the country and Congress.

The disproportionate impact of the elite and the attentive public is a sixth factor that affects the link between opinion and policy. Not all opinions count equally. Some scholars believe that it is the opinions of the **elite**, the country's social, economic, and political leaders, that often determine policy. Similarly, the opinions of the **attentive public**, the 15% to 20% of the people who pay a great deal of attention to politics in general and who, more than most people, are likely to contact policy makers and otherwise participate in politics, may also have disproportional weight in the policy process. Under the adage "squeaky wheels get greased," the attentive public exercises influence beyond its numbers. This distorts public opinion, because the views of the attentive public are often not the same as those of the general public.[116] Immigration policy provides one example. The number of legal immigrants admitted into the United States over the past decade has been nearly a million a year and has not changed despite the fact that most (54%) Americans favor reducing that number. One reason that policy has not followed opinion may be that a survey of the elite found that only 10% support reducing legal immigration.[117]

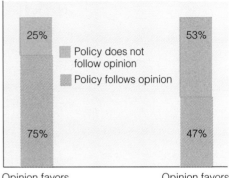

FIGURE 6.9 Variations in the Impact of Opinion on Policy

Public policy is much more likely to follow public opinion when Americans favor the status quo than when they want policy change. This difference partly reflects the fact that it is easier in the U.S. political system to prevent policy change than to institute it.
Data sources: Alan D. Monroe, "Public Opinion and Public Policy, 1980–1993," *Public Opinion Quarterly,* 62/1 (1998): 6–28; and Alan D. Monroe, "Consistency between Policy Preferences and National Policy Decisions," *American Politics Quarterly,* 7/1 (1979): 3–18.

PUBLIC OPINION AND PUBLIC POLICY: WHAT OUGHT TO BE

Most early American leaders doubted the public's ability to govern wisely. They worried about a tyranny of the majority, that is, the possibility of majority opinion forcing the government to adopt policies and take other actions that would violate the rights of those with property and other forms of wealth. The result, as Chapter 2 details, was that most of government was initially insulated from the public, with only the House of Representative directly chosen by the electorate.

Worries about the public have eased in part, and the role of the public in government has expanded considerably since 1787. Members of the Senate and the Electoral College are now elected instead of being appointed. Also, the vote has been extended to all racial groups, to women, and to 18-year-olds. Beginning in the late 1800s, many states instituted limited direct democracy by allowing voters to amend constitutions and decide policy in referendums.

The growth of polling has been yet another part of the democratization process. Since the advent of reliable polling in the 1930s, the number of polls, their perceived validity, and their impact on policy have all increased substantially. This change raises two questions. First, has the increased role of public opinion been a positive or negative development? Second, should the role that opinion plays be expanded, contracted, or kept the same? In broad terms, the debate over what the role of public opinion *ought* to be rests on three considerations: the quality of public opinion, whether public opinion polls are a suitable measure of the will of Americans, and whether Americans want the government to follow their opinions more closely.

What Is the Quality of Public Opinion?

Do Americans merit a significant say in the policy making? The easy answer in a democracy is, "Of course!" However, a perhaps wiser answer is, "Yes, but only insofar as the public meets its responsibility in a democracy of being concerned with and informed about issues and being reasoned in its judgments." To see if the public meets these tests, we can look at two views of the quality of public opinion as a foundation for policy making: deficient and sufficient.

Image I: The Deficient Public

One view of the public is that the average citizen in the United States and every other democracy is unsuited to play a positive role in policy making.[118] Those who take this view disparage public opinion on several counts.

Political apathy is one supposed deficiency attributed to Americans. Sometimes less than half of all eligible adults vote in presidential elections, and the percentage of nonvoters rises sharply in other elections. Beyond that, relatively few Americans contribute to candidates or engage in any other form of campaign activity. This apathy extends to following current political events. Most Americans claim to be interested, but there is evidence that actual attention to the news is much lower than claimed interest. For example, one study asked people if they followed the news about four major policy topics. An average of 61% said they "closely" followed the topics in the press. Then the study asked anyone who said they followed one of the issues closely a series of easy questions about the topic. The respondents fared poorly, correctly answering only 40% of the questions on average.[119] This result casts considerable doubt on the truthfulness of many of the respondents who said they were following the news.

Political ignorance is a second deficient characteristic of Americans, according to critics. One study of responses to more than 2,000 factual questions about politics asked by various surveys over some six decades revealed that the average American scored only 40% correct.[120] Also discouraging is that fact that Americans are generally less knowledgeable about politics in both their country and in the world than are people in most other economically developed countries.[121] Such results have led one scholar to bemoan "a shocking picture" of ignorance about politics and even some "bitter humor" when you realize that "more people know their astrological sign [87%] than know the name of their congressperson [41%]."[122]

Instability is a third negative trait attributed to public opinion by some. The charge is that with such a scant knowledge base, public opinion is subject to unsettling random change. One illustrative study that contacted the same respondents a few months apart and asked them if they favored or opposed 10 policy choices found that for the average issue, 18% of the respondents gave different answers in the two polls even though nothing had occurred that would explain people switching their views.[123]

Easily manipulated is a fourth supposed deficiency of public opinion.[124] The argument is that the social, economic, and political elite in the United States can mold "public opinion . . . in ways that render it compatible with the views of the powerful."[125] This is especially true when there is elite consensus because it ensures uniformity in the messages about an issue that appear in the elite-dominated mass media and other channels of information and opinion to the public.[126]

Image II: The Sufficient Public

Those who argue that the public does have sufficient skills and sophistication to warrant an important role for public opinion in policy making make several arguments.

Sufficiently interested in and informed about politics is one attribute of the public according to its defenders. They contend that the public does acquire enough knowledge to make reasonable policy choices, especially when the news media supply enough information.[127] Those who defend the public also downplay Americans' low-level of specific political facts. From this perspective, the inability of most Americans to, say, name the secretary of state does mean they do not know enough to be for or against the U.S. war in Afghanistan or other major foreign policy choices. Rather than constantly staying up on politics, the argument goes, most people rationally allocate the limited time and energy they can devote to the news to focus on the issues that concern them the most. This arguably is sufficient because, "Politics does not require full-time spectators. Nobody needs to pay attention to everything that stimulates debate in the Washington community."[128]

Sufficiently stable is another positive trait that some scholars attribute to public opinion. They argue that for the most part public opinion is reasonably stable and usually only changes slowly and/or for understandable reasons. This is particularly true for familiar issues in domestic politics. For example, the distribution of opinions on abortion has changed little since before the Supreme Court decided *Roe v. Wade* (1973). Defenders of public opinion also argue that it is reasonably stable on a range of international issues.[129] When asked, "Do you think it would be best for the future of this country if we take an active part in world affairs?" 72% of Americans said yes in 1946, an identical 72% said yes in 2005. Moreover, the percentage of Americans saying yes never varied more than 11% during the intervening six decades. Furthermore, when public opinion does change, it arguably usually does so in an evolutionary way. One area in which this is evident is in attitudes toward gender and racial equality. The share of the public who say they would vote for a qualified woman for president rose slowly but surely from 33% in 1937 to 94% in 1996 and has stayed in the 90% range since then.

Sufficiently reasonable is yet another positive attribute that some scholars apply to public opinion. They reject the claim that public opinion is driven by emotion. The public's defenders argue that to the contrary, it wisely favors pragmatic solutions, instead on those based on one or another ideology. From this perspective, Americans apply their values realistically in light of the specifics of any given issue.[130] "Everywhere we look," one analyst writes, "we have seen a public opinion that responds smoothly and predictably to public events."[131] Several scholars who have examined public opinion on U.S. foreign and national security policy have also come to positive conclusions about the quality of public opinion.[132] For example, one finds that the public is generally "pretty prudent" in its views on using America's armed forces.[133] And what do Americans think of themselves? They agree, although somewhat tentatively, with the "sufficient public" perspective, as detailed in Figure 6.10.

FIGURE 6.10   The Public's Confidence in Its Opinion

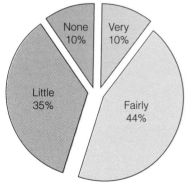

How confident are you in the public when it comes to matching judgments about what direction officials should take?

A thin majority of Americans are confident that public opinion can provide a good guide for policy makers.
Note and data source: The 1% unsure rate was omitted from the figure. Data from the Kaiser Family Foundation survey June 2001, provided by The Roper Center for Public Opinion Research.

Do Public Opinion Polls Reflect the Will of the People?

When trying to decide what role public opinion should play in the policy process, a second consideration is whether poll results closely approximate what Americans think. If polls are greatly and inherently flawed, then the messages being transmitted by them to policy makers may often be wrong. Certainly, as we have seen, polls are not perfect measures. We have also seen though that despite their problems, carefully constructed and conducted polls are reasonably accurate. The bottom-line question is whether polls are good enough to play a vital role in policy making. "Yes," according to one analyst, who characterizes polls as "the only reasonably reliable way to measure public opinion" and the only way that society can "ensure that leaders . . . understand what the public believes and wants."[134] "No," polls are not good enough, writes another scholar, who argues that they "reflect some voices better than others" and are also often "unable to compensate for [the public's] inattentiveness to politics."[135]

This debate is unlikely to be settled soon, but if the public could cast a tiebreaker, it would favor the "yes, good enough" position. The public's view is not based on a naïve belief that polls are precise. When asked if polls accurately reflect what the public thinks," only 33% reply "always" or "most of the time." Yet despite this caution about the quality of polls, 84% of the public believes that they are the best way to communicate public opinion to policy makers.

What Roles Do Americans Want Public Opinion to Play?

Americans think that polls are the best way to communicate public opinion to officials but do not necessarily believe that polls should become unofficial plebiscites (referendums) that public officials should unquestioningly follow. Public opinion on the larger issue of what role polls should play is complex. Examining Americans' attitudes on this issue involves looking first at what they think about the state of democracy in their country and then, in light of that, how Americans think policy should be decided.

What Americans Think about Their Democracy

Americans generally laud at least the ideal of the American democratic system. Yet beneath this acclaim, many think that their democracy is not working as well as it should be. Almost all Americans say they are proud of the way their "democracy works," but only 32% say they are "very proud," while 52% say they are only "somewhat proud."[136] This suggests that Americans do not think the political process is in crisis. It is clear, though, that a very substantial part of the public believes that there are deficiencies, particularly with the country's political leadership. Reflecting that, political trust in government is low. When asked in 2009 if they trusted the federal government, only 41% of Americans said yes.[137] Additionally, only 39% of the public believes that "the government cares much what people like me think."[138] Such sentiments left 77% of Americans expressing frustration with or anger at the government in a 2010 survey.[139]

How Americans Think Policy Should Be Decided

Few Americans would support scrapping their representative form of government and instituting a direct democracy in which the people made all policy by referendum. What Americans do want, however, is a greater voice in their own governance. Indeed, 82% of them said in a 2010 poll that public opinion "has too little power and influence in Washington."[140]

Note that most people do not think that public opinion should be the only factor in decisions. Typically, one poll recorded only 36% saying they wanted officials to pay a "great deal" of attention to public opinion, while 39% said they thought officials should pay only a "fair amount" of attention.[141] Surveys show that the public also wants its leaders to pay heed to their own judgments and to expert advice.

Should There Be Official Polling?

When all is said and done, the issue is how democratic the United States should be. As we have noted, the history of the country has been one of increasing democratization. The following You Decide box presents a way to continue that trend by creating a National Polling Authority.

YOU DECIDE: Create a National Polling Authority?

Polls affect policy, but the blizzard of them, each with questions worded differently and other variations that engender different results, can muddle rather than clarify political debate. One way to ease this problem is to create a National Polling Authority (NPA) to conduct official polls. The NPA's governing board would be non/bipartisan, perhaps with the president and the majority and minority leaders in Congress and, to avoid being Washington-centric, the National Governor's Conference, each appointing some board members. The NPA board would oversee periodic polls that included topics it has authorized and other topics submitted by one of the branches of the federal government, by the agreement of several states, and by petitions signed by, say, 2% of the country's adults. Another possibility would be to conduct state and congressional district polls prior to each election and include topics submitted by candidates. In all cases, though, the NPA staff would shape the questions, and the board would approve them. All polls would be published.

Policy makers would not be legally bound by the NPA poll results, but they would be intensively reported and would carry more weight than current polls do. Officials would almost certainly be quizzed by reporters, constituents, and others about their positions vis-à-vis the poll and would be pressed to explain themselves if they disagreed with a majority of the people.

Would you favor creating the NPA? There are two ways to debate this. One is by discussing the general idea of an official national poll, while leaving the details for later. The second is to draft a proposal for the NPA's structure and procedures, including some of the details mentioned, like the appointment of the board. Your plan should also address such issues as whether polls would be conducted only in English and whether they would interview only citizens. As points of information, about 5% of all legal U.S. residents speak little or no English, and about 8% of U.S. residents are not citizens. A final note is that the idea of government-sponsored polling is not new. A 1946 survey asked if the government should pay for polls to help members of Congress "find out how the citizens feel on important issues," Most (53%) respondents said yes, 33% said no, and 14% were unsure.[142]

SUMMARY

The thoughts that Americans, or any other nation, have about politics can be divided into three main topics: political culture, ideology, and public opinion. Political culture is an amalgam of the nation's core values along the dimensions of individualism ↔ communitarianism, tolerance ↔ intolerance, hierarchy ↔ equality, trust ↔ suspicion, and nationalism ↔ alienation. Americans are generally very individualistic; fairly tolerant, especially compared to other nations; reasonably equalitarian about opportunity and legal standing but not about outcomes and circumstances; suspicious of government, but less so than people in most other countries; and very nationalistic. Individuals are inculcated with political culture values early in life by such agents of political socialization as family, schools, and the media.

Ideology is a view about what society should be like and the role the government should have in achieving that image. Most typically, ideology is analyzed along a liberal ↔ conservative scale, but ideology is actually more complex than that. Whatever ideology's dimensions may be, most Americans are not very ideological. A plurality usually says they are "moderates," and many of those who identify as liberals or conservatives say they are only "slightly" so. The "slightlies" and the moderates combined comprise a majority of Americans, and this middle-of-road orientation makes Americans fairly pragmatic politically.

Political culture and ideology together serve as a foundation for public opinion. More immediately, public opinion is also shaped by experiences, self-interest, the media, and opinion leaders.

Public opinion polling has become an important part of the American political process. Whether this is good or not is controversial. One issue is the accuracy of polling. There are many reasons why the results of even a good poll are arguably only a caricature of American opinion. One is that variations in how poll questions are worded can result in substantial differences in the way the questions are answered. A second of many challenges for polls is reaching a representative sample of adult Americans or, more commonly, adjusting poll results when an accurate cross-section of adults is not queried.

Accurately sampling the population or correctly adjusting poll results when the traits of the poll sample and the population differ is important because opinions vary among different demographic groups. Women and African Americans, for instance, are usually less likely to support the use of military force abroad than are men and whites. An important note is that despite many differences in opinion among groups, the nation's broad consensus on many dimensions of political culture means that the differences among groups are often narrow. Moreover there are many crosscutting currents that leave minority groups and women on different sides of some issues and leave minority groups at odds with one another on other issues.

Public opinion influences policy through a number of channels including voting in elections and in referendums, and policy makers taking public opinion into account when making decisions. It is difficult to link opinion and subsequent policy, but studies do show that policy follows opinion more often than not. Within that overall fact, how often policy follows opinion varies among different types of policy and during different times.

Perhaps the most important question about public opinion is how much it should determine policy. There is a long-standing controversy about whether the public is interested enough, well informed enough, and stable enough to have a major say in policy. As for the public, it feels that its opinion does not have enough influence on policy. However, the public only wants its opinion to be more important, not the sole determinant of policy. One way that might increase the impact of public opinion on policy is to have official national polling.

CHAPTER 6 GLOSSARY

attentive public The 15% to 20% of the public who pay a great deal of attention to politics. These individuals also convey their views to policy makers and otherwise participate in politics more than most Americans.

conservatives Those who believe that government should intervene in society to achieve a more even distribution of circumstances only if inequalities exist because of legal discrimination, not as a result of the economic and social systems.

elite A country's social, economic, and political leaders.

equal opportunity The notion that every person should have the same opportunity to maximize their potential without the assumption that everyone will achieve equally.

equalitarianism The belief that all people are equal.

exceptionalism The belief that one's country is not only good but also has a special mission to spread its values globally for the world's good.

group consciousness Being consciously aware that you are a member of a demographic group.

individualism A political theory based on the belief that each person has rights that cannot be violated in the interests of the society and that individuals have only limited responsibilities to the society.

issue public Those individuals who are intensely interested in and likely to express their opinion on a specific issue.

liberals Those who favor government action to achieve a more even spread of wealth and other circumstances within a society.

nationalism Includes (1) feeling loyal to and proud of your country and (2) seeing your country as the most important part of your political identification.

opinion leaders Individuals who regularly communicate with and influence the opinions of others.

political culture A concept that refers to a society's (a nation's) generally accepted, long-held, and fundamental values.

political efficacy The sense that by participating one can have an impact on politics.

political identification People's perception of who they are politically in terms of a country, an ideology, a demographic group, a political party, or some other factor.

political ideology A set of ideas about the proper purposes and conduct of government and how individuals relate to societies and their governments.

political opinions Individuals' views about current issues, events, leaders, institutions, and other matters, which in aggregate form public opinion.

political salience The perception that there is a relationship between one's group membership or some other factor and politics.

political socialization The process by which individuals acquire their basic political values and orientation toward the political world.

political tolerance The willingness to accept the political participation of individuals who are perceived as being from markedly different groups or who express antithetical opinions.

political trust Belief that the government and other individuals and groups in the political system generally are not conspiring to subvert rights and needs, especially by such illicit means as violence and corruption.

public opinion (American) The distribution of attitudes among adults (in the United States) about contemporary issues, events, leaders, institutions, and other matters.

push poll A public opinion survey that tries to achieve a desired response by preceding questions with value statements or by otherwise intentionally trying to shape responses by its wording.

rally effect The tendency of the public to support the president and the president's policy during times of foreign policy crisis that involve potential or actual military action or other physical threats to Americans.

random sampling A method for selecting respondents to a survey based on the law of averages, which holds that if a large enough percentage of any population is contacted, those people will be representative of the entire population.

sample A subset of a population, such as a nation or a smaller demographic group, that will be contacted and asked questions.

sampling error The percentile range within which the accuracy of a poll probably falls.

INTEREST GROUPS

7

YOU DECIDE: Democracy Distorted?

It was a clash reminiscent of the old "cowboys and Indians" movies. But unlike the typical script of the 1950s, the cowboys lost the 2004 version. The drama pitted the National Cattlemen's Beef Association (NCBA) against the National Congress of American Indians (NCAI), representing more than 500 tribes. The focus of their struggle was William G. Myers III of Idaho, a nominee for a seat on the Ninth Circuit of the U.S. Court of Appeals, which hears cases originating in the 10 westernmost states. When President George W. Bush nominated Myers, he was the top lawyer for the Department of the Interior. He had earlier served as head of the Public Lands Council, a coalition of interest groups, including the NCBA, that favor widespread commercial grazing on public lands. The NCBA and similar interest groups had supported Myers for his administrative appointment, and they also worked to get him a place on the court. More generally, conservatives hoped Myers would moderate the Ninth Circuit Court, which Senator Orrin Hatch (R-UT) called "the most notoriously liberal federal court" in the country."[1]

Native Americans opposed Myers because of decisions he made at the Interior Department. These included allowing gold mining on California lands that the Quechan tribe considered a spiritual site. Based on this and other grievances, the NCAI claimed that Myers had "devoted his career to advancing the interests of grazing and mining industries at the expense of the environment and the rights of Native Americans and tribal governments." To increase its clout, the NCAI sought additional allies, including the Leadership Conference on Civil Rights (LCCR), a potent coalition of more than 180 groups such as the National Association for the Advancement of Colored People, the National Council of La Raza, the National Gay and Lesbian Task Force, the National Organization of Women, and the Organization of Chinese Americans. The LCCR classified defeating Myers' nomination as a top priority. Several environmental groups such as the Sierra Club also joined the fight against Myers because of his frequent support of opening public lands to increased grazing, logging, mining, and other commercial use.

The campaign took its toll. Senate Democrats filibustered to prevent Myers' nomination from coming to a vote. Minority Leader Tom Daschle (D-SD) condemned Myers for his record on the environment and also for showing "a complete lack of understanding of the . . . relationship between the federal government and Indian tribes."[2] In the end, a Republican move to force a vote on the nomination fell seven votes short of the 60 needed to halt a filibuster. This effectively ended Myers' chance of becoming a federal judge. As often happens, the struggle between interest groups had played a key part in determining the fate of a nomination, a proposed law, or some other aspect of policy making. It is up for you to decide as you read this chapter whether these events are simply rough and tumble democracy or a distortion of democracy.

INTRODUCING INTEREST GROUPS

During his inaugural address in 1961, President John F. Kennedy challenged Americans to "ask not what your country can do for you—ask what you can do for your country." It was a noble thought, but it contravened what is for many people, groups, and organizations the essence of politics: pressing the government to favor their interests. This chapter examines the pursuit of those interests. In exploring that topic, the chapter will make the following key points:

★ Analysts disagree about whether interest groups promote or distort democracy, but there is consensus that they are important policy actors and have been so throughout U.S. history.

★ Several factors have combined in recent decades to promote increased interest group formation and activity.

★ Interest groups try to influence policy by direct lobbying, indirect lobbying, and affecting the selection of policy makers.

★ Interest groups work to influence all three branches of government.

★ Interest groups play a policy-making role, but the extent of their influence is debatable.

★ There are significant differences among groups in terms of their strength.

★ Several issue-related variables affect the influence of interest groups.

★ We should carefully evaluate calls to strictly regulate interest group activity.

What Interest Groups Are

All interest groups share two traits: a common interest and political activity to promote that interest. At its broadest, this characterization reflects one specialist's view that interest groups "include every active unit, from the isolated individual to the complex coalition of organizations . . . that engages in interest-based activity relative to the process of making public policy."[3] From this perspective, a single individual can be an interest group if, for instance, that person is a homeowner who is pressing the town to put speed bumps on his or her road to slow traffic. At the other end of the societal spectrum, some scholars include groups based on birth characteristics (such as sex or race) or circumstance (such as wealth and health) in the ranks of interest groups. These are called *nonassociational interest groups* because membership is based on traits rather than on voluntary association. Even though they are not organized, such groups do arguably have interests. Moreover, nonassociational groups can influence policy through spontaneous activity such as demonstrations and even riots. For example, it is impossible to account for the advances in civil rights legislation in the 1960s without factoring in the spontaneous and violent civil unrest in the Harlem area of New York City (1964), the Watts section of Los Angeles (1965), and other inner cities.

Without denying the occasional impact of individuals or mass protests, the overwhelming share of interest group activity is conducted by organizations on behalf of a group or some other stakeholder in the political system. Thus, an **interest group**, as used here, is an organization or a group of organizations that have political goals and try to influence policy. Most interest groups are represented by **lobbyists** who try to change public policy in ways that agree with their group's views. Notice that contrary to the typical use of "group," our definition includes single organizations, such as states, colleges, unions, and corporations. During the 2008 election cycle (2007–2008), for example, a few single organizations and their contributions to various candidates and political parties included AT&T ($5.7 million), the International Brotherhood of Electrical Workers ($4.9 million), and the University of California ($3.5 million).

Interest Groups and American Diversity

Throughout American history, group activity has been important in advancing the rights and status of disadvantaged groups. The American Anti-Slavery Society founded in Philadelphia in 1833 had mostly white members but promoted the interests of the country's black slaves. Blacks themselves established the National Afro-American League in 1890, and it paved the way for the numerous other organized interest groups dedicated to advancing the cause of Americans of color. Similarly, today's women's rights groups can trace their heritage to the American Equal Rights Association established in 1866 by Susan B. Anthony, Lucy Stone, and Elizabeth Cady Stanton.

Such interest groups have helped achieve many victories. These groups have been particularly effective since the 1950s as their numbers have proliferated, and as people of color, women, and other historically disadvantaged groups have gained political power. It is just one measure of the increased presence of organizations representing disadvantaged demographic groups that in 2008 there were 463 such groups lobbying the federal government on behalf of minorities. Women were represented by 109 groups, while 15 were promoting the interests of gays and lesbians.[4] Tempering such numbers is the fact that there are thousands of groups representing businesses. Moreover these pro-business groups have far greater resources than the groups representing minorities and other disadvantaged people.

Interest Groups in a World of Difference

We shall see that globalization has significantly increased the number and types of interest groups. For example, increased international trade coupled with the

FIGURE 7.1
Foreign Interests as a Share of All Interests

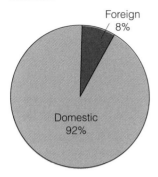

Although domestic interest groups predominate among those that have professional lobbyists working in Washington, foreign interests are also numerous.
Data source: Washington Representatives 2009 (Bethesda, MD: Columbia Books).

status of the United States as the world's largest economy means that virtually every country and a multitude of businesses and other economic enterprises have a powerful interest in trying to shape U.S. policy. As a result, there are over 900 foreign clients that are represented by lobbyists registered with the U.S. government. Moreover, these foreign governments, businesses, and other entities seeking to affect U.S. policy are a notable share of all such lobbyist's clients, as indicated in Figure 7.1.

Even the more than 900 interest groups included in Figure 7.1 are only a fraction of the foreign interests that lobby the U.S. government. Foreign leaders and diplomats, U.S. subsidiaries of foreign corporations, U.S. affiliates for foreign groups, and groups of Americans with ties to other countries are all also part of the "foreign lobby."

WHY INTEREST GROUPS FORM

Interest groups exist worldwide because all countries are complex collectives made up of many types of groups and organizations that have different and sometimes conflicting needs and goals. It is the very nature of politics that these competing groups and organizations struggle with one another to determine whose interests will prevail. In Germany, for example, issues about wages and working conditions often pit business organizations such as the Federation of German Industries against workers' groups such as the German Federation of Trade Unions. This is much like the struggle in the United States between the National Association of Manufacturers (NAM) and the American Federation of Labor-Congress of Industrial Organizations (AFL-CIO). Authoritarian political systems oppress interest groups, but the diversity of society makes complete suppression nearly impossible.

To say that interest groups are natural political phenomenon does not, however, explain when and why specific groups become active. Societal stress and government policy are two important factors that promote interest group formation. Globalization is an increasingly important third factor.

Societal Stress

A 2008 survey conducted in 18 countries found that on average, 63% of all respondents and a majority of people in all but three countries thought that their government was being run to benefit a few big interests.

Group formation and activity can partly be explained by **disturbance theory**. It argues that dramatic changes in a society's social or economic conditions often cause groups whose interests are being adversely affected to become politically active. The 1960s and 1970s were a time of great social upheaval in the United States. The Vietnam War tore the country apart, and the abuses of the administration of President Richard M. Nixon (1969–1974) greatly increased the number of Americans who distrusted their government. One sign of disillusionment, as indicated in Figure 7.2, was the growing number of Americans who thought that government was being run to benefit a few big interests rather than the people as a whole. While this skepticism has eased somewhat, as the figure shows, the public still doubts that they have a government "for the people." Globally, most people in most countries feel the same.[5]

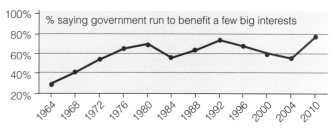

FIGURE 7.2   A Few Big Interests

% saying government run to benefit a few big interests

Americans are much more likely than they once were to believe that government is being run for the benefit of a few big interests rather than for the benefit of all the people.
Data sources: Americans National Election Study, University of Michigan; CBS News/*New York Times* poll; CBS survey report, February 2010.

Amid the growing alienation in the 1960s and early 1970s, numerous groups formed to work to correct the ills that many Americans believed were besetting their country.[6] For example, Ralph Nader, made famous by his 1965 exposé *Unsafe at Any Speed* about the safety deficiencies of American automobiles, founded the consumer interest group Center for Study of Responsive Law (1969). In the same spirit, former Secretary of Health, Education, and Welfare John Gardner established Common Cause (1970) as a "citizens lobby" to help remedy the fact, he said, that "Everybody is organized but the people."[7] Numerous other "citizens lobbies" were also established, including the Environmental Defense Fund (1967) and the Citizen Action Coalition (1974). In the battle for equal rights, the handful of existing organizations were joined by many news ones including the National Organization of Women (1966), the National Council of La Raza (1968), American Indian Movement (1968), the National Gay and Lesbian Task Force (1973), and the Asian American Legal Defense and Education Fund (1974).

Efforts to substantially change the status quo sparked the creation of groups to defend it. Corporations responded to the increased pressures from consumer groups and citizen lobbies by invigorating existing trade groups and creating new ones such as the Business Round Table (1972), which has about 150 member corporations including AT&T and IBM.

Other groups formed to resist social change. The American Family Association (1977), the Christian Voice (1978), and the Moral Majority (1979) were among the first of a host of conservative Christian groups founded to protect "traditional American values." Yet other new

Societal stress during the 1960s and 1970s, the increased importance of social issues, and changes in government policy, such as the legalization of abortion by the Supreme Court in Roe v. Wade *(1973), led to the rise of numerous interest group organizations such as pro-life and pro-choice groups. Here supporters on both sides of the question demonstrate before the Supreme Court. (AP Photo/Ron Edmonds)*

groups focused on specific issues. The anti-abortion National Right to Life Committee (1973), for one, was founded in the same year that the Supreme Court legalized abortion in *Roe v. Wade*. Similarly, the Federation for American Immigration Reform (1978) was formed following passage of laws like the Immigration Reform Act (1965) that increased the number of immigrants from Latin America, Asia, and other "nonwhite" regions and as the annual inflow of new immigrants nearly doubled from about 250,000 in 1960 to almost 500,000 in 1976.

Government Policy

Government action or inaction can also promote interest group formation. Two ways to see that are by examining changes in government spending and the scope of government activity.

Government Revenue and Spending

Markedly increased government spending and taxation spurs interest group growth. Annual federal spending rose especially fast between 1960 and 1990, growing more than 13 times over from $92 billion to $1.2 trillion. This spiral of spending also saw a rapid rise in the number of interest groups and in their activities designed to get favorable tax treatment or to obtain a slice of the growing federal budget pie. This is evident in Figure 7.3, which shows the number of **political action committees (PACs)**, since they were first required to register. PACs are organizations established by interest groups to lobby the government and to raise campaign funds and distribute them to candidates.

FIGURE 7.3 Growth in the Number of PACs

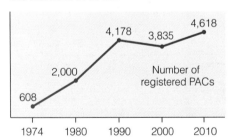

There were only 608 PACs in 1974, the first year they were required to register under the Federal Election Campaign Act of 1971. That number had soared to over 4,000 by 1990 but has been fairly stable since then.
Data source: Federal Election Commission.

Expanding Scope of Government Activity

A second key factor promoting the growth in the number of interest groups and the range of their concerns has been the widening scope of federal, state, and local government activities. As Chapter 1 details, the areas in which government is involved have expanded to the point where today government is involved in virtually all elements of society. A multitude of groups have formed to either promote government involvement in social services and other areas or in response to the government activity in those areas. The directory *Washington Representatives* provides some insight into the range of interests involved. The book's 450-page list of 13,000 groups with professional lobbyists runs the A-to-Z gamut from the American Association of Retired Persons (AARP) through the M&M/Mars Corporation to Zero Population Growth.

Globalization

Increasingly globalization is a third factor promoting the formation of interest groups. Although it has not yet had the impact that domestic factors such as societal stress and government policy have had on interest group formation, globalization is multiplying contacts among countries and otherwise changing the political landscape. National borders are less important than they once were, and a growing number of issues are *intermestic*, with a mixture of *inter*national and do*mestic* components. It might seem, for example, that U.S. arms sales abroad is a foreign policy issue. But arms sales are very much a domestic issue for the U.S. companies that make the weapons, for the workers and their unions at those companies, and for the towns and local businesses that depend on those companies and the workers. Additionally, global interdependence means that such concerns as economic prosperity, a healthy environment, and available and reasonably priced energy are global issues needing global cooperation to achieve solutions.

For these reasons and others, globalization is expanding the interest group universe as governments, companies, and other private groups increasingly lobby across borders. Because of its worldwide economic and political influence, the United States, more than any other country, is the scene of widespread foreign interest group activity. In 2008, there were 937 **registered foreign interest groups** operating in the United States under the Foreign Agents Registration Act (FARA) of 1938 and the Lobbying Disclosure Act (LDA) of 1995.

Foreign businesses, like Japan's Sony Corporation, and industry associations, like the Japanese Steel Information Center, make up a majority of the registrants. Most countries are also listed, and the array of foreign interests goes on to include Iraq's Kurdish regional government; Pakistan's People's Party; the city of St. Petersburg, Russia; King Abdullah University in Saudi Arabia; the Sudan Liberation Movement; Tibet's Dalai Lama; and the Province of Ontario, Canada. Among countries, Canada had the most (118) foreign interest groups operating in Washington in 2008, followed by Great Britain (86), Japan (41), France (26), Mexico (26), Germany (21), Taiwan (29), South Korea (22), China (19), and Saudi Arabia (17).

This roster of registered foreign interest groups is informative, but it has never been and is increasingly less than a complete accounting of all the foreign lobbying that occurs in the United States. *Foreign diplomats* stationed in the United States and *foreign leaders* when they meet with U.S. officials in the United States or abroad all press the

This General Motors sign outside a regional headquarters under construction in Shanghai, China, illustrates economic globalization. This globalization leads American interests to lobby foreign governments and foreign interests to lobby the U.S. government. (Imaginechina via AP Images)

Globalization has increased the number of transnational interest groups that address global issues and have chapters and members in many countries. Greenpeace is one such group. Here three key activists in its anti-whaling campaign are meeting in Yokohama, Japan. They are from left to right: Jun Hoshikawa, executive director of Greenpeace Japan; Pete Bouquet, British captain of the Greenpeace ship Esperanza (Hope) that tries to disrupt whaling at sea; and Karli Thomas of New Zealand, who heads Greenpeace's Ocean Campaign. (AP Photo/Koji Sasahara)

U.S. government for favorable trade terms, more foreign aid, or favorable policy in a wide range of other areas. As one former diplomat has put it, "After all, we lobbied on behalf of our country."[8]

Transnational interest groups are yet another type of lobby.[9] Such groups have affiliates or activity in more than one country and address issues that crosscut national boundaries. Greenpeace USA provides an illustration. It is an affiliate of Greenpeace International, headquartered in The Netherlands and with offices and affiliates in 41 countries. One reason for the proliferation of this type of interest group is that modern communications and travel allow much greater international contact. Second, the number and scope of transnational interest groups has expanded because of the growing realization that global warming and many other issues are global in nature. Therefore, energy policy and many other areas of the domestic policy of every country, especially powerful ones like the United States, have a global impact and are of global interest.

American subsidiaries of foreign-owned multinational corporations are also active in trying to shape U.S. policy. There are thousands of foreign companies that own companies incorporated in the United States and are therefore not subject to FARA registration requirements. Toyota of Japan, for one, owns Toyota of North America, and it in turn owns other subsidiaries such as Toyota Motor Engineering & Manufacturing North America. These firms reported spending more than $12 million in 2010 lobbying the U.S. government on such issues as labor law, environmental standards, and trade regulations.

Ethnic groups of Americans can also be counted as part of the foreign lobby presence. Many Americans have an attachment with the country of their immigrant heritage and think of themselves in such terms as "Italian Americans" or "Vietnamese Americans." This sense of identification with another culture, country, or region has fostered interest groups that try to influence U.S. foreign policy in ways favorable to their homeland and ancestral culture. Such groups often also have close ties to those abroad that they are trying to help. For example, Jewish Americans who support Israel are represented by such organizations as the American-Israel Public Affairs Committee, which declares itself to be "America's Pro-Israel Lobby." Another organization with a keen interest in the Middle East is the Arab American Institute. It lists one of its missions as representing "Arab Americans throughout the United States . . . [on] a variety of public policy issues that concern . . . U.S.–Arab relations." The Cuban American National Foundation, the TransAfrica Forum, the Irish National Caucus, the Polish American Congress, and many other organizations could be added to this list of ethnic interests groups.

WHO THE INTEREST GROUPS AND LOBBYISTS ARE

To begin our detailed analysis of interest groups in the American political process, we will address two questions. What are the categories of interest group? And who are the lobbyists that represent them?

Types of Interest Groups

The diversity of the domestic, foreign, and transnational interest groups that have been mentioned thus far is some indication of the multitude of interest groups and their almost limitless range of concerns. There is no universally accepted way to categorize interest groups, but by classifying them we can advance our knowledge of their origins and political role.

Individual- and Organizational-Membership Groups

One way to categorize organized interest groups is according to their membership base. **Individual-membership interest groups** are made up of people who choose to join as individuals by formally enrolling, by participating in a group's activities, or by contributing money to the group. The National Rifle Association, American Medical Association, AARP, and the Japanese American Citizens League are examples of this type of group. Many of these groups implicitly purport to represent particular demographic groups and try to influence the policy process on their behalf.

One important consideration about the interface between demographic groups and individual membership groups is the **free rider problem**. While a demographic group as a whole may benefit from the activities of a related individual-membership group, most people in the demographic group are not in the membership group. They therefore get a "free ride" by not joining or otherwise supporting the organized group. Americans are "joiners," with 82% of them belonging to at least one voluntary association, a level of membership exceeded by only 3 of the 43 societies surveyed (Iceland, Sweden, and the Netherlands).[10] But with so many possible groups to join, membership in any one is usually very limited. For example, less than 2% of all African Americans are members of the NAACP.

A related issue is the degree to which any individual-membership interest group can legitimately claim to represent the views of its associated demographic group.

AARP has 38 million members, but that is less than half of all people over age 50. Moreover, it is not clear how many people join AARP because of its political activity and how many join simply to get discounts at motels and other benefits that membership offers. Most importantly, the AARP does not submit its policy stands to its members for ratification. Therefore it is unclear how many of AARP members, much less senior citizens generally, support AARP policy preferences. One case where there was disagreement involved heath care legislation. In November 2009, the AARP endorsed the health care legislation pending in Congress even though a plurality (48%) of Americans aged 50 and over opposed it, with just 36% in favor and 16% unsure.[11]

Organizational-membership interest groups have established organizations and institutions as their members. Some of these groups are collectives of *multiple private organizations* such as American Bankers Association and its membership of thousands of U.S. banks. Other organizational-membership interest groups are made up of a *single private organization*. Corporations are the most numerous. Of all interest groups listed under the letter *G* section of *Washington Representatives*, over one third are individual businesses. They range from behemoths such as General Electric to more modest businesses such as the Gibson Guitar Corporation. George Washington University and other single institutions also were on the list.

Yet other organizational-membership interest groups are composed of *public organizations*. Every major federal agency has a congressional liaison staff that lobbies Congress on behalf of its agency and the policies it supports. Additionally, all states and many local governments lobby the federal government, and these efforts affect the flow of money from Washington to the state and local levels.[12] Looking again at the *Washington Representatives G* listing, it includes such diverse units as the State of Georgia; the Territory of Guam; Gary, Indiana; and Gila County, Arizona. Government units can also form associations such as the National Governors Association. Furthermore, as noted above, numerous foreign governments and subnational governments conduct lobby activities in the United States, including Ghana and the British territory of Gibraltar, under *G*.

Public Interest Groups and Self-Interest Groups

Many scholars differentiate between groups that promote their own narrow viewpoints and those that claim to be promoting the general welfare. **Self-interest groups** draw their membership from a limited range of society and organizations and promote specific benefits for themselves or their members. **Public interest groups** draw their membership from the general citizenry and support policies that they claim will benefit the country as a whole. Groups likely to be characterized as public interest groups or citizens lobbies are those involved in areas such as election reform, environmental protection, and consumer safety.

The distinction between public and private interest groups raises an important caution. Do not assume that a policy is good or in the country's interest just because it is backed by a public interest group. One reason is that there are public interest groups representing the entire spectrum of opinions. Such groups tend to be liberal, but there are conservative ones also. One example is the conservative Center for Security Policy. It advocates a high level of military preparedness, or "peace through strength," a phrase often used by President Ronald Reagan. Second, what public interest groups favor or oppose may differ from what the public wants. Like most environmental groups, the Friends of the Earth opposes nuclear power. As such, the organization opposed President Obama's proposal in 2010 to have the government give $55 billion in loan guarantees to encourage the construction of new nuclear reactors. The organization president charged that the reactors and nuclear waste disposal methods were dangerous and urged that, "The future lies in clean energy sources like wind and solar—not nuclear reactors."[13] Perhaps, but most Americans disagreed, with survey showing 52% favoring more government action to build new nuclear power plants, 46% opposed and 2% uncertain.[14]

A third reason not to assume a proposed policy is good simply because a public policy group is advocating it is that what is in the public interest is often not clear. For example, cattle and sheep ranchers in the Public Lands Council argue that grazing their animals on public lands helps keep down the price of meat paid by consumers. The Sierra Club argues that grazing damages vegetation and wildlife and endangers the ability of people to enjoy the natural beauty of the grasslands. It is important to investigate the facts for oneself, but assuming that Americans can have either lower meat prices or pristine prairies, which policy is in the public interest?

Groups by Issue

Interest groups can also be classified according to the types and range of issues they address. Given the huge economic impact of government taxes, expenditures, and regulations, money is a central focus of many groups—whether they are unions, businesses, taxpayer associations, senior citizens groups demanding medical care, or teacher-parent associations pressing to increase school funding. Additionally, there is a nearly endless list of issue types such as the environment and abortion rights that mirror the involvement of the government in nearly every aspect of society.

As for the range of issues that any given group addresses, there are **single-issue interest groups** that concentrate on one issue. Examples include National Right to Life Committee and the opposing National Abortion Rights League. There are also **multiple-issue interest groups** that focus on several issues. For example, the conservative group Concerned Women for America and the liberal group NOW both address a wide range of issues that affect women, even though the two organizations take opposite stands on many of those issues, such as stem cell research and same-sex marriages.

Ideological interest groups are a variety of multiple-issue interest groups that are based on a philosophical perspective rather than an issue orientation. From opposite ideological positions, the American Conservative Union (ACU) and the Americans for Democratic Action (ADA) epitomize this type of group.

The Lobbyists

By one estimate, there are some 25,000 individuals involved in lobbying the federal government alone.[15] To see who they are, we will first look at some of their characteristics, then take up the so-called revolving door.

Some Characteristics of Lobbyists

Of the 25,000 individuals engaged in some form of lobbying, about 10,000 are officers of corporations, trade groups, and other organizations. These people often interact with officials in various ways but are not technically lobbyists. Of the approximately 15,000 people who are full-time lobbyists, about 55% work directly for the organization they represent. The remaining 45% are employed by one of about 1,200 consulting groups or law firms that offer their lobbying services to multiple clients. These firms are often referred to collectively as "K Street," the street in Washington, D.C., where many of their offices are located.

In terms of revenue in 2009, the largest such firm was Patton Boggs, a law firm with lobby-related income of $40.7 million. Patton Boggs' marquee tie-in to official Washington has been through its chairman, Thomas Hale Boggs, Jr., who has been at the firm since the 1960s. He is the son of long-time and powerful Representative Thomas Hall Boggs, Sr. (D-LA, 1941–1972) and Representative Lindy Boggs (D-LA, 1973–1991), who won her husband's seat after his death in 1972. The lobbying part of the huge law firm has more than 100 associates working for one or another of a long and diverse list of over 300 clients that in 2009 included India, Microsoft Corporation, the city of Los Angeles, the University of Wisconsin, Goodwill Industries, the Federal Judges Association, the Chicksaw Nation, and the Major League Baseball Players Association.

About 60% of the professional lobbyists are at least 51 years old, and another 20% are between the ages of 41 and 50. An overwhelming 80% have been lobbying for more than 10 years. Almost all registered lobbyists have at least an undergraduate degree, and law degrees are very common. As for partisan identification, a 2007 survey of lobbyists found 43% reporting themselves as Democrats, 30% identifying as Republicans, 16% saying they were an independent, and 11% declining to answer.

Lobbyists and Diversity

The lobbyist field is male-dominated. For example, men make up two-thirds of the lobbyists at Patton Boggs. There are no statistics about minority lobbyists, but they are rare. The Washington Government Relations Group, an association of black professional lobbyists, has only 100 members and a database listing another 100 or so African American lobbyists. The Hispanic Lobbyists Association is even smaller, with only 60 members. These numbers do not account for all the black and Latino lobbyists, but even if there are triple these numbers, blacks would still be below 3% of all lobbyists and Latinos would be less than 1%.

> No woman headed a Washington, D.C. lobbying firm until 1981 when Anne Wexler, former assistant to the president for public liaison for Jimmy Carter, established what is now Wexler and Walker Public Policy Associates.
>
> AMERICAN DIVERSITY

The Revolving Door

Successful lobbying requires some combination of expertise in the political process, expertise in one or more policy areas, and a range of acquaintances among policy makers and their senior staff. This leads to a steady circular flow of former executive and legislative branch officials and staff members into lobbying and of lobbyists into official policy-making and government positions. This **revolving door** worries many observers.

One concern is that the revolving door gives interest groups too much power because it sometimes puts interest group representatives into government positions where they are policy makers or key staff members to policy makers in the interest group's area. The revolving door also favors interest groups that can afford to hire former officials and their aides who have exceptional access to the current officials with whom they once worked. A third worry is that government policy makers may do favors for an interest group in hopes of later obtaining a high-paying position with that group. Defenders of the revolving door argue that it only makes sense for interest groups to hire former congressional and executive branch personnel who have substantive expertise and who also know how the policy process works. Another argument in defense of the system is that the flow of people from industry, the professions, and other interest groups brings expertise into the government.

These worries came into sharp focus during the massive BP oil spill in the Gulf of Mexico in 2010. One contributor to the disaster according to many sources was the lack of adequate inspections and other oversight of offshore drilling by

This oil-soaked pelican being rescued off the coast of Louisiana in June 2010, is a small symbol of the devastation caused by that year's flood of oil into the Gulf of Mexico from a damaged oil platform. At least part of the blame was attributable to lax oversight by federal government inspectors, many of whom had worked earlier in the oil industry. (AP Photo/Charlie Riedel)

the Minerals Management Service (MMS) of the Department of Interior. Critics of the MMS attributed its failings in part to the revolving door between it and the energy industry, including BP. CBS News reported, for example, that two-thirds of the lobbyists representing BP's U.S. subsidiary, BP America, were former government officials.[16] The congressional connections included former Representative Jim Turner (D-TX). Providing an example on the administration side was Randall Luthi, who moved from his position as MMS director (2007–2009) to soon thereafter becoming the president of the National Oceans Industries Association (NOIA), a trade group promoting the welfare of BP and other offshore drilling interests. Indeed, Luthi replaced Thomas A. Fry, another former MMS director, at NOIA. Some individuals even moved back and forth. Sylvia Baca, for one, held several high-level positions in the Interior Department during the Clinton administration, then went to work as a top executive in for BP America, only to return in 2009 to the Interior Department as deputy assistant secretary for land and minerals management. Lower-level MMS employees also were part of the revolving door. Commenting on what President Obama called the "scandalously close relationship between oil companies and the agency that regulates them," the Interior Department's Acting Inspector General Mary Kendall expressed "particular concern" about MMS inspectors and "the ease with which they move between industry and government."[17]

Such examples are not new, and worries about the revolving door led to a series of reforms beginning in the 1970s. These have established a one-year or in some cases two-year period during which former congressional and executive officials and their top staff are barred from lobbying or have substantial restrictions. Adding to the reforms, President Obama began his administration by signing an executive order significantly increasing the limits on anyone in the administration working on a policy issue on which they had once lobbied or from lobbying the administration once they leave it in the future.

Such restrictions have only been partly effective. President Obama soon discovered that he would have to pass up many individuals he wanted to appoint if he adhered to his own campaign promise to bar former lobbyists from his administration. So he eased his stance, making such appointments as Eric H. Holder, Jr. to be the first black attorney general, even though he was a lobbyist with the powerful firm of Covington and Burlington.

Another problem with revolving door restrictions is the uncertain line between who is and who is not a lobbyist. Certainly, registered lobbyists are just that. But there are many others who are officials of trade groups or hold top positions in other interest groups who are not technically lobbyists and therefore beyond the rules. This allowed, for example, Randall Luthi to go from being director of the

MMS to president of NOIA. He and other top political veterans are in demand by interest groups because, one insider explains, "These are power brokers who make a difference. They are rainmakers. They get their phone calls returned." And organizations are willing to pay."[18]

HOW INTEREST GROUPS OPERATE

Lobbying is big business. In 2009 alone, lobbyists reported spending over $3.2 billion to influence policy, and that sum is just a part of the unknown total. Lobbying is also a growth industry. Both the money lobbyists spent and the number of lobbyists increased substantially between 1998 and 2009, as Figure 7.4 shows. Most interest groups are multitasking organizations. They pursue their policy goals through a number of techniques, often employing several simultaneously. These approaches include direct lobbying, indirect lobbying, and influencing the selection of policy makers. In addition to targeting Congress and state and local legislative bodies, these techniques seek to influence the executive and judicial branches at all levels of government.

FIGURE 7.4 Increases in Number of Lobbyists and Their Spending

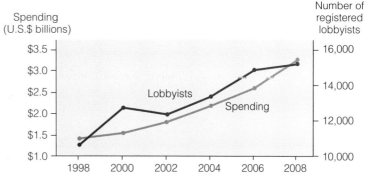

Between 1998 and 2009, the number of lobbyists registered with the federal government grew 42% from 10,693 to 15,138, and their spending grew 127% from $1.43 billion to $3.24 billion.
Data source: Center for Responsive Politics.

Direct Lobbying

Direct lobbying involves individual or small group interactions between interest group representatives and policy makers, and is aimed at gaining the support of the policy makers. Also called "inside lobbying," this approach takes a number of forms.

Testifying before Congress and Executive Agencies
Nearly all interest groups try to influence policy by presenting arguments and evidence to policy makers during formal hearings and other procedures. In Congress, such activity focuses on committees, which usually have considerable influence over bills in their subject area. For instance, hearings in 2009 held by the House Committee on Natural Resources on offshore drilling for oil and gas, drew testimony from the representatives of the following interest groups:

- Gas and oil companies: Shell Oil, BP America, Devon Energy Corporation, ExxonMobil, and Chevron.
- Other business groups: the U.S. Chamber of Commerce, the Outer Banks Visitors Bureau (North Carolina), the St. Petersburg/Clearwater (Florida) Area Convention & Visitors Bureau, and the Pacific Coast Federation of Fisherman's Association.
- Government organizations: the Coastal States Organization and the state governments of California, Louisiana, Maine, and Virginia.
- Environmental groups: Oceana, Ocean Conservancy, Stop Oil Seeps California, and the Center for Coastal Conservation.

Interest groups also submit testimony and other evidence to administrative units. Because the weight and intensity of public opinion matters, agencies usually favor the side that submits the greatest number of comments on controversial matters.[19] When, for example, the Federal Elections Commission recently considered regulating contributions to **tax-exempt groups (TAGs)** that promote their views on policy, they mounted a determined campaign of resistance. Representatives of dozens of these groups spoke at hearings before the FEC, and hundreds of others filed written objections to any regulation (see Chapter 10). Moreover, at the behest of these groups, supporters fired off a barrage of 97,000 messages to the FEC. Faced with a maelstrom of criticism, the FEC deferred its decision.

Meeting Formally with Individual Policy Makers

It is not uncommon for lobbyists to have one-on-one meetings with legislators and agency officials in their offices. In addition to having a chance to present evidence and make their substantive arguments, the private setting permits lobbyists to discuss the political aspects of proposals and to solicit a policy maker's support. When lobbying Congress, interest group representatives spend more of their time on undecided legislators than on supporters, with opponents getting the lowest priority.[20] Lobbyists also spend considerable time gathering information about how a proposal is being received in Congress, the White House, and executive agencies and by the media and public opinion. With this information, lobbyists can help supportive policy makers plan their strategy for advancing a proposal.

Meeting Informally with Individual Policy Makers

One survey of lobbyists found that 90% of them reported that part of their approach is having informal contacts with policy makers in social settings— whether on the golf course, in a Capitol Hill restaurant, or at dinner party.[21] Interest group representatives are usually wise enough not to try a hard sell in such settings. Instead, they use the opportunity to establish a good rapport with policy makers and to practice a more subtle soft sell.

Taking golf as an example, one long-time lobbyist commented, "If you've got a [member of Congress or congressional] staffer in your cart and you're talking for four hours, it's a great way to break the ice. There's only a few places you have that much time. You find out about them, where they went to school, where they live." Another lobbyist pointed out, "You don't get much business done at all on the course." In fact, "It's poor form when people try to start actually lobbying when you're trying to play golf." Instead the "getting-to-know-you" time on the course is valuable because, "It's about getting someone to take your call" in the future.[22]

The advantages of having a good golf swing has led several women's groups to sponsor training courses for women lobbyists to learn golf or sharpen their game. At one such event entitled "In the Swing" and organized by the Women's Networking Forum, a veteran lobbyist explained, "I know a lot of members of Congress because I play golf with them." Another woman lobbyist added that golf in Washington, D.C., is "a professional tool—a very powerful professional tool around town."[23]

Filing Amicus Curiae Briefs

The ability of the courts to create policy through their interpretations of the federal and state constitutions and legislation makes the judiciary a target of lobbying. Lobbyists cannot directly contact judges, but interest groups do file **amicus curiae briefs**.[24] These "friend of the court" briefs are legal arguments submitted by individuals, groups, or organizations that are not a party to a case but do have an important interest in it. Constitutional challenges are particularly likely to draw amicus curiae briefs, sometimes in large number.[25] For instance, interest groups filed a record-setting 107 amicus curiae briefs supporting one side or the other in the *Grutter v. Bollinger* (2003) and *Gratz v. Bollinger* (2003) affirmative action cases involving the University of Michigan, detailed in Chapter 5. Globalization has even led foreign governments to file amicus curiae briefs. A recent example is the brief filed by Mexico supporting the challenge in federal court to Arizona's 2010 law allowing police to do citizenship checks.

Engaging in Corruption

Occasionally interest groups and policy makers engage in illegal activities. Of recent disclosures, some of the most spectacular came to light as a result of the immense 2010 oil spill in the Gulf of Mexico. Subsequent investigations brought out evidence that showed that the Department of the Interior's Minerals Management Service (MMS), which was tasked in part with inspecting offshore drilling operations, had been, in President Obama's words, "plagued by corruption for years."[26]

The immediate revelations did not directly relate to the oil spill, but they did show a troubled bureaucratic unit. According to the *Washington Post*, a 2008 report by the Department of the Interior's inspector general (IG) found that MSS employees had "accepted gifts [from oil and gas companies], steered contracts to favored clients and engaged in drug use and illicit sex with employees of the energy firms." This had occurred, the IG's report charged, "with prodigious frequency."[27]

An even wider recent scandal sent lobbyist Jack Abramoff to prison for six years after guilty pleas or convictions in three different federal courts in 2006 and 2008. Among other felonies, Abramoff gave expensive gifts to legislators, congressional staff members, and executive branch officials and took them on lavish golfing trips and other junkets in exchange for political favors such as changing language in legislation to Abramoff's liking. The investigation also led to the convictions of 12 other lobbyists and public officials, including Representative Bob Ney (R-OH), on such charges as taking bribes and obstructing justice.

Unfortunately, corruption is not new. In fact, it was once more prevalent than it is now, and history is rife with examples of interest group activity, including lavish and often bawdy entertainment, presents, and outright payments to legislators and other political figures. One notorious example involved the effort of Samuel Colt in the 1850s to persuade Congress to extend his patent on the Colt revolver. To that end, he plied legislators with the proverbial "wine, women, and song" and also gave pistols to members of Congress and their families including, according to a congressional report, one legislator's "little son, only eleven or twelve years of age." The report also noted that Colt's main lobbyist maintained that the best way to get a legislators' support was to follow a liquor-dispensing strategy:

> To reach the heart or get the vote,
> The surest way is down the throat.[28]

Indirect Lobbying

In addition to direct lobbying, most interest groups employ **indirect lobbying** (also known as "outside lobbying" or "grassroots lobbying") techniques. This approach includes utilizing intermediary individuals, groups, and organizations to influence policy makers. Techniques include mobilizing members and supporters, shaping public opinion, and promoting public protests. Although indirect lobbying is less common than direct lobbying, there is a rise in interest group efforts to generate support at the **grassroots**, a group's general membership and/or the citizenry at large.[29]

Mobilizing Members and Supporters

Many powerful interest groups have a large base of volunteer members. Some other interest groups, such as businesses, have a built-in core of potential supporters, including employees, stockholders, vendors, and others whose welfare is closely tied to the group.[30] Whatever the source of a group's support, the Web and e-mail have vastly improved communications, making it increasingly easy for interest groups to communicate information to their base and to mobilize it to bring pressure on policy makers. One common informational technique is to compile legislative "scorecards." These rate legislators according to how well their votes parallel a group's policy positions. Testifying to the impact of scorecards, a former House Democratic leader commented that the awareness of legislators that they will be scored is "significant, particularly if there's going to be a close vote. That's part of the lobbying effort, part of putting pressure on members."[31]

Modern communications also make it easy for a group's supporters to contact policy makers. One study of mail received by members of Congress indicated that it had tripled over a recent two-decade period.[32] E-mail traffic has grown even faster. Between 1999 and 2002, inbound messages increased 186% for House members and 69% for senators. Combined, the two chambers received 117 million e-mail messages in 2001, and there is no reason to think that the volume has not risen exponentially since then. This "flood of e-mail," the study concludes, has partly been "fueled by . . . the grassroots activities of lobbyists and e-businesses" that are electronically motivating their supporters to "make their voices heard in Washington."[33]

As part of the effort to utilize supporters, interest groups encourage them to contact their own House and Senate members because elected officials are especially sensitive to the views of their constituents. Groups also take special care to mobilize anyone who has a close connection with a legislator.[34] If the general membership of a group is its grassroots, those members with key contacts are its "grass tops."[35] They include community leaders; family, friends, and business associates of policy makers; key campaign contributors, workers, and other political supporters; and others with access to and influence with a policy maker.

Shaping Public Opinion

Interest groups also spend considerable effort and money appealing to the general public.[36] This strategy has two benefits. First, it may increase core membership. Second, building public opinion support for a group's cause can indirectly influence policy makers.

To shape public opinion, interest groups use several approaches. Paid advertising is one. Less expensive and therefore more common is trying to get favorable stories in the media. Interest group representatives send out press releases and reports, talk to individual reporters, try to get op-ed opinion pieces published in newspapers, and work to have themselves or supporters appear as guest commentators on television and radio programs. The value of such efforts was substantiated by a study that found that about 15% of television news stories that cited a source had used one or more interest groups for background and commentary.[37] Interest groups can also sometimes successfully influence policy by endorsing or opposing measures being decided directly by voters duing referendums.[38]

Perhaps the first think tank was created in 1831 when the Duke of Wellington established the Institute for Defence and Security Studies (now the Royal United Services Institute) in London.

Presenting information and analysis by experts is another way of influencing opinions. This factor has led to a "politicization of expertise" by the creation of a large number of research and analysis centers commonly called "think tanks."[39] These organizations employ analysts with impressive credentials and experience who gather and evaluate information and disseminate it by writing reports, articles, editorials, and press releases that are sent to the media and posted on each center's Website. Think tank representatives also appear on radio and television, testify at congressional hearings, and otherwise present their views to policy makers.[40] One veteran member of Congress comments that "the role of think tanks in this town [Washington, D.C.] is hugely important. They really are an incubator of ideas for policy."[41]

It is important to understand, though, that many think tanks are not neutral. Instead, many have an ideological orientation and employ analysts with the same point of view. The Economic Policy Institute provides liberal economic analysis, for instance, while the American Enterprise Institute has a conservative orientation. Similarly, the liberal Center for Defense Information and the conservative Center for Strategic and International Studies (CSIS) provide differing views on national security. As one measure of the impact of these think tanks, the CSIS annually gets about 700,000 visits to its Website and is cited in more than 1,000 newspapers stories.[42]

Think tanks also serve as a source of policy makers. Among President Obama's initial top appointments, the Brooking Institution provided Budget Director Peter Orszag and U.N. Ambassador Susan Rice. National Security Advisor James Jones came from the internationalist-oriented Atlantic Council; and the liberal Center for American Progress was the source of Melody Barnes, director of the White House Domestic Policy Council.

Taking Direct Action

Taking to the streets in protest and other direct political activity are yet other ways interest groups pursue their goals. Sometimes such activity is spontaneous, but more often one or more organized interest groups is orchestrating the event. Perhaps the largest protest gathering in U.S. history occurred in 2004 when between

800,000 and 1.2 million women and supportive males converged on Washington, D.C., to protest such Bush administration policies as its anti-abortion stance. Sponsored by an alliance of groups such the Feminist Majority, the Black Women's Health Imperative, and the National Latina Institute for Reproductive Health, the "March for Women's Lives" reinforced the commitment of those who attended and drew the support from many political leaders. "Know your power and use it," House Minority Leader Nancy Pelosi (D-CA) exhorted the masses.[43]

Political protest is not uncommon, and it can be effective. One reason is that it attracts attention by the press to a group and its cause.[44] For example, the civil rights movement received a boost from dramatic images such as blacks being arrested for quietly sitting-in at lunch counters that would not serve them and peaceful protestors in Birmingham, Alabama, led by Martin Luther King being attacked in 1963 by police using clubs, dogs, and fire hoses. Writing from his cell, King explained in his famous "Letter from the Birmingham Jail," "nonviolent direct action seeks to create such a crisis and foster such a tension that a community which has constantly refused to negotiate is forced to confront the issue. It seeks to dramatize the issue that it can no longer be ignored."

Influencing the Selection of Policy Makers

Interest groups not only use direct and indirect approaches to attempt to influence policy makers, they also try to have an impact on who the policy makers are. Groups pursue these ends by promoting the nomination and election of sympathetic candidates for office. Interest groups also lobby to secure the appointment of like-minded individuals to administrative and judicial posts. Such activity also can be negative, as when interest groups work to defeat the election or appointment of an unsympathetic official.

Influencing Elections

A key interest group activity is trying to influence who will serve as president and vice president, who will hold the 535 seats in Congress, and who will be among the tens of thousands of elected state and local officials. Interest groups and their members endorse candidates, work on their campaigns, and get out the vote on their behalf.

Interest groups also contribute money to candidates. This funding flow from interest groups to candidates is huge, it moves through multiple channels, and to a degree it is well disguised to avoid public scrutiny and regulation. Political action committees (PACs) established by various interest groups to raise campaign funds and distribute them to candidates are one important source of campaign funds.

FIGURE 7.5 PAC Donations to Federal Candidates

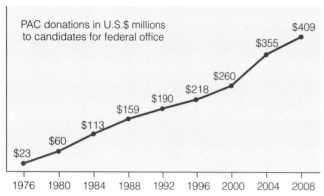

The donations given by political action committees to candidates for federal office during each two-year election cycle (2007 and 2008 = the 2008 cycle) have grown rapidly. *Data sources:* Center for Responsive Politics for 2004 and 2008; Harold W. Stanley and Richard G. Niemi, *Vital Statistics on America Politics 2003–2004* (Washington, DC: CQ Press, 2004) for earlier years.

More than 4,000 PACs are registered with the federal government alone, and many others work at the state and local levels. The number of PACs has risen substantially, as Figure 7.3 on page 242 indicates. Another measure of the growth of PACs, their increasing campaign donations for federal candidates, is detailed in Figure 7.5.

Interest groups additionally spend huge sums waging independent campaigns for or against candidates. To escape campaign finance limits, interest groups give yet more funding to tax-exempt groups (TAGs). These groups are independent of any candidate or party and raise and spend money to advocate policy and even to praise or criticize specific candidates. They are tax exempt as nonprofit groups under sections 501, 503, and 527 of the Internal Revenue.[45] In recent years, TAGs have proliferated because donations to them are not restricted as are donations to candidates and parties. Donation and expenditure reporting requirements are also much less detailed for TAGs. As a result, they took in enough money to spend $488 million in 2007–2008 promoting their points of view. The liberal organization America Votes is an example of a TAG, and it was one of the largest in terms of expenditures ($17 million) during the 2008 election cycle. Headquartered in Washington, D.C., America Votes describes itself as "a coalition of over 40 of the most powerful national groups," such as the AFL-CIO, the Sierra Club, and the NAACP, that support a "broad economic and social justice agenda."

Chapter 10 on elections will take up TAGs in detail, but for now we can note two key concerns about them. One is that the flow of money to these groups has undermined attempts to limit the impact of money on politics. Second, the independence of many TAGs is dubious. Although America Votes is technically nonpartisan, its president is former Representative Martin Frost (D-TX, 1979–2005) and its executive director is Gregory Speed, a former director of communications for the Democratic Congressional Campaign Committee.

Influencing Appointments

Interest groups regularly intervene in the appointment processes by supporting or opposing administrative and judicial appointments. For example, in 2001 groups favoring the commercial utilization of public lands promoted the nomination of one of their own representatives, William G. Myers III, to become solicitor general of the Department of the Interior. Environmental groups warned against him. Three years later, as discussed in this chapter's opening You Decide box, the same forces lined up in favor of or against his appointment to the federal bench. Critics were especially active, with letters of opposition coming from more than 90 groups concerned with civil rights, disability rights, senior citizens, women's rights, human rights, Native Americans, and the environment.

Maneuvering to influence who is on the bench begins even before there is a vacancy on the bench, with groups sometimes basing their electoral decisions on what type of judges presidential candidates are apt to appoint or how U.S. Senate candidates are likely to vote on nominees during the confirmation process. For example, abortion and the probability that the new president would make appointments to the Supreme Court was a key factor in the decision of the National Organization of Women (NOW) to support Barack Obama in 2008. As NOW official Kim Grady put it, "Obama has said 'yes' . . . while John McCain has consistently said 'no' . . . to appointing Supreme Court judges who will uphold women's rights."[46] Grady's logic proved correct, as Obama's nominations to the high court of Sonia Sotomayor in 2009 and Elena Kagan in 2010 showed. And from the opposite perspective, the Republicans' 2010 "Pledge to America" asked for voter support to combat an "overreaching judiciary," whose decisions were "scorning" Americans' "deepest beliefs."

Once a vacancy occurs, groups often try to persuade a president to nominate specific individuals who have views compatible with those of the group. Groups will also seek to undermine potential candidates with whom they disagree. Once a nomination is made, activity intensifies, with groups lining up to support or oppose the nominee. After President Bush nominated Samuel Alito for the Supreme Court, the National Organization for Women, Feminist Majority Foundation, and National Congress of Black Women launched a joint "Enraged and Engaged: Women's Campaign Against Alito" that, among other things, encouraged women across the country to write to their senators and urge them to reject the nomination. Opponents as well as supporting groups also line up to testify against and for nominees at the Senate confirmation hearings.[47] Interest group activity in the selection process is not new, but it has grown. As one scholar explains, "The increased role the judiciary now plays in national policy making has encouraged interest groups to increasingly assert their own distinct (and often competing) interests in the nominee selection process."[48]

While much of the attention to the appointment of judges focuses on the Supreme Court, the lower courts have an important policy role, and interest groups often try to influence appointments at that level.[49] Moreover, interest groups have more impact on lower court appointments. One study of the various factors that determine how quickly the Senate acts on lower court nominations and the likelihood it will confirm them concluded, "Interest group opposition exerts the greatest impact on both confirmation timing and outcomes."[50]

Participating in the Policy-Making Process

In addition to directly and indirectly lobbying the government and trying to influence who policy makers are, interest groups also exert influence by getting involved in policy making as such.

Participating in the Legislative Process

Constitutionally, only members of Congress can propose specific legislation, but in fact interest groups routinely suggest language for pending legislation and sometimes even work closely with friendly legislators to draft entire bills. One common tactic is for a lobbyist to persuade a legislator to slip a "rider," a tangential clause, into a bill. One of the countless times this has occurred is when lobbyist Jim J. Tozzi drafted a two-sentence rider and reportedly got Representative Jo Ann Emerson (R-MO) to insert it virtually unnoticed into a 712-page appropriations bill. "We sandwiched [the rider] in between [funding for] Jerry Ford's library and something else," Tozzi boasted. What the rider did was to give businesses and others the ability to delay and possibly block regulations proposed by a federal agency by challenging any scientific evidence used by the agency to justify its proposal. This allowed, for example, the American Chemistry Council to object to research used by the U.S. Consumer Product Safety Commission to justify its proposed ban on using wood treated with arsenic in playground equipment. Asked later by a reporter about the ethics of such tactics, Tozzi replied, "Is it something that I would do again . . . ? Yes, you bet your ass I would. I would not even think about it, okay? Sometimes you get the monkey, and sometimes the monkey gets you."[51]

In a similar way, lobbyists often persuade legislators to "monkey around" with legislation by attaching so-called earmark or pork-barrel provisions. These provide funding to state and municipal governments, to schools, or to civic groups, all of which are important elements in the universe of organizational interest groups.

During fiscal year (FY) 2010, for instance, Congress enacted legislation containing about 9,500 earmarks that cost approximately $15.9 billion. Universities and other institutions of higher education are among the biggest recipients. They received $2.3 billion in 2008 through 2,306 earmarks. The largest single beneficiary was the University of Alabama, which received $40.6 million, a good return compared to the $360,000 it spent lobbying that year.

Earmarks are so lucrative that some lobbyists specialize in them. "A lobbyist or a consultant like myself comes in handy because I can, as I like to say, show [clients] where to go fishing," observes one such lobbyist. Most government and civic groups seeking earmark funds cannot make campaign donations, but the employees of lobbyist firms that specialize in obtaining the money from Congress regularly make substantial contributions. It is a practice that one critic calls "a total sweetheart deal," in which legislators get campaign contributions from lobbyists and votes from home at election time, lobbyists get substantial fees to represent the special interests, and special interest groups get their pork-fed projects."[52]

Participating in the Administrative Process

Interest group representatives also sometimes participate in the policy-making process by helping help agencies draft bills and regulations. This input comes through the testimony and material that groups submit during hearings, during meetings with administrative policy makers, or by securing seats on the approximately 1,000 **federal advisory committees (FACs)**. These panels, which are meant to increase outside input into the decisions of agencies, serve in part to institutionalize interest group representation in the administrative process.[53] The membership of many FACS includes competing interest groups, public officials, and citizens.[54] Other FACs are less balanced. In 2009 a representative of the America Cane Sugar Refiners' Association was the head of the Department of Agriculture's Advisory Committee for Trade in Sweeteners, and he and officials from sugar producers and refiners held most of the FAC's seats. This dominance is one reason for the U.S. restrictive quota and high tariff on sugar imports, as shown in Figure 7.6, "Protecting Domestic Sugar Producers." The result is a sweet deal for American sugar producers, leaving the 2009 price of U.S. sugar more than 54% higher than the world price. However, the protection is bitter for American consumers, annually costing them an extra $2 billion for sugar and for candy, jam, soda, and other products containing sugar.

FIGURE 7.6 **Protecting Domestic Sugar Producers**

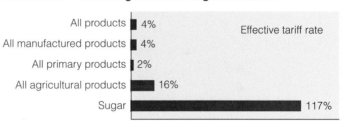

American sugar producers and processors are a powerful interest group that has been effective in keeping a high protective tariff in place. This leaves U.S. sugar above the world market price, giving the sugar industry billions of dollars in added revenue at the expense of American consumers.
Data source: World Development Indicators 09 (Washington, DC: World Bank, 2009); USDA; USTR.

Participating in the Judicial Process

Sometimes interest groups participate directly in the judicial process by filing lawsuits. For example, The Mexican American Legal and Education Defense Fund (MALDEF) filed *Morales v. Georgia Secretary of State Karen Handel* (2008), charging that Georgia was using a database of residents to qualify voters that

Interest groups sometimes pursue their goals through litigation. After an all-white school near the Topeka, Kansas, home of Linda Brown refused to admit the third grader, her parents, backed by the NAACP, filed what became perhaps the most famous of all Supreme Court cases, Brown v. Board of Education *(1954). (AP Photo)*

was inaccurate and incorrectly identifying some Latinos and others as noncitizens and therefore ineligible to vote. The U.S. District and the Circuit Court of Appeals agreed with the MALDEF, thereby protecting the right to vote for many Georgians.

More commonly, interest groups support other plaintiffs and defendants in test cases, legal actions backed by one or more groups to challenge the constitutionality of a law or regulation. For example, *Brown v. Board of Education* (1954), was a test case brought by the NAACP. It chose the plight of a black third-grader Linda Brown in Topeka, Kansas, to challenge racially segregated schools because the facts were unambiguous. Even though there was an all-white school only a few blocks from her home, the child had to walk one mile, partly through a railroad switchyard, to get to her all-black grade school. Additionally, Linda's father had tried to enroll her in the closer white school, but the principal there had refused to admit her. With such a "clean" case, NAACP special council, and later Supreme Court Justice, Thurgood Marshall was able as lead counsel for the Browns to persuade the Court to declare segregated schools to be unconstitutional. This type of interest group legal activity is so common that one scholar concludes, "The majority of important constitutional cases decided by the Supreme Court" are brought to it by "organized interests in the form of test cases."[55] Additionally, as noted earlier, interest groups regularly express their view to the courts by filing amicus curiae briefs.

DIFFERENCES IN INTEREST GROUP INFLUENCE

Clearly there is a huge number of interest groups trying to influence the political process in the United States, and they spend vast amounts of energy and money in that effort. What is less certain is how much influence interest groups actually have. Experts disagree, as is evident in Figure 7.7. It shows an almost even split between the studies that have found significant interest group influence and those that found little or no influence.

One reason for the lack of consensus among scholars about the influence of interest groups is that it is difficult, perhaps impossible, to ascertain and quantify all measures of influence. As one scholar has put it, "Influence is intangible, like faith or patriotism, so it's not easily measurable from one person or group to another."[56] It is clear, for instance, that numerous Native American and environmental groups testified against the judicial nomination of William Myers and otherwise lobbied against him, as

FIGURE 7.7 Analyses of Interest Group Influence

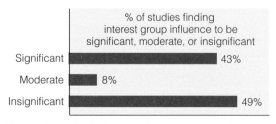

% of studies finding interest group influence to be significant, moderate, or insignificant

Significant	43%
Moderate	8%
Insignificant	49%

Research on the influence of interest groups is inconclusive. One review of 47 such analyses indicated that 43% found significant influence, 49% found little or no influence on policy, and 9% found moderate influence by interest groups.

Data source: Frank R. Baumgartner and Beth L. Leech, *Basic Interests: The Importance of Groups in Politics and in Political Science* (Princeton, NJ: Princeton University Press, 1998).

related in this chapter's opening You Decide box. It is also clear that enough sena-tors opposed Myers to block his nomination. It is unclear, though, whether the pressure from these groups was the reason that enough senators opposed Myers to block his confirmation. Interest group influence was present only if at least some senators who opposed Myers did so because they were persuaded by the interest groups and would have otherwise supported him. On the other hand, if there were no interest group influence, they were only bit players. The senators would have opposed Myers anyway, perhaps even for reasons other than those that motivated the interest groups.

Another reason that scholars differ on interest group influence is that it var-ies. The obvious question that follows is: Varies according to what? The answer involves the strengths of the groups themselves and the nature of the issue being decided, as the next section discusses.

Influence and Group Strength

Interest group strength varies widely. Some groups like the American Associa-tion of Retired People (AARP), the NAACP, the AFL-CIO, and the National Fed-eration of Independent Business (NFIB) wield considerable political clout. The American Beekeeping Federation, the American Coalition of Filipino Veterans, and many other such groups have much more modest influence. Group strength is determined by numerous factors.

Size

Groups with many members like the AARP carry political weight because of the voting power of those members. Additionally, an organized group's strength is enhanced by the size of its associated demographic group. Even though most members of the societal group may not be members of the organized interest group, politicians are aware that the organized group may influence the larger group. In the case of the AARP, politicians know that 32% of all eligible voters are over age 50 and that adults in that age bracket are more than twice as likely to vote as adults under age 30. It should be carefully noted that size alone does not count if there is no effective organized effort to mobilize the membership. For example, cable television consumers are a vast group with identifiable interests. Yet they are more a potential than an actual interest group because they lack an effective advo-cacy organization.

Cohesion and Intensity

Two other factors that help determine the power of an interest group are how cohesive its members are and how intensely active they are. Effective groups such as NOW, the Christian Coalition, the NAACP, and the National Rifle Association (NRA) have members who identify strongly with the group's goals, are likely to be politically active, and are apt to vote in line with the policy positions and candidate endorsements of the group.[57] The intensity with which members of the NRA oppose gun control and convey their views to policy makers helps explain why the group was so effective blocking gun-control measures during the period from the 1960s through 2004 when a majority of Americans, sometimes approaching 80%, favored greater gun control. Now that pro-gun and anti-gun public sentiment is more evenly split, the gun lobby has made progress relaxing former limits, exempting gun manufacturers from liability, and otherwise changing policy to its liking.

Wealth

Money counts in determining group strength. Groups with large treasuries can invest in major public relations campaigns, hire professional lobbyists, and donate heavily to many campaigns. A study of interest group public relations campaigns targeted at Washington, D.C., media outlets, for example, found that during one year alone, 670 groups sponsored more than 5,000 print and television ads at a cost of more than $100 million. The side that spent the most money promoting its view prevailed on 83% of legislative issues reviewed. This would seem to indicate that the side with the most money has an advantage, but other interpretations are possible. The data could also mean that other factors often determined which side would prevail and that one side, knowing it would lose anyway, chose to conserve its money by not engaging in a media battle.

 Of the $3.3 billion in reported lobbying expenditures in 2008, only $48.8 million (2%) was spent by groups advocating for the rights of women, minorities, and others.

Effective Leadership

Like armies, interest groups have a greater chance of mobilizing and then winning victories if they have leaders who are charismatic, able administrators, and good political tacticians. It would be impossible to understand the founding, growth, and successes of the National Farm Workers Union (since 1973, United Farm Workers of America) without accounting for the pivotal role played by its first leader, Cesar E. Chavez. A third-generation Mexican American, he organized farmworkers and became nationally known in the mid-1960s when he led a five-year-long strike against grape growers and organized a national grape boycott that persuaded many Americans not to buy table grapes. In addition to empowering the union, Chavez's efforts raised national awareness of the often-deplorable conditions of farmworkers and served to increase the political awareness of Mexican Americans, a contribution for which he posthumously received a Presidential Medal of Freedom in 1994.

Well-Connected and Knowledgeable Representation

An additional element in interest group success is being represented by professional lobbyists who know how policy making works and who are well connected. As noted, having these traits is why many former legislators, congressional staff members, and agency administrators are among the ranks of Washington's top lobbyists.

Wide Distribution and/or Strategic Location

Political geography is important to group strength. Groups with a large membership that is widely distributed geographically have an advantage because their members are the constituents of many legislators. Teachers are an example. The National Education Association has 2.7 million members, living in every state and more than 13,000 communities; the America Federation of Teachers, has 1.3 million members in 43 states and more than 3,000 localities.

This distributional factor also means that groups gain strength if their membership becomes more widely distributed. One reason that Latinos are receiving increased attention from political leaders is that an increasing number of states are gaining significant Latino populations as that group expands geographically from its traditional base in a few states on the Eastern Seaboard, in the Southwest, and in the West to states in other regions. Hispanics in Illinois, for instance, grew from 3.4% of the state's population in 1970, to 7.9% in 1990, to 15.2% in 2008.

Strategic location is another geographical asset. Groups that are important in the district or state of one of Congress's leaders gain influence from that strategic location. Asian Americans make up only 5% of the national population, but they constitute almost a third of the population of California's 8th congressional district represented by former Speaker of the House Nancy Pelosi.

Similarly, being strategically located with regard to presidential elections enhances a group's influence. Cuban Americans are about 5% of Florida's population. This makes them an important voting bloc in a state that has 27 Electoral College votes—the fourth largest total in the country—and that is considered a swing state that can go either party. One impact of the strategic position of the traditionally anti-Fidel Castro Cuban American community in Florida has been that presidential candidates of both parties, including Barack Obama and John McCain in 2008, have pledged to generally maintain the economic embargo against Cuba despite the fact that such sanctions were long ago lifted from China and Vietnam, which also have communist governments and poor human-rights records. As one

One source of influence for Latinos is that they are a significant part of the population in many parts of the country. In this photo Diana Rios holds up a sign in Chicago urging President Obama to honor his campaign promise to pursue immigration reform. Rios was participating in a nationwide series of demonstrations on May 1, 2010. (AP Photo/Nam Y. Huh)

scholar notes, "U.S. Cuba policy has not been a foreign policy. It's been a domestic policy, based on the Cuban vote in Florida."[58]

Alliances

Winning any contest is always easier with powerful allies, so yet another factor in interest group strength is based on which other political actors can be counted on as allies. More than 75% of interest groups report that they sometimes form alliances with others in what has been called the "dominant lobbying technique among Washington representatives."[59]

Some alliances are short-term. Called **issue networks**, they are temporary coalitions that form around a specific issue or piece of legislation and are composed of interest groups, elected and appointed government officials, and others such as academic policy experts who share an interest in a particular issue area and who interact to shape policy in that area. Often issue networks are on both sides of a major political debate. As we saw in this chapter's opening You Decide box, President Bush's nomination of William G. Myers III for a seat on the Ninth Circuit Court of Appeals prompted the formation of a temporary alliance to oppose it that included Native American groups, environmentalist groups, civil libertarian groups, and others.

Other interest group alliances are relatively permanent. For example, the aforementioned Public Lands Council is a coalition of groups such as the National Cattlemen's Beef Association, the American Farm Bureau Federation, American Sheep Industries, and the National Grasslands Association, all of which favor the use of public lands for grazing and other agricultural pursuits. Another ongoing coalition, and one featured in this chapter's opening You Decide box, is the Leadership Conference on Civil Rights (LCCR) with its more than 180 member groups. Such coalitions have become increasingly common because, as the LCCR's executive director explains, "Coalition politics is the politics of the twenty-first century. No organization has sufficient strength unto itself to move the broad social agenda."[60]

Iron triangles are one type of permanent alliance. An iron triangle is a political alliance among (1) interest groups, (2) bureaucrats, and (3) members of Congress who share a perspective in a specialized area of policy, who cooperate to promote their common view, and who exercise significant policy influence. One classic example is the so-called *military-industrial-congressional complex* that supports military spending. Its *interest group element* includes defense-related corporations, defense plant workers, civilian employees of the military, and the cities and towns in which they reside and shop that are supporters of military spending and foreign sales. Making up the *bureaucratic element* are the defense agencies and the military services. As for the *congressional element*, it is composed of legislators who represent the districts and states with defense plants, military bases, or other activities that benefit from military spending. Many of these members of Congress have seats on the Senate or House Armed Services Committee or the subcommittees for defense spending in the two chambers' Appropriations Committees.[61]

Interest Group Influence and Issues

There are a number of factors related to issues that impact the role of interest groups. Political scientists have advanced an array of theories to explain variations in the role of interest groups in the policy-making process related to difference in issues.[62] To look at issues as a variable in interest group influence, we can explore types of issues, the scope of issues, and issues and change.

Types of Issues

There are numerous ways to classify issues by type. One simple division is between foreign and domestic issues. Interest groups are generally less of a factor on foreign policy issues, such as whether to expand NATO's membership, than on domestic issues, such as health care. Complicating this division are intermestic issues. This third category includes issues with both *inter*national and do*mestic* ramifications. Intermestic issues are becoming increasingly common as globalization blurs the distinction between what is a foreign issue and what is a domestic one. Trade, for example, involves foreign countries but also has a huge impact on jobs, the availability and price of goods, and other domestic concerns. Because of the range of interest groups affected by trade and other intermestic issues, they tend to be treated more like domestic policy than foreign policy.

The second of many ways to classify issues is to distinguish between *crisis policy* involving war, terrorism, rioting, natural disasters, and other events that take or threaten human life and *non-crisis policy*. Scholars of foreign policy have found that decision making during foreign policy crises usually centers on national leaders, with interest groups and other domestic actors being supportive during at least the initial stages of the crisis. There is also some evidence the same pattern initially exists in domestic crises that contain similar threats.[63]

Scope of Issues

Government policy deals with issues that range from very narrow in scope, such as salmon stocking policy, to those that are very broad, such as national health care. Not surprisingly given this range, the number of issue groups involved in any given issue varies considerably. A study of 137 issues and bills before Congress found that the amount of interest group attention each drew ranged widely, from just one group in 22 cases to 1,788 groups active on an omnibus appropriations

FIGURE 7.8 Scope of Issue and Lobbyist Success

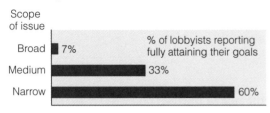

Scope of issue

Broad	7%
Medium	33%
Narrow	60%

% of lobbyists reporting fully attaining their goals

Only a small percentage of lobbyists report fully attaining their goals on broad-scope issues that draw considerable attention by interest groups, the public, and the media. As the scope of the issue narrows, the success of lobbyists increases.
Data source: Christine Mahoney, "Lobbying Success in the United States and the European Union," *Journal of Public Policy,* 27/1 (2007): 35–56.

bill.[64] Of the issues and bills, about one-fourth were very narrow, drawing the interest of just one or two groups. At the other end of the range about another 25% of the issues were very broad and drew the attention of more than 50 interest groups.[65]

The scope of issues and the number of interest groups involved in any one of them is relevant to interest group strength. Moreover, the relative strength or weakness of any individual group is affected in many cases by alliance building among groups on one or both sides of the issue. As seen in the opening You Decide box, for example, Native American groups and environmental groups have created a successful alliance against policies and officials that negatively impact tribal lands and the environment.[66]

Whether interest groups are cooperating in alliances or going it alone, the more that participate, the less likely it is that any one group or alliance can dominate the debate. One factor is the broader the issue, the more likely it is that there will be countervailing interest groups and alliance pressing their views. Broader scope issues also attract more attention from the media and the public, further ensuring that policy makers will take a full range of interests and opinion into account.[67] This impact is evident in Figure 7.8.

Issues and Change

A third issue-related factor that affects the success of interest groups is whether they are defending the status quo or promoting change. Generally, the U.S. political system makes it more difficult to innovate than to maintain current policy. This spills over to interest groups' success rates. Groups lobbying for the status quo report having at least some success 81% of the time. Groups urging change report having at least some success only 41% of the time.[68] Because women, racial minorities, and other disadvantaged groups tend to favor changes in the status quo, this success rate factor works against them.[69]

INTEREST GROUPS: BOON OR BANE?

Amid all the issues about interest groups, perhaps the key question is the degree to which the policy-making role of interest groups supports the democratic process or distorts it. Because there is no consensus among analysts on this issue, one way to address the fit between interest group activity and democracy is to consider a series of questions.

How Do Interest Groups Fit into Democratic Theory?

Although all types of political systems have interest groups, they play a more open and important role in democratic political systems. Indeed, some scholars view interest groups as a necessary and key component of democracy.[70] One analysis argues, for example, that "the advocacy of special interests through lobbying and the challenge and dissent presented through various forms of protest, offers vital links in the democratic chain between the governors and governed."[71] Similarly, the senior member of the Senate, Robert Byrd (D-WV), contended that lobbyists "have a job to do, and most of them do it very well indeed. It is hard to imagine Congress withut them."[72]

Such views are not new. James Madison wrote in the *Federalist Papers* (1788) that the country was "divided into different interests and factions." Recognition of the existence of interest groups and their legitimate role in a democracy led to language in the Bill of Rights ensuring their ability to organize themselves and to advocate their views. Most specifically, the First Amendment bars the government from interfering with the right of people

Article 20 of the UN's Universal Declaration of Human Rights (1948) declares, "Everyone has the right to freedom of peaceful assembly and association."

"peaceably to assemble" or to "petition the government for the redress of grievances." In other words, people have the right to get together and complain. The First Amendment also protects interest group activity by enshrining freedom of speech and other forms of communication. Furthermore, the Supreme Court has ruled that the First Amendment guarantees the **freedom of association**, the right to form and join groups to promote political goals. The key case came in response to efforts in the South to disrupt African American political organizations. Rejecting that, the Supreme Court ruled in *NAACP v. Alabama* (1958) that, "Effective advocacy of both public and private points of view . . . is undeniably embraced by group association. . . . [F]reedom to engage in association for the advancement of beliefs . . . is an inseparable aspect of 'liberty' assured by the [Constitution]."

Whatever theory may hold, many observers argue that the reality of interest groups and their activity do not fit well with democracy. There are two basic objections: (1) the struggle among interest groups is unfair and (2) interest groups play too powerful a role in the political process.

Is the Contest among Interest Groups a Fair Fight?

Most analysts agree that that all interest groups do not all possess equal opportunities. From this perspective, there are vast disparities in wealth and other resources among interest groups that make many contests among them as undemocratically lopsided as pitting the New York Yankees against a Little League team.[73] Typifying

Interest groups have always been part of American democracy. James Madison wrote of their existence in the Federalist Papers in 1788, and the Bill of Rights protects them in a variety of ways. (Library of Congress)

FIGURE 7.9 Lobbying Success

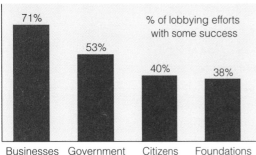

Business lobbyists report having at least some success on a much greater share of their lobbying efforts than lobbyists for other types of groups.

Notes and data source: Businesses combine the corporations and trade groups. Data from Christine Mahoney, "Lobbying Success in the United States and the European Union," *Journal of Public Policy,* 27/1 (2007): 35–56.

this view, one group of scholars writes, "Interest groups tend to reinforce rather than challenge pre-existing inequalities in American society and government." This outcome is attributable to an uneven distribution of group strength that favors those "groups representing the well off, especially business" and that disadvantages those "groups representing broad public interests . . . and the disadvantaged."[74] This view is supported by research on lobbying and campaign expenditures that shows that the playing field is uneven, with a strong tilt in favor of businesses.[75] In 2008, for example, business and trade organizations accounted for 68% of the reported spending on lobbying, campaign donations, and other campaign efforts. Arguably, this unequal ability to spend money leads to unequal success as indicated in Figure 7.9.

It should be carefully noted that some scholars see less inequality among group influence. One extensive study concluded that "no single category of interest groups, be it business organizations, labor unions, or professional associations, proved more successful than others in achieving [their] policy objectives."[76] Those who take this view also argue that the power gap among groups has narrowed, making the process more democratic. For example, one scholar writes, "The mobilization of many new interests over the past several decades, especially the mobilization of many public interest groups, is a highly significant development in terms of the legitimacy of the interest group process."[77] From this perspective, then, American democracy is a rough-and-tumble process that legally protects the ability of all groups to compete even if the struggle among them may be messy.[78]

Are Interest Groups Too Powerful?

Just as American interest groups are as old as the country, so too are concerns about their power. James Madison, for one, worried that one or another group might get the government to adopt policies that were "adverse to the rights of other citizens or to the . . . interests of the community."[79] During the First Congress (1789–1801), one senator fretted that lobbyists were using "every tool . . . that could be thought of" to influence Congress.[80] This dark view of interest groups and lobbying has continued. For instance, President Woodrow Wilson (1913–1921) grumbled that Washington, was so full of lobbyists that, "You can't throw bricks in any direction without hitting one."[81] Even more recently, then candidate Barack Obama assured Americans that as president, "I intend to tell the corporate lobbyists that their days of setting the agenda in Washington are over."[82] Not surprisingly given this drumbeat of criticism, most Americans believe that interest groups are too powerful, as shown in Figure 7.10.

Yet for all the persistent depictions of interest groups selfishly manipulating the political process to their own benefit, research has not yielded an overall picture this dire. Recall, that studies of interest group influence split about evenly on whether it was powerful or not.

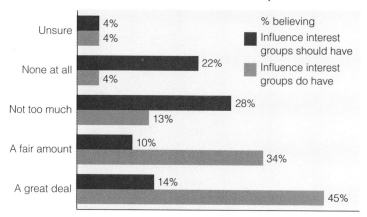

FIGURE 7.10 Public Evaluation of Interest Group Influence

Americans believe that interest groups have more influence than they should.

Data source: Henry J. Kaiser Family Foundation survey, 2003. Data provided by The Roper Center for Public Opinion Research.

Another reason for caution about interest group influence is that within the administrative branch, some evidence suggests that group influence in the bureaucracy has declined in recent decades.[83] A study conducted in 1970 found that 33% of senior civil servants attributed "a great deal of influence" to interest groups. By 1986–1987, only 14% of top ranking bureaucrats took this position. One reason for the decline in influence is that presidents beginning with Richard M. Nixon (1969–1974) have come to emphasize centralized policy making on important issues. This reduction in agency autonomy means that group influence over administrative decisions has decreased. Second, various reforms measures (discussed below) have restricted interest group activity by barring it or at least requiring that it be reported.

As for the judiciary, interest groups have been able to derail some potential judges during the nomination process, but the actual numbers have been relatively small and the impact on the judiciary as a whole has been limited. Similarly, the impact of amicus curiae briefs on the judicial process is very difficult to isolate. Judges certainly read some of the amicus curiae briefs, and court opinions sometimes refer to them.[84] But it is uncertain whether the briefs cited have influenced the justices' decisions or were merely used by justices to bolster their argument. What can be said is that there is no correlation between the number of briefs filed for a position and the court's favoring of that view. In other words, the side supported by the most briefs does not win any more often than the less-supported side.

Do Interest Groups Corrupt the System?

Of all the charges against interest groups, the most damning is that they essentially "buy" support in Congress with their flood of donations to its members.[85] Certainly, as noted earlier, interest groups sometimes do engage in corrupt practices, but such instances that are blatant enough to be prosecuted are uncommon. Discovering more subtle influence is difficult because the link between campaign funding and electoral success is complex. On the one hand, considerable evidence suggests that the flow of money to candidates has more to do with interest groups working to increase their access to policy makers by supporting those who are most likely to win rather than with the flow of money determining who does win. As for the existence of a direct causal link between made or promised campaign funds and how a legislator decides to vote, "the balance of research does not reveal consistent and persuasive evidence that campaign contribution and PAC money cause floor votes."[86]

On the other hand, a great deal of interest group activity occurs while bills are being "marked up" in committee, and that phase of the legislative process is much harder to follow than final votes. It is usually in committees, for example, that "earmarks" or special benefits for one or another interest group are added to legislation. To see how this works and to ponder its legitimacy in at least one instance, consider the case presented in the following You Decide box.

YOU DECIDE: Legitimate Contributions or Corruption?

In 2007, PMA Group, a lobbying firm, hosted a wine-tasting fundraiser for Representative James P. Moran (D-VA), a member of the House Appropriations Committee's subcommittee on defense. Among those solicited to buy tickets were executives of Innovative Concepts, a defense contractor in McLean, Virginia, that employs PMA to lobby on its behalf. In an e-mail exchange, one executive grumbled to another about buying the expensive tickets and complained that he did not even drink wine. The second executive shot back, "You don't have to drink. You just have to pay." Overall, tickets from Innovative Concept executives and other attendees put nearly $92,000 into two campaign funds controlled by Moran. Even though the company is not located in Moran's congressional district, Innovative Concept executives donated a total of $10,000 to Moran's

funds for the 2008 election, and the PMA Group and its executives donated another $47,500. Arguably, the incentive was Moran's subcommittee position overseeing all defense appropriations. That paid off when Moran added an $800,000 earmark for a defense communications system built by Innovative Concepts to the 2008 defense appropriations bill. Note carefully that there is no evidence that Moran illegally sponsored the earmark in exchange for the donations that came to him from Innovative Concepts and its lobby firm, PMA Group. Perhaps the donations were legitimately given because Moran was already supportive of the company. Clearly the line between legal and corrupt is thin. What do you think? Which side of the line were Moran, Innovative Concepts, and the PMA group on?[87]

What Can or Should Be Done about Interest Groups?

Surely the most radical step would be to attempt to outlaw interest groups or ban their activity. Doing so would be very difficult because it would mean amending the Constitution to alter the First Amendment. Even if that could be done, it probably would not be wise because Madison was right that interest groups are inherent to democracy and that the only way to eliminate interest group activity is to eliminate democracy.

A less drastic step is to attempt to regulate interest groups and limit their influence. Efforts to do this are as old as the Republic. After one committee of citizens came onto the Senate floor in 1798 to present a petition regarding U.S. policy toward France, senators banned outsiders from the floor. This began the practice of group representatives gathering in the Senate lobby, thereby earning the name lobbyists. Of course, pushing interest group representatives into the lobby did not end their influence, and ever since there have been regular efforts to regulate lobbying, campaign financing, and other aspects of group activity. Federal legislation has included the Federal Corrupt Practices Act (1925), the Foreign Agents Registration Act (1938), the Federal Regulation of Lobbying Act (1946), and the Lobbying Disclosure Act (1995). Congress also enacted the Federal Election Campaign Act (FECA, 1971) and established the Federal Election Commission to regulate campaign finance, and has enacted further controls on the flow of money from interest groups to candidates, including the Bipartisan Campaign Reform Act (BCRA, 2002). Both houses of Congress also have ethics codes, and there are several presidential directives regulating contact between officials in the executive branch and lobbyists. Among these was an executive order by President Obama in 2009 that no executive branch official could speak with any lobbyists about the administration's economic stimulus plan.

Such efforts have certainly had a positive effect, but not one of them or even all of them combined have provided a cure-all. One problem is that many restrictions contravene constitutional rights. For example, both the American Civil Liberties Union and the watchdog group Citizens for Responsibility and Ethics in Washington joined with the American League of Lobbyists in urging Obama to ease his restrictions on lobbying as violations of the First Amendment and the equal protection clause of the Fourteenth Amendment. Similarly, the Supreme Court has invalidated as unconstitutional parts of both the FECA and the BCRA (see Chapter 10). Another problem relates to the proverbial caution about throwing out the baby with the bathwater. Interest groups and lobbyists come in all stripes, and it is difficult and probably impossible to limit those you disagree with while allowing those that you do agree with to continue their efforts.

Thus, although the system is far from perfect and all reform proposals should be considered, care should be taken in trying to restrict interest groups. Recall

James Madison's conclusion that interest groups, for good or ill, are inherent in a democracy and the only way to eliminate them completely is to dispense with democracy. If he is correct but you still you consider interest groups a problem, what would you do to improve the situation?

SUMMARY

Interest groups are a natural political phenomenon because all societies are complex, with divisions by sex, wealth, race, and numerous other characteristics. Many also argue that interest groups are necessary to democracy because they allow people to organize in order to urge the government to respond to their needs and preferences. Taking this perspective, the Constitution, especially the First Amendment, protects the right of interests groups to organize and operate. Interest groups have always been a major part of the American political process, but their number is growing for several reasons including the impact of globalization, which has prompted more and more foreign governments, companies, and other entities to lobby the U.S. government.

It is possible to classify interest groups according to their membership or their policy focus. These organized groups are represented by both their leadership and by professional lobbyists. One concern is the "revolving door" through which many interest groups leaders move into government positions, and many government officials become lobbyists or leaders of interest groups.

Interest groups use a range of direct and indirect methods to meet their goals. Among the direct methods are testifying during congressional and agency hearings, meeting with individual policy makers, participating in policy formulation, and taking legal action. Indirect lobbying involves such techniques as mobilizing group members and supporters, trying to shape general public opinion, and launching protests and other forms of direct action.

Scholars debate about how powerful interest groups strength is overall in the political process, but there is agreement that there are differences in interest group strength. Among the factors that cause these differences are group size, cohesion and intensity, wealth, leadership and lobbyists' skills, and the distribution of group members. It is also the case that, in general, there are variations in the influence of interest groups as a whole. Factors that cause this ebb and flow relate to the type of policy issue, to how many interest groups are actively concerned, and to whether the policy changes the status quo or maintains it.

Even though interest groups are a natural part of the policy process and arguably should be protected in a democracy, there are many troubling aspects of interest group activity. One problem is that on many issues, the contest among interest groups is not equal. Indeed, it is arguable that in general some interest groups such as those representing business have the resources and organization that make them much more powerful than opposing consumer groups. Most Americans believe that interest groups are too powerful but it is difficult to regulate them. They are protected by the Constitution. Also, care must be taken not to create restrictions on interest groups that undermine their valuable function in a democracy.

CHAPTER 7 GLOSSARY

amicus curiae brief A "friend of the court" legal argument filed with the courts in connection with a particular lawsuit by individuals, groups, or organizations who are not a party to the case but who have an important interest in it.

direct lobbying Individual or small-group interactions between an interest group's representatives and policy makers for the purpose of persuading the policy makers to support the group's positions.

disturbance theory The argument that marked changes in a society's social or economic conditions or important changes in government policy prompt people and organizations whose interests are being affected to become more politically active in a number of ways, including forming new interest groups and invigorating existing ones.

federal advisory committees (FACs) Panels created to increase outside input into the decisions of federal agencies.

freedom of association The right under the First Amendment to form and join groups to promote political goals, as established by the Supreme Court in such cases as *NAACP v. Alabama* (1958).

free rider problem The reliance of the vast majority of people in a demographic group on the relatively few people who join and are active in individual membership groups to protect the interests of those in the larger group.

grassroots The general membership of a group or the general population.

ideological interest groups Interest groups that begin with a philosophical perspective rather than an issue orientation.

indirect lobbying Efforts by interest groups to influence intermediaries, like public opinion, that will then put pressure on officials to support a group's policy preferences.

individual-membership interest group An interest group whose membership is made up of people who choose to join the group by some specific act such as enrolling.

interest group One or more individuals or organizations with a stake in public policy.

iron triangle An ongoing alliance among those with similar economic interests, supportive government agencies, and supportive members of Congress.

issue networks Usually temporary coalitions of interest groups, elected and appointed government officials, and others (such as academic policy experts) who share an interest in a particular policy area and interact to shape policy in that area.

lobbyists Interest group representatives who interact directly with government officials.

multiple-issue interest groups Interest groups that focus on several issues.

organizational-membership interest group An interest group whose membership is composed of one or more private or public organizations and institutions.

political action committees (PACs) Organizations established by various interest groups to lobby the government and to raise campaign funds and distribute them to candidates for office and to lobby.

public interest groups Interest groups that draw their membership from the general population and advocate policies that will benefit everyone equally rather than favor any single individual, group, or organization.

registered foreign interest groups Interest groups centered in another country that operate in the United States to influence public policy and are registered under the Foreign Agents Registration Act of 1938 and the Lobbying Disclosure Act (LDA) of 1995.

revolving door The flow of government policy makers or staff into lobbying positions and the return flow of lobbyists into government policy-making and staff positions.

self-interest groups Interest groups that draw their membership from a limited range of society or organizations and promote specific benefits for themselves or their members.

single-issue interest groups Interest groups that concentrate on one issue.

tax-exempt advocacy groups (TAGs) Groups that are tax exempt under sections 501, 503, and 527 of the Internal Revenue Service (IRS) code and are restricted by law in various ways about the degree to which they may engage in partisan campaign activity.

test cases Legal actions supported by one or more interest groups to challenge the constitutionality of a law or regulation.

transnational interest groups Interest groups with affiliates or activity in more than one country and that address issues that crosscut national boundaries.

THE NEWS MEDIA

8

YOU DECIDE: Should the Gay Rights Case Be Kept in the Closet?

What is almost certain to become a landmark Supreme Court case began its journey through the federal courts in January 2010. The issue is whether state bans on gay marriages violate the U.S. Constitution. California was the immediate battleground. In May 2008, the California Supreme Court ruled the state's prohibition of same-sex marriage violated the state constitution. Six months later, California's voters negated that ruling by passing Proposition 8, a referendum that amended California's constitution to bar same-sex marriages. Gay-rights proponents appealed the validity of Proposition 8 to the state's supreme court on technical grounds but lost there in May 2009.

That set the stage for *Perry v. Schwarzenegger* filed in the U.S. District Court in San Francisco. One unusual aspect of the case is that the defendant, Governor Arnold Schwarzenegger, opposed Proposition 8 and refused to defend it in court. Nevertheless, as governor he was still the defendant in the case brought by plaintiffs Kristin Perry and her partner Sandra Steir of Berkeley. Their attorneys, Theodore Olson and David Boies, provided another interesting twist. The two lawyers had represented the opposing sides in *Bush v. Gore* (2000) when the Supreme Court had refused to order a recount in Florida, thus in effect deciding the presidential election in Bush's favor. Olson had then gone on to represent the Bush administration before the U.S. Supreme Court as U.S. solicitor general. Vaughn R. Walker, the district court trial judge, added to the case's curiosities. In 1979 he represented a club in which he was a member, the all-male Olympic Club of San Francisco, in a suit to bar the gay community from using the word "Olympic" in a sporting event called the Gay Olympics. That had led Democrats to block Walker's nomination by President Ronald Reagan to the federal bench in 1987. Leading the critics, San Francisco representative and future Speaker of the House Nancy Pelosi charged Walker with "insensitivity" to gays.[1] Walker finally got a seat on the bench in 1989 after again being nominated, this time by President George H. W. Bush. By the time the *Perry* case commenced in 2010, Vaughn had become the chief judge for the District Court of Northern California, which meant that he had assigned himself to try the case. It was also widely reported that Walker is gay.[2]

What immediately concerns us here is freedom of the media to broadcast the trial. During pretrial maneuvering, Judge Walker rejected a motion by the plaintiffs to broadcast the trial live but did rule that it could be taped and uploaded later in the day to YouTube for transmission. An attorney for the anti-gay marriage groups that were defending the California constitution in lieu of the governor objected to Walker's ruling and filed an emergency appeal to the U.S. Supreme Court asking it to ban electronically transmitted coverage. The lawyer argued that the trial "has the potential to become a media circus," and he warned that there was considerable evidence showing that supporters of Proposition 8 had suffered "harassment, economic reprisal, threats, and even physical violence. In this atmosphere, witnesses are understandably quite distressed at the prospect of their testimony being broadcast worldwide on YouTube."[3] Acting quickly, the Court by a 5–4 vote barred the trial court from broadcasting its proceedings. The majority decision agreed with the argument that witnesses might be harassed, worried that this might make them "less willing to cooperate," and concluded that "It would be difficult—if not impossible—to reverse the harm of those broadcasts." The four dissenting justices accused the majority of trying to "micromanage" the trial judge and of identifying "no real harm" from broadcasting the trial and concluded that "the public interest weighs in favor of providing [broadcast] access to the courts."[4]

Traditionally, courts have rarely allowed their proceedings to be broadcast for fear that the glare of publicity could affect what happens in the courtroom and could also lead to retribution against witnesses, jurors, lawyers, and court personnel. Critics of this stand argue that banning the news media and now the social media such as YouTube from recording and transmitting court proceedings is a violation of democracy. During her confirmation hearings for the Supreme Court in 2010, Elena Kagan told senators that it would be "a good thing for the Court itself" to televise cases being argued before it.[5] What do you think?

INTRODUCING THE MEDIA AND POLITICS

The purpose of posing the question about transparency in the judicial process is to begin our look at the media's roles in the democratic political process. We will begin with some commentary on the general **mass media**, the organizations that print or electronically convey entertainment, information, and opinion related to politics to the public. However, our focus is the subset of the mass media called the **news media**, or "press." These are the organizations that transmit news to the public. Serving as a link in the political communications system is the most general role of the press in a democracy. The press performs this function in two ways.

Informing the public about political events, issues, and people is the first. Part of this link, especially in the modern, electronic era, is to put Americans at the scene. First radio, then television, and now Internet streaming have provided people with a much greater ability to see and hear events as they occur. When terrorists attacked the World Trade Center (WTC) on September 11, 2001, television coverage was so rapid that millions of Americans saw the second airliner ram into the WTC 18 minutes after the initial attack. Mostly though, what Americans know of events, issues, and leaders depends on **mediated reality**: what they learn second-hand through the press or some other intermediary. Thus, the press plays a key role as a filter and interpreter of political reality based on its ability to decide what to report and how to depict events, people, and issues.

Facilitating two-way communications between the country's citizens and their political leaders is a second communications link provided by the press. President Theodore Roosevelt called his office a "bully pulpit," a platform to present his views to Americans and rally them to his cause. Indeed for presidents and other politicians nearly every speech, press release, interview, and press conference is part of the effort to inform and persuade the public, and they depend on the new media as a carrier. Communications also flow in the opposite direction, with the press helping to carry the views of the people to political leaders. Survey results, for example, are a regular focus of news stories, and they influence political leaders and the policies they pursue.[6]

A final introductory note is that the proposal to use YouTube to transmit the courtroom drama in the gay rights case symbolizes the fact that there are important changes underway in how news and political opinions are being circulated. These shifts are detailed in a later section on the technological setting in which the news media operate. You will see that there has been a decline in the importance of the **legacy news media**, the traditional news sources, which include broadcast and cable television, printed newspapers, the Associated Press and other wire services, and printed news magazines. Newspapers are in particular trouble. Indeed, there are growing doubts about the long-term viability of printed newspapers. There were 200 fewer daily newspapers in 2008 than there were in 1990, the circulation of daily newspapers dropped 14% between 2001 and 2008, and the number of newspaper reporters, editors, and other professional staff plummeted 17% between 2001 and 2009.

In sharp contrast to the ebbing prominence of the legacy news media is the steep increase in the presence of the **Internet news media**. This large group of sources includes the online sites of the legacy news media, news aggregators that gather news from other (mostly legacy) news sources, and exclusively online news sources. Not included here as part of the Internet news media, but included by some observers, are blogs and other Internet platforms for the exchange of information and commentary. Between 1996 and 2008, the share of survey respondents saying they got at least some of their news from the Internet every day grew from 3% to 31%.[7] Some of these sources are simply online versions of newspapers and other legacy media sources, but many other sources are unique to the Internet.

A major change in how the news is delivered is occurring with the traditional methods, especially newspapers, declining in importance and Internet sources rising in importance. (iStockphoto)

In addition to these points, you will see in this chapter that

★ the press plays a central role in political communications and the democratic process.

★ how the press operates is determined in part by its legal, societal, and organizational settings.

★ Internet communications channels are radically reshaping the role and impact of the traditional press.

★ what is deemed newsworthy is based largely on the interaction of what journalists want and what the public wants.

★ there is an extensive range of issues that affect the quality of the news.

★ the press has significant influence in the political process, but that impact is also limited.

★ the press operates neither as well as its defenders claim nor as poorly as its critics charge.

The Media and Demographic Diversity

One factor that affects the role of the press is the place of women and minorities in it. Therefore we will look at the underrepresentation of women and minorities among media owners, editors, and reporters and the impact this limited diversity has on press coverage.

About 25% of U.S. daily newspapers have no minority journalists.

AMERICAN DIVERSITY

More positively, we will also see that there is a growing number of women and people of color who are journalists. Moreover, they are more often playing central roles. One pioneering route to prominence has been the battlefield. Beginning in the late 1960s, African American reporter Ed Bradley built on his success as a war correspondent in Vietnam to become in 1976 the first black journalist to cover the

White House for a TV network (CBS). Two decades later, Christiane Amanpour began her journalistic rise in 1991 with her calm reporting of the Persian Gulf War on live television using an all-woman camera and sound crew despite often being in peril. Now she is CNN's chief international correspondent. In addition to the individual contributions that Bradley, Amanpour, and others like them have brought to journalism, it is important to note that they have also brought a needed perspective to journalism.

The Media in a World of Difference

As is true for all aspects of the American political process, the structure, operation, and impact of the American media can be more fully understood by comparing it with other countries and within the context of globalization.

Global paid newspaper circulation in 2008 was about 540 million copies daily.

Comparing the U.S. and Foreign News Media

One way to enhance our evaluation of the U.S. press is to compare it to its counterparts in other countries. We will see, for instance, that the U.S. press is far freer than the news media in most other countries, but it is not the freest in the world. The comparative perspective also reveals that Americans, like people in every prosperous country and many poor ones, report that television is their most important source of news. Another commonality across national boundaries is that most people including Americans (65%) say that the press has a positive impact on their country.

There are also comparative differences about the operations and status of the media globally. One involves perceived reliability. Only a thin majority of people in a recent survey of 128 countries reported being "confident" in the "quality and integrity" of the media in their country. Oddly, but perhaps out of fear, greater confidence was expressed by people in countries rated by Freedom House as "not free" (50% confident) or only "partly free" (56% confident) than by people in "free" countries (47% confident).[8] Figure 8.1 details public confidence in the media in these free countries, including in the United States where only 32% expressed confidence, compared to 66% who said they were not confident, and 2% who were unsure.

Nations also differ as to which news source is most reliable. Americans are most likely to say the local newspaper. People in most other countries are most confident in national television or national/regional newspapers. There are also differences in the models of news coverage. For instance, many countries have a strong tradition of funding nonpartisan public radio and television; those venues play little role in the United States.

FIGURE 8.1
Comparative Confidence in the News Media

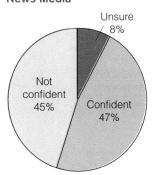

Confidence in the quality and integrity of the media in 40 free countries

Only a narrow plurality of people in 40 countries, including the United States, rated as "free" by Freedom House are confident in the media.
Data source: Gallup Poll report, "Quality and Integrity of World's Media Questioned," December 17, 2007.

Globalization and the Media

Globalization is also affecting the press. The ability of reporters to move quickly around the world and to transmit the news widely and almost instantaneously via the Internet and satellite television has made the top press organizations global in their reach. For example, CNN television airs in 6 languages, BBC Radio broadcasts in over 30, and many countries' major newspapers, such as *China Daily,* are available on the Web in English. Also, as in the United States, the information flow around the world via the Internet is increasingly supplementing and sometimes supplanting the news media. When Iranians took to the streets in 2010 to protest against their government, the government tried to contain awareness of the dissent globally and within the country by banning press coverage. Yet disturbing photos taken by cell phones and other visual recording devices quickly reached the global public via the Internet.

The globalization of the news media is reflected in this photo of a Chinese demonstrator in Beijing protesting CNN's criticisms of press restrictions in China during its hosting of the 2008 Olympic summer games. (AP Photo/Robert F. Bukaty)

As a result, Americans can see much more of the world drama occurring in foreign lands and their people through the very "up front and personal" medium of television and now also increasingly the Internet. This electronic contact has served to humanize other people, especially those in Africa and Asia, continents that not long ago seemed far away and with people very different from Americans. Now more frequent images of other people make them more familiar. They also seem less different because cultural and economic globalization has led people everywhere to increasingly wear the same kinds of clothes, speak English, and use one another's products. All this has important ramifications for U.S. foreign policy. One has been to heighten the sensitivity of Americans to the travails of people elsewhere and to create pressure on Washington to intervene diplomatically, economically, and sometimes militarily. The U.S.-led intervention in Bosnia and then in Kosovo in the Balkans during the 1990s and the U.S. efforts to ease the suffering in Haiti after its devastating earthquake in 2010 provide two examples.

The World and Diversity in Media

The limited extent of demographic diversity in the U.S. media intersects with global realities in a number of ways that we will discuss. There are some comparative points. One is that the press everywhere including the United States gives far less coverage to women than their 49.6% share of the world population warrants. Yet another point about the intersection of diversity in the American media and the surrounding world relates to U.S. coverage of various regions. We will see in a later section, for example, that the U.S. press pays much greater attention to Europe than it does to any other continent and also tends to portray a more positive image of Europe than the rest of the world.

THE NEWS MEDIA AND DEMOCRACY

James Madison had it right when he observed, "A people who mean to be their own governors must arm themselves with the power which knowledge gives."[9] To provide that knowledge without bias or censorship is the essential role of the press. Indeed, many refer to the press as the "fourth branch of government" because of its important role in American politics.

Freedom of the press is far from universal. Indeed, only about 40% of all countries have a truly free press, and even that is a marked improvement over the recent past. Fortunately for Americans and their democracy, freedom of press is the prevailing standard. This is evident in Figure 8.2. It shows the United States ranking twenty-fourth "freest" among countries. According to Freedom House, the United States falls short of having a completely free press only because of a few weak points such as having overly concentrated ownership of media outlets. A final note on comparative freedom of the press is that it is spreading, albeit slowly.

Freedom of the press enjoys strong support among Americans, with two-thirds of them considering it very important to live in a county with a free press. Furthermore, as Figure 8.3 shows, this level of support among Americans is higher than the average for any other global region surveyed. Studies also conclude that a vast majority of Americans supports the freedom of the press to perform its core duties in a democracy, such as being able to publish news stories without government approval (prior restraint), to expose problems, and to criticize public officials.[10]

For all these positive signs of support for a free press among Americans, there are limits. Note in Figure 8.3 that one of every three Americans does not think a free press is very important. Moreover, when that survey compared it to six other factors (free speech, free elections, fair judiciary, civilian control of the military, free religion, and economic prosperity) and asked how important each is to wanting to live in the country, having a free press finished next to last among Americans, besting only civilian control of the military.[11]

Similarly, a third of Americans think the press has too much freedom, and there are even areas where a majority favors restraints. Most people, for instance, oppose

FIGURE 8.2 Comparative Freedom of the Press

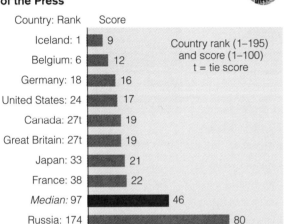

The U.S. press is freer than the news media in most countries. This figure shows some results from Freedom House's 2009 rating of freedom of the press in 195 countries on a scale from 0 (no restrictions) to 100 (no freedom). Iceland was first ("freest") with a score of 9; North Korea was the least free with a 98. The U.S. score of 17 indicates few restrictions and tied it with 2 other countries (the Czech Republic and Lithuania) for the 24th "freest" press.
Data sources: Freedom House, *Press Freedom Ranking 2009.*

FIGURE 8.3 Comparative Perceived Importance of a Free Press

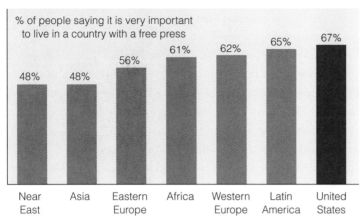

% of people saying it is very important to live in a country with a free press

Near East 48% | Asia 48% | Eastern Europe 56% | Africa 61% | Western Europe 62% | Latin America 65% | United States 67%

Americans value a free press more than people in most of the 36 democracies included in one global survey.

Notes and data source: Germany the only Western European country included. Data from The Pew Research Center, *Global Attitudes Project,* 2002.

allowing the press to televise any courtroom proceedings it wishes, to use hidden cameras, to routinely dig into the private lives of public officials, or to report from war zones without restrictions.[12]

THE SETTINGS IN WHICH THE PRESS OPERATES

How and how well the U.S. press operates depends in part on its complex environment. We will look at five settings in which the press operates: organizational, legal, societal, technological, and global.

The Organizational Setting of the News Media

Organizationally, most of the major news media are businesses. Television and radio news programming, newspapers, and other primary news sources take in over $65 billion in revenue annually. Because the public is best served if the press represents a broad spectrum of perspectives, several questions regarding corporate ownership require exploration. One relates to whether it is too concentrated in the hands of a few corporations. The second question relates to the demographic diversity of the news media's owners and its journalists.

Concentration of Corporate Ownership

The news media, like other types of business, have been undergoing a process of consolidation through mergers and acquisitions into fewer and larger conglomerates. One or another of the 10 largest U.S. newspaper conglomerates, for example, controls 30% of the country's daily newspapers and 54% of the daily circulation. Gannett, the largest conglomerate owns *USA Today* and 84 other daily newspapers with a combined circulation of 6.6 million.

Federal regulations limit the extent to which there can be cross-ownership of media outlets in a single area, but these apply only to radio and television stations that use the public airwaves. Moreover, recent changes in government rules allow more cross-ownership. This means that one company can own, for example, a newspaper and a television station in the same media market.

Some analysts contend that there is "a threat to democracy when a few large companies dominate communications."[13] One often cited example is Clear Channel Communications, which owns 40 television stations and about 1,200 radio stations, and has been accused of such right-wing political censorship efforts as pressuring its stations to drop the music of the Dixie Chicks after they criticized President Bush's invasion of Iraq. For its part, Clear Channel representatives reject charges of censorship and say that station owners are free to make their own programming decisions.

Other analysts argue that although media concentration has increased, it remains "fairly low" by U.S. government standards and in comparison to many other industries.[14] For example, one study applied an antitrust index used by the U.S. Department of Justice. By that index, a score of 1,000 equals a "concentrated" industry that might justify legal action under antitrust laws. Yet on that index, the media concentration scores are low: television (152), newspapers (254), and radio (469).[15] Those who discount some or all of the concern about ownership concentration also argue that owners usually cannot or do not try to impose their political views on the newsrooms in their organization. For example, among the newspapers in the Gannett chain, an average of 44% endorsed the Democratic candidate for president in the five elections from 1996 through 2008, 28% supported the Republican candidate, and 28% endorsed neither.

Increased ownership concentration is also mitigated in part by the proliferation of news sources. Many Americans still have access to the delivery of two or more daily newspapers, and these are supplemented for most people by Internet access to all the major electronic media outlets and to myriad printed news sources. Indeed, the Website of the *American Journalism Review* has links to 1,161 U.S. dailies and more than 1,500 other printed news sources. The number of television news sources has also greatly expanded from the three traditional broadcast networks (ABC, CBS, NBC) to now include PBS (founded 1969), CNN (1980), C-SPAN (1979), FOX (1986), and other sources.

Yet other Internet news sources add further to the availability of news. Some of these sources, like the *Huffington Post*, an online newspaper, and NewMax.TV, which airs news videos, somewhat resemble the traditional media. Other channels such as the White House blog are unique to the cyber world. Whatever their type, online sources had become by 2010 the third most common news source, supplanting newspapers, and trailing only local television and national television. Now a solid majority (59%) of Americans who are daily news consumers report that on a typical day they get news from both online and offline sources.[16]

Additionally, recently established Spanish-language networks such as Univisíon and Telemundo (both 1986) have increased the availability of news to Latinos, and ImaginAsian TV (2004) is striving to do the same for Asian Americans. Foreign language newspapers and radio stations have also increased in number and reach, further serving the diverse American population. Since 1970, for example, the number of Spanish-language daily newspapers has more than quintupled to 33, and their circulation increased from 135,000 to 1.6 million. These news sources are important because they provide two-thirds of Latinos with at least some of their news, as is evident in Figure 8.4.

Ownership by Entertainment Media Conglomerates

A second organizational reality for the U.S. news media is that these news sources, particularly the electronic media, are increasingly owned by huge multimedia conglomerates whose twin emphases are entertainment and profit. The media empire of Sumner Redstone, for example, includes such news and entertainment corporations as CBS and Viacom, which in turn have complete or significant control of the CW Network, 35 television stations, 180 radio stations, Paramount Pictures, Simon & Schuster book publishers, Blockbuster Videos, and the National Amusements Theater chain (1,400 screens); and such cable channels as MTV, CMT, BET, Showtime, VH-1, and Nickelodeon.

One result of this pattern of ownership, according to critics, is increased **tabloid journalism** in the mainstream news media. This type of journalism emphasizes personalities rather than issues, sensationalism rather than careful analysis, and otherwise is designed to appeal to emotions rather than the mind. Critics say the traditional press has responded to pressure from corporate owners to increase audience size and advertising revenue by "dumbing down" its coverage to the point where it is ever harder to distinguish, for example, between the *CBS Evening News* and *Entertainment Tonight*, which follows on many CBS stations.

Demographic Diversity of Ownership and Journalists

In the same way that the balance of the news media's coverage is threatened if its ownership is too concentrated in a few corporate hands, so too is the news media apt to have a limited cultural perspective if its owners and journalists are not demographically representative of their society.

FIGURE 8.4
Use of Spanish–Language Sources of News

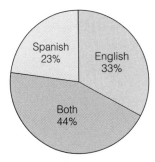

Sources of news for Latinos by language

The increased availability of Spanish-language news broadcasts and newspapers is important to Hispanics, 67% of whom get at least some of their news from such sources.
Data source: Pew Hispanic Center National Survey of Latinos, November 2008.

Demographic diversity among owners is scant. Women and minorities each own just 3% of the radio stations and 1% of the television stations. Furthermore, the diversity of ownership is unlikely to increase much under current conditions. One reason is the wealth gap between women compared to men and minorities compared to whites. Simply put, men and whites control most of the wealth needed to gain control of major media outlets. For example, 91% of everyone making $250,000 or more is white, and 75% of those with net assets worth $20 million or more are men. Changes in law and policy are a second reason that there has been little change in ownership diversity. As discussed below in the legal setting section, changes in federal law since the mid-1990s and Supreme Court decisions about diversity have made it harder to pursue affirmative action in allocating broadcast licenses. The result, according to an FCC report, is the existence of "barriers [that are] nearly insurmountable for small, minority- and women-owned businesses attempting to thrive in or even enter the broadcast industry."[17]

 No woman or person of color had ever been sole anchor of a weekday prime-time news program on a television network until Katie Couric became anchor of *CBS Evening News* in 2006.

Demographic diversity among journalists is better than at the ownership level but still far from proportionate. For example, among newspaper editors and reporters, the core of the press, 87% are white and 63% are male. Adding to the disparity, the presence of women and minority members is particularly small in media with regional and national reach. To cite one example, women are news directors at just 15% of the large television stations, those with staffs of more than 50 people. Furthermore, there has been little progress in diversifying the newsroom. Between 1999 and 2009, the share of minority reporters and editors grew very little. Growth was also marginal for women. Figure 8.5 shows that they as well as minorities are underrepresented among the reporters who air stories on the three major broadcast networks. The figure also indicates the slow increase in the on-air presence of women and minority group members.

There are many reasons why the ranks of journalism remain restricted to women and minorities. For minorities, the factors that have depressed their chances of attending college have also reduced their chances of becoming a reporter. Compounding this problem, the percentage of minority journalists who leave the field is much higher than it is for whites. Some of the causes are related to social barriers. For example, three-fourths of all minority journalists believe that they sometimes "have

FIGURE 8.5 Reporting on National Television by Women and Minority Journalists

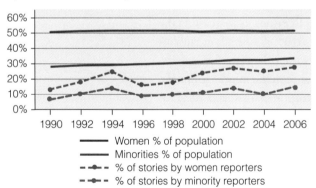

The percent of stories reported on the air by women and minority journalists on ABC, CBS, and NBC increased from 1990 to 2006. However, both groups still cover a lower percentage of stories than their share of the population.
Data source: Center for Media and Public Affairs, *Media Monitor,* Winter 2007.

to work harder than white journalists to get ahead."[18] Others become frustrated after being subject to "racial pigeon-holing," which Pulitzer Prize–winning African American reporter E. R. Shipp describes as being "stuck in the job of urban affairs reporter or race relations reporter."[19]

For reporters in 2010, the median of the salary range for men ($40,726) was 18% higher than for women ($34,219).

Lack of public concern about the racial gap among journalists is yet another part of the problem. A survey in 10 countries around the globe found Americans somewhat more satisfied than average with the representation of minority journalists in their country's press corps. Among the 10 countries, an average of 38% was satisfied, with 43% dissatisfied. By contrast, 48% of Americans were satisfied and 39% were dissatisfied.[20] As for women journalists, their story has been about the same. Their share of the journalist profession has been stalled for a decade or more. For women globally, most of the factors that have created glass ceilings in most professions remain in place and also apply to journalism, both in the United States and abroad.[21]

Impacts of Limited Diversity

There are three reasons why diversity in media ownership and staff matter. *Equity* is one. It is difficult to argue that justice is being served if one group of people or another hold a disproportionate share of the important positions in an institution as powerful as the press while other groups are vastly underrepresented.

Lack of proportionate coverage is the second reason diversity matters. In a later section on the quality of reporting we will see that the share of news coverage that minority groups and women receive is not equal to their share in the population. This coverage gap is partly related to insufficient diversity among media owners and staff, according to an FCC study. It reported that, "Minority-owned stations pay special attention in public affairs broadcasting to events of greater concern to ethnic or racial minority audiences" and to "issues concerning women, particularly health issues."[22] Similarly, another study found, "Increasing the number of minority-owned broadcasting stations increases the amount of minority-oriented programming."[23]

Race, gender, and gay issues were the focus of only 2% of the stories in the U.S. press in 2009 according to the Pew Research Center.

Stereotyping and other inaccuracies are a third reason why the demographic diversity in the press matters. "It's about accuracy," one editor explains. "I can't produce a newspaper that's correct if I don't reflect the community" on the staff.[24] Being correct includes avoiding racial stereotypes. These have declined but persist. One recent study found, for example, a link between how much network news people watch, the likelihood they will perceive blacks in such negative terms as "intimidating," and the chances viewers will express racist attitudes.[25] It is also arguable that negative stereotyping extends to countries and regions populated largely by non-whites. Corroborating that view, one study examined *New York Times* stories about Africa over a 40-year period and found that three-quarters of them were negative.[26]

The Legal Setting of the News Media

A country's laws, administrative regulations, and court decisions related to the press make up its legal setting and influence its operations. For the U.S. press, the most important part of the legal setting is the First Amendment. It prohibits the federal government and, by extension, state and local governments from restricting freedom of the press.

Limits on the Press

Like most of the Bill of Rights, though, this protection is not absolute. Instead, the news media are subject to the law in a number of ways. This fact has opened the way to controversies over what restrictions are allowed and to occasional attempts by the government to interfere in the conduct of the press. Indeed, within a few years of the First Amendment's adoption in 1791, Congress passed the Sedition Act (1798) making it a crime to publish anything meant to bring the federal government or any of its officers into "contempt or disrepute." The law expired in 1801, but many issues regarding the limits to freedom of the press raised by this act persist. In the following sections, we will look at these restrictions and also at how the public feels about them.

The U.S. press enjoys a largely unfettered legal environment, but that is not true for journalists in many countries. Here three staff members of Hammihan (Compatriot), a leading reformist newspaper in Iran, sit dejectedly on the stairs of the paper's offices after learning that the Iranian government had exercised decisive prior restraint by declaring the paper subversive and ordering it closed. (AP Photo/Vahid Salemi)

Prior Restraint   Generally, the government may not impose **prior restraint,** that is, control the press by subjecting it to licensure or to review and censorship prior to publication. Although a few instances of prior restraint had occurred, including President Abraham Lincoln's closing of critical newspapers during the Civil War, the first Supreme Court case on the issue involving the federal government did not occur until the 1970s. In this instance, reporters had obtained a government report dubbed *The Pentagon Papers.* Classified "secret," the document detailed government decision making on the Vietnam War and revealed numerous actions and views embarrassing to President Richard Nixon. His representatives convinced a federal district court judge to bar publication of the report, but the Supreme Court reversed the order in *New York Times v. United States* (1971). Still, the Court did not absolutely prohibit prior restraint. Its opinion said only that the government had not met the "heavy presumption against" prior restraint. Many legal scholars believe that the government might be successful in restraining the publication of such things as wartime battle plans and detailed troop deployments.

Liability for What Has Been Published   Although the press has wide freedom to publish, it can be held liable if it violates certain standards. Most prominently, the press cannot defame an individual by the spoken (libel) or written (slander) word. For public figures, though, the courts construe defamation very narrowly. In one case, the Supreme Court in 1967 rejected a claim by an Alabama official that he had been defamed by a newspaper ad castigating him as a racist. Even though the ad contained errors, the Court ruled that falsehoods about public agencies and officials were protected unless made with a "reckless disregard" for the truth.[27]

Regulation of the News Media as Businesses   Like all businesses, the news media are subject to taxation and certain kinds of regulation by government. For example, the news media must follow labor laws. By contrast, attempts to regulate the actual distribution of the news or to single out the media as a business have been rejected by the Supreme Court. It has held, for instance, that the government may not require permits for sidewalk newspaper vending machines or impose specific taxes on the news media.

Regulation to Achieve Political Balance   The FCC has the authority under the Radio Act (1927) to license radio and television stations that broadcast over the airwaves and to otherwise regulate their use. This power has been used to institute numerous rules that have affected the press. For example, Congress enacted an **equal time rule** in 1934 mandating stations that sold political advertising time or that made free time available to one candidate in an election do the same for other candidates. Another important FCC regulation instituted in 1949 was called the **fairness doctrine**. It required stations to allocate part of their airtime to news and other matters of public importance and also to carry opposing viewpoints on public issues and candidates. The equal time rule remains in place, but the fairness doctrine was repealed in 1987 when the FCC agreed with the broadcast industry's view that the mandate to be fair violated free speech. This change was part of the increased reluctance of the FCC and Congress to regulate any political content, in part because of the broadcaster complaints of prior restraint and also because of suffering an unfair burden in their competition with the less-regulated cable industry.

Regulation to Achieve Diversified Ownership   As early as 1946, the FCC set a goal of ensuring that the stations it regulated "serve significant minorities among our population."[28] Little was done, however, until the 1970s. Then minority ownership began to increase somewhat because of two factors: (1) several laws that increased the possibility that women and minority groups could raise the funds necessary to enter the electronic media market, and (2) the use of affirmative action standards by the FCC to help decide broadcast license applications. This trend halted in the 1990s. In line with a movement to deregulate businesses, Congress made it more expensive to obtain a broadcast license by selling them to the highest bidder. This undercut the ability of less-wealthy groups, including women and minorities, to get licenses. A second new barrier was put in place by the Supreme Court. It ruled in 1995 that federal affirmative action programs must be based on "compelling governmental interests," such as remedying intentional past discrimination.[29] Since this is difficult to establish, the impact was to derail the FCC's use of race and sex as criteria in awarding broadcast licenses.

YOU DECIDE: Shield Reporters' Confidential Sources?

New York Times reporter Judith Miller went to jail in 2005. Her crime was refusing to tell a grand jury who had been her confidential (anonymous) source for a story that she had written. Miller's story had been about who had leaked the fact that Valerie Plame, reputed to be an energy consultant with a private company, was actually a CIA agent. Because disclosing an agent's name is a federal crime, a special prosecutor launched a grand jury probe. He subpoenaed Miller and demanded that she reveal her source. She refused and was jailed for contempt of court. After 85 days detention, Miller was released when I. Lewis Libby (aka "Scooter"), then Vice President Cheney's chief of staff, allowed her to disclose that he had been her source. Almost certainly, Libby's motive for destroying Plame's cover was to retaliate against her husband, former Ambassador Joseph Wilson, for writing an op-ed piece contradicting the administration's assertions that Iraq was importing uranium for its alleged nuclear weapons program.

In addition to a dark story of vindictiveness and criminality within the government, Miller's saga also raises the question of whether journalists should have

to reveal the names of sources after giving them a pledge of confidentiality (anonymity) in exchange for disclosing information. Miller argued she should not be compelled to reveal her sources because (1) it would be very difficult to do investigative reporting without assuring sources of their confidentiality, (2) doing such reporting was the essence of a free press, and, therefore, (3) demands to reveal sources by prosecutors and other officials violated the First Amendment's protection of a free press. Miller's argument failed, though, because the Supreme Court had already rejected such First Amendment claims. In *Branzburg v. Hayes* (1972), for instance, the Court held that while "news gathering is not without First Amendment protections," journalists can be forced to disclose information related to the commission of a crime. A **shield law** that protects reporters from having to divulge the anonymous sources of their stories would have kept Miller out of jail, but the federal government does not have one.

The debate here is whether there should be a federal shield law. Supporters argue, in Miller's words, that, "If journalists cannot be trusted to guarantee

Claims to Special Legal Standing

In addition to using the First Amendment to fend off government control, the press has also tried to claim special constitutional status. This is based on the contention that reporters cannot do their jobs well unless they are sometimes exempt from the laws that apply to other citizens. One such claim relates to shielding confidential sources from disclosure and is discussed in the following You Decide box. Generally, as the box notes, the courts have not recognized such claims to special status. In addition to rejecting claims by reporters that they have a right to keep their sources confidential, the courts have denied journalists' demands to use cameras in courtrooms, to be present during grand jury testimony, and to have unrestricted access to prisoners. Yet the Supreme Court also recognizes that "without some protection for seeking out the news, freedom of the press could be eviscerated."[30] In line with this view, the Supreme Court has struck down several impediments

confidentiality, then journalists cannot function and there cannot be a free press."[31] Opponents make two counterarguments. One is that using anonymous sources obscures an important part of the story because being aware of who is revealing information lets the public judge the source's credibility and also to ask whether the source had an ulterior motive for talking to the press. In the hubbub over Plame, arguably the most important facts for the public were who had leaked her identity and why. Yet Miller kept that to herself. Second, opponents of shield laws say they can allow criminals to escape punishment. For instance, Libby might have avoided prosecution and remained a powerful official if a shield law had been in place.

The ability of the press to shield confidential sources varies around the world. About half the countries with a free press have shield laws, although only a few give journalists absolute protection. While there is no U.S. national shield law, over 30 states have them. Like most countries, most states give only partial immunity, usually by not shielding sources in criminal investigations. Polls show the public about evenly split on shield laws. On the federal level, President Obama has endorsed having a shield law, and in 2009 the House passed a bill shielding sources unless a court finds "the public interest in compelling disclosure of the . . . [source] outweighs the public interest in gathering or disseminating news." Most journalists see this bill as only a limited step forward. For instance, it might not have aided Judith Miller. If you were a U.S. senator, would you vote for the House version, make it stronger, or reject it altogether?

New York Times reporter Judith Miller, seen here leaving U.S. district court, was jailed for refusing to reveal her sources for a news story. The question in this box is whether she and other journalists should be shielded from such probes. (AP Photo/Haraz Ghanbari)

to the press including attempts by judges to bar reporters from courtrooms or to prohibit the press from reporting details of a pending case.

The Societal Setting of the News Media

Societal attitudes also help shape the role of the news media in the political system. As the communications link between the public and politically relevant events and leaders, it is important for democracy that the press conveys sufficient and accurate information to the people and that they pay attention to it.

More than 80% of Americans say that on a typical day they pay some attention to the news.[32] This seemingly positive concern with the news is tempered, however, by several factors. One is that it is probable that more people give what they know is the "correct" answer ("Yes, I follow the news") than actually do so (see Chapter 6 on polling problems). Second, about half of all Americans report that for the most part they follow only the news that particularly interests them. As a result, the level of information that the public has on many topics is modest at best. For example, when presented with a list of 11 questions on current events and multiple-choice answers, only 52% of the respondents on average picked the right answer. Similarly, when given the names of eight prominent American political figures and asked to identify their position or why they were in the news, only 53% of the respondents were on average able to do so correctly. Two nonpolitical Americans, singer Beyonce Knowles and football quarterback Payton Manning, were also included in the 2007 survey, and more people knew who they were than could identify presidential candidate Barack Obama, Speaker of the House Nancy Pelosi, or Secretary of Defense Robert Gates.[33]

Also tempering Americans' assertion that they follow the news are the disparities in attention among various groups. Older adults, those with more education, and those with more income are more likely to follow the news than are younger, less educated, and less wealthy adults. However, there is no gap in those with a high or moderate interest in the news between men and women or between whites and people of color.[34]

The Technological Setting of the News Media

Technology has always been an important factor in how news is conveyed and how widely it is available. During the early 1800s, for instance, development of the steam-powered rotary press vastly increased the speed of printing newspapers and lowered the cost per page. This created the "penny press." By the late 1820s newspapers could be sold for one cent versus an average price of six cents before then. As a result, many more Americans could buy newspapers, and they became the first of the "mass" media. Photography, radio, then television transmissions and other technological advances have each also had an immense impact on delivery of the news. Now the Internet is adding to that history. More than 90% of Americans report having some access to the Internet, with 70% having a connection at home. Over 80% of Americans also have a cell phone, most of which also have access to the Internet. In a trend that is profoundly affecting all political communications including the news, such devices are increasingly used to connect with a growing range of news sites.

Americans' Increasing Use of Internet News Sources

Americans have always used pamphlets, conversations, the mail, and methods other than the organized news media to transmit news. In recent years, though, the growth of Internet communications has begun to dramatically alter the process of disseminating news. Now the traditional sources are being augmented and to a degree supplanted by not only the Internet news media but also by e-mails, blogs, tweets, and other Internet-based communications.

Many of these communications involve opinion formation more than news as such and are covered in Chapter 6; others are more akin to the attempts of political actors such as the president (Chapter 12) to shape public opinion. Still other Internet communications can be classified as news. About 60% of those who check the news daily use the Internet as one of their sources, and 75% say they get at least some of their news from the Internet. Some of these sources are organized operations such as the liberal *Huffington Post*, which was drawing visits from 8.9 million people monthly in mid-2009, the conservative *Drudge Report* (3.4 million visitors monthly), and the less ideological *Politico.com* (6.7 million visitors monthly). There are also organized news aggregators that compile news from various other sites. The largest of these, Yahoo News, had more than 40 million unique visitors in 2009. At the other end of the organizational spectrum are messages and videos posted on YouTube, Facebook, and other sites that handle the billions of e-mail and text messages a day that people use to exchange information.

News is also transmitted via the Internet by politicians and other political figures. These people have usually been covered by the media but now are increasingly able to bypass the traditional media altogether and communicate with the public directly. The Internet-savvy Obama administration provides a prime illustration. While still a candidate for president, Obama formally announced his vice presidential choice by sending out a text message to millions of supporters. Once in the White House, the president used the Internet to stream his press conferences to the public via YouTube. Moreover, he took that channel to a new dimension in February 2010 when he held a "press conference" that did not include the press. Instead, Obama answered some of the 11,000 questions that had been submitted through CitizenTube, YouTube's political Website. According to the White House, it selected those questions that voting on CitizenTube indicated that people wanted answered the most. Indeed, the U.S. government now has its own YouTube channel at www.youtube.com/usgovernment. A third telling illustration occurred in February 2010 when Joseph Stack posted a six-page explanation online about why he was planning to ram an airplane into an Austin, Texas, office building containing an Internal Revenue Service office with some 200 employees. After the deadly attack the White House posted its first comments on its blog site.

Few observers doubt that the new wave of political information is having an impact on the political process, but such ways of transmitting news are so recent and diverse that it is unclear what their overall impact is. We will explore that question later in this chapter. These sources also raise several issues that are taken up later, in the discussion of the quality of the news. For now, though, consider the following additional data about nontraditional sources of news:[35]

- 61% of Americans say they get some news online.
- 31% go online daily to get news.
- 28% of Internet users have customized their home page to include specific news sources and news topics.
- 27% report getting a news story from a friend by e-mail within the last week.
- 14% report sending a news story to a friend by e-mail within the last week.
- 36% read blogs about politics or current events.
- 12% read online magazines such as *Salon* or *Slate*.
- 30% get information about local, national, or international news through social networking sites such as MySpace and Facebook.
- 24% share information about local, national, or international news on a social networking site.

Americans' Continuing Use of Traditional News Soures

There is no doubt that the surge in Internet news is taking a toll on traditional news sources. As noted in this chapter's introduction, the number of daily newspapers, their circulation, and the number of reporters and other professional journalists they employ are declining. Between 1980 and 2008 the number of people watching the national evening news on one of the big three broadcast stations (ABC, CBS, and NBC) dropped more than 50% from about 52 million to 23 million. This decline has been offset a bit by the nearly 4 million people who watch an evening prime-time news program on FOX News, CNN, or one of the other cable networks and the approximately 2 million viewers who watch the news during another time of day on one

The U.S. daily newspaper publication rate at 196 copies for every 1,000 people trails most of the countries of Western Europe (average rate: 291).

of those outlets. In general though, like newspapers, national television news continues to lose its audience.

Yet despite such signs of weakness in traditional news sources, it is far too early to write their obituary. In the first place, Americans still rely heavily on television for news, with 66% saying that it was their main source or tied for their main source of news for the 2010 elections. Newspapers at 31% were a distant second, followed by the Internet (20%), and radio (17%).[36] Television's dominance as a news source is common globally, as shown in Figure 8.6.

Second, some of the most important Internet sources are online extensions of the legacy news media. For instance, the decline in newspaper circulation has been partly offset by the growing use of newspapers' online editions. More than 66 million unique visitors a month accessed the country's newspaper Websites in 2008. With the average individual doing so more than eight times a month, there were about 6.6 billion total visits to newspaper Web editions. All the major television networks also have Websites with "Webcasts" of recent news programs and a host of other news-related features. Millions of people also use the Internet to access other traditional news sources such as the Associated Press, other wire services, and foreign news outlets. Indeed, of the 199 Internet news sites with the most traffic in 2010, 48% were the Websites of traditional newspapers, and another 19% were based on other legacy news media sources, only 33% were online-only news sources.[37]

FIGURE 8.6 Comparative Use of Television as a News Source

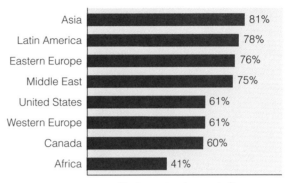

% of people who most often get news from television

Americans, like most people around the world, rely mainly on television for national and international news. Poor sub-Saharan Africa is the only region in which television is not the primary source of news. There, 54% of the people rely first on radio.
Data source: Pew Research Center, *Global Attitudes Project,* 2007.

The Global Setting of the News Media

One of the remarkable changes in the settings within which the news media operate has been the globalization of news: the increased ability of news to move rapidly across borders and even around the world. Americans were once largely isolated from foreign news sources by the country's geographic location. For the same reason, the U.S. news media had little impact on the world and was, in turn, generally isolated from foreign influences. All this has changed to some degree and will change more in the future.

A list of English-language newspapers and other news sites worldwide is at www.world-newspapers.com/.

One change is the increased ability of Americans to get their news from foreign sources. New technology such as cable and satellite television has played a role in this change. British Broadcasting Corporation (BBC) news programming is available on most U.S. cable/satellite carriers, and the Canadian Broadcasting Corporation (CBC) is commonly available on cable systems in states that border Canada. To the south, the news and other programming of Mexico's Grupo Televisa, S.A. flows across the U.S.-Mexico border. Although it has only limited availability because of the current political climate, Al Jazeera, the Arab news network, now broadcasts in English. The Internet has also expanded the availability of other foreign news sources to Americans. English-language editions of foreign newspapers ranging from Russia's *Moscow Times*, through Beijing's *China Daily*, to Egypt's *Al-Ahram* are online.

The ability to get news from foreign sources has important implications. One is that it is possible to access news about foreign policy and world events that is not influenced by the national outlook that shapes the views of the U.S. press. It usually strives to be unbiased, but studies show that "the closer reporters/editors are to a given news event in terms of national interest, the further they are from applying professional news values" such as objectivity.[38]

It is also the case that the ownership of both entertainment and news media is becoming more internationalized. Rupert Murdoch illustrates this trend. He was born in Australia, where he began building a newspaper empire in the 1950s. During the 1960s, Murdoch expanded to Great Britain with such press acquisitions as *The Times*. Then in the 1970s he entered the U.S. media market. He owns or has owned such newspapers as the *Chicago Sun-Times*, *San Antonio Express-News*, *New York Post*, and *Wall Street Journal*. Murdoch became a U.S. citizen in order to enter the television market and proceeded to found the FOX network. He also owns a wide variety of mass media properties including several cable channels, magazines such as *TV Guide*, communications carrier DirectTV, publisher HarperCollins, the tabloid *Star*, film studio Twentieth Century Fox, and Internet venues such as MySpace.

The flow of news is not just one way. The U.S. media have increasingly become important sources of news overseas. CNN has a true global presence, broadcasting in six languages and available at least to some degree by cable/satellite in most of the world's countries.

THE CONTENT AND QUALITY OF THE NEWS

"All the News That's Fit to Print" is the slogan that has adorned the front page of the *New York Times* since 1896. As an ideal it is a nice thought, but in reality no newspaper can come close to mentioning, much less fully reporting everything that might legitimately be labeled "news." The other news media bring the public even less news. For example, the 2,500 to 3,000 spoken words during stories on the average television evening national news broadcast are about the same number as those on just the front page of the *New York Times*. Because space and time limits require journalists to be very selective about what they report, it is important to ask what the press chooses to cover and why.

Deciding What Is News

The place to begin analyzing what makes up the news is at the two ends of the news conduit, the press and the public. The wants and needs of each interact and help structure the news.

What the Press Wants

Three motivations are key to determining what the press wants. *Public benefit* is the first and the one that journalists most often cite. "The most important benefit of being a journalist," the American Society of News Editors advises, is that "you have a chance to do something that is for the public good—inform, explain, reveal unknown and important information, and entertain." This sense of mission means that many journalists work for modest salaries in sometimes difficult and even dangerous conditions to report the news. According to Reporters Without Borders, for instance, 503 journalists were killed and thousands of others were injured or arrested between 2002 and 2009. The impulse in reporters to benefit the public also feeds their desire to be the public's **watchdog**, to protect the public interest by doing **investigative reporting** to expose examples of corruption, neglect, waste, ineptitude, and other transgressions by public officials and other high-profile people.

Business profit is a second factor that motivates the news media. Most of them survive primarily on advertising revenue and other sources of money that are heavily influenced by audience size. This creates a strong economic incentive to report the kind of news that will draw the biggest audience. "The news is principally produced by market forces," one scholar writes, and that pressure stems from what the public wants.[39]

Personal self-advancement is the third motivation that shapes the news. Like people in other professions, journalists seek higher-paying, more prestigious positions in a highly competitive environment. Succeeding depends heavily on reporting the kinds of stories and presenting them in a way that maximizes the audience. As one study explains, "reporters and anchors may not always consciously think about [market forces], but if their actions do not conform to the logic [of the market] they run the risk of losing ratings, raises, or even their jobs."[40]

What the Public Wants

A second part of the equation that determines what is newsworthy is based on what the public wants to know and how it wants it presented. This can be broken down into seven criteria:[41]

- *Impact.* People are most interested in what impacts them directly. That is why when people are asked which parts of the news they pay very close attention to, "the weather" is the answer people give most frequently (48%).[42]
- *Excitement.* People are drawn to stories about crime, violence, and sex because they are exciting. Crime (28%) ranks second to only the weather as the topic people follow very closely.
- *Proximity.* Most people focus on local, national, and world news in that order. Therefore, local television is the news source that Americans are most likely (52%) to visit regularly.
- *Timeliness.* People tend to focus on the present and the immediate future more than the past or the far future. As the adage goes "Nothing is so stale as yesterday's newspaper."[43]
- *Novelty.* Unusual is interesting. As journalist Charles Dana observed over a century ago, "When a dog bites a man, that is not news, but when a man bites a dog, that is news."[44]
- *Familiarity.* Because people devote only a limited time to the news, they are more apt to follow stories about familiar topics because it takes less time to understand them.
- *Brevity.* Most Americans do not seek out in-depth reporting.[45] They devote an average of only 66 minutes a day to the news. Two-thirds of that is spent on television and radio news, both of which feature short news items. That leaves Americans devoting only 22 minutes a day to reading printed newspapers or going online to get more in-depth coverage.[46]

 Belgians spend the most time—54 minutes daily—reading printed newspapers. Americans spend 13 minutes.

The Press, the Public, and the News

It is clear that there is interplay between what the press wants to report and what the public wants to know that helps shape the news. However, there is no formula to determine the weight of each factor. Instead the flow of news is largely decided by **gatekeepers**, the publishers and editors who determine news budgets, assign stories to reporters, and make final decisions about what stories are printed or aired. The Associated Press and other wire services are also important gatekeepers because local news outlets depend on them to supply national and international news stories.

Some decisions are easy for the gatekeepers because what the press wants to report and what the public wants to know are the same. Events such as terrorist attacks, natural disasters, and wars fulfill the urge of journalists to convey major events and also fulfill several of the criteria for what interests the public. When the press and public differ, then the gatekeepers, who are more attuned to the business needs of their paper or station, find themselves under heavy pressure to maintain or increase their audience by catering to the public's tastes. Because excitement appeals to the public, crime is the most frequently covered topic in local television (42% of all stories), metropolitan newspapers (26%), and local radio stations (24%). Responding to the reality that lack of proximity does not sell, the press overall features foreign news that does not involve U.S. foreign policy in only 6% of its stories.[47]

The Quality of the News

Because what constitutes news is partly subjective and because there is a large and increasing number of news sources, it is important to ask about the quality of the news. The need to explore this topic also stems from surveys indicating that neither journalists nor the public is very satisfied with the quality of the news.[48] Precisely measuring quality is challenging, but good quality news is arguably produced by an independent press whose reporting is accurate, objective, balanced, representative, substantive, penetrating, and transparent.

Independent

An independent press is a prime prerequisite to high-quality news. This independence must go beyond legal guarantees, such as those found in the First Amendment, to also include being independent of the news media's corporate ownership, the politicians, and even the public.

Independence from Owners and Advertisers   Journalists must be free to report stories even if they are at odds with the ideological viewpoint of the ownership or offend the advertisers that the owners rely on for revenue. There is some evidence that such restrictions on journalistic independence do occur. For example, one study found that magazines that accepted advertising from tobacco companies were 40% less likely to carry stories linking tobacco and cancer than magazines without tobacco advertisements.[49] Moreover, 25% of journalists say that "corporate owners influence news organizations' decisions about which stories to cover or emphasize" a "fair amount of time" or a "great deal."[50] How widespread this problem is engenders much debate. One source warns that it occurs enough to present a "threat to democracy."[51] Another source disagrees, contending, "There is no solid evidence that media giants squelch anti-business news."[52]

Independence from Politicians   Journalists must also avoid being manipulated by politicians. This creates a **lapdog** press, the opposite of a watchdog press. Press releases, briefings, interviews, documents, and other sources of information provided by government sources make up much of the news that journalists gather. Indeed, one recent study of six news stories in the Baltimore, Maryland, media found that government press releases triggered 62% of the coverage.[53] That is probably considerably higher than typical for national and international news across the country, but it does give some idea of how frequently officials prompt the news.

Sometimes, the press uses this information too readily. Many in the press have blamed themselves for not being more skeptical of information supplied to them by the Bush administration about the threat posed by Iraq as a reason for an invasion. For one, the *New York Times* confessed that it had allowed controversial information from the White House to "stand unchallenged" because the editors had been "too intent on rushing scoops into the paper."[54] In other cases, reporters become too friendly with their sources, and "such coziness may sap journalists' zeal" to investigate matters that might alienate their sources.[55] In addition, politicians sometimes try to intimidate reporters by threatening to cut off their information. "I don't know if there's a physical blacklist," one White House correspondent comments. "But there seems to be a system within the White House of retribution. Basically, if you write something [negative], it's like . . . the message goes out that so-and-so's on the blacklist [and cut off from information]—in some cases for that day, in some cases for that week."[56]

Independence from the Public   The third aspect of journalistic freedom is being willing to publish information that citizens should know even if it makes them angry at the messenger. Such anger can reduce the size of the audience and, by extension, the revenue flow. For example, concern by the press about appearing unpatriotic arguably added to its reluctance to challenge the Bush administration during the run-up to the war in Iraq.[57] This concern by the press about public opinion is not groundless. Americans are closely divided between those who think the press patriotically "stands up" for the country and those who see journalists as "too critical" of the United States.[58] Former CBS evening news anchor Dan Rather has admitted that one reason that he failed to sufficiently probe the Bush administration's case for war in Iraq was because, "Sounding unpatriotic takes strength, strength I didn't always have."[59]

Accurate

High-quality news is accurate. Critics charge that the press often fails to meet this standard, and, a 2009 survey found 63% of Americans saying that news stories are "often inaccurate."[60] Even 31% of reporters are willing to admit that "news reports are increasingly full of factual errors and sloppy reporting."[61] This is generally attributed to the escalating pressure to report stories quickly caused by the proliferation of news outlets competing for audience and revenue.

One notable example occurred during the 2004 presidential campaign when Dan Rather damaged the candidacy of President Bush by reporting that the Texas Air National Guard had given him special treatment during his enlistment in the 1970s. Rather relied on documents supplied by an anonymous source, but they soon proved to be forgeries that had been fabricated and given to CBS by a retired Guard officer who was a virulent critic of the president. Some analysts maintained that CBS had intentionally misled its audience out of liberal animus for Bush, while others agreed with an independent investigation's conclusion that the problem was that CBS had "failed miserably" to authenticate the documents because of competitive pressure and the network's "myopic zeal" to beat the competition by getting the story out first.[62] Eventually CBS apologized for its error, fired four staff members, and forced Rather to resign.

Objective

Good reporting is objective, not subjective. It is policy neutral, nonpartisan, and does not reflect whether journalists like or dislike a candidate or official. How close the press comes to meeting this standard is controversial. It is difficult to agree about how much bias exists and toward what or whom because when the press is subjective it is usually expressed subtly rather than overtly. Whether, for example, a story discusses abortion in terms of "freedom of choice" or a "right to life" may reflect the reporter's personal opinion. Who is interviewed, what sources are cited, and even whether pictures tend to show an individual in a positive or negative light are other subtle ways that subjectivity can come through.

One common charge is that much of the news media has a liberal bias and favors the Democrats. Scholarly studies looking for direct evidence of partisanship are divided. Most find little or no bias.[63] One study argues, for example, that there is "no consistent partisan bias in newspaper coverage" and only "a tiny . . . pro-Democratic . . . bias in television network news."[64] Other scholars disagree. They uniformly find that while the ideological leanings in the press range from such liberal outlets such as CBS, through more neutral one like PBS, to conservative outlets such as the FOX News Channel, there is an overall liberal tendency in the news media.[65]

Some would argue that the 2008 presidential election also demonstrates media bias. Studies by two respected research centers both concluded that Barack Obama received lopsidedly favorable coverage by the major news outlets compared to John McCain.[66] The results of one of the studies are shown in Figure 8.7. Whether this shows partisan

FIGURE 8.7 Tone of Press toward Obama and McCain

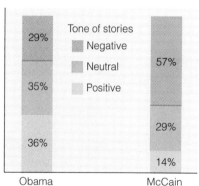

During the 2008 presidential campaign, more than twice as many stories were positive about Barack Obama than about John McCain. More than half the stories about McCain were negative, compared to just over a quarter of the stories about Obama.
Data source: Pew Research Center's Project for Excellence in Journalism, "The Color of News: How Different Media Have Covered the General Election," October 22, 2008.

bias or merely favoritism by the press for one candidate over the other is debatable. In either case, though, it is questionable whether under any circumstances the press should ever lean so decidedly toward a candidate. Moreover, the media's pro-Obama orientation continued into the early days of his presidency. According to the Pew Research Center, "Coverage of Obama's first 60 days in office differed markedly from that of his two immediate predecessors, George W. Bush and Bill Clinton. Not only was Obama's early coverage notably more positive than Bush's and Clinton's . . . but it also focused far more on his personal and leadership qualities than was the case for presidents No. 42 and 43.[67]

There is also a fair amount of indirect evidence supporting suspicions of subjectivity in the press. Some of the indications are:

- Most (64%) journalists agree that the "distinction between reporting and commentary has seriously eroded."[68]
- Journalists are far more likely to be liberal than the average American, as seen in Figure 8.8.
- In every presidential election between 1964 and 2004, journalists voted for the Democratic candidate by margins of at least 2 to 1.[69] For example 68% of journalists said they voted for John Kerry in 2004, 25% voted for George Bush, 1% voted for Ralph Nader, and 5% did not vote or refused to say for whom.
- Journalists are more liberal than the public on many policy issues. They are, for example, almost twice as likely as the public to believe that society should accept homosexuality "as a way of life."[70] Journalists (40%) also favor legal abortion under any circumstances more than the public (25%).[71]
- Fully 74% of the public believes that news organizations "tend to favor one side" on issues and in campaigns. Only 8% think the press deals "fairly with all sides."
- As for which side the public thinks the press favors, 50% saw a liberal bias compared to only 22% saying a conservative bias, with the rest unsure.[72]
- Even 38% of journalists agree that their colleagues "are letting their ideological views show in their reporting too frequently."[73]
- Toward the end of the 2008 presidential election, 70% of the public said it thought that reporters wanted Barack Obama to win.[74]

FIGURE 8.8 Comparing the Political Ideology of Journalists and the Public

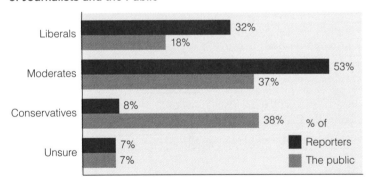

Journalists for national news outlets are decidedly more liberal and less conservative than is the public. Local news journalists are somewhat less liberal/ more conservative than national news reporters but still more liberal/less conservative than the public.
Data sources: Pew Research Center separate surveys of reporters and the public, September 2007.

Many of these findings deserve more analysis than is possible here. For instance, some of the public perception of bias in the press can be attributed to individuals thinking that anything in the press that does not favor their view is evidence of bias.[75] However, this factor does not explain the substantial tendency of those who see bias to see it as liberal or the 45% of independents who see the press as too liberal, while only 19% say it is too conservative, and 30% see no tilt in either direction.[76]

What, then, can we say about allegations of bias in the press? Certainly the jury of scholars and other analysts remains divided. Still, it seems safe to say that the evidence indicates that (1) there is some ideological/partisan bias in the press, that (2) it is more often liberal than conservative, and that (3) whatever bias exists is not nearly as pervasive or one-sided as critics charge.

Represented by this mock-up of headlines, a persistent criticism of the press is that it presents an overly negative image of politics and society, thereby encouraging public alienation and suspicion. (iStockphoto)

Balanced

Because what the public knows about most national and international issues and events is based largely on what the press conveys, it is important for news accounts to be balanced. By its very nature, the news is going to be at least somewhat focused on crime, corruption, violence, and other negative events. However, many critics claim that the press goes overboard by presenting an overwhelmingly negative view of reality.

Presidents of both parties have agreed with this charge. Richard Nixon grumbled, "For the press progress is not news—trouble is news."[77] And Bill Clinton complained that reporters "love to destroy people. That's how they get their rocks off."[78] Most Americans (64%) agree that the press is too negative.[79] Research tends to support these impressions.[80] One indication is how negative press coverage is of presidents even during their first year in office when their popularity tends to be highest. For example, the tone of coverage by the ABC, CBS, and NBC television networks of each of the five most recent presidents (Reagan, Bush, Clinton, Bush, and Obama) during their first year in office was negative, with the percentages of negative stories averaging 68%.[81] President Obama was least battered by the press, with his first year garnering only 54% negative coverage, but that was buoyed by an upbeat January–April 2009 honeymoon period (only 41% negative). After that, though, the press soured on the president, with the share of negative stories rising to 51% during May through June and 61% during August through December.[82]

Congress also fares poorly in the press, with coverage focusing "on scandal, partisan rivalry, and conflict between the House and Senate" rather than on the substance of

A majority of people in 8 of 10 countries and an overall average of 59% in one global survey agreed that their country's press published too many negative stories.

policy.[83] Even many journalists concede the point. One reporter depicts many of his colleagues as "assuming that nearly every public official statement is a lie or a half-truth until proved otherwise."[84]

One reason that the press stresses the negative is that doing so feeds the public's appetite for stories about crime, violence, scandals, and other negative news. A second reason for the high level of negative news is that journalists see themselves as watchdogs for the public. This disposes them to focus on problems.[85] As Jimmy Carter put it, "I never knew of any time when there was an investigative reporter . . . who tried to get the truth about an issue where the truth would be nonscandalous or nonprovocative."[86] This hostility can be circular, with politicians who feel abused by reporters trying to avoid them. Recent presidents, for example, have had fewer press conferences as their time in office has progressed.[87] During his first year in office, for instance, President Obama held 70% of his press conferences during the first six months.

Unbalanced, negative reporting can also have an ill effect on public perceptions of minority groups.[88] The vast majority of Latinos, for example, are law-abiding citizens. Yet according to one analysis of the press and its focus on crime and other problems, what the public has "learned is that Latinos are problem people living on the fringes of U.S. society. Rarely do we see stories about the positive contributions they make."[89] Polls show that this slant has some impact on Americans. One survey asked people to estimate what percentage Latinos were of the U.S. prison population. Over two-thirds of the respondents who answered guessed too high. The average guess (31%), was more than twice the actual rate (15%).[90]

Representative

Yet another factor determining the quality of the press is how well it covers the society about which it is reporting. If the news media pays disproportionate attention to some demographic groups and underreports others, it is not representative. Statistics for this measure of quality show that political minorities receive far less coverage than their proportionate share of the population. This poor coverage regarding Latinos has been documented in the *Brownout Report* sponsored by the National Association of Hispanic Journalists.[91] It found, for instance, that less than 1% of the news stories aired by ABC, CBS, CNN, and NBC focused on Latinos. Moreover, the Latino viewpoint was often absent even from these stories. For example, half the stories about Latinos did not include an interview with one.

The lack of representative coverage also applies to women. They are the focus of only 27% of all U.S. news stories. This share is only somewhat better than cover-

 A global survey of 39 countries found that the average share of women journalists had increased to 38% in 2002 from 27% in 1992.

age in other countries, as is evident in Figure 8.9. The diminution of women is also apparent in other ways. One global study found that women comprised only 14% of the spokespersons and 17% of the experts interviewed by journalists world-wide. The U.S. press was only marginally better, with women making up 21% of the spokespersons and 22% of the experts. Thus, "the news of the day still largely comes from a male perspective."[92]

FIGURE 8.9 Comparative News Coverage of Men and Women

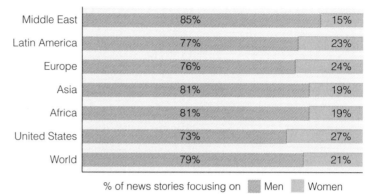

% of news stories focusing on ■ Men ■ Women

Women receive a small minority of the news coverage everywhere, including the United States.
Data source: Who Makes the News: Global Media Monitoring Project 2005 (London: World Association for Christian Communication, 2005).

To a degree, cultural bias also plays a role in foreign news coverage. What foreign news there is tends to emphasize Canada and Europe, except during dramatic events such as conflicts involving U.S. forces or natural disasters. This is evident in a study of how the U.S. press covered 13 countries that were experiencing a civil war or other crisis in 1996. Only one of the 13 countries, Bosnia, was in Europe and largely populated by whites. The other 12 countries were outside of Europe and had predominantly non-white populations. Yet, the media devoted a majority of its attention to Bosnia. Similarly, another study found that—excluding stories about Iraq and the rest of the Middle East—62% of network television news stories about non-U.S. topics were on Europe and Canada. Asia drew 21% of the coverage, Latin America 11%, and Africa 5%.

By contrast, the U.S.-based Spanish-language press takes a very different approach. Its overall coverage of non-U.S. foreign news is relatively high (17% of stories) and focuses heavily on Latin America.[93] In much the same way, the African-American press, such as New York City's *Amsterdam News,* pays more attention to Africa than does the mainstream media.

The first African-American newspaper, *Freedom's Journal,* was published in New York City in 1827.

Substantive

Stories in the press can be divided into two types. **Hard news** is the more substantive of the two and focuses on the operation of local, state, and national government; policy issues; international affairs; and business and finance. **Soft news** includes sports, lifestyle, human-interest, and other such stories. Both types are valid, but the press has to report a significant amount of hard news if journalists are to play their key role in a democracy of informing the public.

The concern is that financial pressures are forcing the news media to stress **info-tainment**. This includes reporting more and more soft news and less and less hard news and also presenting hard news in a format calculated to entertain the public more than inform it. During 2009, for example, President Obama was the focus of more stories in the U.S. press than any other person, but the second ranking went to pop star Michael Jackson and his death. Supreme Court nominee Sonia Soto-mayor, Secretary of State Hillary Clinton, and former Republican vice presidential nominee Sarah Palin trailed in third, fourth, and fifth place respectively.[94]

Another way that infotainment is evident in political news is how much election news is devoted to the electoral **horse race**—who is ahead and behind in the polls, campaign strategy, and related subjects—and how little focuses on issues and other matters of substance.[95] As one analyst explains, "Horse race stories are more fun. Substance stories are more important."[96] Research shows that during presidential elections between 1988 and 2008, the horse race accounted for at least 50% and up to 71% of the news stories about the campaigns.[97] In 2008, despite such pressing issues as the wars in Iraq and Afghanistan, health care reform, and the implosion of the U.S. and world economies, the horse race was discussed in 64% of all stories, while policy was covered in only 31%.[98]

It is easy to criticize the press on this matter, but bear in mind that what the press covers relates to public tastes and to the fact that it must cater to those preferences to survive financially. As Dan Rather ruefully conceded, "Too many of us in hard news are looking for that extra tenth of a ratings point" and trying to get it by "blurring the distinctions and standards between news and entertainment."[99] It is also the case that some scholars argue that soft news plays a positive role by drawing the audience to other, harder news, but this idea is controversial.[100]

Part of the trend toward infotainment is the blurring of the line between the news media and the entertainment media. This shift is represented by this March 2009 photo of Barack Obama explaining his response to the country's deep recession on the Tonight show hosted by comedian Jay Leno. It was the first appearance on such a show by a president while in office. (AP Photo/Gerald Herbert)

A third aspect of infotainment, and one attributable more to the politicians rather than the news media, is the use of the entertainment media by officials, candidates, and other political actors to convey their messages to the public. John McCain, for example, announced his 2008 presidential campaign on the David Letterman show, and another Republican hopeful, former Senator Fred Thompson (TN), launched his campaign on Jay Leno's *Tonight* program. On the Democratic side, future Vice President Joe Biden announced his bid for the presidency on *Good Morning America*, and former Senator John Edwards (NC) chose NBC's morning *Today* show to declare his candidacy. Candidates are not the only ones to use the entertainment media for their political purposes. In March 2009 Barack Obama became the first sitting president to appear on a late-night talk show when he joined Jay Leno to discuss the financial crisis and defend the actions of Secretary of the

Treasury Timothy Geithner. Such uses of the entertainment media are discussed further in Chapters 10 (elections) and 12 (the presidency).

Penetrating

Politics and government are complex topics, and the best reporting reflects that with penetrating coverage that illuminates the intricacies of an event or issue. Although there is no precise measure to judge when coverage is in-depth, statistics indicate that most news reporting is brief and therefore prone to oversimplifying stories. For example, the stories on the presidential campaigns carried by the television broadcast networks have declined in both number and length over the years. One indication is that the average length of television **sound bites** of a candidate's speaking declined from 43 seconds in 1968 to 7 seconds in 2000. Newspapers have more space for in-depth coverage, but even they tend to favor brief stories. One analysis found that 73% of all stories in metropolitan dailies were 500 words or less, and only 1% were more than 1,000 words. As with many of the complaints against the press, what the press does is influenced by what the public wants, in this case brevity. Indeed, journalists would prefer more in-depth coverage, with 78% of them conceding that the press pays too little attention to complex stories.[101]

One suggestion to increase the quality of coverage is to increase the presence of public broadcasting among the U.S. media. The argument for public broadcasting is that it can "afford" to air longer newscasts and more culturally diverse programming than stations driven by market forces. Advocates for more federal funding for public broadcasting also point out that by global standards, U.S. spending is very low. This is evident in one study of government spending during 2006 on public broadcasting in 18 wealthy democracies including the United States. Among these countries, Switzerland annually spent the most per capita ($122), and the average per capita outlay was $63. The United States spent by far the least per capita ($4) on public broadcasting.[102]

Transparent

Journalists and others in recent decades have pressed government to become more transparent in its operations so that the public can evaluate not only policies, but also the process that led up to them. Similarly, press transparency adds to the public's ability to judge the quality of the news. Yet transparency about the sources of news is often missing in journalism. Almost half of all stories that appear in national newspapers or on the national broadcast and cable news programs use at least some anonymous sources. Reporters claim this is necessary to get the news, but the practice also withholds valuable information that would allow people to evaluate the stories.

Those who disagree with using anonymous sources contend the practice negatively impacts the goal of an informed public because often knowing who supplied the information can be helpful in evaluating the context of the story. Some confidential sources are simply public-spirited whistleblowers. But others have a political agenda and are trying to use the press to build support for themselves or their policy preferences. Therefore, it is helpful for the public to know the source when trying to evaluate the information. For example, as related in the You Decide box on shield laws, what turned out to be the most important part of the saga of reporter Judith Miller and CIA agent Valerie Plame was how high in the government the leak was and the reprehensible reason that it had occurred. Yet it took a grand jury investigation to reveal this skullduggery to the public because Miller shielded her source.

Lack of transparency can also lead to inaccurate reporting because someone who is shielded by anonymity is more likely to pass on rumor as fact or even make things up. This occurred in the scandal discussed earlier when Dan Rather used an anonymous source to impugn President Bush's military record. Had the source been known, his strong animus for Bush would have created suspicions that the documents he supplied were what they turned out to be—forgeries.

THE IMPACT OF THE NEWS MEDIA

Perhaps the most important question to ask about the news media relates to the political bottom line: What is the impact of the press on the American political process? To answer that, we will first look at ways that the news media exercise influence, then at limits on that impact.

News Media Influence

"The people don't get it that the press runs the government," President Clinton once exclaimed.[103] That is an overstatement, but it does convey the sense that journalists are actors in, not merely observers of, the political drama. To examine the influence of the news media, the following sections take up their roles in transmitting information, setting the political agenda, framing news topics, and priming us to use one or another standard of evaluation.

Information Transmission

The media's most fundamental source of influence stems from the fact that much of what we know about our political world is what the press tells us.[104] The press is not our only source, but it provides much more political information to the average person than any other source.

Information is not just contained in written and spoken words. Images also are a type of information, and the types of images the media present make a difference. The increasing ability to project images has also arguably changed the political possibilities for various political hopefuls. Being photogenic, for example, is more important for candidates than it once was. From a slightly different angle, you have to wonder if the gaunt Abraham Lincoln with his abnormally long limbs or wheel chair–bound Franklin D. Roosevelt could be elected to office today.

Agenda Setting

Another important role that the press plays is **agenda setting**. This is the process of establishing what the government and public are thinking and talking about, and it relates to our earlier discussion of what constitutes news. Most often, events, political leaders, interest groups, mass movements, and other factors set the political agenda, and the press reactively reports it. Yet even when the press has not launched an item onto the agenda, attention by the press helps determine whether a story remains current or fades. As one scholar notes, "the issues occupying people's minds at any time, on the whole reflect their prominence in the media."[105]

Sometimes, though, the press sets the agenda through investigative reporting. One example is the uproar that arose beginning in 2005 after the press discovered that the Bush administration was secretly monitoring some Americans' communications without judicial authorization. Other traits of media coverage also proactively set the agenda. The focus of the press on crime, for instance, has elevated public concern to a much greater degree than is justified by the country's actual, and in most areas falling, crime rate. This impact is evident, among other places, in the finding that the more people watch television, the more likely they are to overestimate the danger of being a crime victim.[106]

The media not only help set the political agenda for the public, they also do so for the government. Sometimes the press merely brings information to policy makers. "I learn more from CNN than I do from the CIA," President George H. W. Bush once commented, hopefully in jest.[107] At other times, especially during a crisis, media attention pushes government officials to act.[108] As one top advisor to Presidents Carter and Clinton noted, if a dramatic, threatening event "is featured on TV news, the president and his advisers feel bound to make a response in time for the next evening news program." Such pressures to act can be positive or negative. Media reports of the faltering government response to the damage caused by Hurricane Katrina had the positive impact of putting the relief effort at the top of the political agenda for many weeks. But, as former Secretary of State Madeleine Albright has observed, media coverage can also force policy makers "to respond to events much faster than it might have been prudent" to do.[109]

Framing

One factor that influences how the public will perceive events, policies, organizations, and public figures is the way each is characterized or put in context. This is called **framing** or "defining the issue." For example, one way to frame undocumented immigrants is to portray them as filling jobs Americans do not want, paying taxes, and making other contributions. An alternative frame for illegal immigrants is to depict them as undercutting the wages of Americans and adding to the cost of providing education and other benefits.

Politicians, interest groups, and others regularly try to gain an advantage by framing issues in a way that will influence public opinion to agree with their point of view. The press calls this "spin," and those who practice it "spin doctors." But the news media also sometimes frame issues by "reporting the news from a particular perspective so that some aspects of the situation come into close focus and others fade into the background."[110]

Sometimes the press passively helps frame an issue by carrying speeches, press releases, political advertising, and other messages that have spin from politicians and others to the public. At other times, the news media intentionally or unintentionally frames issues by choosing how to portray a topic. One study of public opinion regarding race concluded that media "framing is a significant cause of racial policy preferences."[111] In particular, public support for policies assisting minority groups increases when the press stresses egalitarian values by, among other things, using terms such as "affirmative action" and "equal protection" to describe policies. By contrast, public support for racial advancement policies declines when the press frames them in terms such as "reverse discrimination" and "race-based quotas" that run afoul of values associated with individualism.

Framing and race also intersect in the area for foreign affairs reporting. One illustration is found in a study of news stories about Africa between 1948 and 1979. The analysis revealed that the mainstream U.S. press mostly framed its coverage of Africa in terms of whether one or another African country would become a cold-war ally of the Soviet Union. By comparison, the black-owned press was more apt to frame reports on Africa in terms of its anticolonial struggles and the new countries' social, economic, and humanitarian needs.[112]

Scholars are divided on how often and how much news media frames distort reality and on what the impact on public opinion generally is. Without getting into that complex debate, we can safely say that media framing does make a difference, but it is just one of many factors that influence public opinion. Moreover, framing's impact depends on many "contextual" factors such as whether the media and other opinion leaders are united in how they frame an issue or portray the issue in competing frames.[113] Thus, as one study concludes, it would be misleading to "claim that the media alone drive the framing debates in American politics."[114]

Priming

Another way that the news media exercises influence is through **priming**. This involves how the focus of reporting influences the standards the public uses to evaluate an issue or a public figure. A good example of how priming works relates to presidential job-rating polls, those that ask people whether they approve of the way the president is handling his job. This is a broad question that should include many factors in determining the answer, but studies show that an important determinant of the president's job rating at any given time is his performance related to the one or two most prominent news stories at the time of the poll.[115] George W. Bush did not become markedly more or less competent during his eight years as president. Yet in the fall of 2001, his approval rating averaged 87% because the intensive news coverage of the 9/11 attack and the press's generally positive portrayal of Bush's response to that crisis primed the public to evaluate him positively overall. By contrast, the media's later focus on the U.S. difficulties in Iraq and other problems arguably primed the public to evaluate Bush according to those issues, and his public approval ratings dipped into the mid-twenties. Priming also affects voter behavior because "The priorities that are uppermost in voters' minds as they go to the polls to select a president or a [member of Congress] appear to be powerfully shaped by the last-minute preoccupations of television news."[116]

Framing and priming by the press are inescapable functions of journalism. Usually, one hopes, the orientation is chosen for objective reasons. However, there are times when the press takes a subjective position, either consciously and overtly as in an editorial, or subconsciously and covertly by slanting the news. In either case, the views of the news media are important. There remains a fair amount of disagreement about when and by how much public opinion and voting can be affected by a lack of neutrality in the press, but it does make a difference.[117] As one recent study concludes, "We find concrete evidence that relative editorial slant can influence voters."[118]

Limitations on News Media Influence

Despite the importance of the media's influence, it falls far short of President Clinton's statement that reporters run the government. There are numerous factors that restrain the media's influence.

Limited attention by the public to the news is one factor that restrains press influence. As noted, most Americans are not news wonks. They average only a little more than an hour a day on the news, and many spend most of that time on soft news. Studies also show that the average person absorbs only a minority of the details of the news they do access. Thus the influence of the media is limited by the fact that a good part of their intended audience is paying little or no attention and does not remember a good part of what it does read, see, and hear.

The multiplicity of news sources is a second limit on the press. The news media are extremely diverse and growing more so. This gives Americans access to a range of news sources that would have seemed unbelievable not long ago. The advent of cable and satellite television means that there are at least a half-dozen major television news programs each evening, and numerous channels that are all news, all day. Many people have access to the delivery of at least two daily newspapers and can supplement them with over 3,000 domestic and foreign newspapers and other printed news sources on the Web in English. Blogs are another factor in the recent expansion of sources, and there may be over 3 million of them. This diversity of news sources means, according to one analysis, that "the public cannot easily be pushed around by any particular [news] source."[119]

The selectivity of news consumers is a third limitation on the impact of the media. People are selective about what news sources they access and how they interpret the information and opinions that the news contains. One way that some people are selective is by seeking news that fits their view. One poll found 36% saying they preferred news from like-minded sources. This selectivity is evident in the audience of conservatively oriented FOX News. Most (52%) of its viewers are conservatives, while only 13% are liberal, with the rest describing themselves as moderates. By contrast the viewers of the reputedly liberal CBS Evening News are 46% more likely to be a Democrat than a Republican. Highly ideological programs, like that of Rush Limbaugh, have an even more selective audience, with 77% of his audience conservative and only 7% liberal.[120]

News consumers' rejection of dissonant information and views in the press is a fourth limitation. People who encounter news that does not fit with their views are less likely to believe it than they are news that fits with their preexisting images. This psychological process occurs because people are uncomfortable if they experience *cognitive dissonance*: believing contradictory things. It is for this reason that almost twice as many Republicans as Democrats say they believe all or most of what is reported on FOX, and Democrats are 42% more likely than Republicans to believe CBS news.[121] Studies also show that to avoid cognitive dissonance, people either filter out information they do not agree with or interpret it to conform with their view. During the 2004 presidential debates, for instance, surveys after each found that most Republicans said that George Bush had won the debate and most Democrats said that John Kerry had done so. In sum, people tend to take in information and opinion from the news while subconsciously comparing it to how it fits with what they already know and what they think depending on their ideology, experiences, and personal interests. Compatible information and opinions are usually accepted as reinforcing; contrary information and opinions are suppressed.

Public doubts about the press are a fifth limit on its impact. We have already seen that most Americans see the news media as politically biased and too negative. Also previously noted is that fact that 63% of the public thinks that news stories are "often inaccurate." Other expressions of public skepticism about the press include polls showing that most Americans believe that press organizations "don't care about the people they report on" (58%), "try to cover up" reporting mistakes (62%), and care more about "attracting a big audience" (75%) than "keeping the public informed."[122] Finally, most (73%) think that the independence of the press is at least sometimes compromised by the influence of "powerful people and organizations." By contrast, even though Americans are somewhat skeptical of how much freedom their press has, they trust it more than people in most other regions of the world trust their news media, as shown in Figure 8.10.

FIGURE 8.10   Comparative Trust in the Press

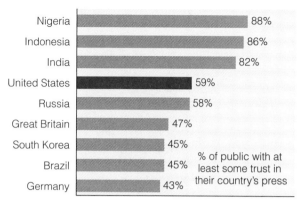

This figure shows the percentage of people in nine countries who said they had "some" or "a lot" of trust in their country's news media "to operate in the best interests of society."
Data source: BBC/Reuters/Media Center poll, "Trust In the Media," 2006.

Evaluating the Impact of Internet News

Evaluating the impact of the press also requires taking note of the Internet media. Gauging the impact of these new news sources is very difficult. One reason is because Internet news is relatively new and rapidly changing. The second reason is the sheer number of Internet news sources. Several things lend support to the idea that Internet news will have a strong impact on the political process. One is that fact that nearly all Americans who follow the news at all get at least some of it from the Internet. Moreover, almost everyone who follows the news closely sometimes uses Internet sources. The Internet is also expanding how news is distributed. Between 1995 and 2008, the share of people who had e-mailed a news item to someone else within the preceding week grew from 8% to 27%.[123] It is also the case that Internet sources are especially attractive to younger adults (ages 18–29); 42% of them say they get news from the Internet regularly compared to 27% of everyone age 50 and up.[124] This probably means that utilization of Internet news will continue to expand, and it is also increasing the number of young adults who follow the news at least sometimes. Yet another impact from Internet news may stem from the variety of sources it offers. Positively, that permits people to get more and countervailing perspectives. However, there is also evidence that many people will choose to focus on media sources that they agree with. This may even

Contrary to the belief that Internet news sources contribute substantially to the factual news available, a sizable majority of the stories and information on the Web has been generated originally by newspapers and other traditional news sources. (© 2009 Joe Heller, the Green Bay Press-Gazette, and PoliticalCartoons.com.)

be part of what many think is a growing political polarization of Americans.

Yet there are offsetting facts that tend to diminish the importance of the rise of Internet news. First, many of the most consulted sources are extensions of the legacy media such as printed newspapers and television networks. Not only do the legacy news media have their own Internet sites, but other Internet news and commentary sites also rely heavily on the legacy news media. A study of current event blogs in 2009, for example, found that 65% of the stories they linked to came from one of just three legacy news sources, the *New York Times*, CNN, and the BBC.[125] Similarly, a study of local news in Baltimore, Maryland, found that about 95% of news first appeared in the traditional media or its Internet subdivisions. Only about 5% came from Internet-only sources, leaving most of the news they did transmit "often brief and derivative of other news accounts."[126] Thus whether and how much this is a new source of news or a repackaged one is debatable.

A second limit on the impact of Internet news relates to its most frequent users, young adults. Despite their higher use of nontraditional news sources, young adults are still much less likely than older adults to pay any attention to the news.

A third limit on the impact of Internet news sources is the reality that Americans trust them even less than traditional sources. On a four-point scale (4 = highly believable to 1 = not believable) about 25% of Americans in 2008 gave television news sources a score of 4, and about 20% assigned that score to printed newspapers and news magazines. Of the Internet-only news sources, news aggregators like Yahoo news and Google received a 4 from only 12% of respondents, and the *Drudge Report*, the *Huffington Post*, and similar sites got a 4 from only about 6% of respondents. As for news being transmitted by social networking sites, only 10% of those who regularly go to these sites reported that they get news from them.[127]

The Press in Perspective

Having reached the end of the chapter, what can we say about the role of the news media in the American democratic political process? Clearly there is a range of opinions, but the view here is that the press is neither the very independent, hard-hitting, unbiased, accurate, watchdog bastion of democracy that it imagines itself to be, nor the profit motivated and personal-advancement driven, biased, inaccurate lapdog of big business and politicians that critics sometimes charge. The truth is somewhere in the middle and the result of a complex range of factors rather than any single cause.[128]

Some of the perceptual divide between press critics and supporters is based on unavoidable cross-pressures on the press. On the one hand, it plays a key role in democracy by informing the public and therefore properly has a certain privileged status under the First Amendment. On the other hand, the news media are businesses, and the people who work for them are employees. These facts introduce the profit motive and personal ambition into the equation and lead to issues about the quality of the news. Many of these concerns exist because the corporate nature of the news media puts pressure on it to provide the people with the news they want, not the news that might theoretically suit an ideal democracy with citizens highly interested in hard news. So while the news does lean to negativism and while a majority of the public criticizes that slant, the reason that crime, violence, corruption, and other such negative stories dominate is that they are what attract an audience. Perhaps, then, it is "we the people" more than "they the news media" who are responsible for negativism, infotainment, and some of the other distortions.

It is also the case that a fair measure of the criticism of the watchdog press comes from those who characterize it as an attack dog when they are dismayed by what appears in the news about them. That reaction is understandable, but it stands in contrast to the 61% of the public that think that investigative journalism and other watchdog roles are good because they "keep political leaders from doing things that should not be done."[129] Even many politicians who have been bitten by press criticism, as most have been, concede that the watchdogs should not be kept on a short leash. Jimmy Carter was so angry at how journalists treated him as president that he wrote an entire chapter in his memoirs lambasting the press for shallow, negative, erroneous, and vindictive reporting. Aides persuaded him to excise the chapter before publication, and after further reflection, Carter admitted, "The adversarial relationship [between politicians and press] is . . . beneficial for our country. . . . I guess that's part of democracy, and it's unpleasant at times, but in balance, good."[130]

Historical perspective also helps when evaluating the news media. To the degree that there is bias in the press, it is certainly less than at times in the past. Indeed, most of the press was once unabashedly partisan. Of the newspapers in the 50 largest cities in 1870, for example, only 13% were independent, compared to 33% that were overtly pro-Democrat, and 54% that were pro-Republican.[131] And while negativism has increased, it is hardly new. At least that is what the sixth president, John Quincy Adams, thought almost two centuries ago when he depicted journalists as "assassins" armed with printing presses and eager to "fire them off for hire or for sport at [anyone] they select."[132]

Evaluating commentary that says that Americans are losing confidence in the fairness and accuracy of the news is helped by another bit of historical perspective. In the early 1970s, an average of 70% of poll respondents said they were confident that the press was reporting "the news fully, accurately, and fairly." By the 1990s, those with confidence had dipped to 54%, and on average remained at that level during 2006 through 2008. Thus it is true that there has been a decline in public trust. That is worrisome, but at least confidence has stabilized, with a majority of Americans still expressing confidence in their news media.

Further offsetting the gloomy evaluations of the press and its standing is the fact that the public's overall evaluation of the news media remains positive. When asked if they saw various media favorably or unfavorably, Americans gave favorable ratings to daily newspapers (80%), local television news (78%), network television news (75%), and cable television news (67%). A majority of the respondents also pronounced each of the three media "believable."[133]

When all is said and done then, the news media—like most of the other institutions, organizations, and individuals in the American political process—are a mixed bag of positives and negatives. Certainly the press does not measure up to the somewhat Olympian image that its defenders sometimes present. It is also true, however, that the news media are not in dire straits, under assault from profit-driven owners, manipulative politicians trying to nullify the First Amendment, plummeting quality standards, and other ills.

SUMMARY

The press plays key roles in the American political system. The most important role is informing the public of political events, issues, and people. The flow of information is not just one way. Instead, the press is a two-way communications link between political leaders and the public. These roles are important to the democratic process, a fact that has generally been recognized by American political leaders and by the public throughout U.S. history. However, there have often been tensions between the press and the nation's leaders. Additionally, the public does not believe in unlimited freedom of the press. Still, the U.S. press is freer than the press in most other countries.

How the press operates is affected first by its organizational setting. The most important organizational fact is that the news media are businesses. Some worry that there is a narrowing number of corporate owners of the news media, but this is offset at least partly by the wide array of news media newly available through the Internet. There are also concerns about the very limited demographic diversity of the media's ownership and staff.

Second, how the press operates is also affected by its legal setting. The core of the legal setting is the First Amendment. It guarantees considerable, but not complete, freedom of the press. Issues about regulating the press center on prior restraint, defamation, fairness of coverage, and demographic diversity of ownership and in the newsroom, and claims by the press of special legal standing.

The social setting (public attitudes toward the press and the news) is a third factor that impacts how the news media operate. Most Americans do not pay much attention to political news. A fourth factor is the technological setting of the news. Most people get news from more than one source, but television continues to be the most important source for most people. The sources, however, are shifting. Americans' use of traditional news media, such as printed newspapers, is declining and its use of nontraditional sources on the Internet and elsewhere is increasing. The global setting of the press is the fifth factor influencing its operation. The process of journalism has been affected by globalization. Among other things, Americans' access to foreign news sources has increased dramatically.

Because it is impossible to convey all the news, what the news media decide is newsworthy is an important issue. What gets reported is based largely on what the press and the public each want and how those desires interact. Press motivations include wanting to bring information and analysis to the public, earning a profit as a business, and advancing personally as individual journalists. What the public wants is news according to seven criteria: impact, excitement, proximity, timeliness, novelty, familiarity, and brevity.

There are several quality standards by which to judge journalism. These include independence, accuracy, objectivity, balance, representative coverage, sophisticated analysis, substance, and transparency. There are concerns in each of these areas that undermine the credibility and impact of the news media. Nevertheless, the news media affect the political process in several important ways. These include being the main source of political information for most people and helping to set the political agenda. Journalists affect public opinion by deciding how to frame the news and to prime the public's evaluation of officials, candidates, issues, and events.

For all the importance of the press, several factors limit its impact. First, most people pay little attention to the news. Second, the impact of any one source is limited by the diversity of news sources that are available. Third, many people are selective about which news sources they use and also are likely to discount interpretations of the news that do not fit with their individual views. Fourth, there is widespread skepticism among people about the press.

CHAPTER 8 GLOSSARY

agenda setting The process of determining which people and issues are the focus of government and public attention.

equal time rule A regulation since 1934 mandating that broadcast stations that sell political advertising time or make free time available to one candidate in an election must do the same for other candidates.

fairness doctrine A Federal Communications regulation in place from 1949 to 1987 that required radio and television stations using the public airwaves to allocate a part of their airtime to news and other matters of public importance and also to carry opposing viewpoints on public issues and candidates.

framing The way that a policy choice or other concern is defined.

gatekeepers Editors and others among the press who play a dominant role in deciding what makes it into print or on to the airwaves and what goes unreported.

hard news News that focuses on the operation of local, state, and national government; politics; international affairs; and business and finance.

horse race Reporting by the press about who is ahead and behind among candidates for office, campaign strategy and conduct, and related subjects.

infotainment An approach to the news that includes reporting more and more soft news and less and less hard news, presenting hard news in a format calculated to entertain the public more than inform it, and generally blurring the line between the entertainment media and the news media.

Internet news media A large group of sources of news including the online sites of the legacy news media, news aggregators that gather news from other (mostly legacy) news sources, and exclusively online news sources. Not included here as part of the Internet news media, but included by some observers, are blogs and other Internet platforms for the exchange of information and commentary.

investigative reporting Proactively conducting an inquiry into a subject, particularly one involving things some organizations wish to keep secret, rather than reactively reporting events.

lapdog A role the press plays when it allows itself to be manipulated by the government to convey specific information and viewpoints, especially if inaccurate.

legacy news media Traditional news sources including broadcast and cable television, printed newspapers, the wire services, and printed news magazines.

mass media The organizations that print or electronically convey entertainment, information, and opinion to the public.

mediated reality What we learn through an intermediary rather than by direct experience.

news media The organizations that disseminate news for public consumption.

priming Establishing the standards the public uses to evaluate an issue or a public figure by shifting the focus of reporting.

prior restraint Subjecting the news media to licensure or to review and censorship prior to publication or broadcast.

shield law A statute that protects the press from having to reveal the identity of an anonymous source used in the story even if demanded by a court or another government body with subpoena power.

soft news Sports, lifestyle, human-interest, and other such news stories.

sound bites Video clips on television or audio clips on radio of a candidate speaking.

tabloid journalism Journalism that emphasizes personalities rather than issues, sensationalism rather than careful analysis, and otherwise is designed to appeal to emotions rather than the mind.

watchdog A role of the press that stresses seeking information about corruption and other malpractices by public officials and institutions and by other prominent people and organizations in the public interest.

POLITICAL PARTIES

9

YOU DECIDE: Is It Time for a Tea Party?

Americans held their first political tea party on December 16, 1773, when about 200 colonists boarded three merchant ships in Boston and dumped their cargo of tea into the harbor. What angered the protestors was a tax on tea imports that Great Britain had imposed on the colonies and, more generally, London's moves to increase its control over its American colonies.

More than 200 years later, tea has once again become the symbol of protest. Sparked by the vast sums spent by the federal government beginning in 2008 to save banks and corporations and by the threat of new taxes to ease spiraling budget deficits and national debt, a movement to send tea bags to Congress as a form of protest emerged in 2009. This quickly led to like-minded people and groups around the country to link together loosely to promote what was soon dubbed the Tea Party. Then in February 2010, some 600 people met at the first national Tea Party Convention in Nashville, Tennessee, with former Republican vice presidential nominee Sarah Palin as the keynote speaker. Thus far, though, "tea baggers" have mostly sought influence by supporting strong conservatives seeking nomination, then election as Republicans. An initial success came in early 2010, when a Republican backed by the Tea Party won a special election to fill the U.S. Senate seat vacated by Teddy Kennedy's death. Later in 2010, Tea Party–backed Republicans had other important successes. Several, for example, beat mainstream Republicans for the nominations for U.S. Senate seats and were elected in November. In two states (Delaware and Nevada) though, such candidates lost in November to Democrats in contests where a more moderate Republican might have prevailed. This arguably cost the Republicans control of the narrowly divided Senate during the 112th Congress (2011–2012). Also worth noting is that while some critics have labeled the Tea Party racist, several candidates it supported in 2010 were minority group members. Among

Tea Party members with the Revolutionary War era flag "Don't Tread on Me" that they have adopted as their symbol are gathered here on April 15, 2010, outside Utah's capitol building in Salt Lake City to demand lower taxes and other changes. Less than a month later, a candidate backed by the group defeated Utah's long-term Republican U.S. Senator in a primary. (AP Photo/The Salt Lake Tribune, Scott Sommerdorf)

these newly elected officials were Florida U.S. Senator Marco Rubio, a Cuban American, South Carolina Governor Nikki Haley, the first Indian American woman elected to state-wide office, and U.S. Representatives Tim Scott (South Carolina) and Allen West (Florida), the first black Republicans elected to Congress from the South in more than a century.

The Tea Party's record as of early 2011 leaves it unclear whether it is best seen as a splinter element of the Republican Party or a loosely connected movement of state and local groups with little national organization or leadership. Yet there are signs that the time is right for a new party to emerge. As we will see, strong third parties have usually arisen during times of turbulence when many people are alienated from government and the existing political parties. That description fits the current situation. When Americans were asked in 2010 whether they trusted the federal government, only 37% said yes.[1] And 56% of Americans agreed in another poll that federal government has become so large and powerful that it poses an "immediate threat to the rights and freedoms of ordinary citizens."[2] This negativism extends to the political parties, which are also in considerable disfavor. In one poll a plurality (48%) expressed anger with both the Republicans and Democrats.[3] Another poll found 90% of Americans agreeing that "Washington no longer works effectively" because of "fighting between parties."[4]

As for the Tea Party, polls in late 2010 showed about one-third each of Americans saying they regarded the Tea Party favorably, unfavorably, or were unsure.[5] Furthermore, Americans were not buying into attacks on the Tea Party as an angry fringe group. To the contrary, 57% of the respondents to one poll agreed that "Tea Party activists are citizens concerned about the country's economic future."[6] What is your view? Most elections are "tea for two": the Republicans and Democrats. Would you welcome political tea party for three?

INTRODUCING POLITICAL PARTIES

The recent emergence of the Tea Party seen in our opening You Decide box raises many questions about the organization and operation of U.S. political parties. Why do political parties exist and what are their roles? As you will see, some analysts believe that national parties are outmoded. A second group of questions surrounds how the party system is structured. Why Americans generally limit their loyalties to one of two parties when most other countries have multiple national parties is a particularly important inquiry. Our task in this chapter is answering these questions and others, and in doing so you will see that:

★ Parties are key political actors in all democracies.
★ The major U.S. parties, like those in other established democracies, are broad-based ideological parties.
★ The Republican Party's future is uncertain because its membership has become increasingly limited to whites in general and white males in particular.
★ Structural, attitudinal, and other factors make the Untied States a two-party system.
★ Third parties occasionally arise because of discontent with the major parties and help shape the future political landscape.
★ American parties are highly fragmented organizationally.
★ There have been several eras of party alignments. Each has been marked by changes in the distribution of party support among various groups and by shifts in the overall strength of the parties among voters.
★ The alignment that began in the 1930s based on economic interests broke down beginning in the 1960s because of the rise of social value issues on the political agenda.
★ There is a debate over whether a new alignment has occurred since the 1970s or whether the parties have become so weak that the electorate has dealigned with them.
★ Party strength has partially recovered since the 1970s, casting doubt on the dealignment theory.
★ Parties play many roles in elections but are not as pivotal to them as they once were.
★ Parties help structure the government and determine policy.

Political Parties and Partisanship

At root, a **political party** in a democracy is an organization of politically like-minded people that presents candidates for election under its name in an effort to gain influence in government and promote its preferred policies. Political parties according to this definition are part of the system inputs (see Chapter 1) that place demands on and give support to the institutions of government. Thus parties are something of a communications link between people and government. Parties are part of the demand structure because they try to capture control of government or at least to gain enough power to have a say in policy making. Parties are also part of the support system because they perform a number of functions that help organize the electoral process and help organize the government. We will take up each of these functions in later sections.

A brief look at terminology will also help put political parties in context. Being **partisan** means supporting a political party. Acting to advance policies your party favors or to strengthen your party politically is partisan behavior or partisanship. Individuals can also be *nonpartisan*. This means that they either do not identify with any party or do not act in a partisan way. You can also be *bipartisan* by working with members of another party on a common cause. Partisanship has gotten something of a bad name because it is commonly used to mean doing what benefits a party even if it harms the public interest. Certainly, partisanship can lead to that, but it is also a key part of a party-based political system and is used here in a neutral way to designate party-related loyalties and activities. In contrast to partisan, the words *nonpartisan* and *bipartisan* have a good connotation. However, these alternatives to partisanship may not always be as attractive as they seem. For example, one view of bipartisanship is that it is "every bit as political as partisanship" and is usually "an electoral strategy that politicians use to broaden their appeal to voters outside of their party—to secure the support of so-called middle-of-the-road or swing voters by establishing a record as moderate and independent public servants."[7]

Parties from a Global Perspective

Taking some time to look at parties from a global perspective is valuable to help understand both the place of parties in the American political system and the specifics of the U.S. party system.

Parties and Democracy

Political parties are not unique to the United States. Parties exist in every democracy because they perform necessary roles. Realistically speaking, the only place it is possible to imagine a democratic system without parties is in a very small community where people know one another. In today's world, however, all countries are far too large to operate democratically without parties. Parties help organize people with similar views, structure electoral contests, and perform other crucial functions. History tends to confirm that all but the smallest democratic political communities have a **partisan political system**, one based in part on the contest between political parties. Tiny Liechtenstein, which is only 62 square miles in size (smaller than Washington, D.C.) with about 35,000 citizens, has three parties with seats in its national parliament.

The American experience also shows the near inseparability of partisan politics and democratic governance. Many of the country's early leaders worried that parties would divide and weaken the country. Most famously, President George Washington warned that having parties would inflame "the animosity of one part against another." Nevertheless, party politics soon secured a permanent place in the American political system. During Washington's years in office, the followers of Secretary of the Treasury Alexander Hamilton and those of Secretary of State Thomas Jefferson coalesced into two parties. By 1796, the election of the president had become a partisan contest. Federalist John Adams defeated Democratic-Republican Thomas Jefferson, who in turn beat Adams in 1800. In his 1801 inaugural address, Jefferson, as many later new presidents would, called for unity. "We are all Republicans; we are all Federalists," he intoned. General partisan unity was not the case then, nor has it ever been.

English political philosopher John Stuart Mill wrote in *On Liberty* (1859), "A party of order or stability, and a party of progress or reform, are both necessary elements of a healthy state of political life."

Party Orientations

Another global commonality is that political parties are all based on achieving political goals. Those goals are, however, often diverse.

Parties Based on Ideology Most of the important parties in the established democracies are ideological parties that support policies that reflect their values across a broad range of issues. Communists, socialist, liberal, and conservative parties are all ideological parties. So are the Democratic and Republican parties in the United States.

Being ideological does not mean that parties are doggedly doctrinaire. To the contrary, the leading parties in the major democracies are all willing to sacrifice some degree of ideological purity to win elections or make policy gains. Democrats and Republicans, for example, try to balance between adhering to a set of principles that appeal to their core supporters, their *base*, and being flexible enough to attract voters from the large centrist segment of American electorate. This balancing act is both difficult and an ongoing part of the story of American parties. Moreover, when one of the major parties has become too doctrinaire, it has courted electoral disaster. This arguably is what the Republicans did beginning in the mid-1990s, leading to electoral debacles in 2006 and 2008 and raising doubts about the party's future.

In countries where ideological parties dominate, power usually moves back and forth between the liberal and conservative parties without either gaining a

FIGURE 9.1 Comparative Shifts in Party Control

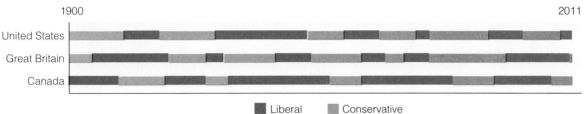

In the United States, Great Britain, and Canada political power, as determined by the president/prime minister's affiliation, shifted between liberals and conservatives an average of 12 times between 1900 and the beginning of 2011. Most periods of dominance were fairly short, with only a few extending more than a decade. Also notice that there is no common pattern in the shifts among the countries, indicating the shifts are driven by domestic factors rather than global trends.

Notes and data source: Short-term control of less than one year not shown. Coalitions classified by party of the prime minister. Data by author's calculations.

permanent upper hand.[8] The frequent power shifts in three leading democracies are evident in Figure 9.1. Also note in the figure that the shifts of power between parties in the three countries have not occurred simultaneously. This implies that a country's ideological orientation at any given time is based more on domestic factors than on global or regional ideological trends.

Parties Based on Other Factors Although most major parties are rooted in a broad-based ideology, there are other foundations. Some countries have *issue parties* based on a single issue or a related number of issues. For example, Germany and some other countries have a Green Party that focuses heavily on the environment. *Religious parties* are also found in many countries. India's second largest party, the Bharatiya Janata Party, wants to reshape India according to traditional Hindu religious and cultural concepts. *Ethnonationalist parties* based on an ethnic or other cultural group are also common and frequently contain at least some degree of separatist sentiment. The Parti Québécois is dedicated to gaining greater autonomy for Quebec Province and its mostly French-heritage population within the Canadian federation.

Nativist parties are yet another type. They are made up of individuals from the dominant cultural group of their country who oppose the dilution of their culture through immigration or other outside influences. The earliest nativist party in the United States, the American Party, established in 1843, was part of the anti-immigrant Know Nothing movement. More than any other factor, changes in immigration patterns that brought a substantial inflow of Roman Catholic immigrants, especially the Irish, motivated the Know Nothings.

The increased movement of people, including immigrants, across national borders has been part of quickening globalization. The inflow of immigrants has caused a negative reaction in the United States and many other countries. During the Netherlands' 2010 national elections, symbolized by this image of a Muslim woman wearing a head scarf passing by election posters and a windmill in Amsterdam, the right-wing, anti-immigration Freedom Party, which pledged to end the "Islamization of the Netherlands," won 16% of the Dutch vote and increased its seats in the 150-member parliament from 9 to 24. (AP Photo/Peter Dejong)

In more recent years, globalization and its greater flow of culture and of immigrants, refugees, and others across national borders have increased anti-foreign feelings. A recent poll taken in 46 countries found that an average of 75% in each country thought that globalization was destroying their traditional way of life, and 73% wanted to protect their traditions.[9] Restricting immigration to do this was favored in all but two countries and by an average majority of 69%. Americans mirrored these feelings, with 73% believing that their way of life was being lost, 62% wanting to protect it, and 75% favoring increased immigration restrictions. One result of such sentiments has been the rise of nativist parties in a number of countries. For example, elections in 2009 saw candidates from such parties in Europe win 5% of the seats in the European Union's European Parliament. Nativism has also increased in the United States, but no related third-party movement has emerged so far.

Number of Important Parties

An additional distinction among party systems is the number of major parties: those parties with significant and ongoing political influence. China and most other countries with a **one-party system** are authoritarian. Occasionally, though, a type of a one-party system called a **dominant-party system** does occur in a democracy.[10] In this type of system, multiple parties exist, but one of them far overshadows the others. South Africa is an example. Thirteen parties have seats in the National Assembly, but the African National Congress has 66% of the seats, and the next largest party has only 17%. As we will see, the United States was a dominant-party system from 1803 to 1823. Most democracies have **multiparty systems**, in which three or more major parties have 5% or more of the seats in the national parliament. Usually such systems have three to six such parties. Examples as of 2009 were Mexico (3), Canada (4), Italy (5), and Germany (6).

A relatively few democratic countries such as the United States, Spain, and Australia have **two-party systems**, with only two parties that regularly play an important role. Distinguishing the U.S. system even more, it is the world's purest two-party system. In 2009, for example, Spain's two dominant parties were joined by eight minor parties in its parliament, and there were two minor parties in Australia's parliament. In the U.S. Congress, by contrast, all but 2 of the 535 senators and representatives were Democrats or Republicans, and the two exceptions, both senators, were independents who caucused with the Democrats.

Political Parties and American Diversity

For most of American history, there has not been a strong connection between political parties and matters of diversity. However, there have been times when diversity and party fortunes were heavily intertwined.

Early Party Involvement with Diversity

The first major intersection between party politics and diversity began in the 1840s with the anti-Roman Catholic sentiment of the Know Nothings and its associated American Party that advocated nativist policies. In the Far West, anti-Chinese and anti-Mexican bias added to Know Nothing strength. The movement peaked in the 1850s when American Party members governed several of the country's largest cities, had majorities in the legislatures of Massachusetts and Maryland, and elected governors in California, Delaware, and Massachusetts. In 1856, former President Millard Fillmore sought to return to the White House by running under the American Party banner. He failed, but received 22% of the national popular vote.

The success of the American Party was also aided by political turmoil in the country that was destabilizing the existing parties. We will take this up later, but for now we can say that the once powerful Whig Party tore itself apart over slavery. With its collapse, several third parties, including the American Party, gained prominence. Simultaneously, a succession of parties including the Liberty Party (1840), the Free Soil Party (1848), and the Republican Party (1854) evolved into a major party. Their supporters favored banning slavery in the territories and, later, abolishing slavery itself. Among the new Republican Party's leaders were such former Whig politicians as Abraham Lincoln of Illinois.

Once the Civil War and the Thirteenth Amendment abolished slavery, the prevailing Democratic and Republican parties put issues of diversity on the back burner for almost a century. Neither party played a key role in advancing women's suffrage. The parties also largely ignored the Jim Crow violations of the rights of Americans of color.

Recent Party Involvement with Diversity

Beginning in the decade after World War II, as discussed in Chapter 5 and elsewhere, the country and its parties began to turn their attention to the prevailing national patterns of discrimination based on race and sex. Since then, the attitudes of the parties—and the public's perception of those attitudes—about demolishing the Jim Crow system and advancing equal opportunity have played an important part in determining political party fortunes. As we will see later in the chapter, for example, the party system was once again destabilized in the mid-twentieth century, this time by the civil rights movement. It split the liberal Democrats in the North and West from the socially conservative Southern Democrats, or Dixiecrats. Many of these Dixiecrats later aligned themselves with the Republicans, empowering that party.

In 1972, Jean Miles Westwood of Utah became the first woman to chair the Democratic National Committee. Later that year, Mary Louis Smith of Iowa became the first woman to chair the Republican National Committee.

Other groups shifted toward the Democrats. Blacks had once favored the Republicans as the party of Lincoln, then in the 1930s had moved more toward the Democrats for economic reasons. Black support of the Democratic Party grew even more decisively in response to Democratic President Lyndon B. Johnson's determined push to improve civil rights. In the same way, women saw the Democrats as more sympathetic to their cause. During the 1960s, women began to shift from usually being Republican voters to favoring the Democrats.

FIGURE 9.2 Party Identification by Race

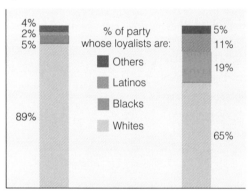

Republicans are in danger of becoming a "white party." Just 11% of all those who define themselves as a Republican are not white. Democrats have better demographic balance, with people of color making up one-third of the party's adherents.
Data source: Gallup poll, May 2009.

These trends have intensified during recent years. A continuing combination of Democratic support of economic policies favorable to disadvantaged groups and the perception that Democrats are more amenable to protecting and advancing the civil rights of women and people of color have kept blacks decidedly Democratic and have also given the Democrats a growing share of the votes cast by women. In 2008, for example, women gave Barack Obama 56% of their votes. Additionally, the policies and perceptions of the Democrats have attracted an increased percentage of Latinos and Asian Americans.[11] Each group favored Obama by an approximately 2 to 1 margin over McCain. Even during the Republicans' huge gains in the 2010 congressional elections, Latinos and Asian Americans continued to markedly favor the Democrats. It is too early to say that the Republican Party has become a white party, but as Figure 9.2 shows, that could be the de facto fate of the Republican Party unless it does something to attract a greater share of nonwhites to its ranks. To a lesser degree, the Republicans have also become a male party. Among the party's already diminished ranks, 53% are men and only 47% are women.

THE STRUCTURE OF THE U.S. PARTY SYSTEM

The most important aspect of the structure of the U.S. party system is that it is strongly two-party. We will begin by explaining why this is so. Then we will turn to third parties, followed by a discussion of the organizational characteristics of the major parties.

The U.S. Two-Party System

The United States is perhaps the most rigidly two-party system in the world. Minor parties have rarely played a strong role in American politics. All U.S. presidents have been either a Democrat or a Republican since 1853 when Zachary Taylor, a Whig, left office. Moreover, Democratic and Republican candidates have received 95% or more of the popular vote during all but 7 of the 36 presidential elections since 1864. The two parties also dominate Congress, where combined they have held 96% or more of the seats for more than 140 years.

The United States has the world's most profoundly two-party system, with the Republicans and Democrats dominating political contests since the Civil War. (Big Stock Photo)

Certainly other parties exist in the United States. During the 2008 presidential election candidates from four minor parties (Independent, Libertarian, Constitution, and Green) were on the ballot in most states, and 17 other small parties were on the ballot in one or a few states. Such parties are called **third parties**, minor parties that have little chance of winning a presidential election or gaining a significant number of seats in Congress. "Little chance" does not, however, mean "no chance," and we will see that third parties have sometimes played an important part in American politics. Overall during the course of American history, the strength of the two parties has balanced out despite some large ebbs and flows. As Figure 9.3 shows, it has been rare for one party to hold more than two thirds

FIGURE 9.3 Party Balance in the House of Representatives

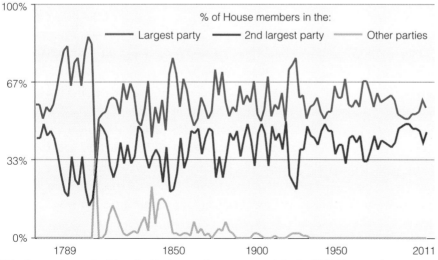

This figure shows the historical balance of party strength in the U.S. House of Representatives. Notice two things: (1) Third parties have rarely been a major factor and not at all since 1867. (2) The two-party system has been relatively well balanced over the long run. Rarely has one party held more than two-thirds of the seats.
Data source: Office of the Clerk, U.S. House of Representatives.

of the seats in the House. Moreover, these periods have been very short, except in the early 1800s. Relative party balance over the long term is also evident in the fact that majority control of the House has switched 25 times including in 2011 from one party to another. The contest for president has also been balanced. No more than four consecutive presidents of the same party have ever been elected, and party control of the presidency changed hands during 22 of the 52 elections between 1792 and 2008.

Americans do not have a two-party system by chance. Instead several factors tend to promote two-party dominance and work against minor parties. These include the election system, the presidential system, the legal environment, inertia, and American pragmatism.

The Election System

The most important two factors promoting the two-party system are the country's almost exclusive use of **single-member districts** and a **plurality elections system.** Single-member districts exist in the United States because most legislative seats are divided among geographical districts with only one person representing each district. Texas, for example, gets 32 seats in the U.S. House of Representatives and divides those seats among 32 congressional districts. States have two senators but function like single-member districts because each seat is filled in separate elections.

Plurality elections are those in which the winner is the candidate who gets the most votes, even if they are not a majority. This approach is more commonly called a **winner-take-all contest,** one in which the winner gets all the prizes and the losers, no matter how close the contest is, get nothing. Plurality elections tend to discourage third parties because they are seldom able to muster a plurality vote and achieve the ultimate reward of an electoral system: electing party members to office. True ideologues continue to run as minor party candidates, but it is hard for them to get less committed individuals to join in because the chances of success are so small. During the 2008 congressional elections, for instance, Libertarian Party candidates won about 1% of the national vote. Yet when the new Congress convened in January 2009, there were no Libertarians in its membership.

This electoral system also discourages minor parties because many people think that voting for a minor party candidate may help elect the major party candidate they like least. For example, Democrats have regularly criticized perennial presidential candidate and liberal populist Ralph Nader for damaging the prospects of the Democrats' presidential nominee.[12] For one, Senator Hillary Clinton (D-NY), a candidate for that nomination in 2008, accused Nader of costing Democrat Al Gore the presidency in 2000 and also charged that Nader's third-party candidacy in 2008 "is not helpful to whoever our Democratic nominee is."[13] Something to think about is whether the single-member district, plurality election approach to choosing legislators is satisfactory or should be replaced. One alternative is proportional representation, an approach you are asked to consider in the following You Decide box.

The Presidential System of Government

Having an independently elected president who serves a fixed term of office also contributes to the two-party system. One reason is that it focuses party politics on building an electoral coalition large enough to capture the country's highest office. This contrasts with countries that have a parliamentary system in which

YOU DECIDE: Adopt a Proportional Representation System?

Many democratic countries elect legislators by a **proportional representation** (PR) system. In its most basic form, a PR system (1) holds elections in multiseat districts with (2) each voter casting one vote for a list of party candidates and (3) each party receiving a share of the legislative seats equal to the percentage of votes its list of candidates received. We can see how a PR system works by applying it to a hypothetical election among Democrats, Republicans, Socialists, and Monarchists.

To keep the math easy, let's assume your state has 10 representatives in the U.S. House. Under a PR system, your state would not be divided into 10 congressional districts as it currently is. Instead, all the seats would be decided on a statewide basis. Each party would present a list of ten candidates, and each voter in the state would cast one ballot for one party's lists, rather than voting for individual candidates. If the statewide voting results were Democrats 40%, Republicans 30%, Socialists 20%, and Monarchists 10%, the state's delegation would be 4 Democrats, 3 Republicans, 2 Socialists, and 1 Monarchist. Typically, the first four candidates on the Democratic list would serve, the top three on the Republican list, and so on.

The main argument for a PR system is that elected representatives better reflect the diverse views of the citizenry because minor parties get seats in the legislature. Typically in a multiparty system, voters get to choose from a wider range of ideological parties, from the pronounced left, through the center, to the distinct right. By contrast, critics say, the choice for the U.S. Congress is either-or. Similarly, a PR system is more likely to give representation to parties based on specific issues, religion, and other factors. The Green Party and the Party for Animals, for instance, hold seats in the parliament of the Netherlands, and the Evangelical People's Party is represented in Switzerland's National Council. Another argument for a PR system is that it avoids the mathematical distortions that often occur in a single-member district. In Connecticut's 2008 U.S. House elections, for example, Democrats received 67% of the votes but 100% of the state's five seats.

An argument against proportional representation is that it can so fragment a parliament that it becomes hard to accomplish anything. Illustrative of this, Israel's 120-member Knesset in 2009 included 13 political parties, and maintaining a delicately balanced majority coalition can make it difficult for Israel's government to make controversial decisions. What do you think and why about replacing single-member districts with a PR system?

the majority party or majority coalition of parties in the parliament selects the head of government (the prime minister). Prime ministers do not have fixed terms; they remain in power only as long as they have the support of a majority of the parliament's members. If the prime minister loses majority support, then new parliamentary elections are usually held and a new government is formed (see Chapter 12).

In such a system, minority parties can gain considerable influence when no one party has enough votes to form a majority and elect a prime minister. One or more of the larger parties then seek support from one or more of the smaller parties by offering them positions in the government and/or promising to support some of the smaller party's policy goals. This rewards small parties, making it easier for them to survive. For example, neither of Great Britain's two dominant parties, the Conservatives and Labour, was able to win a majority of seats in the House of Commons in the 2010 general election. As a result, the country's largest third party, the Liberal Party, was able to install its leader, Nick Clegg, as deputy prime minister and win other concessions in exchange for supporting the Conservatives' David Cameron for prime minister.

Legal Environment

Numerous legal advantages benefit the major parties and sustain the two-party system.[14] There are, for example, legal impediments to minor parties getting on the ballot. In several states, only parties that received at least 5% of the vote in the previous general election are automatically listed on the ballot in the next election. Other parties and independent candidates must petition their way onto the ballot by gathering the signatures of the number of eligible voters equal to at least 1% of the statewide vote in the last election. The major parties also have an advantage where there is public financing for political campaigns. At the national level, the Republicans and Democrats qualify as major parties for full funding of their presidential campaigns as long as each received 25% of the vote in the previous election. Minor parties must have won 5% of the national vote to get funding, and even then they get only a proportionate share. The only time that a minor party has qualified since 1976, the year public funding for presidential campaigns was put in place, was when Ross Perot and the Reform Party qualified in 1996.

Inertia

Inertia in the political system is a fourth factor promoting the two-party system. Part of the inertia is based on the long history of two-party dominance. This has created the idea that third parties cannot win. As a result, potential candidates and party workers shy away from getting involved in what seems an unrealistic quest. Furthermore, money is hard to raise, the press pays little attention to minor party candidates, and many people believe that they will be wasting their vote if they cast it for a minor party candidate. Minor parties remain impotently on the sidelines of American politics because this circular cause-and-effect cycle creates a self-fulfilling prophecy. Adding to the inertia, the vast majority of voters either identifies as Republican or Democrat, or leans toward one of those two parties. These party preferences are usually learned early in life and are slow to change. The result is a gap between what Americans say they want and what they do with regard to the two-party system. A 2007 poll found that 57% of Americans agreed that "it would be good to elect an Independent or third-party president because both the Democratic and Republican parties are disappointments."[15] Yet when the voting booth curtains closed in 2008, 98.6% of the voters cast their ballot for the Democrat or the Republican.

Pragmatism

A fifth factor promoting the two-party system is the generally non-ideological orientation of a significant part of the American public. As Chapter 6 notes, most Americans are not strong ideologues. Instead they tend to be political pragmatists who group toward the center of the ideological spectrum. Only about a quarter of Americans see themselves as "very" liberal or conservative according to a 2009 survey. By contrast, the other three-fourths portray themselves as "moderate," as only "somewhat" liberal or conservative, or as unwilling to express any ideological position. This lack of strong ideology in the electorate prompts candidates from both major parties to move toward the center, especially in close races, thereby leaving little room for a centrist party to arise and position itself between the two major parties. And since most Americans are centrist, more doctrinaire ideological parties to the left or to the right of the major parties have little appeal. For the same reason, when either the Democrats or Republicans have moved sharply toward either ideological extreme, as the Republicans did with the candidacy of Senator Berry Goldwater (AZ) in 1964 or the Democrats did by nominating Senator George McGovern (SD) in 1972, the party has suffered a crushing defeat. If history holds true, the recent rightward shift of the Republican Party carries the same risk.

Third Parties

Our emphasis on the two-party system in the United States does not mean that it is exclusively two-party. There have always been other parties active locally and sometimes regionally or even nationally. Most minor parties have not played a major role, but occasionally one has gained enough strength to have a significant impact on national politics or policy as a third party. On one occasion, a third party even became one of the two major parties. This was in the 1850s when the Republicans supplanted the collapsing Whigs as the second major party.

More often, significant third parties serve to indicate discontent among voters with the two major parties. "Third parties emerge out of the two-party system," one study concludes, "principally because of some broadly recognized failure by the major parties to address an important policy problem and/or because there is a substantial constituency dissatisfied with the policy positions and priorities of the two major parties."[16] As such, voting for a third party is often a protest against the existing parties rather than support for the third party as such.[17] The effect is to put pressure on the one or both major parties to reshape their policy stances in order to draw supporters away from the third party, which then weakens and may disappear altogether.

Segregationist and socially conservative Alabama governor George C. Wallace ran a high-profile presidential campaign in 1968 that prompted Republicans nationwide to adopt a more socially conservative agenda that in turn increased their strength in the South. In this photo, Wallace is campaigning in Maryland in front of a Confederate battle flag. (AP Photo)

The American Independent Party presidential candidacy of Alabama Governor George Wallace in 1968 signified deep distress among conservative Democrats over their party's liberal civil rights and social welfare policies. Wallace received nearly 10 million votes and carried five states with 46 electoral votes. Not only did Wallace do well in the South, he won 5% to 12% of the vote in most of the northern states as well. This prompted the Republicans to move to incorporate Wallace's supporters. The "southern strategy" launched by Richard Nixon emphasized states rights, a strong stance on crime, and other positions designed to appeal to dissatisfied white Democrats, especially in the South. Thus the success of the American Independent Party helped move the Republicans away from their traditional emphasis on economic issues and toward a greater and more conservative stress on social issues. This shift, in turn, dramatically increased the strength of the Republican Party in the South and ended nearly a century of the Democrats' domination of that region.

Party Organization

American parties are largely decentralized organizations. We commonly talk about *the* Republican Party and *the* Democratic Party, but neither exists in a strict sense. Instead, American parties are best described as loosely connected political organizations that share the same name and some similarity in their political views and are allied by a common interest: gaining power. Moreover, American political parties have no control over their membership. In a legal sense, people become members of the Democrats, Republicans, or some other party by declaring they are affiliated with the party on a form submitted to the local registrar of voters in a procedure governed entirely by state law.

The organization of the Democratic and Republican parties mirrors the national-state-local structure of the U.S. federal system. Each party has something of a three-tier system composed of a **national committee**, the Democratic National Committee (DNC) and Republican National Committee (RNC); 50 state party committees; and thousands of local party committees. However, unlike authority in the federal system, where the central government has considerable authority over the states, and they in turn have great authority over local governments, the various layers of the Democratic and Republican parties have much less authority over lower units. Instead each is largely independent. Presidents at the national level and governors at the state level exercise some authority over their party's various committees. Money also plays a role. The funding that flows largely downward from the national party, to state parties, to local parties, gives each higher layer some influence over the lower layers. For the most part, though, the various levels of each party are autonomous, and elected and official and elected part leaders exercise authority more through persuasion than through any other means.

The DNC and RNC are each composed of representatives of the 50 state party committees and various other constituent groups. A chairperson heads each national committee. Typically the president controls who heads his party's national committee. For example, the day after Barack Obama became president in 2009, one of his early backers, Virginia Governor Tim Kane, took over as head of the DNC. The process was very different for the selection the new RNC chairman in 2009. In that case, Maryland's former Lieutenant Governor Michael Steele bested four other hopefuls in a six-ballot contest to become the first African American to head the RNC.

Ronald H. Brown became the first person of color to head either major party when he was elected chairman of the Democratic National Committee in 1989.

AMERICAN DIVERSITY

Beyond the fragmentation that results from the parties' having a federal-state-local structure, numerous other autonomous party units further decentralize the parties organizationally. Each party has a **legislative caucus** of its members in the House and another in the Senate. These four caucuses act autonomously to shape policy positions and legislative strategy (see Chapter 11). Each party caucus also has a campaign organization that recruits candidates, helps devise campaign strategies, and raises and dispenses campaign funds.

PARTIES IN THE ELECTORATE

In a democracy, bringing together citizens who share similar political views is the first step in the process of forming a political party, contesting elections, and if successful, controlling the government. To look at this parties-in-the-electorate function, we will first review the evolution of American parties and their support in the electorate. Then we will turn to the current status of the parties by examining party identification among Americans individually and in groups. As part of this review of the contemporary situation, we will consider the debate over whether the parties have realigned their electoral coalitions or have dealigned, becoming irrelevant as politicians and voters look for other ways to organize and understand the political contest.

Party Alignments in History

The history of American political parties can be roughly divided into several eras, each marked by a particular **party alignment**.[18] This concept includes the significant parties of the time, the policies each backed, and which groups in society were part of each party's coalition of supporters. Each of these *party eras* persists for several decades but each also witnesses its own increasing disintegration as new issues, new groups of voters, and other factors combine to make the old alignment outmoded. A new era is then begun by a **party realignment**, a reconfiguration of the coalitions of voters and other political actors who support each party and either a marked shift in the relative strength of the two parties or the end of one of the old parties and the rise of a replacement party. Sometimes there is a **critical election** in which each party's political power shifts dramatically because of a realignment of each party's supporting coalition. At other times, realignments are more gradual, may be unsteady, and may occur in a series of elections rather than a single critical one.[19] Whether revolutionary or evolutionary, the point is that the pattern of support for the parties, and thus their strength, changes significantly. You will see that these transitions often come during times of considerable societal turbulence and that they are also often accompanied by important third-party activity.

Party Alignments before the Civil War

The *First Party Era* (early 1790s to the mid-1820s) saw the formation of the first two parties, the Federalists and the Democratic Republicans. The Federalists favored a strong central government, high tariffs to protect U.S. industries, and raising revenue to build roads, canals, and other infrastructure to enhance economic development. In foreign policy, the Federalists leaned toward Great Britain because of trade ties and because of the stability of the British monarchy. Federalist strength was strongest along the coast, especially in New England. Opponents to Federalists eventually became known as Democratic Republicans. They were pro-state's rights, pro-farmer, against high import taxes, and pro-republican France. The Democratic Republicans were strongest among southern planters and other farmers, local merchants, and other importers, and were centered in the interior of the country, especially in the South. After electing John Adams president, the

Federalists rapidly declined in strength because of such stands as opposition to the popular purchase of the Louisiana Territory from France in 1803 and the War of 1812.

As a result, the country operated as a dominant-party system between 1803 and the early 1820s. Every president during that period was a Democratic Republican, and they won an average of 76% of the Electoral College vote. Party strength in Congress was also one-sided, with the Democratic Republicans holding an average of 75% of the House seats during the period 1801–1825. Yet beneath the surface, national politics was not as unified as party labels and numbers would make it seem. As the Federalists faded, factions emerged within the Democratic Republicans.

The Second Party Era (mid-1820s to the late 1850s) came into being for two reasons. One was that no one party could be broad enough to encompass all the diverse policy views and interests of Americans. The other reason a second party reemerged was the expansion of who could vote and the increased role of popular elections in choosing the president. Among other things, these changes pitted more traditional political forces against populists who believed in greater equality (among white males) and a greater public say in policy.

These crosscutting forces worked to fragment the Democratic Republicans. In 1824, the leader of one of these splinter groups, John Quincy Adams, won the presidency over three other candidates, each the head of another faction of the Democratic Republicans. Indeed, as often occurs during realignments, there were several elections (1824, 1832, and 1836) during which three or more presidential candidates received electoral votes.

Then in the 1828 election, Andrew Jackson, head of another party faction, ousted Adams. The Jackson faction became the Democratic Party, and the Adams faction along with other Democratic Republicans who were anti-Jackson and the remnants of the Federalists evolved by 1836 into the Whig Party. What united the Whigs was their opposition to Jackson's promotion of a powerful presidency and his anti-business, populist orientation with its emphasis on mass democracy. For a time the Whigs enjoyed success. They captured the presidency in 1840 and in 1848, and held an average of 47% of the seats in the House between 1837 and 1855. However, the Whigs soon disintegrated over two diversity issues: slavery in the territories and whether immigration was destroying American culture. Slavery also split the Democrats, with Southern Democrats defending it, most Northern Democrats hoping to reach a compromise, and a few Democrats opposing it. These antislavery Democrats joined with antislavery Whigs and others to form the Republican Party. Once again, realignment was underway, marked by third parties receiving electoral votes in the presidential elections of 1856 and 1860.

Party Alignments from the Civil War to the Great Depression

The Third-party Era (early 1860s to the 1890s) began as the upstart Republican Party (Grand Old Party, GOP) secured its place as one of the country's two major parties. Indeed the Republicans were the dominant party from the Civil War through the period of Reconstruction (1861–1876). But the Democratic Party regained its strength as the 1870s progressed. The Democrats' resurgence was partly based on the big city political machines that controlled the often-Catholic immigrant vote for the Democrats. They also gained control of the South by ousting Republicans who had been elected in significant part by the votes of newly

enfranchised blacks. The Southern Democrats then ensured their hold by enacting laws that ended most black voting in the South. By 1880 the country had settled into a regional pattern that persisted for several decades, with a solidly Democratic South and a generally Republican Northeast, Midwest, and West interspersed with Democratic-dominated urban centers.

Nevertheless, new issues were beginning to emerge that increasingly splintered the existing Democratic and Republican coalitions. Among other things, increased industrialism accentuated class issues and urban-rural divides. Increased concern about social values put issues such as prohibition on the political agenda. There was also a surge in populism, the belief that a corporate-centered economic elite dominates government and suppresses the interests of the common people. In 1892, the Populist Party candidate won 9% of the electoral votes and 22 electoral votes, and Congress had Populist Party members from 1891 through 1903.

The Fourth Party Era (late 1890s to the early 1930s) was marked by a shift in coalitions that, instead of shifting the dominant party, added to the strength of the already dominant Republicans. One blow to the Democrats was a major economic recession under Democratic President Grover Cleveland. The Republican coalition also grew in response to the seemingly radical economic proposals of three-time Democratic presidential nominee William Jennings Bryan (1896, 1900, 1908). He tried to appeal to the supporters of the Populist Party by adopting many of their views. This convinced most Populists, who also nominated Bryan in 1896. Overall, though, the Democrats' populist tilt backfired because it alienated some demographic groups that usually or sometimes voted Democratic. Among these were German Americans, many of whom rejected populism and turned toward the Republicans.

Soon, however, the Republicans' grip on power was undermined by tensions related to industrialization. The Progressive Party, which dis-

The Fourth Party Era was one of Republican dominance in part because of the Democrats' repeated nomination of William Jennings Bryan for president. He was portrayed as a radical and even as unstable and immature. This Harper's Weekly *cover from 1896 contrasts the Civil War service of the 53-year-old Republican presidential nominee, William McKinley, with the youth of the Democrats' candidate, Bryan, who was 36 at the time. Note the similarity to the comparisons during the 2008 presidential campaign between the older, militarily experienced Republican candidate, John McCain, and the Democrats' younger, nonveteran Barack Obama. The outcomes, however, were very different. (Library of Congress)*

trusted business's impact on the economy and environment and which evolved in part from the Populists, held seats in Congress between 1911 and 1919. Also, former Republican President Theodore Roosevelt got 27% of the popular vote and 88 electoral votes in 1912 running as a Progressive. The Progressive Party was especially active in the Middle West, where numerous states passed laws establishing a direct democracy option through referendums. Also in that region, populism motivated Iowan George Gallup to devise modern public opinion polling to bring the public's sentiments to bear on policy making (see Chapter 6). Even further to the left during this era, the Socialist Party made gains, with its presidential candidate receiving 6% of the popular vote in 1912. The strains in this party era were also evident in 1924 when Senator Robert M. Lafollette (R-WI) ran on both the Progressive and Socialist tickets, winning 17% of the popular vote and 13 electoral votes.

Party Alignments from the Great Depression to the Civil Rights/Vietnam Era

The Fifth Party Era (early 1930s to the late 1960s) began with the Republican collapse and the powerful Democratic victory in 1932. The catalyst for this dramatic shift in party fortunes was the black mark the onset of the Great Depression left on incumbent Republican President Herbert Hoover and his party. By contrast, the Democrats benefited from the appeal to destitute and frightened Americans of Democratic President Franklin D. Roosevelt and his New Deal program of economic reform and recovery. These factors allowed the Democrats to build a dominant **New Deal coalition** based on economic issues that strengthened pro-Democratic partisan leanings among voters in the cities and among union workers, southern and eastern European ethnic groups, and other traditionally supportive groups. Yet other groups, such as small farmers and blacks, that had usually supported the Republicans, moved into the Democratic ranks. They were joined by many who had supported the Progressive and, before that Populist, Parties.

The result was an extended period of Democratic dominance that contrasted sharply with the earlier Republican dominance. During the Fourth Party Era the Republicans won six of the eight presidential elections and controlled both houses of Congress 75% of the time. During this new era, the Democrats won seven of the nine presidential elections from 1932 through 1964 and held majorities in both houses of Congress in all but four years.

Although the Democrats gained a powerful grip on politics beginning in the 1930s, they never created a dominant-party system as the Democratic Republicans had in the early 1800s. Instead, the Republicans began to recover strength in Congress, and between 1931 and 1966 were able to twice win control of both houses of Congress (1947–1948 and 1953–1954) and to elect a president (Dwight

Eisenhower, 1952, 1956). The Republicans were able to remain a significant second party because the Democrats' dominant New Deal coalition began to unravel amid changing issues and the shifting party preferences of various blocks of voters. There is no doubt that by the late 1960s, the Fifth Party Era was over. What came next is a matter of controversy.

The Contemporary Party Era: Realignment or Dealignment?

Most political scientists agree on the broad outlines of the alignments and realignments from the 1790s through the 1960s, but there accord ends. The debate about what occurred next can be roughly divided into the realignment argument and the dealignment argument.

The Realignment Argument

Some scholars believe that another realignment began in the late 1960s that eventually led to a *Sixth Party Era.* This view contends that the coalitions of the two parties, especially that of the Democratic Party, fragmented. A principal cause was the change in the focus of the political agenda from economic issues to social value issues such as civil rights. In turn, the new political agenda reconfigured the composition and strength of each party's coalition. The case for realignment also notes that such shifts in party loyalty and strength occur during times of turbulence, and that the late 1960s and early 1970s were a period of high political stress marked by the Vietnam War, Watergate, urban riots, the assassination of Martin Luther King, and other traumas. Moreover, as during other realignments, third parties were active. George Wallace's candidacy in 1968 was the most important of these, with the Dixiecrat campaign in 1948 and the phantom candidacy of Harry Byrd in 1960 akin to minor tremors before the main political earthquake.

The Dealignment Argument

Scholars with this view argue that what occurred was not realignment, but a **dealignment**. As one recent study put it, "there was no majority realignment." Instead what occurred was a "general dealignment from party affiliation and voting regularity."[20] A dealignment occurs when a large part of the electorate abandons its party loyalties or has them so weakened that most people are not firmly aligned with any party. This argument begins with the numerous changes that have sapped party strength since it peaked in the second half of the 1800s. From that point, parties lost power when civil service rules removed much of the parties' ability to distribute government jobs to loyalists. The power of political parties also once rested on the ability of **party machines** to deliver the vote by manipulating taxes, delivering food and housing to the needy, steering contracts, and engaging in other often corrupt practices that rewarded supporters and punished opponents. Changes such as tougher corrupt practices laws and the coming of the social welfare systems undercut the power of these party machines. Party strength was further undermined by the advent of primaries because they sharply lessen the influence of party organizations on the nomination process.

Dealignment advocates further argue that against this backdrop of already ebbing party strength, many voters discarded or reduced their sense of party loyalty beginning in the mid-1960s. The underlying cause was the increase of political distrust of government among Americans in the aftermath of Vietnam and Watergate (see Chapter 6). This negative sentiment and its impact on the parties are evident in the following:

- In 1966, 65% of Americans said they trusted the federal government to usually try to do the right thing; only 33% felt that way a decade later.
- Amid this distrust, voting declined from an average of 62% during the three presidential elections in the 1960s to 54% in the following three elections.
- Distrust of politics also weakened party identification. In 1964, 38% of the electorate strongly identified with one of the parties. A decade later, only 25% were strong identifiers.
- Weakened party loyalty led to a decrease in straight-ticket voting from 85% in 1964 to 72% in 1980.[21] **Straight-ticket voting** (straight-party voting) means casting all your votes in an election for candidates from one party. **Split-ticket voting** (ticket splitting) is casting your votes for candidates of different parties in the same election.

A Sixth Party Era?

Did a *Sixth Party Era* evolve beginning in the early 1970s? Or had parties become so weak that the electorate dealigned itself from them? It is possible to resolve this by asking seven questions. The first four questions focus on whether the voter alignment in the Fifth Party Era changed. The fifth asks if a critical election occurred. The sixth and seventh questions address whether the parties remained important enough in voter choice to say that realignment, rather than dealignment, occurred. The more questions that can be answered yes, the safer it is to conclude that a new party era occurred.

Question 1: Were There Significant Changes in the National Issue Agenda?
Yes. As occurred during other party eras, old issues faded and new ones emerged. Foreign policy had played virtually no part in the voter realignment that created the Fifth Party Era. However, about half way through it, the onset of the cold war with the Soviet Union in 1946 increased the importance of foreign policy as a factor in party strength and voter alignment. Then the Vietnam War increased the division between those who wanted to be tough on communism and those who

favored a more flexible foreign policy. The domestic political agenda also changed. The country recovered from the Depression and prospered. This decreased the political importance of many of the economic issues that were at the core of the Democrats' New Deal coalition. At the same time, a range of social value issues became increasingly prominent. Civil rights took its place on the political agenda, as blacks, women, and members of other disadvantaged groups escalated their demands for equal treatment. The liberal thrust of the 1960s and 1970s also put abortion, pornography, capital punishment, affirmative action, the separation of church and state, and a range of other social issues onto the political agenda. Moreover, many economic issues became entangled in social value issues. President Lyndon Johnson's "Great Society" program pushed simultaneously for new and increased social welfare programs and for strong civil rights legislations, thereby linking the two efforts in the minds of both supporters and opponents. As Johnson put in 1964, "A Great Society rests on abundance and liberty for all. It demands an end to poverty and racial injustice."[22]

Question 2: Was There Notable Third-Party Activity?

Yes, the weakening alignment of some blocs of voters with their party was accompanied by a rise in third-party activity. Civil rights was the most important fissure line in the New Deal coalition. Gradually, this issue divided the Democratic Party into two factions, Southern Democrats and Northern Democrats. The first overt split occurred in 1948 after President Harry S. Truman, a Democrat, ordered the military to racially integrate its units and also persuaded that year's Democratic National Convention to support integration. Outraged, many southerners temporarily defected from the party, formed the States Rights Democratic Party (the Dixiecrats), and nominated Democratic Governor Strom Thurmond of South Carolina for president. He got only 2% of the national vote, but he was able to win in four southern states with 39 electoral votes. The South rose again in 1960 when 15 presidential electors from Alabama, Mississippi, and Oklahoma voted for Senator Harry F. Byrd (D-VA) even though he was not technically a candidate. A third southern uprising against the civil rights positions and general liberalism of the Northern Democrats occurred in 1968 when Georgia Governor George Wallace ran for president on the American Independent Party ticket, got 14% of the national popular vote, and carried five southern states and their 45 electoral votes.

Question 3: Did Important Changes Occur in the Coalitions Supporting the Two Parties?

Yes, changes in the composition and the strength of the coalitions supporting the two parties did occur between the Fifth and Sixth Party Eras.[23] One shift came midway during the Fifth Party Era. In a reaction to the cold war, there was an increase in Republican voting among some groups, especially Eastern European Americans and southerners, who saw themselves and the Republicans as stronger on defense and tougher on communism than the Democrats. The civil rights movement and the liberal social agenda were even more important to the shift of southern whites from being solidly Democratic to voting heavily Republican. The change, one study concludes, was "driven to a significant degree by racial conservatism in addition to a harmonizing of partisanship with general ideological conservatism."[24] President Nixon's use of these factors to increase the Republican votes was dubbed the "southern strategy."

The liberal-conservative ideological split that divided white Southern Democrats from the rest of the party played out in Congress, especially on civil rights, but also on social issues and national defense. For example, only 2 of 107 Southern Democrats in the House voted for the Civil Rights Act of 1957; only 2 of 118 Northern Democrats voted against it. Republicans supported the act by 168 to 19. Southern Democrats also opposed many of the social welfare policies favored by Northern Democrats, arguably in part because such programs benefited blacks. Typically 14 of 19 Northern Democratic senators favored a measure in 1957 to increase federal aid to housing, while 14 of 17 Southern Democratic senators opposed it. On many such economic policy issues, Southern Democrats voted more like Republicans than like the rest of the Democrats in Congress, creating what was known as the *conservative coalition*.

Social issues also prompted many Christians with strong religious convictions to move toward the Republican coalition because some Christian churches are conservative on abortion and a range of other social-value issues. In 2004, for example, 48% of evangelical Protestants identified as Republicans, while only 23% saw themselves as Democrats.

Civil rights and social issues did not work entirely to the Republicans' advantage, however. Partially off-setting the southern white shift to the Republicans, the percentage of blacks voting Democratic rose in response to President Johnson's Great Society initiative and, more generally, to the increased support of the Democratic Party for civil rights. Adding further to the importance of the shift in party sentiment among blacks was the fact that African Americans began to vote in much greater numbers. These changes are evident in Figure 9.4. A similar pattern emerged for women.

FIGURE 9.4 African American Voting by Party and Turnout

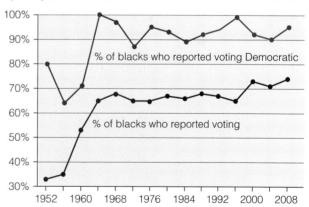

African Americans have become more important to the Democratic coalition because (1) a much higher percentage now vote than once did, and (2) they have become overwhelmingly Democratic voters.

Data sources: American National Election Studies through 2004; exit polls and an average of several polls on reported voting for 2008, data courtesy of The Roper Center.

They were most likely to vote Republican until the mid-1960s. Since then women have become both increasingly more likely to vote Democratic and more likely to vote in general.

Question 4: Were There Marked Changes in the Strength of the Two Parties?

Yes, the Sixth Party Era was heralded by a substantial shift in the political fortunes of the previously existing parties, just as each earlier party era had seen. The election of 1968 brought Republican Richard Nixon to the White House, and he was overwhelmingly reelected in 1972. Indeed, from 1968 through 2004, Republicans won six of the nine presidential elections. Power also shifted in Congress. During most of the 1970s, the Watergate scandal and Nixon's resignation in 1974 slowed the Democrats' decline, but the flood tide of Republican strength resumed in 1980. Republican Ronald Reagan routed Carter, and the GOP also took control of the Senate and held it for 16 of the next 24 years. Republican control of the House of Representatives came last, but once in place after the 1994 elections, it continued for the following 12 years.

In both chambers the end of the once solidly Democratic South and its conversion to a Republican stronghold was particularly important to the upswing of Republican strength.[25] The Republicans went from having 12% of the House seats and 5% of the Senate seats in the South during the 1960s to having over two-thirds of the region's Senate seats and a majority of its House seats even after the Republicans were routed nationally in the 2006 and 2008 elections.

It is true that the Republicans did not gain the dominance that the Democrats had during the Fifth Party Era, but overwhelming dominance is not necessary to denote a party era. There was no dominant party during the Second Party Era, for instance. That period saw five Jacksonian/Democratic presidents and four anti-Jackson/Whig presidents, and while the Democrats usually controlled Congress, the Whigs were a majority in one or both houses after several elections.

Question 5: Did a Critical Election Occur?

No. What was missing from the events signifying other party era changes was a single critical election or sequence of two consecutive elections that significantly changed the political landscape. Nixon's two victories did little to increase Republican strength in Congress. Eight years would pass before the GOP gained a majority in the Senate (1980), and 22 would elapse before the Republicans gained control of the House (1994). The political tide began to flow in the Republicans' direction after 1968, but no single election or series of them proved critical.

Question 6: Did Most Individuals Continue to Identify with a Party?

Yes, most people remained party identifiers, although the evidence is open to debate. The issue over whether the electorate realigned or dealigned after the Fifth

Party Era is complicated by disputes over what percentage of the people are consistent supporters of one of the two major parties.[26] One way to examine this is with the **seven-point party identification scale**. On it, people classify themselves as a strong Republican, a weak Republican, an independent Republican (Republican leaner), an independent, an independent Democrat (Democratic leaner), a weak Democrat, or a strong Democrat. The trick is interpreting the answers. Consider the following three ways of calculating the parties' strength in the electorate:

- If the base of each party consists only of its strong supporters, then the parties are fairly weak, with only a combined 32% of the electorate being solid supporters.
- Adding the parties' combined weak supporters (29%) to their strong supporters (32%) gives the two parties moderate strength with 61% of the electorate.
- Further adding leaners (28%) to the parties' combined strong (32%) and weak (29%) supporters makes the parties strong, with 89% of the electorate.[27]

It is also noteworthy that answers along the seven-point scale will vary according to such factors as whether the survey sample is of all adults or "likely voters," adults who voted in the previous election and say they intend to vote in the coming one. In 2010, for example, the combined percentages of people who declared themselves strong Republicans or Democrats was 26% of the entire adult population sample and 46% of a sample of likely voters. Given these measurement problems and the lack of good data on party identification before the 1950s, it is wise to be cautious about what any data (including that in Figure 9.5, which is based on

FIGURE 9.5   Party Identification, 1952–2008

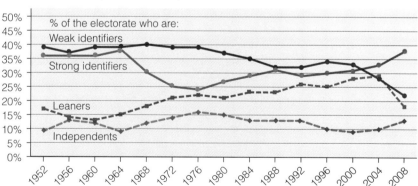

Party identification dropped off sharply in the 1970s, but recovered somewhat in the 1990s. Still the long-term decrease in weak identifiers and increase in leaners indicates that party loyalties are weaker than they once were.

Notes and data sources: Independents include those saying they are apolitical. Data from American National Election Studies except for 2008, which averages several polls using a national sample of all adults. Data for 2008 provided by The Roper Center for Public Opinion.

entire national adult samples) say about realignment and dealignment. Certainly the dealignment camp is correct that party identification declined significantly beginning in the late 1960s. This is especially true when focusing on strong and weak identifiers. Simultaneously, though, the percentage of leaners grew considerably. It is also true that party identification for strong identifiers has recovered to the level found in 1964 and earlier. Moreover, the overall drop-off in the combined totals (of strong, weak, and leaner) was near zero, while true independents rose only about 5% before declining again.

*Question 7: Did Party Identification Remain
an Important Factor in Voter Choice?*

Yes, it did, although party identification during the last three decades of the twentieth century was less pivotal than it once had been in determining how voters cast their ballots. Whatever people say about their party identification, the ultimate test of their connection to the party is how strongly it influences their vote. One way to measure that is to look at ticket splitting. The more there is, the weaker parties are. Conversely, the less split-ticket voting there is, the stronger the parties are. The incidence of ticket splitting between individuals' presidential and congressional votes is shown in Figure 9.6.

Split-ticket voting rose in the late 1960s and peaked at 30% in 1972 as the Fifth Party Era coalition fell apart. After the peak, many southern white voters who had earlier split their ticket by voting Republican for president and Democratic for Congress, switched to voting straight-ticket Republican. As a result, split-ticket voting declined; it was only 17% in 2004 and, preliminarily, about 19% in 2008.

FIGURE 9.6   Split-Ticket Voting

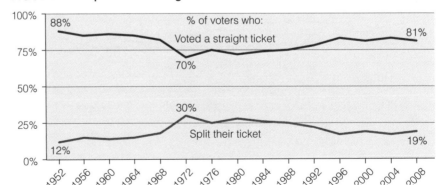

Split-ticket voting, one sign of weak party loyalty among voters, increased to 30% in 1972. However, it has generally declined somewhat since then.
Data sources: The American National Election Studies for 1952–2004; exit polls for 2008.

This indicates that while the impact of party identification on voter choice may be weaker than was once true, it remains too strong to say that there has been a general party dealignment.[28]

The Verdict about a Sixth Party Era

We posed seven questions and argued that the more clearly each could be answered yes, the more it could be confidently concluded that a new party era occurred. We then found that each of these questions except number 5 could indeed be answered yes. As for question 5, the lack of a critical election may have been an anomaly caused by the sharp rise in political alienation and the collapse of the Republican Party in the tumultuous late1960s and early 1970s. By the 1980s, though, political alienation had eased somewhat, the Republicans had recovered, and the positive shift in their electoral fortunes resumed. Therefore, the view here is that a party realignment did occur. Certainly, parties do not have the strength they once did. Nevertheless, they remain important for voter identification and choice. Indeed, there may now be yet another realignment with a Seventh Party Era in the offing.

A Seventh Party Era?

It is difficult to think about the dramatic collapse of the Republican Party's fortunes in the 2006 and 2008 elections without wondering whether a new party realignment is occurring. Most signs indicate that there is a shift underway. Still, the evidence is not definitive, and there are also some counter indications. Among the factors pointing to the advent of a Seventh Party Era are:

- *Time.* Most party eras have lasted 30 to 40 years. If we date the beginning of Sixth Party Era to 1968, it reached its fortieth year in 2008.
- *Party strength/critical election(s).* As true for all but the Third and Fourth Party Eras, there has been a dramatic shift in political power that has changed which party is dominant. If this shift persists, it indicates realignment, with 2006 and 2008 the critical elections.
- *Political turmoil.* There was considerable unease among Americans due to the war in Iraq, the massive recession beginning in 2008, and other factors. Trust in government has once again plummeted.
- *Voters and alignment.* The most important change in recent years is the increase in Latino voters. They were 3% of all voters in 1992 and 9% in 2008. This percentage will continue to rise. The marked preference of Latinos for the Democrats will, if it remains unchanged, be a strong advantage for the Democrats.
- *Issues.* Many of the civil rights and social issues that determined party loyalty during the Sixth Party Era have eased, and other, more traditional economic

issues like health care have emerged. The cold war has disappeared, and unless terrorism or rogue nuclear weapons states (Iran, North Korea) come to the fore, national security will be less important in voter alignment in the future. A rising issue, immigration, is apt to favor the Democrats, given their stands and the growing number of Latino and Asian American voters.

Several other factors cast doubt on whether realignment is taking place. These include:

- *Third-party activity/societal turmoil.* Unlike the other transitional times between party eras, important third-party activity has not been significant, with no major third-party presidential candidate since 1996 (Ross Perot). The turmoil including political violence that has marked some shifts in party eras has also been absent. The Tea Party may become an important third party, but as of mid-2010 that had not yet occurred, as noted in the opening You Decide box.
- *Party strength/critical election(s).* It is not clear whether the Republican disasters in 2006 and 2008 marked a long-term loss of favor or were the short-term result of such issues as the Iraq War and the troubled economy. Certainly, the Republicans' strong comeback in 2010 casts serious doubt on the idea that realignment has occurred. Yet it may be that the Democrats' debacle in 2010 was an anomaly reflecting voter frustration with the party in power for the country's continuing economic difficulties. The 2012 presidential and congressional elections will help sort out which of these possibilities is true.
- *Issues.* Issues could (re)emerge that might move some blocs of voters in the Republicans' direction. Among others, these include terrorism, cultural protectionism, fiscal restraint, abortion, and gay marriage. Depending on party stands, a split between older and younger voters on Medicare, Social Security, and other benefits could affect partisan loyalties.

PARTIES AND ELECTIONS

If for a political party the first step toward controlling the government is building a solid base of support in the electorate, the next step is winning elections. This includes recruiting and selecting candidates, conducting the election campaign, and serving as a symbol for voters. Parties are important in each of these three steps, but not as much as was once true. More than in the past, the election process has become centered on the candidates as individual political entrepreneurs rather than as party representatives. This change, much like the realignment/dealignment debate we have just considered, raises questions about the ongoing vitality of the parties.

Recruiting and Selecting Candidates

One key to party success is presenting voters with candidates who have the political skills and personal attributes to win the election. This function has two parts. The first is recruiting candidates who are willing to run. The second is ultimately choosing which hopeful will be the party's nominee in the general election.

Recruiting Candidates

Most candidates recruit themselves. Indeed, one survey of congressional candidates found that 61% indicated they were self-starters, individuals who had decided for themselves to seek office.[29] However, 14% of the candidates described themselves as having been recruited by party officials to run, and another 25% said that they ran because of a combination of party recruitment and self-motivation. Finding someone, anyone to run is not usually the focus of a party's recruitment effort. Rather it is persuading individuals to run who have the best chance of winning because they already are well-known, have enough personal wealth to help finance a campaign, or are particularly attractive for some other reason.

Parties are important in the electoral process, including recruiting candidates who have name recognition, wealth, or some other asset that improves their chances of being elected. One such successful recruit for the Democrats for Congress in 2006 was former Washington Redskins quarterback and now Representative Heath Shuler. (AP Photo/NFL Photos)

One such recruiting effort focused on former National Football League quarterback Heath Shuler (Washington Redskins, initially). He was one of the 50 or so Democratic candidates for the House in 2006 recruited by Representative Rahm Emanuel (D-IL), head of the Democratic Congressional Campaign Committee (DCCC), his party's campaign committee in the House. Quarterback Shuler is now Representative Shuler, having defeated incumbent Republican Charles Taylor in North Carolina's 11th congressional district with 54% of the vote.

Many party levels do recruiting. The White House is usually a key recruiter for the president's party. Each party in the House and Senate also has a committee dedicated to recruiting candidates for Congress and helping them financially.[30] In addition to the already mentioned NRSC and DCCC, there are the National Republican Campaign Committee (NRCC) in the House and the Democratic Senatorial Campaign Committee (DSCC). The Democratic National Committee, the Republican National Committee, and the various state party committees also join the recruitment efforts. Additionally, special legislative groups like the Congressional Black Caucus and the Congressional Hispanic Caucus also play a recruitment role.

At times the recruiting process can also include trying to persuade a weak candidate to stand aside. One instance involved the role various Democratic party leaders played in the decision of Senator Christopher Dodd (D-CT) to retire. Early polls showed Dodd trailing his potential announced Republican opponents for the 2010 election, and his retirement opened the way for the candidacy of the state's popular attorney general, Richard Blumenthal, in an effort to hold the seat for the Democrats.

Selecting Candidates

It is not uncommon for a party to have to choose among two or more individuals seeking its nomination for an office. There are basically two ways these nominations are decided. The more traditional approach is a **party convention**, a gathering of delegates from geographic subdivisions, such as cities and counties of a state, to nominate a party candidate and sometimes to conduct other party business. The use of conventions was once the dominant method of selecting candidates, but over time **primaries**, elections in which voters choose party nominees, became increasingly widespread. Now almost all states use primaries in one form or another.

Chapter 10 on elections contains a great deal more on the nomination process, but it is important to note here that it has an impact on the parties organizationally. Primaries were introduced as a reform to enhance democracy by taking nominations out of the proverbial "smoke-filled backroom" and allowing all party members and even all voters to have a say. Primaries do that, but they also arguably sap party organizational strength, which is also important to the democratic process. Every organization needs rewards to keep its workers engaged, and for party workers perhaps the most important reward is to be one of the insiders who helps determine the party's nominees and, by extension, who serves in elective office. Primaries undermine that reward system. For instance, a primary by a contender with little or no connection to the party organization can snatch the nomination away from a particular candidate favored by the party workers, those who keep party organizations functioning between elections. Moreover, the nominees and then office holders that are selected by primaries may have few if any ties to the party cadre and may even be at odds with it. This degrades the already limited ability of parties to exercise any organizational or policy control.

The type of primary also affects parties. Nominees selected by a **closed primary**, one in which only those already registered as a party member can vote, have at least been chosen by voters affiliated with the party. By contrast, **open primaries**, those in which members of any party or no party at all may also vote, can lead to a nominee who is not favored by a majority of the party faithful, much less most of the party's workers.

Campaigning

After nominating its candidates, each party turns to helping elect them. This involves fashioning a campaign message, raising campaign funds, and supplying other services. As is true for almost everything about American political parties, the campaign process is fragmented, with the various components of the parties acting quasi-independently. Also, as elsewhere in the electoral process, parties are but one of the actors involved. Individual candidates and their campaign organizations are usually more important than the parties in individual campaigns. As Chapter 10 details, interest groups are also deeply involved in campaigns, especially in their finance.

Persuading the Electorate

As mass parties, both the Democrats and Republicans work to project a general image and to fashion positions on specific topics calculated to simultaneously energize the party's core supporters and to appeal broadly in order to win a majority of votes. This can be difficult because core supporters tend to be much more ideological than are the moderate independents who hold the balance of power in most elections. Moreover the range of views within each party and their fragmented organization make it hard for them to settle on and broadcast a unified campaign theme. During the 2006 campaign, for example, the message of the campaign committee of the House Democrats focused on raising the minimum wage and a few other moderate pledges designed to appeal to the middle of the American ideological spectrum. By contrast, the DNC's campaign theme was decidedly more liberal, highlighting gay rights among other issues. "Wow! That's way off our message," a House Democratic leader in the House exclaimed.[31]

Whether a party's messages are unified or fragmented, it is not clear that they have a great impact. Most Republican candidates for U.S. House seats in 1994 signed the Contract With America committing themselves to support a series of policy proposals and reforms in House rules. Subsequently, the Republicans rolled to an impressive victory, capturing control of the House for the first time in over 40 years. Yet a poll just before the election found that only 29% of Americans had "heard or read anything" about the Contract With America.[32] Similarly, the GOP's Pledge to America prior to the 2010 election seems to have gained little notice. According to one poll, 80% said they had heard "little" or "nothing" about it.[33] It is also the case, though, that the general tone set in Congress by the parties' respective leaders does influence the public's evaluation of the parties and their candidates.[34]

Raising and Spending Campaign Funds

Huge amounts of money are spent on campaigns. During the 2008 election cycle (2007–2008), various Democratic and Republican Party organizations spent about $1.9 billion. Two-thirds of this was spent by the two national committees (RNC and DNC) and the four congressional campaign committees (DSCC, DCCC, NRSC, and NRCC). The rest was spent by state and local party organizations. Preliminary figures for the 2010 election cycle indicate that these various party organizations spent more than $2 billion on the campaign.

Under the adage "money talks," you would think that the huge sums spent by the parties would give them great influence over campaigns and, subsequently the office holders elected with those funds. That is not the case, though, because only about 3% of the money that flows into the congressional campaigns comes from these party funds. The rest of the funds spent by the national party organizations goes to promoting the party in general, paying the expenses of the organization, and raising more money. This is especially true for the DNC and RNC, which give little money to specific candidates. Certainly many of the parties' general expenditures go for voter registration, get-out-the-vote drives, and other efforts that benefit candidates.[35] Yet such impacts are less tangible than a direct contribution to a candidate and therefore less likely to connect candidates and officeholders to party organizations.

Providing Support Services

Campaigns have become increasingly complex technologically and logistically, and party organizations help provide services that would be difficult or cost-inefficient for individual campaigns to duplicate. For example, parties use ad campaigns, phone banks, e-mails, and other techniques to mobilize their core supporters in the electorate.[36]

Serving as a Cue for Voter Choice

One way that people deal with complexities such as the daunting array of offices, issues, and candidates making claims and counterclaims is by using **heuristic devices.**[37] These cues are mental shortcuts that we use to help form opinions and make decisions when we have limited information. Brand names are one type of heuristic device. If we are familiar with and have a good impression of Kellogg's Frosted Flakes, it is easier to pick the box with Tony the Tiger on the front than it is to compare the many sugar-coated corn flake cereals for taste, ingredients, nutritional information, and price per serving. Moreover, the aura of the iconic tiger carries over to boost consumer assumptions about the quality of other Kellogg cereals and products.

Parties as a Heuristic Device in Voting

Political parties provide something of a brand name for candidates and help many voters decide how to cast their ballot.[38] This is especially true for voters who do not know the positions of the candidates.[39] The importance of the Democratic and Republican political brands is partly based on tradition and familiarity. Democrats have been a national party label since 1832 and Republicans since 1856. Also, as Figure 9.7 shows, a substantial majority of Americans believes that the two parties offer important differences in their policy choices and are not just different labels on the same product.[40] Additionally, most voters think it makes a difference which party controls the government.

Even more importantly, most Americans' political preferences are influenced by the differences they see between the parties.[41] As we saw during our discussion of party identification, about 90% of Americans identify with—express brand loyalty to— or at least lean toward either the Democrats or the Republicans. That leaves a mere 10% of Americans expressing no brand preference at all in politics. Most importantly, Americans act on these preferences in the voting booth. Recall from Figure 9.6 that more than 80% of the electorate has shown brand loyalty across offices by voting a straight ticket in recent years. Without taking our brand name analogy too far, such percentages in the commercial world would constitute extremely high brand loyalty.

Furthermore, there are indications that **polarization** is increasing in the electorate, with voters more likely to be viewing politics through a partisan lens. For example, a March 2009 poll found 88% of Democrats but only 27% of Republicans giving President Obama a positive job approval rating. This 61% partisan gap was the highest in 40 years for a president during the first few months of his first elected term and stood in sharp contrast the average 39% partisan gap in evaluating elected presidents in their first term dating back to Richard Nixon in 1969.[42] There are, however, other indications that polarization in the electorate is less pronounced than sometimes reported. One indication is that it appears that ticket splitting in 2008 was somewhat higher than in 2004. Additionally, the overall percentage of party identifiers who voted for their party's candidate for president in 2008 was slightly lower than occurred in 2000 or 2004. Third, while the percentage of adults identifying as "strong" Republicans or Democrats has risen, the increase between 1988 and 2008 was only from 31% to 38% (see Figure 9.5). Fourth, there is evidence, as we will see below, that very strong majorities of Americans are condemning partisanship in Washington and taking a "plague on

FIGURE 9.7 Public Perceptions about Differences between Parties

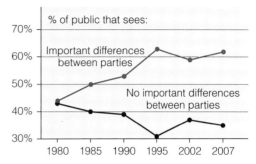

An increasing majority of Americans see important policy differences between the Democratic Party and the Republican Party.
Data sources: Various polls provided by The Roper Center.

both your houses" attitude toward the Republicans and Democrats. Overall then, the evidence on the degree of polarization in the electorate is somewhat mixed. What the future will bring remains to be seen, but partisan polarization in the electorate may be simply returning to the levels present in the 1950s rather than to some uncharted and perilous historic high.

Are Parties a Reasonable Cue for Voting Choice?

Does voting based in part on party labels make any rational sense? Certainly it would be good if every eligible voter went to the polls armed with full knowledge of the qualifications and policy views of each candidate for each office. Short of that, using party as a heuristic device to make a voting choice is not wholly irrational. There are several parts to the connection between party, ideology, and voting choice.

First, people with different ideologies identify with different parties. More than 80% of all liberals define themselves as Democrats; over 80% of all conservatives are Republicans.

Second, people recognize the ideological leanings of the parties. When one survey asked respondents to place the two parties on a 1-to-9 scale with 1 very liberal and 9 very conservative, the average scores were Democrats 3.9 and Republicans 6.6. This showed that the average respondent (1) saw an ideological difference, (2) correctly identified the Democrats as liberal and the Republicans as conservative, and (3) recognized that the Democrats are a left-center party (3.9) not an extreme left party (a 1 or 2) and that the Republicans are a right-center party (6.6), not an extreme right party (an 8 or 9).

Third, most congressional candidates mirror the ideology of their national party. As one study of House candidates between 1874 and 1996 put it, "Throughout this period, congressional candidates . . . primarily espoused the ideology associated with the national party."[43]

Fourth, voting patterns of members of Congress reflect their ideological differences. Using the ratings given by the Americans for Democratic Action, a liberal organization, to legislators' voting records during one recent Congress, the average Democrat received an 85% liberal score, while the average Republican got a distinctly "unliberal" 9% score.

Fifth, once elected to Congress or other legislative bodies, Republicans usually vote like other Republicans, Democrats usually vote like other Democrats, and Republicans and Democrats usually oppose each other on controversial issues. The ideological division between the Republicans and Democrats in Congress is not as distinctive as is the split between major parties in some countries, but it is clearer than the division in other countries. Indeed, there is a trend toward the polarization of the parties in Congress, with the members of each party, especially the Republicans, increasingly coming from the ideologically purist wing of the party and decreasingly from the more moderate/centrist wing of the party.

In sum, if you identify with a party but have little or no information about the candidates in your area, you can still make a partly rational decision by voting for your party's candidate. There is a good likelihood that his or her ideological and policy views are at least somewhat similar to your own.

PARTIES IN GOVERNMENT

Even though parties are not mentioned in the Constitution, they are an important factor in determining how parts of the government are organized. Parties also play a role in shaping policy.

Parties and Government Organization

Parties help shape who is in the government and how it is structured. This is particularly true for Congress, but it also applies to the executive and judicial branches.

Parties and the Organization of Congress

Every member of Congress is elected by a partisan process. Once in office, House and Senate members have come to organize themselves and the House and Senate along partisan lines. By the 1890s under the leadership of Speaker Thomas B. Reed (R-ME), the House began to implement rules that gave the dominant party significant control over the political agenda.[44] Then during the early twentieth century the two chambers took several important steps to formalize the important role of parties. One occurred when both chambers adopted a seating pattern based on party. Still used today, Democrats sit to the presiding officer's left and Republicans to the right. Before that, various other seating arrangements had been used. For example, the House had used a lottery system to determine seating between 1847 and 1913.

Congress also took a number of steps during the early 1900s to recognize the existence in each chamber of a Democratic and a Republican caucus, the members of each

The role of political parties in organizing Congress and making policy are symbolized by this April 2010 photo of President Barack Obama discussing financial reform legislation pending in Congress with Speaker of the House Nancy Pelosi (D-CA) and House Minority Leader John Boehner (R-OH). Following the 2010 elections, Boehner became Speaker and Pelosi minority leader. (AP Photo/Alex Brandon)

party. These caucuses are partisan organizations that discuss legislation and strategy. As part of the acceptance of the partisan role in Congress, the House and Senate formalized the positions of majority and minority leader based on party. The position of Speaker of the House is also partisan. Technically, the whole House elects the Speaker as its presiding officer, but in fact the Speaker is elected by the majority party and is its true leader. When the 111th Congress convened in 2009, the head of the House Democratic Caucus nominated Nancy Pelosi (D-CA) for reelection as Speaker, and the chair of the House Republican Conference (caucus) nominated John Boehner (R-OH) for the position. Then without discussion, every Democrat voting supported Pelosi and every Republican vote went to Boehner.

The partisan organization of Congress that begins with the leadership and seating arrangement extends down through both chambers. Membership on the committees of Congress is apportioned to the parties based on their relative strength in each chamber. The majority party always holds a majority of the seats, and the chairperson of each committee and subcommittee is appointed by the majority party. Furthermore, the parties decide which members of their own party will be on which committees.

The parties in Congress also work to advance their fortunes and to bedevil the other party. As noted, each party has a campaign committee in each house that allocates funds in an effort to maintain or improve the party's strength in Congress.[45] Party leaders will also often support a bill or an appropriation that will help the reelection campaigns of party members.

Parties and the Organization of the Executive and Judicial Branches

Although the executive branch does not have the overtly partisan arrangements common in Congress, party does play a role. The president and vice president are both chosen by a partisan process, and the White House Office and some other parts of the Executive Office of the President are thinly disguised partisan operations dedicated to advancing the political futures of the president and his party. The overwhelming percentage of Cabinet secretaries and other principal executive branch officials that the president appoints are members of his party. Partisanship also figures prominently in the appointment of judges.[46] It is a rarity, for instance, for a president to nominate someone who is not of his party for the Supreme Court or U.S. Court of Appeals.

Parties and Policy Making

Parties also help determine policy. We will see first that the two parties in Congress have distinct policy positions that usually differ from one another on important issues. Then we will take up the idea of party responsibility for government by discussing the contrast between having one party control both the legislative and executive branches and having control of those branches divided between the parties. Our third topic in this section will be the role parties play as opponents of the government.

The Connection between Parties and Policy

Political party is the best gauge of how legislators vote on important issues. This shows the strong link between party and policy. For example, a majority of Republicans and a majority of Democrats oppose one another on a large majority of the most important votes in Congress, as detailed in Figure 9.8. This party link also extends to the White House, with most members of the president's party in Congress usually supporting his major policy proposals and most members of the other party usually opposing them. The connection between party and policy is also evident in the policy that emerges from Congress. One study found, for example, that the survival rate of bills and joint resolutions in the House is only about 1% if most of the members of the majority party are opposed.[47]

Parties and the Responsibility for Government

By combining a wide range of lawmakers and other officials and their view and actions into a group, parties increase the chance that the electorate can affix some level of responsibility for what is occurring in government. This possibility persuades some analysts to favor a **responsible party model of government**, such as found in Great Britain and other *parliamentary systems of government*. Parties in this type of system are under the leadership of the prime minister. The parties and their leadership formulate policy, and party members in the government are under heavy pressure to follow the party's lead. The *presidential system of government* in the United States, which separates the election of the president from the members of Congress, precludes such a responsible-party model of government.

Unified and Divided Government

While party government as such is not possible in the U.S. political system, something similar occurs when one party controls both houses of Congress and the White House. This condition is called a **unified government**. Between 2001 and 2007, for example, the Republicans controlled the House, Senate, and White House. **Divided government** is the opposite state of partisan affairs. It occurs when the president's party is not in control of one or both houses of Congress. During the span of U.S. history, the government has been unified more than 60% of the time. However, as is evident in Figure 9.9, divided government has been the

FIGURE 9.8 Degree of Party Agreement and Disagreement in Congress

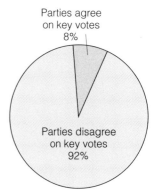

Parties agree on key votes 8%

Parties disagree on key votes 92%

Congressional votes, 2009

During the first session (2009) of the 111th Congress (2009–2010) a majority of Republicans and a majority of Democrats voted on the opposite sides on almost all of the key votes on the most important issues in the House and Senate.
Data source: CQ *Weekly Report* on key votes for 2009.

FIGURE 9.9 Divided Government in U.S. History

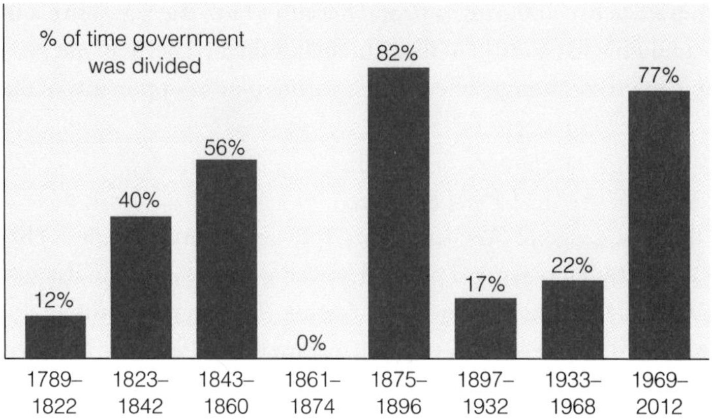

Divided government occurs most often during times of political turbulence or when the strength of a political party is changing markedly.
Data source: Calculations by author.

norm since the late 1960s when the resurgence of the Republican Party marked the advent of the Sixth Party Era.

Unified government was restored with the Democrats in control in 2009, but it lasted just two years. The Republicans took control of the House in 2011, once again dividing the government. Of the new Republicans, many represented the most conservative wing of their party, while most of the Democrats defeated in 2010 were moderate members of their party. This arguably added to the increasing polarization of the parties in government and the electorate, as noted earlier.[48] One typical report depicts the country as "further apart than ever in its political values. . . . Republicans and Democrats have become more intense in their political beliefs."[49]

Polarization adds to the role of parties in government, according to the **theory of conditional party government,** because the parties in government are strongest when there is a high degree of consensus on issues among each party's followers and representatives (*intraparty agreement*) and sharp policy differences between the parties (*interparty disagreement*).[50] Polarization also increases party unity in Congress and mobilizes a party's most ideological supporters to participate in campaigns.[51]

Polarization also has downsides. One is decreasing the possibility of compromise in Congress. Polarization also tends to increase partisan infighting. That along with the policy stalemates that sometime occur when the parties refuse to compromise can also bring retribution from the voters. By 2007, the growing partisanship in Washington left 88% of Americans believing that the "lawmakers in Washington" were putting "partisan politics first," ahead of concern with the public's interests.[52] Moreover, 76% said that "reducing the partisan fighting in government" was a "major" or "important" change that they hoped the next president would achieve.[53] Perhaps the only reason this distress with partisanship did not turn into an important electoral issue is that the public blamed the Bush administration and the Democrats in Congress about equally for partisan excess. The 2008 election and subsequent events in Washington did not change the public's views. A 2010 poll found 82% saying they were "fed up" with partisan conflict.[54] Also as in 2008, however, the political repercussions of that sentiment for the 2010 election appeared to be more an anti-incumbent mood than a negative for either party. The reason is that 67% of Americans were blaming both parties equally for the "gridlock in Washington."[55]

In addition to concerns about polarization, there is considerable controversy over whether divided government is worrisome; that topic is addressed in Chapter 12. We can note here, though, that some argue that the major drawbacks of divided government are that it can lead to stalemate and also can make it harder for voters to determine which leaders and which party should be rewarded for policy successes and which should blamed for failures. The strongest argument for divided government is that it provides a balance between the two parties, strengthening checks and balances. There is also the view that divided government is neither good nor bad because "Congress and the presidency are remarkably able to adapt to changing policymaking contexts and shifts in the balance of influence and power between the branches."[56] As for the public, it is close to evenly divided with 41% in favor of having a divided government, 48% wanting a unified government, and 11% unsure.[57]

Parties and the Organized Opposition

A party is not only important when it governs. When the party is out of power, it also performs a valuable role by creating a center of opposition to the government. The party that controls the House or Senate has to deal with the alternative ideas and criticism of the minority party. Similarly, the president is continuously scrutinized by the other party's members in Congress. Many, even most, of the policy disasters and abuses of power that have been uncovered in the past have been aired and addressed in part based on the criticisms of the party out of power. The Bush administration had a relatively easy time while the Republicans controlled both houses of Congress, but that changed once the Democrats took power in 2007. Soon there were legislative investigations of numerous topics such as the torture of suspected terrorists and other alleged abuses by the White House. When the Republicans took control of the House in 2011, their scrutiny of the Obama administration increased. There is also a downside to party opposition. This occurs when the "out" party goes from playing the legitimate role of watch-dog and policy critic to taking positions based all or mostly on electoral advantage or engaging in partisan witch hunts to embarrass members of the other party.

Evaluating Parties

We should take some time near the end of our exploration of political parties to reflect on them and their role in the political process. One set of questions relates to whether parties play a positive or negative role. George Washington and many other early American leaders warned against parties as divisive elements. Neverthe-less, politicians in the new government soon established two opposing parties, and the two-party system that still exists today was born. Americans remain divided in their thoughts about parties. Many think the party system that exists could be improved, and it is not uncommon to find a majority of Americans favoring the creation of a third national party. Yet most Americans also say that the parties pro-vide distinct alternatives and think that the two-party system is reasonably sound. Moreover, when third parties do appear, none of them has survived, except the Republicans who emerged more than 150 years ago. Whether parties remain an important part of the political system is the second major debate.[58] Some contend that the parties have lost much of their relevance to how voters identify politically and vote. There can be little doubt that parties are not as strong as they once were because of a broad range of developments and public attitudes that this chapter has detailed. Nevertheless, the conviction here is that although weakened, the par-ties remain important elements in the American political process.

What the strengths of the Republican Party and Democratic Party will be and if we are transitioning from the Sixth Party Era to the Seventh remains speculative. The period of unified party government with George Bush in the White House, and Republican majorities in both houses of Congress between 2001 and 2007 led some commentators to predict a dominant Republican majority into the fore-seeable future. The roaring comeback of the Democrats in the 2006 and 2008 elections put that theory to rest, and engendered a counter theory. This one holds that a new Democratic-dominant era is dawning, prompted more than anything by the increased number of minorities, particularly Latinos but also Asian Ameri-cans, among voters. How they structure their party identification and voting will profoundly affect the power and success of the Democrats and Republicans for decades to come.[59] "We have just about maxed out with white men," a key Republican strategist notes. "When you look into the future, all you see is smaller numbers [of them] and more and more Hispanics. Look at Texas. Unless we do something," the strategist worries, "in a decade or so it's going to go the way of California," a once usually Republican and now usually Democratic state.[60] Perhaps, but it may also be that the change in party fortunes one way in 2006 and 2008, then the other way in 2010, showed instead that there is something of a built-in contrariness in American politics that tends to level or reverse the partisan playing field.

SUMMARY

Political parties and partisanship are key elements in the democratic process. Parties exist in all democracies, but they vary from country to country in terms of the basis of their membership, how ideological they are, and how many important other parties they contend with. There is a strong two-party system in the United States for several reasons. These include the use of single-member districts, allowing a plurality of votes to determine an election, having a fixed-term presidency, the existence of many laws favoring the major parties, inertia based on traditional two-party dominance, and the generally non-ideological orientation of Americans. Third parties have been important in a few national elections, but minor parties mostly signal voter dissatisfaction with the major parties and pressure them to change their policy stands.

American parties are decentralized organizations. This reflects the decentralized national-state-local structure of the federal system. As such, the two parties' national committees have only limited authority over state and local parties and even less over the wide range of other autonomous party organizations that further fragment the parties' organizational structure.

One key party role is in the electorate. There parties work to gather a core of supporters and also to win a majority of the voters during elections. The interplay between the parties and the electorate can be roughly divided into several eras, each marked by a particular alignment of various groups in the electorate. Arguably these configurations realign every 35 years or so. Realignments occur because changing issues cause shifts in the degree to which various groups in the electorate support each party. Realignments are also signaled by increased third-party activity. Most importantly, the realignment brings about major and long-term changes in a party's strength in Congress and its chances of electing its presidential candidates.

Scholars generally agree that the Fifth Party Era began in the early 1930s and ended in the 1960s. They disagree over whether what then occurred was a realignment or a dealignment, with most voters no longer closely tied to party identifications. The view here is that realignment did begin in the late 1960s and evolved unsteadily into a Sixth Party Era marked by increased Republican strength. However the realignment was less than classic because the disgrace and resignation of Richard Nixon caused a temporary major setback for the GOP and because sharply increased political alienation among Americans decreased party loyalties. It may be that the Republican disasters in the 2006 and 2008 elections marked the onset of a Seventh Party Era, but that remains unclear.

Parties also play a vital role in elections. They recruit and nominate candidates. Conventions have largely been replaced by several types of primaries and caucuses to nominate party candidates. Both the greater use of caucuses and primaries and which type of primary is used are controversial. Another controversial issue is whether governments should regulate the nomination process or leave it to party regulation. During elections, parties engage in such activities as promoting the party's image and providing get-out-the-vote efforts and other election services, but they give little money to candidates directly.

Parties serve as an important cue for voter choice. Voters with limited information about candidates will often vote according to party. This is not the best idea, but neither is it very irrational. The reason is that there is a degree of ideological difference between and cohesion within the parties. Most voters recognized this and correctly align their political views with the views of the parties. Parties are also connected to policy making. In Congress, members of each party usually vote like one another, and differently from members of the other parties on controversial issues. Also, members of the president's party in Congress usually support him and his policy proposals, and members of the other party are usually opposed. Parties also help provide the watchdog function in government and a measure of accountability to help voters assign praise or blame for what occurs. There is controversy over whether divided government is negative or not.

CHAPTER 9 GLOSSARY

closed primary An election to choose a party nominee in which only eligible voters registered as a party member can vote.

critical election A national, usually presidential, election marked by a significant shift in political power based on a realignment of coalitions supporting each party.

dealignment When a large part of the electorate abandons its party loyalties or has them so weakened that most of the electorate cannot be said to be aligned with any party.

divided government When the White House is in the hands of one party and one or both houses of Congress are controlled by the other party.

dominant party system In this type of system, multiple parties exist in a democracy, but one of the parties has far more electoral support than any other party or even all the others combined.

heuristic devices Mental shortcuts people use to form opinions and make decisions when all the information ideally desirable is not known.

legislative caucus An organization of the members of a political party in one or both chambers of a legislative body.

multiparty system Countries or other political systems in which three or more political parties regularly play an important role in the political process.

national committee The national organizational unit of the two major parties.

New Deal coalition The block of voters that supported the Democratic Party from the early 1930s to the late 1960s because of its economic stands.

one-party system Countries or other political systems in which only one political party regularly plays an important role in the political process.

open primary An election to choose a party nominee in which eligible voters can vote in the primary of any party regardless of party registration.

partisan As a noun, an individual who identifies with a political party and whose voting and policy preferences are determined by that association. As an adjective, making decision based on what is good for the party of one's choice.

partisan political system One based in part on the contest between political parties.

party alignment The strength of each significant party, the policies each supports, and the level and pattern of support of each in the country.

party convention A gathering of delegates from the territorial subunits of an electoral district to nominate a party candidate and sometimes to conduct other party business.

party machine A party organization, usually at the local level, that dominates politics in its area by using political favors and other corrupt practices to ensure its control.

party realignment A reconfiguration of the coalitions of voters and other political actors who support each party. May include the demise of one of the old parties and the rise of a replacement party, a switch in which party is dominant, or a sharp increase in the dominance of an already dominant party.

plurality election system Determining the winner by which candidate receives the most votes, even if it is less than a majority of all votes cast.

polarization A trend that includes a party's members in Congress or other legislative body coming more and more from the ideological purist wing of the party and less and less from the ideologically moderate wing. Polarization can also include the electorate dividing increasingly into two widely split ideological camps.

political party In a democracy, an organization of politically like-minded people that presents candidates for election under its name in an effort to gain influence in government and promote its preferred policies.

primaries Elections in which voters choose party nominees to run for office.

proportional representation A method of conducting elections in multiseat legislative districts that distributes the seats among parties based on their respective voting strength rather than individual contests among candidates.

responsible party model of government A political system in which the majority party in parliament decides and can be held accountable for policy.

seven-point party identification scale A range of self-classifications including strong Republican, weak Republican, independent Republican (Republican leaner), independent, independent Democrat (Democratic leaner), weak Democrat, or strong Democrat.

single-member district An approach to elections that assigns legislative seats to geographical units and has a separate election for each legislative seat.

split-ticket voting (ticket splitting) Voting for one or more candidates of one party for one or more offices and one or more candidates of another party for other offices. The opposite of straight-ticket voting.

straight-ticket voting Voting only for candidates from one party in a given election. The opposite of split-ticket voting.

theory of conditional party government The idea that political parties in government are strongest when they are the most distinct in their policy views.

third party A minor party that has a national or at least important regional following but has little or no chance of winning a presidential election or a significant number of seats in Congress.

two-party system Countries or other political systems in which only two political parties regularly play an important role in the political process.

unified government When one party controls both houses of Congress and the White House.

winner-take-all contest One in which the winner gets all the prizes and the losers, no matter how many, get nothing.

ELECTIONS

10

YOU DECIDE: Make Voting Mandatory?

Two of the things that you will find out in this chapter are that Americans are less likely to vote than the citizens of most other democracies and that voting is not equal across societal groups. Both these facts raise concerns about democracy in America. One solution is to make voting a legal requirement.[1] Australia, Peru, Turkey, and about two dozen other countries do so. Those who do not vote without a valid reason can be fined or even lose their right to vote. Enforcement ranges from strict in some countries such as Singapore to lax in many others.[2]

Proponents of mandatory voting argue it makes democracy more equal. For example, Latinos, Asian Americans, and young adults vote much less often than the general populace, and mandatory voting would increase the presence of these groups in the electoral equation. Another claimed advantage of required voting is that it creates a habit of participation that, in turn, leads to greater interest in politics and to other forms of participation. Opponents of mandatory voting argue that it amounts to government intruding on people's lives by making a privilege into an obligation. More pragmatically, opponents argue that nonvoters are those who are least interested in and informed about politics. Therefore, forcing them to vote would create something akin to random voting with little or no thought behind it.

What would you decide about making voting mandatory for presidential and congressional elections? If you would do so, what penalties would you set for noncompliance? Revisit this debate when you finish the chapter and see if your thoughts have changed.

INTRODUCING ELECTIONS

This chapter considers the conduct of federal elections, who the voters are, and how they decide. To begin our introduction, this section takes up the organization of the U.S. system of elections. Then we will turn to U.S. elections in the global context and to interplay between American diversity and elections.

Following that, the chapter is organized by the five elements of the electoral process. First is the *nomination phase* during which political parties select candidates for various offices. Second is the *electoral campaign*, the effort of the nominated candidates to win office in the general election. Operating concurrently with the first two steps is a third element, *raising campaign money*. The fourth part focuses on *who the voters are and how they decide* to cast their ballots. Fifth and last is the usually, but not always, routine process of *determining the winner*. This includes the Electoral College.

Because elections are intertwined so thoroughly with the U.S. political process, several other chapters contain extensive relevant material. Chapter 9 on political parties covers such topics as the U.S. electoral system compared to those in other countries, the role of parties in campaigns, and the interplay between peoples' party identification and their voting decisions. Chapter 12 on the presidency compares having a separately elected head of government (a president) versus one chosen by the majority in the national legislature (a prime minister). Who is allowed to vote is a key topic in the discussion of civil rights in Chapter 5.

Another note about this chapter's organization begins with the fact that there are similarities in the election process for every office from town council to president of the United States. It is also true, though, that presidential elections have unique aspects. Therefore, each of our five major sections will begin with a general discussion that, given this text's emphasis on the national government, emphasizes congressional elections. Then each section will take up the election of the president. During our exploration, you also will see that:

★ The U.S. electoral system mirrors the federal system of government.
★ All democracies have elections, but there are many different approaches to elections.
★ Women and minorities have done better in the electoral system in recent decades, but still face many obstacles to full equality.
★ Primaries and caucuses rather than party conventions now usually select nominees.
★ Professionals manage most campaigns and rely on paid advertising to get their message out.
★ Campaigns are very costly and rely on large donations from individuals and organizations.
★ Laws trying to limit the flow of big money into campaigns have had only limited success.

★ Americans turn out to vote at lower levels than do citizens in most other democracies.

★ Voting turnout is not equal among various societal groups.

★ Different turnout levels among groups can affect who gets elected.

★ Political party is the most important factor in deciding whom individual voters will support.

★ For Congress, incumbency is a close second to party in determining election outcomes.

★ Candidate characteristics, issues, and the voters' sense of the times also influence voting.

★ The quirky Electoral College will probably remain the process for selecting the president.

Organization of the Electoral System

The U.S. system of elections is fragmented along two dimensions. The *federal/state* divide under the federal system is one. The original Constitution allowed the national government to set the date and some basic procedures for federal elections but left voting qualifications and most other details up to the states. The states still play key roles in the election system, but the federal government has become much more involved. Constitutional amendments have removed racial barriers to voting, given women and 18-year-olds the right to vote, and banned poll taxes. Numerous federal laws have been enacted to ensure these rights, to regulate campaign contributions, and to otherwise regulate elections. The courts have further injected the federal government into the elections system by such decisions as requiring electoral districts to have equal populations.

The *government/political parties divide* is the second dimension of fragmentation. Parties are private organizations, and they are particularly important in determining how candidates are nominated. At first, there was no government supervision of how candidates were selected, but over time, various levels of government have sought greater control. Some states have tried to supersede party rules about when presidential primaries and caucuses can be held. There have also been numerous efforts by states to require parties to open their primaries to independents or even members of other parties. The federal government has also become involved in the nomination process. Among other things, Washington now regulates campaign finance involving nominations as well as the election.

The point of noting these divides is to stress that the U.S. election system is not based on some enlightened process laid down by the Constitution's authors. Instead, it is something of a jury-rigged system in which the national government and the national parties and the governments and the parties of 50 states and the District of Columbia all have some authority.

Elections in a World of Difference

Democratic elections extend at least as far back as 508 B.C. in ancient Athens. Elections and other aspects of the democratic process have been evolving since then, and American practices today are both a product of this global evolution and a contributor to it. Today there is considerable diversity in how elections are conducted around the world, and exploring the options provides insights into the strengths and weaknesses of the U.S. system. As noted above, some of the options such as having a proportional election system are taken up in other chapters.

We will take up additional electoral options found around the world in this chapter. Expanding the **franchise**, the right to vote, is one. All religious barriers to voting were eliminated by 1810, and property requirements were eliminated in most states by the 1820s and were gone everywhere by 1850. The end of these two barriers created nearly universal suffrage for white males.

 Of the 19.5 million U.S. resident adults who cannot vote because they are not yet citizens, about 70% are Latinos or Asian Americans.

As Chapter 5 notes, Americans have been much slower to extend the franchise to other groups including minorities, women, young adults, and others. Currently, the franchise in the United States is fairly inclusive, but it is not as broad as it is in other countries. Some of them, for instance, allow noncitizens to vote.[3] Other countries have set the minimum voting age at 17 or even 16. We will also examine voter turnout in the United States from a global perspective. As the opening box points out, Americans vote less often than do people in most democracies. Yet another global perspective relates to the fact that women in the United States and a growing number of other countries have gone from voting less often than men to more often. Moreover, women around the world, just like those in the United States, are increasingly liberal in their political views and electoral choices. This change could have a significant impact on the ideological orientation of governments worldwide.[4]

The increased participation of women in elections is not only an American phenomenon but also a global one. This 2009 photo from Lebanon, a largely Muslim country, shows two French-language campaign posters by the Free Patriotic Movement Christian Party; the larger one reads "I vote," and the smaller one reads "Be Equal and Vote." (AP Photo/ Hussein Malla)

Elections and American Diversity

We noted earlier that several other chapters contain extensive material related to elections, including the diversity of voters and candidates. To summarize the material discussed in Chapters 1, 5, 6, and 9:

- All minority groups have grown and are projected to continue to add to their share of the electorate (voting-age citizens). Latinos, for one, were 5% of the electorate in 1996 and 9% in 2008.

- The turnout of women and minorities who are voting-age citizens has increased.
- The increased presence of minorities and women in the electorate has helped increase the share of women and minority office holders.
- Data on gay voting and office holding is sketchy, but there appear to be more gay office holders, at least among those who publicly acknowledge their sexual orientation.

Additionally, we have seen or will see in this chapter that:

- Women are increasingly liberal in their politics and more often vote Democratic.
- African Americans and gays overwhelmingly vote for Democrats, and Asian Americans and Hispanics mostly do.
- The Republicans are increasingly a "white" party, and the Democrats a "rainbow" party with significant minority participation.
- Despite advances in participation and white tolerance, few minority members of Congress represent districts in which whites are in a majority.
- Despite advances, women and minority members face a range of electoral disadvantages such as having more limited access to money than whites and males.

THE NOMINATION CAMPAIGN

Candidate selection is a two-step process. The first is the emergence of individuals who are interested in running for election. The second step is determining which of the hopefuls will be on the ballot in the general election.

Overview of the Candidate Selection Process

If you have already read Chapter 9, you will notice some overlap between the material there on the nominating process and the commentary here on that topic. This is consciously done because understanding how parties select candidates is a core topic for both parties and elections. A number of points made in Chapter 9 need only brief reiteration here.

- Most candidates for Congress are self-promoters who are seeking office on their own initiative.[5]
- Political parties and the party caucuses in each house of Congress also help recruit candidates.
- The White House is yet another participant in recruiting candidates for federal elections.
- Interest groups are an additional element in the recruiting process. They sometimes try to persuade like-minded individuals to run for office. For one,

Emily's List describes itself as a pro-choice, pro-Democratic group "committed to recruiting and funding . . . women candidates."

- Especially if there is no incumbent seeking reelection, it is common for several people to seek the nomination for an office.

When a political party does have more than one person seeking the nomination for an office, there are several ways of deciding who the nominee will be. **Party conventions** are one way. They are meetings of delegates from voting districts to choose their party's candidate for the general election and to conduct other party business such as setting its rules. Conventions are still used to pick the presidential nominees at the national level and in some states to choose statewide and local candidates.

Primaries are the second and most common way of deciding nominations. A primary is an election in which voters choose party nominees or choose delegates to a convention that, in turn, selects the nominees. Most primaries decide who the nominee will be. Others, called *indirect primaries,* select delegates pledged to one candidate or another to go a convention that ultimately nominates the candidate. **Closed primaries** are the most common type. They restrict voting to those who are registered with the party that is choosing its nominee. Other states use **open primaries**. These allow independents and in some states even those registered with another party to vote.

There is controversy over the types of primaries. Advocates of open primaries argue that they promote participation. These advocates also point to the fact that there are many electoral districts where one party's candidate almost always wins. Therefore, it can be argued, everyone in such districts should be able to vote in the primary because it is the "real election." Critics of open primaries make many counter arguments. One is that allowing independents and sometimes even members of other parties to help choose another party's nominee will result in blurring the ideological/policy distinctions between the two parties and their candidates.

Embedded in this issue is the question of whether selecting nominees is a party event and therefore the exclusive business of parties or a part of the broader electoral process and therefore open to government regulation. The Supreme Court has occasionally treated primaries as part of the electoral process. For example, it ruled in 1944 that parties cannot use race to exclude people from voting in their primaries.[6] More often the Supreme Court has treated nominations as a party affair. The Court has decided, for instance, that states cannot force parties to accept so-called blanket primaries in which everyone can vote in more than one party's primary.[7] Similarly, state law may not bar a party from opening up its primary to voting by nonparty members.[8]

Caucuses are yet another way for voters to influence candidate selection. This method is less common than primaries but more common than conventions. The caucus process brings people together locally in a face-to-face forum to discuss and ultimately to select delegates pledged to one candidate or another. These local delegates later assemble at a district or state convention to choose nominees or, in the case of the presidential election, to choose yet other delegates to the national conventions. Like primaries, most caucuses are closed, but some are open.

Voter turnout in primaries and at caucuses for offices other than president is almost always quite low. Indeed, a record low was set in 2006 when only 17% of those eligible turned out in the states that had primaries for statewide offices (governor or U.S. senator).[9] Turnout was only slightly better in 2010 at 19%. One reason for the low turnout is that many primaries, such as those against an incumbent, are one-sided, and there is little incentive to vote. However, most eligible voters ignore even hotly contested primaries, with only the rare primary topping a 40% turnout.

Among the impacts of low primary turnout is that Democratic hopefuls tend to take markedly liberal positions and Republican hopefuls tend to take markedly conservative positions during primaries. The reason is that those who do vote in primaries or attend caucuses tend to be the parties' most committed and ideological members. Some analysts cite this as a factor in what they say is the increasingly polar ideological positions of the two parties.

Selecting Presidential Candidates

There is never a shortage of politicians with presidential ambitions. In the 2008 election campaign, a small herd of 10 Democrats and 11 Republicans launched bids for their respective party's presidential nomination.

If one party has an incumbent president running, serious challenges for the nomination are rare. Moreover, the most recent challenges to incumbent presidential candidates (1976, 1988, 1992) all failed. Indeed, no party has denied a sitting president renomination since Chester A. Arthur in 1884. Two partial exceptions occurred when the prospects of a difficult and possibly unsuccessful effort to get renominated helped persuade Harry S. Truman in 1952 and Lyndon B. Johnson in 1968 to announce that they would not seek reelection.[10] To further explore how the parties choose their presidential candidates, the following sections will examine selecting delegates for the national convention and the national convention itself.

Selecting Delegates to the National Conventions

CNN had it right when it observed, "If you think federal income tax forms are complex, try understanding the presidential delegate selection process."[11] What makes the process complex is that for each party, its various national, state, and other electoral units (the District of Columbia and the five U.S. territories) all have some authority over how their delegates are selected. As a result, the process is fragmented and varies significantly between and within parties from state to state.

Each national party adopts a formula to determine how many votes, and therefore, delegates, each state will have at the national convention. For both parties, each state gets a number of votes equal to its House and Senate seats. Each party then adds more seats for party leaders and elected officials (PLEOs). These are commonly referred to as **superdelegates** in the media. Finally each state gets yet more delegates if the party's candidate for president carried the state in the most recent election.

Delegates fall into two groups with regard to how they decide whom to support for the nomination. *Pledged delegates* are the larger group. These delegates are pledged to support one or another of the party's presidential hopefuls as a result of each state's primary, caucus process, or convention results. *Unpledged delegates* are free to choose among the contenders for the nomination. Superdelegates or PLEOs make up most of this second group. At the 2008 conventions, 81% of the Democrats' delegates and 76% of the Republican delegates were pledged. Most states use primaries to allocate pledged delegates among the candidates for nomination. Caucuses followed by a convention decide in almost 30% of the states, and a few states use conventions alone. The Democrats allocate pledged delegates proportionally—according to each candidate's respective shares of the vote in the primary or caucus. The Republicans favor a winner-take-all system, with the candidate who has the most votes winning all the state's pledged delegates.

Scheduling Primaries and Caucuses

Primaries and caucuses have become increasingly important in the presidential nomination for two reasons. First their number has increased. Less than half the states had them as recently as 1972. Now almost every state does. Second, the share of delegates who are pledged delegates has also grown. Therefore, winning them is critical to getting the presidential nomination.

Iowa's caucus and New Hampshire's primary have traditionally led off the schedule, bringing considerable candidate and media attention to the two states and infusing millions of dollars into their economies. Being first also arguably gives the two states a greater impact on the nomination process than warranted given their relatively small and disproportionately rural and white populations. Whatever may be fair, the early contests in these and other states are important because they affect the candidates' efforts to raise money, get media attention, and gain other advantages. Prior to the Iowa caucus on January 3, 2008, Hillary Clinton was widely said by the press to be ahead for the Democratic nomination. But when she finished third and Barack Obama finished first, the momentum began to turn.

One of several scheduling issues related to presidential primaries and caucuses is that the "first in the nation" Iowa caucuses and New Hampshire primary give the small and atypical populations of those two states a disproportionate influence on the presidential contest. (© 2007 Mike Keefe, *The Denver Post, and PoliticalCartoons.com.*)

Nationally, support for Obama among Democrats rose from 27% to 33%. Clinton's support dropped from 45% to 33%.[12] Increased fund-raising was another advantage for Obama. During the last quarter of 2007 Clinton had raised $27 million compared to Obama's $20 million. In January after winning in Iowa, Obama brought in $32 million, and Clinton managed just $14 million.

Reacting to the advantages enjoyed by Iowa and New Hampshire by going early, many other states began **front loading**: moving their primaries and caucuses earlier and earlier to gain influence in the nomination process. In turn, Iowa and New Hampshire moved theirs earlier yet. In 1968, the New Hampshire primary was on March 12. By that date in 2004, John Kerry already had the Democratic nomination sewn up after winning most of the primaries and caucuses in 23 states. All the remaining primaries and caucuses were, in effect, meaningless.

The outcome in 2004 set off a stampede of states trying to gain influence or at least avoid irrelevance by moving their primaries and caucuses even earlier still. In January 2008, the Democrats had caucuses or primaries in 6 states and held them in another 24 states and territories on February 5, "super Tuesday." By that point 60% of the pledged delegates had been chosen.

Several reform plans have been offered to address this scheduling melee among the states. The proposals are presented to you in You Decide: Reform the Presidential Primaries?

YOU DECIDE: Reform the Presidential Primaries?

Respected political columnist David Broder calls the presidential nomination process "True insanity." "None of this helps the country get the best qualified candidates, and none of it helps either party put forward its best candidate," he argues.[13] Those who agree have proposed several plans to modify the process. Each would require Congress to enact a national plan.

A *national primary day* has been talked about since President Woodrow Wilson proposed it in 1913. An advantage is that it might generate increased interest and higher voter turnout in the primaries. A national primary day could also be scheduled later in the year to help shorten the presidential selection process. A disadvantage is that a single primary day would probably favor well-known candidates who could raise substantial funds early.

Regional primaries are a second possibility. A plan proposed by the National Association of Secretaries of State would put states and other jurisdictions into four regional groups. Each would hold its primary during one of the four months between March and June. The order in which the groups hold their primaries could either rotate or be decided by lottery. A plus is that regional primaries would spread out the schedule. Campaigning in regions one at a time would also be less expensive because of reduced travel, media, and other costs and thus might decrease the importance of money in the nomination process. A negative is that the plan might favor or disadvantage candidates depending on which region they were from and when it came in that year's order.

The *Delaware Plan* is a third option. Proposed in 2000 by Delaware's Republican state chairman, the plan would divide the states and other jurisdictions according to their populations into four groups. The group made up of states with the smallest populations would go first in the primary season, and so on, with the group composed of states with the largest populations going last. This would help smaller jurisdictions have a say, but also preserve a major impact for larger states even though they went last. Some of the influence of money might also be eased because it would be less expensive to begin with the smaller states. Grouping states by population rather than region would also avoid the "luck of the draw" impact of being a candidate favored (or disfavored) by the first region to vote. However, like all the proposals, the Delaware Plan would take away freedom of choice from the states and their parties.

What do you think? Would you leave the process the way it is or reform it? If you are a reformer, would you support one of the three plans presented here or do you have an alternative?

Concerns about Presidential Primaries and Caucuses

The increased importance of primaries and caucuses and the front loading that has occurred have created a de facto **permanent campaign for the presidency**. This means that the planning and maneuvering for the next presidential election must begin almost as soon as the last one ends because of the difficulty of building a campaign organization and raising the funds to conduct two national campaigns: one for the nomination, one for the general election. Among the many concerns about this process are its escalation of the importance of money and its sheer length.

Perhaps the most important concern is that the expense of campaigning for delegates across the country increases the role that money plays in elections. Opening up the nomination process to citizen input by adding primaries and caucuses advanced democracy, but doing so also added a de facto second national campaign. That increased the need for funding, which is arguably not good for democracy because it increases the reliance of elected officials on the interest groups and other large donors of campaign funds. During 2008 alone, the 20 candidates still seeking the Democratic or Republican nominations spent about $900 million on that effort.

A second issue with the nomination process is that it has added to the sheer length of the campaign, thereby taxing the interest of Americans in it. There is currently almost two years of intensive campaigning, preceded by another two years or so of positioning by potential candidates. Press speculation also picks up early in the cycle. For example, in mid-October 2008, three weeks before the general election, a *Newsweek* poll was already asking Americans which Republican they wanted to see run in the 2012 election. Gallup was asking the same question by the day after the election, and CNN began in the following month. Some observers worry that Americans become bored with such a long campaign, suppressing eventual voter turnout.

National Party Conventions

Technically, the Republican and Democratic national conventions nominate the parties' presidential and vice presidential candidates and, thus, are the most important part of the candidate selection process. There was a time when this was true, but reality has changed. Now conventions merely anoint the victor of the earlier primary/caucus process. Indeed, 1976 was the last time that a convention actually decided the nomination. That year neither President Gerald Ford nor challenger Ronald Reagan arrived at the convention with a majority of delegates, and it was only after convention politicking that Ford won by 1187 to 1070 votes.

Still, the national conventions continue to have important functions such as gathering the party elite, energizing the party faithful, and symbolizing the existence of the party. To a degree, the demographic distribution of the convention delegates also symbolizes each party's support in society. As Figure 10.1 on the next page shows, whites and males strongly dominated among Republican delegates in 2008, mirroring the party voter base. Similarly, the strongly diverse presence of women and minorities among the Democratic delegates reflected that party's wider demographic base.

The conventions are also often the setting for the presidential nominee to announce his choice for a vice presidential running mate, a selection that the convention dutifully ratifies. Additionally, conventions kick off the general presidential campaign, with both the presidential and vice-presidential nominees giving their first official campaign speeches when accepting the nomination. Speeches at the

FIGURE 10.1 National Convention Delegates

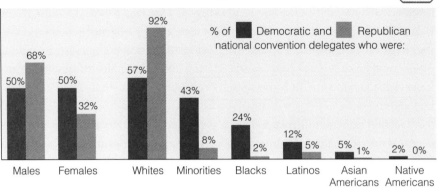

The delegates to the 2008 Republican national convention were overwhelmingly white and mostly male. The delegates to the Democratic national convention were evenly divided among men and women and had a much more diverse representation of minority members.

Data sources: For Democrats, Democratic National Committee. For the Republicans, *New York Times,* September 4, 2008, and *Washington Post,* September 8, 2008.

convention can also help budding political careers. Most recently, little-known then-U.S. Senate candidate Barack Obama won national accolades when he delivered a powerful and nationally televised speech at the 2004 Democratic National Convention.

THE CAMPAIGN FOR OFFICE

Because of the dominance of the two-party system in the United States, most campaigns for office are essentially two-candidate affairs pitting a Democrat against a Republican. As of 2010, every member of the U.S. House of Representatives, 98% of the U.S. senators, 100% of the state governors, and 99.5% of the state legislators were either a Republican or a Democrat. Even if they do not win, minor party candidates occasionally get enough votes to affect which major party candidate wins, but even that is a relative rarity.

Overview of Campaigns

Virtually all candidates create campaign organizations to help them get their message out to the voters, to raise funds, and to otherwise conduct the campaign. In this section and the following one on the overview of presidential campaigns, we will look at that process.

Organizing Campaigns

Modern campaign organization has been evolving since the expansion of the franchise and the advent of mass political parties in the early 1800s. Most campaigns were once fairly basic undertakings largely handled by the candidates assisted by friends and other volunteers. Over time, though, campaigns have gradually grown to sophisticated and extensive operations increasingly staffed by professionals. Indeed, having a talented campaign staff is a key to winning a competitive election. These campaign professionals include general managers, political strategists, and specialists in areas such as fund-raising, advertising, media relations, and polling. Overall, about 40% of the average congressional campaign's expenses go to staff salaries and other administrative costs, and most of the rest of the money that campaigns spend is channeled through professional consultants and their firms.[14]

Getting the Message Out

Candidates face a daunting task in getting the voters' attention and transmitting issue and image messages to them. *Public event appearances* such as having candidates speak at rallies and appear in parades are a traditional method. *Individual contact* is another method. Once this involved approaches such as candidates going door-to-door or shaking hands at factory gates. Now, except for local campaigns, individual contact is more apt to involve sophisticated techniques that gather personal data on voters to create individualized mail, phone, or e-mail messages. Even during non-presidential election years, over half the people report having had some direct contact from a political party or a candidate.[15]

Getting news coverage is another method. Television is the most important news outlet, with 68% of people using it as a main source of campaign news. Next comes the Internet (36%) and newspapers (33%), followed by radio (16%).[16] The national press gives little or no coverage to most congressional campaigns, and even local press coverage is quite limited. During the campaign season of 2004, for example, only 8% of the daily local evening television news programs across the country included a story about a local race for Congress or any other office.[17] Making it even harder for candidates to get their campaign messages out to the voters, the media focus more on the horse-race elements of the campaign—who is winning and losing—than on the issues or the candidates' qualifications.[18]

For these reasons, *commercial advertising* is usually the most effective method for candidates. This is evident when TV ads are compared to TV news coverage (see Figure 10.2). Internet campaign sites and the use of blogs and other social networking media also play a role. It is

FIGURE 10.2 Television News and Political Ads

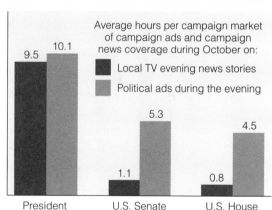

This figure shows the average time in 11 campaign markets devoted to two different kinds of election "coverage"—news stories and paid political advertising—on local evening television news programs during October 2004 for the three main contests of the year.

Data source: Martin Kaplan, Ken Goldstein, and Matthew Hale, "Local News Coverage of the 2004 Campaigns: An Analysis of Nightly Broadcasts In 11 Markets," Lear Center Local News Archive, USC Annenberg School for Communication, February 15, 2005.

not yet clear, though, whether these new capabilities do much to expand the average candidate's support or are more useful to communicate with and reinforce the commitment of those who already support the candidate.

The Presidential Campaign

Presidential campaigns are the most visible of all elections. Most adults know who the Democratic and Republican candidates for president are and follow the contest to some degree.

Organizing Presidential Campaigns

Barack Obama sought to portray his campaign for president as something of a grassroots crusade built on an army of volunteers. There is an element of truth to that, but at its core, the Obama campaign was a professional operation, just like the McCain campaign and other presidential efforts. Obama spent at least $62 million paying staff and political consultants, and about 30% of all his campaign expenses went to such administrative costs and to professional polling.

AMERICAN DIVERSITY The *Boston Herald* reported that the average salaries for the 2008 Obama campaign staff were $54,397 for men and $45,152 for women. Average salaries on the McCain staff were women ($55,878) and men ($53,936).

Getting the Message Out

Presidential campaigns, like others, try to get their message out by mass events, individual contacts, press coverage, and political ads. The presidential debates are also important.

Public Event Appearances Presidential candidates crisscross the country making numerous appearances. During his 2007–2008 quests for the Democratic nomination and the presidency, Barack Obama made 985 campaign appearances.[19] Such stops are important to rally local supporters and to woo local groups ranging from the chamber of commerce to unions. Often more importantly, though, candidate appearances are meant to generate media coverage.

Direct Contacts Presidential campaigns have increasingly moved to using mail/ phone/e-mail operations and to creating persuasive Websites. Additionally, the Obama campaign was the first to emphasize the newest of the electronic channels, interactive, user-generated **social media**. Obama was mentioned three times more often than McCain on blog spots. Obama also had six times more friends on MySpace and Facebook combined than his rival, and his Twitter account had over 118,000 followers, compared to less than 5,000 for McCain. Obama used various techniques to put together 13 million e-mail addresses of possible supporters. Sending them more than 1 billion e-mails helped to raise over $500 million in online contributions and to turn out supporters on election day. "It was a historic marriage, in U.S. politics at least, between digital technology and grassroots [campaigning]," Obama's campaign manager later observed.[20]

Presidential Debates   The premier chance for the presidential candidates to reach out to the voters is the series of nationally televised debates. The first was held in 1960 between John F. Kennedy and Richard M. Nixon, but the next did not occur until 1976. Since then, the debates have been held each election and have become an institutionalized centerpiece of the presidential campaign. Representatives of the two presidential campaigns negotiate the dates, format, and other details of the debates under the auspices of the bipartisan Presidential Debate Commission appointed by the Democratic and Republican national committees. With one exception, the debates have been between just the Democratic and Republican candidates. That exception was in 1992, when H. Ross Perot appeared with Bill Clinton and George H. W. Bush. Critics of excluding third-party candidates say that doing so ensures they will finish poorly. Defenders reply that third-party candidates are destined to lose, so including them with the major-party candidates detracts from the time that voters have to evaluate the "real" candidates.

Certainly the debates draw more public attention than any other part of the presidential campaign. Between 1960 and 2008, an average of 41% of the country's households, or roughly 61% of Americans, have watched at least part of any given debate. Audience size has varied from election to election and from debate to debate depending on several factors, but the most important statistic is that the audience for the debates has declined, as Figure 10.3 indicates. Further reducing the audience, only about half of those who do tune in to any given debate actually watch all of it.[21] The 2004 and 2008 debates saw an uptick in viewership, but whether that is a positive trend or an anomaly remains to be seen.

Of course, the most important question is what difference, if any, the debates make in the final outcome of the election. They do have some impact on increasing the awareness and information of those with relatively little education and/or interest in politics.[22] Similarly, the performance of the

FIGURE 10.3   Audience for Presidential Debates

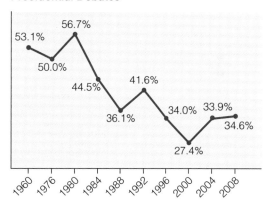

The "Nielsen share" or percent of households owning a television that watched any part of a presidential debate has declined substantially, even though 2004 and 2008 showed an upturn. *Notes and data sources:* No debates were held in 1968 or 1972. Data from the Nielsen Company (1960–2004) and news accounts of Nielsen data (2008).

candidates in the debates themselves and the tone of the media analysis that follows do sway some voters, especially the least well-informed ones.[23] Statistics also show, however, that (1) the debates have little impact on those already committed to a candidate and (2) those who are committed constitute a large majority of the potential voters by the time of the first debate. This limits the possible impact of the debates. In 2008, for instance, the public gave Barack Obama much higher marks than John McCain in each debate. Yet Obama's support among eligible voters increased by only 1% or 2% after each debate. In sum, the debates count, but the impact of any one of them or even all of them combined in most elections is not decisive.

News Coverage   Presidential campaigns get a significant amount of coverage, especially compared to other campaigns, but the impact of that coverage is mitigated by several factors. One is that most Americans are not avid news consumers and on an average day read only a newspaper story or two and watch a few minutes of television coverage of the presidential election. Further reducing the value of these news stories in informing voters is the fact that only about a third of the coverage is about issues, with a majority of stories focusing on who is ahead, campaign strategy, and similar horse-race topics.

Another aspect of media coverage involves the controversy about alleged press bias and its impact. This issue is covered in Chapter 8. It is worth noting, though, that whether the tone of press coverage reflects bias or neutral evaluation, it is common for one candidate to receive more positive coverage than the other. In 2008, the favored presidential candidate by far was Barack Obama. Moreover, among the 100 most widely read U.S. newspapers, 65 endorsed Barack Obama, and 25 endorsed John McCain, with 10 neutral.[24]

Advertising   Methods used for advertising range from billboards to television ads but television, particularly local television, is by far the most important outlet.[25] During the 2008 presidential election, the Obama and McCain campaigns spent over $350 million to air over 200 different commercials more than 300,000 times. Overall, the Obama camps spent far more ($236 million) and produced more television ads (118) than the McCain forces ($126 million spent, 75 ads). The geographic distribution of the ads was far from even. A few hotly contested states such as Florida, Ohio, and Pennsylvania were inundated with ads, while more than half the states—those leaning heavily toward Obama or McCain—had few or no ad placements on their television stations.

The impact of this barrage of advertising is both positive and negative. On the plus side, it tends to stimulate interest in the campaign, to increase familiarity with the candidates and issues, and to increase voting a bit. Moreover, these good effects primarily apply to those with the least political interest and information.[26] There is also evidence that paid ads do their job by influencing the decisions of some voters.[27] On the downside, most ads are one-sided at best and scurrilous misrepresentations of the issues and the other candidate's character at worst. During the 2008 campaign, more than two-thirds of the television ads aired by the Obama and McCain camps were at least partly negative, attacking the record or personal traits of the other candidate. There is frequent commentary that negative campaigning has a variety of bad effects, such as lowering both voter turnout and political trust. However, most research minimizes such impacts. Some even argue that negative campaigning may stimulate voter interest and turnout.[28]

Paid advertising is a crucial part of presidential and many congressional campaigns. Such ads stress emotional appeal over substance, as does this 2008 image of Barack Obama and his daughter Malia during a 30-minute infomercial that was aired during prime time on Oct. 29, 2008, on CBS and NBC television networks at a cost of about $2 million. (AP Photo/Obama Campaign)

RAISING CAMPAIGN MONEY

Almost 80 years ago, comedian Will Rogers quipped, "Politics has got so expensive that it takes a lot of money to get beat." That is true many times over today because of the vastly higher costs of television advertising and other campaign costs. Just one indication of the increased cost of running for office is shown in Figure 10.4. It provides candidate and party campaign expenditures for the House of Representatives from 1974 through 2008. In aggregate, spending by candidates, parties, groups, and individuals on the campaigns for nomination and election for all federal, state, and local offices in 2008 came to about $5.5 billion.

Overview of Campaign Fund-Raising

Being accurate about campaign finance is challenging for several reasons. First, the sums are huge. Second, there is a vast array of organizations and individuals raising money and using it to directly or indirectly influence campaigns. Third, many of these organizations give and get money from one another, and the exact flow cannot be traced. Some of this lack of clarity is intended, part of a cat-and-mouse game to skirt laws that limit contributions and identify donors and amounts.

Our look at campaign finance begins with the direct sources, those that give money to

FIGURE 10.4   Rising Campaign Costs

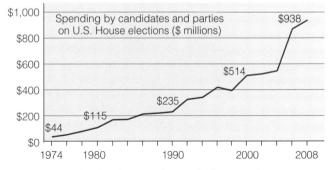

Running for office has become increasingly expensive.
Data sources: Campaign Finance Institute; Center for Responsive Politics.

individual candidates and to political parties. These funds are referred to as **hard money** and are regulated by federal law. Then we will turn to **soft money**. These funds go to and are used by issue advocacy groups that are not regulated by campaign finance law. They are not supposed to try to influence elections in a partisan way, but they often do. Whether the money is hard or soft, most of it comes from "big money" sources associated with interest groups.

Direct Sources of Campaign Money

Candidates and political parties raise hard money from individual contributors, interest groups, congressional power centers, other party organizations, and the candidates themselves.[29]

Individual Contributors The democratic ideal of campaign funding has many individuals giving small amounts to a candidate they support. Reality is much different. Only about 1% of American adults donate money to any campaign or party during an election. Moreover, 79% of the money from individual contributors comes from large contributors donating more than $200 each. Indeed, the 2008 election cycle (2007–2008) saw about 36,000 such contributors give over $10,000 each to candidates and parties, for total contributions of over $900 million.

The law limits how much an individual can annually give to any one candidate ($2,300 in 2008), but there are many ways around these limits. One is to encourage one's family members to contribute. For example, four members of one New Hampshire family gave a combined $425,000 in campaign contributions during the 2008 election. Two family members (sons) were students and a third (grandfather) was retired, yet each gave over $100,000. Representative Virginia Foxx (R-NC) was among the candidates getting a contribution from all four family members, and each of them also donated to at least two PACs and a Republican campaign committee that also funded Foxx's campaign. Perhaps all of these donation decisions were independent, but they at least raise the question about whether they might have all been influenced by the vastly wealthy father. What is clear is that at least 16 donations (4 individual, 8 through the two PACs, 4 through the party committee) flowed to the Foxx campaign in a way that legally complied with the law but certainly violated its spirit.

Interest Group Political Action Committees Through direct donations to candidates and parties, **political action committees (PACs)** of interest groups typically account for 25% to 30% of all congressional campaign funds. However this average disguises the fact that PACs are especially large contributors to the campaigns of Congress's most important members. House Majority Leader Steny Hoyer (D-MD) took in 65% of his campaign funds from PACs. They also supplied 54% of the funding of his Republican counterpart, House Minority Leader John Boehner (R-OH). Indeed, about 90% of PAC campaign contributions go to incumbents. Only 2% goes to their challengers, and 7% goes to candidates in open-seat races. This pattern means that the PACs are seeking to ingratiate themselves with the likely winners, the incumbents. Hoyer, for instance, received more funding from PACs ($2.4 million) than any other member of Congress despite the fact that he was virtually assured of winning reelection to the seat he had held for 27 years and eventually did hold with 74% of the vote while spending $3.4 million compared to his opponents minuscule $28,000. In view of this disparity, it seems clear that what motivated PAC donors was the desire to earn goodwill with Hoyer based on his position as the second highest ranking member of the House. The flow of PAC money to incumbents also means that most PACs give to candidates of both parties. Which party gets the most depends partly on which is in the majority. For 2008, 16 of the 20 biggest spending PACs gave more money to the majority Democrats than to the minority Republicans.

Successful national and statewide campaigns usually cost huge sums. Because money and political influence are closely associated, where campaign funds come from and their impact on elections and later policy making are important and controversial issues. (iStockphoto)

Political Parties   Political parties raise and spend large sums. For the 2008 elections, the Republican National Committee (RNC) took in $428 million and the Democratic National Committee (DNC) raised $260 million. Generally, the two national parties do not give much to individual candidate committees. However, each party donated about $10 million in 2008 to its campaign committees in the Senate and House. The RNC and DNC also gave a combined $113 million to state party committees, and they in turn donated to individual candidates. Additionally, the DNC and RNC help their congressional candidates by sponsoring basic pro-Republican and pro-Democratic ads and by other party-support initiatives.

Congressional Campaign Organizations   Congress has three campaign finance resource centers.

1. *Party campaign committees.* Each party has election organizations in Congress. The two House committees are the National Republican Campaign Committee (NRCC) and the Democratic Congressional Campaign Committee (DCCC). Their Senate counterparts are the National Republican Senatorial Committee (NRSC) and the Democratic Senatorial Campaign Committee (DSCC). They spent a combined $551 million on the 2008 elections, most often through independent efforts on behalf of their party's candidates rather than by giving money directly to individual campaigns.

2. *Leadership PACs.* Many members of Congress run PACs to help their colleagues. There were 376 leadership PACs operating in 2008, and they donated $39 million to congressional candidates. House Majority Leader Steny Hoyer controlled the largest leadership PAC in 2008. It contributed over $1.2 million to about 140 Democratic House candidates.

3. *Candidate committees.* Most incumbents face little chance of defeat and are also able to raise much more money for their campaigns than they really need. Some of the safe incumbents transfer funds from their own campaign fund to those of more embattled current or potential colleagues. During 2008, Representative Hoyer was the top candidate-to-candidate contributor, sending $414,000 to colleagues in addition to his $1.2 million in leadership PAC contributions.

Candidates' Personal Funds   The personal funds of candidates are yet another source of campaign money. In 2008, for example, Colorado Democrat Jared Polis spent $6 million of his own money to win a House seat. But the rich do not always win. Former Ebay president Meg Whitman lost her 2010 bid to become governor of California despite reportedly spending $160 million of her own money. Republican Linda McMahon lost her bid for a Senate seat from Connecticut in 2010 despite spending more than $150 million of her own money. Indeed, only about one-third of the top "self-funding" candidates for Congress in 2010 were victorious.

Indirect Sources of Campaign Money

A second major flow of campaign funding comes from the numerous policy advocacy groups. They are tax-exempt under sections 501, 503, and 527 of the Internal Revenue Service (IRS) code and are referred to here as **tax-exempt advocacy groups (TAGs)**. They are allowed under the law to raise and spend money to advocate policy and in some cases to even support or oppose candidates, but they are not permitted to donate funds to candidates or parties. TAGs spent more than $400 million on federal campaigns during the 2008 election cycle. Much of this money went to partisan electoral activity. Overall, TAGs spent about equal amounts supporting Democrats and Republicans in 2008.[30] In 2010, however, spending by conservative-oriented TAGs was more than twice that of liberal TAGs.

To look in detail at TAGs in the 2008 election cycle, we can focus on the Service Employees International Union (SEIU). As a 501 organization, it spent more than $1 million mobilizing its members to vote in 2008. The SEIU also has an affiliated 527 group, the Political Education and Action Fund (SEIU-PEAF). It spent $28 million in the 2008 election cycle. In a step also used by a number of other interest groups, the SEIU also controls a PAC, the SEIU-PAC. It gave over $2 million directly to federal candidates and spent another $36 million on independent efforts to elect or defeat them in 2008.

To illustrate how TAGs campaign in all but name, the SEIU-527 helped fund another 527 group called Majority Action. Moreover, it has top Democrats and an SEIU official on its board. During the 2008 Senate election in Oregon between incumbent Republican Gordon Smith and Democratic challenger Jeff Merkley, Majority Action ran television commercials in Oregon charging that Smith favored policies that benefited big oil companies and burdened Oregonians with high gasoline prices. The ads stayed within the law by not mentioning the election. Still, the anti-Smith message was clear. He went down to defeat by 59,000 votes out of 1.6 million cast.

The importance of TAGs has grown because donations to them, unlike those to candidates and parties, are not restricted. Also, as explained later, a 2010 Supreme Court decision permits corporations and presumably unions to spend money in various ways, including through TAGs, to campaign for or against individual candidates. Thus, TAGs score twice as part of the "big money" reality in campaign funding. First, they are heavy hitters because the huge amounts they spend helps determine elections. Second, TAGs are a way for individuals to donate huge sums to the campaign effort while getting around the limits on what individuals can give to a candidate, party, or PAC.

Demographics and Campaign Funding

What data there is about race and campaign finance indicates that there are racial differences in campaign giving.[31] Whites are the most likely to contribute to political campaigns and causes, followed by blacks, Asian Americans, and Latinos in that order. Surprisingly, the gaps in giving persist when controlling for age, education, and income.[32] However, the contribution rate of a minority group does increase when a candidate from that group is on the ballot.[33]

There is better data on contributions by sex. For the 2008 elections, we can say that

- 64% of women's contributions went to the Democrats compared to 51% of men's donations.
- a greater percentage of men (0.74%) contributed than women (0.37%).
- the average contribution of men ($2,081) was a bit higher than that of women ($1,808).
- 63% of the large ($200+) individual contributions came from men, 37% from women.
- women have closed the contributions gap, as Figure 10.5 shows.

Concerns about Campaign Money

The rising cost of campaigns and the accompanying steep increase in the money being donated by interest groups and wealthy

FIGURE 10.5 Political Contributions by Sex

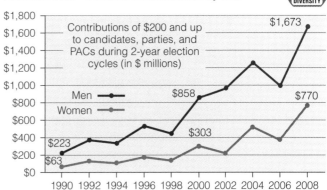

Women have narrowed the gap with men in their campaign contributions from $1:$3.5 in 1990 to $1:$2.2 in 2008. Still, a gap in this area of political participation remains between men and women.

Notes and data source: No data are kept for contribution below $200. Data from Center for Responsive Politics.

individuals directly to candidates and to organizations supporting candidates prompt two troubling questions about the money flow.

First, *how important is money in determining who gets elected?* Analyzing the impact of money on elections is difficult because incumbents run in most races, almost always raise the most money, and almost always win. Therefore it is not clear whether incumbents usually win because they raise the most money or raise the most money because they usually win. One way to avoid this chicken-and-egg problem is to look only at **open-seat elections** (no incumbent) because they are much more likely than average to be competitive. The data from them indicates that money counts. For example, once an open-seat candidate outspends an opponent by 33%, that candidate's chance of winning becomes significant and continues to improve as the spending gap gets get wider.[34] The money factor is even true in races with incumbents who are vulnerable because of scandal or some other factor.[35] To further see the impact of money, consider the following.

Male incumbents running for reelection to the House in 2008 raised an average $196,281 more in campaign funds than women incumbents.

- In the 2008 Senate elections, the candidate who spent the most won every open seat.
- In the 2008 House elections, the candidate who spent the most won 67% of the open seats.
- In contests for open seats in the Senate between 2000 and 2008, the winners spent an average of $56.4 million; the losers spent an average of $33.7 million.
- In contests for open seats in the House between 2000 and 2008, the winners spent an average of $6.8 million; the losers spent an average of $4 million.

It is also the case that the massive flow of campaign funds to incumbents limits competition by discouraging potential challengers who realize they cannot compete with the amounts of money the incumbent can raise.[36] Yet another concern about the high cost of campaigns is that it disadvantages women and members of minority groups because they have, on average, less personal wealth and also have fewer contacts with those who do have substantial funds.

Second, *do campaign donations give large contributors undue access to and influence over the elected officials who receive the funds?* It is certainly true that most of the people and groups that spend billions of dollars to affect elections are hoping to gain influence over policy in a system that Senator John McCain (R-AZ) characterizes as "tainted by the influence of huge big-dollar contributions from special interests on the right and left."[37]

Yet there are several reasons to be wary of overstating the link between money and influence. First, some of the money (37% in 2008) goes to losing candidates. Second, much of the money goes to incumbents who (1) get funds from many donors, (2) are probably going to win anyway and, therefore, (3) are not particularly indebted to any one donor. Third, individuals and groups give money to like-minded candidates. Pro-life groups donate to candidates who oppose abortion, and pro-choice groups give funds to candidates who support it. In this case, the candidate's policy position influences the money flow; the money flow does not influence the candidate's policy position. A fourth caution about overestimating the impact of money on policy is the fact that research has not been able to closely connect the two. As one study concludes, "Recent research shows that campaign contributions have not had much of an effect on legislative voting behavior.[38]

Still, the torrent of money coursing through the political process makes it hard to believe that there is not at least some truth to the so-called "political golden rule": "He who has the gold makes the rules." It may be, for instance, that the connections between money and influence are more subtle than a simple link between contributions to legislators and their subsequent votes. For example, one study found that there was a connection between contributions and the willingness of legislators to exert themselves on behalf of an interest during the crucial committee phase of the legislative process. Although there was "little evidence that PAC money purchased members' votes," the study concluded, campaign contributions "did buy the marginal time, energy, and legislative resources that committee participation requires."[39] Thus the place where money makes a difference may be in the dimmer recesses of committee meetings, off-the-record negotiations among members, and other processes that are far less visible to the press and public than the recorded votes that occur on the floor.

Regulating Campaign Money

Concern about the impact of big money has repeatedly sparked calls for the regulation of campaign finance. Several reform laws have been enacted in response, but they have proven only partly effective.

At the center of the effort to regulate campaign finance are two laws, the **Federal Election Campaign Act (FECA)** of 1971 and the **Bipartisan Campaign Reform Act (BCRA)** of 2002, and one agency, the **Federal Election Commission (FEC)**, that was created in 1974 to oversee campaign finance. The FECA limited hard money contributions by individuals and PACs to political parties and candidates, instituted reporting requirements, and limited what individuals could spend independently to promote themselves or anyone else for office. In time, these contribution restrictions and reporting requirements set off the move to involve tax-exempt advocacy groups in campaigning, and the BCRA (also called the McCain-Feingold Act) was enacted to limit the flow of TAG money to the national political parties, to eliminate campaign ads thinly disguised as issue ads just prior to elections, and to institute other safeguards. The BCRA also tried to offset the advantage the very wealthy can gain from spending unlimited amounts of their own money to promote their own election.

Both acts have had some good impacts, but they also have been limited by the courts. In *Buckley v. Valeo* (1976), the Supreme Court ruled that the FECA's spending limits on people independently promoting themselves or other candidates violated the First Amendment. Initially, the BCRA fared better, with the Supreme Court upholding several of its key provisions in 2003.[40] However, later suits went less well. In one case the Court cited the First Amendment in voiding most of the BCRA's restrictions on political advertising by TAGs.[41] Then in 2008, the Supreme Court dealt the BCRA another blow by striking down the millionaire clause as a restriction of free speech.[42]

Yet another blow by the Supreme Court to campaign finance regulation came in *Citizens United v. Federal Election Commission* (2010). In that decision, the Court struck down as a violation of free speech a provision of the BCRA that prohibited corporations from independently engaging in "electioneering communications." Since the BCRA also barred unions from this activity, it is probable that the Court's ruling applies to unions also. However, the Court did not, as was widely reported by the press and on blogs, strike down long-standing laws that bar corporations (since 1907) and unions (since 1947) from giving money directly to federal candidates and political parties. Nevertheless, by putting corporations (and probably unions) on the same footing as TAGs in their ability to electioneer, *Citizens United* will almost certainly result in increased spending directly by corporations or through contributions to TAGs in an effort to influence elections. That, and perhaps the suspicion that such spending will flow mostly toward Republicans, drew an angry condemnation of the decision by President Obama and a call by him and congressional Democrats to try to fashion a law that would somehow restore the restrictions that the Court had invalidated.

Presidential Campaign Finance

It is not surprising that the quadrennial presidential campaign is by far the most expensive of any election campaign, but the amounts involved are hard to believe. Barack Obama spent more than $750 million and John McCain over $350 million in 2008 seeking their parties' nomination for president and then campaigning against one another. Nine other Democrats and 10 other Republicans collectively spent another $641 million unsuccessfully seeking to be their party's nominee. The Democratic National Committee and the Republican National Committee together spent almost $600 million during the 2008 election cycle, with much of it going to support the presidential campaigns of their respective nominees. Tax-exempt advocacy groups spent $400 million during the 2008 cycle, with a significant part of that funding directed to supporting or defeating either Obama or McCain. Precise numbers are impossible, but all-in-all the 2008 presidential race cost about $2 billion.

Public Funding for Presidential Campaigns

Under the FECA, public funds have been available since 1974 for both the presidential nomination and campaign process. Funding levels of each candidate were established in 1974 at $10 million for the nomination and $20 million for the presidency, adjusted in future campaigns for inflation. Taking the funds is optional, but accepting them requires candidates to abide by a number of limits on fund-raising from other sources. Any party can receive funds, but the eligibility requirements make it difficult for any party but the Democrats or Republicans to qualify.

Public funding was instituted to take big money out of picking the president, and it had some success at first. More recently, though, many of the leading candidates are receiving so much money through their own fund-raising efforts that public funding is being marginalized. Neither George Bush nor John Kerry took public funds for their primary campaigns in 2004. Similarly, Barack Obama, John McCain, and Hillary Clinton all declined the public primary funds in 2008.

Obama further reduced the importance of public funding in 2008 when he became the first presidential candidate to decline it for the general election. Obama had said he would "pursue an agreement with the Republican nominee" to both use public funding, but he changed his mind when he realized that he could raise much more himself than the $84 million he would have received in public funds."[43] McCain did accept the funds, but there are enough loopholes in the regulations that he was able to spend an additional $222 million. Candidates are able to carry over, for example, funds raised during the primaries, and McCain raised $108 million between the time he had locked up the nomination in early March and the convention in early September.

Presidential Campaign Fund-Raising

As is true in congressional campaigns, large donors are responsible for most of the money that flows in to presidential campaigns. The Obama campaign stressed its appeal for small donations as part of its projected image of a "people's campaign." In the end, though, small donors (giving a total of $200 or less) contributed only 26% of the $452 million in individual contributions that Obama received. Moderately large donors ($201–$999) gave 27%, and very large donors ($1,000+) gave 47%. For comparison, small donor contributions to other recent candidates were John McCain (21%), John Kerry (20%), and George Bush (25%).[44]

Further boosting the role of big money in presidential campaigns, multiple channels of money and other factors make it possible for single individuals and groups to directly or indirectly send large sums to support a presidential candidate in ways that violate the spirit, if not the letter, of campaign finance reform laws. For example, individuals can increase their financial importance to a candidate's campaign by soliciting contributions from others and "bundling" these funds to support a candidate or party. Bruce Oreck of the vacuum cleaner family served on the finance committee of the Obama campaign and reportedly bundled over $500,000 for the campaign and the inauguration. Obama soon named Oreck as U.S. ambassador to Finland.

THE VOTERS

Finally, on the first Tuesday after the first Monday in November, the seemingly unending campaigns conclude, and the voters make their collective decisions about who will serve in office. To explore this most democratic of all events, we will first look at who the voters are.

Who Is Eligible to Vote

American history is a story of slowly expanding who can vote. Most economic qualifications to vote were abolished by the 1830s. Barriers to voting based on sex and race persisted much longer before being broken down in law and practice, as detailed in Chapter 5. Other group-related voting restrictions have also been reduced. Age is prominent among these. In 1946, Czechoslovakia became the first country to allow 18-year-olds to vote. The United States did not follow suit until 1971 when the absurdity of 18-year-olds being too young to vote but old enough to fight and often die in Vietnam finally persuaded Congress to pass the **Twenty-sixth Amendment.** The three-fourths of the states needed to ratify it did so in a record 100 days. More recently, an effort to further lower the voting age to 16 has emerged. It has been largely unsuccessful thus far, but some states do now allow 17-year-olds to vote in primaries if they will be 18 by the time of the election.

 Six countries allow 17-year-olds to vote in national elections, and four countries (Austria, Brazil, Cuba, and Nicaragua) set 16 as the minimum voting age.

Reflecting ongoing globalization with people moving between countries at a greater rate, there is also a small but growing movement to allow noncitizens who are U.S. residents, not just visitors, to vote in local elections and even to run for office. This movement is found globally. For example, many countries in the European Union allow residents who are citizens of other EU countries to vote in local elections. There are even a few countries, such as Chile, that permit long-term residents who are not citizens to vote in national elections.[45] In the United States, only a few localities, including Chicago, allow noncitizens to vote in their elections.

As important as who is eligible to vote is the matter of who actually does vote. To determine this, we will look first at overall turnout, then at turnout among demographic groups.

Voter Turnout

Americans are often criticized for being lackadaisical about voting. One way to begin to evaluate this charge is to compare the United States to other countries. To make a fair comparison, it is important to consider only democracies because dictatorships often require people to vote to maintain a false air of legitimacy. It is also important to compare presidential democracies such as the United States to one another, because they average a 6% lower turnout than parliamentary democracies such as Germany.[46]

Americans turned out in 2008 at a higher rate (58%) of the voting age population than in recent presidential elections (average turnout 1992–2004: 53%). That 58% turnout was lower than the global average (68%) for all democracies in recent years. However, as Figure 10.6 shows, the U.S. turnout fares a bit better, if still not well, compared to the average recent turnout (63%) in presidential democracies.

American voting turnout is even less laudable for other types of elections. Turnout for congressional elections in non-presidential election "off years" averaged 17% lower than in presidential years between 2000 and 2010. Except when there is a gubernatorial election, turnout for off-year state and local elections sometimes falls below 30%.[47]

While such numbers are low, a mitigating factor is that the data usually used in the United States and elsewhere to calculate turnout is based on the voting-age population (VAP). The flaw in using VAP is that it includes adults who cannot legally vote for some reason. In the United States, the vast majority of these ineligible voters in 2008 were the country's 19 million noncitizens. They make up 8.6% of the adult population. Moreover, this group has grown from 3.5% in 1980. Excluding them from turnout leaves the voting-eligible population (VEP). Using VEP yields a higher and more accurate turnout. It was 63.7% in 2008. Finally, be cautious of turnout data derived from surveys that ask people if they voted. This voting as reported (VAR) measure is unreliable because more people report that they voted than actually did. In 2008, for example, 5.4% more people told the Census Bureau that they had voted than actually did.

FIGURE 10.6 Voter Turnout in Presidential Democracies

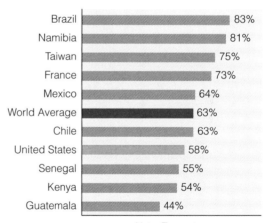

Voter Turnout

Americans' turnout (share of voting age population, VAP) in the 2008 presidential election was the highest in nearly a half-century. Yet it was below the average turnout in other presidential democracies. The VAP turnout in the most recent election in a select list of presidential democracies is shown. *Notes and data source:* Average based on 29 elections, 2005–2009. Data from the Institute for Democracy and Elections Assistance (IDEA).

Factors That Suppress Turnout

Why don't more people vote? The reasons include the costs of voting, lack of interest, and lack of efficacy.[48] Another possible factor is political alienation and negative campaigning.[49]

Costs of Voting

When Americans who have not voted are asked why, more than half cite the **costs of voting**: the time, expense, and energy required to vote. Some reasons for not voting include being too busy, being ill or disabled, being away, having registration problems, and having the polling place inconveniently located. While such voting costs are not huge, neither are the benefits of voting, which mostly consist of psychic rewards. As a result, researchers have concluded that "even small voting costs may deter people from voting."[50]

Registering to vote has been one hurdle, and in the past few decades there have been reforms, including the National Voter Registration Act (NVRA) of 1993, to lower these costs. Steps have included "motor voter" registration through motor vehicle departments when getting a license or conducting other business, mail-in registration, and shortening the time between registration deadlines and elections to allow, in some cases, even election-day registration. Analysts disagree about whether these changes are enough. One scholar concludes that "registration costs cannot go much lower," and that such costs are no longer "responsible for lower turnout in the United States compared to other countries."[51] Other analysts disagree. They point, for instance, to the fact that the seven states that allow election-day registration have turnouts that average about 7% higher than the rest of the country.

The limited time to vote during only a 12- to 14-hour period on one day, election day, has also added to the cost of voting. Changes have eased this problem also.

 In 2007, Estonia became the first country to elect its national government while using the Internet as one means of voting.

Absentee ballots have long been used, but now about two-thirds of the states also allow "no excuses needed" early balloting, sometimes as long as six weeks before election day. Demonstrating the popularity of that option, about 38 million voters, or 29% of all voters, cast early ballots in 2008. Indeed, a majority of the ballots in Florida, Georgia, North Carolina, and Oregon were cast early. Women and minorities are particularly apt to vote early.[52]

Voting can never be cost free, though, and at least some of the costs that remain fall more heavily on some groups than others. For example, the distance between a voter's residence and polling is important for those without automobiles.[53] This circumstance is more common among the poor and among urban residents, populations in which minorities are overrepresented. Urban areas also often have fewer polling stations relative to the population, and this can lead to long lines. Thus even greater efforts to reduce the cost of voting might further increase minority voting, although there is no scholarly consensus on the possible impact.[54]

There are also voices that object to the movement to ease registration and other voting requirements. One complaint is that doing so makes it increasingly easy to commit election fraud such as allowing noncitizens and other ineligible people to vote. Those who take this position favor a national voter identification card. They contend that because a driver's license can be used to register to vote in most states and because some states do not require proof of citizenship to obtain a license, that "it seems likely that voter rolls now contain large numbers of noncitizens—enough in close elections to change the outcome."[55] Opponents counter that there is no evidence of massive voter fraud and that instituting the proposal for a national voter identification card requiring proof of citizenship would be a costly, cumbersome, intrusive procedure that would tend to suppress voting by citizens in an effort to fix a problem that does not exist. Proposals in Congress to require a national ID card have failed. However, several states have tightened requirements for voter identification, and the U.S. Supreme Court has rejected a suit charging that such restrictions violate the NVRA.[56]

Voting turnout has increased as a result of such measures as making it easier to register and allowing early voting in person, as shown here, or by mail before the official election day. (AP Photo/Al Behrman)

Indifference

A second reason often given to explain low voter turnout is lack of interest in politics. It comes in two varieties. Persistent disinterest is one and includes 10% to 15% of the population. The second and larger group of nonvoters includes those who are active only when they find a particular election interesting. For them, the key to prompting interest is competitiveness, how close the race is.[57] Because most congressional districts and most states in presidential elections are not very competitive, many people have little incentive to make the effort to vote for an assured winner and even less motivation to bother to vote for an inevitable loser. Indicating this, an average of over two-thirds of the states with a turnout of 70% or above in 2004 and 2008 had at least one competitive statewide election (president, governor, U.S. senator), while most of the states with turnouts below 60% did not.

Lack of Efficacy

Feelings of political impotence are a third possible cause of low voter turnout. Lack of political efficacy is the belief that your vote or, more generally, the votes of the citizenry and other forms of political participation have little or no impact on the political system. As Chapter 6 notes, Americans' sense of political efficacy has declined since the 1960s, and the sense of not counting is stronger among minorities than whites. Still, it is important not to overstate the impact of efficacy on turnout. A recent survey found that only 3% of Americans said "there is no point in voting" to explain why they did not.[58]

Political Alienation and Negative Campaigning

A fourth contributor to low turnout is political alienation, the feeling that the government cannot be trusted and/or is incompetent. One survey found 12% saying they would not vote because they had "no confidence in government."[59] Like lack of efficacy, political alienation is up since the 1960s and is more common among minorities than whites. Some studies find that personal attacks and other forms of negative campaigning add to Americans' lack of trust in the political system.[60] However, it is not clear that such ads also depress voter turnout. Some studies find that they do.[61] Other studies reveal little or no impact on turnout.[62] Yet other investigations argue that negative campaigning actually increases turnout.[63] Although it is probably not the final word, a recent study that has looked at all the contradictory findings suggests, "It seems reasonable to now conclude that negativity does not reduce turnout," but adds, "It remains an open question as to whether negativity increases turnout or, instead, has no effect."[64]

Turnout Differences among Groups

A second important aspect of American voting patterns is the different turnout levels among groups. Figure 10.7 shows that turnout varies from group to group. Several factors account for these differences in turnout. In addition to those detailed in the figure, turnout in 2008 for people with physical and cognitive disabilities was 57% compared to 65% for those without such challenges.[65]

Education and Income

Level of education is a key variable in voting. People with a college degree were twice as likely to vote in 2008 as those with less than a high school degree. Moreover, education cuts across other categories to help determine voting levels. For example, the more income people have the more likely they are to vote, but the reason is not the wealth. Instead, how much education you have strongly influences both level of wealth and the propensity to vote. Education also usually helps explain the voting turnout of racial and other groups, as we shall see.

Sex

At one time, men turned out to vote more often than women, but that has changed. Beginning with the presidential election of 1980, a larger percentage of

FIGURE 10.7 Demographic Voting Differences

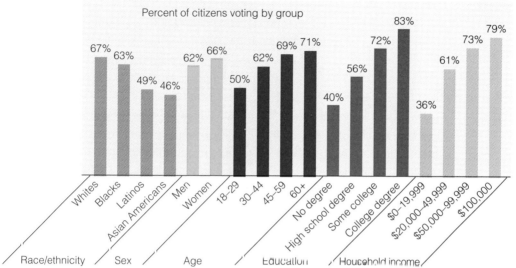

Turnout differs among demographic groups. Usually, the more advantaged a group is within a category, the more likely it is that its members will vote. Sex is the one exception, with women voting more than men.

Note and data sources: The data average the turnout in the voter eligible population (VEP) in 2004 and 2008. Data are from the United States Election Project, the Bureau of the Census, and the Pew Research Center.

women have voted. Moreover the gap has grown, expanding from 0.3% in 1980 to 4.7% in 2008. The gap tends to narrow during off-year elections, and was 2.1% in 2010.

This gender gap to the advantage of the U.S. women is one of the world's widest. Of the few countries that gather data on voting by sex, a majority report that a greater percentage of men vote than women. Scandinavian countries are an exception to that rule, as is the United States. It is also the case that the gender gap has been closing in most countries where a greater percentage of men than women vote.

Race

Figure 10.7 shows that race matters in voter turnout. Black turnout is close to white turnout, but Latino and Asian American turnouts both fall far behind. There are a number of factors that explain the difference in turnout rates of white citizens and Hispanic and Asian American citizens.

Educational differences help explain some of the variation among racial and ethnic groups. For example, the voting gap between all whites and Latinos is cut in half among

In Great Britain, citizens of Asian heritage are the most likely to vote, followed by whites, then blacks. In Canada whites and blacks vote at about the same level, followed closely by Latinos and Asian Canadians.

those in the two groups with college degrees.[66] Asian American turnout also rises with increased education.

Length of citizenship also impacts turnout. One study found that in California only 32% of Latinos who had been citizens for less than 12 years voted compared to 60% of those who had been citizens for a longer time.[67] Among Asian Americans, only 32% of newer citizens compared to 55% of longer-term naturalized citizens voted.[68] Some of the connection between length of citizenship and participation levels is cultural.[69] It takes many immigrants time to become used to exercising their rights as a citizen. This is particularly so for Asian Americans who have emigrated from countries like China with authoritarian governments.[70]

Despite such barriers, minority participation has improved. The growing number of minorities, women, and other historically underrepresented groups who are now on the ballot and serving in office has encouraged voting and eased feelings of political alienation.[71]

Age

Many of the factors that influence minority voting also have an impact on turnout by young adults. Almost by definition, education level also factors into the lower voting level of young adults, many of whom have not yet had time to complete a college degree. In the same sense, length of citizenship, at least unrestricted citizenship, also influences the efficacy and turnout of young adults. Young adults are also more geographically mobile than older adults, and this leads to lower registration levels and less of a sense of investment in the community.

Political participation is learned behavior, and just like the learning curve that leads naturalized citizens to vote more and more often the longer they have been citizens, so too do young adults become more accustomed to the idea that they can and should have a say in politics as each year passes after they are anointed adults at age 18. This trend continues, with each successive age group voting more than the next younger group until age group 75 and over.

The Impact of Voter Turnout

Do turnout levels make a difference? The answer is yes for symbolic reasons and sometimes for practical reasons. Symbolically, the act of voting is an input into the political system, one by which citizens legitimize the government by taking part in the process of selecting it. One testimonial to the symbolic importance of voting is the fact that almost all authoritarian governments hold elections to maintain the fiction of having a popular mandate.

As for the pragmatic impact of voter turnout, it is much debated among scholars. It is safe to say that turnout usually does not count a great deal because most elections are not very close. However, some are close. In them, the impact of higher turnout depends on the pattern of the turnout. Higher turnout would not be significant if the increase was across the board, with all demographic groups increasing by the same percent. However, a change in turnout pattern—with a higher turnout among disadvantaged groups that narrowed or eliminated the turnout gap with the advantaged groups—would have an important impact in close elections. Given the leanings of most low-voting groups toward the Democratic Party, such a change would tend to favor that party's candidates.[72] The most important example in recent years occurred in the George Bush-Al Gore presidential election in 2000, as detailed in Chapter 1. It is clear that Gore would have won Florida's electoral votes and the presidency if there had been only a small increase in the turnout of Florida's young adults, who favored Gore over Bush by a wide margin. A small increase in the turnout of black voters would have had the same result.

Does voter turnout count? For most elections the answer is no because one candidate wins decisively. But changes in the turnout level among groups may count in very close elections. (iStockphoto)

VOTERS AND THEIR DECISIONS

Every campaign comes down to what the voters decide. We will explore how voters decide to cast their votes by looking at five factors: political party, incumbency, candidate qualities, sense of the times, and issues. Before delving into them, be aware that there is no neat formula to calculate the weight of these factors on the overall electoral process. Instead their relative importance varies by level of election, by individual election, and even by individual voter.

Political Party

Most of the time, a candidate's political party determines more votes during an election than any other factor. The impact of party on elections is a result of the influence of voters' party identification on their vote and the existence of party safe districts.

Party Identification of Voters

Most people in most elections vote for the candidate of their party unless some other factor changes their mind.[73] Chapter 9 details party identification and its impact on voting. A summary of that analysis includes the following points:

- About 60% of Americans identify as a Democrat or a Republican. Another 30% admit to leaning toward one of the two major parties. Thus some 90% of all potential voters favor one party or another; only about 10% are true independents.
- On average since 1952, 80% of the electorate has voted a straight ticket, casting ballots for the same party for president and Congress.

FIGURE 10.8 Party and Voting Choice, 2008

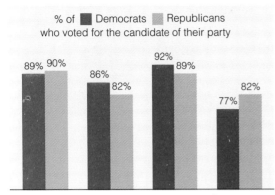

Party is a key to voter choice. On average, 88% of all party identifiers voted for their party's candidate in the contests for the country's highest elected offices in 2008.

Data source: Exit polls on CNN.

• The 2008 elections bore out the importance of party as a norm for voting choice. In the elections for president, the U.S. Senate, the U.S. House of Representatives, and governor combined, Democrats voted for the Democratic candidate 89% of the time, and Republicans voted for Republicans 87% of the time. Figure 10.8 shows this pattern by office.

Party also affects elections because some people who vote for the presidential or gubernatorial candidate at the top of the ballot also tend to vote for that candidate's fellow party members running for Congress and other offices lower on the ballot. The idea that a winning president or governor can thus help other candidates of his or her party get elected when they would otherwise lose is called the **coattail effect**. Presidential coattails exit, but they are limited by the large number of party-safe districts and because incumbents usually win by large margins. Where presidential coattails are most likely to make a difference is in elections in party-competitive districts with no incumbent running. One estimate is that coattails are decisive in deciding the winner in about one-third of the limited number of such competitive races.[74]

None of this means that independent voters are not important in the electoral equation. To the contrary, they are the "swing voters" to a great degree. Because independents are more "up for grabs" than are party identifiers, which way the majority of independents vote determines the outcome of many presidential and competitive congressional elections.

Before leaving the topic of party identification and voting, it should be noted that the propensity of party identifiers to favor the candidate of their party does not mean they are mindless drones who are less attentive or less informed about campaigns than independents. To the contrary, during the 2008 election an average of 62% of Democrats and Republicans said they followed the news regularly. Only 47% of independents did.[75] Reflecting these different levels of interest in the news, a survey that asked 23 questions about current political events found that 36% of independents compared to 31% of Democrats and 26% of Republicans had a "low knowledge" level (could answer less than 10 of the 23 questions).[76] A third indicator is that 26% of independents compared to 21% of Democrats and 20% of Republicans are not even registered to vote. And among those who are registered, 41% of Republicans and 39% of Democrats but just 30% of independents report voting regularly.[77]

Party-Safe Districts

The fact that many congressional districts are **party-safe districts** increases the role of political party on the outcome of elections. These are districts in which voters lean so decisively toward one political party that its candidate is almost certain to be elected.[78] By some estimates, almost half the districts that make up the U.S. House of Representatives are party-safe.[79]

Some party-safe districts exist as an unintended byproduct of the voters who live in the district. Urban districts are a prime example. Typical of many such districts, Democrats outnumber Republicans by 5 to 1 in Speaker of the House Nancy Pelosi's 8th Congressional district in San Francisco. Thus, when the incumbent died in 1987, and Pelosi ran to succeed her in a special election, the issue was not whether Pelosi would win. It was only by how much.

Other party-safe districts are created intentionally by **gerrymandering**. This involves drawing voting district lines to give an electoral advantage to a party. Gerrymandering dates back to the early 1800s when Massachusetts Governor Elbridge Gerry helped design a misshapen district resembling a salamander in an effort to advance his party's electoral fortunes.

The opportunity to manipulate districts is rooted in the constitutional requirement that Congress complete a **reapportionment** of the House of Representatives' seats following the census every 10 years. Once Congress reallocates its seats based on each state's percentage of the U.S. population (with a minimum of one seat per state), then each state legislature draws the boundaries of its congressional districts in a process called **redistricting**. About the only absolute rule is that districts must have approximately equal populations. This was not always the case, but the Supreme Court put an end to unequally populated districts in *Wesbury v. Sanders* (1964) when it established the "one-person, one vote rule." It requires that almost all legislative bodies (except the constitutionally exempt U.S. Senate) have populations that are as nearly equal as possible.

Incumbency

A second key to most congressional races is whether an incumbent is running. These candidates enjoy an **incumbency advantage** over challengers, as Figure 10.9 shows. Even in 2010 when party fortunes were in great flux, 86% of the House incumbents and 80% of the Senate incumbents who were running were reelected.

The power of incumbency is also evident in the **sophomore surge**, a pattern in which members of Congress receive a higher percentage of the vote when they run for a second term than when they ran the first time. Of the 54 House members who were first elected in 2006, 53 ran again, and 48 were reelected in 2008. Of the

FIGURE 10.9   Incumbency and Reelection

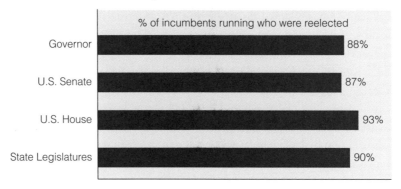

The advantages incumbents have, plus the strong party leanings of many districts and states, mean that incumbents who run for reelection almost always win.

Notes and data sources: Congress is average for 1980–2008; governors are 1996–2008; state legislatures are 1994. Data from CNN, National Conference of State Legislatures, and other sources.

48 winners, 42 increased the percentage of their vote in 2008 by an average of 8% over what it was in 2006.

Advantages of Incumbents

Media exposure and public relations opportunities combine to form one advantage that incumbents enjoy. They receive press attention, attend numerous events in their district as notable guests, and utilize their office in many other ways to advance their image.[80] Atypically in 2010, 23 of the 35 House Democrats first elected in 2008 were defeated in their sophomore campaign by the Republican surge.

Another advantage that incumbent members of Congress have is the ability to provide *constituent services*.[81] Chapter 11 describes these services, but in brief they include bringing federal funds into the district, sponsoring legislation that benefits constituents, and doing "casework" by helping constituents resolve individual problems with federal agencies. For instance, members of Congress inserted 10,160 projects that cost $19.6 billion into various appropriations bills in 2008. Almost all of these "earmarks" or "pork-barrel projects" involved funding for their districts. For example, Senator Tom Harkin (D-IA) secured $1,791,000 for research at Iowa State University on swine odor and manure management. The money earned the senator points in the university community and also brought praise from the state's pig farmers, not to mention residents who lived near the farms.

Campaign fund raising is a third part of the incumbency advantage. As discussed earlier, incumbents almost always raise much more campaign money than their opponents. Part of the funding gap stems from a circular logic. Because incumbents usually win, individuals and groups are more willing to give funds to them and less willing to invest in the race of a challenger. The vast funding gap, in turn, scares off potential challengers and makes it all the more likely the incumbent will defeat any challengers that do emerge. By mid October 2010, with weeks yet to go before that year's congressional election, the average incumbent running for reelection to the House of Representatives had already raised $1.4 million. The challengers seeking to unseat them had taken in an average of only $232,000 each. Senate incumbents seeking reelection had taken in an average of $10.8 million compared to their average challenger's $850,000.

This fictional headline heralds the exception—a close election, rather than the norm, which is a one-sided congressional election because of the power of incumbency and party-safe districts. (iStockphoto)

Serving in a party-safe district is a fourth advantage many incumbents have.[82] This edge begins with the fact that it is very hard for a member of an incumbent's party to challenge the incumbent for their party's nomination. Of the 398 members of the House who sought renomination by their party in 2010, only 4 did not get it. Thus for incumbents in party-safe districts, the nearly zero-chance they can be denied renomination combines with the almost equally minute chance they will be defeated in the general election to mean near electoral invulnerability.

Name Recognition, Positive Image, and Reelection

Over time, the advantages that incumbents have give them a high degree of name recognition within their districts. By contrast, challengers struggle to be known. According to one look at House campaigns with an incumbent running, 79% of the potential voters recognized the name of the incumbent, but only 46% recognized the name of the challenger. This is important because most people who recognize only one of the candidates usually vote for that individual.[83]

Incumbents can also usually build up a favorable image in their district. This helps explain why most people have a better opinion of their own legislators than of Congress. Even amid the anti-Washington atmosphere in 2010, with only 17% of Americans approving of the job Congress was doing, 49% were still favoring reelecting their own members, with another 18% undecided.

Candidate Characteristics

How voters cast their ballots is also influenced by the professional and personal characteristics and images of candidates. Here characteristics do not generally include the kind of "resume factors" that play a role in job applications. There is no indication that which schools candidates have attended, degrees they hold, or jobs they have had count much in voter choice.

What does count are two questions that one political psychologist says are keys to voting decisions: "How do I feel about this candidate's personal characteristics, such as integrity, leadership, and empathy" and even more generally, "How does this candidate make me feel?"[84] To explore these factors, we will take up individual qualities, then turn to demographic traits.

Individual Candidate Characteristics

As the previous discussion suggests, the most important individual characteristic of a congressional candidate, especially for the less visible House of Representatives, is often simply having his or her name recognized by the voters. As for other traits, one survey found that during House elections, a scant 19% could say anything specific about the challenger's characteristics. Even for incumbents, only half were able to comment.[85] This lack of information about candidates is one reason why pre-existing name recognition is often a key asset, especially for challengers and those running for the first time. There can be little doubt, for example, that the 80% name recognition that *Saturday Night Live* comedian Al Franken had among Minnesotans at the time he announced his candidacy for the Senate helped him win the Democratic nomination and then unseat the incumbent Republican senator in 2008.

In some cases, candidate characteristics can be important when a candidate has gotten a lot of negative media attention. For example, Virginia's George Allen was a popular U.S. senator when he lost his huge early lead and his seat in 2006. Allen's self-destruction began when he publicly called an Indian American individual a "macaca," a genus of monkey and also a term used as a racial slur. Adding to Allen's woes, some of his college classmates charged that he had often used the N-word, and his high school yearbook picture showed him wearing a Confederate flag lapel pin. Certainly many factors played a role in Allen's defeat, but prominent among those was the damage he inflicted on his character image.

Demographic Characteristics

A candidate's demographic characteristics can also be a factor in the nomination and election process. For all the success of Barack Obama, it is still very unusual for a person of color to represent a district that has a white majority. Similarly, the important advances that women have made do not mean that they are no longer at a disadvantage when seeking office. For just a few of the facts relevant to race and gender in elections, consider the following about the 2008 elections.

- Fully 86% of the minorities elected to the House won in districts where whites are a minority.
- The 368 House districts with white majorities elected just 11 minority candidates.

- Men were 91% of the 70 Democratic and Republican nominees in the 35 Senate races.
- Eleven of 14 gubernatorial races were male-male; none was female-female.

Issues

Issues count in elections, but less and in different ways than is often portrayed. For elections to the U.S. House of Representatives, state legislatures, and other relatively low-visibility elections, most voters are unlikely to know many if any of the specific positions on issues taken by candidates. In March 2010, for example, a majority (54%) of Americans were willing to admit that they did not know how their representative in Congress stood on health care even after almost a year of protracted debate in the country and Congress on the issue.[86]

Further limiting the impact of issues is Americans' view of what is important in evaluating their representatives. When asked whether their representative's stand on "national issues" or "performance in the district" is most important, people split almost evenly with about 40% for each option. The remaining 20% said both options are important, neither is, or are unsure.[87]

Within these limits, there are three ways that issues are apt have an impact. First, every electoral district has some voters who are very focused on one or a few issues, who find out the candidates' respective positions on those issues, and who cast their votes accordingly. Second, there is an indirect connection between issues, parties, and candidates. When they do not know the candidates' issue positions, people usually vote for their party's candidate. In this case, the voters know the general positions of their party and assume, usually correctly, that the views of their party and their party's candidate are similar. Third, there are times that an issue looms especially large and many voters' decisions are swayed strongly by the positions of candidates and parties on that issue. Iraq was such an issue in 2006. Post-election polls showed that voters, including almost half of all independents, rated Iraq the most important issue in their decision. Moreover, 60% of those who thought Iraq was a top issue voted Democratic for Congress.

Sense of the Times

Yet another factor that influences voting is the electorate's sense of whether times are good or bad. This is called **retrospective voting**. In 2010, 62% of voters thought the country was headed in the "wrong direction," and 75% of them voted Republican. Normally, one analyst argues, retrospective voting makes a difference of "at least several percentage points in most congressional races," enough to make the difference in a close race.[88] By the same logic, retrospective voting will affect the vote received by the president if he is running for reelection or by the party's nominee for president.[89]

Voter Decisions in Presidential Elections

There are both similarities and differences in the importance of the various factors that determine voter decisions in presidential compared to congressional elections.

Political Party and Incumbency

As is true in congressional elections, political party is the most important voting determinant in presidential races. One indication is the timing of voter decisions. By June 2008, two months before the candidates were even officially nominated, 73% of registered voters were already saying they were certain they would vote for Obama (38%) or McCain (35%).[90] More than 90% of the Republicans surveyed said they would vote for McCain and an equally strong majority of Democrats were committed to vote for Obama. These commitments fluctuated some during the campaign, but in the end, as shown earlier in Figure 10.8, 90% of the Republicans who voted in 2008 cast their ballot for McCain, and 89% of the Democrats voted for Obama.

As for incumbency and the voters' decisions, presidents running for a new term are not as safe as their congressional counterparts. Still, of the 18 times between 1900 and 2008 when the incumbent president has sought a new term, he has won 13 of the elections, or 72% of the time.

Candidate Characteristics

Resumes do not count any more for presidential elections than for congressional ones. Of the six presidents elected between 1976 and 2009, only George H. W. Bush had significant national or foreign policy experience. Four of the five others had been state governors, and Barack Obama had served less than four years in the U.S. Senate. Hillary Clinton during the primaries, then John McCain in the election tried but failed to make Obama's limited experience a key issue. Doubts existed, with the public about evenly split on whether Obama had enough experience to be president while also thinking by a wide margin (75%) that John McCain did have the right experience. Yet on election day, experience was not what determined most Americans' vote.

Individual Characteristics   Of all candidates, those for president are the most familiar to Americans. Therefore, their individual qualities are usually more important than for candidates at any other level.[91] During the 2008 presidential election, voters liked McCain for his history. More than Obama, they also thought McCain was "well qualified" to be president and "patriotic." The public gave neither candidate an edge in being honest or a stable leader. Where Obama did well, however, was at the gut level of being emotionally appealing. Voters were more likely to find him "down to earth" than McCain. By an even wider margin, Americans found Obama "inspiring."

In addition to such overall evaluations, voters are swayed by candidate characteristics that seem related to the particular set of circumstances or issues at center stage during an election. During the 2004 election, just three years past the terror attacks of 9/11 and with the country at war in Afghanistan and Iraq, how people viewed the candidates' personal strength and decisiveness was an important image factor. President Bush bested John Kerry by 20% when people were asked which candidate could be better described as a "strong and decisive leader" and by 12% on the question of who would best protect the country.[92] Four years later, who would best protect the country was less important. More people thought McCain (55%) would do so better than Obama (37%).[93] However, change is what people wanted in 2008, and by a wide margin more people thought that Obama would be better able than McCain to bring it about.[94]

Demographic Characteristics   Barack Obama's victory in 2008 proved that most Americans are willing to support an African American for president. That does not mean the election was race neutral, however. Exit polls found that 19% of the voters said that race had played a part in their decision. For 2% it had been the "most important" factor, for 7% an "important" factor, and for 10% a "minor" factor. Of those for whom race was the most important factor, 58% voted for Obama and 41% for McCain. This means that less than 1% of the voters voted for Obama primarily because he was black or voted against him for that reason. How the race factor played out among the remaining 17% is unclear, but Obama's margin of victory makes it clear that he was neither elected president because of his race nor in spite of it. Instead, race cut both ways, and Obama was elected because of the other factors that decide presidential races.

There has also been a greater acceptance of some other groups as presidential possibilities. A 2007 poll found 86% of Americans saying they could support a woman for president, and Hillary Clinton's near-miss campaign for the Democratic presidential nomination provided some support for the truth of that poll finding. The same poll revealed that 87% of Americans said they could support a Latino for president. Additionally, recent polls also show increased possible support for president of candidates who are homosexual (55%), Jewish (92%), and Mormon (72%).

When Johanna Sigurdardottir was chosen as Iceland's prime minister in 2009, she became the first openly gay individual to lead her country's government.

Beyond the overall possibilities of support, there are some particular intricacies. For example, the willingness of voters to support a woman for president rests in part on what issues are the most important to them. For example, people whose top issue is terrorism, homeland security, or overseas military operations are also likely to believe that a male president would be more suited to handling such problems than a female president would be.[95]

Issues

More than at other levels, voters are able to connect the candidates for president and specific issue positions. A majority of voters were able to do this when presented with a range of issues in both 2004 and 2008.[96] It is also the case that the policy preferences of most people generally match those of the presidential candidate who gets their vote. Yet this does not necessarily mean that policy positions drive voters' decisions to a great degree. The reason is that most people and their party's candidate are members of that party because they have the same position on many issues. What this means is that policy positions are important independent determinants of the choice for only a relatively small percentage of voters. However, those voters may be enough to have an important impact on a close presidential election. Issues are particularly important to those who decide whom to support late in a campaign. One survey of undecided voters late in the 2004 presidential campaign found that 76% said that part of their dilemma was that they agreed with Bush on some issues and Kerry on others. Among those individuals who had gone from undecided in early September to favoring Bush or Kerry late in the campaign, the candidates' positions on the issues was most often cited as a reason for the shift.[97]

Sense of the Times

Because Americans tend to see the president as individually responsible for the overall condition of the country, the voters' sense of how good or bad the times are is a factor that helps determine their choice. A great deal of research indicates that how the economy is doing in general and how individuals are doing in particular have an impact of how they will vote.[98] As noted earlier, good times favor incumbents and the president's party; bad times disadvantage them. Good-times/bad-times voting (also called *retrospective voting*) is based on more than economic factors, though. Many other factors also determine whether voters are feeling upbeat or glum. Some factors are weighty, such as the level of casualties if the country is at war.[99] Other factors are trivial and clearly unrelated to presidential policy. One study even found that whether or not a voter's favorite college football team had won on the weekend preceding the election can influence that voter's sense of the times and his or her vote.[100]

Retrospective voting is most pronounced when there is an incumbent president seeking a new term. The flip-side of the coin to retrospective voting is *pro-*

spective voting: voting for those who offer the best hope of continuing good times or improving on bad times.[101]

Voters seemed to be looking in both directions in 2008. As noted above, congressional Republicans were decimated in the 2008 election by a collapsing economy and the mounting casualty count in the Iraq War. President Bush was not running, but the Obama campaign, as the *New York Times* commented, "like[d] to say that electing Senator John McCain would usher in the third term of George W. Bush."[102] That charge stuck, with 54% of Americans saying that McCain "would generally continue George W. Bush's policies"[103] Prospectively, the Democrats also portrayed their candidate as the one who could bring about change. Americans agreed, with 54% replying that Obama was more likely to bring about "the right kind of change," and only 40% saying McCain would.[104] Thus whether retrospectively associating McCain with Bush or prospectively linking Obama with a change in the right direction, the advantage and election went to Obama.

FINAL DECISIONS

On the morning after national elections, the country seems to collectively sigh with relief and think "Whew, it's over." Usually that is true, but not always.

Elections Overall

The one-sided margin by which most elections are decided means that it is unofficially clear who won soon after the polls close. Within a few days local officials such as registrars of voters send the vote count on to state officials, such as secretaries of state, who then officially certify the winners. Very close votes can trigger a recount. Sometimes these occur automatically. In other cases, narrow losers can demand a recount.

A recount usually settles the issue. Occasionally, however, the challenge winds up in the courts or even in the legislative body if it is the ultimate authority on the qualifications of its members. After losing his bid for reelection by 312 votes out of the 2.9 million cast in Minnesota, Republican Senator Norman Coleman launched a series of administrative and legal challenges to the outcome. Victor Al Franken could not take his seat until July 2009 after the state's supreme court unanimously declared that he had won the election. On very rare occasions one of the houses of Congress can get involved in deciding an election. When this occurs, the chamber is the ultimate judge. The most recent instance was in 1984 when the House of Representatives seated Democrat Frank McCloskey after a 1984 election marked by mutual accusations of fraud. Indiana's Republican secretary of state had certified the Republican candidate as the victor by 34 votes, but McCloskey appealed to the House, where the Democrats had a majority. On nearly a straight party vote, the Democratic majority there declared McCloskey the winner by four votes.

Presidential Elections

One of the oddities of the American political system is that the election-day votes of Americans for president are technically and sometimes literally not the deciding factor for who will be president. Instead, the people elect the president indirectly through the **Electoral College**. The process works this way. Each state selects a number of electors equal to its representation in Congress (two senators plus its representatives), and the District of Columbia gets three electors, for a total of 538 electors. The exact process for choosing electors is set by state law and therefore varies, but as a general rule each party or candidate selects a slate of electors. It is for one of these slates that people vote in November. In all states except Maine and Nebraska, there is a "winner-take-all" system. Under it, the slate that receives the most votes wins and thus casts all its state's electoral votes. The official election of the president does not take place until the individual electors cast their separate ballots for president and vice president at meetings in December held in their respective states. The ballots are sent to Congress, where they are counted in early January. It takes a majority (270) of all electoral votes to win.

One concern about the Electoral College is that it is possible for the candidate with the most popular votes to lose the electoral vote. This has occurred on three occasions (1876, 1888, and 2000). It also occurred in 1824, but that year is usually not counted because 6 of the 24 states still did not have popular voting for president and instead had their legislatures decide who to support. Most recently, Al Gore got 51,003,238 votes in 2000 to 50,459,624 votes for George Bush. Yet Bush won 271 electoral votes to 269 for Gore, with one supposedly Gore elector from Washington State refusing to cast his ballot. The most important reason why the popular and electoral votes can differ is that each state gets two of its electoral votes based on its U.S. senators. Therefore, the votes in the Electoral College are only partly based on population.

Another concern with the Electoral College is that it is possible to end up with no president on inauguration day. If no individual receives a majority of the electoral votes, then the House of Representatives selects a president from among the candidates with the three highest electoral votes. This has occurred twice (1800 and 1824). Each state casts one vote in the House, and it requires a majority of the states (26) to win. The Senate, with each member voting individually, chooses a vice president from among the top two electoral vote recipients. It is not possible to detail here all the possible reasons that this process could fail to decide the presidency, but the possibility for a stalemate is real given the fact there are less than three weeks from the time the electoral ballots are officially counted by Congress in early January and the end of the current president's term at noon on January 20.

The Electoral College was established for three reasons. One is that it stressed the role of the states. Indeed, they can choose electors in any way they wish. All states now choose the electors by popular vote, but some states had their legislatures choose them until the Civil War. Second, the Constitution's framers worried that directly electing the president by popular vote would split the country by promoting numerous regional candidates, with no one gaining broad national support. Doubts about the public's wisdom were the third motive for the Electoral College. Illustrating this, Alexander Hamilton worried in *Federalist* No. 68 (1788) that the "general mass" did not "possess the information and discernment" to choose a president.

About 70% of democracies with strong presidencies use a run-off election system to ensure that the final victor has a majority vote.

It is beyond our capacity here to analyze the many arguments for and against the Electoral College and the impact of reform proposals.[105] However, over 700 proposals have been introduced in Congress to reform or eliminate it. Direct election of the president by a plurality of the national vote has been the most frequent alternative suggested. Yet the Electoral College survives. The principal reason is that changing it would probably require a constitutional amendment passed by two-thirds of Congress and three-fourths of the states. Obtaining such supermajorities would be very difficult because the Electoral College appeals to many states. Those with big populations such as California with its 55 electoral votes (more than 20% of those needed to win) believe that they gain political advantage through their hefty share of the electoral votes. States with small populations also see political advantage. Wyoming may have only 55/100ths of 1% of the electoral vote, but that is more than three times the state's 17/100ths of 1% of the U.S. population. States in a middle position come out mathematically about right.

For those who oppose the Electoral College, new hope has arisen in recent years over the progress of a proposal that might change the system without the need for a constitutional amendment. The "national vote proposal" (NVP) asks states to change their law regarding the allocation of their electoral votes and to award them all to the presidential candidate with the most popular votes nationwide. Each state's change is held in abeyance until states with a total 270 electoral votes, a majority, have similarly changed their laws. Once this occurs, then even if some states retained the old system, their electoral votes would not be enough to alter the outcome. As of late 2010 according to the NPV Website (www .nationalpopularvote.com), six states (Hawaii, Illinois, Maryland, Massachusetts, New Jersey, and Washington) combining 73 electoral votes have passed such legislation, and it is making good progress in a number of other states.

SUMMARY

This chapter divides campaigns into six topics: party nominations, campaigning for office, campaign funds, voter characteristics and turnout, voter decisions, and legally determining winners. The chapter looks separately at elections in general and at presidential elections.

During the campaign for nomination, people become candidates mostly through self-selection, but some are recruited by party organizations and interest groups. When there is a contest for the nomination, the choice among candidates is made, in order of importance, by primaries, caucuses, and conventions. Each party has a somewhat different formula for allocating delegates among the states and allocating delegates among the various candidates for the party's presidential nomination. The efforts of states to hold their primaries/caucuses early in the process have led to calls for reform. The primary/caucus process also creates other issues related to money and the sheer length of the presidential selection process. The national party conventions have lost most of their importance because who will be nominated is usually decided by the primary/caucus process long before the convention.

Many primary campaigns and almost all national and statewide election campaigns are run by professionals. Candidates face a daunting task in getting their message out to the voters. Campaigns do so through direct contacts with the voters, getting press coverage, and commercial advertising. The use of a new range of social media channels is the most important recent development in campaigning, but it is not yet clear what the impact of these channels is.

Campaigns are very expensive, and raising funds is a major campaign activity. It is very difficult to trace the flow of campaign funds from donors to recipients. There are concerns about the impact of money on campaigns and policy making. Money does not determine most campaigns, but it is important in close ones. There is little evidence of a significant direct and corrupt influence of campaign finance on later policy making by recipient candidates/lawmakers, but that may be due to the difficulty of connecting money and later political favors. The impact of efforts to regulate campaign finance has been limited due to court decisions and ways of getting around the laws.

Most American citizens 18 and up are eligible to vote, but the United States has a lower voting turnout than the average for other democratic countries. Various reforms to increase turnout have had a positive impact, but it is not clear whether yet more such reforms would have a similar impact because of the presence of other factors including indifference, lack of efficacy, and the lack of competitiveness in most elections. Turnout is higher among those who are wealthier, more educated and older, and among whites and women. Higher voter turnout would not necessarily affect most elections, but it would affect some competitive ones.

Political party is the most important factor in elections because most people vote for their party's candidate. Additionally, most congressional districts are party-safe. Incumbents have huge advantages that usually make them safe at election time. Other factors such as issues and the characteristics of candidates are normally less important factors in elections for Congress. Voter decisions in presidential elections are somewhat different because of the higher level of awareness of the candidates. Most people still vote for their party's candidate, but incumbency plays a smaller role. How people feel about the candidates' various characteristics is important as is the public mood about whether times are good or bad.

Most congressional election outcomes are not controversial, but some wind up in court or being decided by the House or Senate. The legal decision about who will be president is made by the Electoral College. Despite wide criticism, the Electoral College continues to survive because of the difficulty of amending the Constitution.

CHAPTER 10 GLOSSARY

Bipartisan Campaign Reform Act (BCRA) A 2002 law that prohibits federal candidates from having any part in raising or spending soft money, limits the flow of state and local party funds into federal elections, and places new limits on donations to federal campaigns. Other limits imposed by the BCRA on candidate self-financing and independent political committees have been rejected by the Supreme Court.

caucuses These bring party registrants and sometimes others together in local face-to-face gatherings similar to a town meeting to discuss and ultimately, like primaries, to vote on delegates pledged to one candidate or another. These delegates then gather at a convention to choose the party's nominee or, in the case of presidential nominations, to pick delegates to the national convention.

closed primary An election to choose a party nominee in which only eligible voters registered as a party member can vote.

coattail effect The additional votes that lower-level candidates get because some voters who cast their ballot for a party's candidate at the top of the ballot also vote for other candidates of that same party on lower ballot positions.

costs of voting The time, expense, and energy required to vote.

Electoral College The collection of electors from the 50 states and the District of Columbia that have been chosen according to state law to elect the president and vice president of the United States.

Federal Election Campaign Act (FECA) A law originally enacted in 1971, then significantly strengthened in 1974. It limits individual and PAC hard money contributions to political parties and candidates.

Federal Election Commission (FEC) The federal agency that oversees campaign finance.

franchise The legal ability to vote, usually used to designate a group right.

front loading Moving presidential primaries and caucuses earlier and earlier to gain influence in the nomination process.

gerrymandering Drawing voting district lines to give an electoral advantage to one party.

hard money Campaign donations that go directly to a candidate or a political party and that are contributed under the rules of the Federal Election Campaign Act. See *soft money*.

incumbency advantage The factors that make it probable that those in office running for reelection will defeat challengers.

open primary An election to choose a party nominee in which eligible voters can vote in the primary of any party regardless of party registration.

open-seat elections Elections in which no incumbent is running for re-election.

party convention A meeting of delegates from voting districts to choose their party's candidate for the general election and to conduct other party business.

party-safe districts Electoral districts in which voters lean so decisively toward one political party that its candidate is almost certain to be elected.

permanent campaign for the presidency The unceasing activity associated with winning the next presidential election.

political action committees (PACs) Organizations formed by interest groups and others with the specific and stated goal of influencing elections and policy.

primaries Elections in which voters choose party nominees for an office or choose delegates to a party convention to select the nominees.

reapportionment Reallocating the seats in the House of Representatives among the states based on population following the census every 10 years.

redistricting The process by which a state legislature redraws the boundaries of its congressional districts or state legislative districts due to population changes.

retrospective voting Voting based on the past policies and performance of the candidate and/or party and whether one feels times are good or bad.

social media A collection of online sites and techniques that allows users to generate content and interact directly with one another.

soft money Funds that flow to independent political organizations that are not regulated under federal and state campaign finance laws and that are not supposed to try to influence elections in a partisan way but often do so. See *hard money*.

sophomore surge A pattern in which members of Congress receive a larger percentage of the vote when they run for a second term than when they ran for the first time.

superdelegates Term commonly used for people who are delegates to the national conventions based on their status, past or present, as a top party official or a member of the party holding a top elected office (party leaders and elected officials, PLEOs).

tax-exempt advocacy groups (TAGs) Groups that are tax-exempt under sections 501, 503, and 527 of the Internal Revenue Service (IRS) code and are restricted by law in various ways about the degree to which they may engage in partisan campaign activity

Twenty-sixth Amendment A Constitutional amendment adopted in 1971 granting 18-year-olds the vote.

MAKING POLICY
Converting Diverse and Global Inputs to Outputs

CONGRESS

11

YOU DECIDE: Majority-Minority Districts?

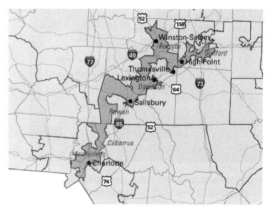

Melvin L. Watt arrived in Washington in January 1993 amid acclaim and controversy as the new member of the U.S. House of Representatives from North Carolina's 12th Congressional District. What brought Watts acclaim was that he and a colleague were the first blacks sent by North Carolina to Congress in the 20th century. What caused controversy was that the districts Watt and his colleague represented had been drawn by the state legislature under pressure from the U.S. Department of Justice using the provisions of the Voting Rights Act (1965) to include a majority of blacks. The aim was to promote the election of black representatives or Latino representatives in states where they had a substantial presence.[1] North Carolina's 12th district, which was 54% African American, elected Watt. Other similarly configured congressional districts also elected blacks or Latinos. Partly as a result of these districts, black representation in Congress increased 66%, and Latino representation doubled between 1990 and 1995.

Two background items merit mention to help evaluate this change. First, and as detailed in Chapter 10, shaping districts for political ends is a widely used and legally accepted practice called *gerrymandering* that dates back to 1812. Second and as discussed further below, whites in the South had earlier long manipulated districts along racial lines to limit the representation of blacks and other minorities.

Despite this background, critics soon challenged the constitutionality of creating such districts. Watt's district became the focus of this debate because of its odd shape. Dubbed the I-85 District because it sometimes included only the lanes of Interstate 85, the 12th snaked southwest from Durham to take in several mostly black areas. The Supreme Court termed the district "bizarre," chided that it had "an uncomfortable resemblance to political apartheid," and rejected its validity by a 5-4 vote in 1993.[2]

After the courts rejected a second attempt, the state drew a third, more compact district in which blacks were 47% of the population. Supporters argued that the district was now designed only to incorporate enough Democrats to be a party-safe seat.[3] Detractors sued yet again, charging that the newest plan did not change the reality that the 12th was a race-based district. This time, the Supreme Court agreed to the plan by a 5 to 4 vote.[4] The Court held that shaping the district to advantage Democrats, even if most were black, was acceptable. Dissenting, Justice Clarence Thomas rejected the new rationale as a sham and charged that that race-based districting "offends the Constitution." What offends others is that between 1966 and 1996, blacks were elected in only 35 of the 6,667 congressional races in white-majority districts?[5] Are race-based districts a reasonable remedy for the under-representation of minorities in Congress?

The darker serpentine area is North Carolina's 12th Congressional District represented by Mel Watt. This box asks whether drawing such a district to promote the election of minority representatives is justifiable. (www.watt.house.gov)

421

FIGURE 11.1 Public Confidence in U.S. Institutions

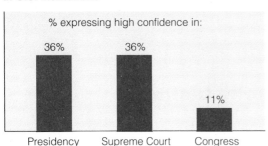

Public confidence in all the branches of the federal government was very low in 2010, but even within this context, a much smaller percentage of Americans expressed high confidence in Congress than in either the presidency or the Supreme Court.
Note and data: The data reflect those who said "great confidence" or "quite a lot of confidence." Data from Gallup poll report, July 22, 2010.

INTRODUCING CONGRESS

Most Americans do not think much of Congress. As Figure 11.1 shows, fewer Americans have confidence in it than either of the other two branches of government. Capturing this negative view of Congress, American humorist Will Rogers once joked, "This country has come to feel the same when Congress is in session as we do when a baby gets hold of a hammer. It's just a question of how much damage [the baby] can do before we take it away from him."

Yet Congress is also more authentically the voice of the people through its 535 locally elected representatives and senators than the farther removed presidency or even more remote judiciary. Moreover, Congress has many supporters, as shown by a recent study entitled, *On Appreciating Congress.*[6] From this perspective, Representative (and future president) Gerald R. Ford once told an audience "Too often critics seem more intent on seeking new ways to alter Congress than to truly learn how it functions." He advised that detractors "might well profit" if they would give up their "preconceived notions" and "sit down before the facts."[7]

This chapter will follow Ford's advice and seek to "truly learn how Congress functions." While doing that, you will find the following basic points:

★ Competition for seats in Congress is limited because most seats are safe for one party or another and/or for the individual who holds the seat.

★ Although the gap has narrowed, the membership of Congress falls far short of representing the gender and racial diversity of Americans.

★ Representation is the most important function of members of Congress, but what that term means is debatable.

★ Congress is a decentralized organization composed of two chambers with leaders of limited power, numerous committees and other units, and 535 often-factious members.

★ Congress legislates through a complex process, often involving negotiations within each chamber, between them, and with the White House, interest groups, and other external actors.

★ Congress is far from an ideal democratic institution, but it is more democratic and effective than many of its critics charge.

Congress in a Global Context

Congress, like the rest of the U.S. government, has been shaped by global trends and events. *The functions of Congress* are one area of impact. Speaker of the House

Joseph Martin (R-MA) recalled being disappointed by being put on the Foreign Relations Committee during his first year in office in 1925. "Foreign affairs were an inconsequential problem in Congress," Martin explained. Indeed, he related, "about the most important issue that came before the committee" in 1925 was the weeklong debate over whether to authorize $20,000 for an international poultry show in Tulsa. "Over the years," Martin further recalled, "the atmosphere changed," and the importance of foreign policy grew vastly because of increasing global involvement of the United States.[8] By the time Martin died in office in 1968, Congress was dealing, among many other things, with a defense budget that had grown from $660 million in 1925 to $82.2 billion and with U.S. trade that had grown from $9 billion to $91 billion as a result of growing U.S. global power and globalization.

Globalization has increased Congress's attention to and role in foreign affairs. Not until 1874 did the first foreign head of state, King Kalakaua of Hawaii, address Congress. Such speeches by foreign leaders were once relatively rare but are now more common. Here the 108th leader to do so, German Chancellor Angela Merkel, speaks to a joint session of Congress in 2009. Among other comments, she pressed for greater U.S. support of policies to curb global warming. "Icebergs are melting in the Arctic . . . we have no time to lose," she warned. Seated behind Chancellor Merkel and listening to her speech translated into English are Vice President Joseph Biden and House Speaker Nancy Pelosi. (AP Photo/J. David Ake)

The structure of Congress also reflects global influences. The creation of the U.S. Senate, for instance, echoed the British House of Lords. One role of the lords was to restrain the popularly elected House of Commons. Expressing the view of many delegates to the Constitutional Convention in 1787, Pennsylvania's John Dickinson said that he hoped the Senate's role would be as "near as may be to the House of Lords in England." To enable this, senators were given longer terms than representatives. Also, how to select senators was left to the states with the general understanding that senators would be appointed, not elected, and chosen from among the country's upper class distinguished by, in Dickinson's view, "their rank in life and their weight of property."[9]

It is also worth exploring the structure of other national legislatures to consider what might be borrowed from abroad to strengthen Congress. We shall see, for example, that most countries have one-house parliaments, not two houses like Congress.

The membership of Congress also has a global context. Women were first elected to a national parliament in Finland in 1907. Ten years later, Jeanette Rankin (R-MT) became the first woman in Congress. Since 1907 the percentage of national legislative seats held by women globally has grown slowly to almost 19% in 2010, as Figure 11.2 shows. The representation of women in the U.S. Congress has also grown, but at 16.8% the United States ranked only 74th in the world, tied with Turkmenistan. At the current rate of improvement, women will not achieve equality in Congress until 2207.

FIGURE 11.2 Women in
the World's Parliaments

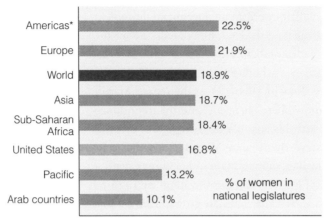

The percentage of women in the U.S. Congress in 2010 was
below the world average and fell to 16.1% in 2011.
Note and data source: * Excluding the United States. Data from the
International Parliamentary Union.

Congress and American Diversity

Diversity in Congress reflects the larger American experience. For most of American history, there were few if any racial minorities or women in Congress. Five years after Rankin took her seat in the House, Rebecca Latimer Felton (D-GA) became the first female U.S. senator. There were minority members of Congress earlier. Sixteen African Americans served in Congress just after the Civil War, but they all came from southern states occupied by the Union army. After the army withdrew, black representation soon vanished. Representation for other minority groups was also nearly nonexistent. One indication of the historical record is that of the 1,930 U.S senators from 1789 through 2011, only 21 have been minority members, and only 39 have been women.

It is also true, though, that the number of minority members and women in Congress has grown more quickly in recent decades. Moreover, members of these groups have also become more prominent in Congress and hold a range of leadership positions. Equal opportunity to serve in Congress remains a goal rather than an achievement, but progress has been made.

WHO THE MEMBERS ARE

A good place to begin examining Congress is with its members. Then we shall turn to how the members got into Congress and have mostly managed to stay there for numerous terms. Table 11.1 contains some basic membership information.

TABLE 11.1 Congress and Its Members

CONGRESS	HOUSE	SENATE
Members	435 voting, 5 non-voting*	100 voting
Term	2 years	6 years
Constituents	±632,000	494,000–33,900,000
Age requirement	25	30
Citizenship requirement	7 years	9 years
Residency requirement	State (but not district)	State

*The five non-voting members of the House represent American Samoa, the District of Columbia, Guam, Puerto Rico, and the Virgin Islands.

The Members

James Madison predicted in *Federalist* No. 57 (1788) that elected legislators would mirror society. The representatives, he wrote, would not be "the rich, more than the poor; . . . the learned, more than the ignorant; . . . the haughty heirs of distinguished names, more than the humble sons of obscurity and unpropitious fortune." As it has turned out, Madison was wrong.

Profile of the 111th Congress (2009–2010)

The membership of Congress is not a cross-section of the American electorate. The average member of Congress is more likely to be white (85%) and a male (83%). Slightly more than half the members are Protestants. The average American over age 25 (the minimum age for service in the House) is 48; the average member is 58. Representative Aaron Schock (R-IL), age 27, was the youngest member when the 111th Congress convened in January 2009. At age 91, Senator Robert C. Byrd (D-WV) was the oldest. Members of Congress are far better off financially than most Americans. The median net worth is about $1.7 million for senators and $675,000 for representatives, compared to a median net worth of $93,000 for American households.

Compared to the 27% of Americans age 25 and older who have at least a bachelor's degree, 95% of the members do. More than half also have a post-graduate degree, mostly law degrees (48%). This makes it no surprise that being an attorney is the most common profession members have ever practiced. Other members have had less common jobs along the way, including riverboat captain, meat cutter, coroner, psychiatrist, deputy sheriff, and casino dealer.

In reality, though, most members are career politicians. There are only a few for whom Congress is their first political job. By contrast, most have served at the state and local levels. Half have been state legislators, 5% have been state governors or lieutenant governors, and 5% are former mayors. About 21% have worked earlier in Congress as interns or staff members. Nearly half the members of the Senate have previous service in the House.

Not only are most members long-time politicians before getting to Congress, they often stay in Congress for many years. At the beginning of the 111th Congress, its average member had already served 11.4 years. Senator Byrd was the longest serving member. He took a seat in the House in 1953 and moved to the Senate in 1959. He served there until his death on June 28, 2010, at which point he was the longest serving member of Congress ever with a total of 56 years, 320 days of combined service. This pattern of having an extensive political résumé before getting into Congress and then serving there for many terms is part of the **professionalization of politics**. This means that top elected and appointed officials are often career politicians rather than citizens temporarily engaged in public service.

Changes in the Composition of Congress

It is also important to note changes in the membership. First, it is getting older. Between 1981 and 2009 the average age of a member of Congress increased from 49 to 58. One cause is that the average age of newly elected members has increased from 43 in 1981 to 51 in 2009. The second reason why the average age of members of Congress has increased is that they tend to stay longer than was once true. This average service of 11.4 years in 2009 was up from 7.0 years in 1981.

A second notable change in the Congress involves its demographic dimensions. Congress remains unrepresentative of the American population, but it is closer than ever before. Increased religious tolerance in the country is reflected in the fact that the 111th Congress had two Buddhists, two Muslims, and an atheist. It was not until 1972 that the first member of Congress acknowledged being gay. There were four openly gay members of the House in 2010. The representation of minorities and women has also increased, as Figure 11.3 shows. The seats in the figure reflect the percentage of seats in the House at the start of the 112th Congress in 2011 held by women (16%), blacks (9%), Hispanics (7%), Asian Americans (2%), and Native Americans (0.2%). The Senate has also become more diverse, although it is usually less so than the House. Women made up 16% of the seats in the Senate in 2011, but there were only four minority group senators.

In addition to increasing their numbers in Congress, women and minorities have also increased their power. Nancy Pelosi (D-CA) was Speaker of the House during the 110th and 111th Congress, and 11 other women served as members

In 1998, Representative Tammy Baldwin (D-WI) became the first openly gay non-incumbent elected to Congress.

As of 2011, Iowa and Mississippi were the only two states never to have elected a woman to either house of Congress.

of their party's leadership or as committee chairs in one of the houses. Minorities are also acquiring more power in Congress. In 2010, for example, African American Charles Rangel (D-NY) chaired the House Ways and Means Committee (taxes and other revenue) and Asian American Daniel Inouye (D-HI) headed the Senate Commerce Committee.

Getting into and Staying in Congress

The legal requirements to serve in Congress are basic. As noted in Table 11.1 earlier, senators must be at least age 30, representatives 25. Senators must have been citizens for nine or more years; representatives need seven years of citizenship. Members of both houses must live in the state they represent. Beyond the legal requirements, politics determines who gets into Congress and who stays there for multiple terms.

FIGURE 11.3 Women and Minorities in the House

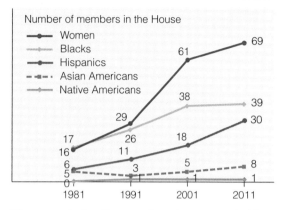

Women and minorities remain under-represented in Congress, but their numbers are increasing.
Data source: Clerk of the House.

The Basic Political Factors

The political aspects of getting elected to and staying in Congress are more complex. Some analysts argue that the fundamental drive in politics is obtaining power by getting into office and holding onto power by staying there.[10] This view may be overly stark, but there is no doubt that getting elected initially to Congress, then getting reelected, is a central concern of most members. Chapter 10 delves into elections, but the process is so important to what motivates the behavior of legislators that some of the basic points warrant also being stated here. These include:

- Most congressional elections are not competitive. Between 2000 and 2008, the victor in 88% of all House elections and 68% of all Senate elections received at least 55% of the vote.
- Many members represent party-safe districts in which their party's members so outnumber the other party that the chances of losing the general election are minimal.
- Incumbents enjoy many opportunities to gain name recognition, cater to their constituency, and otherwise use their office to improve their chance of reelection.
- Most Americans usually disapprove of what Congress is doing, yet most usually believe that their own incumbent representatives deserve reelection.[11]
- The average success rate (2000–2010) of incumbents seeking reelection has been 93% in the House and 84% in the Senate.

- Members running for their second time usually win with a larger percentage of the vote than they received the first time.
- For the 2008 House elections, the average incumbent raised $1.4 million in campaign funds to the average challenger's $335,000. The money gap in Senate elections was: $8.7 million to $1.2 million.
- About 90% of all interest group contributions to congressional candidates go to incumbents.
- Most campaign funds come from large contributions given by individuals and interest groups.
- Only about 1% of incumbents seeking a new term are denied renomination by their party.
- With so many safe incumbents and party-safe districts, specific issues are seldom decisive in most congressional elections.
- Issues can be decisive in competitive seats, when times are especially difficult, or when an issue looms especially large for voters.

Turnover and the Length of Service

Once in Congress, most members use the advantages of incumbency and/or representing a party-safe district to gain repeated reelection. This and the professionalization of politics have decreased the average turnover in Congress markedly from what it once was, as Figure 11.4 shows. Therefore, the average length of time members are in office has increased.

Debating Term Limits

There is an ongoing debate over whether there should be a limit to the number of terms elected officials can serve. For over a century, the issue was somewhat moot because presidents followed the two-term tradition established by George Washington. Also, members of Congress tended to follow the widely accepted idea of the "rotation in office" principle. Then things changed. Franklin D. Roosevelt ignored Washington's precedent and won four terms (1932, 1936, 1940, and 1944). Additionally, the idea of rotation faded, and the average length of service for members grew.

This set off a counter-reaction. The Twenty-Second Amendment limiting presidents to two terms was adopted in 1951. Then in the 1980s the movement to place term limits on Congress strengthened. A constitutional amendment was nearly impossible because members of Congress were unwilling to limit their time in office. Therefore, many states enacted their own limits

FIGURE 11.4 Turnover in the House of Representatives

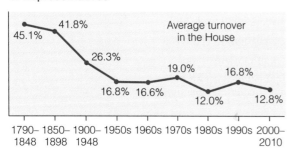

Turnover (the percentage of new members) in the U.S. House of Representatives every two years has declined during U.S. history and even since the 1950s.
Data source: Harold W. Stanley and Richard G. Niemi, *Vital Statistics on American Politics 2007–2008* (Washington, DC, CQ Press: 2008). Some calculations by author.

on their members of Congress. That approach failed, however, when in 1995 the Supreme Court rejected the authority of states to put term limits on Congress.[12]

Those who favor a constitutional amendment to put term limits on Congress most often favor six terms for the House and two for the Senate. These proponents argue that term limits would

- make legislators more responsive to the people by eliminating entrenched incumbents.
- increase the opportunities for underrepresented groups to get into Congress.
- lower the average age in Congress to be closer to the adult average.
- make legislators less inclined to increase public spending to appease interest groups.

Opponents of term limits counter by arguing that term limits on Congress would

- deny citizens' free choice and are therefore undemocratic.
- make members less responsive because they will not be as concerned with public opinion if they do not have to worry about reelection.
- mean the loss of the expertise that senior members acquire, thereby undermining the quality of policy passed by Congress.
- weaken Congress vis-à-vis the presidency by forcing powerful senior members from office.

Studies of state legislatures with term limits have often reached conflicting conclusions on these claims and counter claims. Moreover, the impacts of term limits, whether positive or negative, are modest and inconsistent.[13] For example, the number of women and minorities serving in the legislatures of states with term limits has increased more than those without them, but only sometimes and a little.[14] As for legislators being more attentive to their districts in term-limited states, the evidence is mixed.[15] Also somewhat muddled is evidence about whether Americans support term limits. In the abstract the answer is yes. A 2009 poll found that 70% of its respondents favored putting term limits on both houses of Congress, and an earlier poll recorded 75% of the people opposed to repealing the two-term limit on the president.[16] However, Americans' practice of regularly electing incumbents over and over again seems to undermine the theoretical public support of term limits.

WHAT MEMBERS OF CONGRESS DO

Having seen how members get into Congress and typically remain there for many terms, we can take up what they do. Those tasks are representation, policy making, and constituency service.

Members as Representatives

Representation is the most important function of a member of Congress. Yet despite the central place of representation in a republic, there is no consensus about what representation means.[17] Two sets of theories are especially important for this discussion.

Delegate and Trustee Theories of Representation

Elected officials should undoubtedly act in the interests of the people. But who decides what those interests are? One approach is the **delegate theory**.[18] It holds that representatives should vote in accordance with the wishes of the majority of their **constituents**, the people in their electoral district. The thinking is that that if each representative accurately portrays the views of his or her constituents, then, in aggregate, the public will is served.

An alternative model of representation is the **trustee theory**. One early proponent, British member of Parliament Edmund Burke, argued that representatives should use their own judgment, not popular opinion, to determine the public's interests. As Burke put it speaking to his constituents in 1774, "Your representative owes you . . . his judgment; and he betrays, instead of serving you, if he sacrifices it to your opinion."[19]

To apply these two theories, imagine you are a U.S. senator from Connecticut and have to cast the decisive vote on whether to fund building a nuclear submarine or an aircraft carrier. Your constituents favor the submarine because it will be built in your state's Groton shipyard where many of them work. After careful study, however, you believe that the national interest will be served best by the aircraft carrier, even though it will be constructed in Newport News, Virginia. Moreover you believe that because the carrier will provide greater safety, it is in your constituents' long-term interests, no matter what they think. Should you follow the delegate theory and vote for the submarine or the trustee theory and vote for the aircraft carrier?

Substantive and Descriptive Theories of Representation

The second set of theories addresses the quality of representation. **Substantive representation** theory argues that the best representation is dedicated to advancing the public's substantive interests, whoever determines them, ranging from international security to domestic health care. As such, substantive theory is compatible with both delegate and trustee theory.

While no one disputes the importance of substantive representation, some focus on another, also important concept, **descriptive representation**. This theory holds that the demographic makeup of policy makers should describe the demographic profile of the population. In other words, the major demographic groups should have representation approximately equal to their proportion of the general population.

Instituting Descriptive Representation   There has been a limited effort since the early 1990s to increase minority representation, and thus descriptive representation, by creating **majority-minority districts**. These are electoral districts in which a minority group is a majority of the population. They almost always elect a legislator from that group.[20] Creating such districts or those that are nearly majority-minority is a variation of partisan gerrymandering (see Chapter 10) that is often termed **racial gerrymandering** (or *minority redistricting*). It led to the reconfiguration of the North Carolina district that elected Representative Mel Watt, as described in this chapter's opening You Decide box.

In 2008, blacks were a majority of the population in 27 congressional districts; Hispanics were a majority in 26 others; and Asian Americans were a majority in 1.

Ironically, racial gerrymandering was used during most of U.S. history to minimize the number of minority legislators through a number of processes known as *cracking*, *stacking*, and *packing*. Cracking involved fragmenting minority group influence by dispersing minority voters into many districts. Stacking put concentrations of minority citizens into districts with an even larger white population. Packing refers to crowding as many minority group members as possible into a single district in order to reduce that group's influence in other districts.

Arguments For and Against Descriptive Representation   Advocates of descriptive representation make several arguments. First, they maintain that important demographic groups should be proportionately represented in a democracy. A second argument is that representatives from a demographic group best understand their group's views and, therefore, best promote them. As one study put it, "descriptive representation yields substantive representation."[21] Third, research shows that increased representation of underrepresented groups has such positive effects as encouraging voting and decreasing political alienation.[22] Typifying this, one of Representative Watt's black constituents exulted when Watt was first elected, "Mel Watt gave us an interest in politics and in the process. I never thought we'd get black representation in my lifetime. But when we elected Mel, I thought: Man, this is something special. He gave us a voice."[23]

There are also arguments against the theory or practice of descriptive representation. First, which groups should have representation is a contentious issue. Certainly any scheme would include women and racial minorities, but how about sexual orientation, age, religion, economic class, and other societal divisions? Second, descriptive representation assumes that various groups are monolithic and

Argentina, India, Sweden, Uganda, and some other countries have laws or party rules that require women to be 30% to 50% of candidates or elected officials at one or more levels of government.

can be reflected accurately by a member of the group.[24] Third, instituting descriptive representation would limit democratic electoral choices to a degree. Fourth, some contend that descriptive representation would worsen the country's divisions rather than help to bridge them. Fifth, opponents of descriptive representation claim that it violates what they say is the constitutional requirement that government be race-neutral and sex-neutral.

Yet another question about racial gerrymandering is whether it really does increase minority political activity and influence. Most scholars answer yes to that question.[25] But some scholars disagree.[26] They suggest that diluting minority voting strength in many legislative districts to pack it into a few decreases the number of "minority influence districts."[27] These are districts where a minority group, although short of a majority, has enough voters to ensure that representatives must pay attention to them or risk electoral defeat. Packing minority voters into a few districts may even increase the conservatism of surrounding, now more heavily white districts.[28] It is also the case that majority-minority districts are among the least competitive in the country, and some analysts argue this decreases the quality of their representation.[29]

The Courts and Implementing Descriptive Representation   As noted in the opening You Decide box, the Supreme Court has sometimes allowed the creation of districts that are majority-minority or nearly so and at other times has found the racial factor too blatant. The courts have also rejected diluting majority-minority districts. This occurred in 2006 when the Supreme Court voided an effort by the Republican-dominated legislature of Texas to redraw one district in order to lower the percentage of its Latino population in the hopes of protecting the Republican incumbent.[30] Yet a state may redistrict in a way that reduces the minority population in a district that is heavily minority (39% in the case) but not majority-minority.[31]

Members as Policy Makers

Our review of representation leads to the inquiry, "Which theory describes how members act?" The answer is "all of them," at least in part.[32] To explain this, we will explore several factors that influence which policies members favor and how they vote on the floor and in committees.

Political Party

A member's political party is the best indicator of which policies that member favors and votes for.[33] This is true for foreign and national security policy as well as for domestic policy.[34] The best way to see this is to look at votes on controversial issues. Doing so is better than looking at voting on all measures before Congress because many of them are uncontroversial and draw high or even unanimous support from both parties. In 2010, for example, the House of Representatives voted by 416 to 0 to prohibit mailing private fund-raising letters disguised to resemble 2010 Census forms.

Crucial votes on major policy issues usually show a very different pattern. On them, a majority of Democrats vote one way and a majority of Republicans vote the other. One analysis of such key votes during the 110th Congress (2007–2009) found that a majority of Republicans voted one way and a majority of Democrats voted the other way 57% of the time in the Senate and 80% of the time in the House.[35]

Political Ideology as a Cause of Party Differences Ideological differences are one reason that Democrats and Republicans usually oppose each other.[36] As Chapter 9 details, the two parties have divergent ideologies that shape how party members view policy. This means that shared ideology causes conservatives to become Republicans and also to vote with other Republicans. Similarly, Democrats are Democrats and usually vote alike because of their mutual ideology. Confirming the link between ideology and voting, Figure 11.5 shows that the voting record of the average Democrat gets a high liberal score while the average Republican gets a low score.

The strong connection between a member's ideology, party, and votes helps promote the delegate model of representation.[37] This occurs in part because most people accurately perceive ideological differences between the parties and use that perception as a voting guide if they do not have other strong feelings about the candidates.[38] For this reason among others, studies have found that the opinion of legislators in the House usually parallel those of their constituents.[39]

Party Organization as a Cause of Party Differences When we take up the leadership of Congress later in this chapter, you will find that it is mostly based on party. For example, the Speaker of the House is always a member of the majority party in the House. Party leaders do not have a command relationship with the rank-and-file members of their party and cannot order them to vote one way or another. However, party leaders have a range of tools including incentives and sanctions that give them leverage over members of their party.[40]

FIGURE 11.5 Ideology and Party in Congress

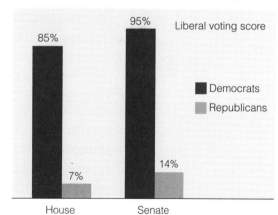

Democrats and Republicans in Congress are ideologically distinct. As this figure shows, the average Democrat in Congress ranks high and the average Republican ranks low on the liberal ranking assigned by the liberal group Americans for Democratic Action based on the voting records of the members of Congress in 2009.

Data source: Americans for Democratic Action.

Moreover, studies indicate that these tools are often used effectively and that pressure from the party as an organization plays a distinct role in congressional voting. It is also true, though, that the influence of the parties varies considerably over time and from issue to issue. The variance over time is caused by factors such as the determination and skills of the party leaders. As for the variance among issues, party pressure tends to be less important on substantive policy votes than on procedural votes, such as whether to continue debate in the Senate or close debate and vote on a measure. Within the range of substantive policy, party pressure is more apt to play a role on taxes and other fiscal issues and least likely to be important on foreign policy and on moral issues such as abortion, and on civil rights.[41] A final point here is that party organization plays a role in both houses of Congress, but stronger in the House than in the Senate.[42]

Constituency

Constituency plays a complex role in the voting decisions of senators and representatives. Three major points stand out.

Constituency influence is powerful. The drive to be reelected helps motivate legislators to care about what the people and various interest groups within their home districts think about issues.[43] Somewhat surprisingly, members from safe districts are just as sensitive to district opinion as members from more competitive districts. This district orientation means that members are apt to adhere to the delegate model of representation and vote in line with the opinion of their constituents when it strongly favors one side or another of an issue.[44] Within this general sensitivity to their districts, members are most responsive to those people and groups who are supporters and those who are "swing voters" and might be supporters in the next election.[45]

Constituency is also limited in its influence. For all the power of constituents, their opinions often have little or no impact on how members vote.[46] One reason is that many bills before Congress have little or no direct impact on the constituents in many districts and therefore generate little constituency interest.[47] A bill on agricultural taxes will be of interest in Nebraska's rural third congressional district, but is unlikely to capture any significant attention in San Francisco's urban eighth congressional district. Second, most people have little or no knowledge of how their members of Congress vote on any issue. In fact, only about a third of eligible voters know who represents them in the House and less than half can name either of their U.S. senators. Nevertheless, it is risky for a member to vote against the strong opinion and interests of his or her district because the legislator's next opponent will surely make the vote a prominent issue.

Legislators often do not know what their constituents think. Even if members think they know what their constituents think, the legislator's "perceptions of district opinion are not strikingly accurate."[48] Members of the House have a particularly hard time gauging opinion. Polls that focus on individual districts are relatively rare. Furthermore, the opinions members receive directly from constituents are often skewed because the type of person who is likely to initiate communications is not representative of the average constituent.[49]

Personal Orientations

Members are also influenced by their personal individual beliefs and other personal factors, and are apt to vote in accordance with them on issues when there is neither strong constituency nor party pressure. One way to identify the personal orientation of legislators is by their affiliation with **congressional membership organizations** (CMOs). There are more than 150 of these informal groups associated with policy issues, for example, the Military Veterans Caucus and the Water Caucus.[50] Yet other CMOs bring together legislators who are members of or supportive of various demographic groups.[51] Among these are the Congressional Asian Pacific American Caucus, the Hispanic Congressional Conference, the Congressional Black Caucus, the Congressional Lesbian, Gay, Bisexual, and Transgender Equality Caucus, and the Congressional Caucus on Women's Issues. Affinity with such groups does not mean that their members always vote alike. Instead, numerous factors determine the votes of minority group legislators, like all other members.[52]

Members as Politicos

To address the question about which theory of representation best describes legislative voting, we examined party ideology, partisanship, concern with constituents, and personal beliefs. It would be gratifying to conclude with a simple answer incorporating these disparate factors. Unfortunately such a simple answer either does not exist or political scientists have yet to discover it. Instead, perhaps the best way to understand legislative voting is to realize that most members of Congress are **politicos**. This term was coined to designate legislators who followed both the trustee and delegate models depending on which best suited the political situation.[53] Others have used *politicos* to describe legislators who maneuver among the pressures of their reelection interests, their ideology, their issue preferences, and party pressures to balance what they believe is right and what is politically expedient. In this sense, most members are politicos, because that is the way to stay in Congress and be effective.

Members as Constituent Advocates

A third role that members play is to serve as advocates for their constituents. Members seek to create goodwill among their constituents by performing three types of services.

Bringing in federal funding is the first service. Most members practice **pork-barrel politics** (also called "earmarking"). This involves bringing federal dollars and projects to the member's district and keeping them there, as detailed in Chapter 10. It notes, for example, that members of Congress inserted 10,160 projects totaling $19.6 billion into various appropriations bills in 2008. For one, Representative John Larson (D-CT) brought in 27 such appropriations totaling $59.4 million that at least partly targeted his Hartford-area district. Among these was $750,000 for equipment at Hartford's new public safety complex.

Members of the majority party in the House and Senate take the lion's share of the pork, but they do allow minority party members to get some. One reason to do this is to win needed votes on legislation.[54] A second reason is to create a reciprocity hedge against the day when the party in the majority and the party in the minority switch. Third, allocating some pork to the minority party deters it from making pork-barrel politics a campaign issue.[55]

Before moving on, three quick notes about pork should be made. One is that it is not synonymous with corruption. There have been instances where pork has been the result of criminal deals, but the vast majority of pork-barrel projects, such as the Hartford public safety complex, arguably fill a legitimate need. Second, the $19.6 billion in pork spending equaled only .006% of the $3.5 trillion budget in 2008. Thus pork is a concern because it does not reflect national priorities and because corruption is sometimes involved. However, pork spending is usually neither wasteful nor illegitimate as such and makes up only a tiny fraction of the budget. Third, earmarks can be defended as a way for Congress to respond to local needs that have been ignored by the federal bureaucrats who are primarily responsible for deciding the details of what the federal government will fund.[56]

One of the many constituent services that most members of Congress offer (via their Websites) is help getting a low-cost American flag ($12–$73) that, like the one pictured here, has been flown over the Capitol in Washington. (iStockphoto)

Sponsoring constituent-oriented legislation that will benefit or otherwise gladden constituents is a second type of service. Some measures are symbolic, such as the resolution that Representative Cynthia Lummis (D-WY) sponsored "congratulating Western Wyoming Community College on the occasion of its 50th anniversary." Other constituent-oriented legislation is more substantive. For instance, Representative Larson, whose district includes the headquarters of Travelers and several other large insurance companies, sought to benefit those companies by introducing a bill to allow affiliated life and non-life insurance companies to file consolidated tax returns, thereby permitting losses by one to offset the profits of the other.

Assisting constituents by doing **casework** is a third service. Constituents who are having problems with or who need something from a federal agency often seek help from their representatives. The offices that all members have in their home district or state are the focal point of this type of constituent service. Typically, Representative Lummis has a section on her Website entitled "Constituent Services" that contains hyperlinks for such services as "Help with Federal Agencies," "Grant Information," "Veterans," "Academy Nominations," "Internships," and being a "Guest Chaplin."

CONGRESS AS AN ORGANIZATION

We often speak of Congress as a unit, as in "Congress passed the bill." Certainly Congress exists as a single structure. It has some centralized units to manage the Capitol and its grounds, and is supported by several congressional agencies and a number of joint committees. Yet despite these, Congress is best understood as a complex and decentralized organization composed of two chambers, a wide array of important committees, and 535 largely independent members.

The Structure of Congress

Several institutional factors impact how Congress works. *The number of houses* is the first. Congress is a **bicameral legislature** made up of the House of Representatives and the Senate. There is nothing sacrosanct about having two chambers.[57] The origin of bicameral legislatures is rooted in monarchial government (such as Great Britain's House of Lords and House of Commons) or in federal systems that have one house based on territorial units and the other based on population (such as Switzerland's Federal Assembly with its National Council and Council of States). As discussed in Chapter 2, the bicameral structure of Congress is linked to both the British example and federalism.

About a third of all national parliaments are bicameral. The rest are unicameral.

Americans seldom think about changing to a one-house **unicameral legislature**, but there are arguments for doing so. Efficiency is one. It is not uncommon for a bill to pass one house of Congress and not pass the other. At other times, the two houses pass different versions of the same legislation, and it has to go to a joint **conference committee**, then back through the chambers for more votes. If one house were to be abolished, it would probably be the Senate. Critics contend that the U.S. Senate is undemocratic because it violates the one-person, one-vote rule that applies to every other legislative body in the country. Unicameral advocates also argue that the United States long ago became a single country economically and socially, making federalism anachronistic. Defenders reply that the Senate is an important component of the federal system and that a two-chamber legislature provides stability by, for instance, protecting Congress from being dominated by one or a few powerful individuals, such as the Speaker.[58]

The different number of members in the two chambers is a second structural factor that affects how Congress works. House membership is more than four times larger than that of the Senate. One impact of this difference is that the procedures of the House are much more formal than those of the Senate. This formality gives the leaders in the House more authority than their counterparts in the Senate. A second impact is that the members of the more numerous House tend to specialize in one or two areas of policy, whereas senators are more generalists.

The national legislative chambers with the most and fewest members are China's People's Congress with 3,000 and the Senate of Saint Lucia with 11.

Different terms of office are a third structural factor that impacts Congress. Senators serve terms that are three times longer than those of House members. Some observers believe that the shorter election cycle for House members makes them more sensitive to the opinions in their home district. By contrast, senators, especially early in their term, have more latitude to ignore public opinion.[59] Whether this is good or not rests on whether you support the delegate model or trustee model of representation discussed earlier.

The different number of constituents is a fourth structural factor. Senators have up to 55 times more constituents than House members. This gives senators a bit more insulation from constituency pressure than representatives because it is unlikely that any single interest group will be as important in a larger, diverse state than in a small, less diverse congressional district.

The Leadership of Congress

Congress has struggled throughout its history with how much power its leaders should have. Members like strong leadership because it makes their chamber more effective by harnessing and directing its activities. At the same time, though, members are independent-minded and resent it when strong leaders impose their will. The result is an ambivalent attitude toward authority. The more hierarchical House has particularly seen the ebb and flow of strong leadership.

As noted earlier, political parties play a strong role in congressional leadership. The leaders of Congress, even the supposedly even-handed Speaker of the House, usually function more as party leaders than as nonpartisan organizational leaders. Moreover, each party in the House and Senate has its own organization that plays an important role in the legislative process.

Leadership of the House of Representatives

The House leadership is composed of four groups of officers: the presiding officer, the floor leaders, the whips, and the conference chairs.

The Presiding Officer   The **Speaker of the House** is the most powerful member in the House, and indeed in Congress. All the members of the House vote for who will be Speaker, but the choice of the majority party always wins on a straight party vote.

Speakers have a wide range of politically important tools. Among these are having some say about which committee will have jurisdiction over proposed legislation, scheduling when legislation will go to the floor for debate and a vote, and making rulings on procedural matters. As a leader of their party, Speakers also have a say over who their caucus appoints as its members on the House's committees, who will chair the committees, who will get funds from their party's campaign committee, and who will get pork-barrel projects.[60]

Such powers make every Speaker a central figure, but Speakers vary in their specific authority. There have been dominant Speakers such as Thomas B. "Czar" Reed and Joseph G. "Uncle Joe" Cannon in the late 1800s and early 1900s, and later Sam Rayburn (1940–1947, 1949–1953, and 1955–1961), Thomas P. "Tip" O'Neill (1977–1987), and Newt Gingrich (1995–1999). Other Speakers have been less effective. Differences in personality and political skills are two factors that account for the variations in the power of individual Speakers. A third factor is the ebbing and flowing desire of the members for strong leadership. There is something of a cycle in which members accept or even desire a powerful Speaker, then eventually find themselves resenting the Speaker's authority over them. In some cases, the members have changed the rules to lessen the power of the Speaker; in other cases they have elected Speakers with less dominating personalities.

Recent Speakers   By most accounts, Nancy Pelosi (D-CA), the Speaker from 2007 through 2010 and the first woman to hold that post, was a fairly powerful Speaker.[61] Her leadership relied mostly on being very hardworking and spending considerable time trying to persuade rather than force the House's Democrats to follow her lead. As one House Democrat comments, "She hasn't put pressure on us, and I respect that."[62]

Pelosi's fundraising has also won her support. She has helped other Democrats raise campaign funds and between 2000 and 2010 has also given them about $6 million from funds she controls. Pelosi has also earned high marks for being attentive to such points as asking about the well-being of members' families. "People remember that kind of stuff," one member observes.[63] Still, Pelosi is something of an iron fist in a velvet glove who occasionally used coercive tactics, including helping to topple a powerful committee chair who opposed a policy she favored. As one member put it with some exaggeration, "Whatever Nancy wants, Nancy gets."[64]

This April 2010 photo shows Speaker of the House Nancy Pelosi and House Minority Leader John Boehner at a Capitol press conference with Afghanistan's President Hamid Karzai. After the elections of 2010, Pelosi and Boehner switched offices. (AP Photo/Harry Hamburg)

One thing Pelosi wanted but did not get was to continue as Speaker. The new Republican House majority elected John Boehner (R-OH) to replace her in 2011. A two-decade House veteran, Boehner's reputation is more of a skilled legislative strategist than an innovative policy thinker. Like Pelosi, his leadership style favors persuasion over coercion, but he too is willing to sanction Republicans who break from the caucus on key matters. Also like Pelosi, Boehner has won support based on his fundraising. He helped other Republicans raise some $46 million during the 2010 election cycle alone and also has given them more than $5 million from his own leadership campaign committee since 2000. How he will operate faced with a Democratic president and Senate during 2011–2012 is yet unclear. His admirers describe him as a political pragmatist who learned how to be patient and compromise while growing up in a household of two parents, 12 children, and one bathroom. His critics paint another picture, with one senior House Democrat describing Boehner as "a very hard-nosed Republican partisan."[65]

Other House Leaders　The floor leaders of the two parties in the House carry the titles of **majority leader** and **minority leader**. They derive their power from such functions as helping assign members of their party to committees, helping schedule the flow of business on the floor, and negotiating agreements among factions within their own party, between the parties, and with the administration. Because the House majority leader is actually the second-ranking member of the majority party after the Speaker, the minority leader is often the more visible and politically important of the two floor leaders. The leader of the party that does not control the White House gains extra prominence for being one of the most visible leaders of his/her party in the press.

Each party in the House also has a **whip** and several assistant whips. They assist their respective leaders as communication links to rank-and-file party members, by trying to get them to support the leader's position, and by taking "nose counts" of how members are apt to vote.

The Republicans and Democrats in both houses each function as a unit through a party organization most commonly called a **party conference** or **party caucus**. Each includes all the members of its party in its chamber, and directly or through party committees performs such functions as coordinating the efforts of the party in the chamber, assigning committee seats to members, conducting media relations, and raising campaign funds. In the House these units are called the Democratic Caucus and the Republican Conference.

Leadership of the Senate

As in the House, the leadership in the Senate is divided among the presiding officer and the various party leaders. There are, however, significant differences between the chambers about how these leaders are selected and what their power and roles are.

Presiding Officer The Constitution designates the vice president of the United States as the presiding officer of the Senate, no matter which party has a majority in that chamber. In practice, vice presidents seldom preside over the Senate and only play a key legislative role in two unusual circumstances. One is making a key parliamentary ruling. On average, vice presidents make such rulings only about once a year, and when they do, they are more likely than not to favor the position taken by the vice president's party in the Senate.[66] The other vice presidential role in the Senate is casting the deciding vote when there is a tie. Through 2010, vice presidents cast 244 such tie votes. Moreover, the frequency of doing so has declined, with only 24 such votes between 1960 and 2010. One pivotal example occurred in 2001 when the party-division in the Senate was 50 Democrats and 50 Republicans and the vote of Vice President Dick Cheney made the Republicans the majority party and gave them all the legislative advantages of majority status.

There is also a **president pro tempore**, who by custom is the longest-serving member of the majority party. In theory the president pro tempore presides in the absence of the vice president. The reality is that neither officer presides very often, with the task usually rotated among junior senators unless a crucial parliamentary ruling or crucial vote is at hand.

Other Senate Leaders The floor leadership of the two parties in the Senate closely resembles that of the House. These include a majority leader, a minority leader, majority and minority whips and assistant whips, and chairs of the party conferences. The biggest difference between the leadership of the two houses is that the Senate's leaders have much less authority, given the Senate's more informal, power-sharing method of operating. Senate leaders have some tools, such as scheduling legislation for debate, but they rely mostly on persuasion to lead their parties. Symbolic of this approach, former majority leader Bob Dole (R-KS) quipped that the "p" had been left out of his title, which should read "majority pleader."[67]

Committees

Congress parcels out its workload to each chamber's numerous committees and subcommittees. There is no other reasonable way for Congress to function given the size, scope, and complexity of the government it is supposed to oversee and the thousands of bills, nominations, treaties, and other business that Congress deals with each year. Signifying the importance of committees, they have been called the "baronies of Congress" and their chairs the "barons." That is no longer as true as it once was, but committees and their chairs do remain powerful players on Capitol Hill.

Types of Committees

There are three types of ongoing committees. **Standing committees** are the most numerous and important. In 2010, there were 16 standing committees and 74 subcommittees in the Senate and 20 standing committees and 103 subcommittees in the House. These committees and their subcommittees are the workhorses of Congress. Almost all bills and other business brought before Congress go first to at least one standing committee in each chamber for consideration.

Each chamber also has a few **select (or special) committees** that are meant to look into some matter of special concern. During the 111th Congress, the House had two such committees (Intelligence and Energy Independence and Global Warming) and the Senate had four (Aging, Ethics, Indian Affairs, and Intelligence). Congress also includes four **joint committees** (Economics, Taxation, Printing, and Library). The first two help provide broad-view analyses in their subject areas; the latter two committees are primarily administrative.

The Role of Committees

Congressional committees are designed to allow Congress to divide its workload among units that have expertise in a particular area. Each committee normally has a very strong say in the success or failure of any bill or other measure that relates to its area of jurisdiction.

Committee Jurisdiction   For the most part, committees are organized around and have jurisdiction over specific policy areas such as agriculture or education and the executive agencies related to those policy realms. There are also a few committees with broad fiscal jurisdiction. Among these are the Senate Committee on Finance and the House Committee on Ways and Means, which concentrate on taxes and other sources of revenue. Additionally, there are the House and Senate Appropriations Committees, which decide how much money to appropriate for the programs authorized by other committees. Each chamber also has a Budget Committee that examines long-term fiscal projections and recommends ways for Congress to exercise budgetary restraint.

Each house has committees that attend to the chamber's administrative concerns, to allegations of wrongdoing against members, and to the chamber's rules.

The most notable of these committees is the House Rules Committee. Before proceeding to the House floor, each bill must have a "rule" specifying such matters as how long it can be debated and if and how it can be amended. These rules are so important to controlling the House's floor debate that two-thirds of its members are of the majority party, and the Speaker directly appoints them and names the committee's chair. As such, the committee acts mostly at the direction of the Speaker. Technically, the House must approve the rule before debate begins, but the vote on the rule is almost always approved on a straight party vote. The Senate committee dealing with its chamber's rules has little power in that area because the Senate does not use a rule to govern floor debates.

Committee Functions   The primary role of most committees is to deal initially with proposed legislation related to the policy areas within its jurisdiction. This "first look" authority includes the ability to hold hearings and otherwise gather information on specific legislation or more general policy concerns. The committee also has the power to send legislation it is considering to the floor without changes for a vote, to amend the legislation, or to kill it by refusing to send it to the floor. As this range of options indicates, committees usually have tremendous say over the legislations that come before them. The Senate and House floors where bills are finally passed or defeated get most of the attention in the media, but it is behind the scenes in the committees where the real action often is. This process has become a bit more transparent because committee sessions that "mark up" (amend) a bill are now on the record. Still, following what goes on is difficult because the formal sessions often merely ratify what has been agreed to in behind-the-scenes bargaining.

Within their areas of expertise, committees also conduct investigations, generally oversee related policies and agencies, and (in the case of the Senate) recommend whether the president's nominees for positions in those agencies should be confirmed or rejected.

Committee Chairs

Committees are always chaired by a member of the majority party caucus. Also, under the **seniority system**, the chair is usually held by the majority party member with the longest continuous service on the committee. The senior member of the minority party is referred to as the "ranking member."

The seniority system was once nearly ironclad, but it has weakened in recent decades, especially in the House. During a reform era in the mid-1970s, Congress instituted various changes to loosen the control of committees over legislation and the control of chairs over their committees. These changes strengthened the parties in Congress and their leaders. In turn, Speakers have sought to gain even greater

Committee chairs are powerful legislative actors.
The financial reform bill passed by Congress in 2010
was shaped in significant part by House Financial
Services Committee Chair Barney Frank, (D-MA)
to the left and Senate Banking Committee Chair
Christopher Dodd (D-CT). The two are seen here
leaving the White House after a meeting on financial
reform with President Obama in March 2010. (AP
Photo/Haraz N. Ghanbari)

power by controlling committees and their chairs even more. One step came in 1995 when the Republican Speaker Newt Gingrich persuaded the House to limit its committee chairs to three consecutive terms. House Democrats under Speaker Pelosi continued that rule when they took power in 2008. Speakers of both parties have also dealt other blows to the seniority system by unseating chairs. In 2003, for example, Speaker Dennis Hastert (R-IL) blocked the appointment of two senior, but dissident, Republicans to committee chairmanships and instead engineered the appointment of two chairs loyal to him. Other chairs took notice. "I think it scared the hell out of them [the chairs]," one House Democrat said.[68] As discussed earlier, Speaker Pelosi did much the same thing for the same reasons and with the same effect when she helped Henry Waxman unseat John Dingell as chairman of the Committee on Energy and Commerce in 2009.

Chairs are also sometimes ousted if they get into ethics or legal problems. That was the fate in 2010 of Charles Rangel (D-NY), the powerful chair of the Ways and Means Committee. He was forced by pressure from the Speaker to step down, after the House Ethics Committee cited him for taking gifts and other ethics violations.

Despite the curbs to their former power, chairs still have considerable power through their strong influence over hiring the committee staff, determining when and even if hearings will be held on a measure, and otherwise shaping the work of the committee. Although chairs cannot use their authority too brazenly, it is also the case, one scholar notes, that, "The barons have not entirely disappeared from Congress."[69]

Committee Membership

Membership on committees ranges from just over a dozen legislators on the smallest to the House's 60-member Committee on Appropriations. The number of members each party has on a committee usually reflects the relative strength of the party in its chamber. During the 111th Congress (2009–2010), for example, Democrats had 61% and Republicans 39% of the 37 seats on the House Appropriations Committee, thereby approximating the House's overall party split of 256 (59%) Democrats and 178 (41%) Republicans.

Committee assignments are a key aspect of a member's congressional service. This is especially true for House members who sit on fewer committees than senators. One reason that assignments are so important is that they help define each legislator's areas of expertise and influence. This occurs because most members remain on the same committees, progressing through the seniority system toward becoming a subcommittee, then committee chair. By contrast, members who switch committees are the most junior members of their new committee.

There are many reasons why members seek a seat on a particular committee.[70] Some are motivated by a special interest or experience in a policy area.[71] Because members tend to specialize in legislation related to their committee assignments, this union of interest and assignment gives those legislators added influence over policy in their area of expertise.

Others seek seats because of the aura of a committee. For example, the Senate Foreign Relations Committee is a plum committee assignment because of the Senate's particular role in foreign policy. Also, some senators see foreign policy expertise as an asset for a possible run for the presidency. It is not surprising, for instance, that Barrack Obama sought a seat on the Foreign Relations Committee when he entered the Senate in 2005.

Other much sought-after seats are those on the committees that determine taxes (the House Ways and Means and Senate Finance Committees) and those that control spending (the Appropriations Committees). These pivotal committees give their members many opportunities to assist their constituents and also the chance to build influence by helping other members with their constituency-related concerns.

Committee assignments can also be important to getting reelected because they influence what a legislator can do for his or her constituency. Thus many members seek assignments that are relevant to their district.[72] Rob Simmons (R-CT) took a seat on the House Armed Services Committee after he was first elected to Congress in 2001. When Joe Courtney (D-CT) defeated Simmons in 2006, the new legislator also sought a seat on the Armed Services Committee. The reason both wanted to be on that committee is the importance of defense spending to the district. Connecticut ranks third among all states in per capita defense spending, and the 2nd District contains the Electric Boat submarine shipyard, the U.S Navy base at New London, the Coast Guard Academy, and other defense industries and facilities.

Indeed, the membership of some committees is dominated by legislators whose districts or states have a strong link to the policy area within the committee's jurisdiction.[73] Therefore, these committees are often not neutral overseers.[74] The armed services committees, for example, tend to be "pro" defense spending and protective of defense industry and the military services.

Support Organizations and Staff

The two chambers, their leaders, their committees and subcommittees, and their members do not work alone. Instead they are assisted by several congressional agencies and a range of staff.

Analysis and Operations Organizations

To generate its own information, Congress has created three analytical support agencies. The largest, the General Accountability Office (GAO), has a staff of over 3,000 that conducts field investigations at the request of congressional committees into such matters as whether federal agencies are spending funds effectively and whether programs are meeting their goals. The Congressional Budget Office (CBO) has about 230 employees who perform a wide range of fiscal analyses ranging from future government income projections to the estimated costs of proposed legislation. The Congressional Research Service (CRS) is a part of the Library of Congress, has a staff of about 750, and performs studies based on historical and current documentation. Individual members as well as committees can ask the CRS for analyses. All three agencies are well respected and generally above criticism for partisanship or other bias. Congress also has a few central functions, such as maintenance and security, that are carried out by the office of the Architect of the Capitol, with a staff of about 5,000.

Usually the important role these agencies play is in the background, but sometimes it is in the spotlight. During the 2009–2010 health-care debate, many votes, especially those of moderate Democrats, hinged on the CBO's analysis of whether the legislation fulfilled President Obama's pledge that health-care reform would not increase the federal deficit.

Leadership, Committee, and Individual Member Staff

Each chamber has its own staff. This includes the administrative heads of the two houses, the Clerk of the House, and the Secretary of the Senate. Each house also has a parliamentarian who advises the presiding officers about the intricate rules of procedure and precedent in the chambers. The various legislative leaders of the two chambers each have staffs attached to their office, and each of the committees also has a staff. Additionally, each of the 535 members has an individual staff that is split between the member's Capitol Hill and district/state offices. Overall these functions employ about 14,500 people, including 11,700 personal staff for individual members, 2,500 committee staff members, and about 300 leadership staff members.

Although the staff labors largely in anonymity, many are important legislative actors who are experts in one or more policy areas, who are skilled in congressional procedure and politics, and who have extensive contacts throughout Congress and in the executive branch. It is not uncommon for members to rely on trusted staff members to analyze legislation, negotiate legislative language, and perform other policy-relevant activities with a fair degree of autonomy.[75] The Senate's Democratic Secretary Lula Davis provides an apt example. She has a distinctly nonclerical position as top aide to the majority party that makes her, according to the *National Journal,* "part drill sergeant, part den mother" to the Senate's Democrats.[76] Davis, who *Roll Call* named to be among its "Fabulous Fifty" top staff members in Congress in 2008, is the second woman and first African American to hold her key position.[77] She is an expert in Senate rules and helps Democratic senators draft legislation and amendments and plan parliamentary strategy. In a humorous tribute to Davis's importance, Senator Mary Landrieu (D-LA) has recalled asking some new staff members whether they had met the "leader." Landrieu meant Senate Majority Leader Harry Reid (D-NV), but one aide replied, "Oh, yeah, we met Miss Lula."[78]

The importance of the congressional staff makes it relevant to inquire into its demographic composition. Congress exempts itself from reporting on diversity, but the information available indicates that the staff of Congress, like its membership, is unrepresentative of society. For example, a 2004 study found that among the staff of individual House members, 9% were black, 7% were Hispanic, and 3% were Asian Americans. Location of the staff was a factor, with the staffs of district offices more diverse than in the Capitol's offices. This led to the conclusion that "Members are concerned with how their staff 'looks' to constituents but not as focused on substantive minority representation among other staff."[79] As for gender, women make up a large percentage of Congress's clerical staff, but only about 20% of the top-ranking professional staff.

CONGRESS: POWERS AND PROCESS

Now that we have examined how members of Congress get elected, who they are, the theories about what their role as representatives should mean, and how Congress is organized, we can turn to exploring the powers of Congress and the process by which they are exercised.

The Powers of Congress

The Constitution grants Congress a wide range of specific **enumerated powers** that form the core of legislative authority. Additionally, Article 1, Section 8 authorizes Congress to "make all laws which shall be necessary and proper" to exercise its enumerated powers and to carry out all the other powers the Constitution gives to the federal government. This **necessary and proper clause** includes a broad range of **implied powers**. For example, if an enumerated power allows Congress to regulate commerce among the states, then it can be argued that Congress also has the implied power to set hygiene standards for meat that is shipped from one state to another.

There are many ways to classify the powers of Congress. One is by their source in the Constitution as illustrated in Table 11.2. Another approach, mirrored in the following sections, is to divide the powers of Congress among a number of often overlapping functions beginning with the power to organize and conduct itself.

TABLE 11.2   The Constitutional Powers of Congress

The Constitution grants a broad array of formidable powers to Congress. To understand how these powers are used, however, requires knowing their historical and political context.

CONSTITUTION	POWERS OF CONGRESS
Article 1, Sections 2, 3	Impeach U.S. officials by vote of the House and try in the Senate.
Article 1, Section 5	Organize itself by having each house:
	• Judge the qualifications of its members
	• Determine its own internal structure and rules of procedure
	• Punish, even expel members for certain reasons
Article 1, Section 7	Override a measure vetoed by the president by a 2/3 vote in each House.
Article 1, Section 8	Raise revenue (such as taxes and tariffs)
	Take other financial actions, such as paying federal debts, borrowing money, creating and regulating money, regulating bankruptcies, fixing weights and measures, and providing for patents and copyrights
	Establish uniform rules of naturalization (becoming a citizen)
	Establish courts below the Supreme Court
	Define and punish crimes
	Declare war
	Raise, support, organize, and regulate military forces
	Organize, arm, and discipline state militias and call them to service to execute U.S. laws, suppress insurrections, and repel invasions
	Create and govern a federal district (Washington, D.C.)
	Take actions "necessary and proper" to carry out enumerated powers
Article 1, Section 9	Appropriate all monies "drawn from the Treasury."
Article 2, Section 1	Decide the order of succession if there is no president or vice president
	Establish procedures if the president is disabled (25th Amendment)
Article 2, Section 2	Ratify or reject treaties (Senate)
	Confirm or reject nominees by the president (Senate)
Article 3, Section 2	Regulate court jurisdictions except as specified in the Constitution.
Article 3, Section 3	Punish treason.
Article 4, Section 4	Make regulations regarding U.S. territories and other property.
Article 5	Propose amendments to the Constitution.

Organize and Conduct Itself

Each house has wide authority to organize and conduct itself largely as it chooses. This ability is central to the independence of Congress from other branches and of each chamber from the other. Such matters of organization and process can have important consequences.

Establishing rules of procedure is one part of this self-organizational authority. With a few exceptions, such as needing a two-thirds vote in the Senate to ratify treaties, each house is free to establish its own rules of procedure. Both chambers have evolved complex, often arcane rules that are important to the legislative process. An example of an important and controversial rule is Senate Rule 22. It bars a measure from going to a final vote if even one senator wishes to continue to debate it. Debate can be closed anyway, but only by a vote of 60 senators. Because achieving this supermajority is difficult, senators can try to derail legislation or force change in it by conducting a filibuster, a tactic that we will take up in detail later.

Creating an organizational structure is a second part of Congress's authority. Other than the Speaker of the House and the president and president pro tempore of the Senate, each house is free to organize its leadership structure as it wishes. Each house has almost complete authority to determine how it will deal with the business before it. We will see, for instance, that both houses have adopted a powerful committee system to handle most legislation.

Policing itself is a third part of each chamber's authority. The Constitution allows each house to censure and otherwise punish its members for "disorderly behavior" and to expel them by a two-thirds vote. Such measures have never been common, and their use has been very rare since 1900. Between then and 2010, only 2 members have been expelled (both from the House) and 12 have been censured (7 senators, 5 representatives). A few others have resigned rather than be punished. Most violations have been clear-cut. For example, the House expelled James Traficant (D-OH) in 2002 by a vote of 240-1 after he had been convicted of taking bribes and other crimes. A few instances have occurred amid charges of partisanship. Most recently, the House censured Representative Joe Wilson (R-SC) in 2009 after he shouted "You lie!" during an address to Congress by President Obama. Wilson apologized to Obama, who accepted the apology, but House Democrats censured Wilson anyway by a vote of 240-179 split largely along party lines.

Make Law

The authority to make law by voting to enact statutes and take other legal actions is a key congressional power. *Passing bills into law* is the most common legislative act. Congress has passed over 48,000 laws since 1789 and annually adds more.

For example, the 110th Congress (2007–2009) enacted 442 laws. The massive number and scope of the laws enacted by Congress make it impossible to catalog them here. However, it is important to note that the power of Congress to legislate has grown considerably for three reasons.

First, the scope of activities in which the government is involved has expanded greatly throughout history, as discussed in Chapter 1. Health care may have been a national imperative in 2010, but in 1819 or even 1910, few would have argued that the government should play a central role in providing health care to private citizens.

Second, the Constitution's necessary and proper clause has been a major factor in expanding the realm of congressional authority because the prevailing view of what is necessary and proper has expanded over time. This has given Congress the authority to legislate on virtually anything that touches on commerce.

Third, the Supreme Court's extension of most of the Bill of Rights to cover state and local governments as well as the national government (as Chapter 3 relates) has also added to the authority of Congress. This nationalization of the Bill of Rights has given Congress the authority to legislate in such areas as civil rights that were once solely within state jurisdiction.

Taking special actions by joint resolution is a second way that Congress makes law. Joint resolutions have the force of law, and they initiate such actions as declaring war, admitting states to the union, approving interstate compacts, and setting the limit on the national debt. Joint resolutions, like bills, must be passed by both houses and signed by the president (or have his veto overridden) to become law.

Spend and Tax

Another cornerstone of legislative authority is the requirement in the Constitution that all money spent from the federal treasury be appropriated by Congress. The sums involved are staggering. Federal spending during the decade between **fiscal year** (FY) 2001 and FY2010 came to $28.1 trillion. The U.S. government's fiscal year (budget year) extends from October 1 to the next September 30, and is numbered by the year in which the October falls. Thus, FY2009 ran from October 1, 2009, to September 30, 2010. Nearly all expenditures are made as a result of either specific dollar amounts appropriated by Congress or according to formulas established by Congress to govern spending on programs such as food stamps.

Congress's budgetary powers also include raising and structuring revenue. During FY2010, the receipts of the federal government came to about $2.3 trillion. Most of the money came from individual income taxes (45%), social security and other retirement taxes (40%), and corporate taxes (8%). Other sources such as excise taxes and custom duties made up the remaining 7%.

The ability to tax includes the ability to structure taxes to create policy. Housing policy is an example. During FY2008, federal spending on housing assistance for the poor came to $41 billion. Even more went to housing indirectly through tax deductions to promote home ownership. These tax benefits came to $141 billion, including deductions for mortgage interest, property taxes, and interest on home improvement loans and for the exemption on capital gains taxes on home-sale profits. The point here is not the implications of relatively well-off home owners receiving a de facto housing subsidy four times larger than that received by the poorest Americans. Rather, the thing to see is that Congress's control over taxes gives it not only the ability to raise revenue but also to structure taxes to promote policy ends.

Organize and Oversee the Government

Congress has the power to create, dissolve, or restructure all federal agencies and most courts and to define their authority. For example, establishing the Department of Homeland Security (DHS) in 2002 involved the largest government reorganization in decades. While the White House was the main architect of the DHS, Congress had a substantial impact on the plan to consolidate 22 agencies. For example many members of Congress worried that moving the Coast Guard from the Department of Transportation to DHS would diminish the Coast Guard's role in boating safety, marine pollution protection, and other traditional functions. In the end, the Coast Guard was moved, but the administration agreed to increase the agency's budget by 28% so that it could meet both its new and old responsibilities.

Congress also possesses **oversight** authority. This involves reviewing how well agencies are implementing the laws enacted by Congress. The oversight function is usually carried out by the committees most closely linked with an agency. For example, the House Judiciary Committee oversees the courts, the Department of Justice, and several other law enforcement agencies.

Congress conducts oversight by such methods as holding hearings at which both agency leaders and outside critics and supporters testify, requiring reports from agencies, and asking the General Accountability Office to look into agencies and their programs. In just one such example, the House Judiciary Committee held oversight hearings in 2002 on the embattled Immigration and Naturalization Service (INS). The title of the hearings, "Restructuring the INS–How the Agency's Dysfunctional Structure Impedes the Performance of its Dual Mission," was a good indication of the committee's mood, and before the year was over the INS had been abolished and its functions dispersed to units in the newly created DHS.

Congress's control of taxes is a major power. During 2010, individual Americans paid almost $2 trillion in federal income taxes and social insurance (Social Security, Medicare) taxes. (iStockphoto)

Investigate

Congress derives yet further power from its ability to investigate anything about which it has the authority to legislate. Especially when an issue captures the headlines, committees will spring into action and launch an investigation. Indeed sharing the headlines is an allure that often spurs more than one committee to begin a probe. Following the economic collapse in 2008, for instance, more than a dozen congressional committees held hearings on why it happened, what could be done to resurrect the economy, and what could be done to avert future economic implosions. In addition to the use of hearings to keep legislators in the news, they also often provide worthwhile information and lead to corrective legislation and policies.[80]

Impeach and Try

Under the Constitution, the House by majority vote can **impeach** the president or any other federal official. An impeachment involves bringing charges, much like an indictment does in the courts. Once an official is impeached, the Senate conducts a trial, with a two-thirds vote required to convict. Only two presidents have been impeached, Andrew Johnson in 1868 and Bill Clinton in 1998. The Senate acquitted both. Nineteen others, mostly judges, have also been impeached. Of these, 6 were acquitted and 12 resigned their office to avoid trial or were convicted. One other, federal judge Thomas Porteous of the Eastern District of Louisiana, was awaiting a verdict by the Senate in late 2010 after being unanimously impeached by the House and then tried by the Senate on charges including perjury and a "long-standing pattern of corrupt conduct," such as taking bribes from lawyers who had clients in cases before him. Conviction by the Senate carries no penalties other than being removed from office and barred from again holding any federal office.

Even the threat of impeachment and removal can be effective. There is little doubt, for example, that the action of the House Judiciary committee recommending that charges be brought against President Richard Nixon was a major factor in his decision to resign from office.

The most controversial aspect of the impeachment and trial process is the grounds for impeachment: "treason, bribery, or other high crimes and misdemeanors." The authors of the Constitution meant the final catchall phrase to imply serious transgressions, but the wording leaves the door open for a partisan attack by Congress on the president and other officials.

Politics clearly motivated the attempt to remove President Andrew Johnson. The articles of impeachment alleged violations of the law, but the charges really stemmed from the disagreement between the Democratic president and the Republican-controlled Congress over how harshly to treat the old Confederate states. Clinton's impeachment also had a partisan element. The root of the charges brought by the House was the president's intimate relations in the White House with a young intern, Monica Lewinsky. Nevertheless, the charges did not include moral turpitude. Instead, the House charged Clinton with committing perjury and obstructing justice while trying to cover up his relations with Lewinsky and another woman, Paula Jones. The impact of partisanship on most members' judgment about the Clinton's culpability was evident in the fact that all the important votes in the House and Senate were nearly straight party tallies. This made the trial in the Senate anticlimactic because if all 45 Democrats voted to acquit Clinton (which they did), the necessary two-thirds vote necessary to convict was not possible.

Consider Nominations

All of a president's nominees for the federal judicial bench and the vast majority of his nominees to senior civilian and military slots in the executive branch must be confirmed by majority vote in the Senate. At first glance it would seem that the Senate's power is little used. Between 1965 and 2008, 89% of the nominees for top posts in the judicial and executive branches were confirmed.[81]

This high confirmation rate does not, however, fully reflect the Senate's authority. One reason is that the Senate distinguishes among types of appointments. In recent years it has confirmed 93% of all nominees to the Executive Office of the President (EOP) or one of the cabinet agencies. This percentage reflects the Senate's view that presidents should have great leeway to decide who serves in their administration. Senators are less willing to easily confirm nominations to regulatory agencies, boards, and commissions because they are supposed to act independently and to have quasi-judicial powers (see Chapter 3). As a result, the confirmation rate to this type of appointee has been 88% in recent years. Because the courts are a separate branch, senators are least willing to defer to the president on nominations to the bench, with a confirmation rate of 75%.[82]

A second aspect of the Senate's confirmation authority is that the potential of not getting a nomination through the Senate gives it a say in who is nominated to begin with. Presidents get suggestions from legislators about who to appoint to fill vacancies and also sometimes consult with congressional leaders about potential

The Senate sometimes helps indirectly decide who will be nominated. One reason that President Obama nominated Elena Kagan for the Supreme Court in 2010 was his expectation that she would be relatively acceptable to some Republicans and would not set off a bitter confirmation fight. This calculation is reflected in this photo of Kagan (center) meeting with Maine's Republican Senator Susan Collins (left) and her chief of staff, Molly Wilkinson (right), soon after Obama announced Kagan's nomination. (AP Photo/Alex Brandon)

nominees.[83] The hurdle of confirmation can also result in a preferred candidate never being nominated. President Bush and Secretary of Defense Robert Gates favored nominating U.S. Marine Corps General Peter Pace for a second term as chairman of the Joint Chiefs of Staff in 2007. It became clear, though, that the Democrats, who controlled the Senate, would assail Pace to show their opposition to the war in Iraq. To avert that, Bush's press secretary said that the president had "reluctantly agreed" to give up on Pace. As Gates explained, "the focus of his confirmation process" on Iraq carried "the very real prospect the process would be quite contentious."[84]

When the Senate does kill a nomination, it usually does so indirectly. As Figure 11.6 shows, only about 6% of the 300 unsuccessful nominations between 1965 and 2008 were caused by a negative vote in the committee that was reviewing the nomination or on the Senate floor. About a quarter of the nominations failed when a nominee withdrew from consideration after unfavorable information came to light and made their confirmation unlikely. For example, President Obama nominated former North Dakota Senator Thomas Daschle to be Secretary of Health & Human Services in 2009, but he had to withdraw when it came out that he had failed to report substantial income between 2005 and 2007. The remaining nearly three-fourths of the failed nominations perished because of what one analysis calls "malign neglect."[85]

FIGURE 11.6   Failed Nominations in the Senate

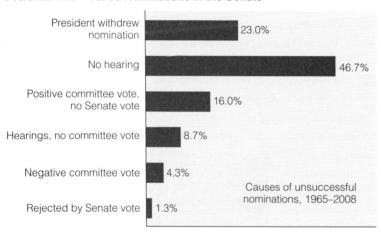

Most unsuccessful nominations die without the full Senate or even the hearing committee taking a negative vote.
Data source: Jon R. Bond, Richard Fleisher, and Glen S. Krutz, "Malign Neglect: Evidence That Delay Has Become the Primary Method of Defeating Presidential Appointments," *Congress & the Presidency,* 36/3 (2009): 226–243.

In most of those cases, the Senate never even held hearings on the nomination. In other cases, the committee that held the hearings refused to vote or the Senate leadership did not schedule a floor vote even if the committee had voted to recommend confirmation.

Consider International Agreements

Over time and particularly in the era of globalization, the United States has made an increasing number of agreements with other countries. These agreements, which are also detailed in Chapter 12, are all made by the president or under his authority. Of these agreements, Congress must approve two types: treaties and congressional-executive agreements.

Treaties   Congressional authority over treaties rests entirely in the Senate, where a two-thirds vote is required to ratify them. It is rare for the Senate to reject a treaty. By one measure, the Senate has formally rejected only 21 of the more than 1,500 treaties it has considered. The most recent of these was the Comprehensive Test Ban Treaty in 1999.[86] Another measure is to add in the treaties that presidents have withdrawn because of Senate opposition and treaties that have never come to a vote. This standard would add about another 125 treaties to the casualty list and bring the rejection rate to about 10%. For example, President Jimmy Carter withdrew the second Strategic Arms Limitations Treaty (SALT II) from Senate consideration in 1979 after it became clear that the Senate would reject it. Carter's move, a U.S. diplomat explained, was "just an easy way for him to recognize the obvious: SALT didn't have a chance."[87] Illustrating a treaty left in limbo, Carter signed the UN Convention on the Elimination of All Forms of Discrimination against Women (CEDAW) in 1980 and submitted it to the Senate. As of 2010, CEDAW remained stuck there, even though 95% of the world's other countries had agreed to it.

In addition to simply accepting or rejecting treaties, the necessity of ratification opens the door to Senate influence in other ways. For instance, the Senate can amend a treaty, thereby requiring that it be renegotiated. Such actions have aborted 43 treaties because either the president or the other government was unwilling to accept the Senate's amendment.[88] Additionally members are sometimes consulted during the negotiation phase, and what is in or not in a treaty sometimes reflects what the president thinks will ease its ratification process.

Congressional-Executive Agreements   International pacts are also made by *executive agreements*. This catch-all category includes all formal U.S. pacts with other countries that do not go through the treaty process. Some executive agreements are made without congressional consent (see Chapter 12). Others, called **congressional-executive agreements**, do require congressional agreement. *Pre-agreement authorizations* by Congress are the most common type. These are created when a treaty ratified by the Senate or legislation passed by Congress authorizes the president ahead of time to conclude executive agreements and preapproves them as long as they are within limits set in the treaty or law. As early as 1792, Congress authorized the president "to make arrangements with . . . any foreign country for the reciprocal receipt and delivery of letters and packets through the post-offices."

Some other congressional-executive agreements require *post-agreement approval*. In this case, Congress authorizes presidents to negotiate an agreement but requires that it be submitted for approval by a majority vote in both houses of Congress. This process is most commonly used for trade agreements. The North American Free Trade Agreement (NAFTA, 1994), for example, was concluded under terms set out by Congress in the Omnibus Trade and Competitiveness Act of 1988. It required the final approval of NAFTA by both houses of Congress. To facilitate that, U.S. trade negotiators met at one time or another with over 400 legislators who aired their views and the demands of interest groups.[89] Such scenarios lead to *two-level negotiations*, those in which U.S. diplomats negotiate simultaneously with both foreign diplomats and members of Congress to reach an agreement satisfactory to all.[90]

Because of the ongoing involvement of Congress, most congressional-executive agreements are approved easily. But they can be contentious when the majority party in Congress has changed or when Congress believes that the president has not paid sufficient attention to congressional input. In 2005, the Central American Free Trade Agreement passed by only 217–215 in the House and 55–45 in the Senate. And as of 2010, U.S. trade agreements with Colombia and Panama have been stalled in Congress for three years.

The Congressional Process

Most of the important and/or even slightly controversial measures that Congress considers go through a multistep process that has been called "the dance of legislation."[91] Perhaps, but it often resembles moshing more than waltzing, with the president, other executive officials, the congressional leadership, committees, interest groups, and others all often intensely involved from the first note to the last on the most important pieces of legislation.

Introduction of Measures

During the two years of the 110th Congress (2007–2008), legislators considered 14,044 bills, resolutions, and other types of measures. Technically a member must introduce all measures other than treaties and nominations that Congress considers. In reality, the White House, agencies, and even interest groups send a great deal of fully drafted legislation to Congress, where one or more supportive members sponsor it. As one example, President Obama sent a 152-page consumer-protection bill to Congress in 2009 that included a proposed Consumer Financial Protection Agency. Representative Barney Frank (D-MA) and 16 co-sponsors introduced the legislation in the House, where it was sent for initial consideration to the Committee on Financial Services, which Frank chairs.

Some measures are introduced in one house and, if they pass, move to the other chamber for consideration. However, the only measures that necessarily follow this path are appropriations bills, which constitutionally must begin in the House. Except for these, most of the important legislation is introduced in and goes through both the House and Senate simultaneously.

Types of Measures   *Bills* are the most common form of legislation, making up about 87% of the measures considered by Congress. A **bill** is a measure introduced in Congress to create, amend, or repeal a statute. To become law, a bill must pass both houses of Congress. Most are also signed by the president, although a few become law without his signature or over his veto, as Chapter 12 details.

Joint resolutions are a second type of legislative measure. They constitute about 1% of all congressional measures and are designed for special actions. Proposals to amend the Constitution are the most common purpose of joint resolutions. Proposed amendments must pass both houses by a two-thirds vote, but do not need the president's signature before being sent to the states for ratification. Other types of actions taken by joint resolution, such as approving interstate compacts, must go to the president for his concurrence or veto.

Concurrent resolutions (4% of all measures) deal with the joint business of Congress, such as establishing joint committees and managing the Capitol grounds. They must pass both houses, but the president has no role.

Simple resolutions (about 8% of all measures) are considered only by the chamber in which they are introduced. Such resolutions usually relate to a chamber establishing its rules and organization or to symbolic statements such as praising veterans.

Motivations for Sponsoring Measures   Congress passes less than 5% of all measures that are introduced. Yet during each two-year session of Congress members each sponsor an average of 17 bills in the House and 35 bills in the Senate. Additionally, most legislators co-sponsor at least another 200 bills. There are three main reasons why members submit so much legislation despite a 95% failure rate.[92]

Legislative focus is one.[93] Members submit legislation on subjects that particularly interest them and are related to their committee assignments. Members do this to begin to build a record that may someday lead to enactment.

Personal commitment is a second and related motivation. Some members believe deeply in promoting some change and persistently file legislation to accomplish it no matter what the odds of success are. West Virginia's Jennings Randolph introduced 11 resolutions in first the House and then the Senate beginning in 1942 to lower the national voting age to 18. He was not successful, though, until 1971 when Congress finally passed the Twenty-Sixth Amendment and sent it to the states.

Electoral motivations are a third reason for sponsoring legislation. Legislators want to appear to be trying to benefit their constituents even if the effort fails. Therefore, legislators submit bills in order to publicize them in their districts, to respond to the requests of interest groups, and to counter potential attacks by future electoral opponents.[94]

Committee Action

Once introduced, measures are sent to one or more committees in each chamber for consideration. The norm is one committee in each chamber, but in recent years the complexity of legislation and the competing demands of committees to take jurisdiction have made multiple referrals more common, especially in the House. Now, the Speaker sends nearly 20% of all bills to more than one committee.[95] It is also not uncommon for multiple bills on a single subject to be introduced and for each to be referred to one or more committees. During the push for national health-care legislation, the final legislation that emerged in 2010 was an amalgam of a range of different bills. Three House committees (Energy and Commerce, Ways and Means, and Education and Labor) and two Senate committees (Finance and Health, Education, Labor, and Pensions) all played a major role, and a half dozen committees played a minor one. The committee system performs three functions.

The complexity of many bills gives committees a strong role in shaping a measure's details. The average bill is only 15 pages long, but some are huge. This photo shows House Minority Leader John Boehner (R-OH) in 2009 with a copy of the then proposed health-care bill. It was 1,990 pages long, and its main body contained 234,812 words, more than the novel, Harry Potter and the Deathly Hallows (198,000 words). (AP Photo/Files)

Providing expertise is the first function. Committees provide expertise through the knowledge that many members and the committee staff have built up. In a system where Congress often has difficulty competing with the executive branch, such expertise is important to Congress's ability to perform its functions as an equal branch of government. The need for expertise is also a reason for the seniority system, despite its otherwise undemocratic reputation. Its proponents argue that the incentive of steadily advancing to the position of committee chair encourages members to remain on a committee and build up expertise.

Acting as a gatekeeper is the second function of committees in the legislative process. Most of the 95% of all bills and joint resolutions that are unsuccessful each Congress die in committee. Committees may hold public hearings on some of these measures, but faced with thousands of them, few pieces of legislation even get that much attention.

Why don't members revolt against such obstructionism? One reason is that the real survival rate is somewhat higher than it appears because multiple bills on the same topic are sometimes merged. Health-care legislation provides a prime example. A second reason is that members sometimes introduce legislation at the behest of an interest group without caring much or at all if it passes. In such cases, members are happy to leave it to one of the committees to do the dirty work. A negative decision by a committee is usually final because it is difficult to bring a measure to the floor if it has not cleared the committee. The process is especially daunting in the House. Its rules require a **discharge petition** signed by a majority (218) of all House members to force a bill out of committee.

Shaping legislation for subsequent action on the floor is a third committee function. Because the committees often have extensive authority over the bills they are considering, there is often intense bargaining over the provisions of a proposal among executive branch officials, the leadership, committee members, interest group representatives, and others during the committee stage over the provisions of the bill.

Intrabranch and Interbranch Negotiations

Especially for important legislation, its movement through Congress does not occur in a vacuum. Instead, the legislation is also shaped in part by negotiations within each House and between each chamber and the White House. As health-care legislation moved toward floor debate in the two chambers in 2010, the leaders of each house along with the White House became increasingly involved in working out the final details that would be presented for debate. The Speaker took personal change of the negotiations in the House, and Senate Majority Leader Harry M. Reid (D-NV) led the negotiations in his chamber. Members of the Obama administration led by White House Chief of Staff Rahm Emanuel also often sat in. Among other concerns, Reid looked for ways to bridge the differences between senators who were determined to have a government-run program as one option and senators who were dead set against it. On the House side, Pelosi had to deal with such issues as the struggle over abortion funding between pro-choice and pro-life members. Both leaders had to deal with cost containment demands by Blue Dog (moderate) Democrats.

Throughout the process the White House was involved in seeking to achieve legislation that would both meet the president's preferences and also be able to pass Congress. At first Obama avoided becoming too closely involved in the details, but as time went on and it appeared that opponents might be able to kill the proposal altogether, Obama went on a public affairs offensive and also became much more closely involved in the negotiations within Congress. The role of the president as legislative leader is detailed in Chapter 12.

Floor Action

House and Senate procedures differ considerably. Although the majority party leaders in both chambers have considerable influence over legislative scheduling, bills favored by the leadership in the House are more likely to move expeditiously to a final vote there than are bills supported by the Senate leadership in its chamber.

The House takes up each bill under a rule specifically crafted for it by the Rules Committee. These rules are important management tools for the Speaker and majority leader, who work closely with the Rules Committee. During the House's consideration of health-care legislation, one pivotal point was when anti-abortion Democrats demanded that the rule governing debate allow them to offer an amendment to tighten the ban on spending public funds for abortions. Over the angry objections of pro-choice Democrats, the Rules Committee at the behest of the Speaker permitted the amendment, which passed on a narrow vote.

In contrast to the House's relatively rigid procedures, the Senate operates under much looser rules. These rule generally emphasize the traditional independent authority of each senator in the legislative process. Two ways of seeing this are to look at amendments and filibusters.

Amendments   Senators have much more freedom than House members to offer amendments because bills there are not governed by a rule on the Senate floor. The result is that many more amendments are offered in the Senate than in the House. During the 110th Congress, for instance, the Senate considered 5,704 amendments. Only 1,185 amendments were offered in the House.

Amendments are usually related to the topic of the bill, but there is a type of amendment called a **rider**, that is extraneous to the legislation. Most riders are attached to appropriations bills as a way of putting opponents to the rider, whether in Congress or by the president, in the position of having to either derail the entire appropriations bill or accept the rider. When, for example, it became clear in 2009 that the Senate would not extend the federal hate crimes act to protect those who are gay, congressional leaders attached the protection to a defense appropriations bill. House Minority Leader John A. Boehner (R-OH) protested that "radical social policy . . . is being put on the defense authorization bill . . . because they [the Democratic leadership] probably can't pass it on its own."[96] Nevertheless, the appropriations measure with its hate-crimes rider passed both houses and was signed into law by the president.

Riders are also used to attach pork-barrel funding to legislation. For example, Senator Debbie Stabenow (D-MI) amended a recent appropriation bill for the Department of Agriculture to "provide market loss assistance for apple producers," who are numerous in Michigan.

Filibusters   Perhaps the most important and controversial example of the individual authority of senators is the chamber's tradition of unlimited debate. This prevents a final vote on a measure or an amendment before the Senate by requiring that debate continues as long as any senator wants to continue presenting his or her views. In effect, this enables a minority of senators, sometimes even one senator, to prevent a vote on a bill by using a **filibuster**.[97] A filibuster is a legislative tactic that involves continuing to debate for the sole reason of trying kill a bill or force changes to it. The Senate has a procedure to invoke **cloture** (end debate), but doing so requires a vote of 60 senators under Rule 22.[98] Because it is difficult to get that many senators to agree to close debate, the filibuster is a powerful parliamentary tactic.[99]

Although the use of filibusters in the Senate dates back to at least 1826, there is growing concern about them because of their increased use in recent years. Prior to 1900, the Senate averaged less than one filibuster a year. That increased to an average of only about two a year between 1900 and the mid-1960s. Then filibuster activity began to increase, mostly due to efforts by conservative Southern Democrats and Republicans to block liberal social and economic legislation. A related change was that the parliamentary maneuvering related to filibusters increased even faster than the number of filibusters. This has been caused by such tactics as not only filibustering to defeat the main bill, but also amendments and other motions. As a result of this, the number of cloture votes has also risen. Another related change has been the success of invoking cloture—stopping debate. Of the 49 cloture votes between 1919 and 1972, only 16% succeeded in ending debate. However, as the frequency of filibuster activity grew, the willingness of senators to support cloture also grew. This has resulted in recent years in about half of all cloture votes succeeding.

In the most recent years, filibuster activity has escalated even more steeply, as indicated in Figure 11.7. Indeed, filibuster activity is now routine on the most important votes ("key votes") in Congress. Cloture petitions were filed for 50% or more of the key votes since 1990, including more than 80% of these votes in 2008.[100]

One probable reason for the escalation of threatened and employed filibusters is the increased partisanship found in Congress. It should be noted that counting filibusters is tricky because there is no announcement that one is underway and therefore no official record that it ever happened unless it is challenged with a

FIGURE 11.7 Cloture Motions in the Senate

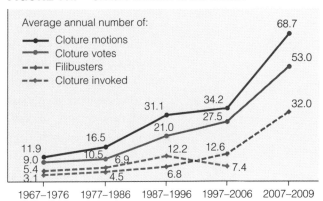

This figure measures the number of filibusters and the intensity of filibustering maneuvering through cloture motions, cloture votes, and the number of times cloture was successfully invoked. Although the annual number of filibusters rose only modestly and even declined between 1997 and 2006, the intensity of maneuvering rose sharply, with many more motions being filed and votes taken. This indicates multiple efforts to filibuster individual bills.

Data sources: For filibusters through 2006, see Lauren Cohen Bell and L. Marvin Overby, "Extended Debate Over Time: Patterns and Trends in the History of Filibusters in the U.S. Senate," paper presented at the Midwest Political Science Association convention, Chicago IL, 2007. For cloture motions and votes, see the Historian of the United States Senate on the Web at http://www.senate.gov/pagelayout/reference/cloture_motions/clotureCounts.htm.

cloture motion. Other approaches to measuring filibuster activity include counting cloture motions and cloture votes, but neither of these measures gives a complete picture.[101] Still, the overall picture clear in Figure 11.7 is that the filibuster
has become an increasingly common method for the minority party in the Senate
to try to block measures or force compromises. This was first notable in the frequent use of filibusters beginning in the 1990s to block judicial nominees and now
has spread to other legislative matters. For example, the main Senate health-care
bill (H.R. 3296) in 2009–2010 saw a level of filibuster activity constant enough to
spark eight cloture motions and three cloture votes.

Some defend the Senate tradition of unlimited debate including the ability to
filibuster as a way of protecting the interests of the few against the tyranny of the
majority. It is also the case though that the Senate has moved at least partially away
from the idea of passing legislation and confirming nominees by a simple majority
(50% + 1) of the senators voting to a de facto requirement of needing 60% of all
senators to pass a measure. This need for a supermajority is questionable as a matter of democracy and also increases the chances for stalemate in the Senate.

The obvious question is, "Why doesn't the Senate change the rule?" The
answer is that whichever party is in the majority and could do so also knows that
it will almost surely someday be the minority party. Then its members will want to
use filibusters to gain leverage in the Senate.

When debate is concluded on a bill or other measures, the item moves to a
vote. There are three kinds of votes: *voice votes*, with the presiding officer deciding
which side is more numerous; *standing votes*, with the presiding officer counting
those for and against; and *roll call votes*. Most important votes are taken by roll call.
During these votes, each member (orally in the Senate, electronically in the House)
records his or her "aye" or "nay." During the 110th Congress, there were 1,876
such votes in the House and 657 in the Senate. These make each member's voting
record easily available. Most citizens do not avail themselves of this wealth of information, but some do (the so-called attentive public), as do many interest groups.

Adjustment and Final Passage

Sometimes the House and Senate pass different versions of the same legislation.
When this occurs, the two versions are sent to a **conference committee**. Because
of the noncontroversial nature of most legislation, less than 20% of all bills and
joint resolutions passed by both houses wind up in a conference committee. But
nearly 50% of the most important and complex legislation does. This results in
about 70 conference committees during an average two-year Congress.

The Speaker and the Senate majority leader have some say over membership,
but 80% of all conference committees are made up exclusively of the chairs and

other senior members of the committees with jurisdiction over the bill in the two houses. Most conference committees have members of both parties, but it is not uncommon when a bill has passed the two houses with one party overwhelmingly in favor and the other equally opposed for the ensuing conference committee to be made up only of members from the majority party. Whatever their membership, conference committees do not operate in a bubble, and not far off stage for many bills, the leaders of the two houses and White House officials are also involved in what the committee decides.

The goal of the conference committee is to reach a compromise that resolves the differences between the Senate and House versions of the legislation. Conference committees can be very important to the final shape of a law because there are many issues on which it is not possible simply to split the difference.[102] When both sets of conferees agree on a compromise version, it goes back to the two houses. Neither house can amend the compromise bill. Each must either pass it, defeat it, or send it back to the conference committee with "instructions" that indicate the chamber's objections. It is not uncommon for a bill to move back and forth between its conference committee and the floor of one or both chambers before final passage.

Presidential Action

Once the House and Senate have passed a unified bill, the final phase on the way to becoming a law involves its being sent to the president. The president's ability to reject legislation by vetoing it gives him considerable leverage in the legislative process, as is discussed in Chapter 12.[103]

When presented with legislation, the president has three options. One is to sign it into law. The second possibility is a **veto**. By this action, the president sends the measure with his objections back to the house where it originated. If both houses **override** the veto by a two-thirds vote, then the measure becomes a law. A third option for the president is to do nothing, to put the measure in his pocket, so to speak. In this case, there are two possible outcomes. If Congress has adjourned, then the bill dies after 10 days by what is called a **pocket veto**. If, however, Congress has remained in session, then after 10 days of presidential inaction the measure become law without his signature by what might be called **pocket passage**.

EVALUATING CONGRESS

We began this chapter with the observation that the American public takes a dim view of Congress and with Gerald Ford's suggestion that people would think better of Congress if they only understood it better. Now that we do know more about

One conundrum when evaluating Congress is that while most Americans, like the people at this 2009 Tea Party rally in Orlando, Florida, disapprove of the job Congress is doing, the same Americans reelected most members who run for reelection. (Big Stock Photo)

Congress, it is fitting to finish this chapter by evaluating some of the criticism leveled at it.[104]

Indictment: Congress is a fragmented, inefficient labyrinth. *Defense:* True, but these traits can also be an asset. Fragmentation arguably gives individuals and groups multiple access points that can be used to try to influence the process. Fragmentation also may be a necessary part of the specialization that Congress utilizes to deal with a complex world. Moreover, whether Congress is slow and inefficient or wisely deliberative is a matter of perspective. China's parliament, the People's Congress, meets only a few days a year and manages to pass lots of legislation very expeditiously, but it is hardly a good model for a democracy.

Indictment: Congress is too self-perpetuating. *Defense:* It is true that the combination of the incumbency advantage and the large number of party-safe districts keeps turnover low. But surveys show that most people believe that their own representatives are doing a good job. Moreover, term limits deny voters the democratic opportunity to elect whomever they want as many times as they want. It can also be said that the low turnover in Congress allows its members to build up the expertise to deal with the complex problems the country faces.

Indictment: Congress is unresponsive and unrepresentative. *Defense:* There is no denying that Congress does not always follow the public will, but those who favor the trustee model believe that is good.[105] Even the general public does not want policy makers to slavishly follow public opinion, as Chapter 6 shows. Perhaps more importantly, studies show that legislators are concerned with public opinion and that especially when there is strong constituency pressure, most members vote as delegates. It is also the case that the policy opinions of members often coincide with opinion in their districts and that legislation passed by Congress parallels national public opinion more often than not. It must also be added that insofar as Congress is not fully responsive, the problem may be with the citizens, most of whom cannot even name all three of their legislators in Congress, much less tell you how any one of them voted on even a single bill. Since we also know that most members carefully watch public opinion, it follows that an active public is almost certainly the best way to ensure a responsive Congress.

Indictment: Congress is too partisan. *Defense:* If taken to the extreme, it is unhealthy to have the parties bickering in Congress and seeking electoral advantage rather than thinking of the national interest. There is particular concern in times of **divided government** when one party has the White House and the other party controls one or both houses of Congress. Yet it can also be said that so-called partisan disagreement is often a matter of the parties disagreeing over what the national interest is, not ignoring it.[106] It is healthy to have parties disagree in a democracy because doing so gives the voters a choice. That is the point of elections. As for the perils of divided government, there is no scholarly consensus on whether or not divided government creates gridlock.[107]

Indictment: Congress is driven by big money. *Defense:* Clearly, immense sums of money from interest groups and other large donors flow into the election coffers of incumbents. It would also be naïve to imagine those dollars are not buying improved access to legislators and some other advantages. That is not ideal, but in the final analysis, as Chapters 7 and 10 point out, no causal link has been established between who gives contributions and how the recipient legislators later vote.[108] There is a relationship between contributions and policy positions, but it may be that groups contribute to members who favor their causes rather than members favoring the causes of contributors.

Indictment: Congress is too often corrupt and unethical. *Defense:* Unfortunately, a Congress rarely goes by without some members or staff winding up in ethical or legal hot water. The year 2009 alone saw two former congressional aides plead guilty to corruption charges, and former Representative William J. Jefferson (D-LA) was convicted of soliciting bribes and money laundering. Should these individual acts cast a shadow on Congress as a whole? Between 1980 and 2010, about 20 members or former members of Congress have been indicted for crimes committed while in office, and 90% have been convicted or plead guilty. At the same time though, all but a tiny fraction of legislators and staff members has served honorably.

When all is said and done regarding the long list of complaints about Congress, it would be fatuous to pretend that it is an ideal democratic institution. Yet it is way too cynical to portray it as corrupt, undemocratic, unrepresentative, and ineffective. Surveys of the public, the ultimate jury, regularly show that it favors one or another reform of Congress. Yet when Americans were asked if Congress worked so poorly that it should be disbanded in favor of a new system of government, four times more respondents wanted to keep Congress than wanted to abolish it.[109] Perhaps therein lies wisdom.

SUMMARY

The chances of being elected to Congress depend all or in part on meeting the constitutional requirements, having the right background, and running in the right place at the right time. The best time and place to run initially is when there is no incumbent seeking reelection because incumbents are very likely to be reelected since they enjoy many advantages, including better name recognition and the ability to raise more campaign funds.

Members of Congress represent the nation but are not representative of a cross-section of the American electorate. Women and minorities are underrepresented, although the representation of both groups is growing. There are various theories about what representation means. The delegate theory holds that members should represent the views of their constituents; the trustee theory argues that representatives should use their own judgment to determine their positions. The idea of substantive representation is that legislators should represent the interests of the general public; the notion of descriptive representation holds that groups are best represented by legislators of the same demographic characteristics. There are a number of factors that influence the decisions of legislators. These include party and ideology, constituency factors, and members' personal beliefs.

Congress is a decentralized organization made up of two chambers, many committees and subcommittees, and independent-minded members. Congress has struggled during its history with how much power its leaders should have. Because the House is larger and more structured, its leaders, particularly the Speaker, are more powerful than the leaders in the Senate. Committees are a key aspect of the organization of Congress.

There are numerous standing and other types of committees. Most committees are organized around and have jurisdiction over specific policy areas and have a very strong say in the success or failure of any bill or other measure that relates to its area of jurisdiction. The chair of each committee is a powerful figure who plays a central role in that committee's operations. Committee assignments are one of the most important aspects of a member's congressional service because these assignments help determine expertise, influence, and ability to do constituency service.

Congress possesses an impressive array of powers, including the power to organize itself internally and conduct its business as it chooses; make laws; appropriate funds; raise revenue and structure taxes; organize and oversee the government; investigate matters within its legislative purview; impeach, try, and remove federal officials; confirm or reject presidential nominees for executive and judicial posts; and ratify or reject treaties. To become law, most bills and other formal legislative actions go through a process that is similar in both houses. Most measures are introduced by one or more members of Congress. They then are reviewed by one or more committees that provide expertise, shape the legislation, and decide whether it will proceed further. Measures that pass committee go to the floor of the two houses for debate and vote. Measures passed by both houses go to the president for acceptance or veto.

CHAPTER 11 GLOSSARY

bicameral legislature A legislative body with two chambers.

bill The most common type of measure that may become law through the legislative process.

casework The activities of legislators that involve dealing with the needs and complaints of individual constituents with federal agencies.

cloture A move to shut off debate in the Senate and move to a vote. It requires a vote of 60 senators to pass.

conference committee A special committee with members of both the House and Senate formed to resolve differences in a piece of legislation passed by the two chambers so that a unified bill can be presented for consideration in each chamber.

congressional-executive agreements International agreements between the United States and other countries that are not treaties but, like treaties, require subsequent congressional consent to be valid. Unlike treaties, which require Senate ratification by a two-thirds vote, congressional-executive agreements require the consent of both houses by majority vote.

congressional membership organizations Unofficial congressional policy-oriented caucuses through which like-minded members promote their related policy agendas.

constituents The people who live in an electoral unit, such as a district or state.

delegate theory The belief that representatives should make policy based on the majority view of their respective constituencies.

descriptive representation The concept that the demographic characteristics that describe the populace should also describe public officials.

discharge petition A demand that a committee discharge a bill for consideration on the House floor. It must be signed by 218 members to succeed.

divided government When the White House is in the hands of one party and one or both houses of Congress are controlled by the other party.

enumerated powers Authority of the federal government that is specifically mentioned in the Constitution, especially in Article 1, Section 8.

filibuster A legislative tactic using an extended speech or series of speeches in the Senate to halt progress on a measure.

fiscal year A budgetary year, which may not correspond to a calendar year. The federal fiscal year is from October 1 to September 30.

impeach An action by majority vote in the House of Representatives to indict a federal official. The trial is conducted by the Senate, with a two-thirds vote required to convict.

implied powers Powers of the federal government Congress that are not specifically mentioned in the Constitution but that are logically derived from the authority that is specified there. See "enumerated powers" and "necessary and proper clause."

joint committee A committee on which members of both the Senate and House sit.

majority leader The leader of the majority party in either the House or Senate.

majority-minority district An electoral district in which an ethnic or racial minority group is the majority.

minority leader The leader of the minority party in either the House or Senate.

necessary and proper clause Wording in Article 1, Section 8 of the Constitution that gives to Congress the authority to "make all laws which shall be necessary and proper for carrying into execution the foregoing [enumerated] powers, and all the other powers vested by this Constitution in the government of the United Sates." See "enumerated powers" and "implied powers."

override A vote by two-thirds of each house of Congress to enact a measure into law over the president's veto.

oversight Congressional review, usually by a committee, of how well agencies are functioning administratively and how they are implementing the laws enacted by Congress.

party caucus See "party conference."

party conference An organization of all the members of a party in one of the houses of Congress. Called a "party caucus" by House Democrats.

pocket passage A process whereby the president allows a bill to become law without signing it by not acting on it within 10 days while Congress is in session.

pocket veto A process whereby the president can prevent a bill from becoming law by not acting on it within 10 days while Congress is not in session.

politicos A term used to describe legislators who maneuver among the pressures of their reelection interests, their ideology, their issue preferences, and party influences to balance what they believe is right and what is politically expedient.

pork-barrel politics Legislators bringing federal funding and projects to their states and districts.

president pro tempore The second ranking member of the Senate after its president, the vice president of the United States. The position is primarily honorary and is filled by the senator of the majority party who has the longest service in the Senate.

professionalization of politics The movement toward elected and appointed officials, especially at the state and national levels, being career politicians rather than citizens temporarily engaging in public service before returning to their private professions and lives.

racial gerrymandering Manipulating the minority population in one or more electoral districts to increase or decrease minority influence and representation.

representation   The core concept in a republic that justifies a few officials making policy on the behalf of those who chose them.

rider   An amendment that is extraneous to the topic of a bill.

select/special committees   Those committees created to consider matters that do not fit well into the jurisdiction of any standing committee or to fulfill a specific purpose, such as conducting an investigation.

seniority system   The practice of selecting committee chairs based on which member of the majority party has the longest continuous service on a committee.

Speaker of the House   The presiding officer and most influential member of the House of Representatives.

standing committees   Permanent committees of Congress, usually with jurisdiction over a policy area.

substantive representation   The concept of elected officials favoring policies whose substance is in the public interest rather than the group from which the official is drawn. See "descriptive representation."

trustee theory   The belief that representatives should make policy based on their own view of the public interest.

unicameral legislature   A parliament with one house.

veto   A formal act by which a president returns a measure to Congress, stating his objections.

whip   An assistant party leader in the House or Senate who is a communications link between the party leaders and members.

THE PRESIDENCY

12

YOU DECIDE: Make Naturalized Citizens Eligible to Become President?

One symbol of American democratic equality is the adage, "Anyone can grow up to be president." In reality, though, many Americans cannot become president. What disqualifies former Secretary of State Madeleine Albright; former Governor Arnold Schwarzenegger of California; Representative Ileana Ros-Lehtinen (R-FL), chair of the House Foreign Affairs Committee, and several other members of Congress; and 38 million other Americans is being a "naturalized citizen" (an immigrant who became a citizen). The Constitution allows only "natural born" citizens (U.S. citizens at birth) to be president.

This limitation sprang from fear that U.S. independence might be subverted if a naturalized citizen who retained loyalty to Great Britain became president. Worry about the loyalty of a foreign-born president continues. "The president of the United States should be a native-born citizen. Your allegiance is driven by your birth," argues Senator Dianne Feinstein (D-CA).[1] Others doubt that immigrants ever fully adopt American culture. Globalization has intensified this view, with the inflow of foreign goods, ideas, and people making some Americans even more defensive of their culture and resistant to a one-time "outsider" becoming president.[2]

Those who favor eligibility for all citizens dismiss the fear of a traitorous foreign-born leader as probably never valid and now absurd. A second contention is that the barrier makes second-class citizens out of the 12% of the population that is foreign-born. Arguably adding to the injustice, these new Americans bear the same responsibilities of citizenship, ranging from paying taxes to military service, as native-born citizens. Advocates of removing the barrier also suggest that while its origin was not racially motivated, its impact has become discriminatory because now over 85% of immigrants are Latinos or other people of color. Therefore, barring naturalized citizens from being president disproportionately limits nonwhites.

Whatever the validity of the various arguments, the natural born citizen clause of the Constitution has proven durable. Congress has refused to approve any of the more than two dozen amendments proposed to change the clause, and two-thirds of the American public supports it.[3] Do you?

INTRODUCING THE PRESIDENCY

The president is the most powerful actor in the U.S. political system, but presidential power is never static. It has ebbed and flowed historically, and it also varies during the tenure of any one president. This chapter will examine these power fluctuations and their impact on the political system. During our exploration of presidential power, you will find that:

★ The presidential model of government concentrates power in a single office and person.

★ Presidential power is linked to the institutional presidency, particularly the increased size and strength of the Executive Office of the President.

★ The trend toward centralization of policy making in the White House raises several concerns.

★ Presidents can be analyzed as a national leader, a partisan politician, and a human being.

★ The power of the presidency has grown absolutely and relative to that of Congress since 1789 and to greater and lesser degrees has been preeminent since the 1930s.

★ How much power any individual president has is based on such factors as his job skills, public opinion, the type of policy at issue, and the situation.

★ The Constitution gives the president considerable formal power as the chief executive officer, commander in chief, head diplomat, and chief legal officer and also restrains those functions.

★ The informal powers of and limits on the president relate to public expectations and his power to persuade.

Introducing the Presidency and Demographic Diversity

Presidential power partly results from the president's status as the "personification and the symbol of the United States"[4] Of course, no single person could accurately personify the demographic diversity of the American people, but legal and societal barriers have limited the pool of Americans from which the president could be chosen. As we have seen, naturalized citizens have not been part of that pool. Even more broadly, the de facto pool historically excluded anyone who was not white, male, Protestant, and heterosexual. The first move toward diversity occurred in 1960 when John F. Kennedy became the first Roman Catholic president. Forty-eight years later another barrier fell with the election of African American Barack Obama as president.

 Victoria C. Woodhull, candidate of the Equal Rights Party in 1872, was the first woman to run for president.

The diversity of the individuals in the leadership circle around the president including vice presidents, top White House officials, and Cabinet members has been only slightly less restricted. That is also changing, however, as we will see later in this chapter.

We will also see that increasing diversity is more than a symbolic advance. It expands and thereby enhances the perspectives of the country's leaders. Colin Powell, the first African American secretary of state, provides an example. American foreign policy has mostly ignored Africa because, as Secretary of State Henry Kissinger saw it, of "the low priority of our interests in the continent."[5] Powell saw the world differently. He increased U.S. attention to and support of Africa and was the "first secretary of state to have any intimate contact with African leaders." Explaining the connection between his race and his policy, Powell stressed that his first duty in dealing with Africa was "to do what is right as secretary of state of the United States of America." But, he added, deciding what was right had been "shaped, to some extent, by fact that [my grandparents] . . . came from somewhere on the west coast of Africa."[6]

Introducing the Presidency in a World of Difference

As this chapter proceeds, we will examine the presidency from a number of international perspectives. Some of these relate to globalization. Others involve comparing the U.S. presidency to the leadership structure in other countries.

National Leadership: U.S. and Global Diversity

Changing American attitudes about race, gender, and other societal categories have been part of global shifts in thinking, as Chapters 5, 6, and others discuss. This is also the case for the demographic diversification of national leaders.

It is still rare, but a few countries now choose leaders from outside the country's dominant racial/ethnic group. In 1997, Guyana, a country of mostly East Indian and African heritage people, elected Janet Rosenberg Jagan, an immigrant white woman (from Chicago), as its president. Alberto Fujimori, whose parents came from Japan to Peru in 1934, served as its president from 1990 to 2000. Nicolas Sarkozy, France's president since 2007, is the child of a Hungarian father and a French mother of Greek descent. Even more than these leaders, Barack Obama is a child of globalization. His father was from Kenya and a Muslim. His white mother was from Kansas, and Obama lived with her and his Indonesian stepfather in Indonesia.

Gender diversification among national leaders is also a global trend. Other than queens, no woman led her country as a fully empowered head of government until Prime Minister Sirivamo Bandaranaike of Sri Lanka took office in

As of April 2010, women were the most powerful government leader in 9 (5%) of the world's 194 countries.

FIGURE 12.1 Women Cabinet Ministers Compared

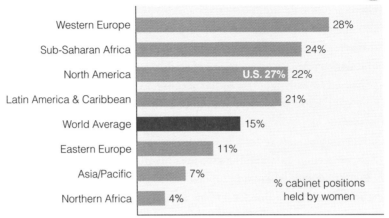

The trend toward greater gender diversification of the U.S. cabinet is part of a global change in that direction.
Notes and data source: Data are for 2007. Women's Environment & Development Organization report, *Getting the Balance Right In National Cabinets.*

1960. Since then, more than 40 other women have risen to the top leadership position in their countries. Commenting on this progress, Norway's Prime Minister Gro Harlem Brundtland noted dryly, "I was the first woman in 1,000 years [to lead my country]. Things are evolving gradually."[7]

The global gender diversification of national leaders is also evident at the ministry/cabinet level of government. Denmark's Secretary of Education Nina Bang was the first woman (1924) named to a national cabinet. Other countries followed, and in 1938 Secretary of Labor Frances Perkins became the first woman in the U.S. Cabinet. By 2007, 15% of the world's cabinet ministers were women. At that point, the United States was ahead of the curve, with 27% of the U.S. Cabinet posts held by women. The share of these posts held by women remained at 27% during President Obama's two years in office. The global status 2007 is in Figure 12.1.

Presidential Power and World Politics

Two changes in the world system have worked to enhance the power of the presidency. *Increasing international danger* is the first. Any illusion that Americans were safely guarded by their flanking oceans was destroyed by being dragged unwillingly into World War I and then World War II. Furthermore, the momentary sense of security that victory in 1945 brought was soon shattered by the onset of the scary cold war confrontation with the Soviet Union. Making matters worse, the ominous dawn of the age of nuclear weapons and intercontinental ballistic missiles meant that national annihilation was possibly minutes away. Some of these fears ebbed with the collapse of the Soviet Union in 1991, but they were replaced by the threat of terrorism symbolized by the 9/11 attacks. All of this has increased presidential power by creating a sense of danger that has cowed Congress and the public into accepting the nearly unilateral power of presidents to decide where and when to use military force and to take other unprecedented steps in the name of national security.

FIGURE 12.2 Growing Importance of Trade to the U.S. Economy

Reflecting globalization, trade has grown as a percentage of U.S. economic activity, measured here by gross national product (GNP). This increase has augmented presidential power over the economy because presidents have more authority over foreign commerce than over domestic economic policy.
Data source: U.S. Bureau of Economic Analysis.

Globalization has also enhanced presidential power. During a time of rapid economic globalization since World War II, for example, trade has expanded greatly as a percentage of the U.S. economy and, therefore, as a factor in American prosperity. This change is visible in Figure 12.2. The increased importance of trade has also expanded the power of presidents because they have a much greater say than does Congress in formulating international trade agreements and making other decisions affecting trade, international investment, and other aspects of U.S. economic foreign policy.

Since World War II, the heightened emphasis on national security and advancing globalization have combined to change the country's global stance from fitful isolationism to full internationalism. This shift has also changed the focus of presidents from what was normally a strong concentration on domestic affairs to a greater foreign policy/national security orientation. Even though President Barack Obama's first year was marked by a staggering U.S. economy and the drive to pass health-care reform, the White House's tabulation of the meetings, speeches, and other events that took up the president's time during 2009 indicated that a plurality of these events (37%) involved foreign policy or national security.

The Presidency in Comparative Perspective

Adopting a global perspective also enables us to compare the U.S. model of executive power with other democratic countries. One way to categorize democratic governments is based on the distribution of power between two key executive roles.[8] One, the **head of government,** is the government's chief operating officer and has a wide array of formal powers to administer the government. The second role is **head of state**. This official is supposed to be "above politics" and to serve as the prestigious symbol of the country and its people.

Parliamentary systems split executive leadership between a head of government, usually called the "prime minister" ("premier," "chancellor") and a head of state, who may be a monarch or a president. In Great Britain, the prime minister is the head of government and has almost all the power. The monarch is the head of state and has a mainly symbolic status. Usually in this type of system, the parliament elects the prime minister. The British House of Commons chooses the prime minister, for example. Additionally, prime ministers serve only as long as they have majority support in the parliament. Thus the term of a prime minister is variable.

Presidential systems vest all executive leadership in one office, the president. This empowers presidents by giving them both the formal powers of a head of government and the symbolic prestige of a head of state. Adding further to the power of presidents, they are usually elected directly by the people. Expressing this advantage, Harry S. Truman asserted that the "only [person] in Washington who represents all the people and is elected by all the people and who is the people's lobbyist is the president of the United States."[9] Prime ministers can make no such claim. Additionally, presidents, unlike prime ministers, serve a fixed-term of office and therefore do not depend on legislative support for their continuance in power.

British Prime Minister David Cameron (left) came to power as the head of a coalition government after his country's parliamentary election in May 2010 and will hold power only as long as he is backed by a majority in the House of Commons. President Barack Obama was elected independently of Congress in 2008 and serves a fixed, four-year term. Cameron shares executive authority with Queen Elizabeth II; Obama holds all U.S. executive authority. Which is more democratic, the British parliamentary system or the American presidential system? (AP Photo/Charles Dharapak)

Which is a better system? Some argue that the presidential model provides the strongest leadership. Having a fixed terms means that presidents, unlike prime ministers, do not have to worry about being brought down by parliament and can even for a time ignore public opinion and other political pressure if they are counter to the national interest. There is some evidence, for instance, that presidents are better able to limit deficit spending than are prime ministers.[10]

Critics of presidential systems argue that democracy is less secure in them than in parliamentary systems because strong presidents may become authoritarian.[11] Another argument against presidential systems is that they allow a leader to persist even if opposed by the public and legislature. Had the United States been a parliamentary system and had George Bush been its prime minister, then the Iraq War would have probably ended his time in office well before 2009, just as British public opposition to the war helped end the 10-year tenure of Prime Minister Tony Blair. A third critique of presidential systems is that they can be stalemated by *divided government*. This occurs when one party controls the presidency and another dominates the national legislature, a circumstance we will explore further below. Since the legislature elects and can unseat the prime minister in a parliamentary system, divided government is unlikely.[12]

It is not necessary to further detail the advantages and disadvantages of the models of executive authority to emphasize the point that how a country structures its executive branch has a significant impact of how government operates.

THE INSTITUTIONAL PRESIDENCY

A first step in our analysis of the U.S. presidency is to explore it as an institution. This entails looking at its organizational structure, then turning to its operation as a political actor.

The Organizational Structure of the Presidency

Although the president is the head of the executive branch, there is a distinction between the *presidency*, which includes the offices of the president, the vice president, and their key advisors, and the larger *executive branch*, which includes the vast assemblage of departments and agencies that make up the federal bureaucracy. Our focus here is on those offices and individuals who are closely linked to the president, rather than those that make up the extended executive branch.

The President

American presidents are the core of the of the U.S. political system. They have vast executive authority over a very large and powerful organization. They also exercise great personal authority as the "personification of the U.S. government" and American people.[13] Ironically, though, the size and scope of the U.S. government also limits presidents because it is too immense for a single individual to control effectively. Because what presidents should know and should do are far beyond the capabilities of any single individual, they rely heavily on the institutional presidency.

For most of American history, presidents had few staff resources to help them oversee the executive branch, formulate policy, communicate with the public, or undertake the other activities necessary to exercise leadership. More recently presidents have been supported by a larger array of offices and advisors within the White House that have added considerably to the power of the presidency. To explore these changes in the institutional presidency, we will take up its components: the vice president and the Cabinet, and its newer parts, the Executive Office of the President and the White House Office. We will also note the often key role of first ladies.

The Vice President

The vice presidency is a curious position. Other than replacing the president if necessary, a vice president's only formal duty is serving as president of the Senate. This limited role is explained in Chapter 11. With so few formal duties, vice presidents have often been marginalized. Many presidents and their vice presidents have not been close politically or personally. Sometimes they have even

John Adams, the first vice president, said of his office: "My country has in its wisdom contrived for me the most insignificant office that ever the invention of man contrived or his imagination conceived." That is an overstatement, but vice presidents still have few formal powers or set duties. (iStockphoto)

been rivals. As such, many presidents have neither consulted their vice presidents nor given them much to do. Indeed, frustrated vice presidents have sometimes disparaged their office. Among them, Texan John Nance "Cactus Jack" Garner (1933–1941) refused a third term, earthily declaring that his office was not "worth a warm pitcher of spit."

Recent presidents have given more responsibility to their vice presidents.[14] A few vice presidents, such as Dick Cheney (2001–2009), have wielded considerable influence. This change has occurred in part because most recent presidents have sought to cope with their job by delegating more authority to their vice president. Some vice presidents have also accrued power because of their individual skills as policy advocates and bureaucratic infighters.

Barack Obama's vice president, Joseph Biden, once called Cheney the "most dangerous vice president we've had probably in American history" because of his quest for power, and Biden pledged to take a more restrained role.[15] Time will tell how Biden fares. His most prominent policy position in 2009 was opposition to increasing U.S. troops in Afghanistan, and he was largely unsuccessful twice, once early in the year, once at the end of the year, when Obama ordered troop increases.

The Cabinet

Another curious institution is the **Cabinet**. It is not mentioned in the Constitution and has evolved mostly by tradition to now include the heads of the 15 executive branch departments. Presidents also designate five or six other "Cabinet-level" officials, such as the director of national intelligence. Like the vice president, the title "Cabinet" is loftier than its role. As Chapter 13 explains, the Cabinet has no authority, and presidents are under no obligation to seek its advice or to follow it. Individual Cabinet members may be influential advisors, but that standing derives more from a personal connection with the president than from an institutional one. Indeed, because each Cabinet member heads a major bureaucracy and sometimes promotes its views, even if they differ from the president's, the White House often views the Cabinet negatively. Richard Nixon once raged, "Screw the Cabinet. I'm sick of the whole bunch."[16] More benignly, President Bill Clinton's chief of staff, Leon Panetta, depicted the Cabinet as a "charade," and commented, "The only time you pull the Cabinet together is when you want to create a PR backdrop for whatever issue the president wants to get out."[17]

The Executive Office of the President

Understandably, presidents feel the need to have aides who are tied personally to them and working solely on their behalf. Congress long provided little or no money for such staff. George Washington's entire administrative staff numbered four. By 1900, the president's administrative staff had grown only to 12. Government continued to expand, however, and by the late 1930s a study called the "Brownlow Report" concluded that, "The president needs help." President Franklin D. Roosevelt used this report to convince Congress to enlarge the institutional presidency in 1939 by establishing the **Executive Office of the President (EOP)**: the personnel and offices that are connected directly to the White House and that focus on supporting the president.

One of Roosevelt's aims was to increase his role in national economic policy. To that end he also persuaded Congress to transfer the Bureau of the Budget from the Department of the Treasury to the EOP. Renamed the **Office of Management and Budget (OMB)** in 1970, this powerful agency prepares the president's annual budget proposal. It also helps oversee the bureaucracy on the president's behalf. One important way OMB does this is by reviewing other agencies' policy proposals, reports, testimony before Congress, and other public presentations for consistency with the president's policy agenda. Adding the Council of Economic Advisors to the EOP in 1946 further strengthened the president in setting national economic policy.

Increased U.S. involvement in world affairs after World War II led to the creation of the National Security Council (NSC) and its inclusion in the EOP in 1949. Although the NSC itself has no formal authority and has seldom been important as such, its staff provides "in-house" expertise for the president. Of particular importance is the head of the NSC staff, who also serves as the assistant to the president for national security affairs, or **national security advisor.** This official coordinates the information coming to the president from the various diplomatic, military, and intelligence agencies and monitors the implementation of international security policy for the president. Most national security advisors have also been important policy advisors, some have been directly involved in diplomacy, and a few have even rivaled or eclipsed the secretary of state. For one, Henry A. Kissinger overshadowed Secretary of State William P. Rogers and negotiated the end of the Vietnam War and the U.S. approach to China during President Nixon's first term. Another mark of the importance of the office is that several national security advisors have later become secretary of state. For one, Condoleezza Rice made that transition in 2005 as the first African American woman to serve as secretary of state.

The White House Office

Although the **White House Office** is legally a part of the EOP, it has its own identity. Whereas most of the EOP's other units have a legislatively mandated mission, the White House Office serves solely as a support system for the president. Various units attend to public relations, legislative liaison, legal matters, policy formation and oversight, and a range of other concerns.[18] The organization of the White

House Office tends to be fluid because each president shapes it to fit his wishes. For instance, President Obama added the Council on Women and Girls in 2009.

The president's **chief of staff** directs the White House Office and, to a degree, the rest of the EOP. Created in 1953, the importance and role of the chiefs of staff have varied depending on several factors.[19] One is how good the chief of staff's relationship with the president is. Another is based on the chief of staff's political and administrative skills.

President Obama's first chief of staff, Rahm Emanuel, was described by the *New York Times* as "perhaps the most influential White House chief of staff in a generation." A former member of Congress and an expert political operative, Emanuel reportedly had "his fingers in almost every decision, like who [got] invited to social events at the White House and how to shape economic and foreign policy." Moreover, his notoriously intense, explicative laden "piledriver" style served, according to another top White House advisor, as a helpful counterbalance to President Obama's more "zen-like" approach to politics and negotiations.[20] Indeed, Emanuel's aggressive style earned him the nickname "Rahmbo." After Emanuel resigned in October 2010 to run for mayor of Chicago, Obama named Peter Rouse as chief of staff. Rouse brought with him many years in various Senate staff positions, including Obama's chief of staff there, and a record of influence that had earned him the informal title, "101st senator." Rouse's quiet demeanor was in such sharp contrast to Emanuel's personality that the president joked, "Obviously these two men have slightly different styles."[21]

Like many who have held the office, White House Chief of Staff Rahm Emanuel, here conferring with President Obama, was one of the most powerful individuals in the government during his tenure (2009–2010). (AP Photo/Charles Rex Arbogast, File)

The First Lady

Although the president's spouse has no formal role in government, some have had substantial influence. Moreover, they have been able to exercise increased influence as the role of women in society has grown.[22] Laura Bush, for one, seemed to have an important measure of influence on "Bushie," as she sometimes calls her husband. As she has put it, "Of course we talk about issues and have influence on each other."[23] Michelle Obama has followed the modern model of an active first lady, with one analyst describing her as "more active and public than any first lady that I can remember."[24] During the president's first year, Ms Obama focused on promoting improvements in health care, education, and advancing the welfare of women and girls. However, she became more active in partisan politics in 2010 as the president's job approval ratings sank (44% in July) while her favorability rating among the public was a lofty 66% and as the congressional elections approached.[25] At first, she avoided overt campaigning, but that changed in October when her travel schedule included an eleven-day trip to raise money and otherwise campaign for electorally endangered Democratic incumbents in nine states. Meeting with a group of endangered Democratic representatives, President Obama conceded that given his poor standing in the polls, "You may not even want me to come to your district." But, he added, "I'll bet you want Michelle."[26]

The Politics of the Institutionalized Presidency

From a handful of aides in 1939, the EOP has grown to a staff of about 2,000 with an annual budget of approximately $400 million. This increase is not exceptional given the expanding size and scope of the government, but there are issues that relate to the accumulation of power, especially in the White Office. Critics of the Brownlow Report argued in 1939 that it would further "Roosevelt's dictatorial ambitions." And even Louis Brownlow conceded that his recommendation for strengthening the institutional presidency had unforeseeable constitutional implications that he compared to a "rabbit stowed in the hat."[27]

The White House Office and Policy Making

One characteristic of the rabbit has proven to be the creation of "a large presidential staff [that] has centralized much policy-making power within the presidency."[28] Recent presidents have regularly designated aides as so-called *czars* to oversee policy in one or another area and have otherwise moved to give their staff important roles in making and implementing policy. President Obama, for example, created the White House's Office of Energy and Climate Change Policy, named Carol M. Browner as its head, and made her his energy and environment czar. That gave Browner de facto authority over such agencies as the Department of Energy and the Environmental Protection Agency. This increasing shift of the policy-making initiative from the Cabinet departments to the White House raises a series of concerns related to the constitutional system of checks and balances, to the quality of policy, and to the isolation of the president.

Check and Balances   The expanded role of the White House staff in making and implementing policy raises two issues about the Constitution's checks and balances. First, most of the top positions in the White House Office are not subject to the Senate confirmation that is required of agency heads. Second, and again unlike agency officials, Congress cannot require White House staff members to testify and submit information. When Congress has tried to do so, presidents have usually refused to allow their aides to appear before Congress or supply documents. When doing this, presidents have claimed **executive privilege**, the asserted right to protect the separation of powers.[29] The result, according to some, is to damage the system of check and balances by undermining the constitutional authority of Congress to check the executive branch by confirming its more important appointed officials and overseeing its agencies. Reacting to the number of czars designated by President Obama, Senator Lamar Alexander (R-TN) labeled the moves "undemocratic," and Senator Robert Byrd (D-VA) protested the "rapid and easy accumulation of power" by the White House staff being achieved by its taking "direction and control of programmatic areas that are the statutory responsibility of Senate-confirmed officials"[30]

Policy Quality   Shifting policy making and even policy implementation to the White House can also arguably hurt policy quality. One worry is that the shift marginalizes whole agencies and the expertise they possess. One Cabinet secretary in the Clinton administration called the White House staff the "arrogant center" and contended that, "from the point of the view of the White House staff, Cabinet officials are provincial governors presiding over primitive territories. Anything of importance occurs in the imperial palace [the White House]."[31]

Another concern is that inserting the White House staff into operational decisions can cause confusion and fragment policy. For example, hearings in 2006 about what went wrong with the federal response to Hurricane Katrina found, among other things, that Michael Brown, head of the Federal Emergency Management Agency, ignored his boss, the Secretary of the Department of Homeland Security (DHS) and instead dealt directly with the White House Office. Brown claimed he wanted to avoid "red tape" in the department, but a DHS official accused Brown of really not wanting anyone "to interfere with . . . what he was doing," Brown called this allegation "just baloney," and the White House bemoaned the "conflicting reports" that it received about the damage Katrina had done.[32] The blame game continued, but the point is that having White House Office staff become part of an alternative chain of command has disadvantages.

Isolation of the President   A third worry is that the White House staff isolates the president. To a degree, isolation is inherent in the office. For one, President Bill Clinton complained that the White House seemed like "the crown jewel in the American penal system . . . because it is so easy to get isolated here."[33] The large White House staff has added to the problem by surrounding the president with a phalanx of aides eager to laud him, demean his opponents, and promote policy based on what is good politically for the president rather than what is good for the country. Additionally, the president's staff sometimes seeks to shield him from problems. One aide to President Bush commented in 2005, "His inner circle takes pride in being able to tell him 'everything is under control,' [even] when . . . it is not." Aides are also averse to disagreeing with the president. Another Bush aide recalls that the first time "I told him he was wrong, he started yelling at me." After retreating from the Oval Office, the aide recalled, "I went and had dry heaves in the bathroom."[34]

Shaping the President's Image

A second function of the White House Office that worries many observers is its heavy focus on acting like the president's personal public relations firm. Presidents understand the importance of their image. "I believe that 90% of this stuff is image," Lyndon Johnson once exclaimed about his ability to lead the public.[35] Understandably then, most presidents have tried to project a positive image. However, they had limited ability through the 1800s to reach out to the public. Then advances in technology began to add to the ability of presidents to increase the attention they receive, to try to shape it, and to seek to capitalize on it politically.

Theodore Roosevelt led the way. He realized that rapid communications through the telegraph and the advent of inexpensive, mass circulation newspapers gave him the opportunity to use his office as a "bully pulpit" to build support among Americans for himself and his polices. Later presidents sought ways to further project their image. Woodrow Wilson held the first scheduled press conference in 1915, and Herbert Hoover appointed the first press secretary in 1929. Radio and then television further added to the ability of presidents to "go public," to regularly and quickly project themselves into Americans' homes in order to sell themselves and their programs.[36]

President Theodore Roosevelt's view of his office as a "bully pulpit" from which he could try to rally public opinion to support his policies was the forerunner of the image campaign that every president now pursues. Here Roosevelt is speaking in New Jersey. (Library of Congress)

From these beginnings, the president's public relations effort has become a complex operation in the White House Office that monitors public opinion and seeks to manipulate the public image of the president and his policies.[37] Under President Obama various White House Office units focusing on this goal include the Office of Public Engagement, the Office of the Press Secretary, the Office of Communications, the Office of Speechwriting, and the Office of Political Affairs.

Some techniques, such as press conferences, have fallen out of favor with the White House because the press has become more adversarial over time and because press conferences are harder to control that some other types of communications. President Obama held 11 solo press conferences during his first six months in office, then none during his second six months. Instead, he has favored longer one-on-one interviews where he feels he can explain his positions in depth. Obama granted 161 such interviews during his first year in office, more than three times the number given by either President Bush or President Clinton during their first year.[38]

Another change has been for presidents to increase their travel around the country. On average, Presidents Kennedy through Reagan spent an average of only 3 of their first 100 days in office traveling outside the metropolitan Washington, D.C., area. By comparison, Presidents Clinton, Bush, and Obama averaged 18 days of their first 100 days in office on domestic travel.[39] Overall during his first year, Obama traveled away from Washington 46 times, visiting 58 cities in 30 states.

Adding yet another new dimension to presidential communications, President Obama has White House sites on Facebook, MySpace, Twitter, YouTube, and other social network sites.[40] The White House also maintains several blog sites. Just one indication of the popularity of these sites is that in September 2009, the White House YouTube site had more than 87,000 subscribers and was recording about 2 million hits a month. Obama has also changed how presidents utilize the more traditional media outlets. For example, he became the first sitting president to appear on a late night talk show when he was a guest on Jay Leno's *The Tonight Show* in July 2009 and the first sitting president to visit a daytime talk show when he appeared on *The View,* hosted by six women including Barbara Walters and Whoopi Goldberg, in July 2010.

All this raises concerns about image trumping substance in White House. Transparency is one victim, and evidence regularly surfaces of attempts by the White House to suppress unfavorable information, sometimes by classifying it as secret. Similarly, explanations of events and proposals issued by the White House are more likely to be the administration's spin, its self-interested view, than to be the truth, the whole truth, and nothing but the truth. Certainly it is naïve to expect any politician, including the president and his staff, to be unflinchingly candid at all times. Yet it also true that a public accustomed to spin has become jaded and suspicious.

Ironically, these efforts to promote the president have not been very successful. One indication is that the media's coverage of the president has become increasingly negative in recent decades, as Chapter 8 discusses.[41] It is also evident from two different ways of looking at **presidential approval ratings**—the share of the public that approves of how the president is doing his job. Over the long term, as Figure 12.3 shows, presidents' ratings have trended lower.

FIGURE 12.3 History of Presidential Approval Ratings

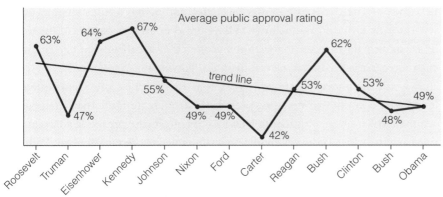

The average public approval of presidents has tended to decline.
Notes and data source: Data drawn from Gallup polls taken in June of each year and averaged for each president. Obama's are for June 2009 and 2010 only.

The second, shorter-term approach to analyzing the public standing of presidents is to look at the approval ratings of each during his time in office. Here again, the general trend is decline. Beginning with Kennedy, every president through George W. Bush except Bill Clinton had a lower approval rating in June of their last full year as president than in June of their first year. Similarly, Barack Obama's popularity began to sag almost as soon as he took office. Neither the long-term nor short-term trends mean that the efforts of presidents to promote themselves always fail. Rather, the trends show that the White House public relations effort is just one of many factors that affect the public's perception of the president and his programs.

THE PERSONAL PRESIDENCY

For all the importance of the institutional presidency, the president is a person. Therefore, it is important to examine what motivates presidents as individuals by examining how presidents act as national leaders, as partisan politicians, and as very human individuals.

The President as National Leader

As national leader, presidents face the same dilemma as members of Congress regarding policy positions. Should a president adhere to the *delegate model* and follow public opinion or adhere to the *trustee model* and support policies that he believes are in the national interest even if the public disagrees. Research shows that presidents usually support policies already favored by the public. According to a study of Presidents Eisenhower through Clinton, they advocated policies that were already favored by a majority of the public an average of 66% of the time.[42] This parallels the delegate model, but it is often the case that the public and president agree, rather than that the president is following public opinion.

It would be a mistake, though, to assume that because presidents often follow public opinion that doing so necessarily detracts from their leadership. One scholar advises against underestimating what he calls the president's "facilitator" role because even if the public wants policy to move in a certain direction, "change is not inevitable, and facilitators make things happen that otherwise would not."[43]

It is also true that presidents see themselves as the national leader and claim that they pursue the country's interest as they see it. Moreover, there are times when presidents proceed despite majority public opposition. President George W. Bush's persistence in Iraq provides a stark example. He defied "public opinion in a way that no modern president has," one analyst has written, because for him, the war was "the defining issue of our times," and he was "hell-bent on avoiding surrender."[44] Times of trouble are especially apt to bring the role of national leader to the forefront. In the aftermath of the 9/11 attacks, President Bush's sense of national leadership was evident when, over the strong objections of his security staff, he flew back to the White House to deliver an address to the nation. "I felt like I had a job as the commander in chief" to show the country "that I was safe . . . not me, George W., but me the president," he later explained.[45]

The President as Partisan Leader

When Ronald Reagan first met with his Cabinet officers, he told them, "We'll take no actions or make [any] decisions that are based on how they might . . . affect an election."[46] Most presidents have made similar proclamations, but in reality, no president is always apolitically high-minded. Sometimes the partisan element in a president's policy is simply a matter of promoting policies that conform to the ideology he shares with his party, rather than the preferences of the public as a whole. At other times, presidents pursue policies primarily to benefit their party's political fortunes. During the years when George W. Bush was in the White House, one scholar has commented, "Creating the basis for a durable Republican [electoral] majority [was] one of the major purposes of the administration's policy agenda."[47] How partisan President Obama will be is not yet clear. However, with Rahm Emanuel, a former Democratic congressman, and Peter Rouse, a long-term Democratic operative, serving as Obama's first and second chief of staff, it is unlikely that Democratic electoral success will not factor into White House policy.

Apart from tailoring legislation for partisan ends, the president's partisan role is also evident in numerous other ways. For example, even for travel between elections, partisan considerations such as past party support and the next congressional elections influence which states a president visits.[48] Also, presidents direct extra federal funding to states that supported them or their party in the last general elections.[49]

The President as Human

Who presidents are as individual humans affects their conduct. According to one former White House official, a "president's 'world view'—his primary, politically relevant beliefs, particularly his conceptions of social causality, human nature, and the central moral conflicts of the time—probably explain as much or more about . . . foreign policy than any other single variable."[50] Arguably, the same could be said about domestic policy. To analyze this aspect of presidential behavior, we will look at intelligence, personality, ego, personal experiences, health, and gender.

Intelligence, or intellectual capacity, involves a president's ability to understand complex issues and options. Presidential IQs have varied considerably. One study that has estimated the IQs of presidents through George W. Bush ranked Thomas Jefferson as the smartest president.[51] It is notable, though, that even those presidents who ranked toward the bottom could hardly be called dumb. George W. Bush fell among the lowest 10% among presidents, yet the study found him "definitely intelligent," with his IQ score "in the upper range of college graduates."[52]

Do smarter presidents perform better? Certainly, they have some advantages. For one, a president's capacity for complex thinking improves the sophistication with which he applies historical lessons to current decisions.[53] Still, IQ is but one factor in overall performance. Jimmy Carter's estimated IQ puts him among the upper ranks for presidents, yet most scholars rate his presidency as among the least successful in the last century.

Personality also impacts presidential behavior.[54] One study correlated personality traits with experts' ratings of presidential performance. It found that superior performance is related to how highly a president scores on 9 standards such as energy, assertiveness, and stress tolerance.[55] Another approach evaluates presidents along two scales.[56] One ranges from active (policy innovators) to passive (those who prefer to preside over government rather than shape it). The other scale ranges from positive (enjoys the give and take of politics) to negative (feels burdened and beset). Active-positive presidents such as Franklin Roosevelt are apt to be the most powerful and successful. By contrast, active-negative presidents such as Richard Nixon are worrisome. The reason is that their high level of activity evokes opposition, but they react by feeling morose and seeing opponents as their enemies and even the country's enemies.

President Obama falls into the active category, but it remains to see where he will fall on the positive-negative scale. Those close to Obama often speak of the impact of his father on his psyche. One early associate remembers Obama relating that his father had returned to Kenya full of ambition to uplift his country "only to devolve into an embittered bureaucrat because he could not find a way to reconcile his ideals with political realities."[57] Obama himself has often repeated the observation, "Every man is either trying to make up for his father's mistakes or live up to his expectations," and has expressed sadness over the way his father's "life ended up unfulfilled, despite his enormous talents."[58] Obama may be a positive who will accept defeats as president as political, not personal. It might also be, though, that he will tend toward the negative and, emulating his father, retreat into bitter recriminations. None of these personality studies is definitive, yet they highlight the impact of personality on presidential performance.[59]

Globalization has led national leaders to meet and negotiate personally on an increasing basis. One early example, pictured here, occurred when British Prime Minister Winston Churchill (left), U.S. President Franklin Roosevelt (center), and Soviet leader Josef Stalin (right) met at the Yalta Conference in February 1945 to negotiate the shape of the post-World War II peace. Some historians argue that Roosevelt was so ill from hypertension, with his blood pressure a perilous 260/150, that he was unable to resist Stalin's demands for domination of Eastern Europe and other concessions. Less than two months after returning home, FDR collapsed and died of a cerebral hemorrhage. (Library of Congress)

Ego is a third personal factor that influences presidents. At least one reason that Richard Nixon and Lyndon Johnson persisted in Vietnam despite flagging U.S. military fortunes there and growing public opposition to the war was their shared aversion to defeat. As Nixon put it in a handwritten note, "won't be 1st P to lose war."[60]

Personal experiences also affect presidents. Family history is one factor.[61] George Bush's resolve to topple Iraqi dictator Saddam Hussein may have partly resulted from a plot by Iraqi agents to assassinate the first President Bush when he visited Kuwait in 1993. Just months before the 2003 invasion, the younger Bush characterized Saddam as "the guy that tried to kill my dad." The White House claimed that Bush did not mean "to personalize" the crisis, but it is hard to dismiss the anger of a son as a factor in the U.S. invasion of Iraq.[62]

Health, both physical and mental, is yet another factor that affects presidential performance. Several presidents have had serious physical health issues such as cancer. Also, a number of presidents have arguably experienced psychological ailments such as depression.[63] Additionally, Richard Nixon and other presidents have abused alcohol, and John F. Kennedy took a questionable array of prescription medicines to ease his chronic back pain. If and how such problems affected specific presidents are subject to considerable controversy, but it would be naïve to believe that a president's health has never affected policy. Part of the story of the defeat of the League of Nations Treaty by the Senate after World War I was Woodrow Wilson's worsening cerebral arteriosclerosis, a condition known to induce the irascibility and obstinacy that he displayed during his failed effort to strong-arm the Senate into ratifying the treaty.

Gender is an additional personal trait that may affect a president's decision making. One indication is the opinion gap that exists between men and women in the United States and in other countries across a range of political issues (see Chapter 6). Women in the United States and other countries, for example, are usually less likely than are men to support going to war. Similarly, as gender equality increases in a country, it tends to become more peaceful internationally and is also less likely to commit human rights abuses.[64] One argument is that males' political aggression and urge to take control are extensions of their sexual behavior.[65] An indication is the frequent use by presidents of sexual imagery use during war.[66] In one earthy instance a reporter asked Lyndon Johnson why he was waging war in Vietnam. In response, the president "unzipped his fly, drew out his substantial organ and declared, 'This is why'."[67] Such evidence leads some scholars to conclude that sex does make a difference in decision making.[68] Yet it would be wise to reserve judgment on the impact of sex on political orientations and decisions. It is, for example, difficult to compare the decision making of male and female national leaders because so few countries have been led by women.

Globally, the number of national leaders who are women is slowly growing, as symbolized by this photograph showing Chile's President Michelle Bachelet (center) and Argentina's President Cristina Fernandez during an official visit to Chile by Fernandez. A fascinating question is whether the increased role of women in politics will lead to important changes in domestic and foreign policy. (AP Photo/Roberto Candia)

Three women prime ministers—Golda Meir of Israel, Indira Gandhi of India, and Margaret Thatcher of Great Britain—have led their countries during a war since 1945. All three were victorious.

PRESIDENTIAL POWER

Presidential power can be divided into two categories. **Formal powers** are those based on Article II of the Constitution or on laws passed by Congress. They mostly include the president's power as head of government. For example, Article II designates presidents as the commander in chief, giving them significant military authority. **Informal powers** stem from the president's political standing, especially his status as head of state, the symbolic embodiment of the country and its people. According to one scholar, "No president can fail to recognize that all his powers are invigorated, indeed are given a new dimension of authority, because he is the symbol of our sovereignty, continuity, and grandeur."[69] As we will see, for instance, the willingness of Americans to give the presidents great license to use military force stems partly from the impulse to rally behind the national leader in time of danger.

To say that there are two sources of presidential power does not mean, however, that in their application they are entirely separate or easily distinguishable. Instead, the authority derived from the two sources can amplify one another. That is why, for one, the president's war power is so extensive. His formal authority as commander in chief is enhanced by the willingness of Congress and the public to defer to presidential leadership as the head of state during crises.

Another key point about the power of the presidency is that it varies over time and from issue to issue for reasons that we will explore. Indeed, presidential power is so variable that presidents sometimes contradict themselves about how much they have. Feeling feisty one day, Harry S. Truman declared that none of the powerful leaders in world history ever "had half the power and influence that the President of the United States has."[70] Yet on another, less ebullient day, Truman sat in the Oval Office bemoaning the fate of his successor, President-elect Dwight D. Eisenhower. "It's going to be tough for Ike," Truman lamented. "He'll sit here and he'll say, "Do this! Do that!' And nothing will happen. Poor Ike!"[71]

The Long-Term Evolution of Presidential Power

It is not accidental that the powers of Congress are spelled out in Article I of the Constitution, while those of the president are found in Article II. That order, with the courts relegated to Article III, generally reflects the order of importance that most of the framers of the Constitution intended and anticipated for the three branches. However, the order does not reflect today's reality. George Washington would be amazed by the power that Barack Obama wields. Several preliminary points to our review of the evolution of presidential power are in order:

- It has grown both absolutely and in comparison with the powers of Congress.
- The growth of presidential power has not been caused by constitutional amendments. To the contrary, the Article II powers remain exactly as they were written in 1787.
- The changes that have occurred are a result of how those powers are interpreted and applied.

- Presidential power has evolved amid numerous and controversial advances and retreats.

Presidential Power, 1789–1932

For about 150 years, presidential power relative to that of Congress grew slowly and fitfully. Notable advances occurred during crises and under strong presidents such as Andrew Jackson, Abraham Lincoln, and Theodore Roosevelt. At other times, presidential power waned somewhat, and Congress regained some of its relative power during times of peace and the tenures of weaker presidents. However, the trend line of relative presidential power was up.

Theodore Roosevelt, for one, advocated the **stewardship theory** of the presidency. He argued that presidents serve as "a steward [caretaker] of the people" and derived power from that role. Among other things, he rejected the view that a president needs specific authority to act. Instead, Roosevelt asserted that he could act unless specifically barred from doing so by the Constitution or law. "I did not usurp power," he wrote, "but I did greatly broaden the use of executive power."[72] Most presidents since Roosevelt have followed his lead.

The Modern Presidency, 1933–Present

Theodore Roosevelt's cousin, Franklin D. Roosevelt (FDR), further expanded presidential power during two crises: the Great Depression in the 1930s and World War II (1939–1945). Indeed, many scholars believe that FDR inaugurated the **modern presidency**, a designation denoting the permanent position of the presidency as the country's dominant political actor. FDR did this by adding to the advances of earlier powerful presidents and by consolidating and institutionalizing "the president's new leadership role in ways that subsequent presidents have continued."[73]

We will take up the powers of the contemporary presidency presently, but four basic points about the modern presidency are in order here. First, presidential power has continued to ebb and flow considerably since FDR. There have been times when presidents seemed so powerful that scholars wrote books with titles such as *The Imperial Presidency*.[74] At other times, the travails of presidents have engendered titles like *The Presidency Under Siege*.[75] Second, whatever the exact degree of its power, the presidency since FDR has remained preeminent. Thus the question is no longer which branch is the most powerful. It is how much more powerful the president is at any given time than is Congress or the courts. Third, presidential preeminence does not mean that Congress and the courts are impotent; they remain powerful. Fourth, the degree of presidential power at any moment depends on numerous variables.

Short-Term Variables in Presidential Power

Presidential power has not only changed over the long term, it also varies from president to president and even from day to day. To help understand these short-term shifts, we can look at the president's job skills, public opinion about him, the type of policy at issue, and situation at hand.

Job Skills

"I wonder whether I've got . . . [the] ability enough to be president," Lyndon Johnson once rhetorically asked a journalist.[76] His self-doubt emphasizes the fact that the skills a president brings to the job help determine how well he uses his powers. Table 12.1 lists four skill areas and shows the average score for each assigned by 90 experts to recent presidents.

Administrative skills include the president's ability to organize and manage the EOP, the bureaucracy, and his own time and energy.[77] President Johnson got top marks in the table based on the substantial degree to which he focused on manipulating executive organizations and "turning them to his advantage."[78] By contrast, President Reagan's hands off approach earned him poor grades. Reagan's first budget director has labeled him a "passive" manager and has recalled that the

TABLE 12.1 Presidential Skills

A president's individual skills add or detract from his powers. This table shows how 90 experts on the presidency evaluated recent presidents. Notice that no president was among either the top three or the bottom three in all skills areas.

PRESIDENT	ADMINISTRATIVE SKILLS	LEGISLATIVE SKILLS	PUBLIC LEADERSHIP QUALITIES	POLICY COMPETENCE	OVERALL AVERAGE
Kennedy	62	58	76	68	67
Johnson	69	80	63	51	66
Nixon	59	44	38	65	42
Ford	53	60	46	49	52
Carter	51	33	54	46	46
Reagan	43	64	79	58	61
Bush	59	52	51	58	55
Clinton	56	36	46	64	51
Average	57	53	57	57	55

Notes and data source: Category scores range from 1 to 100. See data source for calculation of average. Public leadership qualities include public persuasion, vision/setting agenda, and moral authority. Policy competence includes economic management and international relations. Data from C-SPAN Survey of Presidential Leadership at www.americanpresidents.org/survey/.

president "gave no orders . . . asked for no information, expressed no urgency." Faced with discord among his advisors, Reagan's would say, "Okay, you fellas work it out."[79] President Barack Obama's style is considerably less relaxed than was Reagan's but not as controlling and centralized as that of some presidents. A common description of Obama is as a "big picture guy," who listens to his advisors but much prefers brief points rather than the long discussions that reputed "policy wonk" President Clinton enjoyed. One aide recalls that after she repeated a point, Obama interjected, "Yeah, I got it, get on with it" [80]

Legislative skills enable a president to persuade Congress to support him. Here again, Johnson is ranked first in the table. "Lyndon Johnson was a legislative genius," one scholar has written.[81] According to Johnson, his approach was to deal with Congress "continuously, incessantly, and without interruption. . . . I pleaded, I reasoned, I argued, I urged, I warned." Among the reasons that Carter is ranked last on legislative skills is that he lacked Johnson's zeal for dealing with Congress. One aide complained that Carter was reluctant "to call up a congressman and ask for his support on a bill."[82] President Obama's record is still forming, but he had some notable successes, especially getting health care legislation through Congress.

Public leadership qualities focus on a president's ability to win public support through his ability to speak well, to set forth a clear vision and agenda, to project moral leadership, and otherwise to create a positive image of himself and his policies. Reagan earned top honors for his public leadership primarily because of the masterly way the former actor could deliver a speech. Nixon by contrast was a stiff speaker and had something of a disingenuous, "tricky Dick" image with the public. As a speaker, President Obama is well above average but not at the same top level as Reagan and John F. Kennedy. Many observers noted that Obama's public speeches became much less passionate as president than they had been as a candidate and that he had lost some of his ability to galvanize the public. That may have changed during the 2010 elections when, faced with possible massive Democratic losses in Congress, the president reverted to a more shirt-sleeve, emotionally urgent speaking style. Whether that will continue is unclear.

Policy competence, the fourth of our job skills, relates to the president's ability to formulate policy. Kennedy and his policy team ranked first among the eight contemporary presidents in the table. Carter earned low marks for policy competence during a term in which, according to one scholar, "inflation rose and productivity faltered" on the economic front and foreign policy was marked by a "propensity for vacillation and incoherence."[83] The report card is still out on President Obama. His ambitious policy agenda including health care, immigration reform, energy and environmental innovation, and other initiatives has been praised by some as visionary and criticized by others as endangering getting anything done by trying to do too much. In the formulation of health-care reform, Obama's first major policy effort, he chose to concentrate on getting some type of bill passed and to be highly flexible on the details of the legislation. Here again there was praise by some for being able to adapt and win needed votes in Congress, while other chastised the president for lack of leadership and letting the principle of providing health care for all Americans dissolve into a patchwork of half measures and concessions to one or another powerful interest group or member of Congress. Time will tell who is right.

Public Opinion

Presidential popularity is a second power variable. Presidents see a link between their level of public support (presidential approval rating) and their degree of policy success. "Presidential popularity is a major source of strength in gaining the cooperation of Congress" is how Lyndon Johnson put it.[84] Legislators agree. According to one GOP Senator, President George W. Bush's sagging popularity during his second term undermined his influence in Congress because influence "is partly a function of approval ratings. People pay attention [to polls] and start saying, 'Let's take a more independent tack.' It is frankly self-interest, self-preservation."[85] Research confirms that public opinion support is a "source of influence for presidents" and that positive public opinion ratings can embolden presidents, reassure their allies, and make opponents less willing to do battle.[86] It is also true, however, that the link between public opinion and power should not be overestimated. Evidence shows it to exist, but to be less robust than presidents seem to assume.

As might be expected given the ability of declining popularity to diminish a president's influence, President Obama's ability to persuade congressional Democrats to follow his lead declined during his first two years in office as his public approval rating dropped from 68% in January 2009 to 49% in January 2010, and then hovered near that level for the rest of the year. Moreover, an increasing percentage of poll respondents were saying they would vote Republican in the 2010 congressional elections. Adding to Democratic anxiety, Republican candidates won several victories. Most importantly, Republican Scott Brown took what had been Ted Kennedy's Massachusetts Senate seat in January 2010.

All this has made Democrats, especially those from more conservative districts, wary about supporting some of the more liberal aspects of Obama's legislative agenda. "People who had weak knees before are going to have weaker knees now" is how one Democratic legislator put it.[87] The nervousness turned out to be well justified. The Democrats lost more than 50 House seats in November 2010, with Democrats from moderate districts experiencing the vast majority of losses. Speaking soon after the election, one Democratic strategist commented that Obama "had a lot more power [before the election] . . . than he has today and that's just a fact. . . . He's going to have to compromise or get less done."[88]

Policy Type

Different types of policy move through the political process in different ways. This fact is relevant here because the power of the president and the other political actors in the process varies by type of policy. There is, for example, the **two presidencies theory** that distinguishes between the foreign-policy presidency and the domestic-policy presidency.[89] "The difference according to Jimmy Carter, "is that the president has much greater influence in foreign policy. In domestic affairs, yours is just one of a large number of voices. . . . I would guess that the president would not have the most influence. Though on foreign policy, you do."[90] One reason for the difference is that presidents have much greater authority in foreign affairs than in domestic affairs to take unilateral action. For example, presidents can commit troops to battle without congressional authorization. There has been an extended debate over whether or not Congress is more likely to pass foreign policy legislation compared to domestic policy bills favored by presidents.[91] However, that discussion affects only how big the gap is between the president's foreign and domestic policy powers, not whether a gap exists.[92]

Situation

Presidential power also varies according to situation. One commonly recognized situational variable is whether the president is dealing with a **crisis situation** or a non-crisis situation. Crises occur when either a specific event, such as a war or natural disaster, or a longer-term situation, such as the Great Depression or the cold war, causes people to feel that they are threatened or that their nation is endangered. The greater the sense of danger is, the more acute the sense of crisis, and the greater the president's power. This occurs partly because presidents have considerable authority to act quickly, especially in emergencies, and partly because legislators and other political actors tend to be supportive or silent during a crisis.

This support, called the **rally effect**, extends to public opinion in two ways.[93] First, the public usually supports the president's reaction to the crisis. For example, Figure 12.4 shows that the percentage of Americans who supported the president's policy toward Iraq increased as the crisis climaxed, and the U.S. invasion began. Moreover, when those Americans who supported

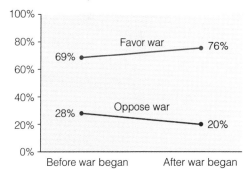

FIGURE 12.4 Public Support of War with Iraq

When a president takes action during a crisis, public support for it usually increases. This is evident here for support for war with Iraq just days before and the day after it began.

Notes and data sources: "Unsure" responses not shown. Data from CBS News polls of March 15–16 and 20–21, 2003, provided by The Roper Center, University of Connecticut.

the war were asked why, 23% said that they were personally unsure if the invasion had been the "best thing to do" but supported President Bush's decision "because he is president?"[94]

Second, the rally effect also increases the president's overall approval rating."[95] Both aspects of the rally effect are particularly pronounced during foreign policy crises because of the "we-they" perception (we, Americans; they, foreign opponents). During 18 such military crises between 1941 and 2003, the president's public approval rating increased in all but one. On average the approval rating increased 10%. The only loss came when President Johnson's rating fell 8% after a U.S. naval vessel, the *Pueblo,* was captured by North Korea in 1968.

However, even if the initial rally effect is strong, it often fades quickly. This is especially true if the public sees the president's reaction as ineffective or weak. President Bush's popularity initially ticked up 1% when Hurricane Katrina struck the Gulf Coast in 2005, but then his uncertain response to the resulting devastation contributed to a 5% decline in his public approval rating during the following two weeks.

FORMAL POWERS AND RESTRAINTS

Even a passive, inept president serving in unfavorable political times is still a powerful force because of the imposing array of constitutional and statutory authority he possesses. Notice two things as we explore these formal powers. First, the list of the president's **enumerated powers**, those that are specifically stated in the Constitution, is very short. Therefore, a great degree of the president's formal authority rests on his **implied powers**, authority that is either inherent in the head of a sovereign country or is derived from such undefined designations as "commander in chief." Second, the president often draws significant strength from his ability to *act*, whereas Congress can only *legislate* and the Supreme Court can only *decide*.

Formal Powers as Chief Executive Officer

Article II of the Constitution gives the "executive power" to the president, and also authorizes him to appoint most executive branch officials and to have them report to him. Although short and vague, this language implies extensive executive authority and establishes the president as the head of government.[96] Presidents have built on this foundation by asserting their prerogatives on many fronts. For example, Thomas Jefferson doubled the size of the country by purchasing the Louisiana Territory from France in 1803 even though nothing in the Constitution clearly allows the federal government to acquire territory. When one Cabinet member questioned the legality of the purchase, Jefferson rejoined, "The less we say about the constitutional difficulties respecting Louisiana the better."[97]

Numerous **delegations of power** by Congress have also expanded the president's executive authority. These occur when Congress authorizes the president to make decisions on matters over which Congress has authority. Congress has often delegated authority over foreign policy and for crisis situations. Legislators also delegated more authority to the president after the significant expansion of government functions and budget that began in the 1930s. Whatever Congress may have wanted, from a pragmatic perspective the vast and complex nature of government today makes it "impossible for every authoritative rule or decision of the government to be approved by the normal legislative process."[98] Now a great degree of legislation establishes general goals and delegates the authority to fill in the gaps to the executive branch. For example, the Americans with Disabilities Act (1990) requires employers to make a "reasonable accommodation" in job functions and physical facilities to avoid discriminating against handicapped workers unless doing so creates an "undue hardship." However, the act leaves it to the executive branch (and also the courts) to decide what "reasonable accommodation" and "undue hardships" are. Some criticize such delegations as undermining the separation of powers.[99]

Personnel Power

All the top policy-making and administrative jobs in the executive branch are filled by presidential appointment. Presidents can also usually fire these individuals at will. This authority gives presidents extensive control over the executive branch officials. Most of the top positions are subject to Senate confirmation, but as Chapter 11 details, it is rare for the Senate to reject or otherwise block presidential nominations for executive branch positions.

Who a president appoints is based on numerous factors. Appointments serve to reward the president's political supporters and to give a voice in the government to various supportive groups. Presidents also seek to enhance the reality and image of expertise in their administration. When President Obama came to office in 2009, he tried to ease concerns about his lack of national security policy experience by reappointing Robert Gates, who President Bush had initially appointed as Secretary of Defense in 2006. For similar reasons, Obama named retired Marine Corps General James L. Jones to the post of national security advisor and retired Admiral Dennis Blair as Director of National Intelligence. Presidents also make symbolic statements through their appointments. One way recent presidents have done this

> The first African American appointed by a president to a diplomatic post was Ebenezer Don Carlos Bassett, U.S. minister to Haiti (1869–1877).

AMERICAN DIVERSITY

FIGURE 12.5 Increasing Cabinet Diversity

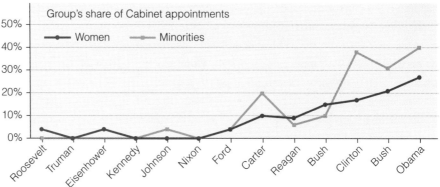

Increased diversity has come slowly but surely to the Cabinet.
Notes and data source: Obama's Cabinet is for 2009–2010. Data from the White House.

is to promote diversity by appointing women and minority group members to top posts.[100] This is detailed in Figure 12.5.

A final note on Cabinet diversity is that women both globally and in the United States are too often pigeon-holed in posts that deal with subjects such as education, health, and labor, that are stereotypically thought to be areas of special interest and expertise for women. Typically, such posts make up 20% to 25% of a country's cabinet ministers. Globally, more than 40% of all female cabinet members hold such ministries. In the United States, more than half of the women who have served in the Cabinet from 1938 to 2010 have been secretaries of labor, of education, of health and human services, or of housing and urban development. Both globally and in the United States women are less often appointed to head core departments (security, foreign affairs, justice), economic departments (agriculture, commerce, treasury), and infrastructure departments (energy, interior, transportation). Something of the same pattern exists for minority appointees to the U.S. Cabinet. They made up 25% of all the Cabinet officers who served between 1990 and 2010, but they were only 10% of those who headed the four most prestigious departments: defense, justice, treasury, and state.

Legislative Power

Early in U.S. history the assumption was that the president would have little to do with the legislative process other than deciding whether to approve or veto measures. Illustrating this, President Washington proposed only three measures to Congress during his two terms, and he considered it improper to intervene in the deliberations of Congress. Soon, however, presidents began suggesting more measures, lobbying for their passage, and generally trying to shape legislation. Doing so has been a regular practice since the time of Franklin Roosevelt. Now, presidents are a key source of legislation, and they also regularly involve themselves in the progress of important bills through the legislative process. Presidents have both formal constitutional and informal partisan roles in the legislative process.

Constitutional Roles   Several parts of Article II enable presidents to involve themselves in the legislative process. One is the requirement that they inform Congress of the "state of the union" and "recommend . . . measures." Technically, a legislator must introduce all bills and resolutions. In practice, though, as Chapter 11 relates, the White House formulates a great deal of legislation, then finds one or more legislators to introduce it. The White House also works with legislative leaders and more generally lobbies Congress to promote, change, or defeat legislation. Presidents rely mostly on argumentation and pleas for support, but they also sometimes offer federal projects in a legislator's district and other incentives to win support. President Carter has recalled, "There were times when [members of Congress] would come to the Oval Office and I would find out what I could do to help them. It was a give-and-take proposition."[101]

Presidents also intervene in the legislative process through their **veto** power. As Chapter 11 also explains, this includes the ability to formally reject a bill with a veto or to informally reject it by a pocket veto. Presidents have vetoed more than 2,500 measures since 1789, with about 60% of the rejections being regular vetoes and the rest pocket vetoes. However, use of the veto has varied considerably among presidents. Over time, vetoes have become more common as presidents shifted from usually vetoing only legislation that they believed to be unconstitutional to vetoing bills that they thought created bad policy. A second factor that determines how often presidents veto legislation is whether their party controls Congress. All of President Clinton's vetoes and 90% of President George Bush's vetoes came during the years when the opposition party controlled Congress. The record of recent presidents is detailed in Figure 12.6.

Vetoes are a powerful tool. One indication is that that Congress has reversed only 107 or 4% of them. Moreover, presidents also use their veto power as a negotiating tool.[102] Threatening to reject a bill puts Congress in the position of compromising with the president or facing a veto. Congress, however, has ways to blunt the veto power. One is by inserting provisions against the president's liking into a bill that he wants a great deal. This maneuver forces presidents either to accept the objectionable provision or to kill the entire measure because the president, unlike most governors, does not have a **line-item veto**, the ability to veto parts of bills.

FIGURE 12.6 Vetoes and Overrides

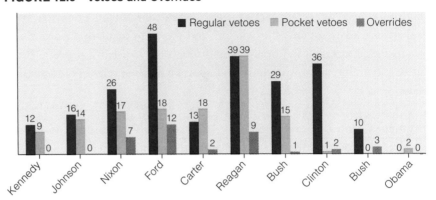

Presidents cast more vetoes and are overridden more when the opposition party controls Congress. Even then, though, Congress seldom overrides a veto.

Notes and data source: Data cover 1961–2010 and are from the Office of the Clerk, U.S. House of Representatives.

Congress gave line-item veto authority over appropriations to the president in 1996, but the Supreme Court ruled it an unconstitutional delegation of power.[103]

Partisan Role Presidents have long sought to enhance their power by establishing themselves as the leader of their party in Congress. Doing so is difficult because presidents have no formal control over who serves in Congress or how they vote. Therefore, presidents exercise leadership through other factors such as shared ideology, a sense of shared political fate, a degree of party loyalty, and the ability to assist party members by raising funds for them and otherwise supporting their reelection. These tools have proven reasonably effective. As Figure 12.7 shows, most members of the president's party support his legislative program, while most members of the other party oppose it. The figure also shows that this partisan divide has generally become sharper over time. Another indication that presidents exercise a reasonable degree of party leadership in Congress is that members of the president's party are more likely to vote to delegate powers to the president than are members of the opposition party.[104]

The President's Effectiveness as a Legislative Leader The most important measure of presidents' legislative power is how effective they are in getting what they want through Congress. Success and failure rates depend on factors such as the persuasive skills of the president and his staff, on how popular the president is with the public, and whether the president's party controls one or both houses of Congress. It is hard, however, to confidently determine how successful a president has been legislatively. One problem is that presidents usually have to compromise

FIGURE 12.7 Presidential Support Scores by Party, 2005–2009

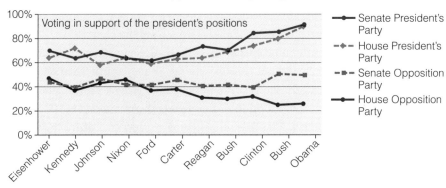

This figure shows the average level of support of the president by members of the president's party and members of the opposition party for votes on issues on which the president had a declared position. Note two things in particular: (1) On average, a majority of the president's party in the House and Senate have been supportive and a majority of the opposition party in the House and (almost always) in the Senate has voted the other way. (2) Note the trend toward greater partisanship. Members of the president's party in both chambers have become more supportive over time, and members of the opposition party in the House have become more likely to be opposed. The Senate opposition party is different from the other three in recent times, in part because opposition senators are more likely to vote for treaties and nominees that the president favors than to support the president on other matters. This lowers the opposition score compared to the House, which votes on neither treaties nor nominees. *Notes and data source:* Obama for 2009 only. Data from *CQ Weekly Report,* January 11, 2010, p. 112.

extensively with Congress, and the result is not clear victory or defeat. President Obama got a health-care bill through Congress in 2010, but it fell far short of what he had initially favored. It is also the case that pressures from interest groups or others may cause a president to profess support for a bill, yet do little to promote it and not really care if it passes or not. Therefore in reviewing the studies on legislative success and the variety measures to gauge it, we can safely say that:[105]

- Congress gives at least a committee hearing to 90% of the legislation that presidents propose.
- Nevertheless, less than half the bills the average president supports become law.
- Often a bill that the president favors dies because the president supports it only to appease a constituency group and therefore gives the bill only token support.
- Even for those bills that do pass, presidents get all of what they want less than a third of the time.
- In bills that pass, presidents get at least half of what they want about two-thirds of the time.
- Measures that the president adamantly opposes are rarely enacted.

Budget Power

Presidents are the driving force behind the country's budget, including revenue (taxes) and expenditures. This was not always true. Until the early 1900s, the various executive agencies submitted spending requests directly to Congress, and legislative committees usually did not consult with the White House when reviewing those requests. This disaggregated system became increasingly unworkable as the budget grew, especially after adoption of the Sixteenth Amendment (1913) permitting a federal income tax. That amendment and World War I drove the federal budget upward by more than 800% between 1910 and 1920. Congress responded by enacting the Budget and Accounting Act of 1921. It required the president to submit an annual budget to Congress. The act also created the Bureau of the Budget (now Office of Management and Budget) to assist in formulating and managing the budget.

Operational and Organizational Power

As chief executive officer, presidents have considerable authority over the organization of the executive branch and even more over its operation. *Presidential directives* are one tool that presidents use to initiate action. These directives are rules promulgated by the president that have the force of law. They are usually called **executive orders**, although they have been issued under many different names such as "national security presidential directives."[106]

Many executive orders are symbolic or deal with routine, but others have important policy impacts. Moreover, the percentage of directives dealing with policy has increased from 26% early in the 1930s to 66% more recently.[107] Abraham Lincoln's Emancipation Proclamation (1863) freeing the slaves in the rebellious states is among history's pivotal executive orders. So was Franklin Roosevelt's executive order in 1942 to confine about 125,000 Japanese-Americans in internment camps during World War II. Yet other executive orders have been used to desegregate the armed forces, ban assassinating foreign leaders, protect endangered species, institute affirmative action, establish U.S. nuclear war fighting plans, and take other key initiatives. Some of these have been challenged in court, but only a few have been invalidated. The most famous instance was when the Supreme Court rejected President Truman's executive order seizing the country's steel mills to avoid a nationwide strike during the Korean War.[108]

Presidents also direct administrative behavior with **presidential signing statements**.[109] These are written statements inserted into the legal record by presidents when they sign legislation. Many are mere rhetorical declarations of the president's views, but others are assertions by the president about the meaning or constitutionality of some aspect of the legislation. These statements are meant to guide federal agencies about how to interpret and implement the law. Although long, signing statements have become controversial because President Reagan and subsequent presidents have used them increasingly to object to various parts of laws.

President George W. Bush set a record by making constitutional objections in about 75% of his signing statements. This evoked sharp criticism from the Democrats in Congress. For one, then Senator Barack Obama (D-IL) condemned Bush's practice as "an abuse." Once he became president, though, Obama's perspective changed, and 63% his own signing statements in 2009 contained an objection.[110] This led several leading House Democrats to fire off a letter to Obama chastising him. "During the previous administration," the letter read, "all of us were critical of the president's assertion that he could pick and choose which aspects of congressional statutes he was required to enforce. We were therefore chagrined to see you appear to express a similar attitude."[111]

Third, and least formally, presidents can simply tell agencies to initiate or change policies. Congress passed a law in 2007 requiring 40% better gas mileage for cars and light trucks by 2020. The Bush administration did nothing to implement that law, but soon after taking office, President Obama directed the Transportation Department to formulate the necessary regulations.

Formal Powers as Commander in Chief

Article II designates presidents as commander in chief, giving them a powerful, if vague, grant of authority. This includes operational control of the military, the authority to deploy the military into combat and dangerous situations, and the authority to make peace.

We will see in the discussion that follows that how the military is used provides a stark and important illustration of the distinction between how what is literally written in the Constitution about the respective powers of the president and Congress differs from what occurs in practice. Congress's impressive enumerated authority in this area includes the power to "declare war," to "make rules concerning captures on land and water," to "raise and support armies," to "provide and maintain a navy," to "make rules for the government and regulation of the land and naval forces," and to "provide for organizing, arming, and disciplining the militia [the National Guard units], and for governing such part of them as may be employed in the service of the United States." By contrast, the president's authority rests mostly on his designation as commander in chief. Presidents may also appoint military officers, but Congress has the authority to reject the president's nominations and, in the case of the most senior officers, even their specific duty assignments. Yet despite all of Congress's specific authority compared to the president's vague grant as commander in chief, it is the president, not Congress, that overwhelmingly decides when and how U.S. military forces will be used.[112]

Operational Control

Presidents do not lead soldiers into battle, but they can make military decisions. One fateful choice was President Truman's decision in 1945 to drop atomic bombs on Japan rather than invade it. During the Vietnam War, Lyndon Johnson regularly reviewed the Air Force's target list in Indochina. Military officers have sometimes chaffed at such control, but they have never successfully resisted it. Most famously, Truman fired General Douglas MacArthur in 1951 after he publicly opposed the president's decision not to expand the Korean War to China.

War Power

Being commander in chief includes the **presidential war power**: the ability to send U.S. forces into combat or into "harms way" (dangerous situations) without authorization by Congress. This power has grown greatly since World War II.

Global Confrontation and the President's War Power   Two wars—one hot, the other cold—dramatically changed U.S. foreign policy. World War II propelled the United States into a full-fledged global role as the dominant world power. Soon thereafter, the onset of the cold war between the United States and the Soviet Union changed U.S. foreign policy:

- U.S. military spending vastly increased. In 1955 with the country at peace, for example, 60% of the federal budget went to defense. That is three times higher than in 2010.
- The large military forces that the United States built gave it the capacity to use them.
- The use of U.S. force abroad grew significantly, as Figure 12.8 indicates.
- The cold war sense of crisis and fear made Americans willing to let the president exercise broad authority as commander in chief to protect national security.

More than any other event, the U.S. response to North Korea's invasion of South Korea in 1950 heralded the change in presidential power. Until then, presidents had usually consulted with Congress and sought some sort of support before using force. In Korea, however, President Truman unilaterally ordered U.S. troops to war. He justified his action by claiming, "The president, as commander in chief of the armed forces of the United States, has full

FIGURE 12.8   **Use of U.S. Force Abroad**

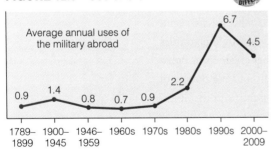

Globalization combined with U.S. power has increased the use of U.S. military forces abroad. This has increased the power of the presidency.
Data source: Congressional Research Service report RL30172, *Instances of Use of United States Armed Forces Abroad, 1798–2009,* January 27, 2010.

control over the use thereof."[113] In the crisis atmosphere of the time, there was hardly a murmur of dissent in Congress, and 75% of the public applauded Truman's action.

Expansion of the War Power Since Truman   Presidents since Truman have repeated his claim to have the authority to initiate military action unilaterally. For example, President Bush encouraged, but did not ask Congress to pass a resolution supporting action against Iraq in 2003.[114] "We don't want, in getting a resolution, to have conceded that one was constitutionally necessary," a White House official explained.[115]

The powers that presidents claim as commander in chief go beyond using military force unilaterally. For example, President Bush also argued after 9/11 that he had the authority to take such antiterrorist actions as authorizing intelligence agencies to intercept, without a court warrant, the communications of Americans contacting suspected terrorists overseas.

Little exists to legally limit the president's war powers. Congress attempted to restrain them by enacting the War Powers Resolution (WPR) in 1973. It directs the president to report to Congress any military action that he orders and to terminate it within 60 days unless he had received legislative authority to continue the action. However, the law has had little effect. All presidents have explicitly or implicitly denied its constitutionality. When George H. W. Bush sent the U.S. military to defend Saudi Arabia in 1990, then to drive Iraq out of Kuwait, the United States was neither under attack nor did it have a defense treaty with either the Saudis or Kuwaitis. Yet Bush asserted that he had the authority to act without congressional support. "I didn't have to get permission from some old goat in the United States Congress to kick Saddam Hussein out of Kuwait," Bush later told an audience.[116]

Many constitutional specialists would disagree with Bush, but challenges to this broad claim of a unilateral war power have failed. Legal challenges have not succeeded because the Supreme Court has refused to take up the matter on the grounds that is a political issue, not a legal issue. Political challenges have failed because of the unwillingness of Congress and the public to say no to the president in times of danger.

A new round of confrontation between the Congress and president over the war power broke out in 2007 when the Democrats took control in both houses. Yet despite this advantage, the Democrats were unable to force the president to alter his policy on Iraq. "I'm the decision-maker," Bush declared, and in practice he was right.[117] Barack Obama has not been as brazen about his war powers as of this writing, but he has exercised them. Most importantly, he gave no indication that he considered the decision about whether to escalate the number of U.S. troops in

Afghanistan anything but his own decision, despite the fact that there was considerable opposition in Congress and in the public to sending more troops.

Peace Power

A third aspect of the president's power as commander in chief is his ability to avoid hostilities and to end them. No president has ever been legally forced to wage a war he opposed. Indeed, peace-minded presidents have sometimes avoided war despite popular and congressional sentiment to the contrary. John Adams, for one, lost any chance of reelection in 1800 when he defied pressure to go to war with France over its raids on U.S. shipping. Adams "understood that his decision for peace meant political suicide, but he persisted anyway."[118]

Presidents can also end hostilities. The Persian Gulf War ended in 1991 when the first President Bush decided to be satisfied with liberating Kuwait and to avoid invading Iraq to topple Saddam Hussein. "We do not want to screw this up with a sloppy, muddled ending," he told aides.[119] Twelve years later, his son made a different decision about invading Iraq. History will judge which president was wiser.

Formal Powers as Head Diplomat

Scattered about in Article II is a smattering of language that gives presidents a variety of diplomatic powers. These include the ability to "make treaties," to "appoint ambassadors," and to "receive ambassadors" (recognize foreign governments). Supplementing these are the implied powers the president has as leader of a sovereign country. This status soon led to assertions of presidential supremacy in foreign affairs. As early as 1800, Secretary of State-designate John Marshall argued that the "president is the sole organ of the nation in its external relations."[120] Echoing those words, the Supreme Court described the president in 1936 as "the sole organ of the federal government in the field of international relations."[121]

Globalization has vastly increased the frequency and importance of U.S. interactions with other countries. This in turn has increased the importance of the president's role as head diplomat. Foreign travel provides one sign of the increasing presidential presence on the world stage. No president had traveled abroad while in office until 1906 when Theodore Roosevelt visited Panama. Barack Obama was in office only 29 days before his first foreign trip (to Canada). Moreover, Obama's 10 trips to 21 countries in his first year in office set new records for first-year presidential trips and countries visited.

International Negotiations

Only presidents and those he designates can negotiate with a foreign government or an international organization on behalf of the United States. Indeed, the Logan

Act of 1798 makes it a criminal offense for anyone else to claim to represent the country.

There are times when whether to negotiate and/or with whom can be controversial. President George W. Bush was reluctant to negotiate directly, especially in bilateral talks, with governments in North Korea, Iran, and elsewhere because he considered them to be rogue regimes supporting terrorism or other unsavory practices. Bush believed that negotiating with such governments gave them an air of legitimacy and served no positive purpose.

Barack Obama criticized this approach while running for president. During an interview, a questioner asked: "Would you be willing to meet separately, without precondition . . . with the leaders of Iran, Syria, Venezuela, Cuba and North Korea. . . ?" Obama responded, "I would. And the reason is this, that the notion that somehow not talking to countries is punishment to them—which has been the guiding diplomatic principle of [the Bush] administration—is ridiculous."[122] Republicans charged that Obama's position reflected his lack of foreign policy experience, and even Hillary Clinton, his then rival for the Democratic nomination, called Obama's position "irresponsible and frankly naïve." "I don't want to be used for propaganda purposes," Clinton explained.[123] The point here is not to decide who was right. Instead, it is to see is that even talking with other governments can be controversial, and presidents control that. As president, Obama has tempered his position, but he has still shown a greater willingness to engage U.S. enemies rather than trying solely to isolate and defeat them.

International Agreements

There are three types of international agreements: treaties, executive agreements, and presidential commitments.

Treaties   George Washington read the Senate's constitutional authority to "advise and consent" to treaties to mean that he should get the Senate's input before making a treaty. However, when he went to the Senate in 1789 to ask its advice about a treaty with the Creek Indians, the experience went so poorly that Washington declared that he would "be damned if he ever went there again."[124] Since then, presidents have sought only the Senate's consent.

One indication of the extent of U.S. global involvement is that it takes 516 pages just to list the U.S. treaties and other international agreements currently in force.

Chapter 11 discusses the Senate record of dealing with treaties, and that analysis need not be repeated here except to make two summary points. First, the Senate rejects or otherwise blocks only about 10% to 15% of all treaties. Second, the sheer necessity for ratification gives the Senate a voice in the negotiation process as officials try to tailor treaties to win ratification.

FIGURE 12.9 Treaties and Executive Agreements

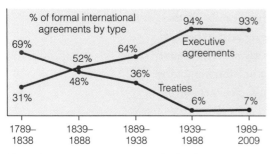

Executive agreements are now by far the most common form of formal agreement with other countries.

Data sources: Congressional Research Service, "Treaties and Other International Agreements: The Role of the United States Senate," January 2001, for data through 1999. Various executive and legislative sources for 2000–2009 data.

Executive Agreements Presidents also reach **executive agreements** with other governments. These include all formal international agreements other than treaties. As explained in Chapter 11, there are two types of executive agreements. *Executive-congressional agreements* are made under the provisions of an existing law or treaty and sometimes need congressional consent of the final accord. *Unilateral executive agreements* are made by presidents under their executive authority and are not subject to congressional approval.

Executive agreements have long existed, but as Figure 12.9 shows, they have become much more common.[125] This has occurred mostly because globalization has caused the volume of international agreements to expand vastly, and it is impossible for the Senate to review them all. It is also the case that presidents sometimes use executive agreements to avoid the Senate ratification process.[126] Most famously, Franklin Roosevelt ignored majority public and congressional opposition to involvement in World War II in 1940 when he committed a near act of war with Germany by making an executive agreement that sent 50 U.S. warships to the British in return for 99-year leases on several British naval bases in the Western Hemisphere.

Presidential Commitments Presidents can additionally pledge the United States to a course of action through presidential commitments. These informal agreements have murky legal standing, but they carry weight because not honoring them would reduce the credibility of president and, by extension, the country. One famous presidential commitment was made by President Kennedy to avoid nuclear war with the Soviet Union in 1962. In that agreement, Moscow committed to withdrawing its nuclear-warhead missiles from Cuba, and in return Kennedy pledged that the United States would never invade Cuba to topple Fidel Castro.

Presidents also have the power to terminate all international pacts, including treaties, at will. This authority was established after President Carter, as part of establishing full diplomatic relations with China, abrogated the U.S. defense treaty with Taiwan. Senator Barry Goldwater (R-AZ) filed suit contesting Carter's authority to do so without Senate agreement. That challenge failed when the Supreme Court declared the issue a political question and refused to hear it.[127]

Diplomatic Recognition

Presidents have the sole authority to decide whether to have diplomatic relations with another country. The president can also decide to break diplomatic relations with a country or to shift recognition from one government to another. This authority is based on the language in Article II empowering the president to "receive ambassadors," that is, to accept the legitimacy of the government they represent. Recognition is usually routine, but it can be very political. President Carter's decision in 1979 to switch U.S. recognition of the government of China from the nationalists in Taipei (on Taiwan) to the communists in Beijing was a major shift in U.S. policy.

Formal Powers as Chief Legal Officer

Presidents are the country's chief legal officer and possess broad power over how laws are administered and enforced. This authority has become increasingly important as the range of matters subject to federal law has grown. Part of this authority rests on the president's ability to appoint and direct the top officials at the Department of Justice and other federal law enforcement agencies. Article II also gives presidents substantial power to preserve or restore domestic peace by requiring that the president ensure that the law is "faithfully executed." This power was recognized in a case that arose in 1890 after U.S. Marshal David Neagle shot a man who was assaulting a federal judge. California authorities arrested Neagle for murder on the grounds that there was no federal law authorizing marshals to protect federal judges.[128] The Supreme Court ruled that no law was necessary because "there is a peace of the United States," and the president's duty to protect it stems "from the Constitution itself."

Discretionary Law Enforcement

Presidents and their appointees have considerable leeway to decide which laws to enforce and how vigorously to do so. Under President Bush the federal government prosecuted individuals in California who thought they were legally using marijuana for medical purposes under California's Medical Marijuana Act (1996). The administration even won a Supreme Court case in 2005 permitting federal control regardless of the state law.[129] There the matter rested until 2009 when the Obama administration announced that it would no longer arrest people for the use of medical marijuana in states that permitted it. Obama had criticized the Bush policy during the campaign, and Attorney General Eric Holder explained, "What the president said during the campaign . . . will be consistent with what we'll be doing in law enforcement. He . . . is my boss. . . . What he said during the campaign is now American policy."[130]

Law Enforcement Tools

Presidents also have an array of tools to enforce the law. These range from demands for legal compliance, through civil suits and criminal prosecutions, to the use of

To enforce the law, presidents can use the military if necessary. This photo shows a man who has been bloodily subdued by soldiers of the 101st Airborne Division who were at Central High School in Little Rock, Arkansas, to protect the black students who integrated the school in 1957. The man had tried to grab the rifle of one of the troops. (AP Photo)

force by the almost 90,000 law enforcement officers in the various federal police agencies. Presidents can even deploy U.S. military forces. In one case, President Kennedy ordered the military into action in 1962 after rioters shot two U.S. marshals who were trying to protect the first black student to enroll at the University of Mississippi. Presidents also deploy military units to keep order during natural disasters and other events that strain the capabilities of local authorities.

Clemency

Yet another aspect of the president's legal authority is his ability to "grant reprieves and pardons for offenses against the United States, except in cases of impeachment." Pardons wipe out a person's guilt and criminal record; reprieves lessen a sentence. They are collectively referred to as *clemency*. Note that pardons and reprieves apply only to federal crimes. Also, pardons can only be issued for acts that have already occurred, but they can come before conviction. Presidents have granted clemency since 1789 in more than 28,000 cases, for an average of almost 200 a year. In recent decades the emphasis on being tough on crime has greatly reduced the incidence of clemency down to a few dozen grants a year. It is also worth noting that among presidents since Franklin Roosevelt, Republican presidents have averaged considerably fewer grants of clemency each year than have Democratic presidents.

Most pardons are given to people who committed minor crimes long ago and have lived exemplary lives since then. But some pardons have been politically important and even controversial.[131] For example, 54% of Americans opposed Jimmy Carter's clemency for those who had evaded the draft during the Vietnam War, and 60% of Americans disapproved of the pardon that Gerald Ford gave to Richard Nixon for his actions in the Watergate scandal.[132]

Formal Restraints

Just as the idea of checks and balances would have it, presidents are restrained as well as empowered by the Constitution and statutory law.

Restraints by Congress and the Courts

Many of the restraints exercised by Congress and the courts are discussed fully in Chapters 11 and 14 and need only to be mentioned here. These include the requirement that the Senate *consent to treaties* and *confirm appointees* and the ability of Congress to *override vetoes* by the president. Additionally, the president's budget power is not as potent as Congress's control over *taxing and spending*, the financial lifeblood of the government. Congress also has *law-making* authority. No president gets everything he wants legislatively from Congress, and some presidential proposals are rejected outright by Congress or are simply left to wither. President Bush began his second term in 2005 by making Social Security reform his top legislative priority. His ideas went nowhere, and his 2006 State of the Union address did not even mention Social Security. Such instances are rare, though, and presidents usually achieve a significant part of their legislative agenda through "bargaining and compromise based on the mutual dependence between the two branches."[133]

Yet it is also true that the relationship between the president and Congress can be very rocky, especially during times of divided government. This occurs when the party that controls the White House does not also have a majority in one or both houses of Congress. Such divisions have existed during 19 of the 37 two-year congresses from the 80th Congress (1947–1948) after World War II to the 112th Congress (2011–2012). Divided government makes it harder for a president to get legislation through Congress. Whether this is desirable or not is subject to a debate that you are invited to join in the following You Decide box.[134]

YOU DECIDE: Is Divided Government Destructive?

For about half the time since World War II, the U.S. government has been divided, with a president of one party and one or both houses of Congress controlled by the other.[135] This alarms some analysts.[136] One worry is that partisanship too often causes gridlock. A second concern is that what policy does emerge is not based on optimal design but lowest-common denominator compromises. A third charge is that divided government makes it hard for the public to pin the tale on the donkey, that is, to know whom to praise or blame for what goes on in Washington.

Proponents of divided government dismiss such concerns and also claim benefits for it.[137] One alleged benefit is that divided government ensures

that a wide range of views will shape policy. A second argument is that divided government helps maintain the separation of power between the executive and legislative branches and thus preserves democracy. As for the public, 55% think that divided government "works well for the country," 37% contend it does not, and 8% are unsure.[138]

What do you think? Is divided government destructive or constructive? Did the government work better under President Obama and a unified government during the 111th Congress during his first two years, or under the divided government that began in 2011? Depending on your answer, what, if anything, should be done to encourage or discourage having a divided government?

Congress's powers of *oversight and investigation* also constrain presidents. During the Reagan administration a Byzantine and illegal scheme to sell weapons to Iran and divert the funds to support the efforts of rebels to overthrow the leftist government in Nicaragua was aired by a congressional investigation and led not only to the end of the practice but also to the convictions of several high-ranking administration officials for lying under oath to Congress and other crimes.

Presidents also face limitations by the courts. The Supreme Court can declare an action by the president to be illegal, as occurred after President Truman's seizure of the steel mills during the Korean War. The courts can also order a president to comply, as it did when it ordered President Nixon to comply with a congressional subpoenas seeking evidence related to the Watergate burglary. Still, these are exceptions to the rule. Overall, the Supreme Court has been cautious about attempts to retrain the president's authority.[139] In fact, between 1789 and 2000, the Supreme Court only overturned actions by the president on 76 occasions, and a third of those were rulings against President Nixon.[140]

Limitations on Continuing in Office

Presidents are also restrained by limits to their time in office. First, presidents may serve only *two terms* under the Twenty-Second Amendment (1953). Advocates of repealing the two-term limit argue, among other things, that "the public ought to have the opportunity to retain or reject" whomever it chooses.[141] Opponents of repealing the Twenty-Second Amendment counter that "a long tenure leads to a dangerous accumulation of power in the president's hands, and also a greater arrogance and tendency to abuse it.[142]

All democracies with a powerful president except France have term limits. Prime ministers are not subject to term limits.

Second, presidents become a *lame duck* once they begin a second term, announce they will not seek another term, or are defeated for reelection. Being a lame duck diminishes a president's power because legislators increasingly focus on the next election and the next president. Meanwhile, the political presence of the current president gradually fades like the Cheshire Cat in *Alice in Wonderland*. For example, President Bush immediately began to lose clout with his own party in Congress after his second election in 2004. "He's discovering the fine line between having a mandate and being a lame duck," a Senate GOP staff member explained.[143] Certainly no lame-duck president is left powerless.[144] Nevertheless, most presidents are strongest early in their terms, with their power slowly declining after that "like a large balloon with a slow leak."[145]

Third, presidents can be *removed from office* by being **impeached** by a majority vote of the House, then tried by the Senate and convicted by a two-thirds vote (see Chapter 11). That has never occurred, but, the near certain impeachment and removal of Richard Nixon drove him from office in 1974. It is also possible under the Twenty-Fifth Amendment to suspend a president from duty when either he alone or the vice president and a majority of the Cabinet together certify to Congress that the president is incapacitated. If the president were to disagree, he would continue his duties unless Congress decided by a two-thirds vote in each house to side with the vice president and Cabinet.

INFORMAL POWERS AND RESTRAINTS

One curiosity about the relative power of the presidency and Congress is that the balance has shifted to the presidency's advantage even though the language in the Constitution about the powers of the two institutions has not changed. How can that be? The answer is the presidency's informal powers. Their existence, one scholar writes, has the effect of creating "two constitutional presidencies." The first relates to the formal powers and restraints in the "original Constitution." The "second constitution" under which presidents govern is based on the changes that have occurred over time in "presidential and public understanding of the constitutional system and of the president's place in it."[146] Thus, the presidency's informal powers are rooted in how Americans, including members of Congress and other politicians, perceive and react to the office and its occupants. This dynamic creates expectations of what presidents should do as leader, and it enhances their ability to persuade others to follow their leadership.

Notice three things as you examine these informal powers. First, they are interrelated. For instance, how well a president is at meeting public expectations overall will add to or detract from his ability to persuade the public, Congress, and other political actors to follow his lead on specific policy issues. Second, the informal powers rest in substantial part on the president's august status as head of state. Third, the factors underlying the president's informal powers are two-edged swords that can diminish as well as enhance his authority. For this reason, each of the following sections will combine both powers and restraints.

Expectations of Leadership

Presidential power has grown in part because Americans have come to expect "active and continuous presidential leadership."[147] Not only have presidents regularly sought greater power, but the public, Congress, and other actors have often willingly agreed and sometimes have even urged presidents to take greater charge. This expectation of strong presidential leadership extends to all aspects of policy, but it is stronger in foreign policy than in domestic policy and also more insistent during crises than in normal times.

Expectations for foreign policy leadership by the president are long-standing, but the demand for strong domestic policy leadership is more recent. The watershed was the Great Depression of the 1930s and President Roosevelt's pledge in his first inaugural address that if Congress failed to act to address the crisis, he would "use broad executive power to wage a war against the emergency." Roosevelt's message was "look to the presidency for leadership." Americans did and still do. As a result, "Everybody now expects the man inside the While House to do something about everything."[148]

The demand for presidential leadership is also evident in how often Congress delegates its authority to the president. One review of grants of emergency authority to presidents found 470 existing laws dating back to 1799. These emergency grants are only part of the overall total through the years. Expectations also make the public willing to accept strong leadership without questioning the president's legal authority. Critics may have berated President Bush for authorizing antiterrorist wiretaps without court warrants, but a majority of the public was less concerned with the legalities than with the president's protecting them against terrorism.

Expectations also have their downside for presidents. One problem is that the public can punish them for what it perceives as weak leadership. Most Americans (57%) were disappointed in Bush's response to Hurricane Katrina in 2005, and this feeling generated a 5% drop in his approval rating during the two weeks following the storm.

More generally, the high expectations for presidential performance may doom all the occupants of the Oval Office to being perceived as inadequate. As early as the 1930s, a panel studying the presidency argued, "The nation expects more of the president than he can possibly do" and that "expecting from him the impossible, inevitably we shall be disappointed in his performance."[149] If anything, the intervening years have increased expectations and added to this concern. Indeed, one informal restraint on the powers of the presidency is the impossibility of anyone having the mental capacity to absorb all the information needed to deal with the mind-boggling array of issues every president faces and the physical stamina to do all Americans expect the president to do. As Lyndon Johnson described it, "The load is unbearable . . . you have to have the physical constitution of a mule."[150]

The Power to Persuade

Perhaps the most widely quoted comment on the power of presidents belongs to scholar Richard Neustadt: "Presidential power is the power to persuade."[151] Or as President Truman grumpily put it, "I sit here all day trying to persuade people to do the things they ought to have sense enough to do without my persuading them."[152] The power to persuade is based on such factors as presidential prestige and the country's focus of attention on the president.

Presidential Prestige

American presidents operate within an aura of prestige that increases their ability to persuade others to follow their leadership. As the U.S. head of government, presidents are the chief operating officer of a multitrillion-dollar enterprise that daily impacts every American in numerous ways. And as head of state, presidents lead the world's most powerful country and are also the living representation of both the people and their country, "the paternal leader of the nation."[153] Presidential prestige is especially effective when presidents project the image of non-partisan leadership in the realm of foreign policy. "Now the way to do that," one former secretary of state has explained, is to assert that party politics should not extend to foreign policy and that "anyone who denies that postulate is a son-of-a-bitch or a crook and not a true patriot. If people will swallow that, then you're off to the races."[154] Attesting to the impact of presidential prestige, one Democratic senator commented after listening to an appeal from Republican President Ronald Reagan, "After sitting down with most powerful person in the . . . whole world, . . . when the president says 'I need your help' that's a rather potent argument."[155]

Deference to the president is much less evident in domestic affairs. Presidents usually enjoy a "honeymoon" period after their election, especially their first one, during which they enjoy strong public opinion support and a willingness in Congress to follow their leadership. That soon fades, however. President Johnson's wife has recalled him telling his staff after his 1964 election that "they would have only six months or so before exhausted, resentful members of the House and Senate began to rebel against the lash of the White House."[156] Nevertheless, even in domestic affairs, the office, if not always the person in it, is accorded great respect.

Focus of Attention

Presidents also gain power to persuade by being the prime focus of Americans' political attention. The center-stage position that presidents enjoy reflects the reality of their power and prestige, as well as the propensity of people to connect better with a person than an institution. This "star power" enables presidents to far outshine either of the other two branches or any other political actor when competing for the attention of Americans.[157] Indeed, presidents get more than twice as much press coverage as the other two branches combined.[158]

One way that the president's central position empowers him is by giving him considerable ability to *set the political agenda*, to determine which issues are at the forefront of political discussions. Being the focus of attention also sometimes allows presidents to *define the situation*, to establish the context of policy. This is particularly true for foreign policy, where competing versions of the situation are less common. To a substantial degree, for example, public support for the invasion of Iraq in 2003 reflected the success of President Bush in defining the situation as one in which military action was necessary to counter an emerging nuclear threat.

A third way that being the focus of attention empowers presidents is by giving them some ability to mobilize public opinion.[159] It would be an error to think, however, that presidents can usually or easily manipulate public opinion. To the contrary, the ability of presidents to increase popular support for their policies is limited. This is especially true when a president is unpopular, when most of the public already opposes a policy, when there are many prominent dissenting views, and when domestic policy, rather than foreign policy, is at issue.[160]

President Obama's nationally broadcast speech on health-care reform to a joint session of Congress and to the country in September 2009 illustrates both the president's ability to influence public opinion and the limits to that influence. The speech did increase public support for health-care reform. Approval among those who watched the speech jumped 14%.[161] However, because only 32 million Americans watched the speech, overall support for heath care rose only a more modest 3% between the day before and the day after the speech. Moreover, that increase soon reversed itself, with public support falling off to its pre-speech within another three days.[162]

Limits to the Power to Persuade

Although the presidency has considerable power to persuade, its ability to do so is still limited. As we have seen, presidents often are unable to convince the public or the Congress to follow them because of such factors as having low public approval, facing an opposition Congress, and possessing poor public relations and legislative relations skills. Even skillful presidents are not political magicians. Instead, "successful presidents," as one scholar notes, are able politicians who achieve their goals by "recognizing opportunities in their environment and fashioning strategies and tactics to exploit them."[163]

EVALUATING THE PRESIDENCY AND PRESIDENTS

As we near the end of this chapter, it is worthwhile to ponder how to evaluate the presidency and its central figure, the president. Coming to definitive conclusions about how the presidency operates is difficult. One reason is that its workings are even less visible than those of the far less than fully transparent Congress and Supreme Court. They at least have votes that can be counted and analyzed, and most of their policy outputs are in written form such as bills or judicial opinions. Another problem in studying the presidency is that how it operates changes from president to president because each incumbent has a different management style. Some, for example, delegate broad authority to subordinates, while others try to micromanage details. Further confounding our ability to evaluate the presidency is the fact that the key element of that institution is the president. Each president has a unique array of abilities, views, experiences, and other idiosyncratic traits. Therefore each presidency is substantially different.

It is no easier to come up with simple statements about the power of the presidency. We can say that the overall power of the presidency has grown as government has taken on ever more functions. Presidential power has also grown relative to that of Congress, and the presidency has become the preeminent political actor. Beyond these statements, evaluations of presidential power are trickier because numerous variables cause it to ebb and flow. Therefore trying to decide questions about the power of the presidency often lead to additional questions about who the president is, what the situation is, and what the issue is.

Evaluating individual presidents may be even harder than analyzing the presidency. It is possible to say simultaneously that there is no consensus on what makes a good president and that the ideal qualifications are so extensive that it is impossible for anyone to have all or perhaps even most of them. Whatever might be reasonable standards for judging presidents, it is clear that, Americans have lost considerable faith in their government, including their presidents. Since the 1960s and early 1970s, the overall average public approval of presidents has trended downward. Moreover, most individual presidents finish their time in office far less popular than when they began it. Additionally, the press shares and amplifies the public's tendency to disapprove of presidents, compounding the difficulty of rallying public support.

The second factor in the poor evaluations that the public gives to presidents centers on the **paradoxes of the presidency**. This involves the public wanting presidents to act in contradictory ways. Americans want the president to lead decisively, yet to also listen to the public. People simultaneously want bold vision and pragmatic compromise. Presidents should get things done but follow the rules, be compassionate but not soft, and innovate but not force unsettling change on us. Needless to say, these conflicting desires put presidents in a no-win situation.[164]

Third, there is an **expectations gap** between what the people expect presidents to do and what they can possibly do given the

Americans' tendency to expect presidents to leap tall buildings at a single bound and otherwise act like superheroes in solving the country's problems leads the public almost inevitably to be disappointed in presidential performance. The very high initial expectations that Americans had for President Obama made the following disillusionment seem particularly profound. (Big Stock Photo)

limits of their power, intellect, and stamina[165]. Given what the nation expects of the White House's occupant, "The probability of failure [of a president in the public's view] is always tending toward 100 percent."[166]

In sum, the presidency is neither imperial nor besieged, as some have described it. Instead its power is complex and shifting. Moreover, because part of the president's power rests on informal sources, he is, to a degree, as powerful or restrained as we want him to be. Similarly, presidents as individual leaders are not, and perhaps cannot be, all that we want them to be. Yet neither are they as flawed as a constantly disappointed public deems them to be.

SUMMARY

The president is the most powerful actor in the U.S. political system, but that power has ebbed and flowed considerably and remains highly variable. One factor enhancing presidential power is that, unlike in most countries, U.S. presidents serve as both head of government and head of state. The president's formal powers are mostly based on his role as head of government. His informal powers draw heavily on his leadership status as head of state.

The presidency is distinct from the larger executive branch. The institutional presidency consists of the offices of president, vice president, the cabinet officers, and the Executive Office of the President. The EOP has grown in size and strength since the 1930s, and its power, especially that of the White House Office, raises a variety of concerns.

Presidents' decisions are based partly on what they see as the national interest. Other decision-making factors include partisan politics and each president's human traits such as personality.

Presidential power is dynamic. Over the long term, the absolute power of the presidency has grown greatly, and the presidency has become the preeminent part of the government. But how preeminent the presidency is varies greatly over the short-term according to such factors as the president's job skills, his popularity, and the situation and issue at hand.

Presidents have an imposing array of enumerated and implied formal powers including being the country's chief executive officer, its commander in chief, its head diplomat, and its chief law enforcement officer. Presidential power is subject to several formal restraints. Congress and the courts exercise a variety of restraints through checks and balances, and there are also limitations to continuing in office that constrain the presidency.

Presidents have informal powers and restraints on them based on political factors. Because the president's formal constitutional powers remain unchanged from what they were in 1789, it is the informal powers that presidents have that are the primary factor in the evolution and expansion of presidential power overall. At this informal level, presidential power is influenced by expectations. Americans expect presidents to be strong leaders and often defer to that leadership. Another informal power of the president is the power to persuade. A president's ability to do that is aided by his considerable prestige, especially as head of state, and by being the prime focus of political attention. Nevertheless, presidents have only limited success persuading others to follow their lead.

CHAPTER 12 GLOSSARY

Cabinet An informal, largely ceremonial advisory board to the president made up of the 15 units of the executive branch that are generally the largest and have the broadest responsibilities.

chief of staff The ranking official in the White House Office who oversees its functions and, to a degree, those of the rest of the Executive Office of the President.

crisis situation A circumstance that arises and is heightened in intensity the more people are surprised, feel individually threatened (especially physically), or believe that there is significant and immediate danger to the country, and in which the time to react to or avert the danger is short.

delegations of power An agreement by one branch of government, usually Congress, to let some of its constitutional authority be exercised by another branch, usually the Executive.

divided government When the White House is in the hands of one party and one or both houses of Congress are controlled by the other party.

enumerated powers Authority of the federal government that is specifically mentioned in the Constitution, especially in Article I, Section 8.

executive agreements All formal agreements other than treaties between the United States and a foreign government. They are made by presidents under their executive authority or under congressional authority.

Executive Office of the President (EOP) The personnel and offices that are connected directly to the White House and that focus on supporting the president.

executive orders Formal presidential directives to the bureaucracy that have legal standing.

executive privilege A right claimed by the executive branch, based on the constitutional principle of separation of powers, to reject some encroachments by Congress and the courts, including demands that executive officials provide particular types of information.

expectations gap The gap between what the people expect presidents to do and what presidents can practically achieve given the limits of their power, intellect, and physical stamina.

formal powers Authority derived from the Constitution and statutory law.

head of government The ranking official with the legal authority to administer the government and carry out its laws and policies.

head of state The ranking ceremonial official who symbolizes the state and its people.

impeach An action by majority vote in the House of Representatives to indict a federal official. The trial is conducted by the Senate, with a two-thirds vote required to convict.

implied powers Powers of the federal government that are not specifically mentioned in the Constitution but that are logically derived from the authority that is specified there. See "enumerated powers" and "necessary and proper clause."

informal powers Authority derived from the president's political standing.

line-item veto The ability to strike out parts of bills, usually appropriations acts.

modern presidency An era beginning in the 1930s and continuing today in which presidents have power that is consistently greater than that which earlier presidents normally wielded.

national security advisor The special assistant to the president for national security affairs and staff director of the National Security Council.

Office of Management and Budget (OMB) An agency within the Executive Office of the President that prepares the president's annual budget proposal and helps oversee the bureaucracy.

paradoxes of the presidency Contradictions in what the public wants from the president, such as decisive leadership yet attention to public sentiment.

parliamentary system A system of government characterized by divided executive leadership involving both a head of state and a head of government, with the head of government elected by the legislature and serving variable terms of office.

presidential approval rating Percent of the public that approves of the way that the president is doing his job.

presidential signing statement A formal written statement sometimes inserted into the record by presidents when they sign legislation. These statements increasingly contain the president's view of his constitutional authority under the new law and otherwise guide executive agencies regarding the meaning and implementation of the law.

presidential system A system of government characterized by a single executive leader, who serves as both the chief executive officer and as the symbolic head of state and who is elected by the voters for a fixed term of office.

presidential war power The ability of the president to commit U.S. forces to combat or to immediate danger without a declaration of war or other authorization by Congress.

rally effect The tendency of the public to support the president and the president's policy during times of crisis, especially foreign policy crisis that involves potential or actual military action or other physical threats to Americans.

stewardship theory The idea first advanced by Theodore Roosevelt that presidents serve as the steward, or caretaker, of the people and are bound to do everything to benefit the people that is not specifically prohibited by the Constitution.

two presidencies theory The idea that in terms of power, the analysis the presidency can be divided between a relatively more powerful foreign policy presidency and a relatively less powerful domestic policy presidency.

veto A formal act by which a president returns a measure to Congress, stating his objections.

War Powers Resolution A joint resolution passed by Congress in 1973 and put into law over the veto of President Richard Nixon that directs the president to report to Congress any military action that he orders and to terminate it within 60 days unless he had received legislative authority to continue the action.

White House Office A unit of the Executive Office of the President that includes the president's closest political staff. Unlike other executive branch officials, those of the White House Office are subject neither to Senate confirmation nor to being required to testify before Congress.

BUREAUCRACY

13

YOU DECIDE: Administrative Justice or Bureaucratic Usurpation?

AMERICAN DIVERSITY

Sometimes government agencies have the power to decide if you even exist. That was true for the 273-member Schaghticoke Tribal Nation (STN) that in 1994 petitioned the Bureau of Indian Affairs (BIA) to become one of the nearly 600 federally recognized American Indian tribes. To be recognized, groups must prove they meet seven standards by presenting specific types of evidence detailed in the *Code of Federal Regulations* (CFR). For the STN, recognition involved acceptance as an historic people. It also meant access to federal funds for recognized tribes and tens of millions of dollars from a casino they hoped to open in Connecticut.

In 2002 the BIA announced its preliminary decision that the STN had failed to meet all the standards and would be denied recognition unless new evidence was presented. Then in 2004 the BIA reversed itself and recognized the STN. A leaked BIA document indicated that its investigators continued to find that the Schaghticokes had not provided the required evidence to meet one of the recognition tests: that the group had exercised "political influence or authority over its members as an autonomous entity from historical times until the present."[1] Nevertheless, the memorandum favored recognizing the STN based on the continuous existence of a state-recognized reservation. The memo conceded that using this fact "would require a change" in what the BIA considered as evidence.[2] Yet doing so was permissible, the memo reasoned, because the CFR's list of acceptable evidence included the catchall phrase, "or by other evidence that the petitioner meets the definition of political influence or authority."[3]

Some saw the outcome as an example of a bureaucracy run amok. Alarmed at the prospect of another casino in Connecticut, the state's entire congressional delegation charged that the BIA had "ignored, overrode, or waived existing criteria" in

a "flawed recognition process."[4] In even stronger language, Connecticut Attorney General Richard Blumenthal thundered, "The BIA is lawless . . . and must be stopped." Others contended that the BIA had acted within its discretion under the CFR and also had made a just decision in light of the deprivations Native Americans have historically suffered. "What happened to the . . . indigenous peoples of New England is now a familiar tale. . . . The Indians were scattered and forced to struggle to survive," one scholar wrote. Given this history, he continued, denying recognition was tantamount to ensuring "that these Indians remain on the path to extinction."[5] As for the BIA, it defended its decision by arguing that the regulations "are permissive and inherently flexible, and therefore afford latitude in the evidence used."[6]

Whatever the truth of the matter, the political outcry against the BIA decision had its impact. After a year of criticism, including Senate hearings on the matter, senior officials at the Department of the Interior reversed the agency's findings once again and denied the STN recognition. The Schaghticokes appealed, but after losing at both the district court then circuit court of appeals levels, their quest for recognition almost certainly ended in 2010 when the U.S. Supreme Court refused to hear their case. Within this controversial tale is the more abstract, but very important point about the ability of appointed administrators to have a profound impact on policy and on people. The saga also raises the issue of what authority administrators should have in a democracy. Regardless of what you think of the specific decision about the STN, do you think that bureaucrats should have the authority to make far-reaching decisions, such as what the rules for recognition are and who meets them?

INTRODUCING BUREAUCRACY

The saga of the Schaghticokes seeking recognition provides insight into the importance of the **bureaucracy**: government agencies and their appointed administrators. In particular, the fate of the Schaghticokes introduces and helps explain why studying the bureaucracy is important.

Why Study Bureaucracy?

One reason to study bureaucracy is that a great deal of policy is the result of the formal rules and the day-to-day decisions made by appointed administrators.[7] This role is reflected in the term *bureaucracy*, which combines *bureau*, the French word for *desk*, with *kratia* or *kratos*, Greek words for *power* or *rule*.

Sometimes, bureaucrats make momentous decisions. Within weeks after President George Bush sent U.S. military forces led by General Tommy Franks into Afghanistan in 2001, the al-Qaeda terrorist group and its host, the Taliban government, had been routed. It was widely thought that Osama bin Laden, other top al-Qaeda leaders, and several thousand of their fighters had fled to the Tora Bora cave complex located in the rugged mountains of eastern Afghanistan. Rather than deploy available elements of the U.S. 10th Mountain Division to cut off bin Laden's escape route to Pakistan and take Tora Bora, General Franks chose to rely largely on an irregular Afghani force of about 2,000 under the control of two area warlords supported by about 90 American commandos and U.S. air power. This tactic failed, and bin Laden escaped.

Why General Franks made his decision is unimportant here. Instead, the thing to see is how a decision made by a career administrator, in this case a general, can have an immense impact. Looking back, a Senate Foreign Relations Committee report in 2009 concluded that the decision "that opened the door for [bin Laden's] escape . . . represents a lost opportunity that forever altered the course of the conflict in Afghanistan and the future of international terrorism, leaving the American people more vulnerable to terrorism [and], laying the foundation for today's protracted Afghan insurgency."[8]

Other examples of bureaucratic decisions and rules are less consequential, but still important to individuals or groups and, in the aggregate, help shape the country. Each day, for example, thousands of police officers stop motorists for traffic violations and decide whether or not to ticket them or just give them a warning. Similarly, each day brings many new federal regulations. On just one randomly selected day, October 9, 2009, the Federal Register recorded 28 new or proposed rules related to such diverse topics as commercial fishing, environmental standards for nuclear power plants, pesticide use, and in-patient Medicare payments.

Military officers, like other career government officials, are bureaucrats, and how they implement policy can have a major impact. Arguably the decisions made by one such officer may have let al-Qaeda leader Osama bin Laden escape capture in 2001. (AP Photo)

A second reason to care about bureaucracy is that it is involved with virtually every aspect of governance (the act or process of governing). At the federal level, one or more of the approximately 200 agencies have a say in nearly every aspect of American society. Some functions, such as the Federal Reserve Board's role in setting interest rates, draw wide notice. Others draw less attention but still affect our daily activities from the time we have breakfast (Food and Drug Administration regulation: "Prevention of Salmonella in Shell Eggs") to the time we go to bed (Consumer Protection Safety Agency regulation: "Standard for the Flammability of Mattresses").

Adding to the omnipresence of the bureaucracy, there are 50 state governments, 5 territorial governments (such as that of Puerto Rico), and more than 89,000 county, municipal, and other local governments. Each has an administrative structure that annually adds what must be hundreds of thousands of rules and billions of implementation decisions to the totality of American governance.

This chapter will continue our examination of the key role of the bureaucracy by exploring administrative authority, the relationship between bureaucratic power and democracy, and what, if any, reforms are needed. During this discussion, you will see that:

★ The bureaucracy is important because of its power and its omnipresence in society.
★ Bureaucracy is a part of government globally.
★ How much discretion administrators do and should have is a key issue.
★ The bureaucracy has evolved by becoming much larger and increasingly insulated from political direction.
★ How the bureaucracy is organized has important policy implications.
★ The actions of bureaucrats are influenced by their personal perspective and by the organizational perspective of their agency.
★ Demographically, the top level of the bureaucracy does not reflect American society.
★ Bureaucrats derive power from their ability to make rules, to adjudicate them, and to implement policy.
★ Bureaucrats also derive power from their expertise, influence over the information flow, public standing, and political alliances.
★ Bureaucratic power is limited by constraints on agency resources and agency actions.

Bureaucracy in a World of Difference

Bureaucracy is not an American invention. Instead, having an administrative structure and staff goes back to the dawn of government. Functionaries became necessary to help govern once government moved beyond settlements whose populations and territories were small enough to be personally overseen by a single leader or council. Ancient records in Mesopotamia, China, and elsewhere speak of the presence and power of the *imy-ras*, or overseers, as the earliest Egyptians entitled their upper- and mid-ranking bureaucrats.

Bureaucracy in the United States and elsewhere has evolved in somewhat similar ways. First, as the size, scope, and complexity of governments and their activities have expanded, it has become ever more difficult for the relative handful of elected and appointed political leaders in any country to exercise effective authority. The result has been an expansion of administrative structures and workforce to provide the expertise and personnel required to cope with modern government. As just one measure, there was only 1 civilian federal employee for every 2,000 Americans in 1792. Now there are 23 federal workers for every 2,000 Americans. Similar growth has occurred in other countries. Now in the average economically developed country, about one in every seven workers is a civilian public employee, as depicted in Figure 13.1.

 At 28%, Norway has the world's highest percentage of government workers in its total workforce.

Second, political leaders have found themselves increasingly frustrated with their reliance on and the difficulty of controlling the administrative structures they head. Although there was little common ground among the leaders of the United States, the Soviet Union, and China during the cold war, they shared a frustration with their limited control over their bureaucracies. "One of the hardest things about being president," President Ronald Reagan (1981–1989) once grumbled, "is to know that down there, underneath, is a permanent structure that's resisting everything you're doing." Similarly, Soviet President Mikhail Gorbachev (1985–1991) complained that his bureaucracy was marked by "conservative sentiments, inertia, [and] a tendency to brush aside everything that does not fit into conventional patterns." Adding his frustration, China's leader, Zhao Ziyang (1987–1989), lamented that the "unwieldiness of government organs, confusion of their responsibilities, and buck-passing" constituted a "serious problem in the political life of our party and state."[9]

FIGURE 13.1 Comparative Government Employment

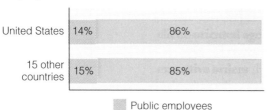

United States 14% 86%

15 other countries 15% 85%

■ Public employees
■ Private employees

One indication of the global extent of bureaucracies is the fact that national, regional, and local public civilian workers now make up an average of 15% of the total workforce in economically developed countries like the United States.
Data source: Organization for Economic Cooperation and Development.

Third, "good government" reforms around the world have included steps to insulate routine administration from political control. This has involved such steps as using tests and other mechanisms to regularize the hiring process, making it illegal for government employees to engage in many forms of politics, and protecting government workers from being fired except for just cause. Such reforms have their advantages, but they have also made it even more difficult for leaders to control the bureaucracy and keep it responsive to the elected leadership and the will of the people.

Fourth, the evolution of bureaucracies in recent decades has included efforts in the United States and other countries to increase diversity in the administrative ranks. Better gender and racial representation among senior officials is particularly important.

Bureaucracy and American Diversity

As just noted, whites and males are overrepresented in the bureaucracy. This is particularly so among top-ranking administrators. However, it is also the case that diversity is improving. Of particular note, the presence of women and minorities among the highest-ranking civil service positions is slowly growing, as is evident in Figure 13.2.

A diverse bureaucracy is particularly important to women and racial or ethnic minorities who have traditionally suffered economic and other disadvantages that often place them in need of government assistance. At the same time, there has also been a history of bias in the administration of federal programs, sometimes from a lack of understanding on the part of bureaucrats and sometimes because of racism or sexism. These factors combine to yield a disproportionate impact on those who are underrepresented in the bureaucratic workforce.

FIGURE 13.2 Diversity Among Senior Executives

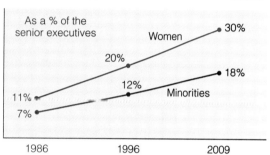

There has been a steady if slow increase in the presence of women and minorities in the highest three grades (GS16–GS18) that make up the senior executive corps in the federal civil service.
Data source: U.S. Office of Personnel Management.

AN OVERVIEW OF BUREAUCRACY

Taken as a whole, the interconnected U.S. federal-state-local bureaucracy is one of the world's largest, most complex, and most powerful organizations. Including those in military uniform, more than 23 million people work directly for the government. Some sense of how many people that is can be gained from the fact that they outnumber the populations of 70% of the world's countries. However, the number of American government workers is not as important as the authority they wield through their ability to make rules and to influence the formation and implementation of policies that touch on virtually every aspect of American society.

Evolution

Bureaucracy in the United States has evolved in two important ways. It has become much larger, and it has generally become more insulated from political direction.

Growth

An important theme in the story of American governments is the steady growth of government, especially over the last century or so. This trend is also found in most of the other economically developed countries. In the United States and elsewhere, there have been marked increases in government spending as a percentage of national economic activity, and the range of societal activities that government programs address has also expanded. This growth of government activity has inevitably increased the number of agencies and the number of government workers.

Organizations   In 1789, the federal bureaucracy was limited to four Cabinet departments (State, War, Treasury, and Justice) and the Post Office Department. Now there are over 65 major operational units, including 15 Cabinet departments, more than 50 major independent agencies and government corporations, another 150 or so medium to small agencies and other units, and 1,000 or so advisory committees. These are detailed further below, but the point here is the upward spiral in the number of organizational units in the federal government.

Personnel   Similarly, the number of government workers has increased. Between 1960 and 2008, for instance, the number of civilian federal workers increased 13%. Many Americans think that such statistics mean the bureaucracy is too large. One survey found 73% of respondents wanting elected officials to give "top priority" to reducing the number of federal employees, while 15% wanted that goal to be a "mid-list" priority, 6% a "toward bottom" of the list priority, and 5% were unsure.[10]

To help judge whether cutting the size of the federal bureaucracy is a worthwhile goal, note several facts. First, as Figure 13.3 indicates, the increase in federal civilian employment has been modest compared to the growth of the U.S. population or the growth of per capita federal spending. Second, the American level of public employment is not unusual compared to other countries. It falls about mid-range for economically developed countries, as documented in Figure 13.1.

Third, most public employees do not work for the U.S. government. It employs only 12% of all civilian government workers. States employ another 23% of these workers, and local governments account for 65%. A similar distribution is found in many countries with a federal system. In Germany, for example, the national

FIGURE 13.3   Population, Federal Employees, and per Capita Spending 1960–2008

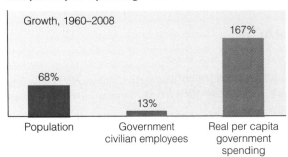

Between 1960 and 2008 the number of full-time civilian employees of the federal government increased much more slowly than did either the country's population or the federal government's per capita spending.
Notes and data sources: Spending in real (constant) dollars (controlled for inflation). Employees include postal workers. Data from the *Statistical Abstract of the United States.*

government employs 12% of the public workforce; the *landers* (states) and local governments employ the other 88%. Under unitary governments, by contrast, subnational governments are more administrative units than policy-making entities. Therefore, the national government employs most government workers. In France, for example, 63% of the public workforce is national and 27% is regional and local.

Fourth, most of the bureaucratic growth in the United States has occurred at the state and local levels. This is shown in Figure 13.4.

FIGURE 13.4 Growth of Public Employees

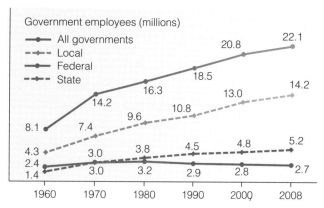

Government civilian employment increased 154% between 1960 and 2008. But most of the increase has been at the local level, which nearly tripled.

Notes and data sources: Civilian employees only. Data from the *U.S. Statistical Abstract*

Increased Insularity from Political Pressure

"To the victor belongs the spoils" is often associated with military victory, but the phrase has also often been applied to American politics. During the early years of the republic, the process of appointing government workers gradually became a **patronage system** (or **spoils system**), one in which elected leaders staffed government agencies with those who provided campaign contributions and other forms of political support. By the time of President Andrew Jackson (1828–1837), according to one senator, it was normal for elected officials to "see nothing wrong in the rule that to the victor belong the spoils of the enemy,"[11] that is, to enrich yourself with offices and other advantages called "spoils" (from the Latin, *spolium*, armor and other valuables stripped from a defeated foe).

Creation of the Civil Service System Frustration with the frequent incompetence, corruption, and other inequities associated with the patronage system led to increasing calls for change. These gathered momentum as part of Americans' general discontent with government and the reform movement during the Progressive Era (about 1880 to 1920). A more immediate impetus for change was the assassination of President James A. Garfield in 1881 by Charles Guiteau, a deranged attorney who had supported Garfield and then unsuccessfully sought appointment as the U.S. counsel in Paris as a reward. A shocked Congress enacted the **Pendleton Act** (1883). It

A major impetus for establishing the modern U.S. civil service was the assassination of President James A. Garfield in 1881 by a former supporter who had not been rewarded with a government job. This drawing from a newspaper at the time shows the scene immediately after Garfield (center, holding back) had been shot in a Washington, D.C., railway station by Charles Guiteau, who is being detained by bystanders (left side of drawing). (Library of Congress)

established a **merit system**, the process of hiring and promoting employees based on education, experience, and competitive examinations. The new law also protected government employees from being fired except for criminality or other specific reasons. Additionally, the legislation created the Civil Service Commission (now the Office of Personnel Management, OPM) to oversee this process. All this laid the foundation for a modern **civil service** with its nonpartisan, professional government administrators. Initially, only about 10% of all federal jobs were removed from the patronage system, but by 1900 about half were under the civil service system. Today, nearly all federal government employees are career civil servants in the general system under OPM or the special systems of the courts and the military, intelligence, and foreign services.

Pros and Cons of the Civil Service System The advantages of insulating most government workers from political pressure are many and obvious. Administrators should decide if you get admitted to a state university, whether your tax return will be audited, and most other matters depending on the merits of the case, not on your party affiliation or some other political consideration. A civil service in which appointment and promotion is based on merit is also more apt to foster technical expertise and administrative competence among civil servants. It is not necessary to extend this list to make its point that apolitical, consistent administration conducted by able career administrators is generally synonymous with good government.

Yet a civil service has drawbacks. One is the insularity of government administrators from political direction. As we will discuss presently, bureaucrats often have their own perspectives on policy. These views can cause administrators consciously or unconsciously to make rules or to implement policy in a way that favors their own preferences rather than those of elected officials. This ability to manipulate policy once led President John Kennedy to tell a visitor who suggested a certain policy direction, "I agree with you, but I don't know if the government will."[12]

Such comments by elected leaders are common and raise a difficult problem for a democracy. What should be the balance between civil servants closely following the political direction of elected officials and the letter of the law, on the one hand, and, on the other, having the flexibility to shape policy based on their expertise and the day-to-day exigencies they encounter while implementing policy? Thinking about this issue can then help shape your opinions about what, if any, reforms are needed. Be careful to keep principles in mind rather than deciding on a case-by-case method to avoid having your favored approach turn out to be a double-edged sword that cuts against your preferences in a different matter and another agency.

Another issue with the civil service system is that it can sometimes shield the incompetent. Less than one-tenth of 1% of federal civilian workers are fired annually for poor performance or for misconduct. The percentage is much lower than for private industry. This matter was a point of controversy when Congress was establishing the 170,000 employee Department of Homeland Security in 2002. Some wanted to dispense with many civil service rules in the agency. For one, Senator Phil Gramm (R-TX) argued that "in the name of national security and personnel flexibility," the president should have the power to "override collective bargaining agreements," that is, to more easily hire, reassign, and fire agency personnel.[13] Some Democrats opposed the president, but in the end the administration got most of the authority it wanted.

Structure

On the surface, discussing government organization may seem bland, but behind it there is often a history of political drama. Organizational arrangements are often hotly contested because they "are not neutral." Instead, one expert explains, they are "one way of expressing national commitment, influencing program direction, and ordering priorities," and they "tend to give some interests and perspectives more effective access" to influence.[14]

Types of Bureaucratic Units

If you were to consult the *U.S. Government Organization Manual*, you would see that various main units of the executive branch are designated by such names as administration, agency, authority, board, bureau, commission, committee, corporation, corps, council, department, foundation, institute, institution, office, service, or system. Many of these terms also designate subordinate units. For example, there are Departments of the Air Force, Army, and Navy within the Department of Defense. What this plethora of overlapping names indicates is that what a unit is called and its status are not necessarily connected. With that said, it is still possible to divide the executive branch into various types of units.

Cabinet Departments   There are 15 **Cabinet departments**. With a few exceptions, they are the largest agencies with the broadest responsibilities. They employ about 60% of all civilian federal workers. Except for the attorney general, who leads the Department of Justice, the heads of these 15 units are called secretaries, and they make up the president's Cabinet. The president appoints the department heads and their principal deputies and can remove them at will.

In addition to the heads of the Cabinet departments, there are other "Cabinet-level" officers. These include the vice president, several top officials from the Executive Office of the President (the White House chief of staff, the director of the Office of Management and Budget, the U.S. Trade Representative, and the chair of the Council of Economic Advisers), one agency head (the administrator of the Environmental Protection Agency), and the U.S. ambassador to the United Nations. The "Cabinet-level" designation adds prestige to various posts but carries no extra authority. Of these officials, only the vice president and the chief of staff regularly attend Cabinet meetings. The other officials may attend Cabinet meetings at the president's invitation but so too may any official the president chooses to invite.

Independent Agencies   A second major component of the executive branch includes the independent agencies. There are about 50 such agencies, which can fall into two subgroups.

Independent regulatory agencies such as the Federal Communications Commission and the Food and Drug Administration compose the first subgroup. These agencies establish regulations and also have a quasi-judicial function that involves determining whether organizations and individuals have met those regulations or have violated them. As such, these agencies are supposed to be independent of partisan control. Their independence rests on the fact that each is governed by a board of 5 to 10 members who have staggered terms and who, although appointed by the president, may be removed only for specific causes, such as corruption. President Franklin Roosevelt tried to assert his control over these boards by claiming that he could fire any presidential appointee. To show that, he fired a member of the board of the Federal Trade Commission, but in the ensuing legal challenge, the Supreme Court rejected Roosevelt's claimed authority.[15]

Many independent regulatory agencies are an important policy force because of the key functions they perform. A prime example is the Federal Reserve System, often called the "Fed." It regulates interest rates and other aspects of monetary body. One testament to the power of the Fed came from the *Washington Post*'s characterization of the chairman of the Fed's Board of Governors as, "Second to the president . . . [as] arguably the nation's most powerful person."[16]

Independent administrative agencies such as the Environmental Protection Agency (EPA) are the second subgroup. They have operational and/or administrative functions that, for one reason or another, were kept apart from the operations of any of the Cabinet departments. When, for example, the EPA was established in 1970, President Richard Nixon favored placing it in the Department of the Interior. However, many strong environmentalists wanted the EPA to be separate as a way of enhancing its status. Environmentalists also worried that the new agency might be undermined if it were controlled by the Interior Department, which has responsibilities for mineral and energy development and is often seen as dominated by commercial interests. A final note about these agencies is that despite their designation, they are not truly independent because their heads are subject to removal by the president.

Government Corporations   There are six **government corporations**. They are structured like a business and provide specific services and charge fees. The oldest is the Tennessee Valley Authority. It was founded in 1933 to supply electricity in its region, and the TVA's more than 40 generating plants are a major source of power. Even more familiar is the United States Postal Service (USPS), which became a government corporation in 1970. It has a budget of over $70 billion (2009), and its 656,000 workers make it the country's second largest civilian employer (after Wal-Mart with 1.4 million U.S. workers). AMTRAK (the National Railroad Passenger Corporation) and the Federal Deposit Insurance Corporation are two other well-known government corporations.

Miscellaneous Units   In addition to these major units, there are numerous others of medium to minor consequence. These include over 60 boards, committees, or commissions; 4 quasi-official institutes (such as the Smithsonian); and over 1,000 federal advisory committees. In sum, there are so many government units and subunits that even the experts who compile the *U.S. Government Organization Manual* are not sure they know them all. As the section listing these miscellaneous organizations puts it, "While the editors have attempted to compile a complete and accurate listing, suggestions for improving coverage of this guide are welcome."

Form Sometimes Follows Function

Master architect Louis H. Sullivan (1856–1924) stressed the principle that form should follow function. This is the idea that a building's structure should be governed by its intended use. To a degree, this principle also applies to governments. Their functions and how those functions have changed are often revealed in organizational charts. The structure or form of the executive branch in 1790 indicates that its activity was weighted much more heavily toward foreign affairs compared to domestic affairs than is true today. Two of the top five appointed officials, the secretaries of state and war, were involved exclusively in foreign affairs. The secretary of the treasury also had a significant external orientation because most federal revenue in 1790 was raised by tariffs. Only the Attorney General and the Post Master General had a mostly domestic orientation. The founding of the Department of Agriculture in 1862 reflected the importance of farming to the country, just as establishing the Department of Housing and Urban Development 103 years later suggests how much the country had changed from a rural to an urban society. More recently, creating the Department of Homeland Security in 2002 reflected yet another new reality in American life, a greater threat of terrorist attacks.

Organizational shifts also indicate changes in the federal government's approach to governance. Initially, the federal government emphasized providing support through units like the Post Office Department (1789) and the Department of Agriculture (1862). Later organizational charts contain the saga of Washington's evolution toward also regulating domestic activity. The first specific regulatory unit, the Interstate Commerce Commission, was established in 1887. Then in 1913, the federal government moved to control monetary policy by creating the Federal Reserve System. Since then, government regulation has spread, and numerous agencies to implement these regulations have been created.

Form Sometimes Follows Politics

Sometimes how the government is organized is less connected to its functions than to the influence of interest groups, public opinion, and other pressures on the government. Many important units of government exist at least in part because one or more interest groups lobbied for their creation. What these groups sought was a major bureaucratic unit that would support their cause and that they could dominate to some degree. Such units are sometimes called **client-oriented agencies**, reflecting their sympathy toward the interest groups they service or regulate and the mutually supportive relationship they have with those groups. Noting that many of the top bureaucrats in his department and many of the leaders in private agriculture had worked together for years, one secretary of agriculture commented that the links formed "a small, incestuous community," in which, "everybody knew each other."[17] Moreover, even when agencies are not specially client oriented, there is evidence that they are not immune from pressure by interest groups, with business groups being particularly successful in exercising influence.[18]

The Department of Education provides an example of an agency created with interest group support. Long-standing efforts by teachers and others to involve the federal government in education gained momentum in the 1950s and 1960s, bringing increased federal aid and the creation of the Department of Health, Education and Welfare in 1953. Still, the National Education Association (NEA) and other teachers' groups wanted a Cabinet department dedicated specifically to their concerns. The opportunity to achieve that goal arose in 1976 during Jimmy Carter's presidential campaign. Reportedly in exchange for a pledge to support creating a new department, the NEA endorsed Carter. Once elected, he pressed Congress to establish the Department of Education in 1979. Thus, as a *Washington Post* columnist put it, Carter backed the agency "largely as a political payoff" for the NEA.[19]

Fragmented Form

Whatever the reasons behind the organization of the executive branch, it is a maze of overlapping responsibilities and crosscutting authority. To a degree this may be inevitable given the government's complex array of functions. Fragmentation is often also the product of the political forces that come into play as agencies and their supporters struggle to preserve the agency's budget and other resources, and its "bureaucratic turf," or realm of responsibility. For example, "foreign intelligence" may sound like a single function, but it is not. To the contrary, the 9/11 Commission's report in 2004 on the events leading up to 9/11 focused on the absence of cooperation, much less coordination, among the FBI, the CIA, the National Security Administration, the Defense Intelligence Agency, and the dozen other units conducting foreign intelligence activities.

To address this problem, Congress created a Director of National Intelligence to coordinate these intelligence units. It is not clear, though, how effective that has been. For example, after Army Major Nidal Malik Hasan shot and killed 13 people and wounded 43 others on the Fort Hood Army base in Texas in November 2009, information came to light that indicated that various government offices were aware that Hasan was acting suspiciously in ways such as communicating with a radical Muslim imam located in Yemen. In the aftermath, Senator Susan Collins (R-ME) lamented, "There were warning signs and red flags galore" about possible terrorist inclinations.[20] Yet nothing was done. Just a month later, another alleged terrorist, Umar Farouk Abdulmutallab of Nigeria, attempted to set off a bomb on a Northwest Airlines flight as it approached Detroit on Christmas day. Yet again, various agencies had not shared information that might have led to revoking Abdulmutallab's visa and putting his name on the no-fly list. Commenting on the progress toward coordination among U.S. antiterrorist operations, former congressman Lee Hamilton, vice-chair of the 9/11 Commission, noted with considerable understatement that the "incident surely illustrates we've got a long ways to go."[21]

A final point is that while fragmentation is usually a problem, sometimes it is a plus. If, for example, the Department of Interior grants permission to an oil exploration company to drill on public lands and the EPA opposes it, then perhaps there are competing voices and eventually a better resolution of differences. Similarly, Secretary of the Interior Ken Salazar responded to the BP oil spill disaster in 2010 by moving to dismantle his department's Minerals Management Service and divide its responsibilities for leasing offshore sites for drilling oil wells and parcels for energy projects, for making and enforcing safety rules, and for collecting royalty payments from the energy companies among three new agencies. "These three missions . . . are conflicting missions and must be separated," Salazar explained.[22]

By this logic, consolidation can sometimes put too much power in one place. Fear of terrorism makes consolidating intelligence functions under a single intelligence "czar" seem attractive, but to be fully effective, that person would require tremendous power over an organization with vast abilities to look into the lives of Americans at home as well as potential enemies abroad. Such czars also tend to be located within the White House office, making it difficult for Congress to exercise its oversight authority, as detailed in Chapter 12. Thus there may be pluses in bureaucratic fragmentation in a democracy.

Bureaucratic Perspective

Max Weber, an early student of bureaucracy, argued that ideal bureaucrats would be "dehumanized" individuals who eliminate "all purely personal, irrational, and emotional elements" from their decisions."[23] Perhaps, but that is an impossible standard as long as people, not machines, staff government agencies. Instead, administrators will continue to approach their jobs based in part on **bureaucratic perspective**. This acts like a mental lens that shapes the information and argumentation that pass through it. The two sources of perspective are (1) each individual's personal perceptions and values and (2) the organizational perceptions and values of the agency in which they work.

Personal Perspective

Each bureaucrat's personal perspective is the product of many factors such as the individual's experiences, ideology, personality, education and expertise, ego, ambition, and even physical and mental health. Examining the ideology of bureaucrats and also their background will illustrate two of the many personal factors that shape each bureaucrat's orientation.

Ideology Administrators who the president appoints to top policy-making posts are often chosen explicitly for their ideology and party connections, and understandably view their jobs from that perspective. But even career civil servants, like most other Americans, have an ideological orientation and a party preference that arguably influence their decisions in many subtle, even subconscious ways. One study of the ideological orientations of bureaucrats found that government workers were more liberal than the general populations in 12 of the 18 countries it reviewed, including the United States.[24] However, in many of these countries, again including the United States, the liberal orientation of the government workforce was not pronounced.

Additionally, bureaucrats are more likely to work in agencies that align with their ideological/partisan perspective rather than differ from it. Figure 13.5 shows, for instance, that conservatives are more apt to be found in the

FIGURE 13.5 Civil Servant Ideology

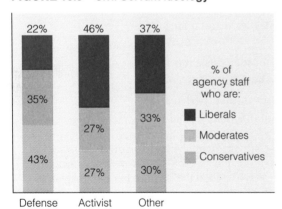

According to one study, conservatives were a plurality of the civil servants in defense agencies, liberals were a plurality in activist agencies, and there was a mix in agencies without a pronounced ideological orientation.

Data source: Robert Maranto and Karen Marie Hult, "Right Turn? Political Ideology in the Higher Civil Service, 1987–1994," *The American Review of Public Administration,* 34/2 (2004), Table 3, p. 207.

Department of Defense and liberals are more common in activist agencies such as the Department of Housing and Urban Development. Workers in less ideological agencies have more of a mix of personal orientations.[25]

Among other impacts, the ideology of these civil servants influenced how they evaluated and interacted with the political administrators who had been appointed by presidents of different parties. Defense Department workers approved of the administrators in that department appointed by President Reagan more than members of the activist agencies approved of his appointees to their departments. With President Clinton in office, this approval shifted. Activist agency personnel were much more likely than Defense Department staff to approve his appointments to administer their respective agencies.[26]

Background Most civil servants spend their career in the bureaucracy, but the top administrators appointed by presidents are often chosen because of their political views and experience. Supporters of this practice argue that it puts in place administrators who will ensure that agencies follow rather than resist the direction of elected leaders. Opponents claim that political appointees are often biased by their background and cannot administer policy with an even hand. Consider such a controversy in "You Decide: Expertise or Bias?"

YOU DECIDE: Expertise or Bias?

Controversy erupted during George W. Bush's presidency when Deputy Secretary of the Interior J. Steven Griles tried to persuade the EPA not to block as "environmentally unsound" a plan by the energy industry to drill up to 80,000 methane gas wells in the Powder River Basin of Wyoming and Montana. Environmentalists charged that Griles had improperly intervened because he had been an executive in and top lobbyist for the energy industry before his appointment. The Friends of the Earth derided Griles as "the Mike Tyson of the coal and oil industry operatives."[27] By contrast, Secretary of the Interior Gale Norton defended Griles's background as providing "enormous institutional knowledge as well as extensive experience" for his job.[28]

In a separate controversy soon thereafter, as related in this chapter's opening You Decide box, critics of the Bureau of Indian Affairs accused it of violating the rules when it granted federal recognition to the Schaghticokes. Deputy Assistant Secretary of the Interior for Indian Affairs Aurene M. Martin made the decision. She is a member of the Bad River Band of Lake Superior Chippewa. Prior to her appointment she had served as senior legal counsel for the Oneida Nation of Wisconsin. This background raised the issue of her neutrality in the minds of some, including Connecticut's attorney general, who charged that "personal agendas" had influenced Martin's decision.[29]

The issue here is whether appointed administrators who have connections with the areas that their agency oversees bring expertise or bias into the policy-making process. If bias, is that always bad? Would you have appointed Griles to his position? How about Martin? You decide.

Organizational Perspective

Bureaucrats also often adopt the viewpoints that their agency holds. James A. Baker, III, who headed both the Treasury Department (1985–1988) and State Department (1989–1992) notes, "In all the bureaucracies in Washington, there are historical positions that the various departments have taken. It's as the old saying goes: where you stand depends on where you sit."[30]

Sense of mission is one factor that determines an agency's perspective. Many agencies are designed to be or come to see themselves as an advocate rather than a neutral organization.[31] The BIA decision about the Schaghticokes was not surprising given the agency's mission statement, which in part reads:

> Once an instrument of federal policies to subjugate and assimilate American Indian tribes and their peoples, the BIA has changed dramatically. . . . As federal policy has evolved away from the subjugation and assimilation of American Indians and . . . into one of partnership and service to them, so has the BIA's mission.

Self-interest also contributes to organizational perspectives. Like private organizations, public agencies have interests and, as Chapter 7 explains, often function as interest groups. Bureaucrats promote their agency's interests because of the tendency of people who work for an organization to identify with it and to believe that a good policy is one that benefits the organization. As such, agency personnel are apt to favor policies that increase or preserve the agency's budget, its autonomy, and its bureaucratic turf (realm of responsibility) and to resist policies that have a negative impact on the agency. From this perspective, it was predictable that after the Soviet Union collapsed in 1991 and the cold war ended that U.S. national security agencies did not agree with those who advocated major cuts to the defense and intelligence budgets. Instead, self-interest combined with sense of mission led the national security agencies to scan the horizon for the next enemy. They soon found one, with a major Defense Department report arguing in 1992 that the military's new mission should be deterring potential "competitors," including U.S. allies, from "challenging our leadership or seeking to overturn the established political and economic order" dominated by the United States.[32]

Inertia is a third factor determining bureaucratic perspective. Agencies are like large ships. They are difficult to get moving, but once moving in a direction they are hard to turn quickly. Presidents since the 1990s have struggled to move the Pentagon away from its orientation toward preparing to fight a major war with the Soviet Union (or perhaps China) as well as its emphasis on high-tech, very expensive weaponry to a more flexible approach suitable for fighting the kinds of insurgencies American forces have faced in Iraq and Afghanistan. Testifying to the challenge of changing the military's direction, Secretary of Defense Robert Gates told an audience, "I have expressed frustration over the defense bureaucracy's priorities and lack of urgency when it came to the current conflicts—that for too many in the Pentagon it has been business as usual." The cause for this inertia, according to Gates, is that "for decades there has been no strong, deeply rooted constituency inside the Pentagon or elsewhere for institutionalizing our capabilities to wage . . . irregular conflict—and to quickly meet the ever-changing needs of our forces engaged in these conflicts."[33]

Personnel

Given the power and omnipresence of the bureaucracy and the impact of bureaucratic perspective, there are also significant stakes in knowing who administrators are.

Who the Bureaucrats Are: Levels of Authority

A significant percentage of everyone who works for the government has some ability to contribute to the countless number of daily decisions that, in aggregate, help form public policy. These workers include top political appointees and civilian and military career civil servants. At the highest level, there are the nearly 900 presidential appointees in key policy-making posts. Over 500 of these are subject to Senate confirmation. The secretaries and principal deputies of the Cabinet departments and the heads and board members of independent agencies are among this group. Such officials would resent being classified as bureaucrats, but they are. Some, such as the military officers who serve as the Joint Chiefs of Staff or who head one of the joint commands are drawn from the ranks of careerists in their service or agency. Others come up through associated bureaucracies. Secretary of Education Arne Duncan was the head of the Chicago school system when President Obama named him to the Cabinet in 2009. Such high-level appointees sometimes have their own policy agendas and may even resist direction from the White House. Former President Jimmy Carter has recalled that his Secretary of Health, Education, and Welfare, Joseph A. Califano, was "excessively independent." According to Carter, "Joe was operating his own shop. He would make major decisions concerning controversial matters and announce them publicly and never inform me."[34] Califano, of course, would never admit to being a rogue Cabinet officer, but he did concede that, as the size of the bureaucracy grows, "the ability of the president to maintain taut control is weakened."[35]

At the next level down are 5,000 or so important administrators. One-third are second-tier political appointees, holding jobs such as an agency's press officer. The other two-thirds are top-ranking career civil servants or senior military officers (admirals and generals). These individuals hold posts that are subject to

Even "street-level" bureaucrats, like this police officer, have the authority to make decisions in implementing the law that can have an important impact on individuals and, in aggregate, on society. Is this officer writing a ticket or just a warning? (iStockphoto)

appointment, but the individuals cannot be fired, only reassigned. Most of these positions are not subject to Senate confirmation, but ambassadorships and some others are. For example, about 70% of all U.S. ambassadors are normally career foreign service officers.

The remaining 99.8% of the people who work in the executive branch are careerists who hold their positions under the civil service system. These individuals have been called **street-level bureaucrats**. They include the federal, state, and local governments' police officers, social services case workers, teachers, health workers, and many other public employees who interact with the public. They do not normally make decisions that, individually, have national major policy implications. Nevertheless, street-level bureaucrats usually have a certain amount of discretion, and their decisions can and do affect other individuals. Moreover, their decisions as a whole are an important element of applied public policy.[36]

Who the Bureaucrats Are: Demographics

Given the authority of the country's administrators, it is important to ask who they are demographically. For one, **representative bureaucracy theory** argues that the principles of democracy are best served if the makeup of the bureaucracy reflects the demographic composition of society.[37] Part of this idea is symbolic, but scholars have also found that better representation of women and minorities in bureaucracies has a number of positive effects. Among these are making the government more responsive to the needs of underrepresented groups and making members of those groups more willing to interact with and trust agencies.[38] For example, studies have shown that as the number of police officers who are women has increased, the willingness of women who have been sexually assaulted to report the crime has also gone up.[39] This reflects the perception of victims that they will be treated more empathetically by police. There is also an international aspect to bureaucratic representation. As one CIA director told Congress, "We are running intelligence collection against a very diverse world, a world in which there are two genders and lots of people of different kinds of races. The CIA will do a better job if it's not a white male fraternity."[40]

Bureaucratic representation is also likely to limit racism and sexism in agencies. It is unsettling to think that bias sometimes affects administrative decisions, but that occurs. For instance, African American farmers won a significant victory in a 1999 class action suit against the Department of Agriculture (USDA) when it admitted that because of "indifference and blatant discrimination" it had denied loans to black farmers while giving them to white farmers under similar circumstances from 1981 to 1996. Two billion dollars was allocated to settle claims, but a study five years later found that the USDA had "willfully obstructed justice" and "deliberately undermined" the "spirit of the settlement" by rejecting most applications for payment and disbursing little of the money.[41]

Membership in the most powerful policy-making strata of the bureaucracy does not closely resemble society and never has. Chapter 12 reviews the progress of women and minorities in the Cabinet from none, to a few, to current levels that approach equality for minorities overall and also show marked increases for women. Within the civil service, statistics indicate that women and minorities are over-represented at the lowest pay/authority levels of the federal workforce and underrepresented at higher levels. The data are presented in Figure 13.6.

Change is underway, though, and diversity in senior ranks has improved. Between 1995 and 2009, women in the Senior Executive Service increased from 19% to 30%, and minorities increased from 11% to 18%. It is also worth noting that the pattern of U.S. gender employment is similar to that found on average in other economically developed countries, as Figure 13.7 details.

Comparative data on racial minorities is generally not available. What there is, though, indicates that, as in the United States, minorities lag

In 2009, Women were 23% of the 120 most senior administrators in the UN's Secretariat.

FIGURE 13.6 Federal Civilian Workforce Diversity

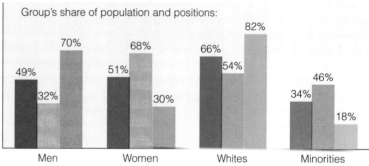

Compared to their share of the U.S. population, women and minorities are overrepresented among the lowest four federal government pay grades (GS 1–4) and underrepresented in the Senior Executive Service, the highest three levels (GS 16–18).
Data source: U.S. Office of Policy Management, Federal Civilian Workforce Statistics for 2009.

FIGURE 13.7 Comparative Gender Diversity in Public Employment

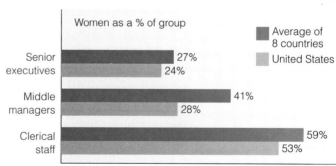

This figure compares data for the United States with eight European countries. Women are underrepresented in middle and senior level jobs everywhere and overrepresented at the lowest levels.
Notes and data sources: Other countries include France, Germany, Greece, Hungary, Ireland, The Netherlands, Portugal, and Sweden. Data are for the national government only. Data for 2006 and from the Organization of Economic Cooperation and Development.

behind the majority group, especially in key positions. About 8% of the population of Great Britain is of Asian or African heritage, yet only 4% of the country's senior civil servants are people of color. Even greater disparity exists in Canada, where so-called visible minorities, based on race (in contrast to "invisible minorities" based on language or religion), make up 16% of the population but only 3% of the senior civil servants.

SOURCES OF BUREAUCRATIC POWER

We remember President Franklin D. Roosevelt as a powerful president, but he did not always see it that way. For instance, trying to control the Navy frustrated him. He once compared trying to shape Navy policy with punching a feather bed. "You punch it with your right and you punch it with your left until you are finally exhausted," he exclaimed, "and then you find the damn bed just as [it was] before you started punching."[42] On another occasion, Roosevelt was startled to learn that the Navy had begun a major shipbuilding program. "Here I am, the commander-in-chief," he grumbled, "having to read about that for the first time in the press."[43] If the Navy was powerful enough to bedevil Roosevelt, we need to explore the sources of the power that agencies have. These sources include legal power and political power.

Legal Sources of Bureaucratic Power

The law provides bureaucracies with a range of ways to influence policy. These methods include making rules, adjudicating them, and implementing policy.

Rulemaking

Agencies gain substantial power from their ability to make legally binding rules. The vast size, scope, and technical intricacies of government make it inevitable that the laws passed by Congress will usually detail only a small portion of the specific rules that govern American society. More commonly, agencies formulate rules to implement the intent of legislation or of directives issued by the president Reportedly, for example, the health-care reform legislation enacted in 2010 "gave sweeping power to federal agencies . . . to fill in gaps lawmakers left in the . . . legislation" by, among other things, referring more than 1,000 times to decisions that federal officials will make about how to implement the law. Therefore, the analysis noted, the second major struggle over health-care reform, "the battle over how to carry out the law is just getting started."[44] To cite one example, Congress required in the law that insurance companies spend at least 80% of the health insurance premiums they receive on "clinical care activities" or on improving "health care quality." However, the legislation does not define either term, leaving it up to the Department of Health and Human Services to sort that out. Huge amounts of money ride on the determination of this issue alone, and soon after the passage of the new law HHS Secretary Kathleen Sebelius characterized her department's struggle with lobbyists from the insurance industry over various rules as "hand-to-hand combat."[45]

Overall, federal agencies issue well over 30,000 rules each year, or more than 160 rules for each law passed by Congress. Most of these rules are very specific and technical and draw little notice beyond those immediately affected. For example, keyboarding the word "pigs" into the *Code of Federal Regulations* (CFR) online site revealed that they were the subject of 190 regulations. A few other topics (and number of regulations in the CFR) were shoes (372), ladders (426), and insecticides (552).

At other times, an agency can move to implement sweeping regulations. Acting under the authority of the Clean Air Act (1990), the EPA issued a "finding" in late 2009 that "the current and projected concentrations of . . . greenhouse gases . . . in the atmosphere threaten the public health and welfare of current and future generations."[46] What the finding did was to create the legal basis for the EPA to begin to regulate green house gas emissions. It remains to be seen what those regulations will be, but they will almost certainly have a significant impact on the U.S. economy and Americans' lifestyle, not to mention the environment.

The authority to make rules includes the ability to change them. In 2004, for example, the Equal Employment Opportunity Commission reversed earlier rules that required agencies to seek to hire and promote political minority members if statistics showed imbalances. The new EEOC directive instructed agencies to deemphasize demographic data about their staffs. Instead, agencies were directed to consider only demonstrable barriers to the advancement of women and minorities. One critic charged it was an effort to "minimize EEO and justice." Others disagreed, with one supporter of the rule change noting that relying on statistics meant, "Sometimes an overrepresented group can be discriminated against."[47] It will not be surprising when the EEOC under the Obama administration once again changes the rules, reverting to the pre-2004 status.

Adjudication

Agencies not only make and change rules, they often exercise a quasi-judicial role. The Food and Drug Administration decides whether medicines can be prescribed and sold. The Internal Revenue Service judges tax returns during audits and also has an appeals process if a taxpayer disagrees with the auditor's findings. Sometimes agencies can even impose penalties for violations. One recent example occurred in 2010 when the National Highway Traffic Safety Administration fined Toyota Motor Corporation $16.4 million for failing to promptly notify car owners of a defect in the gas pedal on some Toyotas that caused them to accelerate uncontrollably.

Implementation

What a policy actually turns out to be is often strongly influenced by its **implementation:** how agencies and even street-level bureaucrats actually carry out policy. At the macro level, as noted earlier, how the Department of Health and Human Service and other federal agencies fill in the numerous blanks left by Congress in the Patient Protection and Affordable Care Act (2010) will have a major impact for tens of millions of Americans on the quality and cost of their health care. At the micro policy end of the spectrum, although the legal speed limit on interstate highways is usually 65 miles an hour, the *real* speed limit is 70, perhaps a little more, because that is usually what patrol officers enforce. So policy and the law diverge in this case because of the way street-level civil servants, the police, implement the law.

The more than $4.6 trillion in annual federal, state, and local spending that the American bureaucracy administers is greater than the gross domestic product (GDP) of any country in the world other than China, Japan, and the United States itself.

Incompetent or hostile implementation can have serious negative consequences. It is clear that part of the fault for the BP oil spill in the Gulf of Mexico in 2010 can be traced to poor enforcement by the Department of the Interior's Minerals Management Service (MMS). The failure of the MMS to adequately inspect the offshore wells and other transgressions (see Chapter 7) was reflected in the angry quip by Representative Edward Markey (D-MA) that "MMS used to stand for Minerals Management Service. It now stands for misconduct, mismanagement and spills."[48]

Political Sources of Bureaucratic Power

In addition to being able to take action, bureaucrats derive power from their ability to influence policymakers and to marshal political support.

Expertise

In a moment of candor, President Warren G. Harding once admitted how taxing he found it to try to understand the implications of revenue policy. "I listen to one side and they seem right," he lamented, "and God! I talk to the other side and they seem just as right! I can't make a damn thing out of this problem." Like Harding, other presidents and top government leaders are not experts in most of the areas in which they make policy. By contrast, each agency is staffed with experts, and generalist policy makers sometimes rely on the advice of those civil servants.

The power of expertise is particularly important in foreign and national security affairs, subjects where there is less expertise outside the bureaucracy than there is on domestic issues. "If someone comes in and tells me this or that about the minimum wage bill," President John F. Kennedy once commented, "I have no hesitation in overruling them. But I always assume that the military and intelligence people have some special skills not available to ordinary mortals."[49] Congress has the same reluctance to challenge bureaucratic experts in foreign and national security affairs. As one chairman of the House Armed Services Committee, put it, "To most congressmen, defense experts are people in uniform, rather than academics in universities or think tanks. Uniforms are identified with expertise."[50]

This source of power is not limited to the U.S. bureaucracy. In a scene that could have just as easily occurred in Washington or many other national capitals, Nikita Khrushchev, the head of the Soviet Union (1953–1964), recalled in his memoirs:

Uniforms, such as the one being worn here by General Stanley McChrystal, former commander of U.S. and allied forces in Afghanistan, with its medals, insignia, and stars, give an aura of authority and expertise that add to the power of the military bureaucracy. McChrystal punctured his own aura (and lost his job) as a result of an injudicious interview he granted to Rolling Stone magazine in 2010. (AP Photo/Kirsty Wigglesworth)

> Some people from our military department come and say, "Comrade Khrushchev, look at this: The Americans are developing such and such a [weapons] system. We could develop the same system, but it would cost such and such." I tell them, "There's no money; it's all been allocated already." So they say, "If we don't get the money we need and if there's a war, then the enemy will have superiority over us." So we discuss it some more, and I end up giving the money they ask for.[51]

Information

"By and large, a president's performance in office is as effective as the information he gets," President Harry S. Truman once remarked.[52] Top policy makers have neither the physical stamina nor the intellectual capacity to read, much less absorb, the huge amount of information that is available on the policy issues they face. Therefore decision makers all rely to some degree on the bureaucracy to gather and evaluate information and to present a manageable amount of it. Such information seldom meets the standard of the "truth, the whole truth, and nothing but the truth," because agencies and individual bureaucrats have perspectives that influence which information they consider valid and important enough to relate. As with expertise, the nature of foreign and national security policy make the information flow more important in external policy than in internal policy.

Usually information is unconsciously filtered because of the biases of the bureaucracy. Sometimes, however, bureaucrats intentionally misrepresent or withhold information.[53] One reason they may not pass on information is that it will damage their agency or the policy they favor. President Kennedy suffered a policy disaster in 1961 when Fidel Castro's forces crushed the U.S.-backed invasion of

Cuba by exiles at the Bay of Pigs. Almost a half-century later, declassified documents indicated that the Soviet Union had learned of the exact date of the invasion and informed Havana. As it turns out, the CIA knew that a leak had compromised the operation and could have avoided a devastating defeat by aborting the invasion. Yet the agency did not tell the president because it suspected that the spy was within its own ranks. At other times, an agency or official may not want to be the bearer of bad news for fear higher ups may want to "kill the messenger." In retrospect, it is clear that from its beginning, the war in Vietnam was going badly for the United States. Yet, to a degree, the White House was not fully informed. One reason was that the CIA and other agencies were reluctant to estimate a communist victory. A top CIA official directed his agency's staff in Vietnam to write reports that would instill confidence in Washington. "There's a lot of ways you can write the English language to make it sound like we're moving ahead," he advised his subordinates.[54]

Political Standing

Agencies work to project a positive image and to publicly promote the policies they favor through press releases, speeches, and other public activities by top personnel. Anonymous interviews, leaked documents, and other covert methods are also used to try to influence official opinion in Washington and public opinion in the country.

Public relations campaigns by agencies are usually most effective in rallying those who are already supportive. The Department of Agriculture, for example, has strong support among agribusiness interests. Drumming up support more broadly is difficult because federal agencies in general are held in low esteem by the public. One recent survey found that only 20% of Americans gave federal agencies a 5 or 4 rating when asked to put their performance on a 5 (excellent) to 1 (poor) scale.[55]

One notable exception to this poor evaluation is the military. It received a 5 or 4 rating from 78% of the public, and such high ratings are typical in surveys. This standing and the military's reputed expertise make it politically risky for presidents to disagree with their uniformed advisers. For example, the power of the military's public standing was evident in President Obama's decision in late 2009 to dispatch more troops to Afghanistan. Amid a great deal of controversy over whether there should be any increase and, if so, how large, the president's options were politically constrained by his commander in the field, General Stanley A. McChrystal. He sent a report to the president in August asking for another 40,000 troops and predicting that without them the U.S. effort in Afghanistan "will likely result in failure." The report was soon leaked to the *Washington Post*.[56] As the White House debated its options, McChrystal turned up the heat again in an October speech,

Among other things, he warned that sending few or no extra troops would lead to "Chaos-istan."[57] Upping the ante even more, ranking members of McChrystal's staff reportedly predicted that the general "would resign before he'd stand behind a faltering policy."[58]

McChrystal's speech "shocked and angered presidential advisors," and he was summoned to meet with President Obama the next day for a reported dressing down.[59] As one constitutional expert described the situation, "It is one thing for some nameless Washington insider to engage in a characteristic power play, quite another for McChrystal to pressure the president in public to adopt his strategy."[60]

General McChrystal denied trying to preempt the president, telling one interviewer, "There was no intent on my part to influence . . . the decision-making process." However, as one news analyst noted, "It's hard to believe that [an experienced] general like McChrystal . . . did not consider how [his statements] . . . coming in the midst of the White House Afghan strategy review might not be seen as a potential public relations campaign to advocate for his policy position."[61]

Whatever his intent, General McChrystal got most of what he wanted. President Obama told Americans in a nationally televised address that he was ordering 30,000 more U.S. troops to Afghanistan. Secretary of Defense Robert Gates later indicated that number was flexible and could actually be 33,000. Additionally, Obama asked other NATO countries to increase their troop strength between 5,000 and 10,000, bringing the total deployment to about or even a bit more than the 40,000 that McChrystal had originally requested. "The key thing is [that] I'm going to get at least 37,000," a satisfied McChrystal noted.[62] It is impossible to know the precise impact of the general's maneuvering on the president's decision. At the very least, though, McChrystal made it difficult for Obama to agree with the anti-increase position of Vice President Joseph Biden, many Democrats in Congress, and others. To do that, Obama in essence would have had to assert that his assessment of the military options was superior to that of one of the country's top generals, indeed the very one that the president had appointed just a few months earlier as his top commander in Afghanistan. Obama could have done that legally, but the standing of the military among the public and in Congress made going along with the general the more likely outcome.

As every general should know, though, there is danger in becoming overconfident. Less than a year later, comments made by McChrystal and his staff were once again headline news. One McChrystal aide told a reporter for *Rollling Stone* that the general had been "pretty disappointed" in President Obama at their first meeting. Other top administration officials fared even less well. Among the scathing comments, National Security Advisor James Jones was described as a "clown" by a McChrystal aide. And the general mockingly dismissed the importance of

Vice President Joe Biden by rhetorically asking, "Who's that?" while another aide added, "Biden? Did you say, 'Bite me'?" When *Rolling Stone* published these comment in its June 2010 edition, McChrystal was once again summoned to meet with Obama. This time the general did not escape unscathed. President Obama relieved McChrystal of his command and forced him into retirement, declaring that the general's scornful commentary "undermines the civilian control of the military that is at the core of our democratic system."[63]

Alliances

Success, the old adage says, is based in part on "who you know," as well as "what you know." This is true in Washington as elsewhere, and agencies and individual bureaucrats are politically empowered if they have strong connections with Congress, interest groups, and other potent political actors.

Bureaucrats, interest groups, and members of Congress who share a mutual perspective in a specialized area of policy are called **iron triangles** (see Chapter 7).[64] These political alliances promote their common view and exercise significant policy influence. Secretary of Health and Human Services Donna Shalala (1993–2001) conceded, "There are iron triangles in government today."[65] The best-known iron triangle is the *military-industrial-congressional complex* supporting defense spending. Another of the iron triangles affects agriculture policy. It features "legislators from farming areas secur[ing] seats on Congress's agriculture committees and work[ing] closely with the Department of Agriculture and organized representatives of farming interests, such as the National Farmers Union, to produce pro-farmer policies."[66]

Yet another iron triangle was revealed in 2010 after an oil drilling platform explosion and the resulting massive oil spill in the Gulf of Mexico off Louisiana. One side of the triangle included the oil industry and the communities, politicians, and others in Louisiana and elsewhere along the Gulf coast that supported drilling because of the jobs, tax revenues, and other benefits it brought to the region. Louisianans annually hold the Shrimp and Petroleum Festival in Morgan City, and undeterred by the oil spill the 75th annual event was held in September 2010. The purpose of the festival, its Website boasted, was to celebrate "the unique way in which these two seemingly different industries [sea food and oil] work hand-in-hand culturally and environmentally in this area of the 'Cajun Coast.' "[67] Similarly, many local officials have supported drilling and continue to do so. In July 2010, with the oil still flooding into the Gulf, Louisiana Governor Bobby Jindal addressed a rally of 10,000 people demanding that the federal government lift its temporary ban on offshore drilling and urged the crowd to "defend our way of life."[68]

The Minerals and Mines Service (MMS) of the Department of the Interior was the second side of the triangle. Faced with a somewhat conflicting mandate to

(1) expedite offshore drilling to add to the country's energy supply and also to the government's money supply through the billions of dollars the oil industry pays to drill and to extract petroleum and natural gas, and simultaneously to (2) protect the environment, the MMS emphasized the former at the expense of the latter. As one analysis put it, "Washington got oil and royalty fees; Louisiana got jobs; and the agency [MMS] got frequent reminders of the need to keep both happy. Adding to that orientation, many of the MMS personal monitoring the Gulf drilling were closely connected to both the oil industry and to the local communities that benefited from the drilling. Inspectors and numerous MMS officials had worked for the oil industry or later did. "Obviously we're all oil industry," one MME district manager in Louisiana conceded. "We're all from the same part of the country. Almost all our inspectors have worked for oil companies out on these same platforms They grew up in the same towns."[69]

Supportive members of Congress made up the third side of the triangle. When the basic law governing offshore drilling was before Congress in 1978, Louisiana's Senator J. Bennett Johnston derided safety concerns and proclaimed, "We need to get on with that drilling."[70] After the spill, Senator David Vitter (R-LA) voiced the same priority. After introducing legislation to end the moratorium on offshore drilling, Vitter explained that the temporary halt was a "huge job killer" that if continued would soon "kill more jobs than the oil [spill] itself [has]."[71] Congress's view of offshore drilling was certainly not harmed by the campaign contributions the oil and gas industry lavished on members of Congress from coastal states. Through July 2010 of the 2010 "election cycle" (2009–2010), the industry had already contributed $14.6 million to members of Congress for their reelection bids. Second among the recipients with $257,600 was Senator Vitter.[72]

Still other alliances including one or more federal, state, or local agencies are more temporary and form around a specific legislative proposal. Whatever the alliance is called, though, and whatever its composition and duration, the important point is that agencies strengthen themselves by making common cause with other politically powerful actors.

CONSTRAINTS ON BUREAUCRATIC POWER

Although the bureaucrats are a powerful force in American governance, they operate within their own system of checks and balances. Presidents and their appointed subordinates in the executive branch have a range of tools to direct and constrain the bureaucracy. Congress and the courts also have considerable authority to check and balance the bureaucracy. For example, President Bush came to office in 2001 promising to restrain bureaucratic regulation, and, for good or ill, he accomplished that. An analysis of regulatory actions taken by federal agencies under Bush and his immediate two predecessors, Bill Clinton and the first President Bush, shows that agencies proposed 25% fewer new rules under the second President Bush than under Clinton and 13% fewer new rules than under the senior Bush during the same periods of their presidencies. Agencies under the second President Bush also withdrew more proposed regulations than they instituted new ones.[73]

Constraints on Resources

Agencies depend on the president and Congress for their core resources. These include the personnel who lead the agencies, operating budgets, and the authority to even exist.

Appointments

With few exceptions, presidents appoint the top agency administrators. Most are subject to Senate confirmation, but they are seldom rejected. Presidents also have considerable authority to fire top administrators. There are a handful of administrators at independent regulatory agencies that cannot be removed except for cause, but beyond this group, all top administrators in the executive branch serve at the president's pleasure.

A volume entitled *United States Government Policy and Supporting Positions,* commonly referred to as the "Plum Book," lists some 6,700 positions in the executive branch (not including the military services) that are considered to be directly involved in or closely supporting policy making and, therefore, not subject to the merit system. While the individuals in these positions are all presidential appointees, they (and their approximate percentage of the 6,700 positions) can be divided into three groups: top political policy makers (35%), most of whom are partisan loyalists to the president; political support personnel (10%), such as public information officers and aides to the top political policy makers; and policy makers who are career civil servants (55%).

The leaders of France, Germany, and Great Britain have only between 100 and 200 political positions to fill.

The top political policy makers include Cabinet department and other agency heads and their immediate subordinates. They have considerable authority but are also subject to White House direction. In part, this is because they see themselves as the president's agents. Secretary of State James A. Baker III (1989–1992) commented that he was aware the departments can "capture you if you're not careful," but he expressed determination "to be the president's man at the State Department, instead of the State Department's man at the White House."[74]

Presidents seek to ensure such an orientation in numerous ways. One is by appointing proven loyalists to many positions. President Bush followed this path after his reelection in 2004 when he favored his inner circle to replace resigning

Cabinet members. However, President Obama's appointments as department secretaries were mostly individuals such as Hillary Clinton (State), Robert Gates (Defense), and Janet Nepolitano (Homeland Security) with considerable individual political standing.

Presidents also seek to control agencies by creating a virtual parallel cabinet in the Executive Office of the President, and staffing it with loyalists who take the lead in forming policy in their area and monitoring associated agencies. Here Obama adhered to the norm, appointing many members of his campaign staff and others with connections to his early days in Chicago politics to the White House staff.

As for the top civil servants who occupy Plum Book positions, the president can relieve them of their job but cannot fire them from government service. As Secretary of State Baker put it, "You can't fire these people, but you can move them."[75]

Budget

Money is the fuel that agencies depend on to operate, and the president and Congress can shape them and their programs through budgetary control. One way the Bush administration sought to restrain government regulation was by cutting the budgets of numerous regulatory agencies. The impact on the Equal Employment Opportunities Commission (EEOC) is shown in Figure 13.8. As you can see, budget restraints reduced the EEOC's staff. These reductions coupled with a growing workload of complaints of discrimination to investigate sharply increased the agency's backlog of cases.

Organizational Authority

Agencies can also be created, reorganized, and abolished through the legislative process or, to a limited degree, by presidential action.[76] Establishing the Department of Homeland Security through the legislative process not only created a new Cabinet department, but did so largely through a massive reorganization of existing units. This included incorporating into the new department such agencies as the Border Patrol, Customs Service, Coast Guard, Federal Emergency Management Administration, Immigration and Naturalization Service, Secret Service, and the Transportation Security Agency.

Presidents also have some authority to unilaterally restructure units and their functions. Reflecting a campaign pledge to improve food safety, President Obama and

FIGURE 13.8 Equal Employment Opportunity Commission 2000–2008

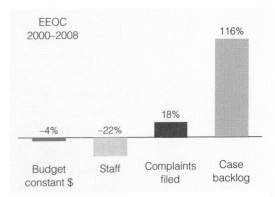

The Bush administration used its budget power to constrain the Equal Employment Opportunity Commission by reducing its budget and cutting its staff. With a rising number of complaints of discrimination filed with the agency, its backlog of cases skyrocketed.

Notes and data source: Budget is in constant dollars (adjusted for inflation). Data from the EEOC.

his newly appointed head of the Food and Drug Administration (FDA) increased the status of the agency's Office of Foods by moving it from being a subunit of the Office of Administration to having its own deputy director who reports directly to the director.

Constraints on Actions

In addition to constraints on who serves in administrative positions, on agency budgets, and on agency organization, the bureaucracy faces a range of limitations on what it can do. These boundaries are created by countervailing executive, congressional, judicial, and administrative authority.

Executive Authority

Article II of the Constitution gives the president and, by extension, his Cabinet officers and other principal political appointees significant authority to direct the bureaucracy. Section 1 declares that "the executive power shall be vested" in the president, and Section 2 makes the president the "commander in chief" of the military. Formally, the president can set policy through such tools as **executive orders**: administrative directives that have legal standing (see Chapter 12). For example, presidents have repeatedly used executive orders to direct the bureaucracy to favor equal opportunity. Two instances of note were President Truman's executive order 9981 in 1948 directing the military to integrate racially and President Nixon's executive order 11478 in 1969 directing agencies to do business only with contractors that met specific hiring goals for minority groups.

If they wish, presidents and their principal subordinates can also become deeply involved in the day-to-day activity of policy implementation. In one recent example, there was considerable off-the-record grumbling among military officers that Secretary of Defense Donald Rumsfeld was micromanaging the planning for the war against Iraq in 2003, "down to the last dog tag," as one Marine Corps general put it. Confirming that view, retired General Norman Schwarzkopf, who had commanded coalition forces in the Persian Gulf War (1991), depicted Rumsfeld as "deeply immersed in the operational planning—to the chagrin of most of the armed forces."[77] Indeed the military has often been so frustrated by what it considers intrusion in its area of expertise that one retired admiral penned a bit of doggerel:

I am not allowed to run the train
    The whistle I can't blow.
I am not allowed to say how fast
    The railroad train can go.

I am not allowed to shoot off steam
    Nor even clang the bell.
But let it jump the goddam tracks
    And see who catches hell.[78]

Presidents also use procedural tools to control the bureaucracy. Recent presidents have required that bureaucracies clear all proposed regulations with the Office of Management and Budget, which is part of the Executive Office of the President. Former Secretary of Agriculture Dan Glickman (1995–2001) has recalled, "OMB exerted a lot of influence over almost all our . . . rules."[79] Adding to that, President Bush issued a directive in 2007 that required each federal agency to create a regulatory policy office to be run by a political appointee. In effect, this made the White House the gatekeeper for any regulation an agency sought to establish, amend, or terminate.

Congressional Authority

Congress has a number of tools it can use to constrain agency actions. Passing laws is one. Laws can create or abolish programs and can at times create detailed regulations and procedures that narrow the discretion of administrators in their implementation.

Congress also has **oversight** authority. According to the House of Representatives, this function "refers to the review, monitoring, and supervision of federal agencies, programs and policy implementation."[80] As detailed in Chapter 11, committees are a key element in oversight. To a degree, the structure of Congress's committees and subcommittees parallels the organization of the executive branch, and committee members monitor the agencies within each committee's jurisdiction. Administrators frequently testify during hearings and supply information. Congress also has a number of agencies, most notably the General Accountability Office, that can independently probe agency activity. The result of oversight can range from high-profile investigations and major legislative initiatives to informal pressure on agencies to adjust their rules and how they are implementing policy.

Congress has taken several actions to improve its oversight ability. One initiative was the Inspector General Act (1978). It and subsequent acts have created inspector generals (IGs) in nearly 60 agencies. These officials have the power to probe all aspects of agency operations and are required to inform both their agency heads and Congress of any deficiencies. Although the president or agency heads appoints the IGs, they have considerable independence because removing them requires a report to Congress explaining why the IG was fired. It is a mark of the effectiveness of IGs that one Defense Department official complained that IGs "are about as welcome as the IRS guy at tax time."[81]

Many countries have officials called *ombudsmen* who investigate complaints from citizens about the bureaucracy.

To gain information, Congress also has enacted numerous *whistleblower laws*. These are meant to protect agency employees who bring information to Congress or to higher executive officials about illegal or other inappropriate activities in the agencies. Such tools are a positive step, but they are not entirely effective. The annual reports filed with Congress by the Office of Special Counsel (OSC), the independent federal agency charged with protecting whistleblowers from retaliation by their agencies, indicates that the OSC agrees with only about 6% of the complaints filed by whistleblower alleging retaliation. It is no surprise, then, that 91% of those who filed complaints in 2008 and answered an OSC survey about its performance said they were dissatisfied with the results.[82] It remains open to question whether this means that most complainants are imagining retaliation that does not exist or that the OSC is sweeping too many retaliatory acts under the rug.

Judicial Authority

Rules generated by agencies, how agencies implement policy, and how agencies adjudicate disputes are all subject to court challenge. In the area of criminal justice administration, for example, the courts' constraint on how street-level of bureaucrats implement the law can range from relatively minor matters to important decisions, such as the famous *Miranda v. Arizona* (1966) decision. In it, the Supreme Court ruled that when police arrest suspects, they must advise them of their constitutional rights to say nothing and to have an attorney. Reflecting on the overall impact of the courts in the criminal justice area, Attorney General Richard Thornburgh (1988–1990) noted that at the Department of Justice, "Our procedures and priorities are shaped by what the courts authorize us to do or forbid us from doing."[83]

Agencies also make innumerable decisions and quasi-judicial rulings every year, and all of these can be appealed to the courts. Such appeals from agencies made up about 25% of all the cases before the various circuit courts of appeals in 2008. At that level, the agencies win about 70% of the time, and the Supreme Court upholds them 60% of the time.[84]

Administrative Authority

It is also worth noting that agencies can sometimes be restrained by other agencies. The issue of commercial development of public lands discussed in the second You Decide box provides an example. By law, such development requires the approval of the Department of the Interior, which often favors such usage. But the law also requires that the EPA sign off, and that agency tends to resist commercial development.

EVALUATING THE BUREAUCRACY

Grumbling about bureaucracy is as American as the Fourth of July. Indeed, discontent with bureaucracy helped incite the American Revolution, with the Declaration of Independence charging King George III with having "erected a multitude of new offices and [having] sent hither swarms of officers [officials] to harass our people." Revolution did not overthrow bureaucracy, though. It merely shifted its ownership to the new American government. Soon its third president, Thomas Jefferson, was protesting, "We have more machinery of government than is necessary, too many parasites living on the labor of the industrious."[85] Some two centuries later, the soon-to-be 44th president, Barack Obama, voiced the same theme. "We cannot meet 21st century challenges with a 20th century bureaucracy," he told cheering delegates at the Democratic National Convention in 2008. "Our government should work for us, not against us. It should help us, not hurt us."[86]

Many Americans agree with bureaucracy bashing. One recent survey found that when asked about the quality of various government institutions and their personnel, few Americans had high praise for agencies and their administrators, as is shown in Figure 13.9.

One mitigating factor is that the scores for federal agencies were not dramatically worse than how Americans evaluated most of the rest of government. Among the other major parts of the federal government, Congress, with a 49% poor and only 18% good rating did even worse than the agencies. The presidency (38% poor, 46% good) and the Supreme Court (22% poor and 35% good) were evaluated more favorably, but barely. Thus, the low score of agencies partly reflects a negative view of government rather than of the agencies as such.

Whether justified or not, the generally negative view that Americans have of their government, including its agencies, has important policy consequences. As we discussed in Chapter 12, presidents have a difficult time rallying public opinion and leading because of Americans' skepticism about their government. Similarly, negative images of the bureaucracy sometimes hamper policy. For example, one of the barriers President Obama faced in moving health-care reform forward was illustrated in a poll that found 78% of Americans saying they were "very" or "somewhat" concerned that the "current efforts to reform the health care system will . . . increase government bureaucracy."[87]

Is all the derision heaped on the bureaucracy just? No is the answer here. It would be untenable to argue that the bureaucracy is flawless or that every bureaucrat is a skilled and dedicated civil servant. It would be equally incorrect, though, to depict the bureaucracy as an unbroken landscape of wasteful red tape and incompetent and uncaring bureaucrats.

It is better to understand several key points about evaluating bureaucracy. First, it is universal. The political history of the world is one of expanding government, and that necessarily means a growing administrative structure. Second, the size of the U.S. bureaucracy falls well within the pattern for wealthy countries. Third, a range of attempts to measure and compare the quality of various countries' administrative structures shows that on a global basis, U.S. public administration is far

FIGURE 13.9
The Public's Evaluation of Federal Agencies

How do you rate the overall performance of federal agencies?

A third of Americans think the federal bureaucracy is doing a poor job, and only 20% think the agencies are doing a good job.
Notes and data source: Survey used a 5-point scale: 1 and 2 were combined for poor here, 3 was fair, and 4 and 5 were good. Data from the *Washington Post*, November 11, 2009, using a Gallup poll.

FIGURE 13.10 Comparative Quality of Public Administration

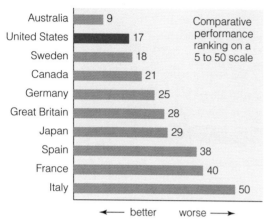

Comparative performance ranking on a 5 to 50 scale

←— better   worse —→

The quality of the U.S. bureaucracy ranks well when compared to those of nine other wealthy countries. These scores are an amalgam of 5 different scoring systems. Each country got a score here of 1 (best) to 10 (worst) based on its ranking compared to the other nine countries on each of the 5 systems. With three first place finishes and two third places, Australia had 9 comparative points and finished first. Italy finished tenth in each of the 5 systems and scored 50 for last place.

Data source: The five scoring system are detailed in Steven Van de Walle, "The State of the World's Bureaucracies," *Journal of Comparative Policy Analysis,* 8/4 (2006): 439–450. Selection of countries and calculations by author.

above average. Even among the wealthy countries, which tend to be better administered, U.S. administration compares favorably, as indicated in Figure 13.10.

A fourth point in evaluating the U.S. bureaucracy is to note that much of the red tape and delays that people complain about are not the fault of the agencies or their workers. Some delays are caused by administrators having to follow procedures that have been mandated by legislators to avoid waste and fraud. Also, as we saw in Figure 13.8, administrative backlogs frequently occur when elected officials do not provide enough funding to hire enough staff to meet the demands on the agency. Similarly, agencies often do not have sufficient funds to carry out the programs they administer and then get blamed for poor quality programs.

Fifth, complaints that presidents and other political executives cannot control the bureaucracy are partly a function of the barriers instituted to protect administration from politics. Americans want most administrative decisions such as the assessment of their property and the taxes on it to be made by neutral administrators who cannot be pressured into political decisions. Of course, it is not acceptable to have bureaucrats defying the country's leaders and the public will, but it is contradictory to try to create a system that simultaneously protects administration from inappropriate political meddling and keeps civil servants perfectly responsive to political direction. In sum, it may be that the famous cartoonist Walt Kelly was right when he had his iconic character, Pogo Possum, counsel a dejected Porky Pine, "Son, we have met the enemy and he is us."

SUMMARY

However one may evaluate bureaucracy, it is a natural and necessary element of government. Bureaucracy is important because a significant amount of public policy is the result of the formal rules and the day-to-day decisions made by appointed administrators. Another reason that bureaucracy is important is because it is involved with virtually every aspect of governance and thus affects everyone daily and in many ways. It is also important to know about the interplay between bureaucracy and democracy, given the ability of nonelected officials to make policy.

Taken as a whole, the interconnected U.S. federal-state-local bureaucracy is one of the world's largest, most complex, and most powerful organizations. The bureaucracy has evolved in important ways. It has grown, with the number of agencies and their realms of responsibility expanding considerably. The number of government workers has also grown greatly, although this is more true at the state and local levels than at the federal level. Another way the bureaucracy has evolved is toward insularity from political pressure. Over time, the bureaucracy has become more representative of the American public demographically, but minorities and women are still underrepresented, particularly among senior career officials.

Symbolized by this photo, bureaucracy is often associated with inertia, red tape, piles of paperwork, and other negative images, and politicians often promise to cut it all back. In reality, all governments need to have an administrative structure, and the U.S. bureaucracy is considered relatively able and efficient by global standards. (iStockphoto)

The organizational structure of the bureaucracy has important consequences. There are many types of bureaucratic units, such as Cabinet departments, independent agencies, and government corporations. In some cases the organizational structure of the bureaucracy reflects government functions. In other cases it is the result of political forces. Agency organization is a maze of overlapping responsibilities and crosscutting authority.

Government administrators approach their jobs based in part on bureaucratic perspective, which may prompt them to promote policies that fit with their own and their agency's perspective rather than with those of elected leaders. Each bureaucrat has a personal perspective based on such factors as the individual's ideology and background. Bureaucrats are also often influenced by their agency's viewpoint, based on such factors as the agency's sense of mission and self-interest.

Because the bureaucracy is important, it is useful to know how agencies are staffed. Almost all bureaucrats have some ability to influence policy, but the significant policy-making power resides with the almost 1,000 political appointees and about 5,000 senior career civil servants. Despite recent progress, the demographic profile of the top strata of the bureaucracy has never and still does not closely resemble society.

Bureaucracies have a number of instrumental sources of power. One is the ability to make rules that have the force of law. Bureaucrats also have the legal authority to adjudicate disputes and to rule on violations. Bureaucrats also derive power from their use of their expertise and informational resources to influence policy makers. Agencies marshal political support through public relations campaigns and by building alliances with members of Congress, interest groups, and other potent political actors. However, there are also constraints on bureaucratic power including limits on resources and the ability of the president, Congress, and courts to check and balance agencies.

CHAPTER 13 GLOSSARY

bureaucracy Government agencies and their appointed administrators.

bureaucratic perspective Administrators' viewpoints on issues and policy based on their personal perceptions and values and on those of the organization in which they work.

Cabinet departments The 15 units of the executive branch that are generally the largest units with the broadest responsibilities. The heads of these are called secretaries, except for the Attorney General, and they make up the president's Cabinet. Sometimes referred to only as departments, although there are non-Cabinet departments.

civil service Nonpartisan, professional government administrators hired and promoted through a merit system and not subject to discharge except for specific causes specified by law.

client-oriented agencies Bureaucratic units that have a mutually supportive relationship with interest groups associated with the unit's mission.

executive orders Formal presidential directives to the bureaucracy that have legal standing.

government corporations Bureaucratic units that are structured to provide specific services, often in a business-like way, including charging fees.

implementation The way in which agencies carry out policy.

independent administrative agencies Bureaucratic units with operational and/or administrative functions that, for one reason or another, are not suitable for being included within the operations of a Cabinet department.

independent regulatory agencies Bureaucratic units that establish regulations and also have a quasi-judicial function that involves determining whether or not organizations and individuals have complied with those regulations.

iron triangle A political alliance among (1) bureaucrats (2) interest groups, and (3) members of Congress who share a perspective in a specialized area of policy, who cooperate to promote their common view, and who exercise significant policy influence.

merit system The process of hiring and promoting employees based on educational and experience qualifications and competitive examinations.

oversight The review, monitoring, and supervision of federal agencies, programs, and policy implementation by Congress.

patronage system An approach to staffing government administration in which elected leaders fill government jobs with workers who are loyal to them and, in general, hire individuals according to political criteria, such as party membership. Synonymous with "spoils system."

Pendleton Act Law passed in 1883 that initiated hiring and promoting employees based on a merit system (including competitive examinations) and protecting them from being fired except for criminality or other specific reasons. Created the Civil Service Commission to oversee this process.

representative bureaucracy theory The idea that the principles of democracy are best served if the makeup of the bureaucracy, especially in top positions, reflects the demographic composition of society.

spoils system See patronage system.

street-level bureaucrats Lower-level government workers who make day-to-day decisions about the implementation of policy during face-to-face interactions or the review of individual cases.

THE FEDERAL COURTS

14

YOU DECIDE: A Representative Court?

Soon after being inaugurated, President Barack Obama faced one of the key decisions that any president makes. Associate Justice David Souter retired from the Supreme Court in May 2009, setting off an intense debate over who should replace him. Part of the debate focused on ideology. Many of the president's supporters favored a distinct liberal to help offset the markedly conservative leanings of President George W. Bush's two appointments, Chief Justice John G. Roberts, Jr. and Associate Justice Samuel A. Alito, Jr. "Unless Obama . . . appoints real progressives to replace not only Souter but [other justices who might retire], our right-wing court may get even more conservative," one liberal advocate worried.[1] However, others warned that picking a very liberal judge would spark a Republican filibuster against the nominee in the Senate that the Democrats might not be able to overcome.

Demographic diversity was another issue. The vacancy left one woman (Ruth Bader Ginsburg), one black (Clarence Thomas), and six white males on the Court. No Latino, Asian American, or Native American was or ever had been a justice. Polls showed that the general public was not very concerned with increasing diversity on the Court, but many groups and individuals felt differently and urged Obama to select a justice from an underrepresented group. The head of one women's group spoke of the "alarmingly low representation of women on the Supreme Court."[2] And as one Latino columnist noted, Latino groups are "ready, and they're due."[3] African Americans, Asian Americans, and other groups also put forth the names of qualified candidates from among their ranks. Yet others decried focusing on diversity because, as one critic wrote, doing so "placed off-limits many [white-male] lawyers and judges whose colleagues regard as some of the best in their profession."[4] In the end, President Obama expanded both the number of women and minorities on the Court by nominating Judge Sonia Sotomayor of the U.S. Court of Appeals. She had laudable credentials, but it was also true that the president did not interview any white males for the position.

Then in April 2010, Obama got a second chance to shape the Court when Justice John Paul Stevens announced he would retire in early summer at the end of the Court's term. Once again, calls for greater diversity were heard, as were objections to using sex or race as a factor in selecting justices. In the end, the president nominated Elena Kagan for the seat, and subsequently the Senate confirmed her as the third female justice on the current Court. At one-third of the justices, women have a greater presence on the Supreme Court than ever but are still short of their proportionate share. If and when President Obama has an opportunity to make another nomination, do you think he should make further increasing diversity on the Court an absolute requirement for picking his nominee, a high priority, just one of many factors, or not a criterion?

President Obama's selection of Elena Kagan for the Supreme Court increased its gender diversity. Yet there was criticism, including this editorial cartoon from U.S. News and World Report, that Kagan, with an Ivy League pedigree (Princeton undergraduate, Harvard Law School) undermined diversity of thought and experience by being yet another justice from a very narrow range of educational and legal training. (© Tribune Media Services, Inc. All Rights Reserved. Reprinted with permission.)

INTRODUCING THE FEDERAL COURT SYSTEM

Few presidential appointments are as significant as those to the Supreme Court. This importance reflects the crucial role that the federal judiciary plays in the American political system. While exploring this role, you will see that:

★ The courts are both a product of the political process and involved in it.
★ Judicial power is based in the Constitution and the American tradition of legalism.
★ For all its authority, the judiciary is the least powerful branch of government.
★ The U.S. legal system is composed of various types of law and courts.
★ There are economic, demographic, and legal restrictions on equal access to the courts.
★ Federal judges do not represent a demographic cross section of adult Americans.
★ Judges are picked based on merit, party/ideology, judicial philosophy, and demographics.
★ The confirmation process in the Senate is complex and partly political.
★ Key factors regarding the Supreme Court's process include how it selects which cases to hear, the presentation of those cases, and the subsequent decisions.
★ Judges' decisions are influenced by the law, ideology, and social and political factors.
★ There is a debate about how well the judicial branch meets democratic principles.

The Federal Courts in a World of Difference

Like the rest of the U.S. government, the American court system and approach to the law have been influenced by foreign sources. British practice and thought have been especially important. As detailed in Chapters 2, 4, and 5, the use of grand juries to restrain prosecutors, the right to trial by a jury of peers, the prohibition of cruel and unusual punishment or double jeopardy, life tenure and other protections for judges, and many other elements of the U.S. legal system can be traced directly back to the common law that evolved in England after the Norman conquest in 1066, to the Magna Carta (1215), and to Great Britain's Bill of Rights (1689).

More contemporaneously, globalization is encouraging national courts to apply global standards. The U.S. Supreme Court, for instance, recently sparked controversy by referring to international norms in a decision when restricting capital punishment. Reflecting the globalization of concepts such as the universality of human rights, other countries' courts are also beginning to look abroad when deciding cases.[5] For example, Australia's High Court cited

"When interpreting the Bill of Rights," South Africa's constitution directs that its courts "must consider international law; and may consider foreign law."

THE FEDERAL COURTS | 563

decisions by the UN's International Court of Justice and by the high courts of Nigeria, Canada, India, New Zealand, and the United States when rejecting the government's authority to take lands from indigenous peoples.[6]

Examining how other court systems work also provides valuable perspectives on the U.S. legal system. For example, to test for constitutionality in the U.S. system, a law must first be passed, then implemented, and then challenged in court. France takes a different approach. Its highest constitutional authority, the Constitutional Council, reviews the constitutionality of changes to some basic laws before they take effect. On less basic laws, France's parliament or its president can ask the Council to rule on legislation before it takes effect. The Council also provides some interesting possibilities about the appointment and tenure of judges. Members on the Council include all former French presidents and another nine members who serve nonrenewable nine-year terms. Three of these members are appointed every third year, with one named by the president of country, one by the Senate, and one by the National Assembly.

American Diversity and the Federal Courts

The demographic profile of U.S. judges resembles that of the top echelons of the other major branches of the government both historically and currently. For most of U.S. history, the federal judiciary was composed entirely of white males. During recent decades, though, presidents have appointed a growing number of women and minorities. During the terms of President John F. Kennedy and Lyndon B. Johnson, women and people of color accounted for only 10% of all their judicial nominees. That share rose to 41% under Presidents Bill Clinton and George W. Bush. Of President Obama's confirmed nominees through mid-2010, half were women and half were minorities. Despite these changes, white males still constitute 59% of the judiciary.

Increased diversity among judges is part of a global trend. This is easiest to see for women. Fifty years ago, almost no women were on the highest court in any country. Now there are more women judges, although they are still a distinct minority. Figure 14.1 shows the status of women on the U.S. Supreme Court, its equivalent

FIGURE 14.1 Gender in the Global Judiciary

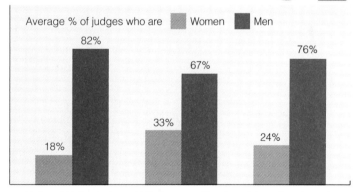

As is true for the U.S. Supreme Court, most of the judges on the highest courts in other countries and on the world's international courts are men.

Notes and data source: Courts reflect a sample of 15 national high courts from around the world and 4 international courts. Data from author's calculations from Websites of various courts in August 2010.

in 15 other democratic countries from around the world, and 4 international courts.[7]

Within the averages shown in Figure 14.1, there was a considerable range of diversity. Among the national high courts, women were most prominent on those in Australia (43%) and Sweden (44%). At the low end of the scale, there were no women on the high courts of India or South Korea in 2010. Diversity on the international courts ranged from the International Criminal Court, where 61% of the judges were women, to the UN's International Court of Justice, with no women justices.

JUDICIAL POWER

President Richard M. Nixon once commented, "Our chief justices have probably had more profound and lasting influence on their times and on the direction of the nation than most presidents."[8] Even if it was an overstatement, Nixon's observation highlights the powerful role that judges play. To see how this is so, we will begin by looking at the scope of judicial power followed by its sources and limitations.

The Scope of Judicial Power

Judicial decisions affect the lives of every American in numerous ways. Impacts include shaping who governs, how power is separated among the branches of the U.S. government, how power is divided between the federal and the state governments, and the direction of public policy.

Who Governs

Federal courts sometimes determine who will be in Congress or even the White House. Nixon's words came back to haunt him when the Supreme Court required him to turn over to Congress audio tapes that proved his involvement in illegal activity and led to his resignation in 1974. A more recent example of the power to shape who governs came during the 2000 presidential election. Florida officials declared that George W. Bush had won the state by about 1,200 votes, but Al Gore, Jr. challenged the count. The outcome was crucial, because whoever received Florida's 25 electoral votes would become president. Florida's Supreme Court ordered a recount, but in *Bush v. Gore* (2000), the U.S. Supreme Court stopped the recount and, in effect, awarded Florida's electoral votes and the presidency to Bush. Court decisions have also settled a number of disputed congressional elections.

Courts also sometimes shape the rules for choosing political leaders.[9] For example, as the country urbanized, rurally dominated state legislatures denied power to the new urban majority by ignoring population when drawing the lines of state and federal electoral districts. One example was Georgia's Atlanta-based congressional district. It had 824,000 residents, while the least-populated of Georgia's rural districts had only 272,000 people. Then in a series of decisions beginning with *Baker v. Carr* (1962), the Supreme Court applied a "one-person, one-vote" standard requiring virtually all electoral districts have equal populations. The only exception is the U.S. Senate, whose state-based representation is mandated by the Constitution.

This standard had a dramatic impact on political power, which then shifted away from rural areas and toward urban ones. By extension, it added to the influence of urban-centered minority groups. For example, two-thirds of all African Americans and about 80% of all Asian Americans and Latinos were living in the underrepresented metropolitan areas in 1960. Policy also changed. With more urban-based members, state legislatures and Congress began to pay more attention to housing, mass transportation, and other issues of concern to metropolitan areas.

Separation of Powers

American political history features an ongoing struggle for power between the president and Congress, and the courts sometimes decide who wins. The Supreme Court has usually supported claims by presidents that they have foreign-policy powers beyond what is found literally in the Constitution."[10] In *U.S. v. Curtiss-Wright Export Corp.* (1936) the Court ruled famously that the president could embargo arms to warring countries without the approval of Congress based on his "exclusive power . . . as the sole organ of the federal government in the field of international relations." Among other impacts, this view helps support the claim of presidents that they have the authority to use military forces without authorization by Congress.[11] Bill Clinton, for one, ordered U.S. air forces to attack Serbia in 1999 "pursuant to my constitutional authority to conduct U.S. foreign relations and as commander-in-chief."[12]

Division of Powers

The courts have also helped determine the outcomes during the historic struggle over the division of powers between the national government and the states (see Chapter 3). One dimension of this conflict has been the meaning of the interstate commerce clause. Traditionally, the Supreme Court interpreted the interstate commerce clause narrowly to mean only the actual transportation of goods. This led the Court to reject various federal laws attempting to expand national control of the economy. Then in the mid-1930s, for reasons discussed later in this chapter, the Court adopted a much broader interpretation of the interstate commerce clause to include the production and distribution of almost everything that moves in or impacts interstate commerce.

This view persists and allows Congress to legislate in areas that were once exclusively within the realm of the states. One recent illustration involved whether California could permit physicians to prescribe marijuana for cancer victims. Based on a U.S. law regulating all drugs under the interstate commerce clause, federal agents seized the prescribed marijuana that a California woman was using to treat her brain tumor symptoms. She sued, arguing the drug had been grown and distributed solely within California and, therefore, was not part of interstate commerce. The Supreme Court disagreed in *Gonzales v. Raich* (2005). It reasoned that although the drug had not crossed state lines, Congress could regulate it because even locally produced pot can "affect price and market conditions" for marijuana that moves in interstate commerce.

Public Policy

Courts also have a policy-making role. This controversial ability is discussed at length below, but abortion policy provides an illustration. It was not elected officials who changed policy in the 1970s and made abortions generally available. Instead, the Supreme Court changed policy when it ruled in *Roe v. Wade* (1973) that most restrictions on a woman's ability to have an abortion during her first two trimesters were unconstitutional. At that point, the U.S. government and 46 states had abortion laws than were more restrictive than the standards mandated by *Roe*.

Sometimes the courts come close to ordering the federal government to make certain policy. When President George W. Bush and the Republican-controlled Congress refused to slow global warming by restricting the emission of carbon dioxide and other greenhouse gases, Massachusetts led a suit against the Environmental Protection Agency (EPA). The EPA argued that it had no authority to regulate these gases. In *Massachusetts v. EPA* (2007), the Supreme Court ruled that greenhouse gases are a pollutant, and, therefore, that the EPA could regulate them under the Clean Air Act (1990). The Court went on to say that the EPA could "avoid promulgating regulations only if it determines that greenhouse gases do not contribute to climate change." The Bush administration ignored the ruling, but in 2009 with President Obama in office, the EPA declared that greenhouse gas emissions "threaten the public health and welfare" and began the process of formulating regulations to restrict them.

Constitutional Sources of Judicial Power

One scholar estimates that only about 10% of all countries, including the United States, have strong judicial systems. Indeed, he writes, "The most common pattern . . . is for the judiciary to be little more than a loyal administrative arm of executive power."[13] This raises the question: What makes the U.S. courts so atypically powerful? In this section we will take up the Constitution as a source of judicial power. Then we will turn to the role of society in empowering the courts.

Judicial Independence

Article III establishes the courts as an independent branch by granting "the judicial power of the United States" to the "Supreme Court" and any lower courts that Congress chooses to establish. This clause ensures that the Supreme Court cannot be abolished short of a constitutional amendment and establishes the presumption of a lower court system. Article III also empowers the judiciary by allowing most federal judges to serve as long as they wish unless Congress removes them from office by impeachment and conviction. This is rare. Of the more than 3,000 judges appointed with life tenure from 1789 to 2010, only 15 have been impeached. Of those, only 10 have been removed from office or have resigned to avoid removal.

These protections have pluses and minuses. An argument for life tenure is that it frees judges from pressure and allows them to make decisions without fear of losing their position. An argument against life tenure is that it insulates judges from the democratic process. Thomas Jefferson, for one, argued that life appointments give judges "a freehold and irresponsibility in office."[14] Another concern is the capacity of aged judges, many of whom are in their seventies and beyond. Between 1975 and Justice Steven's retirement in 2010, the average U.S. Supreme Court justice was 79 years old when he or she stepped down or died. At the extreme, the oldest Supreme Court justice was Oliver Wendell Holmes, who retired at age 90 (plus 9 months) in 1932. On the lower courts, some judges have regularly heard cases until age 95, and Joseph W. Woodrough continued in "senior status" (retired) to hear some cases until he died at age 104 in 1977.

Mandatory retirement is one option frequently suggested. A 2010 survey found 65% of Americans in favor, with a median preference for setting an age limit between 70 and 74.[15] *Term limits* of perhaps 10 years for federal judges are another commonly proposed option. A strong majority (71%) of Americans also support this idea.[16] They would have a huge impact. If, for instance, a 10-year limit had been put into place to coincide with President Obama's inauguration, seven of the nine Supreme Court justices at that time would have been forced to retire.

Justice John Paul Stevens was 90 years (plus 3 months) old and had been on the Court for 35 years when he retired in 2010. Should there be a mandatory retirement age and/or limit on length of service for federal judges? (AP Photo/J. Scott Applewhite)

Jurisdiction

A key to any court's power is its **jurisdiction**: its authority over issues. The Constitution authorizes the federal courts to hear certain types of cases depending on (1) the *parties*: the United States, two or more states, citizens of different states, and foreign governments and officials; and on (2) the *subject*: U.S. constitutional issues, U.S. laws and treaties, and maritime law.

A court can have original jurisdiction, appellate jurisdiction, or both. **Original jurisdiction** courts are the first to hear a case, and they focus on the facts of the case. **Appellate jurisdiction** courts hear claims by the losing side in a lower court that the loss was caused by the judge(s) making errors in applying the law to the case. The Supreme Court has both types of jurisdiction. It has original jurisdiction in cases involving two states and those involving other countries and their diplomats, and appellate jurisdiction in all other federal cases. These come to the Court from a variety of lower courts that we will outline later.

The authority of the Supreme Court to hear its original jurisdiction cases cannot be challenged, but Congress has some ability to limit the jurisdiction of the lower courts. The issue is how far Congress can go. Its authority to shape jurisdiction stems from its power under Article III to create lower courts and to make "exceptions" to and "regulations" about the Supreme Court's appellate jurisdiction over these courts. Such limits are uncommon, but they do exist. For example, the federal courts have jurisdiction over cases "between citizens of different states," but federal law bars cases involving claims below $75,000. Limits of this type are not controversial, but what would happen if Congress barred the federal courts from hearing cases on the constitutionality of state and local law regarding the treatment of gays, the separation of church and state, or abortion? That may sound farfetched, but it is exactly what House bill 539 introduced in 2009 by Representative Ron Paul (R-TX) proposed.

Paul's bill did not pass, just as similar bills have failed, because Congress has sought to limit jurisdiction only rarely and cautiously. For its part, the Supreme Court has upheld some jurisdictional restraints, but it has also warned Congress not to go too far in restricting jurisdiction because of "the 'serious constitutional question' that would arise if a federal statute were construed to deny any judicial forum for a . . . constitutional claim."[17]

A final note on jurisdiction is that presidents have also tried to limit the courts' jurisdiction. For one, President Bush declared that the alleged terrorists being held at the U.S. naval base at Guantanamo Bay were enemy combatants without access to civilian federal courts. In a series of cases culminating in *Boumediene v. Bush* (2008), the Supreme Court disagreed.

Judicial Interpretation

The courts' authority to hear cases includes the power of **judicial interpretation**: the authority to decide the meaning of the language in the Constitution and in laws passed by Congress. Title IX of the Education Amendments Act of 1972 barred discrimination based on sex in schools, and courts soon thereafter interpreted the law to allow women to sue schools for sexual harassment. However, there was little incentive to do so because the law did not explicitly allow victims to ask for monetary damages. The Supreme Court changed that in 1991. It held that the intent of Title IX to protect women meant that penalties for noncompliance logically had to be permissible.[18]

Judicial Review

Yet another cornerstone of the of the courts' power is **judicial review**. This is the ability to decide whether laws, regulations, and executive actions are constitutional. Although this power is not specifically mentioned in Article III, the Supreme Court in *Marbury v. Madison* (1803) found that judicial review was inherent in the authority of the courts and that federal laws and official actions "repugnant to the constitution [are] void." A few years later, the Court also first exercised judicial review of the states in *Martin v. Hunter's Lessee* (1816).

Historically, the Supreme Court has used the power of judicial review with restraint, rejecting fewer than 200 of the nearly 48,000 laws Congress has enacted since 1789. Similarly, the Court has voided relatively few state laws. Still, the impact of judicial review on public policy "is far greater than [the] small percentages suggest."[19] One reason is the ripple effect. When the Supreme Court strikes down one state's law, lower courts use that decision to void similar laws in other states. For instance, *Roe v. Wade* (1973) struck down only Texas's abortion law, but by extension the decision negated the laws in the 45 other states that also had abortion laws more stringent that the standards set forth in *Roe*.

The second reason that judicial review is so important is that the Supreme Court has been more willing since the 1960s to declare laws unconstitutional. Sixty percent of such instances for federal laws and 50% for state laws have occurred since then. One reason for this is that the Court has been at the forefront of expanding civil rights and liberties by negating laws restricting freedoms. Whatever the cause, the assertiveness of the Court has sparked charges of inappropriate judicial activism that we will address later in this chapter.

Societal Sources of Judicial Power

American society is the second source of judicial power. The courts draw power from the Constitution, but that document's strength, in turn, is based on the willingness of the government and people to abide by it and, if necessary, to enforce the law's provisions.

How the people of any country feel about their constitution and laws is rooted in their national political culture, a concept explored in Chapter 6. **Legalism**, a belief in the rule of law, is a strong element of American political culture. When

FIGURE 14.2
Americans' Evaluation
of the Branches of
Government

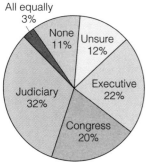

Which branch is the
most trustworthy?

Of the three branches of
the federal government,
Americans normally have
the greatest trust and
confidence in the judiciary.
Data source: Opinion Dynamics
Poll, June 2005. Data provided
by the Roper Center for Public
Opinion Research, University of
Connecticut.

asked in a recent poll if the "rule of law should be followed if that comes at the expense of . . . public safety," 61% of Americans said yes, with only 35% disagreeing, and 4% unsure.[20] Figure 14.2 provides another indication of legalism: Americans normally hold the courts in higher regard and have more confidence in the judicial branch than in either the executive branch or Congress.

Legalism has numerous impacts on the U.S. political system. One is to help protect the courts against any effort by Congress or the president to limit them. After the Supreme Court struck down several laws he supported, President Franklin D. Roosevelt sought to gain control of it in 1937 by proposing an increase in the number of justices from 9 to 15. This would have given him 6 new appointments. However, Roosevelt's "court-packing plan" was so overtly political that it evoked strong negative reactions in the press, public opinion, and Congress that soon killed the idea.

A second impact of legalism is the propensity of Americans to wage policy battles in the courts by looking for constitutional reasons to challenge laws they do not like.[21] As French political observer Alexis de Tocqueville noted in *Democracy in America* (1835), "There is hardly a political question in the United States which does not sooner or later turn into a judicial one."

Some worry about the tendency to make political issues into court cases. Justice Antonin Scalia argues that the courts should more often say, "No, thank you. . . . There is nothing in the Constitution on the . . . issue." His concern is that

As this 1937 cartoon illustrates, President Franklin Roosevelt's effort to get control of the Supreme Court by naming six additional justices met with strong opposition, even from Democrats in Congress, symbolized here by the kicking donkey. (Library of Congress)

by taking such cases, the courts make "themselves politically controversial" and invite political attacks that put "their independence at risk." In sum, Scalia advises, "Everything that is stupid is not unconstitutional."[22]

Limits on Judicial Power

For all its power, the judiciary is the least potent branch of government. Limits to judicial power include: legal limits, constraints on implementation, self-imposed limits, and external pressures.

Legal Limits

Numerous legal restraints on the courts exist under the system of checks and balances. Except for the constitutional requirement that there be a Supreme Court, the courts are entirely dependent on Congress to authorize, structure, and fund them. Congress has occasionally used its power in very political ways. After Abraham Lincoln was assassinated, the Republican-controlled Congress reduced the number of Supreme Court justices from 10 to 7 to block any possibility of Democratic President Andrew Johnson filling vacancies with Democrats. Once Republican President Ulysses S. Grant took office, Congress increased the number of justices to 9, allowing him to appoint replacements. Additional legal limits include the aforementioned ability of Congress to restrict jurisdiction and to remove judges.

Furthermore, there are ways to negate a Supreme Court decision. Passing a constitutional amendment is one. Even though states were using poll taxes to keep poor blacks and Hispanics from voting, the Court ruled in 1937 that these taxes were constitutional because they applied to everyone.[23] That decision stood until 1964 when the country adopted the Twenty-Fourth Amendment barring any tax on voting. Congress can also override the way that the courts interpret statutes by passing new laws.[24] For example, when Lilly Ledbetter sued the Goodyear Tire company under the provision of the Civil Rights Act of 1964 for pay discrimination, the Supreme Court ruled in 2007 that she could not collect damages because she had not met the requirement in the 1964 act that she sue within 180 days of when the discrimination began.[25] Congress fixed the problem in 2009 by amending the 1964 act to extend the time to sue.

Constraints on Implementation

Another limit on the courts is their reliance on the other two branches for **judicial implementation**: putting decisions by the courts into practice. Doing this requires the executive branch to enforce court decisions and Congress to provide funding if needed. In 1830 Georgia made it illegal for whites to live on an Indian reservation without the state's permission. When Georgia arrested two white missionaries for violating the law, they sued, arguing states could not regulate reservations. Eventually the Supreme Court found for the missionaries and ordered the men released.[26] Nevertheless, the governor of Georgia refused to release the missionaries, and President Andrew Jackson refused to enforce the Court's order, supposedly exclaiming, "Well, John Marshall has made his decision, now let him enforce it."

Such open defiance of the courts is rare, but more subtle methods are not. *Bureaucratic delay* is one common barrier to implementation. When, as related earlier, the Supreme Court ruled in 2006 that the Clean Air Act required the EPA to regulate greenhouse gases if they were damaging the environment, the Bush administration stalled. One tactic was to take more than two years to look into the matter, then to have the EPA release a 588-page report that only raised new legal arguments that the EPA had no authority. New suits ensued, but they were overtaken when the newly installed Obama administration finally followed the Court's order in 2009.

Lack of any or sufficient funding is another common barrier to judicial implementation. The courts require that poor criminal defendants have public defenders, but Congress and state legislatures provide limited funds to hire them. The resulting shortage of these attorneys means that they are often overwhelmed by huge case loads that prevent them from giving many of their cases the attention a privately paid attorney could. In Los Angeles County, for one, each public defender handles a yearly average of 138 felony cases and 867 misdemeanor and juvenile cases.

Societal attitudes also limit implementation. Almost 60 years have passed since the Supreme Court ruled in *Brown v. Board of Education* (1954) that separate schools were inherently unequal and therefore unconstitutional. Yet today about 40% of black and Latino children attend schools that are almost completely segregated (with white students 10% or less of enrollment). Moreover, such de facto segregation is up 7% since 1989. A large part of the reason is based on societal attitudes that have included "white flight" to the suburbs and resistance to busing to implement integration in metropolitan school districts where the races live in different areas.

One limit on the courts is their inability to implement the law in the face of widespread opposing social attitudes. The Supreme Court ruled in 1954 that separate schools were inherently unequal. Yet today because of housing patterns, 40% of black and Latino children attend de facto segregated schools. (iStockphoto)

Self-Imposed Limits

Judicial power is also limited by restrictions that the courts place upon themselves. One such self-limitation is holding that some controversies involve **nonjusticiable issues**, those that are not appropriate for judicial resolutions. **Political questions** make up the most common category. Generally the courts have declined to decide issues that they consider political, rather than legal disputes. One example involves the war powers of the president. Numerous suits have challenged "presidential wars" as violations of the Constitution and of the War Powers Resolution (1973), which Congress enacted to limit the president's military authority. However, the courts have rejected these suits because, as one judge put it, they involve "policy considerations . . . [that] are far more suitable for determination by [the other] branches of the government."[27]

The line between what is political and legal is up to the courts, and that line can change. For most of U.S. history, the courts regarded disputes over how state legislatures configured electoral districts to be a "political thicket" and refused to intervene.[28] Then the Supreme Court changed its mind, and in *Baker v. Carr* (1962) and other cases established the one-person, one-vote standard requiring that electoral districts other than the U.S. Senate have approximately equal populations.

Judicial deference is a second self-imposed limitation. One reason that the Supreme Court voids relatively few laws is the tacit assumption that laws passed by elected representatives are constitutional.[29] As Justice Stephen Breyer has put it, "Judicial modesty . . . suggests that" on many matters of policy the "courts should defer to the legislatures' own answers."[30]

This deference extends to the president and is particularly pronounced during crises. One notable example occurred during World War II when the Supreme Court in *Korematsu v. United States* (1944) upheld herding Japanese Americans into detention camps. Even though the government presented no evidence of disloyalty by Japanese Americans, the Court ruled that confining them in remote prison camps was justified because, "We cannot reject . . . the judgment of the military authorities and of Congress that there were disloyal members of that population." It was a policy and decision for which the United States formally apologized to its Japanese American citizens in the Civil Liberties Act of 1988.

External Pressures

Judicial power is also limited by the political environment in which the courts exist. It may be that President Roosevelt's effort at court-packing failed in 1937, but his attack on the Court for having a "horse-and-buggy" mind-set gained him an indirect victory.[31] Many members of Congress and public opinion sided with the president. One poll found 59% of its respondents agreeing that the Supreme Court should be "more liberal in reviewing New Deal measures."[32] Under intense pressure to let the president and Congress address the country's economic emergency, the Supreme Court seemed to give way by adopting a more expansive interpretation of the interstate commerce clause that allowed the federal government to legislate in areas that had been within the exclusive realm of the states.

Overt criticism of the Supreme Court by the president is extremely rare, but it occurred once again in 2010. During his State of the Union message to Congress and other ranking officials, including most of the members of the Supreme Court, President Obama criticized the decision of the Court in *United Citizens v. Federal Election Commission* (2010). The ruling had voided part of existing election laws and thereby allowed corporations to spend funds to independently support or oppose candidates for federal office. Looking directly at the justices sitting in the front rows, and amid applause and cheers by congressional Democrats, Obama chastised the Court for having "reversed a century of law," thereby "open[ing] the floodgates for special interests—including foreign corporations—to spend without limit in our elections."[33] Cameras showed a scowling Justice Samuel Alito, who was part of the majority in *United Citizens*, shaking his head and mouthing "not true." Within days, Chief Justice Roberts joined the fray. During a question-and-answer session with law students at the University of Alabama, Roberts said the State of the Union address had "degenerated into a political pep rally." The Chief Justice added that he found it "very troubling" that Obama had created a situation where there were "members of one branch of government [Congress] standing up, literally surrounding the Supreme Court, cheering and hollering while the [members of the] court—according to the requirements of protocol—ha[d] to sit there expressionless."[34] The exchange between the president and the chief justice may seem restrained compared to the language and volume of many arguments, but given the usually decorous deference among the branches, it was a true firefight. The next overt round may come if Roberts and a number of other justices, or even all of them, break long tradition and decline to attend Obama's State of the Union address in 2011. As for the public, 68%, like Obama, disapproved of the Court's decision. However, the depth of that opinion was put into question when the same survey asked respondents how much they had read or heard about the decision, and 81% said either only "a little" or "nothing at all."[35]

STRUCTURE OF THE LEGAL SYSTEM

Institutionally, the U.S. legal system at the federal level is composed of its various types of law, its courts, and its judges. We will look at each of these components in order.

Types of Law

Laws can be classified by their *relative importance*. **Constitutional law** is at the top, based on the Constitution's declaration it is the "supreme law of the land." **Statutory law**, the thousands of statutes (laws) passed by Congress, is a step down in the hierarchy. Administrative law (decisions made by agencies in accordance with existing laws) and treaty law are subsets of statutory law. **Common law** is subordinate to the other types of law and rests on what the courts have found to be society's practices in cases where no statute applies. Common law is seldom at issue because the vast body of written law leaves little room for common law to apply.

Laws can also be classified by *subject*. **Criminal law** relates to acts against people (such as rape) and property (such as burglary) that disrupt public safety. Federal prosecutors filed 71,000 criminal cases, and convicted 91% of the defendants in 2008. Of those convicted, 80% were sent to prison for an average sentence of more than 5 years. **Civil law** involves business and other noncriminal disputes between individuals, organizations, and/or the government. The federal courts have jurisdiction over a range of civil cases, such as those involving interstate commerce, bankruptcy, and questions about the constitutionality or interpretation of federal laws. Almost 1.8 million civil cases were filed in federal court during 2009, of which about three-fourths involved bankruptcy petitions. There were also more than 57,000 appeals filed in criminal and civil cases that year.

Types of Courts

In addition to classifying courts by their federal-system level (federal, state, local) and their jurisdiction (original and appellate), they can also be grouped by the legal source of their existence. **Constitutional courts** are established by Congress under Article III, and their judges have life tenure. **Legislative courts** are specialized courts that Congress has created using its Article II power. Judges in these courts have limited terms. Both types of courts have full judicial authority, but the constitutional courts form the core of the judicial branch.

Constitutional Courts

U.S. district courts have existed since 1789 and exercise original jurisdiction over most federal cases. There are 94 district courts, with at least one in each state and most territories. They were presided over in 2010 by 663 judges, who were supported by 324 bankruptcy judges handling cases in that area and 466 magistrate judges who deal with misdemeanors and minor civil suits. Magistrate and bankruptcy judges are appointed by the courts themselves for set terms. Each district court also has a **U.S. attorney**, who represents the U.S. government in the district.

Appeals of district court decisions once went directly to the Supreme Court, but in time the number of appeals swamped the Court. In response, Congress created regional "circuit" courts of appeals in 1891. These courts were collectively renamed the **U.S. Court of Appeals** in 1948, although the circuit designator remains common. There are 13 such courts. Eleven are named after their numbered circuit, such as the U.S. Court of Appeals for the First Circuit (Maine, Massachusetts, New Hampshire, Rhode Island, and Puerto Rico). The twelfth is the U.S. Court of Appeals for the District of Columbia (the D.C. Circuit). The thirteenth is the U.S. Court of Appeals for the Federal Circuit. It deals with particular types of cases, such as those involving international trade, government contracts, veterans' benefits, and patents. These appeals courts have 179 judges, ranging from 28 in the busiest circuit (the Ninth, including Hawaii, Alaska, and seven far western states) to 6 in the quietest (the First Circuit). Three-judge panels normally hear cases, but a larger number of judges may hear particularly important cases. The importance of these courts is evident in the fact that they make the final decision for 99% of all appeals cases.

The **U.S. Supreme Court** sits at the apex of the federal judicial structure. Initially, the Judiciary Act of 1789 set the number of justices at six. Since then, the number of justices has ranged from 5 to 10, but it has been stable at 9 since 1869. Eight of the Court's members are associate justices and the ninth serves as chief justice. Most chief justices have not been on the Court when appointed by the president, but if he seeks to appoint one of the existing associate justices as chief justice, then the Senate must confirm that individual in the new position.

Administratively, the chief justice has considerable authority over a range of matters involving the management of the Supreme Court and, indeed, the entire judicial branch. Among other tasks, the chief justice represents the judicial branch in its budget requests. The most important issue raised in recent years has been insistent requests for pay raises for federal judges. Chief Justice Roberts argues that a "constitutional crisis" is impending because the pay of federal judges ($174,000 for district court judges in 2010) falls so short of what a top attorney can make in private practice or teaching law that the quality of the federal judiciary is imperiled by the growing difficulty of persuading the best legal minds to take seats on the federal bench and remain in them.[36] There is no doubt that judges are paid less than the most successful lawyers and that judicial pay rates have lagged inflation for decades. There are counterarguments, however, that salaries are neither an important factor in the recruitment and retention of federal judges nor related to the quality of the work the judges produce.[37]

On the Supreme Court itself, the authority of the chief justice is less august than the title suggests. With a single vote like all other justices, the chief justice exercises leadership based primarily on the force of his intellect and personality. Reflecting this, Chief Justice Rehnquist depicted a chief justice as having some leadership "tools," but added that as only a first among equals, "his stature will depend on how he uses them."[38]

The one other constitutional court is the U.S. Court of International Trade located in New York City. Its nine judges have original jurisdiction in foreign trade cases. Appeals of this court's decision go initially to the United States Court of Appeals for the Federal Circuit.

Legislative Courts

Congress has authorized a range of legislative courts to deal with special legal issues. The earliest of these was using a court martial to try uniformed personnel and others subject to military discipline for crimes committed in the line of duty. Each military service also has its own appeals court, and above them is the U.S. Court of Appeals for the Armed Forces. It consists of five civilian judges appointed by the president for 15-year terms. Other legislative courts include the local courts in the District of Columbia and in U.S. territories, the Court of Appeals for Veterans Claims, the Court of Federal Claims, and the U.S. Tax Court.

Legislative courts seldom receive much media attention, but one recent exception has been the use of court martial-like *military commissions* that President Bush established in 2001 to try suspected terrorists. The effort of the Bush administration to limit the rights that defendants would have in a regular court trial was countermanded in part by several Supreme Court decisions. However, the Court never declared military commissions to be unconstitutional as such. While running for president, Barack Obama called military commissions a "dangerously flawed legal approach," but as president he became less doctrinaire.[39] Obama moved the trial of some detainees to federal district court, but retained military commissions to try other prisoners. Asked about this apparent shift, the White House press secretary reasoned that, "First and foremost, the president of the United States is going to do what he believes is in the best security interest of the people of the United States."[40]

Access to the Courts

In theory, equal justice is available to all Americans. The realty of the judicial system falls short of that ideal. Instead, the evidence shows that Americans' access to the courts and success in them is subject to economic, demographic, and legal restrictions.

Economic Restrictions

Lawyer's fees and other legal expenses make lawsuits expensive. This fact restricts the ability of low- and moderate-income individuals to file civil suits or to defend themselves against suits. The cost of access for plaintiffs in civil suits is sometimes eased in cases that seek substantial monetary damages if an attorney will take the case on contingency, that is, accept his or her fee as a percentage of any damages received. **Class action suits** also aid plaintiffs. These occur when one or a few people sue on behalf of a large number of people with the same complaint. This avoids the expense of separate cases and is attractive to lawyers who can take their contingency fee from the larger overall settlement.

Economic circumstance also plays a role in criminal cases. The Supreme Court ruled in *Gideon v. Wainright* (1963) that poor criminal defendants have the right to a public defender in felony cases, but that has not ensured equal justice. Statistics show that defendants with a privately retained attorney, compared to those represented by a public defender, are more apt to plead innocent or make a plea bargain that reduces the charges and penalties.[41]

Economic circumstances have an even greater impact at the appeals level. Public funding is not generally required for poor people who seek to appeal their cases. Indigent individuals can file their own appeals under *in forma pauperis* (in the manner of paupers) provisions, but such appeals have a vastly lower success rate than do appeals filed by an attorney. Getting a case into the Supreme Court costs tens of thousands of dollars. Therefore, the ability to appeal for most Americans depends on getting the financial backing of an interested group. Also, as with the Court of Appeals, poor individuals may file *in forma pauperis* appeals with the Supreme Court. However, it agrees to hear only about 1 in every 750 such appeals.

Demographic Restrictions

Gender and race also affect access to the courts. One problem is that men and whites are more likely to be able to afford a lawyer than are women and minorities. Therefore defendants in these disadvantaged groups are more apt to have to rely on one of the too few public defenders. This disparity recently led the United Nations' committee responsible for monitoring compliance with the International Convention on the Elimination of All Forms of Racial Discrimination (1969) to urge the United States to "adopt all necessary measures to eliminate the disproportionate impact that persistent . . . inadequacies in criminal defense programs for indigent persons have on defendants belonging to racial . . . minorities."[42]

President Richard Nixon signed the International Convention on the Elimination of All Forms of Racial Discrimination in 1969, but the treaty was not ratified by the Senate until 1994, a quarter century later.

Access is also negatively affected by the limited number of attorneys who are women or people of color. According to the American Bar Association, full and equal access to the courts for women and for people of color depends in part on their "ability to choose a lawyer with whom [they] feel comfortable. . . . Many marginalized members of society understandably put their trust more readily in lawyers who possess a shared background or heritage."[43] However, women and minority groups are underrepresented in the legal profession, as evident in Figure 14.3.

FIGURE 14.3 Demographic Distribution of Attorneys

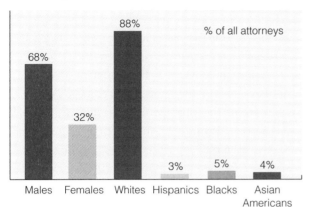

Although the percentage of lawyers who are women or a member of a minority group is growing, the field remains heavily dominated by men and whites.
Data source: U.S. Bureau of Labor Statistics for 2009

FIGURE 14.4 Women Law School Graduates

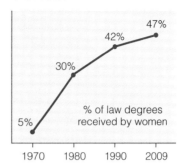

Since 1970 women have increased from 5% to almost half of all new law school graduates.
Data source: U.S. Census Bureau.

Diversity is certainly improving among lawyers, but for most groups it is advancing only slowly. Since 1990, blacks, Hispanics, and Asian American have increased their share of the legal profession by a mere 2% each, and Native Americans have been static at 0.2%. Women represent the brightest spot in diversity. Myra Colby Bradwell became the first woman attorney when in 1869 she passed Illinois' bar examination. However, the state's courts refused to let her practice before them because she was a woman. She appealed to the U.S. Supreme Court, but lost on the grounds that the "natural and proper timidity and delicacy, which belongs to the female sex" made women "unfit" to practice law.[44] Although women slowly gained the right to practice, this view did not begin to change significantly until the civil rights era in the 1960s. Since then, as Figure 14.4 shows, women have scored impressive gains in the percentage of law degrees they are earning.

Language restrictions are another demographic factor that limits equal access to the courts. A significant percentage of Latinos and people of Asian heritage who are living in the United States are immigrants who still do not speak English well. This restricts their ability to operate equally in the legal system. There is progress toward addressing this problem, but it is slow. Federal and state courts are supposed to have translators available under various federal civil rights laws, but budget restrictions keep the number of translators limited.

Legal Restrictions

A variety of legal restrictions also limit access to the courts. *Legislative barriers* are one type of legal restriction. Numerous laws bar civil suits altogether on some matters or set other restrictions. For instance, the Protection of Lawful Commerce in Arms Act (2005) bars lawsuits against gun manufacturers, importers, and dealers based on claims that their product caused injury or death. *Sovereign immunity* is another legal restriction. This doctrine allows governments to exempt themselves from being sued without their permission on many civil matters and is based on the idea that the monarch, or sovereign, could not be held accountable in court. In practice, though, this mostly applies to suits seeking monetary damages and does not extend to suits claiming that a law or administrative action is unconstitutional.

Standing is a third legal restriction. You must have a particular, immediate, and substantial interest to sue. For example, you do not have standing to challenge a federal law solely because you disagree with it philosophically or object as a taxpayer to supporting it. Who has standing can have important consequences. When President Jimmy Carter terminated the U.S. defense treaty with Taiwan as a preliminary step to establishing diplomatic relations with China, Senator Barry Goldwater (R-AZ) led a group of senators that filed suit. They claimed that since the Senate had ratified the treaty with Taiwan, ending it also needed the Senate's consent. In *Goldwater v. Carter* (1979), the Supreme Court, in effect, upheld the president by refusing to hear the case on the grounds that the senators lacked standing. As the Court's opinion put it, "Congress, by appropriate formal action" could have sued in this case, but "small groups or . . . individual members of Congress" could not.

THE JUDGES

There are over 2,000 federal judges in the constitutional and legislative courts. Given the power that the courts have, it is important to understand who the judges are and how they are selected.

Who the Judges Are

There are no formal requirements to be a federal judge. Like Supreme Court Justice Robert H. Jackson (1941–1954), you do not even need a law degree. Given the lack of formal qualifications, who the judges are depends mostly on political and societal factors. All federal judges now possess a law degree, and most also have had a political appointment or have held an elected office. Judges tend to be well off financially when appointed, with about half having net assets above $1 million. The average federal judge is in his or her late 40s when appointed, with the Supreme Court justices on the bench in late 2010 averaging 52 years old when appointed. The average female judge is a bit younger than her male counterparts when appointed, less wealthy, less likely to have been active politically, and more apt to have come from a career in public service. [45]

FIGURE 14.5 Demographic Composition of the Federal Judiciary

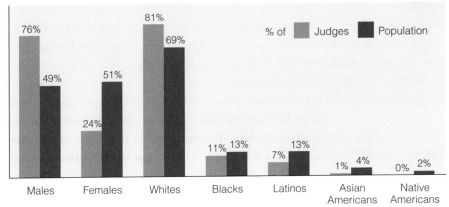

The percentage of white and male federal judges far exceeds those groups' share of the general population.

Notes and data source: Data as of August 2009 and for active judges on the district courts and the Court of Appeals only. There were no Native Americans among these 768 judges. Data from Russell Wheeler, *The Changing Face of the Federal Judiciary* (Washington, DC: Brookings, 2009).

Degree of Diversity

Judges also little resemble American society in terms of gender and race, as evident in Figure 14.5. For instance, the composition of the Supreme Court in late 2010 included five white males, two white female, one Hispanic female, and one African American male.

As is true for positions in the rest of the government, political minorities were long generally excluded in practice from the federal bench. The first woman did not take her seat until 1934. African Americans waited until 1950, Latinos until 1961, Asian Americans until 1971, and Native Americans until 1994 before the first member of their group became a federal judge. Recent years have seen a growing number of women and minorities appointed to the federal bench, but change remains slow. For instance, at the current rate, it will take women another 80 years before they achieve an equal number of appointments to the bench.

Impact of Diversity

To open this chapter, a You Decide box asked if it was important for President Obama to continue to increase the diversity of the Supreme Court. Those who advocate that he do so make several arguments. *Equity* is one. "Gender equality [is] based on equity and legitimacy; . . . equal participation of men and women in the justice system is an inherent and essential feature of a democracy," one advocate argues.[46]

Symbolic impact is a second argument for diversity. In part because of the scarcity of minority judges, most blacks (87%) and Hispanics (72%) believe members of their groups are at least sometimes treated less fairly than are whites by the courts. Even most whites (63%) agree that inequity exists.[47] Arguably, having more minority judges would ease this sense of unequal treatment.

Substantive impact is a third argument for diversity. Do women and judges who are people of color decide differently than do male and white judges? To a limited degree, the answer is yes.[48] For instance, women judges are more likely than male judges to be sensitive to a woman's point of view on sexual harassment and other issues of particular importance to women.[49] Similarly, women on courts of appeals tend to vote more liberally in civil rights and liberties cases than male judges.[50] Male and female judges also differ in their voting in criminal procedure cases.[51] None of this means that male and female judges always differ or do so radically where they do diverge. To the contrary, most differences are modest, and there are no significant gender differences on many matters, such as tax law.[52]

In 1960, Supreme Court Justice Felix Frankfurter refused to interview Ruth Bader Ginsburg, the valedictorian of her law school class at Columbia University, to be his law clerk because she was a woman. In 1993 she took a seat on the Court.

A second reason why women judges make a substantive difference is that they influence male judges with whom they serve. One indication is that male judges on multi-judge appeals court panels that included female judges decided for women in sexual harassment cases twice as often as male judges on all-male panels.[53]

Race also has some influence on judicial decision making. African American judges are more apt than their white colleagues to agree with charges of police misconduct.[54] Yet, at the same time, black judges sentence convicted felons, both black and white, to longer jail terms than do white judges.[55] Latino and white judges also sentence somewhat differently.[56] Yet another study that looked at the combination of race and gender on appeals court decisions concluded that "minority female judges . . . are significantly more likely than minority males, Caucasian females, and Caucasian males to support criminal defendants' claims."[57]

It must be added, though, that even where race-based and gender-based differences among judges' decisions exist, they are limited. For example, minority female judges were most favorable to the defendant's position, but (1) they still supported it only 25% of the time, and (2) that was only 6% more than the toughest group of judges, minority males. Thus it can be said that the backgrounds of judges who are women or minority members count, but only on some issues, and, even then, only to a small degree.

How Judges Are Selected

All federal judges are appointed by the president, and are among his most important legacies. One reason is the power that the courts wield. Second is the life tenure of the judges. Third, the turnover rate among judges is high enough to give most presidents an important role in shaping the courts' future by appointing a large number of judges. At the end of President Bush's term in 2009, he had appointed 22% of the then sitting Supreme Court justices, 34% of the judges on the Court of Appeals, and 39% of the district court judges. As for who is selected for the bench, the importance of the courts, their appointment by an elected president, and their confirmation or rejection by an elected Senate all combine to make the process intensely political.[58] The factors involved include the partisanship/ideology of potential judges, their judicial philosophy, their merit, and their demographic characteristics.

Partisanship/Ideology

A potential judge's political party and the associated political ideology combine for one criterion. Presidents typically choose about 90% of their judicial appointees from their own political party. Supreme Court appointments are particularly partisan. Since 1945, the only justice nominated to the Court who was not a member of the president's party was Lewis F. Powell, a conservative Democrat nominated by Richard Nixon.

Adding to the partisan imprint on the judiciary, it is common for judges to have served in state legislatures or Congress or as political appointees in the executive branch. Of the nine Supreme Court justices in late-2010, all but Anthony Kennedy and Ruth Bader Ginsburg had earlier served in at least one such position. The partisan factor is reinforced for district court judges by the tradition of **senatorial courtesy**.[59] If the senator of the state in which there is a vacancy is of the president's party, then senatorial courtesy requires the president to defer to the senator's choice for the court. Failure to do so is apt to lead to the Senate rejecting the nomination. Another way that partisanship affects who becomes a judge is by influencing when vacancies occur. It is not the norm, but some judges do opt for politically *strategic retirement* by waiting to step down until a president of their own party or ideological inclination is in the White House.[60] Liberal stalwart Justice John Paul Stevens all but admitted he would strategically retire when in March 2010 he commented that he thought that President Obama was doing "a good job of filling vacancies" and told a reporter, "You can say I will retire within the next three years [while Obama would be in office]. I'm sure of that."[61] Just a few weeks later, Stevens made good on his assurances and announced he was stepping down.

Yet, despite the role that party and ideology play in the appointment of judges, there are no guarantees about what judges will be like ideologically once on the bench. Most judges adhere to their ideological roots, but some do not. Despite being a ranking Republican politician, Earl Warren became a liberal chief justice (1953–1969), leading Republican President Dwight Eisenhower to call his appointment of Warren the "biggest damn-fool mistake I ever made." President John Kennedy expected Justice Byron White (1962–1993) to be liberal, but he regularly sided with conservatives. Most recently, conservatives were disappointed with Justice David H. Souter, who President George H. W. Bush appointed in 1990. "We thought Justice Souter would vote differently," explained a White House official, but "You can never predict or control how they'll vote. That's just absolutely a fact a life."[62]

Judicial Philosophy

Presidents understandably appoint judges who also share their views about the proper role of the courts. Judicial philosophy involves the debate over whether the courts should follow the model of judicial restraint or judicial activism. Advocates of **judicial restraint** believe that judges should avoid making policy, leaving that entirely to the elected officials of the legislative and executive branches. According to this approach, judges should adhere to several standards. First, they should respect the democratic legislative process by giving a constitutional "benefit of the doubt" to statutory laws passed by the people's elected representatives. Second, they should follow a policy of constitutional **strict constructionism**. This means interpreting the Constitution or a statute by emphasizing its literal text and the **original intent** of its authors. Supporting original intent, Chief Justice Roger B. Taney wrote long ago in the *Scott v. Sandford* (1857, the Dred Scott case) that the Constitution should be read with "the same meaning and intent" it had "when it came from the hands of its framers."

Those who favor **judicial activism** believe that judges should consider the Constitution a "living document." This means interpreting it in light of contemporary circumstances and even breaking new policy ground in judicial decisions, especially when protecting civil rights and liberties. A classic expression of this view is the argument of Justice Oliver Wendell Holmes in *Missouri v. Holland* (1920) that the Constitution should be interpreted "in light of our whole experience and not merely in light of what was said a hundred years ago."

The historic debate over these two approaches was intensified by what many saw as the markedly liberal activism of the Supreme Court in the 1960s and 1970s and by the subsequent efforts of Republican presidents to rein the Court in by nominating strict constructionist judges. Abortion has been the single greatest flash point of the debate since 1987 when President Reagan nominated a strict constructionist, Robert H. Bork, to the high court. He condemned the Supreme Court's *Roe v. Wade* (1973) decision expanding abortion availability as "a serious and wholly unjustifiable usurpation of state legislative authority."[63] In the end, Bork's outspoken opposition to the *Roe* decision allowing abortions, to the Civil

Rights Act of 1964, and other changes associated with the civil rights revolution of the 1960s and 1970s galvanized ferocious opposition from women, blacks, and others and led the Senate to reject his nomination by a vote of 58 to 42.

That did not end the judicial restraint-judicial activist debate, though. It was clearly on the mind of President Bush in 2005 when he told an audience that his nominee for the Supreme Court, John Roberts, "will strictly apply the Constitution and laws, not legislate from the bench."[64] Not surprisingly, President Obama applied a different standard in choosing Sonia Sotomayor for the high bench. As one senior White House official explained, Sotomayor met all of Obama qualifications "including his goal of selecting someone with the empathy factor—real-world, practical experience and understanding of how the law affects real people."[65] Of course, the "you-never-can-be-sure" rule governs Sotomayor like every other judge. One analysis of her 226 majority opinions as an appeals court judge found that only 38% were unmistakably liberal, while 49% were clearly conservative. Within these overall figures, she tended to be liberal on civil rights and liberties questions and conservative on criminal appeals.[66]

A final note is that in practice the original intent versus living document debate is not as stark as it is often portrayed. Few advocate relying absolutely on original intent because it is often impossible to know what the framers meant. Even if you can find out, the world has changed too much for original intent to be the sole standard of interpretation. Conversely, almost no one argues that the text of the Constitution and what the framers intended should be ignored. Thus, the debate for most is more a matter of degree than an "either-or" controversy.

One reason that President Obama named Sonia Sotomayor to the Supreme Court was his belief that her "real world" experience growing up in public housing in the Bronx section of New York City would add to her empathy as a justice. Whatever the impact on her judicial views, her childhood made her a New York Yankees fan. Here Justice Sotomayor achieves a fan's dream as she accompanies catcher Jorge Posada to the mound in Yankee Stadium in September 2009 to throw out the first pitch in a game between the "Bronx Bombers" and the Boston Red Sox. Adding to her day, the Yankees won 3-0. (AP Photo/Henny Ray Abrams)

Merit

Objective merit also usually plays an important role. Most appointees are reasonably qualified to serve as a judge and perform adequately once seated. Among other indicators that merit is an important factor in selecting judges are the ratings that the American Bar Association (ABA) gives nominees for the federal bench based on their experience. Since President Carter, the ABA has rated 58% of all nominees as "well qualified" and another 41% as "qualified."

All current judges have law degrees, and Supreme Court justices in recent decades have typically come from a few elite private undergraduate and law schools. For example, all nine justices of the justices serving in late 2010 went to one of just three Ivy League law schools: Harvard (5). Yale (3) and Columbia (1), and five of the justices also received their undergraduate degrees from an Ivy League university. Most federal judges have also had successful careers in private practice, government service, or academia. Additionally, many have been judges on state courts, and it is common for Supreme Court justices to also have served on lower federal courts.

As far as experience, the most notable trend in the appointment judges is that a decreasing share of appointees has come from private practice and an increasing number have been in the public service as a judge or government lawyer at the time of appointment. During the Eisenhower administration, the private sector supplied 67% of the new district court judges, while public service supplied 33%. By the administration of George W. Bush, the numbers were nearly reversed, with 64% of new district judges coming from public service and only 36% from private practice.[67] Appointments of the U.S. Court of Appeals are even more likely to come from the public sector.[68] A review of judges in a selection of six circuits found that 75% of them had come from the public service. Of those, a majority (51%) had been elevated from district court seats, 25% had been state court judges, and the remainder had been elected or appointed government lawyers.[69] The Supreme Court epitomizes this trend of drawing from public service. Indeed, eight of the nine justices as of late 2010 came to the high court from seats on the Circuit Court of Appeals.

At least one explanation for this trend is that as political polarization has increased the emphasis on the ideology of judges, presidents have increasingly made appointments from the public sector because those individuals are more likely to have an established record of positions on divisive issues and are therefore less likely to surprise the appointing president with their subsequent rulings.

Whatever the cause of the de facto narrowing of the pool of potential judges, the trend concerns some observers. For one, Senate Majority Leader Harry Reid has urged that the president consider "people with some real-life experience . . . rather than people who walk around in these black robes all the time."[70] Or, as Vice President Joseph R. Biden once put it, "We have enough professors on the bench. I want someone who ran for dog catcher."[71] Perhaps that is a valid criticism, but overall no single qualification determines merit. For example, 39 of the 110 Supreme Court justices appointed from 1789 to 2010 had no prior experience as a judge. The list includes such chief justices as John Marshall, Earl Warren, and William H. Rehnquist.

Demography

A potential nominee's demographic characteristics are a fourth selection criterion. *Geographic balance* was once a concern, but that died out by the early 1900s. *Religion* is a second all but vanished criterion. Historically, almost 75% of all Supreme

Court justices have been Protestant, but there has been at least one Catholic on the Supreme Court almost continuously since 1894 and usually a Jewish justice since 1916. Symbolizing the end of Protestant domination of the Court and the current lack of concern with religion, the retirement of Protestant Justice Stevens in 2010 and his replacement by Jewish Justice Elena Kagan left the Court with six justices who are Roman Catholic, three who are Jewish, and for the first time in history no Protestants.

Gender has been a criterion since Ronald Reagan pledged during the 1980 presidential campaign to appoint a woman to the Supreme Court and honored that by naming Sandra Day O'Connor in 1981. Ruth Bader Ginsburg joined her on the Court in 1993. When O'Connor retired in 2006, President Bush named Harriet Miers to replace her but turned to a male after Miers withdrew. This left Bader Ginsburg as the only woman on the Court until Sonia Sotomayor joined her in 2009, followed by Elena Kagan in 2010. *Race* is yet another criterion. There has been an African American justice ever since 1967 when Thurgood Marshall became the first African American on the Supreme Court. Justice Sotomayor is the Court's first Hispanic member.

Thurgood Marshall, who became the first African American justice of the Supreme Court in 1967, is pictured here in his official court portrait. (Library of Congress)

The Confirmation Process

Presidents submit their judicial nominations to the Senate. There the Judiciary Committee reviews most of them, but simply ignores a few for one reason or another. If the committee proceeds, it can vote against a nomination, which almost always kills it, or vote for it and send it to the full chamber. Some troubled nominations are never scheduled for a debate or are derailed by a filibuster. Finally, if a nomination does come to a vote, senators confirm or reject the nominee by majority vote. The length of this process for a Supreme Court nomination averages about two months but has ranged from the same day for Edward White in 1910 to five months for the first Jewish justice, Louis Brandeis, in 1916.

Nominations for lower courts have traditionally received much less Senate scrutiny than those for the Supreme Court, but that has changed somewhat in recent decades. Now many Court of Appeals nominations and even some district court nominations are the subject of considerable conflict in the Senate.[72] One indication is that the time involved in the confirmation process has grown longer and longer. Simultaneously, the share of judicial nominees getting confirmed has decreased. Both these trends are clear in Figure 14.6. Most of the nominations that have failed have not been rejected outright. Instead the nominations have been "buried" in the Senate by various legislative tactics (see Chapter 11). Partisanship and ideological polarization have been the primary cause of the changes in the

FIGURE 14.6 Trends in the Length of the Confirmation Process and Success Rates

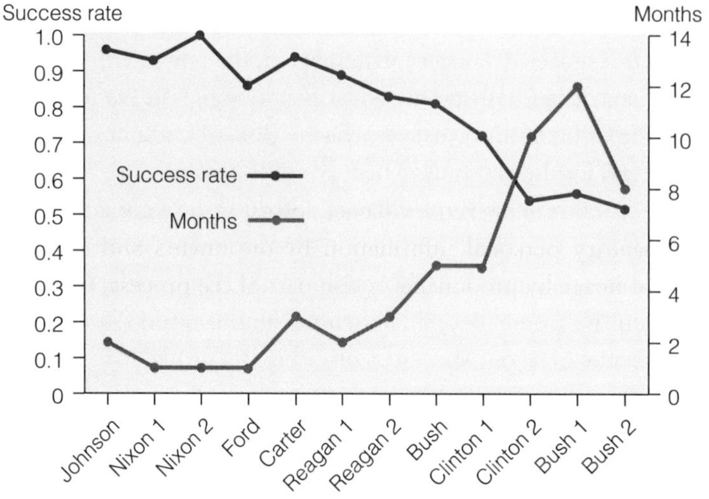

This figure shows that the Senate's confirmation process for judges has become more contentious. The right vertical axis shows that the number of months the average nomination is under consideration in the Senate has grown much longer. At the same time, as the vertical axis on the left shows, the success rate of nominees being confirmed has trended downward.

Notes and data source: The numbers 1 and 2 after a president's name indicate first and second terms. Data from Jon R. Bond, Richard Fleisher, and Glen S. Krutz, "Malign Neglect: Evidence That Delay Has Become the Primary Method of Defeating Presidential Appointments," *Congress & the Presidency,* 36/3 (2009): 226–243.

Senate's willingness to confirm judges. As late as Clinton's first term, the reasons senators gave for opposing a nominee were about evenly split between accusations of poor qualifications or wrongdoing and charges of ideological extremism. From that point through the Bush presidency, ideological objections outnumbered those based on merit by more than two to one.[73]

While the nominations for the various courts have some differences, we will concentrate here on Supreme Court nominations to explore the confirmation process.[74]

The Preliminaries

After a president has announced the nominee for the Supreme Court, there is usually a delay of several weeks before the beginning of the Judiciary Committee's hearings. During this time, nominees submit to the Judiciary Committee a long questionnaire about their qualifications and views. The nominee also meets informally with the Senate's leadership, members of the Judiciary Committee, and other key senators.

Beyond the Senate, proponents and opponents of the nominee gather information, marshal their forces, and may launch public relations campaigns. Soon after Chief Justice Roberts was nominated, for example, the National Abortion Rights Action League bought television ads charging Roberts with sympathy for "violent fringe groups and a convicted clinic bomber," and arguing, "America can't afford a justice whose ideology leads him to excuse violence against other Americans."[75]

Looking for derogatory personal information by opponents and fashioning a positive personal image by proponents is also part of the process. Clarence Thomas barely survived charges of sexual harassment in 1991, and the nomination of Douglas Ginsburg to the Supreme Court collapsed in 1987 because he had smoked marijuana many years earlier. By contrast, images of Samuel Alito as a hard-shell conservative were softened by portrayals of him as a baseball enthusiast who coached Little League, who had a team poster of his beloved Philadelphia Phillies in his office, and who had once attended a baseball fantasy camp. Alito's affable image aided his cause. As one dejected Democrat conceded, "He's a nice guy, and he doesn't drool."[76]

Similarly, Elena Kagan's affable testimony eased her confirmation process. By one count the quips and lighter comments made during her more than eight hours of testimony before the Senate Judiciary Committee engendered 30 moments of laughter.[77] In one instance a senator was trying to ask her where she stood on a controversy over when the suspect of a terrorist attempt to set off a bomb aboard a commercial flight in Detroit on December 25, 2009, had been read his Miranda rights. Jumbling his words, the senator inquired, "Where were you on Christmas Day?" Reportedly, "a gleam appeared in Kagan's eye. She laughed out loud, [and replied], 'You know, like all Jews, I was probably in a Chinese restaurant,' as the hearing room "erupted in laughter followed by applause."[78]

Committee Hearings and Recommendation

Once the preliminaries are completed, the Judiciary Committee holds several days of high-profile hearings. This is a relatively modern practice. No Supreme Court nominee met formally with the committee until 1925, and only some did before 1955. Now all do. Even more recently, nominees for the Court of Appeals have also appeared regularly before the committee.

More than any factor, this intensification of the confirmation process is a result of the increasing role of the judiciary in deciding important policy questions. The particular turning point involved Chief Justice Earl Warren. He received a recess appointment to his post in 1953 by Dwight Eisenhower, then was nominated and confirmed in early 1954 without even appearing before the Senate. Soon thereafter, he wrote the Court's opinion in *Brown v. Board of Education* (1954) outlawing officially segregated schools. Southern Democrats in the Senate were so outraged that they subjected Eisenhower's next nominee to a full-scale hearing, and that approach continues today.

To begin the hearings, the nominee makes an opening statement followed by statements by all or most of the committee members. They then spend a day or two questioning nominees about their qualifications, views on the Constitution, and other legal issues. This becomes something of a cat-and-mouse game, because nominees try to avoid giving specific answers about how they would vote, on the grounds that prejudging an issue would require them to withdraw from hearing future cases on the matter. Avoiding such questions also deprives opposition senators and groups of ammunition. In addition to the nominees, an evenly divided selection of supporters and opponents appear before the committee. Confirmation hearings of recent nominees have each had about 30 such witnesses split between supporters and opponents.

Nominees for most posts usually must receive a positive recommendation by a majority of the committee to move forward, but Supreme Court nominations are always sent to the Senate floor. With rare exceptions, the committee's recommendation is positive, in part because nominees who are in trouble withdraw rather than face a negative vote. One exception involved Clarence Thomas in 1991. Because of the charges of sexual harassment noted earlier, the committee tied 7-7 and sent his nomination without a recommendation to the floor, where he was confirmed by a narrow 52-48 vote. The only negative recommendation ever from the committee was on Robert Bork in 1987, and the full Senate then rejected him.

How Senators Decide

Three factors are most apt to determine how a senator votes on a nominee. They are ideology/partisanship, legal qualifications, and judicial demeanor.

Ideology/partisanship prompts senators to usually vote for nominees who share their party affiliation and who otherwise have a similar ideological outlook. The partisan connection is particularly strong for senators of the president's party. They rarely vote against his nominees. Indeed, members of the president's party cast only 4 of the 155 Senate votes cast against the confirmation of one or another of the Supreme Court justices on the bench in late 2010.[79] Of the 57 Democrat senators voting on Kagan's confirmation, for example, only one, Ben Nelson of Nebraska, voted against her.

Legal qualifications such as experience on the bench also play a strong role in determining how senators vote. Because most nominees are at least reasonably well qualified, their basic merit is seldom in doubt. For example, Justice Sotomayor's solid record during 17 years as a federal judge (11 on the Court of Appeals, 6 on a district court) was an important asset in her hearings. But there have been nominees who raised doubts. Most recently, many senators from both parties questioned President Bush's characterization of Harriet Miers in 1995 as "exceptionally well suited" for the Supreme Court.[80] Trent Lott (R-MS), for one, expressed concern about whether she "had enough experience in the constitutional area to be on the Supreme Court."[81] These and a variety of other objections soon led Miers to withdraw.

Supreme Court nominations have become more subject to partisan battles in recent years than was once the case. (© 2009 Dave Granlund and PoliticalCartoons.com.)

Judicial demeanor is a third and related qualification. All judges have political views, but proper judicial demeanor requires that they decide cases based on the law rather than personal beliefs. Justice Alito certainly has a marked conservative ideology, but what helped persuade some Democratic senators to support him was confidence that, as one observer said of Alito, "When engaging cases, he wouldn't start with the result and work his way backwards."[82]

Judicial demeanor also requires that judges not be intolerant of other demographic groups, make decisions based on their religious convictions, or otherwise approach cases with a bias. In addition to his dubious legal competence, the Senate rejected G. Harold Carswell in 1970 because of alleged racism. Among other evidence, Carswell had boasted to a group in Georgia that "I yield to no man in the firm, vigorous belief in the principles of white supremacy."[83]

Senate Debate

Debate on the Senate floor regarding nominations, as on bills and other matters, is largely symbolic because most senators usually have decided how to vote before debate begins. Therefore the speeches are primarily used by senators as statements of conscience or to explain their position on the nominee to the voters and interest groups at home. By the time the nomination of Samuel Alito moved to the Senate for debate in 2006, for instance, enough senators had announced how they would vote to ensure that he would be confirmed. Yet about two-thirds of them spoke on the floor.

Speeches on the floor are also sometimes used to **filibuster** a nomination. As detailed in Chapter 11, a filibuster is an effort to defeat a measure by having one or more members continue to talk, thus halting Senate business unless the matter is withdrawn from consideration or 60 senators vote for cloture, that is, to close the debate and vote on the matter.[84] Filibusters can also be used as a threat. As noted, the announcement by Justice Stevens in 2010 that he was retiring was soon followed by warnings from several Senate Republicans that the president faced a filibuster if he nominated a liberal activist to replace Stevens. That was an especially potent threat because there were several important measures that Obama favored, such as reforming the regulation of the country's banks and other financial institutions, that could be derailed by an extended stalemate in the Senate. Time would be even more limited because Congress would be in recess most of the fall to allow members to campaign for the November elections. Such concerns were reportedly one of the several factors that led President Obama to nominate Elena Kagan, who, while undoubtedly liberal, had voiced or written few views that could serve as a lightning rod for opponents. That strategy worked. Republican opposition to her was more pro forma than passionate, and she was confirmed in a relatively quick three months.

The use of filibusters with regard to judicial nominations has become highly controversial in recent years. Democrats used the tactic, for example, to derail several of Bush's judicial nominees during his first term. In response, angry Republicans charged that the Democrats were acting undemocratically by blocking Senate votes. After considerable partisan maneuvering, a compromise was reached in 2005. The Republicans agreed not to change the basic rules that permitted filibusters in the first place, and the Democrats agreed to filibuster judicial nominees only in "extraordinary circumstances." The first major test of the agreement came during the debate over Samuel Alito's 2006 nomination for the Supreme Court. Senator Ted Kennedy (D-MA) tried to lead a filibuster but lost a cloture motion, allowing the Senate to confirm Alito.

The first move against an Obama judicial nominee came in late 2009 when Senator Jeff Sessions (R-AL) tried to block a nominee for the Seventh Circuit of the Court of Appeals in the Midwest. "The new rule is that filibusters are legitimate, but only if there are extraordinary circumstances. That's where we are," Sessions commented. However, not enough Republicans agreed with him. Debate was closed by a vote of 70 to 29, and the nominee was confirmed.

A final note is that the views of most senators on filibusters and other delaying tactics depend on circumstances. For instance, Senator Kennedy condemned Republican delays of President Clinton's nominees in 1999 as a "gross perversion of the confirmation process."[85] Taking the opposite view four years later while seeking to block President Bush's nominees, Kennedy defended his delaying tactics as a way "to protect the country from the tyranny of the majority."[86]

Confirmation, Rejection, Withdrawal

Judging how successful presidents are in having their Supreme Court picks confirmed is difficult. Overall, the confirmation process would seem fairly benign because more than 77% of all nominees to the Supreme Court have been confirmed, and the confirmation rate for lower court judges has been even higher. Indeed, the confirmation rate for Supreme Court justices has usually been even higher than the historical average because a third of all failed nominations occurred during the tenure of just three troubled presidents: John Tyler, Millard Fillmore, and Grover Cleveland (second term). If the records of these three are factored out, the confirmation rate is 85%, and 93% of all Supreme Court nominees were confirmed between 1896 and 1963. How to judge the record during the most recent decades (1964–2010) depends in part on what its confirmation rate (77%) is compared to. It is exactly the same as the overall historical rate, but noticeably lower than the 93% rate of the nearly six previous decades.

Whatever the apparent success rate of any era or president, evaluations must be tempered by factoring in potential justices who a president might have wished to nominate but did not because of likely Senate opposition. There was speculation in 2005, for instance, that President Bush would nominate Attorney General Alberto R. Gonzales to become the first Latino justice on the Supreme Court. But strong conservatives objected because of what they considered Gonzales's overly liberal record on abortion and other matters while he was a justice of the Supreme Court of Texas, and liberal Democrats grumbled about the attorney general's defense of the alleged torture of accused terrorists and prisoners in Iraq and Afghanistan. With senators of both parties expressing doubts, Gonzales's chances vanished.

Whatever standard is used, most analyses agree that the current nomination process is considerably more contentious than it has been at most times in history. There is also considerable agreement that part of this increased conflict has been caused by the rise in partisanship, with senators increasingly deciding how to vote based on a nominee's party and ideology rather than on competence alone.[87]

Options in the Selection and Confirmation Process

There are other ways to fill judicial positions. *Electing judges* is one option. Voters in many U.S. states and a few other countries including Switzerland and Japan select some judges. The advantage of electing judges is that citizens have a direct say in who is on the bench. The worry about electing judges is that it interjects politics into the judicial process even more than now exists. *Voter confirmation* of judges is another option. One possibility would be to have the Senate conduct an interim confirmation process, then submit the ratification of judges to voters in the next general election for final confirmation or rejection. This option is very much like the retention-election system used in 15 states.

THE SUPREME COURT PROCESS

Having examined how the justices are selected, we can now turn to how the Supreme Court functions. Most cases begin and end in trial courts, those with original jurisdiction, but perhaps 5% are appealed to higher courts. Of the more than 60,000 appeals filed annually with the intermediate federal courts of appeals, about half are rejected for procedural reasons and half are decided on their merits. As noted earlier, up through this "first-appeal" level, almost everyone has a guaranteed ability to have their case heard as long as they meet court procedures and can afford the legal costs. Open access does not extend to the Supreme Court. Except for its rare original jurisdiction cases, the Supreme Court picks the cases it will hear.

Selecting Cases

In recent times, the Supreme Court has averaged one or two original jurisdiction cases and more than 9,000 appeals each term, which traditionally begins on the first Monday in October and usually extends to late June. These appeals are petitions seeking a **writ of certiorari**. A writ is a court order, and petitioning for certiorari means asking the higher court to review the decision of the lower court. Of the petitions, about 75% are *in forma pauperis* cases and 25% are "regular" or "paid" appeals filed by attorneys. The justices have complete discretion to decide which appeal cases to hear.

Procedure

Initially, the appeal petitions are divided among the justices, who in turn rely heavily on their law clerks to do a first screening to decide which ones have some merit. This step eliminates the vast majority of the petitions. Which of the remaining petitions are selected depends on having at least one justice decide a petition should be brought to the other justices for discussion. During their weekly meetings, the justices have very brief discussions and quick votes to further winnow the list. "Bam! Bam! Bam!" is how one justice described the process.[88] For a writ of certiorari to be issued, the Court's **rule of four** requires that four justices vote to have the Court take the case. These elimination rounds discard 99% of the petitions, with the justices finally selecting only about 85 cases for a full hearing. About half these cases involve constitutional issues. The rest relate to other matters such as statutory interpretation and whether lower courts have followed proper procedures. As for the source of the cases on the Court's final docket, one or two are typically original jurisdiction issues, and a few more come from the microscopic percentage of *in forma pauperis* petitions that the Court agrees to hear. The rest of the cases are drawn from the regular appeal petitions. Even for this type of petition, the acceptance rate recently has hovered around 4%, the lowest rate in history. Part of this decline reflects the nearly tripling of regular appeals to the Supreme Court since 1940. Another factor is the declining number of cases that the Court has been willing to take, as evident in Figure 14.7.

While the selection rate is very low, two factors mitigate it to some degree. First, most *in forma pauperis* petitions are "nothing to lose" attempts by convicts to get out of jail and have no merit. Second, the Court sometimes makes *de facto* decisions by not taking up cases that, after preliminary review, the justices believe were probably decided properly. This action, in effect, upholds the lower court. Indeed, cases that the justices suspect may not have been properly decided are much more likely to be heard. It is for this reason that in those cases where the Supreme Court during its 2009–2010 term clearly agreed or disagreed with lower court decisions, the high court reversed or vacated the lower court 78% of the time.

FIGURE 14.7 Cases Decided by the Supreme Court

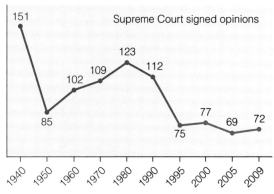

Between 1980 and the mid-1990s, the number of signed opinions issued by the Supreme Court each term declined sharply and has remained very low by historical standards.

Notes and data sources: Year denotes beginning of term. Thus 2009 is the 2009–2010 term. Data from U.S. *Statistical Abstract* and ScotusWiki.

Selection Criteria

Because the Court does not explain why it accepts or rejects cases, it is not possible to be precise about its standards. Nevertheless, petitions that have a better chance than others of being granted a review involve cases in which:

- Two or more circuits of the Court of Appeals issue contradictory decisions.
- The federal government is the petitioner asking for review.
- A federal law has been ruled unconstitutional by a lower federal court or state supreme court.
- The issue is of national significance.

Most of these criteria are self explanatory, but the fourth needs elaboration. National significance has to do with overall impact on the political system and, to a degree, urgency. It would have been unthinkable, for instance, for the Court to decline to hear *Bush v. Gore* (2000), on which the presidential election hung. Another measure of importance is the number of **amicus curiae briefs.** These are formal legal arguments (briefs) filed by a "friend of the court" (amicus curiae) to support one side or the other by individuals, groups, and organizations interested in the case.[89] For example, *Grutter v. Bollinger* (2003) and *Gratz v. Bollinger* (2003), companion cases related respectively to the University of Michigan's undergraduate and law school affirmative action admission policies, collectively drew over 150 amicus curiae briefs.

In addition to the above list, court watchers often note several other standards. One is called *ripeness*. This means waiting to take a case until its issue has been contested in the political and judicial system for a time. For example, the Court is unlikely to quickly take a case regarding a new law. Instead the justices prefer to wait to see how the law is implemented and how challenges to it in various lower courts are decided. A second factor has to do with the *national political agenda*, or what the dimensions of political conflict are. In recent decades, the Court has been prone to take civil rights and civil liberties cases, reflecting the social issues that are prominent on the political agenda. During the first part of the twentieth century, the Court was more apt to hear cases involving the economic authority of the federal government, which was then at the top of the political agenda.

Political discretion is a third possible factor. Some observers claim that the Court often avoids deciding issues that could subject it to serious political attack. One recent example occurred when the justices refused to hear a claim that the phrase "one nation under God" in the Pledge of Allegiance violated the establishment of religion clause in the First Amendment. Technically, the Court rejected the case on the grounds that the plaintiff had no standing, but many observers thought the Court was really just avoiding a political hot potato. It was a "way out for the court," one analyst commented. "It was politically impossible to strike [the reference to God] down, and legally impossible to uphold it."[90]

Hearing Cases

Once the Court agrees to take a case, all the parties are notified and a hearing date is scheduled. For *in forma pauperis* cases, the Court appoints an attorney to represent the petitioner. Each case usually receives an hour for oral arguments, with the time divided equally between the opposing attorneys. If one of the parties is the U.S. government, it is usually represented by the **solicitor general**, a senior official in the Department of Justice. In addition to arguing before the Court, solicitor generals have an important say in deciding (1) which cases the government will appeal from lower courts and (2) whether to submit amicus curiae briefs in cases where the government is not a party. Since the federal government is a direct party to or files an amicus brief in more than half of the cases that the Court hears, the solicitor general is the only attorney with an office in the Supreme Court.[91]

Arguing before the Court can be a disconcerting experience for attorneys, who often find themselves peppered with questions by the justices. During a case about whether school districts could require student athletes to submit urine samples for drug testing, Justice Breyer asked the student's lawyer why providing a sample should be considered intrusive when urination was a natural act. The nervous attorney conceded that urinating was natural and gasped, "In fact, I might do so here."[92] Such humorous moments aside, the questioning is important. For example, justices often probe how a decision one way or the other would affect the country as a whole, rather than how it would affect just the parties to that particular case.

Deciding Cases

Within a few days of oral arguments, the justices meet behind closed doors to decide a case's fate. Each justice expresses his or her opinion in order of descending seniority, then votes in the same order. What determines how individual justices vote? Chief Justice Roberts, for one, has argued that "judges wear black robes because it doesn't matter who they are as individuals—that's not going to shape their decision. It's their understanding of the law that will shape their decision."[93] By contrast, Justice William O. Douglas (1939-1975), wrote, "At the constitutional level where we [justices] work, 90 percent of any decision is emotional. The rational part of us supplies the reasons for supporting our predilections."[94] Reality lies somewhere between these two extremes, with the law, the judges' ideology and other personal views, and social and political factors all influencing decisions. Subjective factors play a greater role in highly charged constitutional cases than in lower-key cases regarding business law and other such topics.[95]

The Law

The frequency with which all or nearly all of the justices agree is a good indicator that the law can often be determined objectively and is a key factor in Court decisions.[96] Notice in Figure 14.8 that about two-thirds of the Supreme Court decisions are made unanimously or with only one or two justices disagreeing about what the law is. Determining what the law is involves four elements: text, intent, precedent, and legal reasoning.

Text   Part of interpreting the law involves the *textualist approach,* a straightforward reading of what the Constitution and statutes say. Sometimes the law is clear, as when the Supreme Court ruled unanimously in 2005 that providing services and software that allowed computer users to download music without paying royalties to its producers violated the federal Copyright Act.[97]

At other times, the text of the law is not clear. In *Ledbetter v. Goodyear Tire & Rubber Co.* (2007), Lilly Ledbetter sued her employer on the grounds that she

FIGURE 14.8
Vote Pattern in the Supreme Court

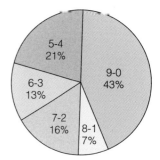

This figure shows the average vote pattern of the Supreme Court during its 2003–2004 through 2009–2010 terms. From one perspective, the Court was usually divided, with at least one justice disagreeing 57% of the time. The other perspective is that the Court is seldom closely divided (5–4), with justices agreeing by at least a 2 to 1 margin (a 6–3 vote) in 79% of all cases.
Note and data source: Data include only those votes in which all nine justices participated. Data from various news sources and ScotusWiki.

had long been getting less pay than males with equal experience and responsibilities. The issue before the Court was whether she had met the requirement in the Civil Rights Act of 1964 that complaints of discrimination be filed within 180 days "after the alleged unlawful employment practice occurred." Justice Ginsburg argued that (1) because Ledbetter had received paychecks within 180 days prior to filing a complaint, and (2) because the pay in those checks "was substantially less than the pay of men doing the same work," then (3) the checks constituted ongoing discrimination. This, Ginsburg concluded, satisfied the 180-day standard. However, a majority of the justices disagreed. They interpreted the law to mean that the 180-day clock began when the discrimination first occurred and therefore dismissed Ledbetter's complaint.

Intent   Because of frequent imprecision in the text of the Constitution and laws, courts are also interested in what their authors intended. As discussed earlier, *original intent* refers to what the authors of the Constitution or one of its amendments meant. A second standard is **legislative intent**: what Congress intended when enacting a piece of legislation. It was this standard that Ginsburg was using when she wrote that upholding Ledbetter's claim would be "more respectful of the [act's] purpose." Using legislative intent is less controversial than original intent because statutes are almost always more contemporary than the Constitution and its amendments. Nevertheless, the fact that all legislation must go through so many steps involving so many legislators before becoming a law makes ascertaining legislative intent tricky.

Precedent   When interpreting the law, judges look to **precedent**, what higher courts, especially the Supreme Court, have ruled on an issue, to guide decisions in subsequent similar cases. This occurs under the common law doctrine of *stare decisis* (let the decision stand). Lower courts are bound to follow the precedent of higher courts, and even the Supreme Court almost always cites its own earlier decisions to help justify a current decision.

Although precedent plays a powerful role in court decisions, there are several things to note about its limits. One is the Supreme Court has overturned precedent over 250 times since 1789. Moreover, about 60% of those have been since the 1950s. Second, which cases should serve as precedent for a pending decision is debatable.[98] The majority opinion and dissenting opinion in many Supreme Court cases both claim to be following precedent but have chosen different cases to cite. Third, arguing that precedent should be considered sacrosanct can be a two-edged sword. A liberal, for instance, would probably contend that the precedent set by *Roe v. Wade* should apply to all future abortion-rights cases. But that same individual would also probably applaud the *Lawrence v. Texas* (2003) decision because it overturned the precedent set in *Bower v. Hardwig* (1986) upholding state laws punishing gay sex. Fourth, when to overturn precedent is more a function of the ideological views of the justices on the Supreme Court at any given time than any abstract legal principle.[99] It is not surprising, for example, that when the liberal Warren Court overturned precedent, it overwhelmingly did so to substitute a liberal interpretation for an earlier conservative one. Similarly, when the more conservative Rehnquist Court overturned precedent, it overwhelmingly substituted a conservative interpretation for an earlier liberal one.[100] The same can be said of the current Roberts Court. This record has led some scholars to conclude that the impact of *stare decisis* on Supreme Court decision is overestimated.

Legal Reasoning   Judges often look beyond precedent to other sources for guidance. What other federal and state courts have said on a legal issue is one source. For example, the Supreme Court is likely to follow "the reasoning process adopted by the majority of [the Court of Appeals] circuits involved in the conflict" over an issue and also to pay particular attention to the "position endorsed by prestigious circuit court judges."[101] Articles by legal scholars in law journals are another, if declining, source of legal thinking for the courts.[102] On occasion, judges also consider the legal reasoning of international courts and the courts of other countries. Justice Ginsberg has explained that while foreign sources cannot establish precedent, "they can add to the store of knowledge relevant to the solution of trying questions, and it only makes good sense to learn what we can from the experience and good thinking foreign sources may convey."[103]

Ideology and Other Personal Traits

Supreme Court justices are humans, not legal robots. Therefore they and other judges usually retain the liberal or conservative views that often led presidents to appoint them in the first place. It is true that Earl Warren and a few other justices have undergone ideological conversions once on the bench. Mostly though, Democrats appointed by Democratic presidents make liberal decisions and Republicans appointed by Republican presidents make conservative decisions. It is not partisanship, as such, but ideology that influences how judges decide.[104]

The role of ideology on the Supreme Court is demonstrated in Figure 14.9. It begins with Justice Clarence Thomas, who has been rated the most conservative justice since 1937, then calculates how often each of the other eight justices fully agreed with him on cases decided by non-unanimous votes during the Court's

FIGURE 14.9 Voting Alignment of Justices

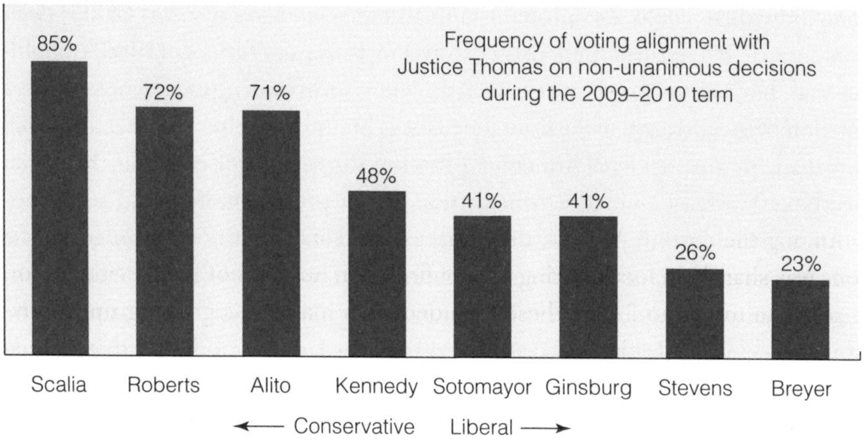

Ideology on the Supreme Court is clear in this figure depicting how often on split-vote decisions justices agreed with the Court's most conservative justice, Clarence Thomas, during the 2009–2010 term.
Data source: ScotusWiki.

2009–2010 term.[105] Note that there was a four-member conservative faction composed of Thomas and the three justices who agreed with him at least 71% of the time. Opposing them was a liberal group of four justices who agreed with Thomas 41% or less of the time. Justice Kennedy occupied the middle, agreeing with Thomas about half the time.

Arguably another indication of the importance of ideology on the Court and its politicization is the increased percentage of cases decided by one vote. Until 1940, such cases averaged about 5% annually. Since then the average percentage of 5-4 decisions has more than quadrupled. During the chief justiceship of Harlan Stone (1941–1946), 11% of the decisions were 5-4. Under Chief Justice Fred Vinson (1946–1953), one-vote decisions reached 16% on average, and beginning with the tenure of Chief Justice William Rehnquist (1986–2005) and continuing with Chief Justice John Roberts (2005–present), over 20% of the Court's decisions have been 5-4 splits.[106]

In addition to ideology, the personal characteristics and life experiences of judges can affect opinions. As noted earlier, gender and race have some impact on how judges rule. Financial background also has some influence, with wealthier appointees to the federal bench tending to be more conservative than less wealthy appointees.[107] Some studies have also found a correlation between religion and judicial decisions. For example, Catholic and Baptist judges have been less strict about separating church and state than judges of other religions.[108] Another suggestive finding is that of the Supreme Court justices who served between 1937 and 2006, six of the nine Roman Catholics were among the most conservative one-third of the justices.[109] By contrast, six of the seven Jewish justices were among the most liberal one-third of the justices. Yet, it is also clear that religion is but one factor. For example, Justice William J. Brennan, the only Catholic on the Supreme Court in 1973, voted with the pro-abortion majority in *Roe v. Wade*.

Among the current justices, the impact of personal factors on a judge's decisions was sharply in focus during the confirmation hearings of Justice Sotomayor. In addition to sex and race, these included such matters as growing up in poverty. Faced with questions about how much her background would influence her decisions, Sotomayor tried to split the difference between saying she would be unbiased and would ignore her personal history. As she put it, "Life experiences do influence us [judges] in good ways. That's why we seek the enrichment of our legal system from life experiences, but that's not what drives a result [the decision]."[110]

Societal and Political Factors

Societal and political considerations are a third group of factors that influence judges. It would be an error to say that the courts routinely calculate their own political standing or follow public opinion when making decisions. But it would also be wrong to ignore the interaction of the courts with their environment.[111] A classic example of political pressure impacting the court is the "court packing" story discussed earlier. Studies of more recent decisions by the Court indicate that it continues to be sensitive to political pressures.[112]

It is also the case that changes in judicial views parallel changing societal values.[113] In 1986, a poll that asked Americans if they thought "homosexual relations between consenting adults should be legal" found only 32% saying yes.[114] That year in *Bower v. Hardwig* (1986), the Supreme Court upheld a state law criminalizing gay sex. Society's views changed, however, and when a poll asked the same question in 2003, 60% said gay sex should be legal.[115] The Court changed, too, reversing its 1986 decision by striking down a state sodomy law in *Lawrence v. Texas* (2003). It is unclear exactly how society's attitudes are linked to judicial opinions, but there is no doubt that there is a correlation between public opinion and court decisions.[116]

In recent years, there are even indications that U.S. courts sometimes react to international values. This has created a controversy for you to evaluate in the following You Decide box.

YOU DECIDE: Should Global Values Influence U.S. Courts?

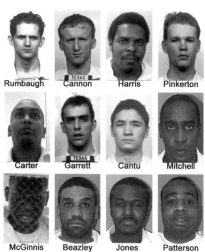

Globalization is much more than just an economic trend. It also includes the transnational spread of cultural values. One place this is evident is in the U.S. Supreme Court decision in *Roper v. Simmons* (2005). In it, the Court ruled that executing individuals for crimes committed while still a juvenile was unconstitutional because it violated the Eighth Amendment's ban on "cruel and unusual punishments." One justification offered by the Court was "the stark reality that the United States is the only country in the world" to legally follow the practice. The Court noted that "the overwhelming weight of international opinion against the juvenile death penalty" provides "respected and significant confirmation for the Court's determination that the penalty is disproportionate punishment for offenders under 18." Proponents hailed the ruling and the Court's sensitivity to world values. Opponents were outraged by what they saw as yet another example of globalization undermining U.S. sovereignty (independence). What do you think? Should American judges pay attention to global opinion and the laws of other countries?

These 12 men were all executed by Texas between 1973 and 2002 for crimes they committed while still juveniles. Others met the same fate in other states. Such sentences were ruled unconstitutional as cruel and unusual punishment by the Supreme Court in 2005. The justices relied in part on global practice to reach their conclusion. (AP Photo/Texas Dept. of Criminal Justice, File)

FIGURE 14.10 Public View of the Court's Role

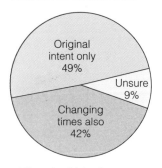

What should the Supreme Court consider when making decisions?

Americans are narrowly divided about whether the Supreme Court should look only to original intent to determine the meaning of the Constitution or should also interpret it in light of changing times.
Data source: Quinnipiac University poll, April 2010. Data provided by the Roper Center.

Public Opinion about Judicial Decision Making

What does the public think about what standards the justices should use in making decisions? Generally, Americans are closely divided on the issue of whether judges should follow the judicial constraint/strict constructionist approach or the judicial activist/living constitution approach. When asked if the Supreme Court should consider only legal issues or also public opinion to decide cases, 49% of Americans said "only legal issues," 42% favored also including public opinion as a factor, and the rest said it depends or were unsure. On a related question shown in Figure 14.10, Americans were also narrowly divided over whether judges should look only to original intent when deciding what the Constitution or a law means or should follow the living constitution approach by incorporating contemporary thinking and realities into account.

As for what Americans think that judges do in practice, 78% of the respondents to one poll said they thought that judges let their personal political views influence their decisions.[117] Nevertheless, a plurality of Americans (46%) believe that the Court is "balanced" in the decisions it makes, while 26% view the Courts as too liberal, 21% see it as too conservative, and 7% are unsure.[118]

Decisions and Opinions

Rulings by the Supreme Court have two parts, a decision and an opinion. The vote of the justices determines the **decision**: the Court's ruling on the specific case before it. While the decision is important to the parties involved, it is less important to the country's legal system than the **opinion**, which explains the Court's legal reasoning in the case. Opinions are significant because they establish precedent, thus influencing future decisions in similar cases by all state and federal courts including the Supreme Court.

If the chief justice is in the majority, he decides which justice who is also in the majority will write the opinion. When the chief justice is in the minority, the senior associate justice in the majority assigns the opinion. Because the precedent established by the Court's opinion is strongest when there is a lopsided majority of justices who agree on the legal reasoning of the decision, the justice writing the *majority opinion* seeks to write one that has the support of at least five, and optimally more, of the justices. To do this, the justice who is drafting the opinion circulates it among other justices, often modifying its language at the suggestion of other justices in order to persuade as many justices as possible to sign the opinion.

However, justices sometimes decide the same way for different reasons. In such cases, some justices may write **concurring opinions**. These support the decision but make their own legal argument.[119] Opinions agreeing with the decision but signed by four or fewer justices are *plurality opinions*. They were once very unusual but have increased since the mid-1950s and now average about 6% of the Supreme Court's decisions each term. One reason for the increase is that the Court in recent decades has dealt with a relatively high percentage of socially divisive cases on subjects such as affirmative action and capital punishment. On these cases, judges, like the rest of society, are often "unable to form a majority to support a particular rationale."[120] Whatever their cause, plurality decisions are a problem because they do not set precedent to guide the lower courts.

Justices who disagree with the majority often write **dissenting opinions**, separately or together. Dissents have no immediate legal impact, but those who write them feel it necessary to voice their objections. As Justice Ginsburg had explained, "Dissents speak to a future age." They are not meant "simply to say" to other justices that they "are wrong and I would do it this way." Instead, Ginsburg notes, "The greatest dissents do become court opinions and gradually over time their views become the dominant view. So that's the dissenter's hope: that they are writing not for today but for tomorrow."[121]

It is common for the press to describe the Supreme Court as "the court of last resort" or to otherwise imply an ultimate finality of the Court's decisions on U.S. law and political practice. This image is misleading. In fact, Supreme Court decisions seldom decisively resolve contentious policy issues. More often, new rounds of legal cases erupt because of claims that particular situations vary in some way from the rule decided by the Court. Moreover, as also noted earlier, U.S. courts have limited ability to implement their decisions, and sometimes the political system resists court decisions. Yet for all these limitations, the profound impact of the Supreme Court's decisions in *Brown v. Board of Education*, *Roe v. Wade*, and many other cases makes it clear that the American judiciary plays a key role in shaping policy. For that reason, a final important issue about the courts is: How well they fit into a democracy.

THE COURTS AND DEMOCRACY

It is evident that U.S. courts sometimes make policy. A prime example is *Roe v. Wade*, which toppled many existing federal and state laws. It is also clear that, to a degree, judges' decisions are based on subjective factors such as ideology

There are important questions about how the Supreme Court and the rest of the U.S. judicial system fit with democracy. (iStockphoto)

rather than on a purely objective reading of the law. Yet another reality is that most judges are selected in part because of their political views. These ties between politics and the law prompt five questions about the courts and democracy.

Is there equal justice for all in the United States? "No" is the distressing answer. Everyone may be equal before the law in theory, but in reality equal access to the courts is limited. Economics is one factor. Poor people are disadvantaged compared to wealthier individuals and organizations when it comes to initiating a civil suit, mounting a defense in a civil or criminal case, or appealing the decision in either type of case. There are also demographic inequalities stemming from such factors as the relatively small number of attorneys drawn from minority groups and from language difficulties for people who do not speak English well or at all.

Is the U.S. judicial branch a democratic institution? "Only partly," is the answer. Americans have no direct say in choosing federal judges. Moreover, the lifetime tenure of federal judges and the infinitesimal chance they will be removed by the Senate means that the people have nearly zero say about whether a judge should remain on the bench. A third issue is the continuing underrepresentation of women and minority group members on the bench. Important progress in diversifying the judiciary has been made, but reality still falls short of democratic ideals.

What is the proper role of the courts in a democracy? The core of this question is how far the courts should be able to go in the policy-making realm. Of course there is no objective "right" answer, but it can be said that Americans are not alarmed by the courts' policy-making power. This view does not reflect naiveté about the role of the courts.[122] To the contrary, 87% of Americans recognize that the Supreme Court has a "very" or "somewhat" important policy role.[123] Americans are also aware that they have a very limited say in what the courts do. Only 34% of Americans think that public opinion had a "great deal" or "some" impact on court decisions.[124] Yet despite their sense of a powerful judiciary and only marginal public influence, most Americans do not favor reining in the courts, as Figure 14.11 indicates.

Is reform needed? The answer to this question depends on how you feel about the preceding questions. However, if you are like most Americans, then you are relatively satisfied with the court system. Polls show that the public trusts the judicial branch more than either of the other two branches of government (see Figure 14.2).

If reform is needed, what should be done? Critics of the judicial system have made numerous reform proposals. The pros and cons of terms limits for judges and some other suggestions to make the courts arguably more responsive to the society have already been discussed. Other reform proposals focus on diminishing the courts' power, especially their policy role. One possibility is giving Congress the power to override a court decision by a two-thirds vote of both chambers, just like it can override a presidential veto. Another approach would be to change the voting formulas for the Court of Appeals and the Supreme Court to require a two-thirds margin of the judges voting to declare an act of Congress or a state law unconstitutional. Such ideas would certainly reduce the power of the judiciary, as some wish to do, but in doing so the "reforms" would weaken the checks and balances system. It would also affect the federal system by making it more likely that state laws would withstand constitutional challenge in the federal courts.

FIGURE 14.11 Views of Supreme Court Power

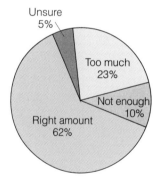

Public view of the Supreme Court's power

Despite recognizing that the Supreme Court plays a powerful role in making policy and the belief that the public has little influence over the Court's decisions, less than one in four Americans believes that the Supreme Court is too powerful. Most Americans are satisfied with its power. *Data source:* Associated Press/Ipsos-Public Affairs Poll, November 2004. Data provided by the Roper Center.

Which of these options or combination of them, if any, provides the right answer? Do you have any other suggestions? As has been true throughout this text for all the issues facing Americans, You Decide!

SUMMARY

The judiciary can have a powerful impact on the structure of the American government system by sometimes deciding who governs, how power is distributed among the three branches of government, and how power is divided between the national and state governments. The courts can also have a major impact on policy.

The courts draw their power from the U.S. Constitution and societal forces. Article III of the Constitution establishes the courts as an independent branch of government and also gives the courts jurisdiction over certain types of cases. Under the Constitution, the courts have the power of judicial interpretation and the power of judicial review. Judicial power is also derived from American political culture and its commitment to the rule of law and the legal process.

For all its importance, the judicial branch is the least powerful of the three branches of government. The courts are restricted by constitutional and statutory legal limits, they impose limits on themselves, and they are subject to external pressures.

Laws can be classified according to their source (constitutional, statutory, common law) and according to their subject (civil and criminal). Courts can be classified by their jurisdiction (original, appellate) and by the principal source of their existence (Articles II and III of the Constitution). The three tiers of the Article III courts are the core of the judicial branch. Access to the courts is in practice not equally open to all. Instead, access is limited by economic factors, demographic factors, and restrictions on who may sue in court. Federal judges do not represent a cross section of American society in terms of gender or race. The lack of demographic diversity among judges has symbolic and substantive consequences.

The president nominates federal judges based on political party/ideology, judicial philosophy, merit, and demographic characteristics.

Senate confirmation of judges has become an increasingly partisan political process because of the importance of the courts in policy and the growing polarization and partisanship in Congress and elsewhere. From the time a nominee is named, supporters and opponents maneuver for advantage as the nominee proceeds through the preliminary stages of public and congressional scrutiny, testifies during the Senate Judiciary Committee hearings, and ultimately is the subject of debate and final vote in the Senate. Senators' decisions on a nominee reflect a mix of merit and political considerations. Few judges are overtly rejected by the Senate, but numerous nominees fail because of more subtle ways in which the Senate influences appointments.

The Supreme Court hears only about 1% of the cases appealed to it. Cases with some characteristics are more likely to be heard by the Supreme Court than are others. Oral arguments before the Court are short but important. A plurality of cases is decided unanimously, but many others (especially recently) are 5-4 decisions. The text and intent of the law and existing precedent are important factors in court decisions. Ideology, other personal and societal values, the courts' standing, and additional factors also influence how justices decide. Rulings by the Supreme Court have two parts, a decision and an opinion. Opinions are more important because they establish precedent governing future decisions. There is a debate over how well U.S. courts fit democratic principles.

CHAPTER 14 GLOSSARY

amicus curiae brief A "friend of the court" legal argument filed with the courts in connection with a particular lawsuit by individuals, groups, or organizations who are not a party to the case but who have an important interest in it.

appellate jurisdiction The authority of appeals courts to review the work of lower courts to determine whether the conduct and decisions of those courts were based on a proper application of the law.

civil law Relates to contracts and other business matters and is considered a dispute between individual groups, organizations, or people.

class action suits Civil suits in which one or a few plaintiffs sue on behalf of a large number of similarly affected people.

common law A society's general understanding of what is legal and perhaps fair as determined by a judge.

concurring opinions Opinions by judges who support the majority decision of a court but who make their own legal argument and disagree with some or all of the legal reasoning in the main opinion.

constitutional courts Those courts, including the main federal courts, established under Article III of the Constitution. They have numerous protections such as unlimited terms for judges.

constitutional law What the Constitution requires, permits, or prohibits.

Court of Appeals (U.S.) The intermediate appellate court at the federal level, consisting of 11 numbered circuit courts, the D.C. Circuit Court, and the Court of Appeals for the Federal Circuit.

criminal law Relates to assaults on persons (such as murder and rape) and property (such as burglary and fraud) that are so disruptive of public safety and order that they constitute offenses against the people as a whole and their government.

decision A ruling of the court as to the specific case before it.

dissenting opinions Opinions by judges who disagree with the majority decision of a court and who make a legal argument faulting the legal reasoning of the court in its opinion.

district courts (U.S.) The basic federal trial courts. They exercise original jurisdiction over the vast majority of federal civil and criminal cases.

filibuster A legislative tactic using an extended speech or series of speeches in the Senate to halt progress on a measure.

in forma pauperis Appeals that are filed by people who do not have the funds to hire an attorney and that are acceptable to the various federal appeals courts even though the appeals do not meet the many exacting standards required of "paid" appeals.

judicial activism An approach to the role of judges that stresses interpreting the Constitution in light of contemporary circumstances and being willing to break new policy ground in decisions, especially if elected officials are not doing enough in such areas as protecting minority rights. Because of its extensive use on behalf of civil rights, judicial activism is often identified with political liberalism, but currently conservative judges are also being called judicial activists because of their decisions overturning precedent in such areas as campaign finance. Judicial activism is the antithesis of judicial restraint.

judicial implementation Putting decisions by the courts into practice.

judicial interpretation The authority of the courts to decide on the meaning of language in the Constitution and laws passed by Congress.

judicial restraint An approach to the role of judges that contends that it is solely the responsibility of legislatures to make law and that judges should avoid making policy by interpreting the Constitution only in terms of its literal words and the intentions of the document's authors. Judicial restraint is the antithesis of judicial activism. See strict constructionism.

judicial review The authority of the courts to rule that legislation or actions of government are unconstitutional and void. See *Marbury v. Madison* (1803).

jurisdiction The authority of a court to hear certain types of cases.

legalism A political culture orientation that emphasizes organizations, rule, agreements/contracts, procedures, and other such formal structures to govern conduct.

legislative courts Those courts established under Article II of the Constitution. There are only a few such courts, and they do not have all the protections afforded the principal federal courts. See constitutional courts.

legislative intent What the sponsors and supporters in Congress of various statutes intended when they wrote and passed a law.

Marbury v. Madison (1803) Landmark case in which Chief Justice John Marshall, delivering the opinion of the Supreme Court, declared that the courts have the authority to strike down laws or executive actions that they deem unconstitutional.

nonjusticiable issues Controversies that are not appropriate for judicial resolution.

opinion The legal justification of a court for its decision.

original intent What the authors of the Constitution and its amendments intended their clauses to mean.

original jurisdiction The authority of trial courts to hear cases in the first instance and to apply the law and make decisions based on the facts of the case.

political questions Issues that the courts consider political, not legal, disputes and therefore nonjusticiable—beyond the authority of the courts to decide.

precedent A standard established by a Supreme Court opinion that shapes the rulings of lower courts and to which the Supreme Court looks for guidance in its subsequent decisions.

rule of four The rule of the Supreme Court that requires the vote of four justices to place a case on the Court's docket for a hearing.

senatorial courtesy An informal tradition whereby senators of the president's party in a state where a vacancy occurs on the U.S. District court control who is nominated to fill the open seat.

solicitor general The third-ranking official of the Department of Justice and the one who usually handles federal involvement in cases before the Supreme Court.

stare decisis Meaning "let the decision stand," this doctrine holds that decisions in current cases should follow decisions in earlier cases. See *precedent*.

statutory law What acts (statutes) passed by a legislative body into law require, permit, or prohibit.

strict constructionism Also called original-intent theory, this approach favors interpreting the Constitution only in terms of its literal words and the intentions of the document's authors. See judicial restraint.

Supreme Court (U.S.) The highest court in the United States and the only one specifically established or required by the Constitution.

U.S. attorney The federal government's primary attorney in the area served by a district court in federal criminal prosecutions and in cases when the U.S. government is either the defendant or plaintiff in a civil suit.

writ of certiorari A court order directing that cases from a lower court be presented for review.

NOTES

CHAPTER 1

1. ABC News/Harris Survey, January 1980; and Gallup/CNN/*USA Today* poll, December 2001. Data provided by The Roper Center for Public Opinion Research, University of Connecticut.
2. Address to the American Society of Newspaper Editors, January 17, 1925.
3. *Reynolds v. United States*, 1879.
4. *Employment Division v Smith*, 1990.
5. Vito Tanzi and Ludger Schuknecht, *Public Spending in the 20th Century: A Global Perspective* (New York: Cambridge University Press, 2000); Robert Higgs, *Crisis and Leviathan: Critical Episodes in the Growth of American Government* (New York: Oxford University Press, 1987); and Charlotte Twight, *Dependent on D.C.: The Rise of Federal Control over the Lives of Ordinary Americans* (New York: Palgrave Macmillan, 2002).
6. This quote is from the Website of National Youth Rights Association at www.youthrights.org/. All other quotes in this box are from the *Cleveland Plain Dealer*, November 4, 2008.
7. John Stuart Mill, *Considerations on Representative Government* (1861).
8. Joseph Marie De Maistre, letter of August 15, 1811 in *Lettres et Opuscules Inedits du Comte J. De Mastrie* (1869).
9. Public Agenda Foundation poll, 1998. Data provided by The Roper Center. There was a 2% "don't know" reply rate.
10. ABC News/Facebook poll, December 2007. Data from The Roper Center.
11. Harris Poll news release, "More People Alienated," July 2008. Data average for 1990–2008.
12. Pew Research Center, "Public Knowledge of Current Affairs Little Changed by News and Information Revolutions," April 15, 2007.
13. Pew Research Center, "News Audiences Increasingly Politicized," June 8, 2004.
14. Gabor Toka, "Citizen Information, Election Outcomes and Good Governance." *Electoral Studies*, 27/1 (2008): 31–44.
15. D. Clayton Brown, *Globalization and America Since 1945* (Wilmington, DE: Scholarly Resources, 2003).
16. Robert A. Denemark and Matthew J. Hoffmann, "Just Scraps of Paper? The Dynamics of Multilateral Treaty-Making," *Cooperation and Conflict*, 43/2 (2008): 185–219.
17. CNN.com, May 31, 2003.
18. Central Intelligence Agency, *The Global Infectious Disease Threat and Its Implications for the United States* (2000).
19. Miles Kahler and Barbara F. Walter, eds., *Territoriality and Conflict in an Era of Globalization* (New York: Cambridge University Press, 2006); and Gerald Schneider, Katherine Barbieri, and Nils Petter Gleditsch, *Globalization and Armed Conflict* (Lanham, MD: Rowman & Littlefield, 2003).
20. Chicago Council on Foreign Relations, "Global Views 2004: American Public Opinion and Foreign Policy," 2004.
21. *New York Times*, August 25, 1992.
22. The quote is from Greenspan's 2007 book *The Age of Turbulence: Adventures in a New World*, quoted in the *Los Angeles Times*, September 17, 2007.
23. Henry A. Kissinger, "The Next Steps with Iran: Negotiations Must Go Beyond the Nuclear Threat to Broader Issues," op-ed in the *Washington Post*, July 31, 2006.
24. MSNBC, February 4, 2009.
25. Sherri L. Wallace and Marcus D. Allen, "Survey of African American Portrayal in Introductory Textbooks in American Government/Politics: A Report of the APSA Standing Committee on the Status of Blacks in the Profession," *PS: Political Science & Politics*, 41/1 (2008):154.
26. ABC News/Washington Post poll, September 2003. Data provided by The Roper Center. Also, see Lee Sigelman, Steven A. Tuch, and Jack K. Martin, "What's in a Name? Preference for 'Black' versus 'African-American' among Americans of African Descent," *Public Opinion Quarterly*, 69/3 (2005): 429–438.
27. Pew Hispanic Center/Kaiser Family Foundation, "2002 National Survey of Latinos," December 2002.
28. "2002 National Survey of Latinos."
29. Natalie Masuoka, "Political Attitudes and Ideologies of Multiracial Americans: The Implications of Mixed Race in the United States," *Political Research Quarterly*, 61/2 (2008): 253–267.
30. Robert Charles Smith and Richard Seltzer, *Contemporary Controversies and the American Racial Divide* (Lanham, MD: Rowman & Littlefield, 2000), Chapter 3.
31. Pew Hispanic Center, "Survey of Latino Attitudes on a Possible War with Iraq," February 18, 2003.

CHAPTER 2

1. John Chester Miller, *The Wolf by the Ears: Thomas Jefferson and Slavery* (Charlottesville: University Press of Virginia, 1995), p. 184.
2. Quoted in Peter R. Henriques, " 'The Only Unavoidable Subject of Regret': George Washington and Slavery," unpublished paper, July 25, 2001.
3. Washington's Farewell Address, September 1, 1796.
4. Poll taken by Peter D. Hart Research Associates, November 1997, on the Web at www.hrusa.org. The question was: "Suppose America's Founding Fathers came back to the present day. Do you think they would generally approve of the way things are going in the country, or do you think that they would be generally disappointed?"
5. Wallace Brown, *The Good Americans: The Loyalists in the American Revolution* (New York: William Morrow: 1969).
6. Ellen Gibson Wilson, *The Loyal Blacks* (New York: Putnam's, 1976).
7. George Rogers Clark to the governor of Virginia, November 27, 1872, on the Web at www.intercom.net/local/richardson/Linder.html.
8. Quoted in Thomas G. Paterson, J. Garry Clifford, and Kenneth J. Hagan, *American Foreign Relations: A History*, Vol. I., *To 1920* (Boston: Houghton Mifflin, 2000), p. 13.
9. George Washington to Jabez Bowen, January 9, 1787.
10. Gerry's remark was made while he was a delegate to the Constitutional Convention and is widely quoted. It can be found, among other places, in Charles R. Kesler, "The Founders' Views of Direct Democracy and Representation," on the Website of the Ethics and Public Policy Center at www.eppc.org/publications/xq/ASP/pubsID.1255/qx/pubs_viewdetail.htm.
11. Widely attributed to Washington, but not fully documented.
12. Thomas Jefferson, letter to Samuel Kercheval, July 12, 1816.
13. T. Harry Williams, Richard N. Current, and Frank Freidel, *A History of the United States to 1877*, 2nd ed. rev. (New York: Alfred E. Knopf, 1964), p. 178.
14. Gordon S. Wood, "The Origins of the Constitution," on the Website of the American Political Science Association at www.apsanet.org/CENnet/thisconstitution/wood2.cfm.
15. Williams, Current, and Freidel, *A History of the United States to 1877*, p. 179.
16. Charles A. Beard, *An Economic Interpretation of the Constitution*, rev. ed. (New York: Macmillan, 1935), p. 324. Beard's book was originally published in 1913. A more recent study that supports the notion of economic interests being important is Robert A. McGuire, *To Form a More Perfect Union: A New Economic Interpretation of the United States Constitution* (New York: Oxford University Press, 2002).
17. George Washington to John Jay, August 1, 1786.
18. A fine essay on the *Federalist Papers* is Jean Yarbrough, "The Federalist," on the Website of the American Political Science Association at www.apsanet.org/CENnet/thisconstitution/yarbrough.cfm.
19. Williams, Current, and Freidel, *A History of the United States to 1877*, p. 191.
20. Letter to William S. Smith, November 13, 1787.
21. Williams, Current, and Freidel, *A History of the United States to 1877*, p. 189.
22. James Bruce, *The American Commonwealth* (London: Macmillan, 1898), Vol. 1, p. 530.
23. Edward S. Corwin *The President: Office and Powers, 1787–1957* (New York: New York University Press, 1957), p. 171.
24. Charles Evans Hughes, speech before the Chamber of Commerce, Elmira, New York, May 3, 1907. Available in *Address and Papers of Charles Evans Hughes, Governor of New York, 1906–1908* (New York: GP Putnam's Sons, 1908), p. 139.
25. Jacqueline Jones, Peter H. Wood, Thomas Borstelmann, Elaine Tyler May, and Vicki L. Ruiz, *Created Equal: A Social and Political History of the United States* (New York: Longman, 2003), p. 281.
26. All quotes are from the *Philadelphia Inquirer*, July 3, 2003.
27. Hamilton speaking to the Continental Congress, June 21, 1788.
28. James Madison letter to Thomas Jefferson, October 10, 1787; and *Federalist* No. 63.
29. *Federalist* No. 62.
30. Joseph J. Ellis, *American Sphinx: The Character of Thomas Jefferson* (New York: Alfred A. Knopf, 1997), p. 91.
31. Thomas Jefferson to Horatio Gates, July 11, 1803, on the Website of the School of Cooperative Individualism at www.cooperativeindividualism.org/jefferson_i_02.html.
32. Christian B. Keller, "Philanthropy Betrayed: Thomas Jefferson, the Louisiana Purchase, and the Origins of the Federal Indian Removal Policy," *Proceedings of the American Philosophical Society,* 144 (2000), p. 39.

CHAPTER 3

1. R. Daniel Kelemen, "Globalization, Federalism, and Regulation," in David Vogel and Robert Kagan, eds., *Dynamics of Regulatory Change: How Globalization Affects National Regulatory Policies,* University of California International and Area Studies Digital Collection, Vol. I (Berkeley: University of California Press, 2002), p. 1.

2. The interpretations in this figure are those of the authors. They were informed in part by Ronald L. Watts, *Comparing Federal Systems*, 2nd ed. (Montreal, Canada: McGill-Queen's University Press, 1999) and by the comments on initial drafts of the figure by Professors Richard Vengroff and Cyrus Ernesto Zirakzadeh, both of the Department of Political Science, University of Connecticut.

3. James Madison to Thomas Jefferson, October 24, 1887, in Philip B. Kurland and Ralph Lerner, eds., *The Founders Constitution* (Chicago, IL: University of Chicago Press, 1986). Web edition at http://press-pubs.uchicago.edu/founders/.

4. Jean Yarborough, "Federalism in the Foundation and Presentation of the American Republic," *Publius: The Journal of Federalism*, 6/1 (1976): 34–53.

5. Ellis Katz and G. Alan Tarr, eds., *Federalism and Rights* (Lanham, MD: Rowman and Littlefield, 1996).

6. Lilliard E. Richardson, Jr. and David J. Houston, "Federalism and Safety on America's Highways," *Publius: The Journal of Federalism* 39/1 (2009):117–37.

7. James Madison to Edmund Randolph, April 8, 1787, in Kurland and Lerner, *The Founders Constitution*.

8. Federal Farmer, no. 17, January 23, 1788, in Kurland and Lerner, *The Founders Constitution*.

9. David B. Walker, *The Rebirth of Federalism*, 2nd ed. (New York: Chatham House, 2000), p. 58.

10. Walker, *Rebirth of Federalism*, p. 59.

11. For the division of U.S. history into eras of federalism, the authors owe a debt to Walker, *Rebirth of Federalism*.

12. Concurring opinion of Justice William Johnson in *Gibbons v. Ogden* (1824).

13. Richard S. Randall, *American Constitutional Development*, Vol. I, *The Powers of Government* (New York: Longman, 2002), p. 72.

14. Quoted in Randall, Vol. I, *The Powers of Government*, p. 70.

15. *Briscow v. Bank of the Commonwealth of Kentucky* (1837).

16. Quoted in Walker, *Rebirth of Federalism*, p. 67.

17. Quoted in Randall, Vol. I, *The Powers of Government*, p. 91

18. Walker, *Rebirth of Federalism*, p. 73.

19. Deil S. Wright, *Understanding Intergovernmental Relations* (Pacific Grove, CA.: Brooks/Cole, 1988), pp. 115–116.

20. Walker, *Rebirth of Federalism*, p. 77.

21. Gary B. Nash, Julie Roy Jeffrey, John R. Howe, Peter J. Frederick, Allen F. Davis, and Allan M. Winkler, *American People: The Creating of a Nation and a Society*, Vol. II: *Since 1865*, 6th ed. (New York: Longman, 2004), p. 600.

22. Note on Eisenhower's White House memo stationary, undated by probably about September 24, 1957, located on the Web at www.eisenhower.Utexas.edu/d/littlerockdocuments.html.

23. Walker, *Rebirth of Federalism*, p. 107.

24. Walker, *Rebirth of Federalism*, p. 326, uses the term for the current state of federalism. Also see Shelly Arsneault, "Welfare Policy Innovation and Diffusion: Section 1115 Waivers and the Federal System," *State and Local Government Review*, 32/1 (2000): 49–60; and Michael D. Reagan and John G. Sanzone, *The New Federalism*, 2nd ed. (New York: Oxford University Press, 1981).

25. *Katzenbach v. McClung* (1964).

26. Randall, Vol. I, *The Powers of Government*, p. 481.

27. Charles Davis, "Preemptive Federalism or Regulatory Dismantlement? The Bush Administration's Implementation of the Federal Coal Mining Reclamation Program," *Politics & Policy*, 36/3 (2008): 400–418.

28. Alex Conant, quoted in the *New York Times*, March 10, 2006.

29. Joseph F. Zimmerman, "Congressional Preemption During the George W. Bush Administration," *Publius: The Journal of Federalism*, 37/3 (2007): 432–452.

30. Michael Greve, head of the Federalism Project at the American Enterprise Institute, quoted in the *Washington Times*, January 3, 2004.

31. Thornburg's comment was during testimony during hearings on the "Overcriminalization and the Need for Legislative Reform" held by the Subcommittee on Crime, Terrorism, and Homeland Security, Committee on the Judiciary, U.S. House of Representatives, July 22, 2009.

32. Task Force on the Federalization of Criminal Law, Edwin Meese, chairman, *Report on the Federalization of Criminal Law* (Chicago: American Bar Association, 1998.)

33. Chief Justice William H. Rehnquist, "1998 Year-End Report on the Federal Judiciary," published in the *Newsletter of the Federal Courts* 31 (1999) on the Federal Judiciary Website at www.uscourts.gov.

34. *United States v. Lanza* (1922).

35. *United States v. Wheeler* (1978).

36. *Garcia v. San Antonio Metropolitan Transit Authority* (1985).

37. *Washington Post*, March 15, 2005.

38. General Accountability Office, *Unfunded Mandates: Analysis of Reform Act Coverage,* Report to the Chairman, Subcommittee, on Oversight of Government Management, the Federal Workforce, and the District of Columbia, Committee on Governmental Affairs, U.S. Senate, May 2004, GAO Report GAO-04-637, May 2004, p. 36.

39. Mitchell Pickerill and Cornell W. Clayton, "The Rehnquist Court and the Political Dynamics of Federalism," *Perspectives on Politics*, 2/2(2004): 233–248.

40. Senator Patrick Leahy (D-VT), comment during hearings on "Narrowing

the Nation's Power: The Supreme Court Sides with the States," before the U.S. Senate, Committee on the Judiciary, October 1, 2002.

41. A review of the court's approach to federalism during the period is Timothy J. Conlan and Francois Vergniolle De Chantal, "The Rehnquist Court and Contemporary American Federalism," *Political Science Quarterly*, 116/2 (2001), pp. 253–275.

42. Christopher Banks and John Blakeman, "Chief Justice Roberts, Justice Alito, and New Federalism Jurisprudence," *Publius: The Journal of Federalism*, 38/3 (2008): 576–600. Also see, Simon Lazarus, "Federalism R.I.P.? Did the Roberts Confirmation Hearings Junk the Rehnquist Court's 'Federalism' Revolution?" March 2006, on the Website of the American Constitution Society for Law and Policy at www.acslaw.org/.

43. Banks and Blakeman, "Chief Justice Roberts, Justice Alito, and New Federalism Jurisprudence," p. 576.

44. Ann O'M. Bowman and George A. Krause, "Power Shift: Measuring Policy Centralization in U.S. Intergovernmental Relations, 1947–1988," *American Political Research*, 31 (May 2003): 301, 316.

45. Walker, *Rebirth of Federalism*, p. 171.

46. Robert F. Nagel, *The Implosion of American Federalism* (New York: Oxford University Press, 2002), p. 12.

47. Richard Briffault, "A Fickle Federalism: The Rehnquist Court Hobbles Congress—and the States, Too, *The American Prospect*, 14/3 (March 2003). Online edition at www.prospect.org/print/.

48. "Statement on Signing the Executive Order Establishing the Presidential Advisory Committee on Federalism," April 8, 1981, *Public Papers of the Presidents of the United States, Ronald W. Reagan (1981)*.

49. John Dinan and Shama Gamkhar, "The State of American Federalism 2008–2009: The Presidential Election, the Economic Downturn, and the Consequences for Federalism," *Publius: The Journal of Federalism,* 39/3 (2009): 373, 369–407.

50. The statement, made in late 1995, was quoted in the *Washington Times*, January 3, 2004.

51. Tim Conlan and John Dinan, "Federalism, the Bush Administration, and the Transformation of American Conservatism," *Publius: The Journal of Federalism*, 37/3 (2007): 279–303.

52. Presidential Memo Regarding Preemption, May 20, 2009, on White House Website at www.whitehouse.gov

53. Robert P. Grimesey, superintendent of schools in Orange County, Virginia, quoted in the *New York Times*, August 16, 2009.

54. Diane Ravitch, research professor at New York University's Steinhardt School of Education and former U.S. Assistant Secretary of Education, quoted in the *New York Times*, August 16, 2001.

55. The expert was David Osborne, a former senior adviser to then-Vice President Al Gore, quoted in the *Washington Times,* December 3, 2008.

56. Letter to Ambassador Robert Zoellick, United States Trade Representative, September 23, 2003. On the Website of the Forum on Democracy and Trade at www.forumdemocracy.net.

57. Richard L. Cole and John Kincaid, "Public Opinion on U.S. Federal and Intergovernmental Issues in 2006: Continuity and Change," *Publius: The Journal of Federalism*, 36/3 (2006): 443.

58. John Kincaid and Richard L. Cole, "Public Opinion on Issues of Federalism in 2007: A Bush Plus?" *Publius: The Journal of Federalism*, 38/3 (2008): 469–487.

59. Council for Excellence in Government. Methodology, 1995. Data provided by The Roper Center for Public Opinion Research, University of Connecticut.

60. Kincaid and Cole, "Public Opinion on Issues of Federalism in 2007."

61 For example, see the discussion in Robert S. Erikson and Ken L. Tedin, *American Public Opinion*, 6th ed. (New York: Longman, 2003), pp. 313–318.

62. William Riker, *Federalism: Origin, Operation, Significance* (Boston: Little Brown, 1964), p. 155.

63. Brandis's dissenting in *New State Ice Co. v. Liebmann* (1932).

64. Harold Meyerson, "Fed Up with Federalism," *The American Prospect*, December 2, 2009. Online edition at www.prospect.org/print/

CHAPTER 4

1. *Washington Post*, April 11, 2007.

2. *Boston Globe*, April 12, 2007.

3. CNN.com, April 10, 2007.

4. Reuters dispatch, April 13, 2007.

5. *Wall Street Journal* poll, October 1986. Data provided by The Roper Center for Public Opinion Research, University of Connecticut.

6. *New York Times* poll, June 1983. Data provided by The Roper Center.

7. Survey by National Public Radio, Henry J. Kaiser Family Foundation, and Harvard University's Kennedy School of Government, August 2002. Data provided by The Roper Center.

8. National Constitution Center poll, July 2002. Data provided by The Roper Center.

9. Princeton Survey Research Associates/*Newsweek* poll, November 2001. Data provided by The Roper Center.

10. Fox News/Opinion Dynamics poll, June, 2006. Data provided by The Roper Center.

11. John C. Domino, *Civil Rights & Liberties in the 21st Century* (New York: Longman, 2003), p. 142.

12. Senator John Cornyn (R-TX), Testimony during hearings on "Beyond the Pledge of Allegiance: Hostility to Religious Expression in the Public Square," U.S. Senate Committee on the Judiciary, June 8, 2004.
13. *Davis v. Beason* (1890).
14. *Torcaso v. Watkins* (1961).
15. *Employment Division, Department of Human Resources of Oregon v. Smith* (1990).
16. *Wisconsin v. Yoder* (1972).
17. *Goldman v. Weinberger* (1986).
18. *O'Lone v. Shabazz* (1987).
19. *United States v. Seeger* (1965).
20. Letter of Abraham Lincoln to Erastus Corning and others, June 12, 1863, quoted in Josiah Gilbert Holland, *The Life of Abraham Lincoln* (Lincoln, NE: Bison Books, 1998), p. 415. Originally published in 1866.
21. *United States v. O'Brien* (1968).
22. *Chaplinsky v. New Hampshire* (1942).
23. *R.A.V. v. City of St. Paul* (1992).
24. *West Virginia Board of Education* (1943).
25. *Wooley v. Maynard* (1977).
26. *Roth v. United States* (1957).
27. Madison's address to the House of Representatives, June 8, 1789.
28. *Bill of Rights*, Chapter 9 "Property Rights," U.S. Department of State at http://usinfo.state.gov/products/pubs/rightsof/property.htm.
29. *Wilkinson v. Leland* (1829).
30. The author gratefully acknowledges the influence of material supplied by Professor Pei-te Lien of the University of California, Santa Barbara, on the section "Civil Liberties and Criminal Justice."
31. American Civil Liberties Union poll, February 21–February 1989, and *USA Today* poll, April 1985. Provided by The Roper Center.
32. *Dickerson v. United States* (2000).
33. *Berghuis v. Thompkins* (2010).
34. *Benton v. Maryland* (1969).
35. *Trop v. Dulles* (1958).
36. *Robinson v. California* (1962).
37. *Graham v. Florida* (2010).
38. Eric Neumayer, "Death Penalty: The Political Foundations of the Global Trend Towards Abolition," *Human Rights Review*, 9/2 (2008): 263.
39. *McClesky v. Kemp* (1987).
40. *New York Times*, April 29, 2008.

CHAPTER 5

1. Branwen Gruffydd Jones, "Race in the Ontology of International Order," *Political Studies*, 56/4 (2008): 907–927.
2. United Nations Development Programme, *Human Development Report, 2009*.
3. *Boston Globe*, January 15, 2003. Faculty members at the University of Chicago Graduate School of Business and the Massachusetts Institute of Technology conducted the study.
4. Frederick Douglass, "British Influence on the Abolition Movement in America: An Address Delivered in Paisley, Scotland, on April 17, 1846." Renfrewshire *Advertiser*, April 25, 1846. Found in John Blassingame et al, eds., *The Frederick Douglass Papers: Series One—Speeches, Debates, and Interviews*. New Haven: Yale University Press, 1979. Vol. I, p. 215, online.
5. Office of Public Opinion Research poll, 1945. Data provided by The Roper Center for Public Opinion Research, University of Connecticut.
6. William D. Carrigan and Clive Webb, "The Lynching of Persons of Mexican Origin or Descent in the United States, 1848 to 1928," *Journal of Social History*, 37/2 (2003): 411–438.
7. Harris poll, 1971. Data provided by The Roper Center.
8. Quoted in Asian Pacific American Historical Timeline Details (1875 to 1899)," on the Website of U.S. Asians.net. at http://us_asians.tripod.com/index2.html.
9. *United States v. Thind* (1923).
10. Lt. Gen. J. L. De Witt, *Final Report, Japanese Evacuation from the West Coast, 1942*, June 5, 1943, quoted by Justice Frank Murphy dissenting in *Korematsu v. United States* (1944).
11. Secretary of the Interior Harold Ickes quoted in Smithsonian Institution, *A More Perfect Union: Japanese Americans & the U.S. Constitution: Internment: Permanent Camps*, on the Internet at http://americanhistory.si.edu/perfectunion/non-flash/internment_main.html.
12. Jake Page, *In the Hands of the Great Spirit: The 20,000-Year History of American Indians* (New York: Free Press, 2003), p. 277.
13. *Federal Education Policy & Off-Reservation Schools, 1870–1933*, a presentation of the Clarke Historical Library, Central Michigan University, online http://openlibrary.org/books/OL3285790M/Federal_education_policy_off-reservation_schools_1870-1933.
14. Steven Shapin, "Man with a Plan: Herbert Spencer's Theory of Everything," *New Yorker*, August 13, 2007, online.
15. Herbert Spencer, *Principles of Biology* (1864).
16. All quotes from Mike Hawkins, *Social Darwinism in European and American Thought, 1860–1945: Nature as Model and Nature as Threat* (Cambridge, UK: Cambridge University Press, 1997), pp. 201–202.
17. League of United Latin American Citizens Website at www.lulac.org.
18. *Gayle v. Browder* (1956).
19. Harris poll, 1965. Data provided by The Roper Center.
20. National Opinion Research Center poll, 1956 and Harris poll, 1963. Data provided by The Roper Center.
21. Harris poll, May 1965. Data provided by The Roper Center.
22. Marilyn Lake and Henry Reynolds, *Drawing the Global Colour Line: White Men's Countries and the Inter-*

national *Challenge of Racial Equality* (Cambridge, UK: Cambridge University Press, 2008).

23. James H. Meriwether, *Proudly We Can Be Africans: Black Americans and Africa, 1935–1961* (Chapel Hill: University of North Carolina Press, 2002).

24. Roger A. Davidson, Jr., "A Question of Freedom: African Americans and Ghanaian Independence," *Negro History Bulletin*, July/September, 1997, online.

25. "The Birth of a New Nation," sermon delivered by Martin Luther King, Jr. at Dexter Avenue Baptist Church in Montgomery, Alabama, April 7, 1957.

26. "Martin Luther King Inspired by 1959 Journey to India," February 4, 2009, entry on the "American Life" section of the Website of the U.S. Department of State.

27. *Congressional Record*, August 25, 1965, p. 21783.

28. *Guinn v. United States* (1915) and *Smith v. Allwright* (1944).

29. Nick Kotz, *Judgment Days: Lyndon B. Johnson, Martin Luther King, Jr., and the Laws that Changed America* (Boston: Houghton Mifflin, 2005).

30. Chandler Davidson, "The Voting Rights Act: A Brief History" in Bernard Grofman and Candler Davidson, eds., *Controversies in Minority History: The Voting Rights Act in Perspective* (Washington, DC: Brookings Institution, 1992).

31. Michael Jones-Correa, "Language Provisions Under the Voting Rights Act: How Effective Are They?" *Social Science Quarterly*, 86/3 (2005): 549–564.

32. David T. Cannon, *Race, Redistricting, and Representation* (Chicago: University of Chicago Press, 1999). Research indicates that blacks are of mixed mind on racial gerrymandering. They support changes in electoral laws to increase black representation, but they do not support

overtly creating majority–minority districts. On this point, see Katherine Tate, "Black Opinion on the Legitimacy of Racial Redistricting and Minority-Majority Districts," *American Political Science Review*, 97(2003): 45–57.

33. Pei-te Lien, Dianne M. Pinderhughes, Carol Hardy-Fanta, and Christine M. Sierra, "The Voting Rights Act and the Election of Nonwhite Officials," *PS: Political Science and Politics*, 40/3 (2007): 489–494.

34. For state legislatures, *Reynolds v. Sims* (1964); for local districts, *Board of Estimate of City of New York v. Morris* (1998).

35. Nixon's "Statement about the Busing of Schoolchildren," August 3, 1971.

36. *Keyes v. School District No. 1* (1973)

37. *Milliken v. Bradley* (1974).

38. *Parents Involved in Community Schools v. Seattle School District No. 1* (2007).

39. *Grove City College v. Bell* (1984).

40. Johnson's commencement address at Howard University, June 4, 1965.

41. Jewerl Maxwell. "Presidential Executive Orders and Equal Employment," Paper presented at the Midwest Political Science Association convention, Chicago, IL, April 2008, online at http://www.allacademic.com/meta/p265875_index.html.

42. *Griggs v. Duke Power Co.* (1971).

43. *Washington v. Davis* (1976).

44. *CBOCS West v. Humphries* (2008).

45. Kenneth Y. Chay, "The Impact of Federal Civil Rights Policy on Black Economic Progress: Evidence from the Equal Employment Opportunity Act of 1972," *Industrial and Labor Relations Review*, 51/4 (1998): 608–632.

46. Sara Wakefield and Christopher Uggen, "The Declining Significance of Race in Federal Civil Rights Law: The Social Structure of Employment Discrimination

Claims," *Sociological Inquiry*, 74/1 (2004): 128–157.

47. C. Elizabeth Hirsh, "Settling for Less? Organizational Determinants of Discrimination-Charge Outcomes," *Law & Society Review*, 42/2 (2008): 239–274.

48. Kevin Stainback, Corre L. Robinson, and Donald Tomaskovic-Devey, "Race and Workplace Integration: A Politically Mediated Process?" *American Behavioral Scientist*, 48/9 (2005): 1200–1228.

49. Risa Goluboff, *The Lost Promise of Civil Rights* (Cambridge: Harvard University Press, 2007).

50. World Public Opinion.org, "Publics Around the World Say Governments Should Act to Prevent Racial Discrimination," March 20, 2008.

51. Anthony F. Heath, Catherine Rothon, and Elina Kilpi, "The Second Generation in Western Europe: Education, Unemployment, and Occupational Attainment," *Annual Review of Sociology*, 34 (2008), p. 211.

52. Organization for Economic Co-Operation and Development, "Ending Job Discrimination," *Policy Brief*, July 2008, p. 1.

53. Judith Wellman, *The Road to Seneca Falls: Elizabeth Cady Stanton and the First Woman's Rights Convention* (Urbana: University of Illinois Press, 2004).

54. *Minor v. Happersett* (1875).

55. *New York Times*, August 19, 1920.

56. Claudia Goldin and Lawrence F. Katz, "Career and Marriage in the Age of the Pill," *The American Economic Review*, 90/2 (2000): 461–465.

57. John R. Vile, "Permitting States to Rescind Ratifications of Pending Amendments to the U.S. Constitution," *Publius: The Journal of Federalism*, 20/2 (1990): 109–122.

58. Louis Bolce, Gerald De Maio, and Douglas Muzzio, "The Equal Rights

Amendment, Public Opinion, and American Constitutionalism," *Polity* 19/4 (1987): 551–569.

59. David B. Hill, "Women State Legislators and Party Voting on the ERA," *Social Science Quarterly*, 64/2 (1983): 318–326.

60. Merit Report poll, 1982. Data provided by The Roper Center.

61. *Corning Glass Works v. Brennan* (1974) and *Meritor Savings Bank v. Vinson* (1986).

62. Judith Evans, *Feminist Theory Today: An Introduction to Second Wave Feminism* (London: Sage, 1995).

63. Quoted in Sandra Dijkstra, "Simone de Beauvoir and Betty Friedan: The Politics of Omission," *Feminist Studies*, 6/2 (1980): 293.

64. Charlotte Bunch, executive director, Center for Women's Global Leadership, Rutger's University, quote in the *New York Times*, June 13, 2000.

65. *Time*/Yankelovich, Skelly & White poll, March 1978. Data provided by The Roper Center.

66. Gallup poll, 1983. Data provided by Roper Center.

67. Gallup poll, 1999. Data provided by Roper Center.

68. CNN/Opinion Research Corporation poll, May 25, 2010. Data provided by Roper Center.

69. *Romer v. Evans* (1996).

70. *Boy Scouts of America v. Dale* (2000).

71. *Hernandez v. Robles* (2006).

72. Quoted in the *New York Times*, November 11, 2008.

73. Rose McDermott, professor of political science, University of California at Santa Barbara quoted in "To Tell or Not? Disclosing Candidate Health Issues," reported by Joanne Silberner on NPR, March 4, 2008, online at http://www.npr.org/templates/story/story.php?storyId=88789897.

74. National Council on Disability, *The Impact of the Americans with Disabilities Act: Assessing the Progress Toward Achieving the Goals of the ADA* (Washington, DC: National Council on Disability, July 26, 2007).

CHAPTER 6

1. Various Pew, Fox, and Gallup polls, December 2006. Data provided by The Roper Center for Public Opinion Research, University of Connecticut.

2. *Washington Post*, January 15, 2007.

3. *Discourse on Method* (1637).

4. William G. Jacoby, "Core Values and Political Attitudes," in *Understanding Public Opinion*, Barbara Norrander and Clyde Wilcox, eds. (Washington, DC: CQ Press, 2002), p. 177.

5. Speech, "The American Moment" to the Chicago Council on Global Affairs, Chicago, IL, April 23, 2007.

6. ABC News, Jan. 13, 2009.

7. CNN exit poll.

8. *Gender & Multicultural Project Survey, 2006–2007*. Also, Pei-te Lien, Carol Hardy-Fanta, Christine Marie Sierra, and Dianne M. Pinderhughes, "Exploring Dimensions of Interracial Connections between Asian and Other Nonwhite Elected Officials," Paper presented at the Association for Asian American Studies Convention, New York, April 2007.

9. Pew Research Center and Chicago Council on Foreign Relations, *America's Place in the World, 2005*.

10. Public Agenda Foundation, September 1998. Data provided by the Roper Center.

11. American Civil Liberties Union survey, February 1989. Data provided by The Roper Center. Of respondents, 63% agreed the pledge should be required, 33% disagreed, and 4% were unsure.

12. David L. Paletz, *The Media in American Politics: Contents and Consequences* (New York: Longman, 2002), p. 147.

13. Julianna Sandell Pacheco, "Political Socialization in Context: The Effect of Political Competition on Youth Voter Turnout," *Journal of Political Behavior*, 30/4 (2008): 415–436.

14. Gallup polls, September 30, June 16, and October 13, 2009 respectively.

15. *New York Times*, April 13, 1994.

16. James L. Gibson, "Intolerance and Political Repression in the United States: A Half Century after McCarthyism," *American Journal of Political Science*, 52/1 (2008): 96–108.

17. Gallup poll, December 1958 and *Newsweek* poll, June 2007. Data provided by The Roper Center.

18. Gallup polls, January 1937, September 1958, and December 2007. Data provided by The Roper Center.

19. Pew Global Attitudes Project 2003.

20. *Newsweek* poll, October 2001. Data provided by The Roper Center.

21. Pew Research Center, "Independents Take Center Stage in Obama Era," May 21, 2009.

22. Robert S. Erikson and Kent L. Tedin, *American Public Opinion*, 6th ed. (New York: Longman, 2003), p. 147.

23. Rodolfo O. de la Garza, Louis DeSipio, F. Chris Garcia, John Garcia, and Angelo Falcon, *Latino Voices: Mexican, Puerto Rican, and Cuban Perspective on American Politics* (Boulder, CO: Westview Press, 1992), p. 82. Also see Michael Corbett, *Political Tolerance in America: Freedom and Equality in Public Attitudes* (New York: Longman, 1982); and Richard Seltzer and Robert C. Smith, "Race and Civil Liberties," *Social Science Quarterly*, 66 (1985): 155–162.

24. Pew Research Center poll, January 2007. Data provided by the Roper Center.

25. *Washington Post*/Kaiser/Harvard Racial Attitudes Survey, March–April 2002 on the Web at www.washingtonpost.com/wp-srv/nation/sidebars/polls/race071101.htm.

26. *Public Perspective*, 4/3 (March 1996), p. 34.

27. Everett C. Ladd, "*E Pluribus Unum* Still: The Uniting of America," *Public Perspective*, 1/4 (May 1992): 7. Also see, Rodolfo O. de la Garza, Angelo Falcon, and F. Chris Garcia, "Will the Real Americans Please Stand Up: Anglo and Mexican American Support of Core American Political Values," *American Journal of Political Science*, 40/2 (1996).

28. Roper Center poll, August 1994, *Public Perspective*, 6/2 (February, 1995), p. 35.

29. American National Election Study for data through 2004. Data for 2004 from Joseph Gershtenson and Dennis L. Plane, "Trust in Government: 2006 American National Election Studies Pilot Report." April 10, 2007, unpublished paper located at www.electionstudies.org/resources/papers/Pilot2006/nes011890.pdf. Data for 2008 from Gregg Van Ryzin, "Outcomes, Process and Citizens Trust Of The Civil Service," paper prepared for the 10th National Public Management Research Conference, John Glenn School of Public Affairs, Ohio State University, Columbus, Ohio, October 1–4, 2009. Data for 2010 from CBS/*New York Times* poll, February 2010.

30. Tom W. Smith and Lars Jarkko, "National Pride: A Cross-National Perspective," unpublished paper (Chicago: National Opinion Research Center/University of Chicago, 2001).

31. *Time*, February 15, 2020.

32. Ladd, "*E Pluribus Unum* Still."

33. Brian D. Silver and Kathleen M. Dowley, "Measuring Political Culture in Multi-ethnic Societies: Reaggregating the World Values Survey," *Comparative Political Studies*, 33/4 (2000), p. 522. Similar findings are found in Smith and Jarkko, "National Pride."

34. Comment to a reporter, *Los Angeles Times*, April 28, 2009.

35. Remarks to the Chicago Council on Global Affairs, April 23, 2007 at www.thechicagocouncil.org/.

36. White House, *National Strategy of the United States of America*, September 2, 2002.

37. Pew Research Center report, *U.S. Position in the World*, January 2009, citing a 2008 survey.

38. CNN/*USA Today*/Gallup polls found on the Website of www.PollingReport.com.

39. *Washington Post*, May 1, 1997.

40. George Washington University, "Battleground 2008 Survey," July 2007. Data from the Roper Center.

41. Ole R. Holsti and James N. Rosenau, "The Domestic and Foreign Policy Beliefs of American Leaders," *Journal of Conflict Resolution*, 32/2 (1988): 248–294. Also, William O. Chittick, Keith Billingsley, and Rick Travis, "A Three-Dimensional Model of American Foreign Policy Beliefs," *International Studies Quarterly*, 39/3 (1995): 313–332.

42. Adam J. Berinsky, *Silent Voices: Public Opinion and Political Participation in America* (Princeton, NJ: Princeton University Press, 2004), p. 3.

43. James A. Stimson, *Tides of Consent: How Opinion Movements Shape American Politics* (New York: Cambridge University Press, 2004), p. xvi.

44. Robert S. Erikson and Kent L. Tedin, *American Public Opinion* (New York: Longman, 2003), p. 87.

45. Joe Soss, Laura Langbein, and Alan R. Metelko, "Why Do White Americans Support the Death Penalty?" *Journal of Politics*, 65/2 (2003): 397–422. Also Byron D'Andra Orey, "White Racial Attitudes and Support for the Mississippi State Flag," *American Politics Research*, 32/1 (2004): 102–116.

46. *Washington Post*/Kaiser Family Foundation/Harvard University Racial Attitudes Survey, March–April 2002.

47. *Washington Post*/Kaiser Family Foundation/Harvard University Racial Attitudes Survey, March 2002.

48. Kenneth E. Wald, *Religion and Politics in the United States* (Washington, DC: Congressional Quarterly Press, 1997).

49. Laura R. Olson, Wendy Cadge, and James T. Harrison, "Religion and Public Opinion about Same-Sex Marriage," *Social Science Quarterly*, 87/2 (2006): 340–360.

50. Americans Talk Security poll, September 1988. Data provided by The Roper Center.

51. Americans Talk Security poll, December 1988. Data provided by The Roper Center.

52. Andrea Louise Campbell, "Self-Interest, Social Security, and the Distinctive Participation Patterns of Senior Citizens," *American Political Science Review*, 96/3 (2002): 565–574.

53. NPR/Kaiser/Kennedy School Education Survey, 1999.

54. Pew Research Center, "Attitudes Toward Immigration: In Black and White," April 2006.

55. Jennifer Jerit, Jason Barabas, and Toby Bolsen, "Citizens, Knowledge, and the Information Environment." *American Journal of Political Science*, 50/2 (2006): 266–287.

56. Christine H. Roch, "The Dual Roots of Opinion Leadership," *Journal of Politics*, 67/1 (2005): 110–131.

57. Arthus Lupia and Tasha S. Philpot, "Views from Inside the Net: How Websites Affect Young Adults' Political Interest," *Journal of Politics*, 67/4 (2005): 1122–1142.

58. Kathleen A. Frankovic, "Reporting 'The Polls' in 2004," *Public Opinion Quarterly*, 69/5 (2005): 682–697.

59. Tom Rosenstiel, "Political Polling and the New Media Culture: A Case

of More Being Less," *Public Opinion Quarterly*, 2005 69/5 (2005), p. 698. Pp. 698–715.

60. Kenneth Dautrich, director of the Center for Survey Research and Analysis at the University of Connecticut, quoted in Lori Robertson, "Poll Crazy," *American Journalism Review*, 25/1 (2003), p. 42.

61. Quoted in Kathleen A. Frankovic, "The Truth About Push Polls," nd. CBSNews.com.

62. Thomas E. Patterson, "Of Polls, Mountains U.S. Journalists and Their Use of Election Surveys," *Public Opinion Quarterly*, 69/5 (2005): 716–724.

63. Bill McInturff and Lori Weigel, "Servants of the People: Political Leadership and the Public Voice," *Public Perspective*, 12/4 (2001), p. 18.

64. Real Clear Politics, "Election 2008 National Head-to-Head Polls," at www.realclearpolitics.com.

65. David C. Wilson, David W. Moore, Patrick F. Mckay and Derek R. Avery, "Affirmative Action Programs for Women and Minorities: Expressed Support Affected by Question Order," *Public Opinion Quarterly*, 72/3 (2008): 514–522.

66. In order of the questions, the polls were a Gallup poll, June 2003; a Pew Research Center poll, April 2003; and a Quinnipiac University poll, February 2003.

67. CBS News/*New York Times* poll, CBS survey report, February 2010.

68. CNN/*USA Today* poll, January 2006. Data provided by The Roper Center.

69. NBC News/*Wall Street Journal* poll, September 2008.

70. George F. Bishop, Robert W. Oldendick, Alfred J. Tuchfarber, and Stephen E. Bennett, "Pseudo-Opinions on Public Affairs," *Public Opinion Quarterly*, 44/1 (1980): 198–209.

71. Jeffery J. Mondak and Mary R. Anderson, "The Knowledge Gap: A Reexamination of Gender-Based Differences in Political Knowledge,"

Journal of Politics, 66/2 (2004). Also, Scott L Althaus, *Collective Preferences in Democratic Politics: Opinion Survey and the Will of the People* (New York: Cambridge University Press, 2003).

72. NBC News/*Wall Street Journal* poll, December, 2008. Data provided by The Roper Center.

73. Emily W. Kane and Laura J. Macaulay, "Interviewer Gender and Gender Attitudes," *Public Opinion Quarterly*, 57/1 (1993):1–28.

74. Henry J. Kaiser Family Foundation poll, January 2001. Data provided by The Roper Center.

75. NBC News/*Wall Street Journal* poll, December, 2008. Data provided by The Roper Center.

76. American National Election Studies, Frequency Codebook for the Advance Release of the 2008–2009 ANES Panel Study.

77. Justin Lewis, *Constructing Public Opinion: How Political Elites Do What They Like and Why We Seem to Go Along with It* (New York: Columbia University Press, 2001), p. 28. Also, Eric Shirev and Richard Sobel, *People and Their Opinions: Thinking Critically About Public Opinion* (New York: Longman, 2006), Table 2.2, p. 26.

78. *Washington Post*, April 11, 2006.

79. Maurice Mangum, "Testing Competing Explanations of Black Opinions on Affirmative Action," *Policy Studies Journal*, 36/3 (2008): 347–366.

80. Natalie Masuoka, "Political Attitudes and Ideologies of Multiracial Americans," *Political Research Quarterly*, 61/2 (2008): 253–267.

81. Ron Walters of the University of Maryland quotes in the *Washington Post*, March 25, 2003.

82. Pew Hispanic Center, "Survey of Latino Attitudes on a Possible War with Iraq," February 18, 2003.

83. Carole Jean Uhlander and F. Chris Garcia, "Latino Public Opinion," in

Norrander and Wilcox, eds., *Understanding Public Opinion*, p. 99.

84. Barbara Norrander and Clyde Wilcox, "The Gender Gap in Ideology," *Political Behavior*, 30/4 (2008): 503–523.

85. Pamela Johnston Conover and Virginia Sapiro, "Gender, Feminist Consciousness, and War," *American Journal of Political Science*, 37/4 (1993): 1079–1099.

86. Pew Research Center report, "U.S. Needs More International Backing," February 20, 2003.

87. Clyde Wilcox, Lara Hewitt, and Dee Allsop, "The Gender Gap in Attitudes toward the Gulf War: A Cross-National Perspective," *Journal of Peace Research*, 33/1 (1996): 67–82.

88. Tom W. Smith, "The Polls: Gender and Attitudes Toward Violence," *Public Opinion Quarterly*, 48/1 (1984): 384–396.

89. R. Michael Alvarez and Edward J. McCaffery, "Are There Sex Differences in Fiscal Policy Preferences?" *Political Research Quarterly*, 56/1 (2003): 5–17.

90. Gregory M. Herek, "Gender Gaps in Public Opinion About Lesbians and Gay Men," *Public Opinion Quarterly*, 66/1 (2002): 40–66.

91. Virginia Sapiro, "It's the Context, Situation, and Question, Stupid: The Gender Basis of Public Opinion," in Norrander and Wilcox, eds., *Understanding Public Opinion*, p. 41.

92. All data from CNN Election Center 2008.

93. Pets: ABC News/BeliefNet poll, June 2001; Reincarnation: FOX News/Opinion Dynamics poll, October, 2001; ghosts: CBS News poll, October 2005. Data provided by The Roper Center.

94. Jeff Manza and Fay Lomax Cook, "The Impact of Public Opinion on Public Policy: The State of the Discipline," in *Navigating Public Opinion: Polls, Policy, and the Future of*

American Democracy, Jeff Manza, Fay Lomax Cook, and Benjamin I. Page, eds. (New York: Oxford University Press, 2002), pp. 17–18.

95. Robert M. Eisinger, *The Evolution of Presidential Polling* (New York: Cambridge University Press, 2003). Also, Diane J. Heith, "One for Al: Using Focus Groups and Opinion Polls in the George H.W. Bush White House," *Congress & the Presidency*, 30/1 (2003): 81–94.

96. Philip J. Powlick, "The Sources of Public Opinion for American Foreign Policy Officials," *International Studies Quarterly*, 39/4 (1995): 427–452.

97. Pew Research Center, "Trust in Government Study," February 1998.

98. Pew Research Center, "Washington Leaders Wary of Public Opinion," April 1998. The data is an average of the three categories of officials, not all the officials individually. Also see Philip J. Powlick, "The Attitudinal Bases for Responsiveness to Public Opinion American Foreign Policy Officials," *Journal of Conflict Resolution*, 35/4 (1991): 611–641.

99. Brandice Canes-Wrone, *Who Leads Whom? Presidents, Policy, and the Public* (Chicago, University of Chicago Press, 2006), p. 156.

100. Pew Research Center, "Trust in Government Study."

101. Erikson and Tedin, *American Public Opinion*, p. 272.

102. George C. Edwards, III and Stephen J. Wayne, *Presidential Leadership in Congress* (New York: St. Martin's, 1995), p. 97.

103. Christopher A. Cooper and Lilliard E. Richardson, Jr., "Multi-member Districts and Representational Roles in U.S. State Legislatures," paper presented at the 2004 State Politics Conference at Kent State University, Kent, Ohio, May 2004.

104. Powlick, "The Attitudinal Bases," p. 624.

105. *Washington Post,* February 1, 2002.

106. Christopher Wlezien, "Patterns of Representation: Dynamics of Public Preferences and Policy," *Journal of Politics*, 66/1 (2004): 1–24. Also, Paul Burstein, "Public Opinion and Congressional Action on Labor Market Opportunities, 1942–2000," in *Navigating Public Opinion.*

107. Robert Y. Shapiro, The Dynamics of Public Opinion and Public Policy, Ph.D. dissertation, University of Chicago, 1982, reported in Lawrence R. Jacobs and Robert Y. Shapiro, "Politics and Policymaking in the Real World," in *Navigating Public Opinion*, p. 56.

108. Alan D. Monroe, "Public Opinion and Public Policy, 1980–1993," *Public Opinion Quarterly*, 62/1 (1998): 6–28; and Alan D. Monroe, "Consistency between Policy Preferences and National Policy Decisions," *American Politics Quarterly*, 7/1 (1979): 3–18.

109. Sara Binzer Hobolt and Robert Klemmemsen, "Responsive Government? Public Opinion and Government Policy Preferences in Britain and Denmark," *Political Studies*, 53/2 (2005): 379–402.

110. Vincent L. Hutchings, *Public Opinion and Democratic Accountability* (Princeton, NJ: Princeton University Press, 2003), p. 141. Italics in the original.

111. Powlick, "The Attitudinal Bases," p. 624.

112. Thomas Riess-Kapan, "Public Opinion, Domestic Structure, and Foreign Policy in Liberal Democracies," *World Politics*, 43/4 (1991): 510.

113. Representative Earl Pomeroy (D-ND) quoted in the *Washington Post*, May 5, 2003.

114. Alan D. Monroe, "Public Opinion," and "Consistency."

115. Jacobs and Shapiro, "Politics and Policymaking in the Real World," Table 3.1, p. 56; Monroe, "Public Opinion"; and Monroe, "Consistency."

116. Martin Gilens, "Inequality and Democratic Responsiveness," *Public Opinion Quarterly*, 69/5 (2005): 778–796.

117. Chicago Council on Foreign Relations, *Global Views 2004.*

118. Bryan Caplan, *The Myth of the Rational Voter: Why Democracies Choose Bad Policies* (Princeton, NJ: Princeton University Press, 2007).

119. Pew Research Center, "Ten Years of the Pew News Interest Index," May 1997.

120. Michael X. Delli Carpini and Scott Keeter, *What Americans Know About Politics and Why It Matters* (New Haven, CT: Yale University Press, 1989), Chapter 2.

121. John R. Baker, Linda L. M. Bennett, Stephen E. Bennett, and Richard S. Flickinger, "Citizens' Knowledge and Perceptions of Legislatures in Canada, Britain, and the United States," *The Journal of Legislative Studies*, 2/2 (1996): 44–62.

122. W. Lance Bennett, *Public Opinion and American Politics* (New York: Harcourt Brace Jovanovich, 1989), p. 44. The percentage knowing their astrological sign is from an ABC News/*Washington Post* poll, May 1988. Data provided by The Roper Center. The percentage knowing the name of the representative in the House is from a *Washington Post* poll, January 1996. Data provided by The Roper Center.

123. Erikson and Tedin, *American Public Opinion*, p. 58.

124. Kathleen M. McGraw, "Manipulating Public Opinion," in Norrander and Wilcox, eds., *Understanding Public Opinion.*

125. Justin Lewis, *Constructing Public Opinion: How Political Elites Do What They Like and Why We Seem to Go Along with It* (New York:

Columbia University Press, 2001), pp. xi and 86.

126. G. William Domhoff, "The Power Elite, Public Policy, and Public Opinion," in *Navigating Public Opinion*.

127. James H. Kuklinski, Paul J. Quirk, Jennifer Jerit, and Robert F. Rich, "The Political Environment and Citizen Competence," *American Journal of Political Science*, 45/2 (2001): 410–424.

128. Stimson, *Tides of Consent*, p. 15.

129. Donald L. Jordan and Benjamin I. Page, "Shaping Foreign Policy Opinions: The Role of TV News," *Journal of Conflict Resolution*, 36/2 (1992): 227–241.

130. William G. Jacoby, "Core Values and Political Attitudes," in Norrander and Wilcox, eds., *Understanding Public Opinion*.

131. Stimson, *Tides of Consent*, p. 158.

132. Benjamin I. Page and Robert Y. Shapiro, *The Rational Public: Fifty Years of Trends in American's Policy Preferences* (Chicago: University of Chicago Press, 1992). Also, John Mueller, "American Foreign Policy and Public Opinion in a New Era: Eleven Propositions," in Norrander and Wilcox, eds., *Understanding Public Opinion*.

133. John R. Oneal, Bradley Lian, and James Joyner, Jr., "Are the American People 'Pretty Prudent'? Public Responses to U.S. Uses of Force, 1950–1988," *International Studies Quarterly*, 40/2 (1996), p. 274 (pp. 261–279). Also, Bruce W. Jentleson, "The Pretty Prudent Public: Post-Vietnam American Opinion on the Use of Military Force," *International Studies Quarterly*, 36/1 (1992): 49–73.

134. Humphrey Taylor, "The Value of Polls in Promoting Good Government and Democracy," in *Navigating Public Opinion*, p. 316.

135. Althaus, *Collective Preferences in Democratic Politics*, p. 177.

136. General Social Survey 2004 poll, August 2004. Data provided by The Roper Center.

137. Fox News poll, February 2009. Data provided by The Roper Center.

138. General Social Survey 2004 poll, August 2004. Data provided by The Roper Center.

139. Harris poll, November 2005. Data provided by The Roper Center.

140. Harris poll, February 2009. Data provided by The Roper Center.

141. Henry J. Kaiser Family Foundation poll, September 2001.

142. Gallup poll, June 1946. Data provided by The Roper Center.

CHAPTER 7

1. Statement during "Judicial Nomination" hearings before the U.S. Senate Committee on the Judiciary, February 5, 2004.

2. *Rapid City Journal*, July 18, 2004.

3. Robert H. Salisbury, "Interest Structures and Policy Domains: A Focus for Research," in *Representing Interests and Interest Group Representation*, William Crotty, Mildred A. Schwartz, and John C. Green, eds. (Lanham, MD: University Press of America, 1994).

4. *Washington Representatives 2009* (Bethesda, MD: Columbia Books, 2009).

5. World Public Opinion.org, survey report, May 12, 2008.

6. Theda Skocpol, Rachael V. Cobb, and Casey Andrew Klofstad, "Disconnection and Reorganization: The Transformation of Civic Life in Late-Twentieth-Century America," *Studies in American Political Development*, 19/1 (Fall 2005): 137–156.

7. Quoted on the Common Cause Website, www.commoncause.org.

8. "New Trade of Old Diplomats," *Euro*, February 2, 2007.

9. Diane Stone, "Global Public Policy, Transnational Policy Communities, and Their Networks," *Policy Studies Journal*, 36/1 (2008): 19–38.

10. Ronald Inglehart, Miguel Basañez, and Alejandro Moreno, *Human Values and Beliefs: A Cross-Cultural Sourcebook* (Ann Arbor: University of Michigan Press, 1998).

11. Pew Research Center survey report, September 2, 2009.

12. Robert C. Lowry and Matthew Potoski, "Organized Interests and the Politics of Federal Discretionary Grants," *Journal of Politics*, 66/2 (2004): 513–533.

13. Friends of the Earth press release, February 25, 2010, at www.foe.org.

14. ABC News/*Washington Post* poll, August 2009. Data from Polling Report.com.

15. "Characteristics of a Federal Lobbyist," a white paper, September 11, 2008, on the Website of Lobbyists .info.

16. CBSNews.com, June 1, 2010, at www.cbsnews.com.

17. Obama's quote is from the *New York Times*, May 27, 2010; the second quote is from the *Hartford Courant*, May 25, 2010.

18. Bara Vaida, "Salary Survey: Higher and Higher," *National Journal* online, February 15, 2008.

19. Amy McKay, "Interest Group Competition on Federal Agency Rules," *American Politics Research*, 35/3 (2007): 336–357. Also, Susan Webb Yackee, "Sweet-Talking the Fourth Branch: The Influence of Interest Group Comments on Federal Agency Rulemaking," *Journal of Public Administration Research and Theory*, 16/1 (2006): 103–124.

20. Beth L. Leech and Frank R. Baumgartner, "Lobbying Friends and Foes in Washington," in *Interest Group Politics,* 5th edition, Allan J. Cigler and Burdett A. Loomis, eds. (Washington, DC: CQ Press, 1998), pp. 217–233; Kenneth M. Goldstein, *Interest Groups, Lobbying, and Par-*

ticipation in America (New York: Cambridge University Press, 1999), chapter 4.

21. Baumgartner and Leech, *Basic Interests,* Table 8.1, p. 152.

22. "Rules of the Game," *The Hill,* July 19, 2005.

23. "It's Tee Time for Women Lobbyists," *Roll Call,* August 8, 2005.

24. Keven R. den Dulk and J. Mitchell Pickerill, "Bridging the Law Making Process: Organized Interests, Court-Congress Interaction, and Church-State Relations," *Polity,* 35/3 (2003): 419–430.

25. Thomas G. Hansford, "Information Provision, Organizational Constraints, and the Decision to Submit an Amicus Curiae Brief in a U.S. Supreme Court Case," *Political Research Quarterly,* 57/1 (2004): 219–230.

26. *Washington Post,* May 26, 2010.

27. *Washington Post,* September 11, 2008.

28. U.S. Senate, "Lobbying," on the Website of the U.S. Senate at www .senate.gov/legislative/ common/ briefing/Byrd_History_Lobbying .htm#1.

29. Goldstein, *Interest Groups,* p. 24.

30. David Lowery, Virginia Gray, Jennifer Anderson, and Adam J Newmark, "Collective Action and the Mobilization of Institutions," *Journal of Politics,* 66/3 (2004): 684–705.

31. *CQ Weekly,* April 19, 2003, p. 924. The legislator was former Representative David E. Bonior (D-MI), who served as House Democratic whip.

32. Goldstein, *Interest Groups,* p. 25.

33. Kathy Goldschmidt, "E-mail Overload in Congress—Update," a report of the Congress Online Project, August 7, 2002.

34. Goldstein, *Interest Groups,* p. 62.

35. Among other studies in which the term is used is William P. Browne, *Groups, Interests, and U.S. Public Policy* (Washington, DC: Georgetown University Press, 1998).

36. William P. Browne, "Lobbying the Public: All-Directional Advocacy," in Browne, ed. *Groups, Interests, and U.S. Public Policy,* pp. 343–363.

37. Lucig H. Banielian and Benjamin I. Page," The Heavenly Chorus: Interest Group Voices on TV News," *American Journal of Political Science,* 38 (1994): 1056–1078. For the place of interest groups in the news, also see John M. Berry, *The New Liberalism: The Rising Power of Citizen Groups* (Washington, DC: Brookings, 1999), chapter 6.

38. Elisabeth R. Gerber and Justin H. Phillips, "Development Ballot Measures, Interest Group Endorsements, and the Political Geography of Growth Preferences," *American Journal of Political Science,* 47 (2003): 625–640.

39. Frank Fischer, "American Think Tanks: Policy Elites and the Politicization of Expertise," *Governance,* 4/3 (2005): 332–353.

40. Andrew Rich and R. Kent Weaver, "Advocates and Analysts: Think Tanks and the Politicization of Expertise," in Browne, ed., *Groups, Interests, and U.S. Public Policy,* pp. 235–253.

41. Former 34-year Representative Lee Hamilton (D-IN) quoted in Lee Michael Katz, "American Think Tanks—Their Influence Is on the Rise," *Carnegie Reporter,* 5/2 (2009), online.

42. Fairness and Accuracy in Reporting ezine *Extra!,* March/April 2008; DomainTraddicRank.com

43. AP, April 29, 2004.

44. Berry, *The New Liberalism,* p. 122.

45. Robert G. Boatright, "Situating the New 527 Organizations in Interest Group Theory," *The Forum* online, 5/2 (2007): Article 5.

46. National Organization for Women Political Action Committee (NOW PAC) press release, "National Organization of Women National Organization for Women PAC

Endorses Obama-Biden, September 16, 2008.

47. Karen O'Connor, "Lobbying the Justices or Lobbying for Justice," in *The Interest Group Connection: Electioneering, Lobbying, and Policymaking in Washington,* Paul S. Herrnson, Ronald G. Shaiko, and Clyde Wilcox, eds. (Chatham, NJ: Chatham House Publishers, 2003) Table 16.2, pp. 273, 267–288).

48. David Alistair Yalof, *Pursuit of Justices: Presidential Politics and the Selection of Supreme Court Nominees* (Chicago: University of Chicago Press, 1999), p. 18.

49. Richard L. Hall and Kristina C. Miler, "What Happens After the Alarm? Interest Group Subsidies to Legislative Overseers," *Journal of Politics,* 70/4 (2008): 990–1005

50. Nancy Scherer, Brandon L. Bartels, and Amy Steigerwalt, "Sounding the Fire Alarm: The Role of Interest Groups in the Lower Federal Court Confirmation Process," *Journal of Politics,* 70/4 (2008), p. 1035.

51. All quotes in this paragraph are from the *Washington Post,* August 16, 2004.

52. *CQ Weekly,* Feb. 7, 2004, p. 324. The source of the first quote was anonymous; second quote is by Jill Lancelot, President of Taxpayers for Common Sense.

53. Lowery and Brasher, *Organized Interests,* pp. 210–213.

54. Steven J. Balla and John R. Wright, "Interest Groups, Advisory Committees, and Congressional Control of the Bureaucracy," *American Journal of Political Science,* 45 (2001), pp. 799–812.

55. O'Connor, "Lobbying the Justices or Lobbying for Justice," p. 277.

56. William Browne, "Asking the Right Questions," in *Groups, Interests, and U.S. Public Policy,* p. 5.

57. Christopher Kenny, Michael McBurnett, and David Bordua, "The Impact of Political Interests in

the 1994 and 1996 Congressional Elections: The Role of the National Rifle Association," *British Journal of Political Science* 34 (2004): 331–344.

58. Shannon O'Neil, the Douglas Dillon Fellow for Latin America Studies at the Council on Foreign Relations, quoted in *The Washington Independent*, December 12, 2008.

59. Frank R. Baumgartner and Beth L. Leech, *Basic Interests: The Importance of Groups in Politics and in Political Science* (Princeton, NJ: Princeton University Press, 1998), Table 8.1, p. 152. The quotation is from Kevin W. Hula, *Lobbying Together: Interest Group Coalitions in Legislative Politics* (Washington, DC: Georgetown University Press, 1999), p. 2

60. *Detroit News*, July 18, 2004.

61. Barry S. Rundquist and Thomas M. Carsey, *Congress and Defense Spending: The Distributive Politics of Military Procurement* (Norman: Oklahoma University Press, 2004).

62. This section is greatly informed by Richard A. Smith, "Interest Group Influence in the U.S. Congress," *Legislative Studies Quarterly,* 20/1 (1995): 89–139; and John P. Heinz, Edward O. Laumann, Robert L. Nelson, and Robert H. Salisbury, *The Hollow Core: Private Interests in National Policy Making* (Cambridge, MA: Harvard University Press, 1993).

63. Allan McConnell, "Overview: Crisis Management, Influences, Responses and Evaluation," *Parliamentary Affairs*, 56/3 (2006): 363–409; Arjen Boin, "Lessons from Crisis Research," *International Studies Review*, 6/1 (2004): 165–194; and Uriel Rosenthal, Michael T. Charles, and Paul 't Hart, "The World of Crises and Crisis Management," in *Coping with Crises: The Management of Disasters, Riots, and Terrorism*, Uriel Rosenthal, Michael T. Charles,

and Paul 't Hart, eds. (Springfield, IL: Charles C Thomas, 1989).

64. Frank R. Baumgartner and Beth L. Leech, "Interest Niches and Policy Bandwagons: Patterns of Interest Group Involvement in National Politics," *Journal of Politics*, 22/4 (2001), p. 1202.

65. Baumgartner and Leech, "Interest Niches," pp. 1191–1213.

66. Mik Moore, "Coalition Building between Native American and Environmental Organizations in Opposition to Development: The Case of the New Los Padres Dam Project," *Organization & Environment*, 11/3 (1998): 287–313.

67. Christine Mahoney, "Lobbying Success in the United States and the European Union," *Journal of Public Policy*, 27/1 (2007): 35–56.

68. Mahoney, "Lobbying Success."

69. Suzanne Dovia, "Theorizing Women's Representation in the United States," *Politics & Gender*, 3/2 (2007): 297–319.

70. Grant Jordan and William A. Maloney, *Democracy and Interest Groups: Enhancing Participation?* (London: Palgrave Macmillan, 2008).

71. Collin Hay, Gerry Stoker, and Andy Williamson, 'Revitalising Politics: Have We Lost the Plot?' Unpublished memo (2008) quoted by William Maloney in "Interest Groups and the Revitalization of Democracy: Are We Expecting Too Much?" Paper presented at the Revitalizing Politics Conference, London, UK, November 5–6, 2008

72. U.S. Senate, "Lobbying."

73. The classic expression of this view is E. E. Schattschneider, *The Semisovereign People* (New York: Holt, Rinehart and Winston, 1960).

74. Larry M. Bartels, Hugh Helco, Rodney Hero, and Lawrence R. Jacobs, *Inequality and American Governance, A Report of the Task Force on

Equality and American Democracy (Washington, DC: American Political Science Association, 2004), pp. 26, 44.

75. Jason Webb Yackee and Susan Webb Yackee, "A Bias Towards Business? Assessing Interest Group Influence on the U.S. Bureaucracy," *Journal of Politics*, 68/1 (2006): 128–162.

76. Heinz, Laumann, Nelson, and Salisbury, *The Hollow Core*, p. 369.

77. John R. Wright, *Interest Groups and Congress: Lobbying, Contributions, and Influence* (New York: Longman, 2003). Originally published in 1995.

78. The classic example is David B. Truman, *The Governmental Process: Political Interests and Public Opinion* (New York: Alfred A. Knopf, 1951).

79. James Madison, "Vices of the Political System of the United States," April 1787; James Madison, *Federalist* No. 10, 1789.

80. William Maclay (PA) quoted in "Lobbying" on the Website of the U.S. Senate at www.senate.gov/ legislative/common/briefing/Byrd _History_Lobbying.htm#1. This historical discussion of lobbying draws on that document.

81. U.S. Senate, "Lobbying." A variation of the quote is in Don Wolfensberger, "Woodrow Wilson, Congress, and the Income Tax," An Introductory Essay for the Congress Project Seminar on "Congress and Tax Policy," Woodrow Wilson International Center for Scholars, March 16, 2001.

82. Comment in December 2007 on a New Hampshire Public Radio program quoted by Trudy Lieberman in "Obama's Lobbyist Line," *Columbia Journalism Review* online, February 15, 2008.

83. This paragraph relies heavily on William T. Gormley, Jr., "Interest Group Intervention in the Administrative Process," in *The Interest Group Connection: Electioneering, Lobbying, and Policymaking in Washington*,

Paul S. Herrnson, Ronald G. Shaiko, and Clyde Wilcox, eds. (Chatham, NJ: Chatham House Publishers), pp. 217–219.

84. Lowery and Brasher, *Organized Interests*, p. 240.

85. David J. Jackson and Steven T. Engel, "Don't Bite the PAC that Feeds You: Business PAC Punishment over the China Vote," *American Politics Research*, 31 (2003): 138–154.

86. Bartels, Helco, Hero, and Jacobs, *Inequality and American Governance*, p. 35.

87. The quote and some information from the *Washington Post*, March 6, 2010. Other information from the Center for Responsive Politics and Earmark Watch.org.

CHAPTER 8

1. SFGate.com (*San Francisco Chronicle*), February 2, 2010.

2. SFGate.com, *Chronicle* Op-Ed, "Gay Judge Has Proven Record of Impartiality," February 2, 2010.

3. *Los Angeles Times*, January 10, 2010.

4. Majority and minority opinion quotes from the *Los Angeles Times*, January 14, 2010.

5. *New York Times*, June 29, 2010.

6. Philip J. Powlick, "The Source of Public Opinion for American Foreign Policy Officials," *International Studies Quarterly*, 39/5 (1995): 427–451.

7. Gallup Poll report, December 15, 2008.

8. Gallup Poll report, December 17, 2007.

9. James Madison, letter to W. T. Berry, August 4, 1822, found in most compilations of Madison's writing.

10. David A. Yalof and Kenneth Dautrich, *The First Amendment and the Media in the Court of Public Opinion* (New York: Cambridge University Press, 2002).

11. Pew Research Center, Global Attitudes Project 2002.

12. State of the First Amendment survey June, 2003; and Pew Research Center survey, February, 2006. Data provided by The Roper Center for Public Opinion Research, University of Connecticut.

13. "Media Fact Sheet," The Free Expression Policy Project, Brennan Center for Justice, New York University Law School.

14. Eli Noam, "How to Measure Media Concentration," *Financial Times*, August 30, 2004.

15. Noam, "How to Measure Media Concentration."

16. Pew Research Center, Project for Excellence in Journalism report, March 1, 2010.

17. Ivy Planning Group, *Whose Spectrum Is It Anyway: A Historical Study of Market Entry Barriers, Discrimination and Changes in Broadcast and Wireless Licensing, 1950 to Present*, a report to the Office of General Counsel, Federal Communications Commission (Rockville, Maryland, December 2000), p. 80.

18. Lawrence T. McGill, *News Room Diversity: Meeting the Challenge* (Arlington, VA: Freedom Forum, 2003), p. 3.

19. Quoted in David Pritchard and Sarah Stonbely, "Racial Profiling in the Newsroom," *Journalism & Mass Communication Quarterly*, 84/2 (2007), p. 235. "Racial pigeonholing" is Pritchard and Stonbely's term.

20. BBC/Reuters/Media Center poll, "Trust in the Media," 2006.

21. Gertrude J. Robinson, *Gender, Journalism, and Equity: Canadian, U.S., and European Perspectives* (Cresskill, NJ: Hampton Press, 2005); Maurine H. Beasley and Sheila J. Gibbons, *Taking Their Place: A Documentary History of Women and Journalism* (State College, PA: Strata Publishing, 2003); and Bettina Peters, *Equality and Quality: Setting Standards for Women in Journalism*, IFJ Survey on the Status of Women Journalists (Brussels: International Federation of Journalists, 2001).

22. Christine Bachen, Allen Hammond, Laurie Mason, and Stephanie Craft, "Diversity of Programming in the Broadcast Spectrum: Is There a Connection Between Owner Race or Ethnicity and News and Public Affairs Programming?" a report to the Federal Communications Commission (Santa Clara, CA: Santa Clara University, December 1999), p. 20.

23. Jeff Dubin and Matthew Spitzer, "Testing Minority Preference in Broadcasting," *Southern California Law Review*, 68/3 (1995), p. 841.

24. Richard Oppel, editor of the *Austin American-Statesman* and president of the American Society of News Editors, quoted in Cheryl Arvidson, "Editors Welcome Minority Recruitment Help," Freedom Forum Online.

25. Travis L. Dixon, "Network News and Racial Beliefs: Exploring the Connection between National Television News Exposure and Stereotypical Perceptions of African Americans," *Journal of Communication*, 58/2 (2008): 321–337.

26. Peter J. Schraeder and Brian Endless, "The Media and Africa: The Portrayal of Africa in the *New York Times* (1955–1995)," *Journal of Opinion* 26/2 (1998): 29–35, especially Table 5, p. 32.

27. *New York Times v. Sullivan* (1964).

28. Federal Communications Commission staff report, *Public Service Responsibility of Licensees*, 1946.

29. *Adarand Constructors v. Peña* (1995).

30. *Branzburg v. Hayes* (1972).

31. *New York Times*, July 7, 2005.

32. Pew Research Center report, "Audience Segments in a Changing News Environment," August 2008.

33. Pew Research Center report, "What Americans Know: 1989–2007," April 2007.

34. Pew Research Center report, "News Audiences Increasingly Politicized," June 2004.

35. Pew Research Center, "Biennial Media Consumption Survey 2008."

36. TVB Media Comparisons Study 2008 at TVB.org.

37. Pew Research Center, *State of the News Media 2010*.

38. Hillel Nossek, "Our News and Their News: The Role of National Identity in the Coverage of Foreign News," *Journalism*, 5/3 (2004), p. 343.

39. James T. Hamilton, *All the News That's Fit to Sell* (Princeton, NJ: Princeton University Press, 2004), p. 1.

40. Hamilton, *All the News*, p. 262.

41. This section relies substantially, but not entirely, on Doris A. Graber, *Mass Media & American Politics*, 7th edition (Washington, DC: CQ Press, 2005), pp. 98–102.

42. Pew Research Center survey report, August 17, 2008. All data in bulleted points for 2008.

43. Attributed to Morrill Goddard, editor of the *American Sunday Magazine* in 1896 and quoted in Calvin Woodward, "Rough Seas," *The American Editor*, October/November 1999.

44. Dana's article, "What Is News" appeared in 1882 in the *New York Sun* and is quoted in John T. Rourke, Ralph G. Carter, and Mark A. Boyer, *Making American Foreign Policy* (Guilford, CT: Brown & Benchmark, 1996), p. 351.

45. Pew Research Center, "Press Biennial Media Consumption Survey," April 2004.

46. Pew Research Center, "Online News Audience Increasingly Politicized," June 2004.

47. Pew Research Center, Project for Excellence in Journalism's annual report, "State of the News Media 2006."

48. Pew Research Center "2007 Survey of Journalists," March 2007, and "News Audiences Increasingly Politicized," June 2004.

49. Cited in Robert L. Craig, "Business, Advertising, and the Social Control of News," *Journal of Communication Inquiry*, 28/3 (2004): 233–252.

50. Pew Research Center, "2007 Survey of Journalists."

51. "Media Fact Sheet," The Free Expression Policy Project, Brennan Center for Justice, New York University Law School.

52. Graber, *Mass Media and American Politics*, p. 48.

53. Pew Research Center Project for Excellence in Journalism, "How News Happens," January 11, 2010.

54. *New York Times*, May 25, 2004.

55. Graber, *Mass Media and American Politics*, p. 258.

56. Nicholas Confessore, "Does the White House Have a Blacklist?" *American Prospect*, March 11, 2002.

57. Robert M. Entman, *Projections of Power: Framing News, Pubic Opinion, and U.S. Foreign Policy* (Chicago: University of Chicago Press, 2004).

58. Pew Research Center, "Public More Critical of Press, But Goodwill Persists," June 2005.

59. *Hartford Courant*, October 3, 2004.

60. Pew Research Center report, September 13, 2009.

61. Pew Research Center report, September 13, 2009.

62. *Washington Post*, January 11, 2005.

63. Robert M. Eisinger, Loring R. Veenstra, and John P. Koehn, "What Media Bias? Conservative and Liberal Labeling in Major U.S. Newspapers," *Harvard International Journal of Press/Politics*, 12/1 (2007): 17–36; Jeffrey S. Peake, "Presidents and Front-page News: How America's Newspapers Cover the Bush Administration, *Harvard International Journal of Press/Politics*, 12/4 (2007): 52–70. David Niven, "Objective Evidence on Media Bias: Newspaper Coverage of Congressional Party Switchers," *Journalism and Mass Communication Quarterly*, 80/2 (2007): 311–326; S. Robert Lichter, "A Plague on Both Parties: Substance and Fairness in TV Election News," *Harvard International Journal of Press/Politics*, 6/3 (2001): 8–30.

64. Dave D'Alessio and Mike Allen, "Media Bias in Presidential Elections: A Meta Analysis," *Journal of Communication*, 50/4 (2000), p. 150.

65. Tim Groseclose and Jeff Milyo, "A Measure of Media Bias," *Quarterly Journal of Economics*, 120/4 (2005): 1191–1237; Jim Kuypers, *Press Bias and Politics* (Westport, CT: Praeger, 2002); David P. Baron, "Persistent Media Bias," unpublished paper, Stanford University, August 2004; Ricardo Puglisi, "Being the *New York Times*: The Political Behavior of a Newspaper," working paper, London School of Economics, 2004.

66. The two research groups were the Center for Media and Public Affairs at George Mason University and the Pew Research Center's Project for Excellence in Journalism.

67. Pew Research Center, *State of the Media 2010*.

68. Pew Research Center, "2007 Survey of Journalists."

69. Robert Lichter, Stanley Rothman, and Linda Lichter, *The Media Elite, America's New Powerbrokers* (Bethesda, MD: Adler & Adler, 1977); Kenneth Walsh, *Feeding the Beast: The White House versus the Press* (New York: Random House 1996); Stanley Rothman and Amy E. Black, "Media and Business Elites: Still in Conflict?" *Public Interest*, 143 (Spring 2001): 72–86; Department of Public Policy, University of Connecticut, press release, "Press Freedom in the U.S.: A National Survey of Journalists and the American Public," May 16, 2005.

70. Pew Research Center survey, December 2004. Data provided by The Roper Center; and Pew Research Center, "How Journalists See Journalists," March/April 2004.

71. David H. Weaver, Randal A. Beam, Bonnie J. Brownlee, Paul S. Voakes, and G. Cleveland Wilhoit, *The American Journalist in the 21st Century: U.S. News People at the Dawn of a New Millennium* (New York: Routledge, 2006).

72. Pew Research Center report, September 13, 2009.

73. Pew Research Center survey, July 2007.

74. Pew Research Center report, October 22, 2008.

75. Tien-Tsung Lee, "The Liberal Media Myth Revisited: An Examination of Factors Influencing Perceptions of Media Bias," *Journal of Broadcasting & Electronic Media*, 49/1 (2005): 43–64; William P. Eveland, Jr. and Dhavan V. Shah, "The Impact of Individual and Interpersonal Factors on Perceived News Media Bias," *Political Psychology*, 24/1 (2003): 101–123.

76. Gallup Poll report, October 1, 2009.

77. David L. Paletz, *The Media in American Politics* (New York: Longman, 2002), p. 59.

78. From Dick Morris, *Behind the Oval Office* (New York: Random House, 1996), quoted in a book review, *Columbia Journalism Review*, March/April 1997.

79. Pew Research Center survey, July 2007.

80. Niven, "Bias in the News"; Robert K. Goidel and Ronald E. Langley, "Media Coverage of the Economy and Aggregate Economic Evaluations: Uncovering Evidence of Indirect Media Effects," *Political Research Quarterly*, 48/2(1995): 313–328; Thomas E. Patterson, "Bad News, Period," *PS: Political Science and Politics*, 29/1 (1996): 17–20.

81. Center for Media and Public Affairs, *Media Monitor*, July/August 2004; and press release, January 25, 2010.

82. Center for Media and Public Affairs, press release, January 25, 2010.

83. Mark J. Rozell, "Press Coverage of Congress, 1946–1992," in *Congress, the Press, and the Public*, Thomas E. Mann and Norman J. Orenstein, eds. (Washington, DC: American Enterprise Institute and Brookings Institution, 1994), p. 186, quoted in Paletz, *The Media and American Politics*, p. 245.

84. Dan Oberdorf, correspondent for the *Washington Post* from 1958 to 1993, quoted in his article, "Government and the Media: Dependence and Distrust," *Washington Post National Weekly Edition*, April 26–May 2, 1993.

85. Amy McKay and David L. Paletz, "The Presidency and the Media," in *Handbook of Political Communication Research*, Lynda Lee Kaid, ed. (Mahwah, NJ: Lawrence Erlbaum Associates, 2004).

86. "Final Edited Transcript, Interview with Jimmy Carter," Carter Presidency Project, November 29, 1982, p. 41.

87. Martha Joynt Kumar, "*Source Material*: 'Does This Constitute a Press Conference?' Defining and Tabulating Modern Presidential Press Conferences," *Presidential Studies Quarterly*, 33/1 (2003), especially Table 4, p. 231.

88. Franklin D. Gilliam, Jr. and Shanto Iyengar, "Prime Suspects: The Influence of Local Television News on the Viewing Public," *American Journal of Political Science*, 44/3 (2000): 560–573; Robert M. Entman and Andrew Rojecki, *The Black Image in the White Mind: Media and Race in America* (Chicago: University of Chicago Press, 2000).

89. *Network Brownout Report 2005* (Washington, DC: National Association of Hispanic Journalists, 2005), p. 18.

90. Center for Survey Research & Analysis, University of Connecticut, 2000. Data provided by The Roper Center.

91. *Network Brownout Report 2005*.

92. Pew Research Center, Project for Excellence in Journalism, "The Gender Gap: Women Are Still Missing as Sources for Journalists," (n.d.) at www.journalism.org.

93. Pew Research Center, Project for Excellence in Journalism's annual report, "State of the News Media 2006."

94. Pew Research Center, *The State of the Media 2010*.

95. Julianne F. Flowers and Audrey A. Haynes, "The Media, the Campaign, and the Message," *American Journal of Political Science*, 47/2 (2003): 259–273.

96. Stephen Hess of the Brookings Institution, quoted on PBS, October 20, 2004.

97. Thomas E. Patterson, "Of Polls, Mountains: U.S. Journalists and Their Use of Election Surveys," *Public Opinion Quarterly*, 69/5 (2005): 716–724.

98. "Election Watch: Campaign 2008 Final," *Media Monitor*, 23/1 (Winter 2009), Center for Media and Public Affairs, George Mason University.

99. *New York Times*, March 8, 1994.

100. Markus Prior, "News vs. Entertainment: How Increasing Media Choice Widens Gaps in Political Knowledge and Turnout," *American Journal of Political Science*, 49/3 (2005): 577–592. Also, Henrik Örnebring and Anna Maria Jönsson, "Tabloid Journalism and the Public Sphere: A Historical Perspective on Tabloid Journalism," *Journalism Studies*, 5/3 (2004): 283–295.

101. Pew Research Center, "2007 Survey of Journalists."

102. Nordicity Group, "Analysis of Government Support for Public

Broadcasting and Other Culture in Canada." Prepared for the CBC, 2006.

103. From Dick Morris, *Behind the Oval Office* (New York: Random House, 1996), quoted in a book review, *Columbia Journalism Review*, March/April 1997.

104. Jennifer Jerit, Jason Baraba, and Toby Bolsen, "Citizens, Knowledge, and the Information Environment," *American Journal of Political Science*, 30/2(2006): 266–282.

105. Paletz, *The Media in American Politics*, p. 157.

106. Graber, *Mass Media and American Politics*, p. 198.

107. Rourke, Carter, and Boyer, *Making American Foreign Policy*, p. 366.

108. B. Dan Wood and Jeffrey S. Peake, "The Dynamics of Foreign Policy Agenda Setting," *American Political Science Review*, 92/1 (1998): 173–184.

109. The top official was Lloyd Cutler. His quote and that of Madeleine Albright are from Graber, *Mass Media and American Politics*, p. 344.

110. Graber, *Mass Media and American Politics*, p. 160.

111. Paul Lellstedt, "Media Frames, Core Values, and the Dynamics of Racial Policy Preferences," in *Framing American Politics*, Karen Callaghan and Frauke Schnell, eds., pp. 174, 179.

112. Keith S. Petersen, "U.S. Black Newspaper Coverage of the UN and U.S. White Coverage, 1948–1975, *International Organization*, 33/4 (1979): 525–539.

113. James N. Druckman, "Political Preference Formation: Competition, Deliberation, and the (Ir)relevance of Framing Effects," *American Political Science Review*, 98/04 (2004): 671–686.

114. Karen Callaghan and Frauke Schnell, "Framing Political Issues in American Politics," in Callahan and

Schnell, eds., *Framing American Politics*, p. 11.

115. Joanne M. Miller and Jon A. Krosnick, "News Media Impact on the Ingredients of Presidential Evaluations: Politically Knowledgeable Citizens Are Guided by a Trusted Source," *American Journal of Political Science*, 44/2 (2009): 295–309.

116. Shanto Iyengar and Donald R. Kinder, *News That Matters: Television and American Opinion* (Chicago: University of Chicago Press, 1987), p. 110.

117. Alan S. Gerber, Dean Karlan, and Daniel Bergan, "Does the Media Matter? A Field Experiment Measuring the Effect of Newspapers on Voting Behavior and Political Opinions," *American Economic Journal: Applied Economics*, 1/2 (2009): 35–52; Stefano Della Vigna and Ethan Kaplan, "The Fox News Effect: Media Bias and Voting," *Quarterly Journal of Economics*, 122/3 (2007): 1187–1234; and Kim Fridkin Kahn, and Patrick J. Kenney, "The Slant of the News," *American Political Science Review*, 96/2 (2002): 381–394.

118. James N. Druckman and Michael M. Parkin, "The Impact of Media Bias: How Editorial Slant Affects Voters," *The Journal of Politics*, 67/4 (2005), p. 1045.

119. Donald L. Jordan and Benjamin I. Page, "Shaping Foreign Policy Opinions: The Role of TV News," *Journal of Conflict Resolution*, 36/2 (1992), p. 237.

120. Pew Research Center survey report, "News Audiences Increasingly Politicized," June 2004.

121. Pew Research Center, "News Audiences Increasingly Politicized."

122. Much of the data on doubts about the press in this section are from a CBS News/*New York Times* poll, January 2006. Data provided by The Roper Center.

123. Pew Research Center report, August 17, 2008.

124. Pew Research Center report, August 17, 2008.

125. Pew Research Center, *State of the Media 2010*.

126. Pew Research Center, Project for Excellence in Journalism's report, January 11, 2010.

127. Pew Research Center report, August 17, 2008.

128. Kathleen Hall Jamison and Paul Waldman, *The Press Effect: Politicians, Journalists, and the Stories That Shape the Political World* (New York, Oxford University Press, 2004).

129. Pew Research Center, "Public More Critical of Press." Data based on the averages from 13 surveys between 1985 and 2005.

130. "Final Edited Transcript, Interview with Jimmy Carter," Carter Presidency Project, November 29, 1982, p. 11.

131. Hamilton, *All the News That's Fit To Sell*, Table 2.1, p. 53.

132. John Quincy Adams, diary entry, September 7, 1820.

133. CBS News/*New York Times* poll, January 2006. Data provided by The Roper Center.

CHAPTER 9

1. Fox News/Opinion Dynamics poll, February 2010. Data provided by the Roper Center for Public Opinion Research, University of Connecticut.

2. CNN/Opinion Research Corp. poll, February 2010. Data provided by the Roper Center.

3. CNN/Opinion Research Corp. poll, January 2010. Data provided by the Center.

4. Ipsos-Public Affairs/McClatchy poll, February 2010. Data provided by the Center.

5. Various polls taken in October and November 2010. Data courtesy of The Roper Center.

6. National Review Institute Political Attitudes Survey, January 2010. Data provided by The Roper Center.

7. Peter Trubowitz and Nicole Mellow, " 'Going Bipartisan: Politics by Other Means'," *Political Science Quarterly*, 120/3 (2005), p. 433.

8. Samuel Merrill, Bernard Grofman, and Thomas L. Brunell, "Cycles in American National Electoral Politics, 1854–2006: Statistical Evidence and an Explanatory Model," *American Political Science Review*, 102/1 (2008): 1–17.

9. Pew Global Attitudes Project, "World Publics Welcome Trade—But Not Immigration," 2007.

10. Kenneth F. Greene, *Why Dominant Parties Lose: Mexico's Democratization in Comparative Perspective* (New York: Cambridge University Press, 2007).

11. P. See Lim, Colleen Barry-Goodman, and David Branham, "Discrimination that Travels: How Ethnicity Affects Party Identification for Southeast Asian Immigrants," *Social Science Quarterly*, 87 (2006): 1158–1170.

12. Solon J. Simmons and James R. Simmons, "If it Weren't for Those ?*!&*@!* Nader Voters We Wouldn't Be in This Mess: The Social Determinants of the Nader Vote and the Constraints on Political Choice," *New Political Science*, 28/2 (2006): 229–224.

13. CNN.com, February 25, 2008.

14. Lisa Jane Disch, *The Tyranny of the Two-Party System* (New York: Columbia University Press, 2002).

15. Harris poll, July 2007. Data provided by The Roper Center.

16. Ronald B. Rapoport and Walter J. Stone, *Three's a Crowd: The Dynamic of Third Parties, Ross Perot, and Republican Resurgence* (Ann Arbor: University of Michigan Press, 2005), p. 223.

17. Neal Allen and Brian J. Brox, "The Roots of Third Party Voting: The 2000 Nader Campaign in Historical Perspective," *Party Politics*, 11/5 (2005): 623–637.

18. Joel H. Silbey, "American Political Parties: History, Voters, Critical Elections, and Party Systems," *The Oxford Handbook of American Political Parties and Interest Groups*, L. Sandy Maisel and Jeffrey M. Berry, eds. (New York: Oxford University Press, 2010). Also, Norman Schofield, Gary Miller, and Andrew Martin, "Critical Elections and Political Realignments in the USA: 1860–2000," *Political Studies*, 51/2 (2003): 217–240.

19. Stephen Weatherford, "After the Critical Election: Presidential Leadership, Competition and the Consolidation of the New Deal Realignment," *British Journal of Political Science*, 32/2 (2002): 221 256.

20. Demetrios James Caraley, "Three Trends over Eight Presidential Elections, 1980–2008: Toward the Emergence of a Democratic Majority Realignment?" *Political Science Quarterly*, 124/3 (2009), p. 444.

21. Barry C. Burden and David C. Kimball, *Why Americans Split Their Tickets: Campaigns, Competition, and Divided Government* (Ann Arbor: University of Michigan Press, 2002).

22. Johnson's speech was delivered on May 22, 1964, at the University of Michigan.

23. Harold W. Stanley and Richard G. Niemi, "Partisanship, Party Coalitions, and Group Support, 1952–2004," *Presidential Studies Quarterly*, 36/2 (2006): 172–299.

24. Nicholas A. Valentino and David O. Sears, "Old Times There Are Not Forgotten: Race and Partisan Realignment in the Contemporary South," *American Journal of Political Science*, 49/3 (2005), p. 672.

25. Byron E. Shafer and Richard G. C. Johnston, "The Transformation of Southern Politics Revisited: The House of Representatives as a Window," *British Journal of Political Science*, 31/3 (2001): 601–625.

26. Barry C. Burden and Casey A. Klofstad, "Affect and Cognition in Party Identification," *Political Psychology*, 26/2 (2005): 869–906.

27. John Richard Petrocik, "Measuring Party Support: Leaners Are Not Independents," *Electoral Studies*, 28/4 (2009): 562–572. Data averages reports of the American National Election Studies for 2000, 2002, and 2004.

28. Larry M. Bartels, "Partisanship and Voting Behavior, 1952–1996," *American Journal of Political Science*, 44/1 (2000): 35–50.

29. Thomas A. Kazee and Mary C. Thornberry, "Where's the Party? Congressional Candidate Recruitment and American Party Organizations," *Western Political Quarterly*, 43/1 (1990): 61–80.

30. Kira Sanbonmatsu, "The Legislative Party and Candidate Recruitment in the American States," *Party Politics*, 12/2 (2006): 233–256.

31. *Time*, June 12, 2006.

32. CBS News/*New York Times* poll, October 1994. Data provided by The Roper Center.

33. Pew Research Center poll and Gallup/CNN/*USA Today* poll, October 1994. Data provided by The Roper Center.

34. L. Marvin Overby, "Public Opinion Regarding Congressional Leaders: Lessons from the 1996 Elections," *Journal of Legislative Studies*, 12/1 (2006): 54–75.

35. Daniel E. Bergan, Alan S. Gerber, Donald P. Green, and Costas Panagopoulos, "Grassroots Mobilization and Voter Turnout in 2004," *Public Opinion Quarterly*, 69/5 (2005): 760–777.

36. Scott D. McClurg, "Indirect Mobilization: The Social Consequences of Party Contacts in an Election Campaign," *American Politics Research*, 32/4 (2004): 406–443.

37. Monika McDermott, "Candidate Occupations and Voter Information Shortcuts," *Journal of Politics*, 67/1 (2005): 201–219.

38. Craig Goodman and Gregg R. Murray, "Do You See What I See? Perceptions of Party Differences and Voting Behavior," *American Politics Research*, 35/6 (2007): 905–931. Also Sharon E. Jarvis, *The Talk of the Party: Political Labels, Symbolic Capital, and American Life* (Lanham, MD: Rowman & Littlefield, 2005); and Cindy D. Kam, "Who Toes the Party Line? Cues, Values, and Individual Differences," *Political Behavior*, 27/2 (2005): 163–182.

39. Brian F. Schaffner and Matthew J. Streb, "The Partisan Heuristic in Low-Information Elections," *Public Opinion Quarterly*, 66/4 (2002):559–581.

40. Pew Research Center poll, April 2006. Data provided by The Roper Center.

41. Thomas M. Carsey and Geoffrey C. Layman, "Changing Sides or Changing Minds? Party Identification and Policy Preferences in the American Electorate," *American Journal of Political Science*, 50/2 (2006): 464–477.

42. Pew Research Center report, "Partisan Gap in Obama Job Approval Widest in Modern Era," April 2, 2009. Elected presidents factors out Gerald Ford.

43. Stephen Ansolabehere, James M. Snyder, Jr., and Charles Stewart, III, "Candidate Positioning in U.S. House Elections," *American Journal of Political Science*, 45/1 (2001), p. 136.

44. Gary W. Cox and Mathew D. McCubbins, *Setting the Agenda: Responsible Party Government in the U.S. House of Representatives* (New York: Cambridge University Press, 2005).

45. Timothy P. Nokken, "Ideological Congruence Versus Electoral Success: Distribution of Party Organization Contributions in Senate Elections, 1990–2000," *American Politics Research*, 31/1 (2003): 3–26.

46. Lisa A. Solowiej, Wendy L. Martinek, and Thomas L. Brunell, "Partisan Politics: The Impact of Party in the Confirmation of Minority and Female Federal Court Nominees," *Party Politics*, 11/5 (2005): 557–577.

47. Mathew and McCubbins, *Setting the Agenda*, p. 251.

48. Alan I. Abramowitz and Kyle L. Saunders, "Is Polarization a Myth?" *The Journal of Politics*, 70/2 (2008): 542–555. Also, Sean M. Theriault, "Party Polarization in the U.S. Congress: Member Replacement and Member Adaptation," *Party Politics*, 12/4 (2006): 483–503.

49. Pew Research Center report, "Evenly Divided and Increasingly Polarized," November 2003, p. 1.

50. Jeffrey W. Ladewig, "Conditional Party Government and the Homogeneity of Constituent Interests," *Journal of Politics*, 67/4 (2005): 1006–1029.

51. Kyle L. Saunders and Alan I. Abramowitz, "Ideological Realignment and Active Partisans in the American Electorate," *American Politics Research*, 32/3 (2004): 285–309.

52. NBC News/*Wall Street Journal* poll, November 2007. Data provided by The Roper Center.

53. George Washington University Battleground 2008 Survey, July 2007. Data provided by The Roper Center.

54. Fox News/Opinion Dynamics poll, February 2010.

55. Quinnipiac University Poll, February 2010. Data provided by The Roper Center.

56. Richard S. Conley, *The Presidency, Congress, and Divided Government: A Postwar Assessment* (College Station: Texas A&M University Press, 2005).

57. George Washington University Battleground 2010 Survey, December 2009. Data provided by The Roper Center.

58. Jeffrey E. Cohen, Richard Fleisher, and Paul Kantor, eds., *American Political Parties: Decline or Resurgence?* (Washington, DC: CQ Press, 2001).

59. R. Michael Alvarez and Lisa Garcia Bedolla, "The Foundations of Latino Voter Partisanship: Evidence from the 2000 Election," *Journal of Politics*, 65/1 (2003): 31–50.

60. *Washington Post*, December 23, 2003.

CHAPTER 10

1. Lisa Hill, "Low Voter Turnout in the United States: Is Compulsory Voting a Viable Solution?" *Journal of Theoretical Politics*, 18/2 (2006): 207–232.

2. This box relies extensively in information on the Website of the International Institute for Democracy and Electoral Assistance.

3. Ron Hayduk, *Democracy for All: Restoring Immigrant Voting Rights in the United States* (New York: Routledge, 2006).

4. Ronald Inglehart and Pippa Norris, "The Developmental Theory of the Gender Gap," *International Political Science Review*, 21/4 (2000): 441–463.

5. Thomas A. Kazee and Mary C. Thornberry, "Where's the Party? Congressional Candidate Recruitment and American Party Organizations," *Western Political Quarterly*, 43/1 (1990): 61–80.

6. *Smith v. Allwright* (1944).

7. *California Democratic Party v. Jones* (2000).

8. *Tashjian v. Republican Party of Connecticut* (1986).

9. The 20% is an estimate by the author based on a turnout of 15% of eligible voters, a national total of 79% of eligible adults registered to vote, and a check of registration data in a sample

of 11 states showing that 75% of all registrants had indicated a party affiliation, making 59% of all eligible adults registered with a party.

10. Wayne P. Stegner, "Presidential Renomination Challenges in the 20th Century," *Presidential Studies Quarterly*, 33/4 (2003): 827–853.

11. "The delegate selection process," *America Votes 2004: The Primaries*, on the Website of CNN.com.

12. Gallup polls, December 14–16, 2007, and January 4–6, 2008.

13. Cox Newspapers, May 20, 2007.

14. *Campaign Consultants: The Price of Democracy* (Washington DC: The Center for Public Integrity, 2006).

15. Pew Research Center poll, November 2006. Data provided by The Roper Center for Public Opinion Research, University of Connecticut.

16. Pew Research Center poll, November 2008. Data provided by The Roper Center.

17. Martin Kaplan, Ken Goldstein, and Matthew Hale, principle investigators, "Local News Coverage of the 2004 Campaigns: An Analysis of Nightly Broadcasts in 11 Markets," Lear Center Local News Archive, USC Annenberg School for Communication, February 15, 2005.

18. Thomas E. Patterson, "Of Polls, Mountains: U.S. Journalists and Their Use of Election Surveys," *Public Opinion Quarterly*, 69/5 (2005): 716–724. Also see, Kim Leslie Fridkin and Patrick J. Kenney, "Do Negative Messages Work? The Impact of Negativity on Citizens' Evaluations of Candidates," *American Politics Research*, 32/5 (2004): 570–605.

19. *Washington Post* Campaign Tracker at http://projects.washingtonpost.com/2008-presidential-candidates/tracker/candidates/barack-obama/states/.

20. David Plouffe quoted in *The Guardian*, June 25, 2009.

21. Kate Kenski and Natalie Jomini Stroud, "Who Watches Presidential Debates? A Comparative Analysis of Presidential Debate Viewing in 2000 and 2004," *American Behavioral Scientist*, 49/2 (2005): 213–228.

22. Thomas M. Holbrook, "Presidential Campaigns and the Knowledge Gap," *Political Communication*, 19/3 (2002): 437–454.

23. Kim L. Fridkin, Patrick J. Kenney, Sarah Allen Gershon, Karen Shafer, and Gina Serignese Woodall, "Capturing the Power of a Campaign Event: The 2004 Presidential Debate in Tempe," *Journal of Politics*, 69/3 (2007): 770–785.

24. The American Presidency Project.

25. Paul Freedman, Michael Franz, and Kenneth Goldstein, "Campaign Advertising and Democratic Citizenship," *American Journal of Political Science*, 48/4 (2004): 723–741.

26. Freedman, Franz, and Goldstein, "Campaign Advertising and Democratic Citizenship." Also, Ted Brader, "Striking a Responsive Chord: How Political Ads Motivate and Persuade Voters by Appealing to Emotions," *American Journal of Political Science*, 49/2 (2005): 388–405.

27. Gregory A. Huber and Kevin Arceneaux, "Identifying the Persuasive Effects of Presidential Advertising," *American Journal of Political Science*, 51/4 (2007): 957–977. Also, Michael M. Franz and Travis N. Ridout, "Does Political Advertising Persuade?" *Political Behavior*, 29/4 (2007): 465–491.

28. Richard R. Lau, Lee Sigelman, and Ivy Brown Rovner, "The Effects of Negative Political Campaigns: A Meta-Analytic Reassessment," *Journal of Politics*, 69/4 (2007): 1176–1209. Also, Deborah Jordan Brooks, "The Resilient Voter: Moving Toward Closure in the Debate over Negative Campaigning and Turnout," *Journal of Politics*, 68/3 (2006): 684–696; and Daniel Stevens, John Sullivan, Barbara Allen, and Dean Alger, "What's Good for the Goose Is Bad for the Gander: Negative Political Advertising, Partisanship, and Turnout," *Journal of Politics*, 70/1 (2008): 507–541.

29. Robert G. Boatwright, "Campaign Finance in the 2008 Election," in *The American Elections of 2008*, Janet M. Box-Steffensmeier and Steven E. Schier, eds. (Lanham, MD: Rowman & Littlefield, 2009).

30. Amounts are based on Campaign Finance Institute report, *Soft Money: Political Spending by 501(c) Nonprofits Tripled in 2008 Election*, February 25, 2009, at www.cfinst.org/ on 501(c) groups; and on Center for Responsive Politics, *527s: Advocacy Group Spending in the 2010 Elections*, which includes 2008 data at www.opensecrets.org/527s.

31. Peter Francia, John Green, Paul Herrnson, Wesley Joe, Lynda Powell, and Clyde Wilcox, "Donor Dissent: Congressional Contributors Rethink Giving," *Public Perspective* (July 2000), p. 30.

32. S. Karthick Ramakrishnan and Mark Baldassare, *The Ties That Bind: Changing Demographics and Civic Engagement in California* (Public Policy Institute of California, 2004). Also see, Karlo Barrios Marcelo, Mark Hugo Lopez, and Emily Hoban Kirby, *Civic Engagement Among Minority Youth* (College Park, MD: Circle, the University of Maryland's School of Public Policy, 2007).

33. Wendy K. Tam Cho, "Tapping Motives and Dynamics Behind Campaign Contributions: Insights from the Asian American Case," *American Politics Research*, 30/4 (July 2002): 347–383.

34. Christopher M. Duquette, "Does Money Buy Elections? Evidence from Races for Open-Seats in the U.S. House of Representatives, 1990–2004," unpublished paper, Center for Naval Analyses, The CNA Corporation, Alexandria, VA, February 2006.

35. Gary C. Jacobson, "Campaign Spending Effects in U.S. Senate Elections: Evidence from the National Annenberg Election Survey," *Electoral Studies*, 25/2 (June 2006): 195–226.

36. Alan I. Abramowitz, Brad Alexander, and Matthew Gunning, "Incumbency, Redistricting, and the Decline of Competition in U.S. House Elections, *Journal of Politics*, 68/1 (2006): 75–88.

37. Press release, the Senate Website of John McCain, November 14, 2001.

38. Thomas Stratmann, "Some Talk: Money in Politics. A (Partial) Review of the Literature," Public Choice, 124/1 (2005), p. 144. Also for studies that do not find a link, see Stephen Ansolabehere, John M. de Figuieredo, and James M. Snyder, "Why Is There So Little Money in U.S. Politics?" *Journal of Economic Perspectives*, 17/1 (2003): 105–130; and Gregory Wawro, "A Panel Probit Analysis of Campaign Contributions and Roll-Call Votes," *American Journal of Political Science*, 45/4 (2001): 563–579. One study that does find a substantial link is Thomas Stratmann, "Can Special Interests Buy Congressional Votes? Evidence from Financial Services Legislation," *Journal of Law and Economics*, 45/2 (2002): 345–374.

39. Richard L. Hall and Frank W. Wayman, "Buying Time: Moneyed Interests and the Mobilization of Bias in Congressional Committees," *American Political Science Review*, 84/3 (1990), p. 814.

40. *McConnell v. Federal Election Commission* (2003).

41. *Federal Election Commission v. Wisconsin Right to Life, Inc.* (2007).

42. *Davis v. Federal Election Commission* (2008).

43. *New York Times*, June 20, 2008.

44. Campaign Finance Institute press release, "Reality Check: Obama Received about the Same Percentage from Small Donors in 2008 as Bush in 2004," November 24, 2008.

45. Daniel Munro, "Integration Through Participation: Non-Citizen Resident Voting Rights in an Era of Globalization," *Journal of International Migration and Integration*, 9/1 (2008): 63–89. Also David C. Earnest, "Neither Citizen nor Stranger: Why States Enfranchise Resident Aliens," *World Politics*, 58/2 (2006): 242–275.

46. Margit Tavits, "Direct Presidential Elections and Turnout in Parliamentary Contests," *Political Research Quarterly*, 62/1 (2009): 42–54. Also, Bryan J. Dettrey and Leslie A. Schwindt-Bayer, "Voter Turnout in Presidential Democracies," *Comparative Political Studies*, 42/10 (2009): 1317–1338; and Peter Selb, "A Deeper Look at the Proportionality–Turnout Nexus," *Comparative Political Studies,* 42/4 (2009): 527–548.

47. Zoltan L. Hajnal and Paul G. Lewis, "Municipal Institutions and Voter Turnout in Local Elections," *Urban Affairs Review*, 38/5 (2003): 645–668.

48. Benny Geys, "Explaining Voter Turnout: A Review of Aggregate-Level Research," *Electoral Studies,* 25/4 (2006): 637–663.

49. James Adams, Jay Dow, and Samuel Merrill, "The Political Consequences of Alienation-Based and Indifference-Based Voter Abstention: Applications to Presidential Elections," *Political Behavior*, 28/1 (2006): 65–86.

50. Benjamin Highton, "Voter Registration and Turnout in the United States," *Perspective on Politics*, 2/3 (2004), p. 508.

51. Highton, "Voter Registration and Turnout in the United States," p. 511.

52. Martha Kropf and Angela Cooke, "Early Voting and the 2008 Elec-

tion," paper presented at the Ninth Annual State Politics and Policy Conference, Chapel Hill and Durham, NC, May 22–23, 2009.

53. Moshe Haspel and H. Gibbs Knotts, "Location, Location, Location: Precinct Placement and the Costs of Voting," *Journal of Politics*, 67/2 (2005): 560–573.

54. Adam J. Berinsky, "The Perverse Consequences of Electoral Reform in the United States," *American Politics Research*, 33/4 (2005): 471–491.

55. Dan Stein, president of the Federation for American Immigration Reform, testimony before the U.S. House of Representatives, Committee on House Administration, hearings on "Non-citizen Voting," June 22, 2006."

56. *Purcell v. Gonzales* (2006).

57. Michael P. McDonald, "Rocking the House: Competition and Turnout in the 2006 Midterm Election," *The Forum*, 4/3 (2006): 1–18.

58. Pew Research Center, "Regular Voters, Intermittent Voters, and Those Who Don't," October 18, 2006.

59. Pew Research Center, "Regular Voters, Intermittent Voters, and Those Who Don't."

60. Diana C. Mutz and Byron Reeves, "The New Videomalaise: Effects of Televised Incivility on Political Trust," *American Political Science Review*, 99/1 (2005): 1–15.

61. Stephen Ansolabehere and Shanto Iyengar, *Going Negative: How Political Advertisements Shrink and Polarize the Electorate* (New York: The Free Press, 1995).

62. Joshua Clinton and John Lapinski, " 'Targeted' Advertising and Voter Turnout: An Experimental Study of the 2000 Presidential Election," *Journal of Politics*, 66/1 (2004): 69–96.

63. Robert A. Jackson and Jason C. Sides, "Revisiting the Influence of Campaign Tone on Turnout in Sen-

ate Elections," *Political Analysis*, 14/2 (2006): 206–218. Also, Kim Fridkin Kahn and Patrick J. Kenney, *No Holds Barred: Negativity in U.S. Senate Campaigns* (Upper Saddle River, NJ: Pearson Education, 2004).

64. Deborah Jordan Brooks, "The Resilient Voter: Moving Toward Closure in the Debate over Negative Campaigning and Turnout," *Journal of Politics*, 68/3 (2006), p. 696.

65. Lisa Schur and Douglas Kruse, *Fact Sheet: Disability and Voter Turnout in the 2008 Elections* (New Brunswick, NJ: School of Management and Labor Relations, Rutgers University, nd).

66. Cindy D. Kam, Elizabeth J. Zechmeister, and Jennifer R. Wilking, "From the Gap to the Chasm: Gender and Participation among Non-Hispanic Whites and Mexican Americans," *Political Research Quarterly*, 61/2 (2008): 205–218.

67. Jack Citrin and Benjamin Highton, "Latino Political Integration Follows European Pattern," *Public Affairs Report*, 43/4 (2002), online.

68. Anil G. Jacob, "Asian American Political Participation: Research Challenges for an Emerging Minority," *PS: Political Science & Politics*, 39/1 (2006): 103–106.

69. Luis R. Fraga and Gary Segura, "Culture Clash? Contesting Notions of American Identity and the Effects of Latin American Immigration," *Perspectives on Politics*, 4/2 (2006): 279–287. Also, Gary Segura, Stephen P. Nicholson, and Adrian D. Pantoja, "Explaining the Latino Vote: Issue Voting among Latinos in the 2000 Presidential Election," *Political Research Quarterly*, 59/2 (2006): 259–271.

70. Jun Xu, "Why Do Minorities Participate Less? The Effects of Immigration, Education, and Electoral Process on Asian American Voter Registration and Turnout," *Social Science Research*, 34/4 (2005): 682–702.

71. Claudine Gay, "The Effect of Black Congressional Representation on Political Participation," *American Political Science Review*, 95 (2001): 589–602; Jane Mansbridge. "Should Blacks Represent Blacks and Women Represent Women? A Contingent 'Yes,' " *Journal of Politics*, 62 (1999): 628–657; Susan A. Banducci, Todd Donovan, and Jeffrey A. Karp, "Minority Representation, Empowerment, and Participation," *Journal of Politics*, 66/2 (2004): 534–556; Karen M. Kaufmann, "Black and Latino Voters in Denver: Responses to Each Other's Political Leadership," *Political Science Quarterly*, 118/1 (2003): 107–112.

72. Christopher R. Ellis, Joseph Daniel Ura, and Jenna Ashley-Robinson, "The Dynamic Consequences of Nonvoting in American National Elections," *Political Research Quarterly*, 59/2 (2006): 227–233; Zoltan Hajnal and Jessica Trounstine, "Where Turnout Matters: The Consequences of Uneven Turnout in City Politics," *Journal of Politics*, 67/2 (2005): 515–535; Michael D. Martinez and Jeff Gill, "The Effects of Turnout on Partisan Outcomes in U.S. Presidential Elections 1960–2000," *Journal of Politics*, 67/4 (2005): 1248–1274; Jack Citrin, Eric Schickler, and John Sides, "What If Everyone Voted? Simulating the Impact of Increased Turnout in Senate Elections," *American Journal of Political Science*, 47/1 (2003): 75–90; Benjamin Highton and Raymond E. Wolfinger, "The Political Implications of Higher Turnout," *British Journal of Political Science*, 31/1 (2001): 179–233.

73. Mark D. Brewer, "The Rise of Partisanship and the Expansion of Partisan Conflict within the American Electorate," *Political Research Quarterly*, 58/2 (2005): 219–229.

74. Franco Matteia and Joshua Glasgow, "Presidential Coattails, Incumbency Advantage, and Open Seats: A District-Level Analysis of the 1976–2000 U.S. House Elections," *Electoral Studies*, 24/4 (2005): 619–641.

75. Pew Research Center report, October 22, 2008.

76. Pew Research Center report, April 15, 2007.

77. Pew Research Center report, October 18, 2006.

78. For the continuing importance of partisan loyalties in congressional elections, see Larry M. Bartels, "Partisanship and Voting Behavior, 1952–1996," *American Journal of Political Science*, 44 (2000): 35–50.

79. Alan I. Abramowitz, Brad Alexandera, and Matthew Gunning, "Incumbency, Redistricting, and the Decline of Competition in U.S. House Elections," *Journal of Politics*, 68/1 (2006): 75–88.

80. Markus Prior, "The Incumbent in the Living Room: The Rise of Television and the Incumbency Advantage in U.S. House Elections," *Journal of Politics*, 88/3 (2006): 657–692.

81. David W. Romero, "What They Do *Does* Matter: Incumbent Resource Allocations and the Individual House Vote," *Political Behavior*, 28/3 (2006): 241–258.

82. Alan I. Abramowitz, Brad Alexander, and Matthew Gunning, "Incumbency, Redistricting, and the Decline of Competition in U.S. House Elections," pp. 75–106.

83. Barbara Hinckley, "House Re-Elections and Senate Defeats: The Role of the Challenger," *British Journal of Political Science*, 10/3 (1980): 441–460.

84. Drew Weston, *The Political Brain: The Role of Emotion in Deciding the Fate of the Nation* (Cambridge, MA: Perseus Books, 2007), p. 418.

85. Jennifer Wolak, "The Consequences of Concurrent Campaigns for Citizen Knowledge of Congressional

Candidates," *Political Behavior*, 31 (2009): 211–229.

86. CBS News poll, March 18–21, 2010. Data provided by The Roper Center.

87. NBC News/*Wall Street Journal* poll, June, 2006. Data provided by The Roper Center.

88. Steven S. Smith, Jason Roberts, and Ryan Vander Wielen, "Congressional Elections and Policy Alignments," chapter 4 of *The American Congress*, 3rd edition (Boston: Houghton Mifflin, 2002).

89. Herbert F. Weisberg, "The One Thing You Need to Know about Voting in American Presidential Elections," Paper prepared for presentation at the Conference in Honor of Richard G. Niemi, Rochester, NY, November 3, 2007.

90. CNN poll, June 2008. Data from The Roper Center.

91. Martin P. Wattenberg, "Elections: Reliability Trumps Competence: Personal Attributes in the 2004 Presidential Election," *Presidential Studies Quarterly*, 36/4 (2006): 705–713.

92. All poll questions in this section are drawn from polls by national organization after the third presidential debate in October 2004. Data provided by The Roper Center.

93. George Washington University Battleground Survey, October 2008. Data provided by The Roper Center.

94. IPOS-Public Affairs/McClatchy poll, October 2008. Data provided by The Roper Center.

95. Erika Falk and Kate Kenski, "Issue Saliency and Gender Stereotypes: Support for Women as Presidents in Times of War and Terrorism," *Social Science Quarterly*, 87/1 (2006): 1–23. Also Michele Swers, "Building a Reputation on National Security: The Impact of Stereotypes Related to Gender and Military Experience," *Legislative Studies Quarterly*, 32/4 (2007): 559–595.

96. Kenski and Jamieson, "Issue Knowledge and Perceptions of Agreement in the 2004 Presidential General Election."

97. Pew Research Center report, October 27, 2004.

98. Richard Nadeau and Michael S. Lewis-Beck, "National Economic Voting in U.S. Presidential Elections," *Journal of Politics*, 63/1 (2001): 159–181.

99. Douglas A. Hibbs, Jr., "Bread and Peace Voting in U.S. Presidential Elections," *Public Choice,* 104/1 (2000): 149–180.

100. Andrew J. Healy, Neil A. Malhotra, and Cecilia Hyunjung Mo, "Euphoria and Retrospective Voting," May 12, 2009; unpublished paper available at SSRN: http://ssrn.com/abstract=1403606.

101. Kristin Michelitch, Marco Morales-Barba, Andrew Owen, and Joshua Tucker," Old Wine in a New and Improved Bottle: Prospective Economic Voting in the 2008 US Presidential Elections," Unpublished draft paper prepared for NYU in-house workshop, December 8, 2009, on the Web at http://politics.as.nyu.edu/docs/IO/12796/in_house_120809.pdf.

102. *New York Times,* June 17, 2008.

103. CBS News poll, October 2008. Data provided by The Roper Center.

104. Democracy Corps poll October 2008. Data provided by The Roper Center.

105. Darshan J. Goux and David A. Hopkins, "The Empirical Implications of Electoral College Reform," *American Politics Research*, 36/6 (2008): 857–879.

CHAPTER 11

1. Tinsley E. Yarbrough, *Race and Redistricting: The Shaw-Cromartie Cases* (Lawrence: University of Kansas Press, 2002).

2. *Shaw v. Reno* (1993).

3. On the debate over whether racial gerrymandering actually helps the Republican Party, read Kenneth W. Shotts, "The Effect of Majority-Minority Mandates on Partisan Gerrymandering," *American Journal of Political Science*, 45/1 (2001): 120–135; and Kenneth W. Shotts, "Does Racial Redistricting Cause Conservative Policy Outcomes? Policy Preferences of Southern Representatives in the 1980s and 1990s," *Journal of Politics*, 65/1 (2003): 216–227.

4. *Easley v. Cromartie* (2001).

5. David T. Cannon, *Race, Redistricting, and Representation* (Chicago: University of Chicago Press, 1999). Research indicates that blacks are of mixed mind on racial gerrymandering. They support changes in electoral laws to increase black representation, but they do not support overtly creating majority-minority districts. On this point, see Katherine Tate, "Black Opinion on the Legitimacy of Racial Redistricting and Minority-Majority Districts," *American Political Science Review*, 97/1 (2003): 45–57.

6. Louis Fisher, *On Appreciating Congress: The People's Branch* (Boulder, CO: Paradigm Publishers, 2010).

7. Gerald R. Ford, address at the University of Florida, Gainesville, November 3, 1966, published in Michael V. Doyle, ed., *Gerald R. Ford Selected Speeches* (Arlington, VA: R. W. Beatty, 1973), p. 114.

8. Quoted in John T. Rourke, Ralph G. Carter, and Mark A. Boyer, *Making American Foreign Policy* (Guilford, CT: Dushkin, 1994), p. 234.

9. Quotes are from the Records of the Constitutional Convention found in Daniel Wirls and Stephen Wirls, *The Invention of the United States Senate* (Baltimore, MD: Johns Hopkins Press, 2004), pp. 87–88.

10. David R. Mayhew, *The Electoral Connection* (New Haven, CT: Yale University Press, 1974).

11. Gerhard Loewenberg, *On Legislatures: The Puzzle of Representation* (Boulder, CO: Paradigm Publishers, 2010).

12. *U.S. Term Limits, Inc. v. Thornton* (1995).

13. Edward J. López, "Term Limits: Causes and Consequences," *Public Choice*, 114/1 (2003): 1–56.

14. John M. Carey, Richard G. Niemi, Lynda W. Powell, and Gary F. Moncrief, *Legislative Studies Quarterly*, 31/1 (2006): 105–134; Leslie A. Schwindt-Bayer, "The Incumbency Disadvantage and Women's Election to Legislative Office," *Electoral Studies*, 24/2 (2005): 227–244; Stanley M. Caress, Charles Elder, Richard Elling, Jean-Philippe Faletta, Shannon K. Orr, Eric Rader, Marjorie Sarbaugh-Thompson, John Strate, and Lyke Thompson, et al., "The Effect of Term Limits on the Election of Minority State Legislators," *State and Local Government Review*, 35/3 (2003): 183–95.

15. Monica P. Escaleras and Peter T. Calcagno, "Does the Gubernatorial Term Limit Type Affect State Government Expenditures?" *Public Finance Review*, 37/5 (2009): 572–595; H. Abbie Erler, "Legislative Term Limits and State Spending, *Public Choice,* 133/3 (2007): 479–494; Rebekah Herrick and Sue Thomas, "Do Term Limits Make a Difference? Ambition and Motivations among U.S. State Legislators," *American Politics Research*, 33/5 (2005): 726–747.

16. Fox News polls, March 2009 and June 2003. Data provided by the Roper Center.

17. An excellent discussion of the theories of representation is available in Hanna F. Pitkin, *The Concept of Representation* (Berkeley: University of California Press, 1967).

18. Donald J. McCrone and James H. Kuklinski, "The Delegate Theory of Representation," *American Journal of Political Science,* 23 (1979): 278–300.

19. Burke's widely quoted "Speech to the electors of Bristol" can be found in *The Works of the Right Honorable Edmund Burke*, Vol. II (New York: Oxford University Press, 1906).

20. The ironic view that packing, concentrating minorities in a few districts, actually lessens their influence in other districts to such a degree that, overall, the minority group loses influence in Congress can be found in David Lublin, *The Paradox of Representation: Racial Gerrymandering and Minority Interests in Congress* (Princeton, NJ: Princeton University Press, 1999).

21. Christian R. Grose, "Beyond the Vote: A Theory of Black Representation in Congress," paper presented at the meeting of American Political Science Association, August 2002, Boston, MA, p. 1. Also see Katherine Tate, "The Political Representation of Blacks in Congress: Does Race Matter," *Legislative Studies Quarterly,* 26/4 (2001): 622–638; and Kenny J. Whitby and George A. Krause, "Race, Issue Heterogeneity and Public Policy: The Republican Revolution in the 104th US Congress and the Representation of African-American Policy Interests," *British Journal of Political Science*, 31/3 (2001): 555–573.

22. L. Marvin Overby, Robert D. Brown, John M. Bruce, Charles E. Smith, Jr., and John W. Winkle, III, "Race, Political Empowerment, and Minority Perceptions of Judicial Fairness," *Social Science Quarterly*, 86/2 (2005): 444–469; Claudine Gay, "The Effect of Black Congressional Representation on Political Participation," *American Political Science Review*, 95 (2001): 589–602; Adrian D. Pantoja and Gary Segura, "Does Ethnicity Matter? Descriptive Representation in the Statehouse and Political Alienation among Latinos," *Social Science Quarterly*, 84/2 (2003): 441–460; Lonna Rae Atkeson and Nancy Carrillo, "More is Better: The Impact of Female Descriptive Representation on Citizen Attitudes toward Government Responsiveness," *Gender and Politics*, 3/1 (2007): 79–101; and Jane Mansbridge, "Should Blacks Represent Blacks and Women Represent Women? A Contingent 'Yes'," *Journal of Politics*, 62 (1999): 628–657.

23. *The Charlotte Observer*, February 21, 1997.

24. Suzanne Dovi, "Preferable Descriptive Representatives: Will Just Any Woman, Black, or Latino Do?" *American Political Science Review,* 96/4 (2002): 729–743.

25. Robert R. Preuhs, "The Conditional Effects of Minority Descriptive Representation: Black Legislators and Policy Influence in the American States," *Journal of Politics*, 68/3 (2006): 585–599; Susan A. Banducci, Todd Donovan, and Jeffrey A. Karp, "Minority Representation, Empowerment, and Participation," *Journal of Politics*, 66/2 (2004): 534–556; John R. Petrocik and Scott W. Desposato, "The Partisan Consequences of Majority/Minority Redistricting in the South, 1992 and 1994," *Journal of Politics*, 60/4 (1998): 613–633.

26. For those expressing doubt about the efficacy of majority-minority districts, see Jason Barabas and Jennifer Jerit, "Redistricting Principles and Racial Representation," *State Politics and Policy Quarterly*, 4/4 (Winter 2004): 415–435.

27. David Lublin. *The Paradox of Representation, p. 121.*

28. L. Marvin Overby and Kenneth M. Cosgrove, "Unintended Consequences? Racial Redistricting and the Representation of Minority

Interests," *Journal of Politics*, 58/2 (1996): 540–550. Rejecting this view is Shotts, "The Effect of Majority-Minority Mandates on Partisan Gerrymandering"; and Shotts, "Does Racial Redistricting Cause Conservative Policy Outcomes?

29. John D. Griffin and Michael Keene, "Are African Americans Effectively Represented in Congress?" *Political Research Quarterly*, forthcoming in vol. 63 (2010), but with an abstract available online at http://prq.sagepub.com/content/early/2009/07/17/1065912909340894.abstract.

30. *League of United Latin American Citizens v. Perry* (2006).

31. *Bartlett v. Strickland* (2009).

32. Stephen Ansolabehere, James M. Snyder, Jr., and Charles Stewart, "The Effects of Party and Preferences on Congressional Roll-Call Voting, *Legislative Studies Quarterly*, 26/4 (2001): 533–572.

33. Roger H. Davidson and Walter J. Olezek, *Congress and its Members*, 8th edition (Washington, DC: Congressional Quarterly Press, 2002), p. 274.

34. C. James Delaet and James M. Scott, "Treaty-Making and Partisan Politics: Arms Control and the U.S. Senate, 1960–2001," *Foreign Policy Analysis*, 2/2 (2006): 177–201.

35. *Congressional Quarterly Weekly Report*, January 23, 2009, and February 3, 2008.

36. Keith T. Poole and Howard Rosenthal, *Ideology and Congress* (New Brunswick, NJ: Transaction Publishers, 2007).

37. Stephen Ansolabehere, James M. Snyder, Jr., and Charles Stewart, III, "Candidate Positioning in U.S. House Elections," *American Journal of Political Science*, 45/1 (2001): 136–159.

38. NES Guide to Public Opinion and Electoral Behavior, surveys from 1960–1992.

39. Robert S. Erikson, "Constituency Opinion and Congressional Behavior," *American Journal of Political Science*, 22/3 (1978): 511–535. Also see Alan Monroe, "Consistency Between Public Preferences and National Policy Decisions," *American Politics Quarterly*, 7/1 (1979): 3–19.

40. Eric D. Lawrence, Forrest Maltzman, and Steven S. Smith, "Who Wins? Party Effects in Legislative Voting," *Legislative Studies Quarterly*, 31/1 (2006): 33–69; Gary W. Cox and Mathew D. McCubbins, *Setting the Agenda: Responsible Party Government in the U.S. House of Representatives* (New York: Cambridge University Press, 2005); Gary W. Cox and Keith T. Poole, "On Measuring Partisanship in Roll-Call Voting: The U.S. House of Representatives, 1877–1999," *American Journal of Political Science*, 46/3 (2002): 477–489.

41. James M. Snyder, Jr., and Tim Groseclose, "Estimating Party Influence in Congressional Roll-Call Voting," *American Journal of Political Science*, 44/2 (2000), pp. 193–211; Nolan McCarty, Keith T. Poole, and Howard Rosenthal, "The Hunt for Party Discipline in Congress," *American Political Science Review*, 95/3 (2001): 673–687.

42. Nathan W. Monroe, Jason M. Roberts, and David W. Rohde, *Why Not Parties? Party Effects in the United States Senate* (Chicago: University of Chicago Press, 2008).

43. The classic study of the relationship of members and their constituencies is Richard F. Fenno, Jr., *Home Style* (Boston: Little Brown, 1978). Also valuable is R. Douglas Arnold, *The Logic of Congressional Action* (New Haven, CT: Yale University Press, 1990).

44. Warren E. Miller and Donald E. Stokes, "Constituency Influence in Congress," *American Political Science Review*, 57/1 (1963): 45–57. Also, John E. Jackson, *Constituencies and Leaders in Congress* (Cambridge, MA: Harvard University Press, 1974).

45. Benjamin Bishin, "Constituency Influence in Congress: Does Subconstituency Matter?" *Legislative Studies Quarterly*, 25/3 (2000): 389–415.

46. Joshua D. Clinton, "Representation in Congress: Constituents and Roll Calls in the 106th House," *Journal of Politics*, 68/2 (2006): 397–419. Also, Jeff Manza and Fay Lomax Cook, "A Democratic Polity? Three Views of Policy Responsiveness to Public Opinion in the United States," *American Politics Research*, 30/6 (2002): 630–667.

47. Paul Burstein, "Why Estimates of the Impact of Public Opinion on Public Policy are Too High: Empirical and Theoretical Implications," *Social Forces*, 84/4 (2006): 2273–2289.

48. James H. Kuklinski, "Representative-Constituency Linkages: A Review Article," *Legislative Studies Quarterly*, 4/1 (1979), p. 132.

49. Martin Gilens, "Inequality and Democratic Responsiveness," *Public Opinion Quarterly*, 69/5 (2005): 778–796.

50. A list of CMOs can be found on the Website of House Committee on Administration at www.house.gov/.

51. Neil Pinney and George Serra, "A Voice for Black Interests: Congressional Black Caucus Cohesion and Bill Cosponsorship," *Congress and the Presidency*, 29/1 (2002): 69–86.

52. Michael S. Rocca, Gabriel R. Sanchez, and Joseph Uscinski, Personal Attributes and Latino Voting Behavior in Congress," *Social Science Quarterly*, 89/2 (2008): 392–405.

53. Heinz Eulau, John C. Wahlke, William Buchanan, and Leroy C. Ferguson, "The Role of the Repre-

sentative: Some Empirical Observations on the Theory of Edmund Burke," *American Political Science Review*, 53/3 (1959): 742–756.

54. Diana Evans. *Greasing the Wheels: Using Pork Barrel Projects to Build Majority Coalitions in Congress* (New York: Cambridge University Press, 2004).

55. Steven J. Balla, Eric D. Lawrence, Forrest Maltzman, and Lee Sigelman, "Partisanship, Blame Avoidance, and the Distribution of Legislative Pork," *American Journal of Political Science*, 46/3 (2002): 515–525.

56. Scott A. Frisch and Sean Q. Kelly, *Cheese Factories on the Moon: Why Earmarks Are Good for American Democracy* (Boulder, CO: Paradigm Publishers, 2010).

57. Philip Norton, "How Many Bicameral Legislatures Are There?" *Journal of Legislative Studies*, 10/4 (2004): 1–9; George Tsebelis and Jeannette Money, *Bicameralism* (New York: Cambridge University Press 1997).

58. A study that finds bicameralism contributes to stability is William P. Bottom, Cheryl L. Eavey, Gary J. Miller, and Jennifer Nicoll Victor, "The Institutional Effect on Majority Rule Instability: Bicameralism in Spatial Policy Decisions," *American Journal of Political Science*, 44/3 (2000): 523–540.

59. Rose K. Baker, *House and Senate*, 2nd edition (New York: W. W. Norton, 1995).

60. Kenneth N. Bickers and Robert M. Stein, "The Congressional Pork Barrel in a Republican Era," *Journal of Politics*, 62/4 (2002): 1070–1057.

61. Cindy Simon Rosenthal and Ronald M. Peters, Jr., "Who Is Nancy Pelosi?" *PS: Political Science & Politics*, 41/1 (2008): 57–62.

62. Representative Gene Taylor (D-MS), quoted in the *Miami Herald*, April 8, 2009.

63. Representative John Larson (D-CT), quoted in John Bresnahan, "Pelosi's Power Reigns Supreme," Politico.com, November 12, 2008.

64. Unidentified House Democrat quoted in Bresnahan, "Pelosi's Power Reigns Supreme."

65. *Time*, November 15, 2010.

66. Anthony Madonna, "Questions of Order in the U.S. Senate: Moving Towards a Static Interpretation of Precedent," paper presented at the annual meeting of the Southern Political Science Association, New Orleans, LA, 2007.

67. Lee Hamilton, "Power in Congress," Center on Congress at Indiana University, n.d., on the Web at http://congress.indiana.edu/outreach/opeds/oped33.htm.

68. *Washington Post*, January 13, 2003. The House Democrat was David Obey (D-WI).

69. Julian E. Zelizer, "Congress Taps Forgotten Power," *Washington Independent*, September 25, 2008.

70. Scott A. Frisch and Sean Q. Kelly, *Committee Assignment Politics in the U.S. House of Representatives* (Norman: University of Oklahoma Press, 2006), especially chapter 3.

71. Jonathan Woon, "Issue Attention and Legislative Proposals in the U.S. Senate," *Legislative Studies Quarterly*, 34/1 (2009): 29–54.

72. E. Scott Adler, "Constituency Characteristics and the 'Guardian' Model of Appropriations Subcommittees, 1959–1998," *American Journal of Political Science*, 44 (2000): 104–114.

73. Thomas M. Carsey and Barry Rundquist, "The Reciprocal Relationship Between State Defense Interest and Committee Representation in Congress," *Public Choice*, 99/3 (1999): 455–463.

74. Mark S. Hurwitz, Roger J. Moiles, and David W. Rohde, "Distributive and Partisan Issues in Agriculture Policy in the 104th House," *American Political Science Review*, 95/4 (2001): 911–922.

75. Christine DeGregorio and Kevin Snider, "Leadership Appeal in the U.S. House of Representatives: Comparing Officeholders and Aides," *Legislative Studies Quarterly*, 20/4 (1995): 491–511.

76. Alexis Simendinger, "Davis Marshals the Majority in the Senate," *National Journal*, October 3, 2009, online.

77. Roll Call.com, "The Roll Call Fabulous Fifty," Sept. 22, 2008, online at www.rollcall.com/features/Guide-to-Congress_2008.

78. Simendinger, "Davis Marshals the Majority in the Senate."

79. Curt Ziniel, "Descriptive Representation in Congressional Offices, " paper presented at the annual meeting of the Western Political Science Association, Las Vegas, Nevada, March 8, 2007, p. 18. Also, Christian R. Grose, Maurice Mangum, and Christopher Martin, "Race, Political Empowerment, and Constituency Service: Descriptive Representation and the Hiring of African-American Congressional Staff," *Polity*, 39/4 (2007): 449–478.

80. Daniel Diermeier and Timothy J. Feddersen, "Information and Congressional Hearings," *American Journal of Political Science*, 44/1 (2000): 51–65.

81. Jon R. Bond, Richard Fleisher, and Glen S. Krutz, "Malign Neglect: Evidence That Delay Has Become the Primary Method of Defeating Presidential Appointments," *Congress & the Presidency*, 36/3 (2009): 226–243. The 2,610 posts were judges on the Supreme Court and Court of Appeals, Cabinet officers, top Executive Office officials of the President, and independent agency and government corporation heads.

82. Bond, Fleisher, and Krutz, "Malign Neglect."

83. Brandon Rottinghaus and Daniel E. Bergan "The Politics of Requesting Appointments: Congressional Requests in the Appointment and Nomination Process," *Political Research Quarterly,* forthcoming in volume 63 (2010), but with an abstract available online at http://prq.sagepub.com/content/early/2009/08/26/1065912909343582.abstract.

84. *Washington Post,* June 9, 2007.

85. Bond, Fleisher, and Krutz, "Malign Neglect."

86. Terry L. Deibel, "The Death of a Treaty," *Foreign Affairs,* 81/5 (2002): 142–161.

87. Dan Caldwell, "The Carter Administration, the Senate, and SALT II," in *Jimmy Carter: Foreign Policy and Post-Presidential Year,* Herbert D. Rosenbaum and Alexej Ugrinsky, eds. (Westport, CT: Greenwood Press, 1994), p. 352.

88. David P. Auerswald, "Senate Reservations to Security Treaties," *Foreign Policy Analysis,* 2/1 (2006): 83–100.

89. Frederick W. Mayer, *Interpreting NAFTA: The Science and Art of Political Analysis* (New York: Columbia University Press, 1998). Also, Sharyl Cross, "Congress, the Executive and the United States-Mexico Free Trade Agreement," *Presidential Studies Quarterly,* 26/2 (1996): 425–434.

90. Robert D. Putnam, "Diplomacy and Domestic Politics: The Logic of Two-level Games," *International Organization,* 42/4 (1988): 427–460.

91. Eric Redman, *Dance of Legislation* (Seattle: University of Washington Press, 2000). First published in 1974 by Simon and Schuster. Also see, Barbara Sinclair, *Unorthodox Lawmaking: New Legislative Processes in the U.S. Congress* (Washington, DC: Congressional Quarterly, 1997).

92. Jeffery C. Talbertal and Matthew Potoski, "Setting the Legislative Agenda: The Dimensional Structure of Bill Cosponsoring and Floor Voting," *Journal of Politics,* 64/4 (2002): 864–891.

93. Jonathan Woon, "Issue Attention and Legislative Proposals in the U.S. Senate," *Legislative Studies Quarterly,* 34/1 (2009): 29–54; Glen S. Krutz and Justin Lebeau, "Recurring Bills and the Legislative Process in the U.S. Congress," *Journal of Legislative Studies,* 12/1 (2006): 98–109; Andy Baker and Corey Cook, "Representing Black Interests and Promoting Black Culture: The Importance of African American Descriptive Representation in the U.S. House," *Du Bois Review,* 2/2 (2005): 227–246.

94. Michelle A. Barnello and Kathleen A. Bratton, "Bridging the Gender Gap in Bill Sponsorship," *Legislative Studies Quarterly,* 32/3 (2007): 449–474; Wendy J. Schiller, "Building Careers and Courting Constituents: U.S. Senate Representation, 1889–1924," *Studies in American Political Development,* 20/2 (2006): 185–197; James C. Garand and Kelly M. Burke, "Legislative Activity and the 1994 Republican Takeover: Exploring Changing Patterns of Sponsorship and Cosponsorship in the U.S. House," *American Politics Research,* 34/2 (2006): 159–188; and Tracy Sulkin, *Issue Politics in Congress* (New York: Cambridge University Press, 2005).

95. Roger H. Davidson, Walter J. Oleszek, and Thomas Kephart, "One Bill, Many Committees: Multiple Referrals in the U.S. House of Representatives," *Legislative Studies Quarterly,* 13/1 (1988): 3–28.

96. *Washington Post,* October 8, 2009.

97. Gregory J. Wawro and Eric Schickler, *Filibuster: Obstruction and Lawmaking in the U.S. Senate* (Princeton, NJ: Princeton University Press, 2006).

98. David R. Mayhew, "Supermajority Rule in the U.S. Senate," *PS: Political Science & Politics,* 36/1 (2003): 31–36.

99. Alison B. Alter and Leslie Moscow McGranahan, "Reexamining the Filibuster and Proposal Powers in the Senate," *Legislative Studies Quarterly,* 25/2 (2000): 259–284. For an analysis of when filibusters are used, consult Sarah A. Binder, Eric D. Lawrence, and Steven S. Smith, "Tracking The Filibuster, 1917 To 1996," *American Politics Research,* 30/4 (2002): 406–422.

100. Testimony of Steven S. Smith and Kate M. Gregg during hearings before the Committee on Rules and Administration, United States Senate, May 19, 2010.

101. For filibusters through 2006, this section relies on Lauren Cohen Bell and L. Marvin Overby, "Extended Debate Over Time: Patterns and Trends in the History of Filibusters in the U.S. Senate," paper presented at the Midwest Political Science Association convention, Chicago Illinois, 2007. For cloture motions and votes, the source is the Historian of the United States Senate on the Web at www.senate.gov/pagelayout/reference/cloture_motions/. In addition to the problems counting filibusters mentioned in the main commentary, there are also problems with using cloture motions and cloture votes to measure filibuster activity. Neither of these measures gives a complete picture either because Senate parliamentary maneuvering means that some filibusters evoke no cloture motion or vote and some evoke more than one cloture motion and cloture vote. Additionally, some cloture motions that never come to a vote are meaningless tactical maneuvers, while other may not come to a vote because one side or the other gives way.

102. Jeffrey Lazarus and Nathan W. Monroe, "The Speaker's Discretion:

Conference Committee Appointments in the 97th through 106th Congresses," *Political Research Quarterly*, 60/4 (2007): 593–606. Also, Elizabeth Rybicki, "Conference Committee and Related Procedures: An Introduction," Congressional Research Service Report for Congress, No. 96–708, November 6, 2007.

103. Charles Cameron, *Veto Bargaining: Presidents and the Politics of Negative Power* (New York: Cambridge University Press, 2000).

104. A good analysis of American attitudes toward Congress is John R. Hibbing and Elizabeth Theiss-Morse, *Congress as Public Enemy: Public Attitudes Toward American Political Institutions* (New York: Cambridge University Press, 1995).

105. Patricia A. Hurley and Kim Quaile Hill, "Beyond the Demand-Input Model: A Theory of Representational Linkages," *Journal of Politics*, 65/2 (2003): 304–327.

106. James Shoch, *Trading Blows: Party Competition and U.S. Trade Policy in a Globalizing Era* (Chapel Hill: University of North Carolina Press, 2001).

107. David R. Mayhew, *Divided We Govern: Party Control, Lawmaking, and Investigations, 1946–1990* (New Haven: Yale University Press, 1991); Sean Kelly, "Divided We Govern: A Reassessment," *Polity*, 25/3 (1993): 475–484; and Sarah H. Binder, "The Dynamics of Legislative Gridlock, 1947–1996," *American Political Science Review*, 93/3 (1999): 519–534.

108. Gregory Wawro, "A Panel Probit Analysis of Campaign Contributions and Roll-Call Votes," *American Journal of Political* Science, 45/3 (2001): 563–579.

109. ABC News poll, September 1994. Data provided by The Roper Center. The actual results were 19% of respondents wanted to abolish Congress, 79% want to continue it, and 2% were undecided.

CHAPTER 12

1. Unattributed, "Not Born in the USA: Should Foreign-Born Citizens Be Allowed to Run for President?" *Current Events*, online, January 14, 2005.

2. Sarah P. Herlihy, "Amending The Natural Born Citizen Requirement: Globalization as the Impetus and the Obstacle," *Chicago Kent Law Review*, 81 (2006): 275–300.

3. *USA Today*/CNN/Gallup poll, November 2004. Data provided by The Roper Center for Public Opinion Research, University of Connecticut.

4. Bartholomew H. Sparrow, "Who Speaks for the People? The President, the Press, and Public Opinion in the United States," *Presidential Studies Quarterly*, 38/4 (2008), p. 578.

5. Quoted in David F. Schmitz, *The United States and Right-wing Dictatorships, 1965–1989* (New York: Cambridge University Press, 2006), p. 83.

6. All quotes from Charles Cobb, Jr., "Considering Colin Powell and Africa," *Foreign Service Journal*, March 2003, pp. 29–32.

7. *New York Times,* January 28, 1998.

8. Bert A. Rockman, "The American Presidency in Comparative Perspective: Systems, Situation, and Leaders," in *The Presidency and the Political System*, 11th edition, Michael Nelson, ed. (CQ Press: Washington, DC, 2006), pp. 28–56; Robert Elgie, "Semi-presidential: Concepts, Consequences, and Contesting Explanations," *Political Studies Review*, 2/3 (2004): 314–330; Alan Siaroff, "Comparative Presidencies: The Inadequacy of the Presidential, Semi-Presidential and Parliamentary Distinction, *European Journal of Political Research*, 42/3 (2003): 287–312.

9. Truman's remarks during a speech in Johnstown, Pennsylvania, October 22, 1952.

10. José Antonio Cheibub, "Presidentialism, Electoral Identifiability, and Budget Balances in Democratic Systems," *American Political Science Review*, 100/2 (2006): 353–368.

11. Pippa Norris, *Driving Democracy: Do Power Sharing Regimes Work?* (New York: Cambridge University Press, 2008).

12. Richard S. Conley, "Presidential Republics and Divided Government: Lawmaking and Executive Politics in the United States and France," *Political Science Quarterly,* 122/2 (2007): 253–285.

13. Bartholomew H. Sparrow, "Who Speaks for the People?" p. 578.

14. Joel K. Goldstein, "The Rising Power of the Modern Vice Presidency," *Presidential Studies Quarterly,* 38/3 (2008): 374–389.

15. Reuters, November 5, 2008.

16. Andrew Rundalevige, "The President and the Cabinet," in *The Presidency and the Political System*, p. 535.

17. Daily Briefing, January 27, 2003, GovExec.com.

18. George C. Edwards, III and Stephen J. Wayne, *Presidential Leadership*, 6th edition (New York: St. Martin's Press, 2003).

19. David B. Cohen, Chris J. Dolan, and Jerel A. Rosati, "A Place at the Table: The Emerging Foreign Policy Roles of the White House Chief of Staff," *Congress & the Presidency*, 29/2 (2002): 119–150.

20. All quotes from the *New York Times*, August 15, 2009, and the *Washington Post*, April 9, 2009. The White House official was senior political advisor David Axelrod.

21. Reuters, October 1, 2010.

22. Jerome L. Short, Colleen J. Shogan, and Nicole M. Owings, "The Influence of First Ladies on Mental Health Policy," *White House Studies*, 5/1 (2005): 65–76.

23. CNN.com, July 30, 2001.

24. *Politico*, February 4, 2009. The analyst was Mary Finch Hoyt, press secretary for Rosalynn Carter and a first ladies historian.

25. Gallup poll reports of July 28 and July 22, 2010.

26. *Boston Globe*, August 1, 2010.

27. Kenneth R. Mayer and Thomas J. Weko, "The Institutionalization of Power," in *Presidential Power: Forging the Presidency for the Twenty-First Century*, Robert Y. Shapiro, Martha Joynt Kumar, and Lawrence R. Jacobs, eds. (New York: Columbia University Press, 2000), p. 181.

28. John P. Burke, "The Institutionalized Presidency," in *The Presidency and the Political System*, p. 390.

29. Louis Fisher, "White House Aides Testifying before Congress," *Presidential Studies Quarterly*, 27 (Winter 1997), 135–152; Congressional Research Service, "Presidential Advisers' Testimony Before Congressional Committees: An Overview," document # RL31351, prepared by Harold C. Relyea and Jay R. Shampansky, April 14, 2004.

30. All quotes from the *Washington Post*, September 16, 2009.

31. Robert B. Reich, "Locked in the Cabinet," in *Understanding the Presidency* (New York: Longman, 2003), James Pfiffner and Roger H. Davidson, eds., p. 216.

32. *Washington Post* and *Baltimore Sun*, February 9, 2006.

33. White House, Office of the Press Secretary, transcript of "Remarks by the President in Live Phone Call to 'Imus in the Morning' Radio Talk Show, February 14, 1994.

34. Both quotes are from *Time*, September 19, 2005.

35. Johnson conversation with Attorney General Nicholas Katzenbach, April 17, 1965, quoted in Michael Beschloss, ed., *Reaching for Glory: Lyndon Johnson's Secret White House Tapes, 1964–1965* (New York: Simon & Schuster, 2001), p. 270.

36. Samuel Kernell, *Going Public: New Strategies of Presidential Leadership*, 3rd edition (Washington, DC: CQ Press, 1997).

37. Brandon Rottinghaus, " 'Dear Mr. President': The Institutionalization and Politicization of Public Opinion Mail in the White House," *Political Science Quarterly*, 121/3 (2006): 451–476. Also, Martha Joynt Kumar, "Communications Operations in the White House of President George W. Bush: Making News on His Terms," *Presidential Studies Quarterly*, 33/2 (2003): 1–29.

38. Fox News, February 10, 2010. Based on data gathered and conveyed Martha Joynt Kumar, who scrupulously tabulates presidential communication as a political science professor at Towson State University.

39. Data from the American Presidency Project.

40. Diana Owens and Richard Davis, "Presidential Communication in the Internet Era," *Presidential Studies Quarterly*, 38/4 (2008): 658–673.

41. Jeffrey E. Cohen, "If the News Is So Bad, Why Are Presidential Polls So High? Presidents, the News Media, and the Mass Public in an Era of New Media," *Presidential Studies Quarterly*, 34/3 (2004), especially Figures 1 and 2.

42. Brandon Rottinghaus, "Rethinking Presidential Responsiveness: The Public Presidency and Rhetorical Congruency, 1953–2001," *Journal of Politics*, 68/3 (2006): 720–732.

43. George C. Edwards, III, *The Strategic President: Persuasion and Opportunity in Presidential Leadership* (Princeton, NJ: Princeton University Press, 2009), p. 15. Also, Erwin C. Hargrove, *The Effective Presidency: Lessons on Leadership from John F. Kennedy to George W. Bush* (Boulder, CO: Paradigm Publishers, 2007).

44. Bruce Buchanan of the University of Texas, quoted a Reuters dispatch, January 3, 2007.

45. *Washington Post*, January 27, 2002.

46. Cabinet meeting of March 30, 1981, quoted in Rowland Evans and Robert Novak, *The Reagan Revolution* (New York: E.P. Dutton, 1981).

47. Gary Jacobson, a political scientist at the University of California at San Diego, quoted in the *Washington Post*, January 30, 2005.

48. Brendan J. Doherty, "The Politics of the Permanent Campaign: Presidential Travel and the Electoral College, 1977–2004," *Presidential Studies Quarterly*, 37/4 (2007): 749–773.

49. Valentino Larcinese, Leonzio Rizzo, and Cecilia Testa, "Allocating the U.S. Federal Budget to the States: The Impact of the President," *Journal of Politics*, 68/2 (2006): 447–456.

50. John J. Dilulio, "Inside the Bush Presidency: Reactions of an Academic Interloper," a paper presented at a conference, The Bush Presidency: An Early Assessment, at the Woodrow Wilson School, Princeton University, Princeton, NJ, May 27, 2003.

51. Dean Keith Simonton, "Presidential IQ, Openness, Intellectual Brilliance, and Leadership: Estimates and Correlations for 42 U.S. Chief Executives," *Political Psychology*, 27/4 (2006): 511–526.

52. Simonton, "Presidential IQ, Openness, Intellectual Brilliance, and Leadership," p. 520.

53. Stephen Benedict Dyson and Thomas Preston, "Individual Characteristics of Political Leaders and the Use of Analogy in Foreign Policy Decision Making," *Political Psychology*, 27/2 (2006): 265–293.

54. George R. Goethals, "Presidential Leadership," *Annual Review of Psychology*, 56 (2005): 545–570. Also, David G. Winter, "Things I've Learned about Personality from Studying Political Leaders at a Distance," *Journal of Personality*, 73/3 (2005): 545–570.

55. Steven J. Rubenzer and Thomas R. Faschingbauer, *Personality, Character, and Leadership in the White House: Psychologists Assess the Presidents* (London: Brassey's, 2004).

56. James D. Barber, *The Presidential Character: Predicting Performance in the White House* (Englewood Cliffs, NJ: Prentice-Hall, 1992).

57. Gerald Kellman, quoted in Stanley A. Renshon, "Psychological Reflections on Barack Obama and John McCain," *Political Science Quarterly*, 123/3 (2008), p. 398.

58. An early reporting of the use of the first quote is in the *Washington Post*, December 14, 2007. The second quote is from CBS News, December 14, 2007.

59. Thomas Preston, "The President's Inner Circle: Personality and Leadership Style in Foreign Policy Decision-making," in *Presidential Power*, Shapiro, Kumar, and Jacobs, eds. Also, Felix J. Thoemmes and Lucian Gideon Conway, III, "Integrative Complexity of 41 U.S. Presidents," *Political Psychology*, 28/2 (2007): 193–226.

60. Michael A. Genovese, *The Nixon Presidency* (Westport, CT: Greenwood, 1990), p. 117.

61. Robert E. Gibert, "President Ronald Reagan's Presidency: The Impact of an Alcoholic Parent," *Political Psychology*, 29/5 (2008): 737–765.

62. *Albany Times-Union*, November 10, 2002.

63. Jonathan R. T. Davidson, Kathryn M. Connor, and Marvin Swartz, "Mental Illness in U.S. Presidents Between 1776 and 1974: A Review of Biographical Sources," *Journal of Nervous & Mental Disease*, 194/1 (2006): 47–51.

64. Mary Caprioli, "Gendered Conflict," *Journal of Peace Research*, 37/1 (2000): 51–68; Mary Caprioli and Mark A. Boyer, "Gender, Violence, and International Crisis," *Journal of Conflict Resolution*, 45/4 (2001): 503–518; and Erik Melander, "Political Gender Equality and State Human Rights Abuses," *Journal of Peace Research*, 42/1 (2005): 149–166.

65. Harvey C. Mansfield, *Manliness* (New Haven, CT: Yale University Press, 2006); and Ivan Kenneally, "Mansfield, Harvey C., *Manliness*," (book review), *Perspectives on Political Science*, 35/2 (2006): 104–106.

66. Robert D. Dean, *Imperial Brotherhood: Gender and the Making of Cold War Foreign Policy* (Amherst, 2001), 221–224; and Randolph W. Baxter, "Butch vs. Femme During the Early Cold War: Deconstructing Hyper-Masculine Ideologies," *Peace & Change*, 30/4 (2005): 540–547.

67. The incident was related by former Supreme Court justice and Johnson's ambassador to the United Nations, Arthur Goldberg, and is quoted in Robert Dallek, *Flawed Giant: Lyndon and His Times, 1961–1973* (New York: Oxford University Press, 1988), p. 491.

68. Francis Fukuyama, "Woman and the Evolution of Politics," *Foreign Affairs*, 77/5 (1998): 24–40.

69. Rossiter, *American Presidency*, p. 18.

70. Quoted in "Harry Truman Speaks," observations by President Harry S. Truman compiled by Raymond H. Geselbracht, and found at the Harry S. Truman Presidential Library at www.trumanlibrary.org.

71. Quoted in Richard E. Neustadt, *Presidential Power: The Politics of Leadership* (New York: Wiley, 1960), p. 9.

72. Quoted from *The Autobiography of Theodore Roosevelt*, excerpted in Pfiffner and Davidson, eds., *Understanding the Presidency*, 3rd edition, p. 30.

73. Sidney M. Milkis and Michael Nelson, *The American Presidency: Origins & Development, 1776–1998*, 3rd edition (Washington, DC: CQ Press, 1999), p. xii.

74. Arthur M. Schlesinger, Jr., *The Imperial Presidency* (Boston: Houghton Mifflin, 1973).

75. Gary L. Rose, *The American Presidency Under Siege* (Albany: State University of New York Press, 1997). Also see Thomas M. Franck, ed., *The Tethered Presidency: Congressional Restraints on Executive Power* (New York: New York University Press, 1981).

76. Quoted in Hugh Sidey, *A Very Personal Presidency: Lyndon Johnson in the White House* (New York: Atheneum, 1968), p. 283.

77. Charles E. Walcott and Karen M. Hult, "White House Structure and Decision Making: Elaborating the Standard Model," *Presidential Studies Quarterly*, 35/2 (2005): 303–318. Also, David Mitchell, "Centralizing Advisory Systems: Presidential Influence and the U.S. Foreign Policy Decision-Making Process," *Foreign Policy Analysis*, 1/2 (2005): 181–206.

78. Mayer and Weko, "The Institutionalization of Power," p. 190.

79. David Stockman, quoted in James P. Pfiffner, *The Modern Presidency* (New York: St. Martin's Press, 1994), p. 73.

80. Christina Romer, head of the Council of Economic Advisers, quoted in the *Wall Street Journal*, August 9, 2009.

81. Michael A. Geneovese, *The Power of the American Presidency, 1789–2000* (New York: Oxford University Press, 2001), p. 157.

82. Quoted in Paul Quirk, "Presidential Competence," in *The Presidency and the Political System*, p. 153.

83. The first quote is by Genovese, *Power of the Presidency*, p. 173. The second quote is by Quirk, "Presidential Competence," p. 148.

84. Lyndon B. Johnson, *The Vantage Point: Perspective of the Presidency, 1963–1969* (New York: Holt, Rinehart & Winston, 1971), p. 443.

85. Senator John Thune (R-SD), quoted in the *Washington Post*, January 25, 2005.

86. Lyn Ragsdale, "Personal Power and the President," in *Presidential Power*, Shapiro, Kumar, and Jacobs, eds., p. 41. Also, Douglas D. Roscoe, "Electoral Messages from the District: Explaining Presidential Support in the U.S. House of Representatives," *Congress & the Presidency*, 30/1 (2003): 37–54.

87. Representative Bill Pascrell (D-NJ), quoted in *Politico*, November 5, 2009.

88. The strategist was Joe Trippi, quoted in the *Hartford Courant,* November 13, 2010.

89. Aaron Wildavsky, "The Two Presidencies," *Transaction*, 4 (1966): 7–14.

90. "Final Edited Transcript, Interview with Jimmy Carter," Carter Presidency Project, November 29, 1982, p. 54.

91. Richard Fleisher, Jon Bond, Glen Krutz, and Stephen Hanna, "The Demise of the Two Presidencies," *American Politics Quarterly*, 28/1 (2000): 3–25; Steven A. Shull, ed., *The Two Presidencies: A Quarter Century Assessment* (Chicago: Nelson-Hall, 1991).

92. Bryan W. Marshall and Richard L. Pacelle, Jr., "Revisiting the Two Presidencies: The Strategic Use of Executive Orders," *American Politics Research*, 33/6 (2006): 895–898; Brandice Canes-Wrone, William G. Howell, and David E. Lewis, "Executive Influence in Foreign versus Domestic Policy Making: Toward a Broader Understanding of Presidential Power," unpublished paper, 2005.

93. Sophia Moskalenko, Clark McCauley, and Paul Rozin, "Group Identification under Conditions of Threat: College Students' Attachment to Country, Family, Ethnicity, Religion, and University Before and After September 11, 2001," *Political Psychology*, 217/1 (2006): 77–98.

94. CBS News/*New York Times* poll, March 20–24, 2003. Data provided by The Roper Center.

95. Patrick James and Jean-Sebastian Rioux, "International Crises and Linkage Politics: The Experiences of the United States, 1953–1994," *Political Research Quarterly*, 51/3 (1998): 781–812. Also Marc J. Hetherington and Michael Nelson, "Anatomy of a Rally Effect: George W. Bush and the War on Terrorism," *Political Science and Politics*, 36/1 (2003): 37–42.

96. Harold J. Krent, *Presidential Powers* (New York: New York University Press, 2005), especially chapter 1.

97. Quoted in Thomas G. Paterson, J. Garry Clifford, and Kenneth J. Hagan, *American Foreign Relations*, 5th edition, Vol. 1: *A History to 1920* (Boston: Houghton Mifflin, 2000), p. 62.

98. David K. Nichols, *The Myth of the Modern Presidency* (University Park: Pennsylvania State University Press, 1994), p. 108.

99. Jasmine Farrier, *Passing the Buck: Congress, the Budget, and Deficits* (Lexington: University of Kentucky Press, 2004).

100. Donald R. Kinder and Corrine M. McConnaughy, "Military Triumph, Racial Transcendence, and Colin Powell," *Public Opinion Quarterly*, 70/2 (2006): 139–165.

101. "Final Edited Transcript, Interview with Jimmy Carter," November 29, 1982, p. 29.

102. Rebecca E. Deen and Laura W. Arnold, "Assessing Effectiveness of Veto Threats in the Bush Administration (1989–1993): Preliminary Evidence from Case Studies," *Congress & the Presidency*, 29/1 (2002): 47–68.

103. *Clinton v. the City of New York* (1998).

104. David Epstein and Sharyn O'Halloran, "The Institutional Face of Presidential Power: Congressional Delegation of Authority to the President," in *Presidential Power*, Shapiro, Kumar, and Jacobs, eds.

105. Andrew W. Barrett and Matthew Eshbaugh-Soha, "Presidential Success on the Substance of Legislation," *Political Research Quarterly*, 60/1 (2007): 100–112; Andrew W. Barrett. "Are All Presidential Legislative Successes Really Victories? Examining the Substance of Legislation," *White House Studies*, 5/2 (2005): 133–152; Andrew Rudalevige, *Managing the President's Program: Presidential Leadership and Legislative Policy Formulation* (Princeton, NJ: Princeton University Press, 2002), especially Table 7.2; and George C. Edwards, III, and Andrew Barrett, "Presidential Agenda Setting in Congress," in *Polarized Politics*, Jon R. Bond and Richard Fleisher, eds. (Washington, DC: CQ Press, 2000).

106. Congressional Research Service, *Presidential Directives: Background and Overview*, prepared by Harold C. Relyea, report #98-611, updated February 10, 2003.

107. Adam L. Warber, *Executive Orders and the Modern Presidency: Legislating from the Oval Office* (Boulder, CO: Lynne Rienner, 2005).

108. *Youngstown Sheet & Tube v. Sawyer* (1952).

109. Christopher S. Kelley and Bryan W. Marshall, "The Last Word: Presidential Power and the Role of Signing Statements," *Presidential Studies Quarterly*, 38/2 (2008): 248–267.

110. Obama's first eight presidential signing statements through November 2009.

111. Letter from Representatives Barney Frank, David Obey, and others to President Obama, quoted in the *New York Times*, August 8, 2009.

112. For a range of views on the war powers of the president and Congress, see Kenneth B. Moss, *Undeclared War and the Future of U.S. Foreign Policy* (Johns Hopkins University Press, 2008); William G. Howell and Jon C. Pevehouse, *While Dangers Gather: Congressional Checks on Presidential War Powers* (Princeton, NJ: Princeton University Press 2007); John Yoo, *The Powers of War and Peace: The Constitution and Foreign Affairs after 9/11* (University of Chicago Press, 2006); and Louis Fisher, *Presidential War Power* (Lawrence: University Press of Kansas, 2004).

113. "Authority of the President to Repel the Attack in Korea," (U.S.) *Department of State Bulletin*, 23 (July 31, 1950), p. 173, quoted in John T. Rourke, *Presidential Wars and American Democracy: Rally 'Round the Chief* (New York: Paragon House, 1993), p. 90.

114. Gary R. Hess, "Presidents and the Congressional War Resolutions of 1991 and 2002," *Political Science Quarterly*, 121/1 (2006): 93–118.

115. *Washington Post*, August 26, 2002.

116. Bush's comment was to the Texas State Republican Convention on June 20, 1992, quoted in Joles Lobel in testimony during hearings on "War Powers for the 21st Century: The Constitutional Perspective," before the Subcommittee on International Organizations, Human Rights and Oversight of the Committee on Foreign Affairs, U.S. House of Representatives, April 10, 2008.

117. *Washington Post*, January 27, 2007.

118. Paterson, Clifford, and Hagan, *American Foreign Relations*, Vol. I., *A History to 1920,* p. 58.

119. *New York Times*, October 23, 1994.

120. Quoted in "The President's Constitutional Authority to Conduct Military Operations Against Terrorists and Nations Supporting Them," Memorandum Opinion for the Deputy Counsel to the President, September 25, 2001.

121. *United States v. Curtiss-Wright Export Corp* (1936).

122. CNN, July 24 2007.

123. MSNBC, July 24, 2007.

124. Gordon S, Wood, "The Greatness of George Washington," *Virginia Quarterly Review*, 68 (1992), p. 192.

125. Glen S. Krutz and Jeffrey S. Peake, *Treaty Politics and the Rise of Executive Agreements: International Commitments in a System of Shared Powers* (Ann Arbor: University of Michigan Press, 2009).

126. Kiki Caruson and Victoria A. Farrar-Myers, "Promoting the President's Foreign Policy Agenda: Presidential Use of Executive Agreements as Policy Vehicles," *Political Research Quarterly*, 6/1 (2007): 631–644.

127. *Goldwater v. Carter* (1979).

128. *In Re Neagle* (1890).

129. *Gonzales v. Raich* (2005).

130. *Huffington Post,* February 26, 2009.

131. H. Abbie Erler, "Executive Clemency or Bureaucratic Discretion? Two Models of the Pardons Process," *Presidential Studies Quarterly*, 37/3 (2007): 427–448.

132. CBS News/*New York Times* poll, January 1977; and Harris Poll, September 1974. Data provided by The Roper Center.

133. Matthew J. Dickinson, "The President and Congress," in *The Presidency and the Political System*, p. 456.

134. Stephen P. Nicholson, Gary M. Segura, Nathan D. Woods, "Presidential Approval and the Mixed Blessing of Divided Government," *Journal of Politics,* 64/3 (2002): 701–720.

135. Paul J. Quirk and Bruce Nesmith, "Divided Government and Policy Making: Negotiating the Laws," in *The Presidency and the Political System*.

136. James L. Sundquist, "Needed: A Political Theory for a New Era of Coalition Government in the United States," *Political Science Quarterly*, 103/4 (1989): 613–635.

137. David R. Mayhew, *Divided We Govern: Party Control, Lawmaking, and Investigations, 1946–1990* (New Haven: Yale University Press, 1991).

138. NBC News/*Wall Street Journal* poll, December 1999. Data provided by The Roper Center.

139. David A. Yalof, "The Presidency and the Judiciary," in *The Presidency and the Political System*.

140. Lance T. LeLoup and Steven A. Shull, *The President and Congress: Collaboration and Combat in National Policy Making* (New York: Longman, 2003), Table 2.3, p. 51.

141. House Majority Leader Steny Hoyer (D-MD), quoted in U.S. State Department, "Term Limits Help Prevent Dictatorships," information paper, August 7, 2007.

142. Gideon Maltz, "The Case for Presidential Term Limits," *Journal of Democracy*, 18/1 (2007), p. 131.

143. *Washington Post*, January 28, 2005.

144. William G. Howell and Kenneth R. Mayer, "The Last One Hundred Days," *Presidential Studies Quarterly*, 35/3(2005): 533–551.

145. James P. Pfiffner, *The Strategic Presidency: Hitting the Ground Running* (Lawrence: University of Kansas Press, 1996), p. 5.

146. Jeffrey K. Tullis, "The Two Constitutional Presidencies," in *The Presidency and the Political System*, pp. 57–58.

147. Tullis, "The Two Constitutional Presidencies," pp. 57–58.

148. Neustadt, *Presidential Power*, p. 7.

149. Brownlow Committee, quoted in Richard W. Waterman, Hank C. Jenkins-Smith, and Carol L. Silva, "The Expectations Gap Thesis: Public Attitudes Toward the Incumbent President," *Journal of Politics*, 61/4 (1999): 944–966.

150. Sidey, *A Very Personal President*, p. 281

151. Richard E. Neustadt, *Presidential Power: The Politics of Leadership from FDR to Carter* (New York: Wiley & Sons, 1980), p. 10. First published in 1960 under a slightly different title.

152. Neustadt, *Presidential Power: The Politics of Leadership from FDR to Carter*, p. 9.

153. Harold F. Bass, Jr., W. Craig Bledsoe, Christopher J. Bosso, Daniel C. Diller, Dean J. Peterson, and James Brian Watts, *Powers of the Presidency* (Washington, DC: CQ Press, 1989), p. 182.

154. Dean G. Acheson, secretary of state under Harry Truman, quoted in John T. Rourke, Ralph G. Carter, and Mark A. Boyer, *Making American Foreign Policy*, 2nd edition (Madison, WI: Brown & Benchmark, 1996), p. 235.

155. Senator John Glenn (D-OH) on the issue of selling warplanes to Saudi Arabia, quoted in Mitchell Bard, "Ethnic Groups Influence on Middle East Policy—How and When," in *The Domestic Sources of American Foreign Policy: Insights and Evidence*, Charles W. Kegley, Jr. and Eugene Wittkopf, eds. (New York: St. Martin's, 1988), p. 59.

156. Quoted in Beschloss, *Reaching for Glory*, p. 425.

157. Doris A. Graber, *Mass Media & American Politics* (Washington, DC: CQ Press, 2006), Table 9-2, p. 253. Also see Roger E. Gilbert, "President Versus Congress: The Struggle for Public Attention," *Congress & the Presidency*, 16/1 (1989): 91–102.

158. Cohen, "If the News Is So Bad, Why Are Presidential Polls So High," pp. 493–515. Also Gary Young and William B. Perkins, "Presidential Rhetoric, the Public Agenda, and the End of Presidential Television's 'Golden Age,'" *Journal of Politics*, 67/4 (2005): 1190–1205.

159. Michael Bailey, Lee Sigelman, and Clyde Wilcox, "Presidential Persuasion on Social Issues: A Two-Way Street?" *Political Research Quarterly*, 56/1 (2003): 49–58.

160. Brandice Canes-Wrone, *Who Leads Whom? Presidents, Policy Making and the American Public* (Chicago: University of Chicago Press, 2005); George C. Edwards, III, *On Deaf Ears: The Limits of the Bully Pulpit* (New Haven: Yale University Press, 2003). Also, Reed L. Welch, "Presidential Success in Communicating with the Public through Televised Addresses," *Presidential Studies Quarterly*, 33/2 (2003): 347–365; and Jeffrey E. Cohen and John A. Hamman, "The Polls: Can Presidential Rhetoric Affect the Public's Economic Perceptions?" *Presidential Studies Quarterly*, 33/2 (2003): 408–529.

161. CNN, September 10, 2009.

162. Rasumssen Report, health-care opinion tracking poll.

163. Edwards, *The Strategic President*, p. 188.

164. Thomas E. Cronin and Michael A. Genovese. *The Paradoxes of the American Presidency* (New York: Oxford University Press, 1998); Stephen J. Wayne, "Evaluating the President: The Public's Perspective Through the Prism of Pollsters,"

White House Studies, 3/1 (2004): 35–30.

165. Thomas E. Cronin, *On the Presidency: Teacher, Soldier, Shaman, Pol* (Boulder, CO: Paradigm Publishers, 2008).

166. Theodore J. Lowi, *The Personal President* (Ithaca: Cornell University Press, 1985), p. 11, quoted in Richard G. Waterman and Hank C. Jenkins-Smith, "The Expectations Gap Thesis: Public Attitudes toward an Incumbent President," *Journal of Politics*, 61/4 (1999), p. 945.

CHAPTER 13

1. *Code of Federal Regulation*, Title 25, Section 83(c).

2. Quotes from the BIA memorandum are from the *Hartford Courant*, March 12, 2004.

3. *Code of Federal Regulation*, Title 25, Section 83(c).

4. Letter to Secretary of the Interior, *Hartford Courant*, March 17, 2004.

5. Robert Odawi Porter, law professor and director of the Center for Indigenous Law, Governance & Citizenship, Syracuse University, in an op-ed piece, "A Modern Indian War in the Making," *Hartford Courant*, May 2, 2004.

6. Letter from the inspector general, Department of the Interior to Senator Christopher Dodd, quoted in the *Hartford Courant*, September 1, 2004.

7. Sean Nicholson-Crotty, "Bureaucratic Competition in the Policy Process," *Policy Studies Journal*, 33/3 (2005): 341–368.

8. Staff, Committee on Foreign Relations, *Tora Bora Revisited: How We Failed to Get Bin Laden and Why It Matters Today*, A Report to Members of the Committee on Foreign Relations in the U.S. Senate, 111th Congress, November 20, 2009, p. 1.

9. Quoted in John T. Rourke, *Making Foreign Policy: United States, Soviet Union, China* (Pacific Grove, CA: Brooks/Cole, 1990), p. 131.

10. Democratic Leadership Council/ Greenberg Research survey, November 1994. Data provided by The Roper Center for Public Opinion Research, University of Connecticut.

11. Senator William Marcy's (NY) statement was in 1832, quoted in William Safire, *Safire's New Political Dictionary* (New York: Random House, 1993), p. 745.

12. Richard Rose, *The Post Modern President: The White House Meets the World* (Chatham, NJ: Chatham House, 1988), p. 162.

13. CNN.com, September 3, 2002.

14. Harold Seidman, *Politics, Position, and Power: The Dynamics of Federal Organization*, 5th edition (New York: Oxford University Press, 1998), p. 12.

15. *Humphrey's Executors v. U.S.* (1935).

16. *Washington Post*, March 27, 1997.

17. Secretary of Agriculture Dan Glickman (1995–2001), quoted in William T. Gormley, Jr., and Steven J. Balla, *Bureaucracy and Democracy: Accountability and Performance* (Washington, DC: CQ Press, 2004), p. 103.

18. Jason Webb Yackee and Susan Webb Yackee, "A Bias Towards Business? Assessing Interest Group Influence on the U.S. Bureaucracy," *Journal of Politics*, 68/1 (2006): 128–139.

19. D. T. Stallings, *A Brief History of the United States Department of Education, 1979–2002* (Durham, NC: Center for Child and Family Policy, Duke University, 2002). The columnist was David Broder.

20. CBS News, November 18, 2009.

21. CBS News, December 29, 2009

22. *Washington Post*, May 19, 2010.

23. Max Weber, "Bureaucracy," in *From Max Weber: Essays in Sociology*, H. H. Gertz and C. Wright Mills, eds.

24. Jason L. Jensen, Paul E. Sum, and David T. Flynn, "Political Orientations and Behavior of Public Employees: A Cross-National Comparison," *Journal of Public Administration Research and Theory*, 19/4 (2009): 709–730.

25. Robert Maranto and Karen Marie Hult, "Right Turn? Political Ideology in the Higher Civil Service, 1987–1994," *American Review of Public Administration*, 34/2 (2004): 199–222.

26. This finding is this text's interpretation of the findings reported in Maranto and Hult, "Right Turn?"

27. Friends of the Earth press release, May 16, 2001.

28. U.S. Department of the Interior press release, March 9, 2001.

29. *Hartford Courant*, May 4, 2004.

30. Gormley and Balla, *Bureaucracy and Democracy*, p. 132.

31. Daniel W. Drezner, "Ideas, Bureaucratic Politics, and the Crafting of Foreign Policy," *American Journal of Political Science*, 44/4 (2000): 733–749.

32. *Arizona Republic*, March 8, 1992.

33. *New York Times*, September 29, 2008.

34. Final edited transcript, Interview with Jimmy Carter, November 29, 1982, Plains, Georgia, in association with the Carter Presidency Project.

35. Richard Rose, *The Post Modern President*, p. 88.

36. Michael Lipsky, *Street-Level Bureaucracy: Dilemmas of the Individual in Public Services* (New York: Russell Sage, 1980).

37. Sally Coleman Selden, Jeffrey L. Brudney, and J. Edward Kellough, "Bureaucracy as a Representative Institution: Toward a Reconciliation of Bureaucratic Government and Democratic Theory," *American Journal of Political Science*, 42/3

(1998): 717–744. Also, Katherine C. Naff. "Representative Bureaucracy," in *Encyclopedia of Public Administration and Public Policy*, 2nd ed., edited by Jack Rabin and T. Aaron Wachhaus, published online, April 15, 2008; and Julie A. Dolan and David H. Rosenbloom, eds., *Representative Bureaucracy: Classic Readings and Continuing Controversies* (Armonk, NY: M. E. Sharpe, 2003).

38. David W. Pitts, "Representative Bureaucracy and Ethnicity in Public Schools: Examining the Link between Representation and Performance," *Administration & Society*, 39/4 (2007): 497–526.

39. Kenneth J. Meier and Jill Nicholson-Crotty, "Gender, Representative Bureaucracy, and Law Enforcement: The Case of Sexual Assault," *Public Administration Review*, 66/6 (2006), 850–860. Also on gender, see Lael Keiser, Vicky M. Wilkins, Kenneth J. Meier, and Catherine A. Holland, "Lipstick and Logarithms: Gender, Institutional Context, and Representative Bureaucracy," *American Political Science Review*, 96/3 (2002): 553–564.

40. R. James Woolsey, quoted in *Time*, August 1, 1994.

41. *Washington Post*, July 20, 2004 and October 3, 2004.

42. Robert E. DiClerico, *The American President* (Englewood Cliffs, NJ: Prentice-Hall, 1979), p. 107.

43. Robert Sherrill, *Why they Call It Politics* (New York: Harcourt Brace Jovanovich, 1979), p. 217.

44. *USA Today*, April 27, 2010.

45. Politico.com, May 5, 2010.

46. Environmental Protection Agency statement, "Endangerment and Cause or Contribute Findings for Greenhouse Gases under the Clean Air Act," December 7, 2009.

47. *Washington Post*, October 7, 2004. The critic was NAACP board member Leroy W. Warren, Jr., Roger

B. Clegg, counsel for the Center for Equal Opportunity, was the supporter.

48. CNN.com, May 27, 2010.

49. Lucien S. Vandenbroucke, *Perilous Options: Special Operations as an Instrument of U.S. Foreign Policy* (New York: Oxford University Press, 1993), p. 113.

50. Representative Les Aspin (D-WI), quoted in James M. Lindsay, "Congressional Oversight of the Department of Defense: Reconsidering Conventional Wisdom," *Armed Forces & Society*, 17 (1990), p. 16.

51. Quoted in John T. Rourke, *Making Foreign Policy: United States, Soviet Union, China* (Pacific Grove, CA: Brooks/Cole, 1990), p. 125.

52. George C. Edwards and Stephen J. Wayne, *Presidential Leadership in Congress* (New York: St. Martin's, 1985), p. 198.

53. Roger Larocca, "Strategic Diversion in Political Communication," *Journal of Politics*, 66/3 (2004): 469–491.

54. Richard Helms, quoted in Joseph Finder, "The Spy in the Gray Flannel Suit," *New York Times Book Review*, October 23, 1994.

55. *Washington Post*, November 17, 2009.

56. *Washington Post*, September 21, 2009.

57. All quotes from the *Telegraph* (UK), October 5, 2009.

58. McClatchy Newspapers, September 18, 2009.

59. *Telegraph* (UK), October 5, 2009.

60. Bruce Ackerman, Sterling Professor of Law and Political Science at Yale University in an op-ed piece, "A General's Public Pressure," *Washington Post*, October 2, 2009.

61. *Politico*, December 8, 2009.

62. *Washington Independent*, December 8, 2000.

63. All quotes in the paragraph are from the *Washington Post*, June 23, 2010.

64. Michael T. Heaney and Scott D. McClurg, "Social Networks and American Politics: Introduction to the Special Issue," *American Politics Research*, 37/5 (2009): 727–741. Also, Paul M. Hallacher, *Why Policy Issue Networks Matter: The Advanced Technology Program and the Manufacturing Extension Partnership* (Lanham, MD: Rowman & Littlefield, 2005).

65. Gormley and Balla, *Bureaucracy and Democracy*, p. 88.

66. Gormley and Balla, *Bureaucracy and Democracy*, p. 88.

67. The home page of the festival is at http://www.shrimp-petrofest.org/home.htm.

68. *New York Times*, August 8, 2010.

69. *Newsweek*, May 29, 2010.

70. *New York Times*, August 8, 2010.

71. Politico.com, July 18, 2010.

72. Contributions as reported by the Center for Responsive Politics at http://opensecrets.org/.

73. The analysis was done by *Washington Post* staff, and reported in the *Washington Post*, August 15, 2004.

74. *Time*, February 13, 1989.

75. Gormley and Balla, *Bureaucracy and Democracy*, p. 65.

76. David E. Lewis, "The Politics of Agency Termination: Confronting the Myth of Agency Immortality," *Journal of Politics*, 64/1 (2002): 89–108.

77. *Time*, January 19, 2003.

78. Quoted in William J. Taylor, Jr., and David H. Petraeus, "The Legacy of Vietnam for the U.S. Military," in *Democracy, Strategy, and Vietnam: Implications for American Policymaking*, George K. Osborn, Asa A. Clark, IV, Daniel J. Kaufman, and Douglas E. Lute, eds. (Lexington, MA: Lexington, 1987), p. 254.

79. Gormley and Balla, *Bureaucracy and Democracy*, p. 68.

80. "The General Principles of Congressional Oversight," a document on the Website of the Committee on Rules, U.S. House of Representatives at www.house.gov/rules/.

81. *Washington Post*, October 5, 1992.

82. U.S. Office of Special Counsel, *Fiscal Year 2008 Annual Report*.

83. Gormley and Balla, *Bureaucracy and Democracy*, p. 76.

84. Joseph L. Smith, "Presidents, Justices, and Deference to Administrative Action," *Journal of Law, Economics, and Organization*, 23/2 (2007): 346–364.

85. Thomas Jefferson to William Ludlow, September 26, 1824, quoted in *The Jeffersonian Cyclopedia: A Comprehensive Collection of the Views of Thomas Jefferson*, John P. Foley, ed. (New York: Funk & Wagnalls, 1900) located in the Thomas Jefferson Collection Electronic Text Center, University of Virginia Library.

86. *New York Times*, August 21, 2008.

87. ABC News/*Washington Post* poll, June, 2009. Data provided by The Roper Center.

CHAPTER 14

1. Jeff Cohen, founding director of the Park Center for Independent Media at Ithaca College, quoted in the *New York Times*, May 26, 2009.

2. Jennifer Maree of the Women's Bar Association of the District of Columbia, quoted on CNN, May 25, 2009.

3. Ruben Navarrett, quoted on CNN, May 25, 2009.

4. Benjamin Wittes, senior fellow at the Brookings Institution, quoted in the *Washington Post*, May 2, 2009.

5. Cody Moon, "Comparative Constitutional Analysis: Should the United States Supreme Court Join the Dialogue?" *Washington University Journal of Law and Policy*, 12 (2003): 229–247.

6. *Mabo v. Queensland* (1992).

7. The 15 other countries are Argentina, Australia, Brazil, Canada, France, Germany, Great Britain, India, Italy, Japan, Philippines, South Africa, South Korea, Sweden, and Turkey. The four international courts

are the International Court of Justice, the International Criminal Court, the European Court of Justice, and the International Criminal Tribunal for the former Yugoslavia.

8. Quoted by Senator Max Baucus, *Congressional Record,* September 14, 2005, p. S10032.

9. Richard L. Hansen, *The Supreme Court and Election Law: Judging Equality from Baker v. Carr to Bush v. Gore* (New York: New York University Press, 2003).

10. Robert Dudley, "Judicial Control of the Presidency: Stability and Change," in *Understanding the Presidency,* 3rd ed., James Pfiffner and Roger H. Davidson, eds. (New York: Longman, 2003), p. 325.

11. Louis Fisher, "Judicial Review of the War Power," *Presidential Studies Quarterly,* 35/3 (2005): 466–496.

12. Letters to the President of the Senate and Speaker of the House of Representative, March 26, 1999.

13. James N. Danziger, *Understanding the Political World,* 6th ed. (New York: Longman, 2003), p. 150.

14. Letter to Monsieur A. Coray, October 31, 1823, online edition of *The Founder's Constitution,* edited by Philip B. Kurland and Ralph Lerner.

15. Fox News/Opinion Dynamics poll, April 2010. Data supplied by the Roper Center for Public Opinion Research, University of Connecticut.

16. *Los Angeles Times* poll, June 1991. Data provided by The Roper Center.

17. *Webster v. Doe* (1988).

18. *Franklin v. Gwinnett County Public Schools* (1991).

19. Richard S. Randall, *American Constitutional Development,* Vol. I, *The Powers of Government* (New York: Longman, 2002), p. 81.

20. Associated Press/National Constitution Center poll, September 2009. Data provided by The Roper Center.

21. Robert A. Kagan, *Adversarial Legalism: The American Way of Law* (Cambridge, MA: Harvard University Press, 2001).

22. Associated Press, October 23, 2006.

23. *Breedlove v. Suttles* (1937).

24. Jeb Barnes, *Overruled?: Legislative Overrides, Pluralism, and Contemporary Court-Congress Relations* (Palo Alto, CA: Stanford University Press, 2004).

25. *Ledbetter v. Goodyear Tire & Rubber Co.* (2007).

26. *Worcester v. Georgia* (1832). See Stephen Breyer, "The Cherokee Indians and the Supreme Court," *Journal of Supreme Court History,* 25/3 (2000): 215–227.

27. Federal District Court judge rejecting in 1977 a motion to dismiss charges for failure to report for the draft in *United States v. Sisson* (1970).

28. *Colgrove v. Green* (1946).

29. Testimony of Professor David A. Strauss, The University of Chicago School of Law, during hearings on "Federalism and States' Rights: When Are Employment Laws Constitutional?" before the Senate Committee on Health, Education, Labor and Pensions, April 4, 2001.

30. Stephen Breyer, "Our Democratic Constitution," address at the New York University Law School, October 22, 2001.

31. Remarks at a press conference, May 31, 1935.

32. Gallup poll, November 1936. Data provided by The Roper Center.

33. A transcript of the address is in the *New York Times,* January 28, 2010.

34. Roberts, quoted in the *Washington Post,* March 10, 2010.

35. Pew Research Center poll, February 2010. Data provided by The Roper Center.

36. *New York Times,* January 19, 2009.

37. Stephen J. Choi, G. Mitu Gulati, and Eric A. Posner "Are Judges Overpaid? A Skeptical Response to the Judicial Salary Debate," *Journal of Legal Analysis,* 1/1 (2009): 47–117. Also, Scott Baker, "Should the Salaries of Federal Judges Be Raised?" *Boston University Law Review,* 88 (2008): 63–112.

38. Justice Ruth Bader Ginsberg quoting Rehnquist, CNN, September 4, 2005.

39. *Wall Street Journal,* May 18, 2009.

40. CNN, May 15, 2009.

41. Stephanos Bibas, "Plea Bargaining Outside the Shadow of Trial," *Harvard Law Review,* 117/8 (2004): 2469–2545.

42. This paragraph, including the quote, relies on Robin L. Dahlberg, senior staff attorney, Racial Justice Program, American Civil Liberties Union, testimony during hearings on "The State of Public Defense Services in Michigan," before the Subcommittee on Crime, Terrorism and Homeland Security, Committee on the Judiciary, U.S. House of Representatives, March 26, 2009.

43. American Bar Association, *amicus curiae* brief in *Grutter v. Bollinger,* February 2003.

44. *Bradwell v. Illinois* (1873).

45. Sheldon Goldman, Elliott Slotnick, Gerard Gryski, and Gary Zuk. "Clinton Judges: Summing Up the Legacy," *Judicature,* 84 (2001): 228–254.

46. Kate Malleson, "Justifying Gender Equality on the Bench: Why Difference Won't Do," *Feminist Legal Studies,* 11/1 (2003), p. 1.

47. David B. Rottman, Randall Hansen, Nicole Mott, and Lynn Grimes, *Perceptions of the Courts in Your Community: The Influence of Experience, Race and Ethnicity,* Final Report (Williamsburg, VA: National Center for State Courts, 2003), Table 3.7, p. 41.

48. Virginia A. Hettinger, Stefanie A. Lindquist, and Wendy L. Martinek, "Separate Opinion Writing on the United States Courts of Appeals," *American Politics Research,* 31/3 (2003): 215–250.

49. Barbara Palmer, "Women in the American Judiciary: Their Influence and Impact," *Women & Politics,* 23/3 (2001): 89–99; and David Songer and Kelly Crews-Meyer, "Does Judge Gender Matter? Decision Making in State Supreme Courts," *Social Science Quarterly,* 81/3 (2000): 750–762.

50. Tajuana Massie, Susan W. Johnson, and Sara Margaret Gubala, "The Impact of Gender and Race in the Decisions of Judges on the United States Courts of Appeals." Paper prepared for delivery at the Midwest Political Science Association convention, Chicago, Illinois, April 2002.

51. Massie, Johnson, and Gubala, "The Impact of Gender." Also, Madhavi McCall, "Structuring Gender's Impact: Judicial Voting Across Criminal Justice," *American Politics Research,* 36/2 (2008): 264–296.

52. Daniel M. Schneider, "Statutory Construction in Federal Appellate Tax Cases: The Effect of Judges' Social Backgrounds and of Other Aspects of Litigation," *Journal of Law and Policy,* 13 (2003): 257–304; and Songer and Crews-Meyer, "Does Judge Gender Matter?"

53. Jennifer L. Peresie, "Female Judges Matter: Gender and Collegial Decisionmaking in the Federal Appellate Courts," *Yale Law Journal,* 114/7 (2005): 1759–1790; and Richard Fox and Robert Van Sickel, "Gender Dynamics and Judicial Behavior in Criminal Trial Courts: An Exploratory Study," *The Justice System Journal,* 21 (2000): 260–280.

54. Nancy Scherer, "Blacks on the Bench," *Political Science Quarterly,* 119/4 (2004): 655–675.

55. Darrell Steffensmeier and Chester L. Britt, "Judges' Race and Judicial Decision Making: Do Black Judges Sentence Differently?" *Social Science Quarterly,* 82/4 (2001): 749–763.

56. Malcom D. Holmes, Hareon M. Hosch, Howard C. Daudistel, Dolores A. Perez, and Joseph B. Graves, "Judges' Ethnicity and Minority Sentencing: Evidence Concerning Hispanics," *Social Science Quarterly,* 74/3 (1993): 496–506.

57. Todd Collins and Laura Moyer, "Gender, Race, and Intersectionality on the Federal Appellate Bench," *Political Research Quarterly,* 61/2 (2008), p. 225. Also, Frank B. Cross, *Decision Making in the U.S. Courts of Appeals* (Stanford, CA: Stanford University Press, 2007), especially chapter 3.

58. David Alistair Yalof, *Persuit of Justices: Presidential Politics and the Selection of Supreme Court Nominees* (Chicago: University of Chicago Press, 1999).

59. Sarah A. Binder, "Where Do Institutions Come From? Exploring the Origins of the Senate Blue Slip," *Studies in American Political Development,* 21/1 (2007): 1–15. Also, Tonja Jacobi, "The Senatorial Courtesy Game: Explaining the Norm of Informal Vetoes in Advice and Consent Nominations," *Legislative Studies Quarterly,* 30/2 (2005): 193–218.

60. Alan Rozzi and Terri L. Peretti, "Modern Departures from the U.S. Supreme Court: Party, Pensions, or Power? (July 17, 2009), a research paper available from SSRN at http://ssrn.com/abstract=1307845.

61. Jeffrey Toobin, "After Stevens," *The New Yorker,* March 22, 2010.

62. All quotes from the *St. Petersburg Times,* July 3, 2005. The White House official was C. Boyden Gray, counsel to the president in 1990.

63. Quoted in "Bork Confirmation Battle," a historic document from September 15, October 9, and 13, 1987, CQ Press.com.

64. *New York Times,* July 20, 2005.

65. CNN, May 26, 2009.

66. The analysis by Professor Stefanie Lindquist of the University of Texas at Austin law school was reported in *Time,* June 11, 2009.

67. Russell Wheeler, *The Changing Face of the Federal Judiciary* (Washington, DC: Brookings Institution, 2009).

68. Elisha Carol Savchak, Thomas G. Hansford, Donald R. Songer, Kenneth L. Manning, and Robert A. Carp, "Taking It to the Next Level: The Elevation of District Court Judges to the U.S. Courts of Appeals," *American Journal of Political Science,* 50/2 (2006): 478–493.

69. Research and calculations by author using the active judges as of April 2010 on the First, Third, Fifth, Seventh, Ninth, and Eleventh Circuits. Included among public service judges were those who had less than two years private practice after long government service prior to being first appointed to the bench.

70. MSNBC.com, May 7, 2009.

71. *Time,* April 13, 2010, quoting a Biden remark in 1997.

72. Jon R. Bond, Richard Fleisher, and Glen S. Krutz, "Malign Neglect: Evidence That Delay Has Become the Primary Method of Defeating Presidential Appointments," *Congress & the Presidency,* 36/3 (2009): 226–243.

73. Bond, Fleisher, and Krutz, "Malign Neglect."

74. Joyce A. Baugh, *Supreme Court Justices in the Post-Bork Era: Confirmation Politics and Judicial Performance* (New York: Peter Lang, 2002); and Timothy R. Johnson and Jason M. Roberts, "Presidential Capital and the Supreme Court Confirmation Process," *Journal of Politics,* 66/3 (2004): 663–689.

75. *Hartford Courant,* September 10, 2005.

76. *Time,* November 14, 2005.

77. *Time,* June 30, 2010.

78. *Christian Science Monitor,* June 30, 2010.

79. Lee Epstein, Jeffrey A. Segal, Nancy Staudt, and René Lindstädt, "The Role of Qualifications in the Confirmation of Nominees to the U.S.

Supreme Court," August 3, 2004, unpublished paper.

80. Press conference, October 3, 2005.

81. CNN, October 28, 2005.

82. Michael Stein of Harvard Law School, quoted in *Time*, November 14, 2005.

83. John W. Dean, *The Rehnquist Choice: The Untold Story of the Nixon Appointment That Redefined the Supreme Court* (New York: Free Press, 1991), excerpted in the *Washington Post*, November 19, 2001.

84. Mitchel A. Sollenberger, "The Law: Must the Senate Take a Floor Vote on a Presidential Judicial Nominee?" *Presidential Studies Quarterly*, 34/2 (2004): 420–436.

85. *Congressional Record*, September 21, 1999, p. S11102.

86. *Congressional Record*, March 12, 2003, p. S3678.

87. Lee Epstein, René Lindstädt, Jeffrey A. Segal, and Chad Westerland, "The Changing Dynamics of Senate Voting on Supreme Court Nominees," *Journal of Politics*, 68/2 (2006): 296–324.

88. "Choosing Cases," WashingtonPost.com, 2001.

89. Paul M. Collins, Jr., *Friends of the Supreme Court: Interest Groups and Judicial Decision Making* (New York: Oxford University Press. 2008). Also, Paul M. Collins, Jr., "Friends of the Court: Examining the Influence of *Amicus Curiae* Participation in U.S. Supreme Court Litigation," *Law & Society Review*, 38/4 (2004): 807–832.

90. Douglas Laycock, a law professor at University of Texas at Austin, quoted in the *Christian Science Monitor*, June 15, 2004.

91. Michael A. Bailey, Brian Kamoie, and Forrest Maltzman, "Signals from the Tenth Justice: The Political Role of the Solicitor General in Supreme Court Decision Making," *American Journal of Political Science*, 49/1 (2005): 72–99.

92. "Oral Arguments," WashingtonPost.com, 2001.

93. *Los Angeles Times*, September 13, 2005.

94. William O. Douglas, *The Court Years, 1939-1975* (New York: Random House, 1980), p. 8.

95. Isaac Unah and Ange-Marie Hancock, "U.S. Supreme Court Decision Making, Case Salience, and the Attitudinal Model," *Law & Policy*, 28/3 (2006): 295–320.

96. Michael A. Bailey and Forrest Maltzman, "Does Legal Doctrine Matter? Unpacking Law and Policy Preferences on the U.S. Supreme Court," *American Political Science Review*, 102/2 (2008): 369–384.

97. *Mayer Studios v. Grokster, Ltd* (2005).

98. Mark J. Richards and Herbert M. Kritzer, "Jurisprudential Regimes in Supreme Court Decision Making," *American Political Science Review*, 96/2 (2002): 305–321.

99. Harold J. Spaeth and Jeffrey A. Segal, *Majority Rule or Minority Will: Adherence to Precedent on the U.S. Supreme Court* (New York: Cambridge University Press, 2001).

100. Saul Brenner and Harold J. Spaeth, *Stare Indecisis: The Alteration of Precedent on the Supreme Court, 1946-1992* (New York: Cambridge University Press. 1995).

101. Stefanie A. Lindquist and David E. Klein, "The Influence of Jurisprudential Considerations on Supreme Court Decisionmaking: A Study of Conflict Cases," *Law & Society Review*, 40/ (2006), p. 135.

102. Adam Liptak, "When Rendering Decisions, Judges Are Finding Law Reviews Irrelevant," column in the *New York Times*, March 19, 2007.

103. Ruth Bader Ginsburg, " 'A Decent Respect to the Opinions of [Human] kind': The Value of a Comparative Perspective in Constitutional Adjudication," speech, Constitutional Court of South Africa, February 7, 2006, on the U.S. Supreme Court Website at www.supremecourtus.gov/publicinfo/speeches/.

104. Jeffrey A. Segal and Harold J. Spaeth, *The Supreme Court and the Attitudinal Model Revised* (New York: Cambridge University Press, 2002); Theodore W. Ruger, Pauline T. Kim, Andrew D. Martin, and Kevin M. Quinn, "The Supreme Court Forecasting Project: Legal and Political Science Approaches to Predicting Supreme Court Decisionmaking," *Columbia Law Review*, 104 (2004): 115–209; and Virginia A. Hettinger, Stefanie A. Lindquist, and Wendy L. Martinek, "Comparing Attitudinal and Strategic Accounts of Dissenting Behavior on the U.S. Courts of Appeals," *American Journal of Political Science*, 48/1 (2004): 126–137.

105. William M. Landes and Richard A. Posner, "Rational Judicial Behavior: A Statistical Study," *Journal of Legal Analysis*, 1/2 (2009): 775–831.

106. David Paul Kuhn, "The Polarization of the Supreme Court," *Real Clear Politics*, July 2, 2010, online at http://www.realclearpolitics.com/articles/2010.

107. Frank B. Cross, *Decision Making in the U.S. Courts of Appeals* (Palo Alto, CA: Stanford University Press, 2007).

108. Barbara M. Yarnold, "Did Circuit Courts of Appeals Judges Overcome Their Own Religions in Cases Involving Religious Liberties?" *Review of Religious Research*, 42/1 (2000): 79–86.

109. Landes and Posner, "Rational Judicial Behavior: A Statistical Study."

110. CBS News, July 14, 2009.

111. Kevin T. McGuire, "The Institutionalization of the U.S. Supreme Court," *Political Analysis*, 12/1 (2004): 128–142.

112. Brett W. Curry, Richard L. Pacelle, Jr., and Bryan W. Marshal, "An Informal and Limited Alliance: The

President and the Supreme Court," *Presidential Studies Quarterly*, 38/2 (2008): 223–247. Also, Mario Bergara, Barak Richman, and Pablo T. Spiller, "Modeling Supreme Court Strategic Decision Making: The Congressional Constraint," *Legislative Studies Quarterly*, 28/2 (2003): 247–280.

113. Barry Friedman, *The Will of the People: How Public Opinion Has Influenced the Supreme Court and Shaped the Meaning of the Constitution* (New York: Farrar, Straus and Giroux, 2009).

114. Gallup poll, July 1986. Data provided by The Roper Center.

115. Gallup poll, May 2003. Data provided by The Roper Center.

116. Michael W. Giles, Bethany Blackstone, and Richard L. Vining, "The Supreme Court in American Democracy: Unraveling the Linkages between Public Opinion and Judicial Decision Making," *Journal of Politics*, 70/2 (2008): 293–306. Also, Kevin T. McGuire and James A. Stimson, "The Least Dangerous Branch Revisited: New Evidence on Supreme Court Responsiveness to Public Preferences," *Journal of Politics*, 66/4 (2004): 1018–1041.

117. Quinnipiac University poll, April 2010. Data provided by The Roper Center.

118. ABC News/*Washington Post* poll, April 2010. Data provided by The Roper Center.

119. Adam S. Hochschild, "The Modern Problem of Supreme Court Plurality Decision: Interpretation in Historical Perspective," *Journal of Law & Policy*, 4 (2000): 262–287.

120. Pamela C. Corley, Udi Sommer, and Artemus Ward, "Extreme Dissensus: Explaining Plurality Decisions on the United States Supreme Court," unpublished paper (July 14, 2009), p. 27. Available at SSRN: http://ssrn.com/abstract=1433742/.

121. National Public Radio, "Ruth Bader Ginsburg and Malvina Harlan—Justice Revives Memoir of Former Supreme Court Wife," May 22, 2002.

122. John M. Scheb, II and William Lyons, "Judicial Behavior and Public Opinion: Popular Expectations Regarding the Factors That Influence Supreme Court Decisions," *Political Behavior*, 23/2 (2001): 181–194.

123. Nine percent answered "not that important or "not important at all," and 2% were unsure. NBC News/*Wall Street Journal* poll, July 2005. Data provided by The Roper Center.

124. Three percent were unsure. Associated Press/Ipsos-Public Affairs poll, November 2004. Data provided by The Roper Center.

SCHOLARS CITED

As noted in the acknowledgements, the author owes a great debt to the scholars whose research has been published in books and articles, presented at academic conventions, or posted on the Internet. These research contributions are a key part of the foundation of this text. The listing of the scholars below is meant to specifically recognize each of these scholars and to also give readers a sense of the breadth of research on which this book, like all political science offerings, rests. Each of these academicians along with the one or more studies that they have published and that have informed this text can also be found in the bibliography. To save printing costs, and thus to keep the price of this book down for students, the bibliography is found on the book's Web site at

www.paradigmpublishers.com/books/BookDetail.aspx?productID=274091

For those who are interested in pursuing one or another topic further, the studies listed here are also meant to serve as an "additional reading" source.

Marisa Abrajano
Alan I. Abramowitz
James Adams
E. Scott Adler
Brad Alexander
Dean Alger
Barbara Allen
Marcus D. Allen
Mike Allen
Neal Allen
Dee Allsop
Alison B. Alter
Scott L. Althaus
R. Michael Alvarez
Jennifer Anderson
Mary R. Anderson
Stephen Ansolabehere
Kevin Arceneaux
R. Douglas Arnold
Laura W. Arnold
Shelly Arsneault
Jenna Ashley-Robinson
Lonna Rae Atkeson
David P. Auerswald
Derek R. Avery
Christine Bachen
Michael A. Bailey
Andy Baker
John R. Baker
Ross K. Baker
Scott Baker
Mark Baldassare
Steven J. Balla
Susan A Banducci
Lucig H. Banielian
Christopher Banks
Jason Barabas
James D. Barber
Katherine Barbieri
Mitchell Bard

Michelle A. Barnello
Jeb Barnes
David P. Baron
Andrew W. Barrett
Karlo Marcelo Barrios
Colleen Barry-Goodman
Brandon L. Bartels
Larry M. Bartles
Miguel Basañez
Harold F. Bass Jr.
Joyce A. Baugh
Frank R. Baumgartner
Randolph Baxter
Randal A. Beam
Charles A. Beard
Maurine H. Beasley
Lisa Garcia Bedolla
Lauren Cohen Bell
Linda L. M. Bennett
Stephen E. Bennett
W. Lance Bennett
Daniel E. Bergan
Mario Bergara
Adam J. Berinsky
John M. Berry
Michael Beschloss
Stephanos Bibas
Kenneth N. Bickers
Keith Billingsley
Sarah A. Binder
Benjamin Bishin
George F. Bishop
Amy E. Black
Bethany Blackstone
John Blakeman
W. Craig Bledsoe
Robert G. Boatwright
Arjen Boin
Louis Bolce
Toby Bolsen

Jon R. Bond
David Bordua
Thomas Borstelmann
Christopher J. Bosso
William P. Bottom
Ann O'M. Bowman
Mark A. Boyer
Paul Brace
Ted Brader
David Branham
Kathleen A. Bratton
Saul Brenner
Mark D. Brewer
Stephen Breyer
Richard Briffault
Chester L. Britt
Deborah Jordan Brooks
D. Clayton Brown
Robert D. Brown
Wallace Brown
William P. Browne
Bonnie J. Brownlee
Brian J. Brox
James Bruce
John M. Bruce
Thomas L. Brunell
William Buchanan
Ian Budge
Barry C. Burden
John P. Burke
Kelly M. Burke
Paul Burstein
Wendy Cadge
Peter T. Calcagno
Dan Caldwell
Karen Callaghan
Charles Cameron
Andrea Louise Campbell
Brandice Canes-Wrone
David T. Canon

Bryan Caplan
Mary Caprioli
Demetrios James Caraley
Stanley M. Caress
John M.Carey
William D. Carrigan
Nancy Carrillo
Thomas M. Carsey
Ralph G. Carter
Kiki Caruson
Michael T. Charles
Kenneth Y. Chay
José Antonio Cheibub
John Cheslock
William O. Chittick
Wendy K. Tam Cho
Stephen J. Choi
Sung-Chang Chun
Jack Citrin
Cornell W. Clayton
J. Garry Clifford
Joshua D. Clinton
Charles Cobb Jr.
Rachael V. Cobb
David B.Cohen
Jeffrey E. Cohen
Richard L. Cole
Paul M. Collins
Todd Collins
Nicholas Confessore
Timothy J. Conlan
Richard S. Conley
Kathryn M. Connor
Pamela Johnston Conover
Lucian Gideon Conway III
Corey Cook
Fay Lomax Cook
Angela Cooke
Christopher A. Cooper
Michael Corbett

Pamela C. Corely
Edward S. Corwin
Kenneth M. Cosgrove
Gary W. Cox
Stephanie Craft
Robert L. Craig
Kelly Crews-Meyer
Thomas E. Cronin
Frank B. Cross
Sharyl Cross
Richard N. Current
Brett W. Curry
Dave D'Alessio
Robert Dallek
James N. Danziger
Howard C. Daudistel
Kenneth Dautrich
Chandler Davidson
Jonathan R. T. Davidson
Roger H. Davidson
Allen F. Davis
Charles Davis
Richard Davis
Robert D. Dean
Francois Vergniolle De Chantal
Rebecca E. Deen
John M. de Figuieredo
Christine DeGregorio
Terry L. Deibel
C. James Delaet
Rodolfo O. de la Garza
Michael X. Delli Carpini
Gerald De Maio
Keven R. den Dulk
Robert A. Denemark
Louis Desipio
Scott W. Desposato
Bryan J. Dettrey
Matthew J. Dickinson
Robert E. DiClerico
Daniel Diermeier
Sandra Dijkstra
Daniel C. Diller
John J. Dilulio
John Dinan
Lisa Jane Disch
Travis L. Dixon
Brendan J. Doherty
Chris J. Dolan
John C. Domino
G. William Domhoff
Todd Donovan
William O. Douglas
Suzanne Dovi
Jay Dow
Kathleen M. Dowley
Michael Doyle
Daniel W. Drezner
James N. Druckman
Jeff Dubin
Robert Dudley
Christopher M. Duquette
Stephen Benedict Dyson
David C. Earnest
Cheryl L. Eavey
George C. Edwards III

Richard C. Eichenberg
Robert M. Eisinger
Charles Elder
Robert Elgie
Richard Elling
Christopher R. Ellis
Joseph J. Ellis
Brian Endless
Steven T. Engel
Robert M. Entman
David Epstein
Lee Epstein
Robert S. Erikson
H. Abbie Erler
Monica P. Escaleras
Matthew Eshbaugh-Soha
Heinz Eulau
Diana Evans
Judith Evans
William P. Eveland Jr.
Angelo Falcon
Jean-Philippe Faletta
Erika Falk
Victoria A. Farrar-Myers
Jasmine Farrier
Thomas R. Faschingbauer
Timothy J. Feddersen
Richard F. Fenno Jr.
Leroy C. Ferguson
Frank Fischer
Louis Fisher
Richard Fleisher
Richard S. Flickinger
Julianne F. Flowers
David T. Flynn
Richard Fox
Luis R. Fraga
Peter Francia
Thomas M. Franck
Kathleen A. Frankovic
Michael M. Franz
Paul Freedman
Peter J. Frederick
Frank Freidel
Kim L. Fridkin
Scott A. Frisch
Francis Fukuyama
Shama Gamkhar
James C. Garand
F. Chris Garcia
John Garcia
Claudine Gay
Michael A. Genovese
Alan S. Gerber
Elisabeth R. Gerber
Sarah Allen Gershon
Joseph Gershtenson
Benny Geys
Sheila J. Gibbons
James L. Gibson
Robert E. Gilbert
Martin Gilens
Michael W. Giles
Jeff Gill
Franklin D. Gilliam Jr.
Joshua Glasgow

Nils Petter Gleditsch
George R. Goethals
Robert K. Goidel
Claudia Goldin
Sheldon Goldman
Kathy Goldschmidt
Joel K. Goldstein
Kenneth M. Goldstein
Risa Goluboff
Craig Goodman
William T. Gormley Jr.
Darshan J. Goux
Doris A. Graber
Joseph B. Graves
Virginia Gray
Donald P. Green
John Green
Kenneth F. Greene
John D. Griffin
Lynn Grimes
Bernard Grofman
Christian R. Grose
Tim Groseclose
Gerard Gryski
Sara Margaret Gubala
G. Mitu Gulati
Matthew Gunning
Kenneth J. Hagan
Zoltan L. Hajnal
Matthew Hale
Melinda Gann Hall
Richard L. Hall
James T. Hamilton
John A. Hamman
Allen Hammond
Ange-Marie Hancock
Stephen Hanna
Randall Hansen
Richard L. Hansen
Thomas G. Hansford
Carol Hardy-Fanta
Erwin C. Hargrove
James T. Harrison
Paul 't Hart
Moshe Haspel
Mike Hawkins
Ron Hayduk
Audrey A. Haynes
Andrew J. Healy
Anthony F. Heath
John P. Heinz
Diane J. Heith
Hugh Helco
Peter R. Henriques
Gregory M. Herek
Sarah P. Herlihy
Paul Herrnson
Rebekah Herrick
Rodney Hero
Gary R. Hess
Marc J. Hetherington
Virginia A. Hettinger
Lara Hewitt
John R. Hibbing
Douglas A. Hibbs Jr.
Robert Higgs

Benjamin Highton
David B. Hill
Kim Quaile Hill
Lisa Hill
Barbara Hinckley
C. Elizabeth Hirsh
Sara Binzer Hobolt
Adam S. Hochschild
Matthew J. Hoffmann
Thomas M. Holbrook
Malcom D. Holmes
Ole R. Holsti
David A. Hopkins
Hareon M. Hosch
David J. Houston
John R. Howe
William G. Howell
Gregory A. Huber
Kevin W. Hula
Karen Marie Hult
Patricia A. Hurley
Mark S. Hurwitz
Vincent L. Hutchings
Ronald Inglehart
Shanto Iyengar
David J. Jackson
John E. Jackson
Robert A. Jackson
Anil G. Jacob
Lawrence R. Jacobs
Gary C. Jacobson
William G. Jacoby
Patrick James
Kathleen Hall Jamison
Lars Jarkko
Sharon E. Jarvis
Julie Roy Jeffrey
Hank C. Jenkins-Smith
Jason L. Jensen
Bruce W. Jentleson
Jennifer Jerit
Wesley Joe
Susan W. Johnson
Timothy R. Johnson
Richard G. C. Johnston
Branwen Gruffydd Jones
Jacqueline Jones
Michael Jones-Correa
Anna Maria Jönsson
Donald L. Jordan
Grant Jordan
James Joyner Jr.
Robert A. Kagan
Miles Kahler
Kim Fridkin Kahn
Martin Kalan
Cindy D. Kam
Brian Kamoie
Emily W. Kane
Paul Kantor
Ethan Kaplan
Martin Kaplan
Dean Karlan
Jeffrey A. Karp
Ellis Katz
Lawrence F. Katz

Karen M. Kaufmann
Thomas A. Kazee
Michael Keene
Scott Keeter
Christian B. Keller
Christopher S. Kelley
Sean Q Kelly
Ivan Kenneally
Christopher Kenny
Patrick J. Kenney
Kate Kenski
Thomas Kephart
Samuel Kernell
Elina Kilpi
Pauline T. Kim
David C. Kimball
John Kincaid
Donald R. Kinder
Emily Hoban Kirby
David E. Klein
R. Daniel Klemen
Robert Klemmemsen
Casey Andrew Klofstad
H. Gibbs Knotts
John P. Koehn
Nick Kotz
George A. Krause
Harold J. Krent
Herbert M. Kritzer
Martha Kropf
Jon A. Krosnick
Douglas Kruse
Glen S. Krutz
James H. Kuklinski
Martha Joynt Kumar
Jim Kuypers
Everett C. Ladd
Jeffrey W. Ladewig
Marilyn Lake
William M. Landes
Laura Langbein
Laura Langer
Ronald E. Langley
John Lapinski
Valentino Larcinese
Roger Larocca
Richard R. Lau
Edward O. Laumann
Eric D. Lawrence
Geoffrey C. Layman
Jeffrey Lazarus
Simon Lazarus
Justin Lebeau
Chungmei Lee
Tien-Tsung Lee
Beth L. Leech
Paul Lellstedt
Lance T. LeLoup
David E. Lewis
Justin Lewis
Michael S. Lewis-Beck
Paul G. Lewis
Bradley Lian
Linda Lichter
S. Robert Lichter
Pei-te Lien

P. See Lim
Stefanie A. Lindquist
James M. Lindsay
René Lindstädt
Michael Lipsky
Steven Livingston
Gerhard Loewenberg
Edward J. López
Mark Hugo Lopez
David Lowery
Theodore J. Lowi
Robert C. Lowry
David Lublin
Arthus Lupia
William Lyons
Laura J. Macaulay
Anthony Madonna
Christine Mahoney
Neil A. Malhotra
Kate Malleson
William A. Maloney
Gideon Maltz
Forrest Maltzman
Maurice Mangum
Jane Mansbridge
Harvey C. Mansfield
Jeff Manza
Robert Maranto
Bryan W. Marshall
Andrew D. Martin
Christopher Martin
Jack K. Martin
Wendy L. Martinek
Michael D. Martinez
Laurie Mason
Tajuana Massie
Natalie Masuoka
Franco Matteia
Elaine Tyler May
Frederick W. Mayer
David R. Mayhew
Kenneth R. Mayer
Ian McAllister
Michael McBurnett
Edward J. McCaffery
Madhavi McCall
Nolan McCarty
Clark McCauley
Scott D. McClurg
Corrine M. McConnaughy
Allan McConnell
Donald J. McCrone
Mathew D. McCubbins
Monika McDermott
Michael D. McDonald
Michael P. McDonald
Lawrence T. McGill
Leslie Moscow McGranahan
Kathleen M. McGraw
Kevin T. McGuire
Robert A. McGuire
Bill McInturff
Amy McKay
Patrick F. Mckay
Erik Melander
Nicole Mellow

James H. Meriwether
Samuel Merrill
Alan R. Metelko
Harold Meyerson
Kristin Michelitch
Sidney M. Milkis
Kristina C. Miler
Gary J. Miller
Joanne M. Miller
John Chester Miller
Warren E. Miller
Jeff Milyo
David Mitchell
Cecilia Hyunjung Mo
Roger J. Moiles
Jeffery J. Mondak
Gary F. Moncrief
Jeannette Money
Alan D. Monroe
Nathan W. Monroe
Cody Moon
David W. Moore
Mik Moore
Marco Morales-Barba
Alejandro Moreno
Smosophia Mockalenko
Kenneth B. Moss
Nicole Mott
Laura Moyer
John Mueller
Daniel Munro
Gregg R. Murray
Diana C. Mutz
Douglas Muzzio
Richard Nadeau
Robert F. Nagel
Gary B. Nash
Michael Nelson
Robert L. Nelson
Bruce Nesmith
Eric Neumayer
Richard E. Neustadt
Adam J. Newmark
David K. Nichols
Stephen P. Nicholson
Sean Nicholson-Crotty
Richard G. Niemi
David Niven
Timothy P. Nokken
Barbara Norrander
Pippa Norris
Philip Norton
Hillel Nossek
Karen O'Connor
Sharyn O'Halloran
Robert W. Oldendick
Walter J. Oleszek
Laura R. Olson
John R Oneal
Byron D'Andra Orey
Gary Orfield
Henrik Örnebring
Shannon K. Orr
L. Marvin Overby
Andrew Owen
Diana Owens

Nicole M. Owings
Julianna Sandell Pacheco
Richard L. Pacelle Jr.
Benjamin I. Page
Jake Page
David L. Paletz
Barbara Palmer
Costas Panagopoulos
Adrian D. Pantoja
Michael M. Parkin
Thomas G. Paterson
Thomas E. Patterson
Jeffrey S. Peake
Jennifer L. Peresie
Terri L. Peretti
Dolores A. Perez
William B. Perkins
Bettina Peters
Ronald M. Peters Jr.
Keith S. Petersen
Dean J. Peterson
David H. Petraeus
John R. Petrocik
Jon C. Pevehouse
James P. Pfiffner
Justin H. Phillips
Tasha S. Philpot
J. Mitchell Pickerill
Dianne M. Pinderhughes
Neil Pinney
Hanna F. Pitkin
Dennis L. Plane
Keith T. Poole
Eric A. Posner
Richard A. Posner
Matthew Potoski
Lynda W. Powell
Philip J. Powlick
Preston Thomas
Robert R. Preuhs
Markus Prior
David Pritchard
Ricardo Puglisi
Robert D. Putnam
Kevin M. Quinn
Paul J. Quirk
Eric Rader
Lyn Ragsdale
S. Karthick Ramakrishnan
Richard S. Randall
Ronald B. Rapoport
Michael D. Reagan
Eric Redman
Byron Reeves
Robert B. Reich
Stanley A. Renshon
Henry Reynolds
Andrew Rich
Robert F. Rich
Mark J. Richards
Lilliard E. Richardson Jr.
Barak Richman
Travis N. Ridout
Thomas Riess-Kapan
William Riker
Jean-Sebastian Rioux

Leonzio Rizzo
Jason M. Roberts
Lori Robertson
Corre L. Robinson
Gertrude J. Robinson
Michael S. Rocca
Christine H. Roch
Bert A. Rockman
David W. Rohde
Andrew Rojecki
David W. Romero
Jerel A. Rosati
Douglas D. Roscoe
Gary L. Rose
Richard Rose
James N. Rosenau
Tom Rosenstiel
Cindy Simon Rosenthal
Howard Rosenthal
Uriel Rosenthal
Catherine Rothon
Stanley Rothman
Brandon Rottinghaus
David B. Rottman
Ivy Brown Rovner
Mark J. Rozell
Paul Rozin
Alan Rozzi
Steven J. Rubenzer
Andrew Rudalevige
Theodore W. Ruger
Vicki L. Ruiz
Barry S. Rundquist
Elizabeth Rybicki
Robert H. Salisbury
Kira Sanbonmatsu
Gabriel R. Sanchez
John G. Sanzone
Virginia Sapiro
Marjorie Sarbaugh-Thompson
Kyle L. Saunders
Brian F. Schaffner
E. E. Schattschneider
John M. Scheb II
Nancy Scherer
Eric Schickler
Wendy J. Schiller
Arthur M. Schlesinger Jr.
David F. Schmitz
Daniel M. Schneider
Gerald Schneider
Frauke Schnell
Norman Schofield
Peter J. Schraeder
Ludger Schuknecht
Lisa Schur
Leslie A. Schwindt-Bayer
James M. Scott
David O. Sears
Jeffrey A. Segal
Gary M. Segura
Harold Seidman

Peter Selb
Richard Seltzer
George Serra
Dhavan V. Shah
Byron E. Shafer
Karen Shafer
Robert Y. Shapiro
Robert Sherill
Eric Shirev
James Shoch
Colleen J. Shogan
Jerome L. Short
Kenneth W. Shotts
Steven A. Shull
Alan Siaroff
Jason C. Sides
Hugh Sidey
John Sides
Christine Marie Sierra
Lee Sigelman
Joel H. Silbey
Brian D. Silver
James R. Simmons
Solon J. Simmons
Dean Keith Simonton
Barbara Sinclair
Theda Skocpol
Elliott Slotnick
Charles E. Smith Jr.
Joseph L. Smith
Richard A. Smith
Robert Charles Smith
Steven S. Smith
Tom W. Smith
Kevin Snider
James M. Snyder Jr.
Richard Sobel
Mitchel A. Sollenberger
Lisa A. Solowiej
Udi Sommer
Donald R. Songer
Joe Soss
Harold J. Spaeth
Bartholomew H. Sparrow
Pablo T. Spiller
Matthew Spitzer
Kevin Stainback
D. T. Stallings
Harold W. Stanley
Nancy Staudt
Darrell Steffensmeier
Wayne P. Stegner
Amy Steigerwalt
Robert M. Stein
Daniel Stevens
Charles Stewart
James A. Stimson
Donald E. Stokes
Sarah Stonbely
Diane Stone
Walter J. Stone
John Strate

Thomas Stratmann
Matthew J. Streb
Natalie Jomini Stroud
John Sullivan
Tracy Sulkin
Paul E. Sum
James L. Sundquist
Marvin Swartz
Michele Swers
Jeffery C. Talbertal
Vito Tanzi
G. Alan Tarr
Katherine Tate
Margit Tavits
Humphrey Taylor
William J. Taylor Jr.
Ken L. Tedi
Cecilia Testa
Sean M. Theriault
Elizabeth Theiss-Morse
Felix J. Thoemmes
Sue Thomas
Lyke Thompson
Mary C. Thornberry
Gabor Toka
Donald Tomaskovic-Devey
Jeffrey Toobin
Rick Travis
Jessica Trounstine
Peter Trubowitz
David B. Truman
George Tsebelis
Steven A. Tuch
Alfred J. Tuchfarber
Joshua Tucker
Jeffrey K. Tulis
Charlotte Twight
Christopher Uggen
Carole Jean Uhlander
Isaac Unah
Joseph Daniel Ura
Joseph Uscinski
Nicholas A. Valentino
Steven Van de Walle
Gregg Van Ryzin
Lucien S. Vandenbroucke
Ryan Vander Wielen
Robert Van Sickel
Loring R. Veenstra
Jennifer Nicoll Victor
Stefano Della Vigna
John R. Vile
Richard L. Vining
Paul S. Voakes
John C. Wahlke
Sara D. Wakefield
Barbara F. Walter
Charles E. Walcott
Kenneth E. Wald
Paul Waldman
David B. Walker
Sherri L. Wallace

Kenneth Walsh
Artemus Ward
Adam L. Warber
Richard G. Waterman
Martin P. Wattenberg
James Brian Watts
Ronald L. Watts
Gregory J. Wawro
Frank W. Wayman
Stephen J. Wayne
Stephen Weatherford
David H. Weaver
R. Kent Weaver
Clive Webb
Max Weber
Lori Weigel
Herbert F. Weisberg
Thomas J. Weko
Reed L. Welch
Judith Wellman
Chad Westerland
Drew Weston
Russell Wheeler
Kenny J. Whitby
Clyde Wilcox
Aaron Wildavsky
G. Cleveland Wilhoit
Jennifer R. Wilking
T. Harry Williams
David C. Wilson
Ellen Gibson Wilson
John W. Winkle III
Allan M. Winkler
David G. Winter
Daniel Wirls
Stephen Wirls
Christopher Wlezien
Jennifer Wolak
Don Wolfensberger
Raymond E. Wolfinger
B. Dan Wood
Gordon S. Wood
Peter H. Wood
Gina Serignese Woodall
Nathan D. Woods
Jonathan Woon
Deil S. Wright
John R. Wright
Jun Xu
Jason Webb Yackee
Susan Webb Yackee
David A. Yalof
Jean Yarborough
Tinsley E. Yarbrough
Barbara M. Yarnold
John Yoo
Gary Young
Elizabeth J. Zechmeister
Julian E. Zelizer
Joseph F. Zimmerman
Curt Ziniel
Gary Zuk

INDEX